THE PAPERS OF

WOODROW WILSON

VOLUME 1

1856-1880

SPONSORED BY THE WOODROW WILSON
FOUNDATION
AND PRINCETON UNIVERSITY

THE PAPERS OF

WOODROW WILSON

ARTHUR S. LINK, *EDITOR*

JOHN WELLS DAVIDSON AND DAVID W. HIRST
ASSOCIATE EDITORS

T. H. VAIL MOTTER, *CONSULTING EDITOR*

JOHN E. LITTLE, *EDITORIAL ASSISTANT*

Volume 1 · 1856-1880

PRINCETON, NEW JERSEY
PRINCETON UNIVERSITY PRESS
1966

FOREWORD

THE idea of publishing the letters and papers of Woodrow Wilson developed almost spontaneously among some of the members of the Board of Directors of the Woodrow Wilson Foundation. The group, as I now recall it, consisted of August Heckscher, Arthur M. Schlesinger, Jr., Philip C. Jessup, Francis Sayre, Jonathan Daniels, Harold Dodds, John B. Oakes, Julie Herzog, and myself. Later Timothy Pfeiffer entered the picture very effectively, but Frank Altschul was really the man who pushed the matter through. These associates of mine asked me to serve as chairman, presumably because I had been a student of Woodrow Wilson's at Princeton University in the early years of the century.

The first action that our group or committee took—and it was our happiest action—was to appoint a man of uncommon ability to act as Editor—Dr. Arthur S. Link. Dr. Link was at that time connected with Northwestern University as professor of history, but our committee felt that the work on the letters and papers should be centered at Princeton, where Wilson had taken his place as one of the foremost educators of his generation. Consequently arrangements were made with Princeton University—and with Northwestern—by which Dr. Link was transferred to the New Jersey institution with the same rank, and he entered on his new duties with us in 1958.

Dr. Link brought with him talents of unusual distinction. He was not only a scholar who was already deeply involved in writing his monumental work on the life of Woodrow Wilson, but he was a natural administrator, too, and he seized upon the new opportunity we offered him with precision and dispatch, getting the system organized and in operation in a few months' time. Shortly afterward, he selected two men of excellent qualifications —Dr. John Wells Davidson and Dr. David W. Hirst—as his associates. These three men constituted the core of the staff, and while additional personnel were later added, it was this closely knit group that really launched and guided the project from the beginning.

In undertaking this work our committee naturally felt very strongly that the records of a man of Woodrow Wilson's place in his generation should be preserved for posterity. The overriding claims of history to the inspiration and recuperative values of the past cannot wisely be denied. It is the vision of the past that makes the present livable, and no era should be prevented from learning its secrets.

This is a point of view that had already been widely accepted, and the growing collections of personal letters and papers in the Library of Congress and elsewhere are an eloquent testimonial to this new attitude toward privacy. With the passage of years privacy becomes at best a relative term. There is a kind of statute of limitations which, after a reasonable period, allows us to unlock the secrecies and intimacies of a given generation without embarrassment or lack of taste. We are not shut off from the richness of the past because of modesty or a sense of inappropriateness which, however valid at the time, has probably outlived its relevance and meaning.

With this principle our committee was thoroughly in agreement, and it is this principle, too, which has guided the editors of all the new books that are today giving us the letters of men like Thomas Jefferson, Alexander Hamilton, Benjamin Franklin, the Adams family, and many others.

The many volumes of letters and papers in this particular collection are a monument to Woodrow Wilson. But in a deeper sense they are also a monument to people everywhere—people whose ideals and principles he shared and understood. They cover his many contributions to mankind, particularly his gift of the idea of a definite system of international relationships. No one before him ever left the world so priceless a legacy. That is why his name is in a sense immortal. That is why the generations which follow us will never forget him.

But Wilson brought other gifts, too—and his students at Princeton recall them with an affectionate gratitude. Wilson lit a lamp for us which time has never been able to put out. We remember him as the inspiring teacher who introduced us to the kingdom of the mind, and who held up before our eyes what Whitehead later called "an habitual vision of greatness."

If to future generations these volumes have meaning and significance, it will be because they have been lighted by that spark of genius and fired by that incandescent vision of greatness.

RAYMOND B. FOSDICK

December 15, 1964

GENERAL INTRODUCTION

THE WILSON PAPERS

W OODROW WILSON himself made the single greatest contribution to the preservation of his papers. He did this not because he preserved copies of his personal letters—indeed, he usually saved no copies of his private correspondence—but rather because he grew up during a generation that reverenced the raw materials of history, and he rarely threw away anything he thought to be of possible importance, at least after childhood. He seems to have begun consciously and methodically to save his papers during the summer of 1874, just after his withdrawal from Davidson College. From this time until his death in 1924, Wilson carefully accumulated what would become the Wilson Papers. Thus the collection is not only large but varied and, in addition to correspondence, includes scrapbooks, notebooks, class notes, drafts of undergraduate essays, articles, books, lecture notes, drafts of speeches, and official materials of many kinds. In addition, even from boyhood Wilson saved his books. His substantial library is now housed in a special room in the Library of Congress.

Ray Stannard Baker, journalist and close associate of President Wilson, took the first steps toward arrangement of the Wilson Papers by grouping such of the Peace Conference materials as were then available to him preparatory to writing *Woodrow Wilson and World Settlement* in 1921-22. Subsequently, in 1925, Mrs. Wilson entrusted what she then believed to be the entire collection to Mr. Baker, and it remained in whole or in part in his possession until 1939. During this period he and his research assistant, Miss Katharine E. Brand, took further steps toward organization. Mrs. Wilson deposited the papers in the Library of Congress in 1939, converting the deposit to a deed of gift in 1945. Meanwhile, Miss Brand, working with the staff of the Manuscript Division of the Library of Congress as Mrs. Wilson's representative, had arranged the papers in nine major series. For descriptions, see Katharine E. Brand, "The Woodrow Wilson Collection," *Library of Congress Quarterly Journal of Current Acquisitions*, II (February 1945), 3-10, and "Woodrow Wilson, in His Own Time," in the same *Quarterly*, XIII (February 1956), 61-72, and also her "The Man in History," Em Bowles Alsop (ed.), *The Greatness of Woodrow Wilson* (New York, 1956), pp. 183-205. David W. Hirst's "Preliminary Survey of Woodrow Wilson Manuscripts," *Woodrow Wilson Centennial Celebration Commis-*

sion (Washington, 1958), pp. 223-24, also describes the papers. Mrs. Wilson made frequent additions to the Wilson Papers, the most important being in 1949 and 1952. Her own papers, given to the Library of Congress in 1959, are an important supplement. Finally, a group consisting of some 18,000 items was transferred from the Wilson house in Washington to the Library of Congress in 1963. At the present writing, the entire collection is being reorganized.

This constitutes the major core of the Wilson Papers. However, Wilson, in addition to keeping no copies of his personal letters, rarely kept copies of official letters that he wrote either by hand or on his own typewriter. The largest volume of such official letters is to be found in the National Archives in departmental files, particularly in the State Department records. The latter include numerous diplomatic dispatches, correspondence with Secretaries of State, and so on. The Princeton University Library has gathered a collection of original Wilson letters that is significant particularly for the pre-presidential period. This collection is supplemented by a variety of related materials that document Wilson's long association with the University. The Yale University Library owns, among others, the originals of President Wilson's letters to Colonel House, most of which Wilson typed himself. The University of Virginia Library has the important group of letters that Wilson wrote to his lifelong friend, Richard Heath Dabney. Davidson College has a small but important collection. The remaining Wilson documents are widely scattered in libraries, historical societies, and in private hands throughout the world.

Wilson's writings and speeches were widely published and circulated during his lifetime. For a list, see Laura S. Turnbull, *Woodrow Wilson Bibliography* (Princeton, N. J., 1948), pp. 9-15. The first serious effort to publish Wilson's public papers and addresses was made by Albert Shaw (ed.), *President Wilson's Papers* (New York, 1917), later expanded into *The Messages and Papers of Woodrow Wilson* (2 vols., New York, 1924). Next came Ray Stannard Baker's selection of Peace Conference materials in *Woodrow Wilson and World Settlement* (3 vols., Garden City, N. Y., 1922), the third volume of which consists entirely of documents. The most important of all collected editions appeared between 1925-27: R. S. Baker and William E. Dodd (eds.), *The Public Papers of Woodrow Wilson* (6 vols., New York, 1925-27), commissioned by Mrs. Wilson. It ranged chronologically from Wilson's undergraduate days to the last years of his life and brought together for the first time many fugitive items, along with more obvious ones. It remains an indispensable tool. However, Baker and Dodd included only items that were readily available at that time in the Wilson Papers or which had already been published. It was, inevitably, fragmentary. The only important additions to this record were T. H. Vail Motter (ed.), *Leaders of Men* (Princeton, N. J., 1952), and John Wells Davidson (ed.), *A Crossroads of Freedom: The 1912 Campaign Speeches of Woodrow Wilson* (New Haven, Conn., 1956).

No one, before the present editors began their task, has undertaken to prepare a comprehensive edition of Wilson letters. Mr. Baker, in his authorized biography, *Woodrow Wilson: Life and Letters* (8 vols., Garden City, N. Y., 1927-39), printed but a small portion of the total, even though the last two volumes of this biography consisted in large part of letters. Mrs. Wilson, retaining close control of the use of her husband's papers, did not approve widespread publication of Wilson letters until she gave her blessing to *The Papers of Woodrow Wilson* in 1958. President Wilson's daughter, Eleanor Wilson McAdoo, published a selection of the letters between her mother and father under the title *The Priceless Gift, The Love Letters of Woodrow Wilson and Ellen Axson Wilson* (New York, 1962).

THE GENESIS OF THIS SERIES

The Papers of Woodrow Wilson is one of the outgrowths of the Wilson Centennial Year of 1956. Biographers and specialists in the field of American history had long recognized and acutely felt the need for a comprehensive edition of President Wilson's papers. That need became more generally apparent as statesmen, scholars, and educational leaders set out in 1956 to recall the Wilsonian contribution in the light of historical perspective. This was a massive re-evaluation, and the dimensions of President Wilson's contributions to political science and historical literature, educational theories and practice, the formation of modern domestic policies, and the building of a peaceful international community became evident as never before. More important, the re-thinking of the Centennial Year revealed, for those persons who had forgotten, the fact that the twenty-eighth President lives on in his principles and the things for which he stood and fought, and lives with perhaps greater influence and power than during his days upon the earth.

It soon became evident as this re-evaluation proceeded that a full-scale edition of President Wilson's papers was urgently needed. Scholars pointed to the absence of any edition of letters and to the incompleteness of *The Public Papers of Woodrow Wilson.* David W. Hirst, in his survey made for the Woodrow Wilson Centennial Celebration Commission, revealed that Wilson letters were widely scattered, and he pointed to the large volume of Wilson materials that had become available since Baker completed the authorized biography in 1939. Public men and specialists alike agreed that a comprehensive edition of President Wilson's papers would be the surest safeguard of the vitality and strength of his ideals, particularly since memories dim and men would soon have to rely entirely upon the written word for their knowledge of the man. And everyone agreed that there could be no more fitting monument to a great American.

The challenge was taken up by the Woodrow Wilson Foundation of New York. It had been the principal agency in disseminating President Wilson's ideals since its founding in 1922. The Board of Directors, in response to a recommendation of the Woodrow Wilson Centennial Celebration Commission, voted on May 16, 1957, "Resolved, That the Woodrow Wilson Foundation sponsor and promote the publication of the Woodrow Wilson Letters and Papers." A Publications Committee consisting of Raymond B. Fosdick, Chairman, August Heckscher, Vice Chairman, Jonathan Daniels, Harold W. Dodds, Philip C. Jessup, John B. Oakes, Francis B. Sayre, and Arthur M. Schlesinger, Jr., surveyed the problems involved and appointed Arthur S. Link, then Professor of History at Northwestern University, as Editor on February 20, 1958. The Board of Directors ratified the appointment on March 19, 1958.

The Publications Committee, assisted by Timothy N. Pfeiffer, Fund-Raising Chairman, next set to work to raise funds to launch *The Papers of Woodrow Wilson* auspiciously. Contributions were received from the Rockefeller Foundation, the Ford Foundation, the Cleveland H. Dodge Foundation, the Avalon Foundation, the United States Steel Corporation, the State of New Jersey, Mrs. Woodrow Wilson, John D. Rockefeller, 3rd, Bernard M. Baruch, and many other individuals. Princeton University, which became a co-sponsor of the project when the Woodrow Wilson Foundation accepted the University's request to participate in the project in 1959, assumed a large financial burden in housing the Papers of Woodrow Wilson and helping to care for its staff.

Clarification of the dimensions of the task of collecting and editing soon revealed that this support, generous and indispensable though it was, would not suffice to guarantee the success of an undertaking that would require many years for completion. The Board of Directors of the Woodrow Wilson Foundation, as an earnest of good faith, on November 12, 1959, adopted a resolution affirming "that the Board was not only determined to see the Project through but was prepared in principle to spend capital funds to implement the work." The Board of Directors, following a recommendation by its Executive Committee made on December 3, 1962, voted on January 23, 1963, to cease its traditional activities and devote its full resources to the Papers of Woodrow Wilson for so long as might be necessary to complete the published series.

GATHERING WILSON'S PAPERS

The work of selecting and cataloguing had meanwhile gone forward. It began on September 1, 1958, when John Wells Davidson, appointed Associate Editor on March 21, 1958, took up his post in Study Room 128 in the Library of Congress Annex. Offices were opened at 132 Third St., S. E., Washington, D. C., on September 1, 1959, at which time David W. Hirst joined the staff as Assistant Editor. From this time on until the major work in Washington was completed in 1963 and the editorial staff moved to Princeton, the editors and their assistants sifted the entire body of the Woodrow Wilson Papers in the Library of Congress, along with some seventy collateral manuscript collections in the same depository. In addition, they combed the holdings of all libraries known to possess Wilson documents or related materials and conducted a nationwide search for Wilson letters still in private hands. The fruit of this labor is the collection of photocopies, typescripts, shorthand transcripts, and additional papers now housed in Firestone Library at Princeton University. It fills nineteen large filing cabinets and brings together for the first time most of the widely scattered corpus of the Wilson Papers. It includes, besides, catalogues, inventories, and other control apparatus.

The following persons assisted the editors in the work of the Washington office during the first phase of the history of this project: Helga Sandburg, Naomi Proff, and Evelyn Roberts, administrative assistants; Charles M. Bacon, Valerie Berman, John Boettjer, Rachel Dach, Janice Hepworth, Bruce Horney, John E. Little, Diane Nester, Margaret Pearce, and George Treasure, research assistants; and Serena Cox, Sara Jane Gaston, Mary Kanacopoulos, Diane Parr, and Rosemary Zaloznik, typists and secretaries. Carole Alsup, Margaret Cazin, Donna Gunderson, Mary

P. Krueger, and Helen Spiro have served as secretaries in the Princeton office. Dr. T. H. Vail Motter joined the staff as Consulting Editor in 1964.

An editorial Advisory Committee, appointed in 1959, contributed (and continues to contribute) generously in insights and guidance. It consisted during the first five years of the project of Samuel Flagg Bemis, Katharine E. Brand, Henry Steele Commager, August Heckscher, Richard W. Leopold, and Arthur M. Schlesinger, Jr. Professor Bemis resigned in 1964 and was succeeded by David C. Mearns.

EDITORIAL OBJECTIVES AND METHODS

The editors hope to publish a comprehensive edition that will include all important letters, articles, speeches, interviews, and public papers by Woodrow Wilson. These volumes, when complete, should make available to readers all the materials essential to understanding Wilson's personality, his intellectual, religious, and political development, and his careers as educator, writer, orator, and statesman. The editors also hope that these volumes will be useful to scholars and others in various fields of history between the 1870's and the 1920's.

It would perhaps be ideal if the editors could set as their goal publication of every document by or relating to Wilson. They have concluded for a number of reasons that this goal is neither feasible nor desirable. There is first the fact of the huge bulk of documentary materials now available. Most of Wilson's career fell in the period when the typewriter was in general use. This technological advance combined with a rapid increase in population and governmental activities to cause a much larger volume of letters and documents to pour into the White House during Wilson's time than earlier. The editors estimate that they have photocopied about 250,000 documents, totaling considerably more than 500,000 pages. Clearly, it is not feasible to think of publishing all these documents, not even all documents by Wilson. Furthermore, it is doubtful that they would want to print all documents by Wilson even if it was possible to do so. For example, it would hardly advance the cause of scholarship to include in this series all of Wilson's perfunctory replies and form letters to well-wishers and patronage-seekers. Letters of this type will be represented by samples.

More specifically, the editors intend:

1. To publish all letters by Wilson that are essential to understanding his thought and activity. These, they think, have the

highest priority. This first volume includes all of Wilson's letters thus far discovered for the period that it covers. Selection of letters for future volumes will obviously depend upon their quality and significance. The editors, when necessary, will also publish incoming letters or extracts from or digests of such letters, particularly when they provide the only indications concerning Wilson's missing replies or furnish the only information about events in Wilson's life. The first two or three volumes, which cover a hitherto sparsely documented period, will include a substantial proportion of incoming letters.

2. To print a selection of Wilson's speeches. Public speaking was for Woodrow Wilson a very important form of communication, and the editors will not neglect it. But Wilson made hundreds of speeches during his lifetime, and publication of all of them would consume disproportionate space. It seems advisable, therefore, to publish in full only the most important speeches, and to edit others by eliminating inordinate repetition.

3. To print as much as seems wise of a wide variety of Wilson manuscripts. Diaries will be published in full, but only samples of Wilson's voluminous classroom and lecture notes will be included. Additional items, such as commonplace books, memoranda, lists, accounts, records of organizations in which Wilson participated, and marginal notes in books, will be printed in whole or in part depending upon importance. However, the editors will describe the contents of all important Wilson documents (e.g., scrapbooks, notebooks, and copybooks) that they do not print in full.

4. To publish all of Wilson's important articles, because the journals in which they appeared are in many cases unavailable even in good libraries.

5. To publish from among Wilson's books only *Congressional Government* and *Constitutional Government in the United States*, on the ground that they are so central in the development of his political thought that they cannot be omitted from a comprehensive edition of his papers.

6. To publish all items in as strict chronological order as possible. The editors believe such arrangement necessary because of the intimate relationship between letters, speeches, and other writings. Documents are presented in chronological order. Enclosures are printed with the letter in which they were enclosed. Attachments appear in chronological order.

These, then, are the general objectives that the editors have in view for *The Papers of Woodrow Wilson*. They would add a further word about the specific task of clarifying and annotating documents. The editors have concluded that it is not possible for them to do all the things that a biographer and historian would ordinarily do. They conceive their most important task to be the presentation of a reliable Wilson text. In addition, they believe that this text must be accompanied by as much editorial treatment as is necessary to make it meaningful in its context. Hence they will employ the following editorial practices:

(a) Each document will be given a descriptive heading. Titles, headings, and so on that are part of the document will be printed in the type used for documentary text.

(b) Each document will be dated, either exactly or approximately.

(c) Each document will be briefly described physically and its location given. It will be apparent from these descriptive-location notes whether the document is being printed from a manuscript or from a printed source.

(d) That the reader may be assured that he is seeing the document as it stands, each document, whether manuscript or printed, will be reproduced *exactly* as it appears in the original, with the exceptions noted hereafter. The editorial *sic* will be reduced to the minimum and used only in cases where absolutely necessary for clarity. Completion of words and alterations of punctuation marks, including the use of single and double quotation marks, will likewise be resorted to (enclosed in square brackets) only for the sake of clarity. The only silent alterations employed will be in letters, where, for the sake of clarity, periods in salutations will be changed to commas, periods will be substituted for dashes when the dashes would ordinarily be read as periods, and superior letters will be lowered to the regular line.

(e) Each document will be annotated when this is necessary for identification of individuals and events. The editors, when possible, will briefly identify casual friends, subjects, and events. They will provide longer biographical notes for subjects whose relationships with Wilson stretched over a number of years and were important to him. The main purpose of these notes is to signal to the reader the importance of that relationship. It is not their function to provide full biographies of persons or definitive accounts of events involved. Fortunately, in most cases the documents speak for themselves about the character and significance of these relationships. Well-known historical personages and literary figures, as well as writings and events, will not ordinarily be identified. Except in unusual cases, the editors will not cite the standard biographical and other references used for information

afts of let-
ginal notes
overed for
most confi-
nt volumes
transcrip-
rican prac-
uation has

s of one of
ted States,
n, born in
e same edi-
d. He sub-
man began
the present
ave worked
n to express

In addition,
am expert,
d materials

e following

loo, for en-
under their

Foundation
porting this
of president
ugust Heck-
e Executive
niel L. Mon-
ations Com-
k, great Wil-

foundations
ssible, finan-

niversity, for

ve bibliographical data. They will
o biographers.
upplied when the briefer and more
fficiently indicate the importance
e context of the document.
ts are grouped under a single edi-
etters from . . ." or "Three Items
ne descriptive-location note. This
nt in the group, and will describe
qually. In this case such an ab-
a plural. But if this note does not
uments included under the com-
ch document so included, whose
s in any respect from the final
ve-location note. This innovation
e hope that, without sacrificing
eliminating unnecessary repeti-

between references to incoming
hose that are not included, ref-
that are not printed in whole or
tive and location abbreviations
abbreviations will be omitted if
the series.
sought original documents for
xistence of the central core of
ry of thousands of original Wil-
ed the editors' task. Wherever
r copies are available, the copy
original will be used. Wherever
checked against the originals
ing taken to indicate significant

utset master files consisting of
ribing documents according to
ronology, sender and recipient,
ding to date and location.

'S SHORTHAND
anscription of the voluminous
ials scattered throughout the
which will be discussed else-
have had more than 2,000

pages of transcripts made, including transcripts of dr
ters, speeches, lectures, articles, state papers, and mar
in books and on documents. They have, they think, red
posterity the main body of Wilson's writings in this
dential form. Transcripts printed in this and subseque
approximate as closely as possible what Wilson's own
tion would have been, except that contemporary Ame
tices in spelling have been followed. Wilson's punct
been retained.

The editors were fortunate in obtaining the service
the foremost Graham shorthand experts in the Uni
Clifford P. Gehman of Denver, Colorado. Mr. Gehma
1875, the year that Wilson entered Princeton, used th
tions of shorthand textbooks that Wilson himself use
sequently won many honors in his profession. Mr. Geh
work on Wilson shorthand materials in October 1959;
writing finds him still at the task. The editors, who h
with him during the past five years, take this occasior
their gratitude for his notable contribution to history

The editors have carefully checked all transcripts.
Marjorie Sirlouis of Washington, D. C., another Gral
has further read and checked most of the shorthan
in this first volume.

ACKNOWLEDGMENTS

The editors express their profound gratitude to tl
institutions and individuals:

Mrs. Woodrow Wilson and Eleanor Wilson McA
couragement, support, and access to Wilson materials
control.

The Board of Directors of the Woodrow Wilson
of New York, for launching and wholeheartedly sup
project, particularly these men who held the office
during the period 1957-1965: Philip C. Jessup, A
scher, Ernest A. Gross, and Pendleton Herring; th
Director, 1957-63, Julie C. Herzog; the Treasurer, Da
roe; and the members of the aforementioned Public
mittee. Special tribute is paid to Raymond B. Fosdic
sonian and guiding spirit.

The Rockefeller and Ford Foundations, and other
and individuals mentioned earlier, for making it po
cially, to launch this project.

The Board of Trustees and officers of Princeton U

providing an academic home for the Papers of Woodrow Wilson, and for assuming the burden of administration, particularly Robert F. Goheen, President; Ricardo A. Mestres, Vice President; J. Douglas Brown, Dean of the Faculty; W. M. Young, Controller; Joseph R. Strayer and Jerome Blum, Chairmen of the History Department; Alexander Leitch, Secretary of the University; and Samuel C. Howell, Assistant Dean of the Faculty.

The following members of the staff of the Princeton University Library for hospitality and assistance: William S. Dix, Librarian; James M. Keels, Assistant Librarian; Howard C. Rice, Jr., Alexander P. Clark, and Wanda Randall, of the Department of Rare Books and Special Collections.

The Archivist of Princeton University, M. Halsey Thomas, who gave unstinting help in the search for materials and read this volume before it went to press.

The staff of the Manuscript Division of the Library of Congress, particularly David C. Mearns, Chief; Robert H. Land and Daniel Reed, Assistant Chiefs; and Joseph Vance, C. Percy Powell, John de Porry, and Russell Smith, staff members.

The Photoduplication Service of the Library of Congress, particularly Donald C. Holmes and Elmer King.

The staffs of the National Archives and National Historical Publications Commission, in particular Philip M. Hamer, Oliver W. Holmes, Herman Kahn, and Judy Carroll.

The staffs of the New Jersey State Library, particularly Roger McDonough and Kenneth Richards, and of the New Jersey Tercentenary Commission, particularly David Davies and Pauline Callahan.

The aforementioned members of the Editorial Advisory Committee, for general guidance and for a critical reading of the manuscript of this first volume; also Henry W. Bragdon, for reading the manuscript; in addition Leonard W. Larabee, Editor of *The Papers of Benjamin Franklin*; Julian P. Boyd, Editor of *The Papers of Thomas Jefferson*; and Elting E. Morison and John M. Blum, Editor and Associate Editor of *The Letters of Theodore Roosevelt*, for sharing experiences and knowledge.

The staff of Princeton University Press, particularly Herbert S. Bailey, Jr., Director; R. Miriam Brokaw, Managing Editor; P. J. Conkwright, typographer; and Marjorie Putney, copy editor for this first volume, for producing a handsome series worthy of the subject.

The editors of course accept responsibility for whatever errors remain.

The following institutions and libraries, for helpful information and copies of letters and other documents: Alabama Department of Archives and History, Allegheny College Library, American Academy of Arts and Letters, American Jewish Archives, Archdiocese of Baltimore, Argentine Ministry of Foreign Affairs, Augusta-Richmond Public Library, Berea College Library, Bodleian Library of Oxford University, Boston Public Library, Brown University Library, Bucks County (Pennsylvania) Historical Society, Bryn Mawr College Library, University of Buffalo Library, St. John's Seminary Library of Camarillo, California, University of California (Berkeley) Library, University of California (Los Angeles) Library, Chicago Public Library, Chicago Historical Society, University of Chicago Library, Canadian Public Archives, Colby College Library, Colgate University Library, Columbia University Libraries, Connecticut State Library, Connecticut Valley Historical Museum, Cornell University Library, Creighton University Library, Dartmouth College Library, Davidson College Library, University of Delaware Library, Detroit Public Library, Dickinson College Library, Duke University Library, The Filson Club, Ford Motor Company Archives, University of Georgia Library, Harper & Brothers, Hartford Seminary Foundation, Harvard University Library, Haverford College Library, Rutherford B. Hayes Library, Hispanic Society of America, The Historical Foundation, Montreat, North Carolina, Historical Society of Pennsylvania, The Hoover Library, The Huntington Library, Illinois State Historical Library, Indiana Historical Society, Indiana State Library, Indiana University Library, Indianapolis Public Library, Iowa State Department of History and Archives, Jersey City Public Library, Jewish Community Council of Essex County, New Jersey, The Johns Hopkins University Library, Kent State University Library, University of Kentucky Library, The Lawrenceville School, Lehigh University Library, Library of Congress, Lincoln Memorial University Library, London School of Economics Library, Louisiana State University Library, University of Louisville Library, Massachusetts Historical Society, Michigan Historical Commission, University of Michigan Library, Minnesota Historical Society, Missouri Historical Society, Monmouth County (New Jersey) Historical Association, Pierpont Morgan Library, Morristown National Historical Park Library, National Archives, Newberry Library, New Jersey State Library, New Jersey Historical Society, New-York Historical Society, New York Public Library, New York State Library, North Carolina Department of Archives and History, University of North Carolina Library, University of Notre Dame Library, Ohio Historical Society, Ohio Historical and Philosophical Society, Paterson (New Jersey) Public Library, Pennsylvania State University Library, Presbyterian Historical Society, Princeton Theological Seminary Library, Princeton University Library, Randolph-Macon Woman's College Library, William Marsh Rice University Library, University of Rochester Library, Will Rogers Memorial Commission, Rome (Georgia) Public Library, Franklin Delano Roosevelt Library, Rutgers University Library, University of the South Library, University of South Carolina Library, Stanford University Library, Swarthmore College Library, Tennessee State Library and Archives, University of Texas Library, Trenton Public Library, Tuskegee Institute Department of Records and Research, Union Theological Seminary Library, Richmond, Virginia, University of Vermont Library, Virginia Historical Society, Virginia State Library, University of Virginia Library, Washington State University Library, Western Reserve University Library, Wildwood (New Jersey) Historical Society, Williams College Library, Wisconsin State Historical Society, University of Wisconsin Library, Woodrow Wilson Foundation, Yale University Library, and Yivo Institute for Jewish Research.

For very recent help: Atlanta Public Library, Fordham University Library, Newark Public Library, Savannah Public Library, and Wilmington (North Carolina) Public Library.

The editors also thank the following individuals for supplying information and copies of letters and other documents:

J. S. Armentrout, Jr., Benjamin P. Axson, Edward E. Barthell, Jr., Mrs. Henry A. Barton, Edward C. Beall, Julian B. Beaty, Richard Bender, George C. Benfer, Florence Berryman, Ray A. Billington, Robert K. Black, Thomas M. H. Blair, Marian B. Bothe, Harry L. Bowlby, Henry W. Bragdon, Thomas W. Brahany, William M. Brodhead, Bernard M. Baruch, R. A. Burkholder, J. Morgan Calhoun, David F. Chapman, J. Rives Childs, James T. Clark, Mrs. John Maurice Clark, Francis O. Clarkson, Cyril Clemens, Hennig Cohen, Rowland L. Collins, H. Bartholomew Cox, John R. Craft, Bernard Crick, C. C. Crittenden, George E. Cutley, Jr., Virginius Dabney, Helen B. Davison, Mrs. Harold M. DeLorme, John H. DeRidder, Sander Diamond, Allen W. Dulles, David C. Duniway, Robert F. Durden, Walter N. Eastburn, Mrs. R. C. Egbert, Woodrow Eichorn, Margaret Hale Ely, Dr. George L. Erdman, Francis P. Fentress, Mrs. W. P. Fentress, Charles E. Feinberg, Irving M. Fisher, David Flanzman, A. Hugh Frazier, Lysbeth Geran, Jackson A. Giddens, Arthur J. Goldberg, Mrs.

Edward F. Goltra, Howard B. Gotlieb, Cary T. Grayson, Jr., Gordon Grayson, William Grayson, James S. Green, Richard F. Green, William Harlan Hale, Edward S. C. Handy, Pauline Hardwick, Charles Heath, Mark Heefner, George W. Hervey, Leo H. Hirsch, Jr., Lindsay Hoben, Richard Hooker, Herbert Hoover, Richard B. Hovey, William D. Hoyt, Jr., T. Russell Hungerford, Edwin C. Hutten, S. Kelvin Johnson, Warren F. Johnson, Owen D. Jones, Anthony S. Kalina, Earl Kaplan, James Kerney, Jr., Mrs. Benjamin King, Thomas D. Lee, Jessica Lobel, Mrs. Bradford B. Locke, Arthur W. Machen, Jr., Donald R. MacLaren, Dean Mathey, Eleanor W. McAdoo, Bruce McClellan, Alice Wilson McElroy, Lawrence H. McGill, Charles H. McIlwain, Stiles A. Martin, Mrs. Thomas N. Mays, Harvey W. Mortimer, Ralph G. Newman, Eva Newton, William B. Northrop, Oscar Otto, Timothy N. Pfeiffer, Catherine J. Pierce, Clarence Poe, Mrs. John Prentiss Poe, John A. Potter, Jr., William S. Powell, Harold Ray, Siegfried Ray, Chauncey W. Reed, Frank T. Renick, Leon Reussille, Mrs. A. Harrison Reynolds, J. Sherrard Rice, Helen M. Rietheimer, William H. Robinson, Walter S. Rogers, Mrs. Alexander S. Salley, Eleanor Sayre, Francis B. Sayre, William Schiela, Louis L. Schlosser, Jr., Marguerite D. Seamans, Charles Seymour, Albert Shaw, Jr., Mrs. Hugh L. Shaw, Mrs. David B. Skillman, Samuel R. Spencer, Jr., Alexander Sprunt, Jr., James L. Sprunt, Sr., James L. Sprunt, Jr., Walter P. Sprunt, Jr., Rupert M. Stewart, Mary Strohecker, Reed Stuart, John M. Taylor, Mrs. Perry W. Terhune, Mrs. Homer A. Thompson, Bascom Timmons, Horatio W. Turner, Frederick R. Vincent, Charles C. Wagner, Lydia P. Walker, Arthur Walworth, Horace V. Wells, Jr., Mrs. Ralph W. Wescott, Susan Colston Wilson, Mrs. Woodrow Wilson, Emily Winn, John T. Winterich, Alvin Witt, Robert F. Wood, John S. Woodbridge, Adeline J. Woodman, James Woodrow, Lawrence C. Woods, Jr., M. S. Wyeth, Gerald E. Young, and Richard Young.

For recent help, also, Doris Fielding Reid, Francis B. Sayre, Jr., and Arthur P. Dudden.

A NOTE ABOUT THE FIRST VOLUME

The documents in this volume cover the period between Woodrow Wilson's birth in 1856 and his withdrawal from the University of Virginia in December 1880. The Wilsonian documentary record before 1873 is virtually nonexistent. It begins sparsely just before Wilson went to Davidson College in September 1873 and becomes increasingly rich and revealing after he matriculated at the College of New Jersey in September 1875. Documentation after this date is varied and unusual in character. The documents in this volume are here first presented in a scholarly edition, except for Wilson's essays on Bismarck, Chatham, cabinet government, Bright, and Gladstone, the report of his debate on Roman Catholicism, extracts from a few of his letters to Robert Bridges and Charles A. Talcott, and a few extracts from the minutes of the American Whig Society.

Woodrow Wilson as a youth and young man truly lives for the first time in the printed record in these pages. We see the immature boy at Davidson College, the student at Princeton as he first comes into his intellectual, literary, and oratorical powers, and the impatient law student at the University of Virginia, eager to move into the world of affairs. We are often able to see him day by day in his most intimate reflections, reading, habits, religious concerns, and relationships with friends and classmates. Moreover, we can observe the whole range of his self-motivated activities that from childhood revealed his ceaseless drive for knowledge, the improvement of his powers to mold and lead opinion, and his capacity for self-criticism. Most strikingly, we see for the first time the remarkable relationship between Wilson and his father and can now understand why Woodrow Wilson afterward said that his father was incomparably his greatest teacher, guide, and friend.

THE EDITORS

Princeton, New Jersey
February 22, 1966

CONTENTS

ILLUSTRATIONS

Following page 306

ABBREVIATIONS

ALI	autograph letter initialed
ALS	autograph letter signed
att.	attached
enc.	enclosure, enclosed
env.	envelope
hw	handwritten, handwriting
JRW	Joseph Ruggles Wilson
JWW	Janet Woodrow Wilson
miscl.	miscellaneous
sh	shorthand
shLS	shorthand letter signed
shP(S)	shorthand postal (signed)
WW	Woodrow Wilson
WWhw(S)	Woodrow Wilson handwriting or handwritten (signed)
WWsh	Woodrow Wilson shorthand
WWshL(S)	Woodrow Wilson shorthand letter (signed)
WWshP(S)	Woodrow Wilson shorthand postal (signed)

ABBREVIATIONS FOR COLLECTIONS AND LIBRARIES

Following the National Union Catalogue of the Library of Congress

DLC	Library of Congress
MdBJ	Library of The Johns Hopkins University
Meyer Coll., DLC	Meyer Collection, Library of Congress
NcDaD	Davidson College Library
PCarlD	Dickinson College Library
NjP	Princeton University Library, including the Archives of Princeton University
RSB Coll., DLC	Ray Stannard Baker Collection of Wilsoniana, Library of Congress
RSB Papers, NjP	Ray Stannard Baker Papers, Princeton University Library
ScU	University of South Carolina Library
ViU	University of Virginia Library
WC, NjP	Woodrow Wilson Collection, Princeton University Library
WP, DLC	Woodrow Wilson Papers, Library of Congress

SYMBOLS

[blank]   blanks in the text

[- - - -]   undecipherable words in text, each dash representing one word

[* *]   undecipherable shorthand, each asterisk representing one shorthand outline

[   ]   word or words in original text which Wilson omitted in copying

⟨   ⟩   matter deleted from manuscript by Wilson and restored by editors

†   used in the *Index Rerum* to indicate WWhw in the source

[Sept. 8, 1879] publication date of a published writing; also date of a document when date is not part of text

[*Sept. 8, 1879*] latest composition date of a published writing

[[Sept. 8, 1879]] delivery date of a speech if publication date differs

THE PAPERS OF

WOODROW WILSON

VOLUME 1

1856-1880

THE PAPERS OF
WOODROW WILSON

From the Wilson Family Bible

[Feb. 28, 1822-Jan. 4, 1868]

Family Record

Births

Joseph R. Wilson[1] Born in Steubenville O. on the 28th day of February, 1822.

Jessie Wodrow[2] was born in Carlisle, England, on the 20th day of December, 1830

Marriages

1849—June 7th—by Rev. Thomas Woodrow[3]—Joseph R. Wilson and Jessie E. Woodrow.

Deaths

1 *James Wilson,*[4] our beloved father, departed this life on the 17th day of October 1850, at 10 A.M.—of *cholera*—after a severe sickness of 11 hours—aged 63.

Births

1. *Marion M.* [W.][5] Born in Chartiers' Manse, Washn Co., Pa., on 20th Oct. 1851, at 1 3/4 o'clock in the afternoon.—Was baptised in the college church Prince Edward Co. Va., on the 15th day of November 1851, by Benj. H. Rice, D.D.

2. —At Hampden Sidney College, September 8th 1853, at 8 3/4 o'clock. A.M.—*Annie*[6]—and baptised by Dr. B. H. Rice in the College ch., Pr. Ed. Co. Va., in the month of November 1853.

3. In Staunton, Virginia on the 28th December, 1856 at 12 3/4 o'clock at night[7]—*Thomas Woodrow*—and baptized April 1857 by Rev. J. H. Smith of Charlottesville.

[4.] 1867 *Joseph R.*[8] In Parsonage Augusta, Georgia, on the 20th day of July 1867, at 4 o'clock in the morning. Baptized by Rev. Thos Woodrow D.D. on Saturday [Jan. 4] before 1st Sab. in January 1868.

Hw entries in family Bible (Woodrow Wilson Birthplace Foundation, Staunton, Va.).

[1] Joseph Ruggles Wilson, father of WW, born at Steubenville, Ohio, Feb. 28, 1822, son of Anne Adams and James Wilson. Attended Steubenville Academy and Jefferson (now Washington and Jefferson) College, being graduated valedictorian from the latter in 1844. Taught at Mercer, Pa., and then studied at Western Theological Seminary, 1845-46, and Princeton Theological Seminary,

1846-47. Taught at Steubenville Male Academy, 1847-49. Married Janet, or Jessie, Woodrow, June 7, 1849. Licensed by Steubenville Presbytery, 1848; ordained by Ohio Presbytery, 1849. Pastor, Chartier's Church, Pa., 1849-51; Professor of Rhetoric, Jefferson College, 1849-50. Professor of Chemistry and Natural Science, Hampden-Sidney College and stated supply, Walker's Church, Va., 1851-55. Pastor, First Presbyterian Church, Staunton, Va., 1855-57, and of First Presbyterian Church, Augusta, Ga., 1857-70. Professor, Pastoral and Evangelistic Theology, Columbia Theological Seminary, 1870-74. Pastor, First Presbyterian Church, Wilmington, N. C., 1874-85. Professor of Didactic, Polemic, and Historical Theology, Southwestern Presbyterian University, 1885-93. Resident, Columbia, S. C., Richmond, Va., and Princeton, N. J., 1893-1903. Died Princeton, Jan. 21, 1903. D.D., Oglethorpe University, 1857.

JRW was one of the founders of the Presbyterian Church of the Confederate States of America, re-named the Presbyterian Church in the United States in 1865, and commonly referred to as the southern Presbyterian Church. He was Permanent Clerk of the General Assembly, 1861-65; Stated Clerk, 1865-98; and Moderator, 1879-80. See "Memorial Address Delivered before the General Assembly of 1886 by Joseph R. Wilson, D.D. . . . ," Columbia (S. C.) *Southern Presbyterian*, Aug. 19, 1886, for JRW's reminiscences of the first General Assembly of the southern Presbyterian Church. Theologically, JRW was in the mainstream of nineteenth-century Presbyterian orthodoxy, scholasticism, and pietism. He was noted as a learned and powerful preacher, widely read in political as well as theological questions. Two of his sermons are Joseph R. Wilson, D.D., *Mutual Relation of Masters and Slaves as Taught in the Bible, A Discourse Preached in the First Presbyterian Church, Augusta, Georgia, on Sabbath Morning, Jan. 6, 1861* (Augusta, Ga., 1861); and his moderatorial sermon in 1880, printed in the Wilmington *North Carolina Presbyterian*, May 21, 1880.

JRW was easily the most important influence on the development of WW's character, education, and thought. The letters printed in this and following volumes reveal the relationship between father and son in vivid detail.

² Janet E. Woodrow, mother of WW, born in Carlisle, Eng., Dec. 20, 1830, daughter of the Rev. Thomas Woodrow and Marion Williamson. Middle name unknown. Often called Jessie and sometimes Jeanie. She moved with her family to New York and Canada in 1835-36, and from Canada to Chillicothe, Ohio, in 1837. Attended the Female Seminary in Chillicothe and married JRW on June 7, 1849. Died April 15, 1888. Her love and concern for WW, along with details of family life, are revealed in her letters printed in this and subsequent volumes.

³ The Rev. Thomas Woodrow, grandfather of WW, born Paisley, Scotland, 1793. M.A., University of Glasgow. Pastor, Annetwell Street Congregational Church, Carlisle, Eng., 1820-35. Married Marion Williamson, who died in 1836; married Isabella Williamson. Moved to America with family in 1835-36, preaching in Poughkeepsie, N. Y., and Brockville, Canada, 1836-37. Pastor, Presbyterian Church, Chillicothe, Ohio, 1807-48; Worthington, Ohio, Presbyterian Church, 1849-57; Nicholasville, Ky., Presbyterian Church, 1857-61; Scioto Presbyterian Church, Columbus, Ohio, 1862-65. Retired, 1866-77. Died, April 25, 1877.

⁴ James Wilson, grandfather of WW, born near Strabane in northern Ireland, Feb. 20, 1787. Migrated to Philadelphia, 1807. Married Anne Adams, Nov. 1, 1808. Worked on Philadelphia *Aurora*, 1807-15. Moved in 1815 to Steubenville, Ohio, to assume editorship of *Western Herald and Steubenville Gazette*. Active as Democrat in Ohio politics, serving several terms in Ohio General Assembly and as associate judge of Court of Common Pleas. Became a Whig in 1840. Died Oct. 17, 1850.

⁵ Marion Williamson Wilson, sister of WW, born Chartier's Manse, Pa., Oct. 20, 1851. Little is known of her life until her marriage to the Rev. Anderson Ross Kennedy Oct. 29, 1872. Died in Batesville, Ark., Aug. 14, 1890, three months after the death of her husband. For further details, see note on A. R. Kennedy, p. 66.

⁶ Annie Josephine Wilson, sister of WW, born Hampden-Sidney College, Va., Sept. 8, 1853. Married George Howe, M.D., of Columbia, S.C., in 1876. Died Sept. 16, 1916.

⁷ For additional evidence that WW may have been born on Dec. 29, 1856, see JWW to WW, Dec. 29, 1877.

⁸ Joseph R. Wilson, Jr., brother of WW, born Augusta, Ga., July 20, 1867. A.B., Southwestern Presbyterian University, 1888; married Kate Wilson, 1892. Editor, Clarksville (Tenn.) *Leaf-Chronicle*, 1895-1904; on staff of the *Nashville Banner*,

Drawing on inside front cover in John Brocklesby, *Elements of Physical Geography* (Wilson House, S Street, Washington). There is a different line-up on the inside back cover of this book and a diagram of a baseball diamond on the front cover.

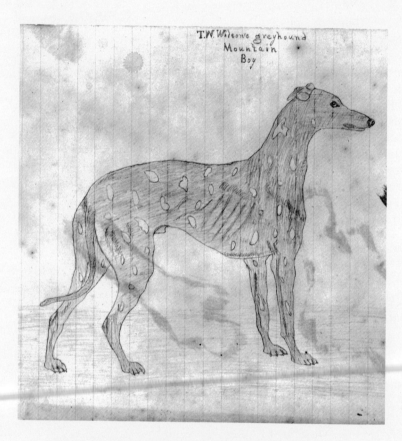

Drawing on loose page in John Brocklesby, *Elements
of Physical Geography* (Wilson House).

1904-13. Executive, United States Fidelity and Guaranty Co., Baltimore, Md., 1913-21, and of Maryland Casualty Co., Baltimore, Md., 1921-27. Died Feb. 26, 1927.

Janet Woodrow Wilson to Thomas Woodrow

My dear Father,   Staunton Va. April 27th 1857
. . . Since the birth of our little son (who is now nearly four months old) I have had very little leisure for writing until within the last month—and I have only been waiting till I could feel sure that you have gotten settled in your home in Kentucky, so that I could address my letter there. . . . The boy is a fine healthy fellow. He is much larger than either of the others were—and just as fat as he can be. Every one tells us, he is a *beautiful* boy. What is best of all, he is just as *good* as he can be—as little trouble as it is possible for a baby to be. You may be sure Joseph is very proud of his fine little son—though he used to say daughters were so much sweeter than sons. . . . Our boy is named *"Thomas Woodrow"*—Your affectionate daughter[1]   Jeanie Wilson

ALS (WP, DLC).
[1] The elipses in this and other letters not written by WW indicate parts omitted because they shed no important light on WW.

Scrapbook of Miscellaneous Items

Inscribed on front flyleaf (WWhw):   [c. 1872-74]
    "Thomas Woodrow Wilson   Columbia South Carolina"
Followed by WWsh, transcript of which reads:
    "Thomas W. Wilson, Wilmington, North Carolina. Phonographer to be. Graham's system above all others, no comparison in my estimation. Munson's[,] Pitman's[,] humbugs—Thomas W. Wilson"[1]

Contents:
    (a) Newspaper clippings, news stories and illustrations *re* sporting events (such as regattas, intercollegiate rowing contests, and horse racing), ships, and nautical scenes. One section with heading, "Navy Department," with pictures of British, French, and American warships.
    (b) Clippings from *The Student's Journal*.
    (c) Originals of letters and postcards (mostly in Graham shorthand) from Andrew J. Graham and Joseph F. Snipes to WW, 1873-75, pasted in scrapbook.
    (d) Clippings of articles on "Phonography" (with WWhw and WWsh marginal notes) from *Frank Leslie's Boys' and Girls' Weekly*, XIII-XIV (Nov. 23, 1872-Oct. 11, 1873).

(WP, DLC).
[1] See the editorial note below for information about Andrew J. Graham, Joseph F. Snipes, and WW's practice of Graham shorthand.

EDITORIAL NOTE
WILSON'S STUDY AND USE OF
SHORTHAND, 1872-92

AN admirer of President Wilson's prose style once asked him to reveal the secrets of his technique of writing. "I begin," Wilson replied, "with a list of topics I want to cover, arranging them in my mind in their natural relations—that is, I fit the bones of the thing together; then I write it out in shorthand. I have always been accustomed to writing in shorthand, finding it a great saver of time. This done, I copy it on my own typewriter, changing phrases, correcting sentences, and adding material as I go along."[1]

This statement stresses Wilson's lifelong interest in shorthand, which may be said to have begun with his discovery of a series of articles by Joseph F. Snipes, a stenographic law and news reporter of New York City. The first of these, which were based almost entirely on Andrew J. Graham's[2] *Hand-Book of Standard or American Phonography*, appeared in the November 1872 issue of *Frank Leslie's Boys' and Girls' Weekly*. That Wilson's interest in this series was immediate and sustained is evidenced by his pasting forty-six of these articles in one of his scrapbooks[3] and by his initiation of a correspondence with Snipes in August 1873 when Wilson was only sixteen.[4]

Snipes, who recommended to his readers certain "new departures" to improve the Graham system, was an enthusiastic advocate of the new system. It was, he said, beautiful, provided mental discipline and training, and would yield a "pecuniary profit." Perhaps it was the compactness and beauty of Graham shorthand, as described by Snipes, or even its aura of the unusual, that aroused Wilson's interest. But it is more likely that the practical advantages of becoming an expert phonographer appealed to him most. "To save time is to lengthen life," is a maxim that he wrote in the front of one of his shorthand books. He also put it (in shorthand) at the center of the rather elaborate illustration he drew for the heading of the shorthand diary he kept while a student at Princeton.[5]

It is not possible to determine how much time Wilson devoted to the study of shorthand before he entered Davidson College in the autumn of 1873, but his interest was keen enough in August of that year to

[1] Ida M. Tarbell, "A Talk with the President of the United States," *Collier's*, LVIII (Oct. 28, 1916), 6.

[2] Andrew Jackson Graham (1830?-1894) was an American shorthand reporter who developed a modified form of phonography, the phonetic system of shorthand devised in the 1830's by the Englishman Isaac Pitman. Graham, who was most active between 1866 and 1894, popularized his system by publishing periodicals and textbooks. He claimed that his "Standard Phonography" was superior to Pitman's "Old Phonography" mainly because of its more accurate representation of vowel sounds. Although his son-in-law, Chandler Sexton, continued for a time to carry on Graham's business after his death, Graham shorthand began to lose ground rapidly in the early twentieth century to the more cursive Gregg system. Now almost extinct, it is still used by a few stenographers and reporters.

[3] See scrapbook described immediately above. Henceforth all MSS cited in this Editorial Note, unless otherwise indicated, are to be found in WP, DLC.

[4] Snipes to WW, Aug. 9, 1873.

[5] See illustration on p. 131.

prompt him to question Snipes about how certain words should be written in shorthand.[6] Later in the same month, he placed an order for
Graham's *Hand-Book*, a basic textbook that set forth in detail the fundamental principles of Graham's Corresponding Style and also included
a short section on the briefer, more difficult, Reporting Style. That Wilson soon began to exhibit signs of progress can be inferred from a letter
he received from Snipes. It assured him that his shorthand was "easy
to read."[7]

Despite all his eagerness and diligence, Wilson did not master the
Graham system in one year. The pressures of school work and partici-

A Page of Wilson's Early Shorthand Practice

[6] Snipes to WW, Aug. 9, 1873.
[7] Snipes to WW, Aug. 29 and Sept. 10, 1873.

pation in extracurricular activities at Davidson College probably allowed him little time for the study of shorthand. In the shorthand draft of a letter to John W. Leckie, his roommate at Davidson (c. July 4, 1875), there is an indication that there were lapses in his practice of shorthand: "The great mistake that I made was that I had to commence over again every time because I did not stick to what I learned."

Eventually, however, Wilson did find the time to acquire a proficiency in shorthand. The opportunity came when his parents decided not to send him back to Davidson but to keep him out of college for a year, mainly to prepare him for Princeton. Wilson was free from the demands of a formal school routine during the fifteen months between June 1874 and September 1875. He spent part of his time studying such basic subjects as Greek, Latin, and mathematics. He also indulged his taste for adventure by reading such books as Scott's *The Pirate* and wandering along the banks of the Cape Fear River. This still left him time for studying and practicing his shorthand.

His longhand notation on the flyleaf of his copy of Graham's *Hand-Book*[8] marks the beginning of a period of self-imposed drill: "Recommenced July 17/74." And the shorthand marginal notes which he wrote in this book indicate that he systematically subjected himself to a rigorous routine. The transcript of one of these is: "Read each of the following exercises three times, copy them twice. Except when a page then do not copy them at all.—Thomas W. Wilson." Another reads: "Write each of the following exercises three times if not over a page long. When over that, for one page and a half, twice; for over page and a half, once." One has only to look in his notebooks for July, August, and September 1874, to see how faithfully he applied his rules when he copied twenty-five exercises from Graham's *Hand-Book*.

That he was well advanced in his study of shorthand by August 1874 is indicated by his placing an order for Graham's *Second Standard Phonographic Reader*, a manual of instruction for students who might want to acquire a detailed knowledge of the Reporting Style.[9] And a little later he wrote in one of his notebooks: "Commenced the corresponding style on July 17th and finished it on Sept. 9th 1874."[10] At about the same time, he subscribed to a new Graham periodical, *The Student's Journal*, which, in addition to proclaiming the merits of Graham shorthand, carried articles on such varied subjects as literature, music, philology, hygiene, and bibliography. He also sent for issues of *The Standard-Phonographic Visitor*, a Graham publication that had been discontinued in 1871.[11]

By October 1874 Wilson seems to have been concentrating on the more difficult Reporting Style with the hope of increasing his speed. On one page of his copy of the *Second Reader*[12] he copied in shorthand a portion of a letter from Graham urging him not to be content with writing a page of that book "once or twice" but to "write it from reading . . . *50 to 100 times*." The Reporting Style differs from the Cor-

[8] WW's copy, published by Graham in 1858, is in his library at DLC.
[9] Graham to WW, Aug. 15, 1874.
[10] Entry in WW's notebook described at Sept. 29, 1873.
[11] Graham to WW, Sept. 7 and 16, 1874.
[12] WW's copy, published by Graham in 1861, is in his library at DLC.

responding Style in its (1) omission of vowel symbols, (2) greater emphasis on the position of shorthand outlines in relation to a base line, (3) use of a greater variety of word-signs and contractions, and (4) more frequent resort to "phrasing," the representation of two or more words by an unbroken outline.

Wilson's enthusiasm for Graham shorthand did not wane during the winter of 1874-75. His letter to Graham in the January issue of the *Student's Journal* tells of his admiration for "Standard Phonography" and of his having memorized "lists of reporting word-signs," probably those in the 1858 edition of the *Hand-Book*.

Wilson spent a considerable amount of time copying into his notebooks shorthand articles from the fifth volume of *The Visitor* in April 1875. Among other things, he copied an entire series of articles entitled "Geology," which Graham had had engraved on plates in his Corresponding Style. But rather than copy these exactly as they had been reproduced, he chose to recast them into the Reporting Style. They occupy in his notebook just a little short of fourteen legal-sized pages of closely written shorthand, including his copies of the accompanying illustrations. At the end of this lengthy exercise, he wrote, partly in shorthand: "Finished 4/10/75." At about the same time, he also copied into the same notebook forty-six of Snipes's articles on shorthand, putting all of the comments and directions into the Reporting Style. On April 24, 1875, according to one of his shorthand notations, he completed a shorthand abstract (in the Reporting Style) of thirty-two pages from Richard Chenevix Trench, *On the Study of Words*, which he had studied at Davidson College and would use again as a student at Princeton. His shorthand draft of a letter to Graham, written near the end of the same month, gives additional evidence of how deeply engrossed he had become. "I am spending all the time I have to spare," he wrote, "and more too I am afraid, on the study of Phonography and am now pretty deep in the Reporting Style." Confident that he could "already write the Corresponding Style with considerable ease," he asked Graham to consider giving him private lessons in shorthand during the summer vacation following his first year at Princeton. Graham excused himself on the ground that he was too busy.[13]

During the spring of 1875 Wilson also used the Reporting Style to copy into another notebook a number of articles from *The Student's Journal*, being careful to choose those that interested him most. A large portion of these were on the uses of shorthand and techniques of writing it, but others were on such varied subjects as "Self-Deception," "The Poet Moore," "A Novelty in Color-Printing," and "Objects of Interest in Constantinople." He also copied the shorthand exercises in Graham's *Second Reader*, all of which were already in the Reporting Style. His own shorthand notations at the end of each section suggest a conscious effort on his part to increase his speed in shorthand. For instance, he wrote at the end of a selection entitled "The Infallibility of the Church": "1122 words about six minutes work for a good reporter. 5/1/75. Thomas W. Wilson." And when he finished copying these exercises, he wrote at the end of the last one: "3,468 words about 17 minutes work for a

13 Graham to WW, April 30, 1875.

good reporter. Copy finished 5/26/75. Total number of words in Second Reader 26,192, making about 200 hours [*sic*] and 4 minutes work for a reporter."

Regardless of whether Wilson meant to write "200 hours" or "20 hours," which is more likely, the copying of these exercises required a great deal of self-discipline and probably would have been very onerous but for the clearly defined goal he had in mind. "Phonography," he wrote about the time he finished this long stint, "will be of great use to me in college. Expect to be a good reporter by the end of the summer."[14]

He did indeed make good use of his shorthand at Princeton, as can be seen from an examination of the large quantity of class notes, nearly all in shorthand, which he wrote between September 1875 and May 1879. A large proportion of these, it is true, are in outline form or in elliptical sentences, but he seems often to have recorded verbatim, or nearly so, the words of his professors. Of his Princeton classroom notes still extant, those taken in Professor Theodore W. Hunt's English course on October 16, 1875, are the earliest. His notes for this lecture on oratory consist mostly of short sentences and should not be considered a verbatim record. Compared with some that he wrote during his senior year, when he had become more proficient in note-taking and had more meaty fare than that offered by Hunt, they are rather sketchy. For example, he seems to have tried to preserve as much as possible the important parts of the lecture delivered by Professor Lyman Atwater on November 1, 1878, which dealt with such questions as papal infallibility and the reading of the Bible in public schools. On the other hand, he was content to put down in outline and elliptical form only the substance of Professor James O. Murray's lecture on Wordsworth, May 14, 1879.

While a student at Princeton, Wilson continued on a larger scale his practice of writing shorthand marginal notes in his books, mostly in those which were not required reading. He obviously intended many of these marginalia to serve merely as jogs to his memory. But there were others of a more critical nature, often very lengthy, showing approval or disagreement.

His fondness for reading and eagerness to develop a felicitous prose style may account for his beginning in February 1876 an *Index Rerum*, a commonplace book into which he copied, mostly in shorthand, selections from his reading. And, emulating Samuel Pepys, he commenced on June 3, 1876, a shorthand diary, the most important document now extant relating to his undergraduate years.[15] The first part of this diary —consisting of twenty-four pages of closely written shorthand, averaging thirty-two lines to a page—he kept without a break until November 23, 1876. On this day he discontinued it "for want of time" but later resumed it sporadically during 1877 and 1878.

What eventually proved to be, in the light of Wilson's future career, a more practical application of his shorthand than the writing of class notes and the keeping of a diary was his drafting of a speech and an essay. The draft of the speech, entitled "The Union," is crude both in

<hr/>

[14] WW to Leckie, May 28, 1875.
[15] WW wrote this diary in ink but most of his many shorthand notes were written with sharp, hard lead pencils.

organization and phraseology. But the draft of the essay, "William Earl Chatham," written during his junior year, is similar enough in its text to the version of it published in the *Nassau Literary Magazine* to be considered a good working copy. Both of these drafts are significant because they are in extended form rather than in elliptical or outline form. Also he made shorthand outlines of two speeches in one of his pocket notebooks:[16] one entitled "Independent Conviction," the other "Thomas Carlyle." These shorthand notes represent all that has been preserved of these two speeches that he wrote during the summer of 1877.

There is extant no shorthand draft of Wilson's article, "Cabinet Government in the United States," but it is possible that he attempted one. When this essay was near completion in the latter part of his senior year, his father advised him how to employ his shorthand to the best advantage as a drafting tool, as follows:

"You are perhaps correct in thinking that long-hand writing is more favorable than shorthand, to composition which ought, like a tree, to grow rather than, like a house to be built. You should use your shorthand as a rapid limner rather than a filler-in of details. . . . When you first are studying a given subject, place it upon paper in shorthand:— then make no direct use of that, but, quitting it altogether, commence afresh in long-hand as if you had not previously written at all. The one operation would give you the advantage of rapid and connected *study* —the other that of slow and connected expression."[17]

This suggests that Woodrow Wilson had tried at first to draft his article in shorthand and afterwards had written to his father about the disappointing results. This, of course, is conjectural, but he did write in shorthand the revision of a few sentences on the back of the envelope of a letter from his father. In any event, Joseph Ruggles Wilson's advice is significant even though his son eventually used his shorthand in ways never envisaged by his father.

There is no certain evidence that Wilson made it a practice to draft letters in shorthand during his undergraduate years. There is extant only one well-composed shorthand draft of a letter he wrote during this period: the one to his classmate Robert Harris McCarter on "originality."[18] But we do know that in later years he made extended shorthand drafts of letters that required special care in the choice of words. There are in his papers six of these written in 1883: one to Professor Atwater and another to President James McCosh of Princeton, asking them to recommend him for graduate work at The Johns Hopkins University; three to close friends—Robert Bridges, Hiram Woods, and Richard Heath Dabney; and, adding a romantic touch, one to his future wife, Ellen Louise Axson.

Insofar as the editors have been able to make textual compari-

16 By the time WW entered Princeton, he had formed the habit of carrying pocket notebooks in which he jotted notes in shorthand, as well as in longhand. He included such items as quotations from books and articles, sometimes even short drafts of letters.
17 JRW to WW, Feb. 25, 1879.
18 WWsh draft of letter to McCarter, c. July 18, 1877.

*Wilson's Shorthand Draft of a Letter to Robert Harris McCarter,
c. July 18, 1877*

sons, they have found the shorthand drafts to be very similar in content, mode of expression, and sentence structure to the recipients' copies of these letters. Although only a comparatively few of these extended shorthand drafts of letters written before 1892 have been preserved, they are enough to indicate that Wilson continued to use his shorthand in this manner from time to time. It seems safe also to assume that there were other drafts of his letters that were either destroyed or misplaced.

Wilson, while a student at the Law School of the University of Virginia in 1879-80, continued his practice of writing classroom notes in shorthand. His two sets of notes for Professor Stephen O. Southall's courses on international and constitutional law, averaging slightly over six hundred words per page when transcribed, are neatly arranged with brief topical notes in Wilson's longhand in the lefthand margins. For some of these lectures Wilson's notes are very brief. In one instance he was content to put down merely a quotation from Edmund Burke with a few prefatory comments.[19] But other lectures did not receive such cavalier treatment. Such a one was the tenth in Constitutional History, delivered March 9, 1880, in which Southall set forth his reasons for believing that the Constitution of the United States was formed by the people of the several states, not by the whole people. Wilson's notes on

[19] Lecture Seventeen, c. April 8, 1880, on constitutional provisions for suffrage qualifications.

this lecture, which he put down in complete sentences, run to approximately 850 words. It was undoubtedly a live subject to the young man who had been reared in the South during the Civil War and Reconstruction. Less interpretive, but in the end more significant, were Southall's lectures on international law in which he discussed such subjects as the right of intervention, the nature of treaties, and the rights of neutrals—questions that the future President of the United States would have to face eventually. However dry they may have seemed to him then, he took rather full notes on them. His notes for the lecture on treaties run to almost eight hundred words.

Much more significant in relation to Wilson's later careers as educator, historian, and statesman are the classroom notes that he kept for his graduate courses at The Johns Hopkins University, where he specialized in history and political economy from September 1883 to June 1885. These cover Herbert Baxter Adams's courses in the Sources of American Colonial History, European Constitutions, the History of Politics, and Modern Constitutions; Richard T. Ely's, in Political Economy, Commerce, Administration, and Finance; and George Sylvester Morris's, in the Philosophy of the State. For the course Wilson took under G. Stanley Hall, Professor of Psychology and Pedagogics, there remain only the notes for four lectures. Missing entirely from the Wilson Papers in the Library of Congress are his classroom notes for the course on English constitutional history taught by John Franklin Jameson, who in time became an outstanding historian and Wilson's close friend. Also unaccounted for are any of the shorthand notes he might have made in the regular meetings of Adams's celebrated Friday evening Historical Seminary, which he occasionally served as secretary. The absence of these, however, is partially compensated by the preservation of the shorthand notes he wrote in the course on the Sources of American Colonial History, which was actually a weekly "extra session" of Adams's regular Historical Seminary.

These notes made at The Johns Hopkins University are unusually brief at times, often written in outline and elliptical form. We may account for this in part by recalling that graduate students often write rather sketchy classroom notes. But one should also remember that Wilson's high degree of sophistication probably made him more selective in his note-taking than he had been at Princeton and the University of Virginia.

Nevertheless, these shorthand classroom notes furnish clues as to the kind and quality of the teaching at The Johns Hopkins during Wilson's graduate years. They may also help to explain why Wilson at first complained that Adams was permitting his students to starve "on a very meagre diet of ill-served lectures" but later hailed him as "a captain in the field of systematic organized scholarship," whose work with doctoral candidates "set the pace for university work in history throughout the United States."[20] One can only wish that Wilson had regularly put into his shorthand notes the "prolegomena" on current topics of

20 WW to Ellen Axson, Feb. 17, 1884, WC, NjP; Richard T. Ely, "A Sketch of the Life and Services of Herbert Baxter Adams," *Herbert Baxter Adams, Tribute of Friends* (Baltimore, 1902), p. 46.

public and academic interest with which Adams often prefaced his lectures, and that he had kept a fuller record of the seminar reports of his fellow students.

Apparently Wilson found much substance in the lectures of George Sylvester Morris on the Philosophy of the State. His shorthand notes for this course are fuller, on the whole, and consist of more complete sentences than the notes he made for the lecture courses of Adams and Ely. The following extract from the transcript of Wilson's notes covering a lecture on Hobbes, delivered on October 29, 1884, gives the impression of being the exact words Morris uttered in the classroom:

"What is the notion of liberty that is involved in a mechanical conception of the State as developed by Hobbes? It is a negative conception, a purely ephemeral conception, not substantial. What does 'substantial' liberty mean? That is the necessary conception with which to start. It consists in the absence of any authority or regular power over the individual to do as he likes. It is a state in which the law of man has no law. Every man having a right to all things and being judge of the means by which he may secure all things. Freedom, so far as it exists, is freedom from some extraneous power or authority."

Wilson left The Johns Hopkins in June 1885 and began his teaching career at newly established Bryn Mawr College three months later. With this change in role, he sought to use his shorthand to prepare his classroom lectures, even though his classes were small. Among his papers are shorthand notes for his courses on American, French, and Roman history, along with one set for his course on the Renaissance.

However uninspiring and unprofitable Wilson may have found lecturing to the young women of Bryn Mawr, his shorthand notes (supplemented by others in longhand) indicate that he prepared his courses conscientiously and systematically. He did not compose lengthy formal lectures for the purpose of reading them to his students but usually wrote out in shorthand a summary of about seven hundred words on the topic he planned to discuss. It is quite likely that his chief purpose in writing these shorthand summaries was to organize his thoughts and fix in his mind the essential points he wished to convey.

By the time Wilson began teaching at Wesleyan University, in the autumn of 1888, he may have decided to abandon his method of preparing his academic lectures in shorthand. The one set of his lecture notes that can be exclusively identified with his two years at Wesleyan—"Histories of England and France"—is written partly in longhand and partly on his Caligraph (a typewriter purchased in 1883) in detailed outline form. And most of the academic lectures that he prepared as a Princeton professor were also written in longhand or on his typewriter, shorthand being used only for revision or change of pace. However, for some reason, perhaps for security, he quite often drafted his examination questions in shorthand.

Meanwhile Wilson was also engaged in other activities that gave him an opportunity to use his shorthand. During the years between his graduation from Princeton and his return to his alma mater as a professor in 1890, he had won wide acclaim as the author of *Congressional*

Government, The State, and several articles on politics and government. But he also felt the need "to loosen the joints" of his prose style by writing on purely literary subjects. "I have more than one story," he wrote to his friend Bridges, "longing to be told and no less than a dozen essays on literary subjects struggling towards utterance—some of them partly uttered in *ms.*"[21]

Unpublished manuscripts composed by Wilson during this period suggest that he, like many other successful writers, entertained ambitions never fully realized. In the field of politics and government, for instance, he completed but failed to get published a long article on French politics and an extended essay, "Government by Debate," parts of which he finally incorporated into *Congressional Government.* Among these unpublished literary remains are such items as a short story entitled "The World and John Hart" and an essay, "The Eclipse of Individuality," both of which were rejected by the *Atlantic Monthly* in 1887.

Anyone who examines these and other Wilson manuscripts of this period will not have to strain his imagination to visualize how he worked to prepare drafts and revised copies of articles, short stories, and books. Some of these, like "Government by Debate," he first drafted in longhand and then copied in his legible hand for submission to publishers. Others, like *Congressional Government,* he first drafted in longhand and then typed on his Caligraph. In the case of *The State,* however, part of his preliminary work does not fit into this pattern. During 1887 and 1888 he drafted, mostly in shorthand, a set of lectures for a course on political science at Bryn Mawr College, but there are certain indications that he might have intended this work to aid him in writing this book. Though this manuscript consists of fifty-two pages of shorthand (a considerable number of which are only partially filled), it should not by any means be considered an extended draft.[22]

Not long after his return to Princeton, he began writing *Division and Reunion,* a volume in the *Epochs of America* series under the editorship of Albert Bushnell Hart of Harvard University. The method he used in writing this, his third book, is important, for the evidence is conclusive that he first drafted in extended form most, if not all, of it in shorthand. Why he decided to depart from his usual practice of writing the first drafts of a work of this kind in longhand is a question that cannot be answered with certainty now, but it is likely that he sought to ease the pressures of a heavy load of teaching, lecturing, and writing by a greater use of his shorthand.

The study of two basic documents, in conjunction with a few of his personal letters, makes it possible to trace with reasonable certainty the steps Wilson employed in the writing of *Division and Reunion.* The first of these documents, in reality Wilson's first draft, consists of thirteen chapters of an extended draft, numbered nine through twenty-one, and totals 114 pages of closely-written shorthand. Originally it consisted of twenty-one chapters, probably all in shorthand, but the first

21 WW to Bridges, Nov. 5, 1887, WC, NjP.
22 The dating of this MS is made possible by two composition dates: one on p. 3, "10/14/87"; the other partially in sh on the verso of p. 52, "lectures completed May 31, 1888."

eight are missing. The second of these documents is Wilson's Caligraph typescript, the draft that went to Hart for editing and later to the publisher, Longmans, Green and Company. On it are both Hart's editorial changes and the printers' marks, including the usual ink smudges.

Wilson's method of composition, briefly described, was first to make a detailed shorthand draft of each chapter, each full page of which averaged about 650 words. Then from his shorthand draft he made a Caligraph typescript, which became his unrevised second draft, although he referred to it in his letters as his first draft. When he finished this second draft, in the autumn of 1892, he found that he had a typescript of approximately 575 pages. Consequently he proceeded to cut it by eighty pages in order to bring it closer to the limit set by the publisher.[23] This reduction he was able to make by a judicious use of scissors and paste and a certain amount of retyping. This revised second draft, or printer's copy, still bears in some parts the marks of the pagination Wilson used for the longer, unrevised draft.

The Last Page of Wilson's Shorthand Draft of a Chapter in DIVISION AND REUNION

Of the extant thirteen chapters of the first draft of *Division and Reunion*,[24] the last eight bear Wilson's composition dates showing that he wrote chapters fourteen, fifteen, and sixteen in July 1892, and chapters seventeen through twenty-one in August of the same year, when he was pushing hard to have a finished draft by early October. Other notations on his shorthand draft provide a basis for estimating the size of his unrevised second draft: in most instances he recorded as he progressed

[23] WW to Hart, Oct. 25, 1892, TCL, RSB Coll., DLC.
[24] The env. containing the extant chapters of this WWsh draft (WP, DLC) bears the WWhw notation: "Epoch 9– 1st MSS."

the total number of pages in his typescript, as well as the number of typed pages each shorthand chapter made when transcribed. Thus the editors have been able not only to estimate that each full page of short-hand (written on 5″ x 8″ pages) made approximately 3.4 pages of type-script, or approximately 650 words; but also that Wilson's unrevised second draft amounted to about 575 pages of typescript, thus confirming Wilson's statement that he cut about eighty pages from his unrevised second draft.[25]

For some unaccountable reason, Wilson wrote no composition dates at the end of chapters nine through thirteen. But he did indicate at the end of chapter twelve that his typescript had reached 308 pages; and at the end of chapter thirteen, 328 pages. Since he wrote to Bridges, on September 22, 1891,[26] that during the preceding summer he had finished "something over three hundred pages of mss." of Division and Reunion, we can safely assume that chapters nine through twelve were written in the summer of 1891, thus leaving in doubt only the year that chapter thirteen was drafted.

Wilson, in his correspondence with Hart, made no mention of his shorthand draft but more than once referred to his unrevised typescript as his first draft. Not having mentioned his shorthand draft in his earlier letters, he may have decided not to refer to it at all in order to avoid making a lengthy explanation to Hart, who was of a rather inquisitive nature. This is probably the reason for his qualifying his reference to his unrevised typescript in his letter to Hart, August 24, 1892, when he called it "in a sense my first draft."[27]

It is noteworthy that this extended shorthand draft of Division and Reunion represents a radical departure by Wilson from the advice of his father that shorthand for literary composition should be a "rapid limner rather than a filler-in of details." But the chief significance of this first example of Wilson's drafting in shorthand on an extensive scale is that he had reached a point in his development of this particular skill where he could draft in detail with rapidity and at the same time produce a prose with a certain amount of literary quality. His shorthand had become a more flexible and effective instrument—one that would stand him in good stead in the years ahead.

[25] The typescript, or printer's copy, is in WP, DLC, and totals 498 pages.
[26] WC, NjP.
[27] TCL, RSB Coll., DLC.

Notebook and Exercise Book

Inscribed on cover (WWhw):   [c. Jan. 5, 1873-c. Feb. 11, 1875]
    "Note, Exercise book &c.
       Thomas W. Wilson   Columbia, So. Ca."
Inscribed on front flyleaf (WWhw):
    "Thomas W. Wilson   Columbia, South Carolina"

Contents (all in WWhw unless otherwise noted):
    (a) Notes, "Programme for tomorrow," printed at Sept. 1, 1873.
    (b) List of furniture for WW's room at Davidson College, printed at Sept. 4, 1873.

(c) Outline of four-year course at Davidson College, printed at Sept. 1, 1873.

(d) Notes for letters, printed at Nov. 18 and Dec. 5, 1873.

(e) Memorandum about the vessels of "Her Britannic Majesty's Flying Squadron. Commander in chief, Vice-Admiral Lord Thomas W. Wilson, Marquis of Huntington."

(f) Lists of Graham shorthand books desired, or already owned by him, printed at Aug. 1, 1873, and Feb. 11, 1875.

(g) General Orders No. 1,000 for "Royal Lance Guards," printed at Jan. 5, 1873, and Special Orders No. 100, printed at Sept. 1, 1873.

(h) List of officers of "Royal Lance Guards," printed at Aug. 25, 1873.

(i) General Orders No. 1,570 for "Her Majesty's Royal Rifle Brigade," printed at Aug. 28, 1873.

(j) Other general and special orders.

(k) List of officers of the Veteran Lancers, "organized in the year 1750 by Lord Wilson, Duke of Eagleton."

(l) Practice Graham shorthand, some of it possibly written by J. W. Leckie.[1]

(m) Practice arithmetic; Greek and Latin exercises.

(n) List of horses of the Marquis of Huntington.

(o) Descriptions of ships belonging to the Atlantic and Great Western Steamship Line and the operations of the company, "Lord Thomas W. Wilson, Marquis of Huntington, President and owner."

(p) Miscellaneous writing and scribbling, most in WWhw.

(WP, DLC)

[1] John William Leckie of Columbia, S.C., WW's roommate at Davidson College, 1873-74, and a pre-ministerial student. Though of WW's class standing ('78) he was listed as an "eclectic student." For an account of his tragic and violent death in 1877, see JWW to WW, Nov. 5 and c. Nov. 10, 1877, and Annie Wilson Howe to WW, Dec. 20, 1877.

EDITORIAL NOTE
WILSON'S IMAGINARY WORLD

IN childhood and youth most boys dream up imaginary worlds in which they spend many happy hours. Tommy Wilson's environment in Augusta, Columbia, and Wilmington encouraged the boy to spin out the world of his imagination. In these semirural cities life moved at a leisurely pace, and amusements were largely self-devised. Wilson was not taught to read until he was about nine. A premium was thus placed on the fertility of his mind even as it had begun to develop. At the same time, from within his family came lively intellectual stimulation. His mother was a woman of considerable intelligence and many interests, and there was a great deal of reading aloud in the family circle. But most important was his exposure to the flow of thoughts and ideas from his father's wide-ranging and vigorous mind. The letters in this volume reflect this intimate relationship once Wilson was in college; they also reveal something about the storehouse of learning and experience from which the boy's mind had earlier drawn rich nourishment.

Wilson probably began to sketch his imaginary world during his

early teens in Augusta. Unfortunately, no materials have been found
which illustrate his play-world activity during these years. The extant
manuscripts fall in the period 1873-75, when the Wilsons lived in Columbia and Wilmington. There are approximately thirty handwritten
items in the Wilson Papers, scattered among four notebooks and one
scrapbook, representing some of the dream worlds that seem to have
fascinated the boy most. A majority are more than a page in length; a
few run as much as ten pages. Wilson's principal obsession seems to
have been with naval affairs. The longest and most detailed items concern the organization of a naval squadron, a yacht club, and two commercial steamship lines. But there are also about a dozen entries dealing with military units and one list of race horses, "arranged by age and
speed." As the selections printed indicate, Wilson's play world, although
romantic in conception, was constructed with striking realism and me-
ticulous attention to detail. He also took the leading role in each as vice
admiral, commander in chief, lieutenant general, Duke of Eagleton,
Duke of Arlington, and Marquis of Huntington. The commanders of
his vessels and officers of his regiments seem, for the most part, to have
been friends or relatives in Augusta, Columbia, and Wilmington, but
a few bear historical names. Another characteristic is striking: without
exception the organizations are English in structure, probably reflecting Wilson's developing admiration of things British.

There is an interesting connection between this play-world documentation and Wilson's scrapbook of clippings. It includes a large number
of illustrations of warships and other vessels, and many newspaper
stories about ships and yacht racing clipped mainly from British week-
lies and monthlies. Wilson drew some descriptive material from these
and similar articles. The names of several of his yachts were borrowed
from the illustrations. The one manuscript item in the notebooks representing Wilson's interest in horses also has its counterparts in the
many clippings of illustrations and stories on racing at Ascot, Saratoga,
Monmouth and Long Branch in New Jersey, and other prominent
tracks.

The imaginary characters assumed by Wilson in every document described thus far were British. On one occasion, however, he did portray
himself as an American admiral who performed heroic exploits. William Bayard Hale saw this manuscript while he was writing his biography of Wilson in 1911. Since the manuscript seems to have been lost,
Hale's description is worth noting. After mentioning Wilson's youthful
penchant for exercising his imagination, Hale wrote:

"Thus for many months he was an Admiral of the Navy, and in that
character wrote out daily reports to the Navy Department. His main
achievement in this capacity was the discovery and destruction of a
nest of pirates in the Southern Pacific Ocean. It appears that the Government, along with all the people of the country, had been terrified by
the mysterious disappearance of ships setting sail from or expected at
our Western ports. Vessels would set out with the precious freight,
never to be heard from again, swallowed up in the bosom of an ocean
on which no known war raged, no known storms swept. Admiral Wilson
was ordered to investigate with his fleet. After an eventful cruise they

overtook, one night, a piratical looking craft with black hull and rakish rig. Again and again the chase eluded the Admiral. Finally the pursuit led the fleet to the neighborhood of an island uncharted and hitherto unknown. Circumnavigation seemed to prove it bare and uninhabited, with no visible harbor. There was, however, a narrow inlet which seemed to end at an abrupt wall of rock a few fathoms inland. Something, however, finally led the Admiral to send a boat into this inlet— and it was discovered that it was the cunningly contrived entrance to a spacious bay, the island being really a sort of atoll. Here lay the ships of the outlawed enemy and the dismantled hulls of many of their victims. And it may be believed that the brave American tars, under the leadership of the redoubtable Admiral, played a truly heroic part in the destruction of the pirates and the succor of such of their victims as survived."

Unlike others which are found in the Wilson Papers, this was a story with a plot as well as American heroes. In other ways it was very similar, as is indicated by Hale's comment on "the verisimilitude with which the details relating to the great adventure were set forth in the daily 'reports.'" William Bayard Hale, *Woodrow Wilson, The Story of His Life* (Garden City, N. Y., 1912), pp. 44-46.

From a Wilson Notebook

[Jan. 5, 1873]

General Orders—No. 1,000. Sergeant Thomas T. Williams, Sergeant Major, Royal Lance Guards, having retired from the service on account of illhealth, resulting from old age, I hereby, by right of Parliament granted me on the 1st of January 1872, promote Alexander T. J. Evans to the rank of Sergeant-Major, Royal Lance Guards. January 5th 1873.

(Signed) Thomas W. Wilson, Lieutenant-General, Duke of Eagleton, Commander-in-chief Royal Lance Guards.

WWhw entry in notebook described at Jan. 5, 1873. Representative of the many "Orders" which WW drew up for his "Guards."

From the Minutes of Session, First Presbyterian Church

Columbia, S. C. July 5th 1873

Session met at the call of the Moderator in the Church—previous to the services preparatory to the Lords Supper—members present Dr Jos R Wilson[,] Elders Muller, Duffie & Stenhouse[.] The business before Session was to receive applications for church membership. Douglas McKay,[1] Thos W Wilson & Samuel H Simonton[2] presented themselves—(three young men out of the Sunday School & well known to us all,)—& after a free conversation during which they severally exhibited evidences of a work of grace begun in their hearts—were unanimously admitted into the membership of this church. The ordinance of baptism was administered to Mr Douglas McKay who had not been baptised in infancy. . . .

E Stenhouse   Clerk.

Hw entry, First Presbyterian Church, Columbia, S. C., "Session Book, 1847-1874," p. 322. (ScU).
1 One of WW's close friends in Columbia.
2 Another of WW's boyhood friends in Columbia.

Notebook of Miscellaneous Items

[c. Aug. 1, 1873]

Inscribed on front flyleaf (WWhw):
"Thos. W. Wilson, Standard Phonographer, Wilmington, N. C."
Contents:
(a) Index partially in WWhw.
(b) WWsh copies of his letter to Andrew J. Graham, c. April 30, 1875, and Graham's reply, printed at April 30, 1875.
(c) WWsh copies of the letters from Joseph F. Snipes, printed at Aug. 9 and 29, 1873; and of letters from Andrew J. Graham, 1874-75. Two of these are printed at May 18, 1875.
(d) WWhw memoranda of purchases, printed at July 13, 1875.
(e) WWhw lists of expenses at Princeton, Sept. 1875-June 1876, printed at Sept. 7, 1875 and Jan. 10, 1876.
(f) "My Phonographic Library," WWhw list of Graham shorthand books purchased by him, printed at Feb. 11, 1875.
(g) WWsh and WWhw copies of extracts from James Hadley, *Greek Syntax*; exercises written by WW in Greek characters, from Thomas Kerchever Arnold, *Greek Composition*.
(h) WWsh copies of items from Andrew J. Graham's publications (*The Student's Journal, The Visitor*, and *The Phonographic Reader*); also copies or summaries of such items as "Her Britannic Majesty's 'Flying Squadron'" and "The Royal Circumnavigation Steamship Company."
(i) "The Royal United Kingdom Yacht Club," and "Rules and Regulations," printed at July 1, 1874.
(j) WWhw minutes and accounts, "Minutes of the General Assembly for 1875" and "General Assembly in act. with Thomas W. Wilson." WWhw notation, p. 151: "The above copied and sent to Father 1/13/76."
(k) Drawings and scribbling by a child, added after WW's entries.
(l) List of clothing, printed at Sept. 7, 1875.

(WP, DLC). WW ink pagination in addition to penciled pagination in another hand.

From a Wilson Notebook

[c. Aug. 1, 1873]

Books that I desire to send for as soon as possible, i.e. as soon as I can get the money:

1. The Phonographic Dictionary.
2. The First Phonographic Reader.
3. Graham's Reporter's Manual.
4. Large Blank Book for Phonographic, and other, uses.

WWhw entry in notebook described at Jan. 5, 1873.

From Joseph F. Snipes

Dr. Sir: New York, Aug 9th 1873
Your favor of 2d. has been rec'd. Glad you are so much interested in the beautiful study of Short Hand.
The words you desire written are:
Purity, period, variety, Albany, melody, enigma. . . .[1]
When more *advanced* you can write them without any vowels, thus: . . .[2]
Suppose I send you the Instruction book. Price $2.20 postage included.   Very truly   J. F. Snipes

ALS (WP, DLC). Pasted in scrapbook described on p. 5.
  [1] Snipes wrote the shorthand characters beneath each word.
  [2] Here follows Snipes' abbreviated shorthand of the six words referred to in note 1.

Two Items from a Wilson Notebook

August 25th 1873.
List of the officers of the Royal Lance Guards, organized in the year 1750 by Lord Wilson, fifth Duke of Eagleton, Field-Marshall, consisting of 2000 men divided into 20 companys of 100 men each.
Commander-in-chief—Lord Thomas W. Wilson, sixth Duke of Eagleton, Lieutenant-General, Count Schkloffe, Knight of the Gartor, Knight of the Star of India, Knight of Bath, M. P.
Lieutenant-Commander—Lord Douglas McKay, Marquis of Woodstock, Major-General, Knight of the Star of India, Knight of Bath, M. P.
Colonel—Lord George J. Evans, Vicount Montfort, Brigadier-General, Knight of Bath, M. P.
First-Major—Sir Richard Howard, Bart, Knight of Bath, Colonel.
Second Major—Sir Robert Clive, Knight of Bath, Colonel.
1. Captain-Major Alexis Collingwood.
2. Captain-Major George Howe.
3. Captain-Major Charles Howard.
4. Captain-Major Baldwin Lacy.
5. Captain-Major Frank J. Brooke.
6. Captain-Major Howard McAlpine.

7. Captain-Major James Blackwood.
8. Captain-Major Hubert De Filburne.
9. Captain-Major Osborne Wilcox.
10. Captain-Major Walter Wilson.
11. Captain-Major Charles Evans.
12. Captain-Major Edward Caroll.
13. Captain-Major John Cambell.
14. Captain-Major James Campbell.
15. Captain-Major John Harkaway.

This is one of several entries describing in detail naval squadrons and military companies devised by WW in Columbia. Most of the names were those of WW's friends.

General Orders—No. 1,570.   Headquarters, Aug., 28th, 1873.
   (To the officers & men of) Her Majesty's Royal Rifle Brigade, Stationed at York, Yorkshire Co., England. To Colonel James Atwood.
   You are hereby commanded to be at these headquarters with your whole brigade, 1,000 men, on the 10th of September next, with tents and campaigning outfit.
   (Signed) Thomas W. Wilson, Lieutenant-General, Duke of Eagleton, Commander-in-cheif Royal Lance Guards & Royal Rifle Brigade.

WWhw entries in notebook described at Jan. 5, 1873.

From Joseph F. Snipes

Dr Sir: New York, Aug 29 1873.
   Yr favor and enclosure rec'd. today. Book will be sent tomorrow. Wish you success.
   In haste.   Yr friend in Science   J. F. Snipes
Is Columbia built up!
Answer in shorthand [after you have studied sufficiently to write].

ALS (WP, DLC). Pasted in scrapbook described on p. 5.
Portion in brackets transcribed from WWsh copy in notebook described at Aug. 1, 1873.

Student Notebook
                    [c. Sept. 1, 1873]-Mar. 24, 1875
Inscribed on flyleaf (WWhw and WWsh):
   "Thomas W. Wilson, Davidson College North Carolina
   9 Ground Floor   North Wing.[1]
   Lectures on Mathematics by Professor Chas. Phillips of Davidson[2]
   College of North Carolina   Davidson College   Session of 1873-4"

Contents:

(a) Lecture notes on algebra course.

(b) Lecture notes on geometry course.

(c) WWhw notation about taking final exam in Professor Phillips' course, printed at June 18, 1874.

(d) WWsh practice notes copied from the *Standard Phonographic Visitor*, the *Hand-Book of Standard or American Phonography*, *The Student's Journal*, and the *New York Daily Tribune*.

(e) WWhw and WWsh drafts of letter to Joseph F. Snipes, about which see descriptive note to Snipes' letter of Sept. 10, 1873.

(f) WWhw notes and ciphering on algebra problems.

(WP, DLC).

[1] Of Old Chambers, first used as the main building of the College in 1860. It burned on November 28, 1921.

[2] Charles Phillips, born Harlem, N. Y., July 30, 1822. B.A., University of North Carolina, 1841; M.A., same institution, 1844; D.D., same institution, 1868; LL.D., Davidson College, 1876. Tutor in mathematics, Professor of Engineering, and Professor of Mathematics, University of North Carolina, 1844-68, 1875-79. Professor of Mathematics and Engineering, Davidson College, 1869-75. Died May 10, 1889.

Four Items from a Wilson Notebook

Course at Davidson College[,] North Carolina.

Freshman Year. First Term.   [c. Sept. 1,] 1873

Bible,—Old Testament History, Chronology, and Geography.

English.—Fowler's Grammar.

Latin.—Gildersleeve's Grammar; Cicero de Senectute (C & S); Gildersleeve's Exercise book, Course 1st.

Greek.—Hadley's Grammar, throughout course Xenophon's Anabasis, books III and IV (Owen); Composition

Mathematics.—Towne's Algebra.

Second Term.

Bible.—See first term.

English.—Trench on the Study of Words; Harts Composition and Rhetoric, to chapter IV.

Latin.—Cicero de Amicitia (C. S.); Satires & Epistles of Horace (C & S); Composition, II.

Greek.—Xenophon's Memorabilia (Robbin's); Herodotus (Johnson); Composition.

Mathematics.—Algebra; Pierce's Geometry.

Sophomore Year. First Term.

Bible.—New Testament in Greek, Harmony of the gospels.

English.—Hart completed.

English Literature.—Shakspeare's Julius Caes.

French.—Ahn's Method; Otto's Reader.
Latin.—Cicero's Tusculan Disputations (C & S); Exercises, course III.
Greek.—Plato's Apology of Socrates (Tyler); Composition.
Mathematics.—Pierce's Geometry.

Second Term.

Bible.—See first term.
Logic.—Bowen; Lectures.
French.—Reader; Exercises; French Drama.
Latin.—Livy, books XXI and XXII (C. & S); Horace's Odes, Epodes, and Art of Poetry (C & S) Exercises, IV.
Greek.—The Crito of Plato (Tyler); Homer's Iliad (Owen); Composition.
Mathematics.—Trigonometry and its Applications (Lomis).

Junior Year. First Term.

Bible.—New Testament in Greek, Epistles. Evidences of christianity.—Alexander.
Latin.—Cicero de Oratore (Kingsley); Composition.
Greek.—Demostenes on the Crown (Champlin).
Mathematics.—Analytical Geometry.
General Chemistry.—Lectures; Roscoe.

Second Term.

Bible.—See first term.
Rhetoric.—Whately.
Political Economy.—Champlin; Lectures.
Latin.—The Germannia & Agricola of Tacitus, (Tyler); Terence (Davies); Composition.
Greek.—Thucydides (Owen); Greek Drama; Com.
Mathematics.—Diferential & Integral Calculus.
Physics.—Snell's Olmsted.
General Chemistry.—Lectures; Roscoe.

Senior Year   First Term.

Bible.—New Testament in Greek, Epistles.
Mineralogy.—Lectures & specimens.
Practical Chemistry.—Qualitative Analysis.
Metaphysics.—Hamilton (Brown).
Physics.—Rational and Applied Mechanics.
Law.—Constitutional (Townsend); International.
Rhetoric.—Original Speeches.

Second Term.

Bible.—See first term.
Evidences of Christianity.—Butlers Analogy.
Geology.—Lectures; Fossils; Dana.
Practical Chemistry.—Qualitative Analysis.
Astronomy.—Descriptive and Physical.
Metaphysics.—Cousin's True, Beautiful, & Good; Alexander's
Moral Science; Bp. Butler's Sermons.
Rhetoric.—Original Speeches.

Finis.

Special Orders—No. 100.

To the Officers of Her Majesty's Royal Lance Guards.

I've heard lately, much to my displeasure, that some of the junior officers of this regiment have openly violated the rules, not only of the regiment, but also of the service, by appearing in citizen's clothes. Therefore, all the officers of this regiment are warned that if such a breach of disapline is again committed by any officer, or officers, of this regiment, they will immediately be lowered one grade in rank & put under arrest for the space of one month.

(Signed) Thomas W. Wilson, Lieutenant-General, Commanding.

Programme for tomorrow.

September 1st 1873.

Study: First, Chauvenets Geometry; Second, Goodwin's Greek Grammar; Third, Arnold's Greek Prose Composition; Fourth, thoroughly memorize the Forty-second lesson of Joseph F. Snipes' edition of Graham's Phonography, and practice well on it. Next day, September 3rd, study same as above and the Forty-third lesson in Snipes' course, thoroughly, and practice well on it.

To be translated.   Can't translate it.

After you have studied sufficiently to write.[1]

Sept. 4th. [1873]

Inhuman vārious!

Furniture already gotten for room at college: Washstand; Basin; Water Bucket; Study table; Wardrobe; Bookcase. Things that I will be examined on at college. *Virgil; Xenophon's Anabasis;* Algebra & 5 books of Chauvenet; *English Grammar;* Trench on the Study of words; *Hart's Composition & Rhetoric.*

Furniture still needed!

Bed, iron; Wash-tub; Large chair; Looking glass; Desk, small; &c; &c.

WWhw entries in notebook described at Jan. 5, 1873, the fourth entry partly obscured by scribbling.
1 Transcript of WWsh, copied from J. F. Snipes to WW, Aug. 29, 1873.

From Joseph F. Snipes

New York September 10, 1873

Mr. Wilson Columbia South Carolina
Dear Sir

Your letter received. Your book was sent you duly. Hope you have received it by this time. The dictionary costs $4.40 which includes the postage[,] a very valuable book indeed and the best authority on Phonography. The accented syllable governs the position of the sign[,] the rest of the word follows where it will. Your phonography was easy to read.

Reporting Style

The city [Columbia] is building up very fast indeed and there is little or no trace of the fire to be seen now and it is about three times as fine a city as it was before the war. There are some buildings going up on or near the main street which would do great credit to any street in New York except Broadway.

Respectfully   J. F. Snipes

Transcript of shLS (WP, DLC). Pasted in scrapbook described on p. 5. The last paragraph is Snipes' recasting into Graham's reporting style of WW's sh reply in the corresponding style, to Snipes' letter of Aug. 29, 1873. There are also sh and hw drafts in the notebook described at Sept. 1, 1873, item (e).

Student Notebook

[Sept. 29, 1873-Sept. 8, 1874]

Inscribed on cover (WWhw): "Standard Phonography"
Contents (in WWhw unless otherwise noted):

(a) Schedule of freshman class, Davidson College, 1873-74, printed at Sept. 29, 1873.

(b) Sh exercises, Oct. 9, 1873-Sept. 9, 1874, with a memorandum printed at Sept. 9, 1874.

(c) Records of the corresponding secretary, Eumenean Society,[1] 1874-75, printed at May 23, 1874.

(d) Phonography by WW from Graham's Hand-Book, printed at July 17, 1874.

(e) List and prices of furniture in room at Davidson College, printed at Sept. 29, 1873.

(f) List of books to carry home from Davidson, printed at June 1, 1874.

(g) List of officers of the "Royal Lancer Guard and the Royal Dragoon Guards."

(h) Article, "Her Britannic Majestys Squadron 'Flying Squadron,'" printed at April 5, 1874.

(i) Two versions of article, "H. M. S. 'Renown,' flag-ship of H. M. 'Flying Squadron.'"

(j) Third version of article, in loose pages, printed at April 5, 1874.

(k) Practice conjugation of Greek verbs.

(l) Poem, "The Prayer," from the Columbia (S.C.) *Southern Presbyterian*, printed at Nov. 6, 1873.

(m) List of books to be withdrawn from library of Eumenean Society, printed at Nov. 6, 1873.

(n) Lists of the baseball nines of Davidson College, printed at May 1, 1874.

(o) Memorandum reminding WW to beg his father for permission to attend business college after graduation from Davidson, printed at June 1, 1874.

(p) List of correspondents, printed at Jan. 1, 1874.

(q) "Addresses of Ponography," printed at June 1, 1874.

(r) List of clothing brought to Davidson College, printed at Oct. 3, 1873.

(s) Laundry accounts, Sept. 29, 1873-c. June 15, 1874.

(NcDaD).
1 See at Oct. 4, 1873, note 1.

Three Items from a Wilson Notebook

Davidson College, Sept. 29th 1873

Schedule of the Freshman Class,—: 1873-4.

	1st Hour;	2nd Hour;	3rd Hour
Monday	Blake;[1]	Phillips;	Winn.[2]
Tuesday	Richardson;[3]	Phillips;	Anderson[4]
Wednesday	Richardson;	Phillips;	Winn.
Tursday	Richardson;	Winn;	Anderson.
Friday	Richardson;	Winn;	Phillips.

Prices of furniture now in my room:

[c. Sept. 29, 1873]

Wardrobe	4.00	Two chairs	1.00 for [?] paid
Book-case	1.00	Bucket, new,	50
Wash stand	25	" old,	15
Bowl	25		

Memoranda of Clothes Brought.

Oct. 3rd 1873.

Eight pair of Socks.	Twelve Pocket Hankerchiefs.
Three Flannel Shirts.	6 New Pleated Shirts.
Twelve Face Towels.	4 Plain Front Shirts.

One Open Front Shirts.
4 Night Shirts.
4 pair Drilling Drawers.
4 Pair Canton Flannel Drawers.
12 Shirt Collars.
4 Sheets.
3 Pillow Cases.
1 Bed Spread.
2 Curtains.
2 Overcoats.
1 Blue Dress Coat.
1 Black Alpacca Coat.
1 Pair Blue Pants.
1 Blue Vest.

1 Pair Dark Cas. Pants.
1 Grey Summer Suit.
1 Pair Pearl Colored Pants.
1 Black Broad-Cloth Coat.
1 Heavy Grey Sack Coat.
6 Napkins.
1 Pair Heavy High-quartered Shoes.
1 Pair low-quartered Gaiters.
1 Pair High-quartered Gaiters.
1 Pair Heavy Shoes, (Old).
1 Pair Cloth Slippers.
1 Pair Leather Slippers.
(Total 103 pieces.

WWhw memoranda in notebook described at Sept. 29, 1873.
   [1] John R. Blake, Professor of Natural Philosophy and Astronomy and Chairman of the Faculty.
   [2] Paul P. Winn, Adjunct Professor of Languages.
   [3] W. G. Richardson, Professor of Ancient and Modern Languages.
   [4] The Rev. J. Monroe Anderson, Troy Professor of English and Political Philosophy.

From the Minutes of the Eumenean Society[1]

Regular Meeting   Oct. 4th 1873.

The members assembled at the usual hour. Roll called and Messrs. Baird, Craig, Moore, Reedy, G. Smith, T. Whaling and Titcomb were noted absent. Divine blessing was invoked, and minutes of the last Regular Meeting read.

Special business was called for. The names of Messrs. F. J. Brooke, J. W. Leckie, T. W. Wilson, L. M. Hensell, B. H. Rice, H. P. Eagleton, S. Eagleton, R. H. Lapsley, S. E. Bishop, Louis Sharpe, T. Dixon, V. Caldwell, Miller, Stuart, were proposed for membership & were on motion unanimously elected.

Messrs. Baird and Moore were appointed as a com. to escort the gentlemen into the Hall. The Vice President made the request that the members would pay their dues, as the Society was needing the money. It was moved to dispense with the exercises of the morning, seconded. *Lost.*

The President requested the newly elected members to present themselves before the Vice Pres. stand. They were all then with the exception of Mr. Bishop, (who was absent) duly initiated, after hearing a part of the constitution read, and took their seats as regular members. . . . Motion was made to appoint a com. of three to transcribe our constitution, list of Honorary Members, and catalogue of Books in the new books obtained for the purpose. Seconded, carried. Messrs. Bryan, Brooke & S. Wilson were appointed on this com. . . .

Appointments for to-day two weeks are as follows:

Comp,	Select Speaking	Orig' Speaking
McKeown	T. Wilson	G. Smith
McLees,	Williamson	W. Wilson
Norris,		T. Whaling
Ready,		Bryant
D. McQueen		H. Whaling[2]

Hw entry, bound ledger book (NcDaD).

[1] The Eumenean Society, founded in 1837, was one of the two undergraduate debating and literary societies at Davidson College. According to its constitution, it had as its objective "the acquirement of literary knowledge, the promotion of virtue, and the cultivation of social harmony and friendship." In fact, the list of topics for debate indicated a keen interest in political as well as social and cultural affairs. The extracts from the minutes have been chosen not only to reveal the part that WW played, but also to shed light on an important phase of undergraduate life at Davidson College in which WW was involved.

[2] These undergraduates not previously identified were Edwin M. Baird, '75, Samuel E. Bishop, '77, Francis J. Brooke, '77, William S. Plumer Bryan, '75, David B. Bryant, second-year scientific, Robert V. Caldwell, first-year scientific, Thomas B. Craig, '76, Thomas W. Dixon, '77, Horace P. Eagleton, first-year scientific, Samuel E. Eagleton, Jr., '77, Lawrence Hensell, '77, Robert A. Lapsley, '77, Calvin B. McKeown, '74, James A. McLees, '75, Donald McQueen, Jr., '74, Robert M. Miller, Jr., '76, William R. Moore, '74, Alexander E. Norris, '75, Howard Reedy, '75, Bolling H. Rice, '75, Louis Sharpe, first-year scientific, Edward G. Smith, '76, Calvin L. Stewart, '77, Joseph A. Titcomb, '76, Horace M. Whaling, eclectic, John T. C. Whaling, Jr., '76, James L. Williamson, '75, Samuel L. Wilson, '76, William C. Wilson, '75.

Regular Meeting of Eumenean Society

Nov. 1st 1873

Members assembled at ringing of the bell. . . . Appointments for to day two weeks are as follows

Composition	Select Speaking	Orig.
Smith	S. Wilson	McQueen
A. Simpson	T. Whaling	Reedy
W. Simpson	L. Sharpe	Brooke
T. Wilson	H. Reedy	Miller
Titcomb	H. Whaling	Moore
Williamson		Rice
		Mebane

A. E. Norris[1] R. S. pro. tem.

[1] The undergraduates listed above, heretofore not identified, were Leonard A. Simpson, '75, William C. Simpson, eclectic, and Benjamin W. Mebane, '75.

Two Items from a Wilson Notebook   [c. Nov. 6, 1873]

Books to be gotten from the Eumenean Library.

1. *Victories of Wellington and British Armies*—Maxwell, She'f. 50.
2. *Art of Extempore Speaking*—   33.
3. *Letters of the British Spy.*   35.
4. Present College System—   96.
5. Select Speeches—Canning—   56.
6. *Columbian Orator*—   93.

Books still left to be gotten out:

1. Present College System—   96.
2. Select Speeches—Canning—   56.

From the "Southern Presbyterian" of Nov. 6, 1873.

The Prayer.

The way is dark, my Father! Cloud on cloud
Is gathering thickly o'er my head, and loud
The thunders roar above me. See, I stand
Like one bewildered! Father, take my hand,
    And through the gloom
    Lead safely home
      Thy child.

The day goes fast, my Father, and the night
Is drawing darkly down. My faithless sight
Sees ghostly visions, fears a spectral hand.
Encompass me. O Father! Take my hand,
    And from the night
    Lead up to light
      Thy child.

The way is long, my Father, and my soul
Longs for the rest and quiet of the goal;
While yet I journey through this weary land,
Keep me from wandering, Father, take my hand
    Quickly and straight,
    Lead to heaven's gate
      Thy child.

The path is rough, my Father; many a thorn
Has pierced me, and my weary feet—all torn
And bleeding—mark the way; yet Thy command

Bids me press forward. Father, take my hand,
 Then safe and blest,
 Lead up to rest
  Thy child.

The throng is dark, my Father; many a doubt,
And fear, and danger compass me about,
And foes oppress me sore; I cannot stand
Or go alone. O Father! take my hand,
 And through the throng
 Lead safe along
  Thy child.

The cross is heavy, Father; I have borne
It long and still do bear it. Let my worn
And fainting spirit rise to that blest land
Where crowns are given. Father, take my hand
 And, reaching down,
 Lead to the crown
  Thy child.

The Answer.

The way is dark, my child, but leads to light;
I would not always have thee walk by sight;
My dealings now thou canst not understand;
I meant it so, but I will take thy hand,
 And through the gloom
 Lead safely home
  My child.

The way is long, my child, but it shall be
Not one step longer than is best for thee.
And thou shalt know at last, when thou shalt stand
Safe at the goal, how I did take thy hand,
 And quick and straight,
 Led to heaven's gate
  My child.

The path is rough, my child, but oh! how sweet
Will be the rest, for weary pilgrims meet,
When thou shalt reach the borders of that land
To which I lead thee as I take thy hand;
 And safe and blest,
 With me shall rest
  My child.

The throng is great, my child, but at thy side
Thy Father walks. Then be not terrified
For I am with thee—will thy foes command
To let thee freely pass. Will take thy hand
    And through the throng
    Lead safe along
      My child.

The cross is heavy, child, yet there was One
Who bore a heavier for thee—My Son,
My well beloved. For him bear thine, and stand
With him at last, and from Thy Father's hand,
    Thy cross laid down,
    Receive a crown,
      My child.

                              Copied by T. W. Wilson

WWhw entries in notebook described at Sept. 29, 1873.

From the Minutes of the Eumenean Society

                      Regular Debate   November 7th 1873
   House met. Roll called and Messrs. M. Davis,[1] T. Dixon, Mc-
Keown, Mebane, Miller, and McQueen noted absent. Divine blessing was invoked. Minutes read. Special business was called for.
Mr Baird requested that he be granted indulgence in the payment
of his Society dues until Christmas. Motion made and carried that
his request be granted. A request was presented from the ladies of
the village that the meeting next Friday night be suspended to allow the members to attend some charades to be held that night for
the benefit of the Memphis sufferers.[2] Motion to that effect was
made and carried. . . . The question "Was the execution of Mary
Queen of Scotts justifiable?" was debated at some length. The
Committee and House both decided in the negative. Mr Leckie was
fined ten (10¢) cents for talking.
   The question for tonight two weeks reads as follows. "Is the
existence of two great political parties beneficial to a republic."

   [1] Robert M. Davis, '75.
   [2] In August 1873 Memphis, already reeling from smallpox, cholera, and the
"epizootic," an equine malady, was struck by yellow fever. Of the population
of 40,000, all but 15,000 fled. By Thanksgiving, cold weather had ended the
epidemic; but of 5,000 stricken, 2,000 died. See Gerald M. Capers, Jr., *The Biography of a River Town* (Chapel Hill, N.C., 1939), pp. 187-93.

Regular Meeting of the Eumenean Society   November 15th 1873

The meeting was called to order at the usual hour. . . . The Vice Presd't stated that it was his painful duty to prefer the charge of profanity against Mr L. Sharpe. Mr Sharpe being called to answer the charge pled guilty. He then retired and the house proceeded with the trial. The President having put the question to the house, "guilty or not guilty,["] the house decided he was guilty. As it is evident that Mr. Sharpe is trying to break himself of this habit it was moved and carried that the Presd't censure Mr Sharpe lightly. Mr Sharpe was then called in and the Presd't administered the censure lightly. . . . The following fines were imposed, viz Mr. Looney[1] 10 cts for talking, Mr Moore ten cents for spitting. Messrs T. Wilson, Rice and Baird ten cents (10 cts) each for sitting on the rostrum. Mr Mebane twenty (25) five cents for looking at notes while speaking. Mr Latimer[2] seventy five cents (75¢) for absence without excuse and twenty cents (20) for spitting on the floor. . . .

[1] Christopher T. Looney, '77.
[2] Albert G. Latimer, '75.

From a Wilson Notebook

Notes for letters.   Nov. 18th 1873.

The boys' mumps; weather snow; visit to the Anderson's;[1] tableaux; Dr. Howe's[2] letter; Dr. Phillips' mode of teaching, disgusting; Prof. Winn's mode of teaching, programme; the boys whose acquaintance I have made, their looks and manners; Speaking; English Grammar; Mr. Mac; Roll of Freshman class. Health.

Again.   Nov. 21st 1873.

Visit to the Anderson's; tableaux, my keen on Dr. Phillips; speaking; Health; our wrestling & general tuslings;

WWhw memoranda in notebook described at Jan. 5, 1873.
[1] Probably the family of the Rev. J. Monroe Anderson.
[2] The Rev. George Howe, D.D, professor at Columbia Theological Seminary and father of WW's brother-in-law, George Howe, M.D.

From the Minutes of the Eumenean Society

Regular Debate of the Eumenean Society   November 21st 1873

. . . The question for tonight two weeks reads as follows, viz: "Which is the better form of government Republicanism or Limited Monarchy" to discuss which the following gentlemen were appointed

on the Affirmative	on the Negative
Messrs. T. Whaling	Messrs. T. Wilson
Rice	H. Whaling
Brooke	Titcomb
Williamson	S. Wilson
	F. J. Brooke, R. S.

From a Wilson Notebook

[Notes for Letters—*continued*]

Again. Nov. 25th 1873.

The boys whose acquaintance I have made.

Dec. 5th [1873]

How I will have to do if I come home. Breaking of the laws &c. None of the other Columbiads coming. Our laziness this morning. Box last night. How late we sat up. The boys' trick in chapel this morning.

WWhw memoranda in notebook described at Jan. 5, 1873.

From the Minutes of the Eumenean Society

Regular Debate   Decr 5th 1873

The house was called to order at the usual hour by the Vice Presd't. . . . Messrs. M. Davis, Mebane, and T. Dixon were appointed a committee to decide on the debate. The question "Which is the better form of government Republicanism or Limited Monarchy," was then debated. The Committee and House both decided in favor of the Affirmative.

The question for tonight two weeks reads as follows "Ought the Missouri compromise to have been adopted"? . . .

Regular Debate   Decr 12th 1873

The House met at the usual hour. . . . The Vigilance Committee stated that they were instructed by Mr Norris to deney the rumor that he had been intoxicated and asked, in his name, that the Society further investigate the matter. Motion was made to turn the investigation over to the Vigilance Committee. Carried. Motion made to have a Called meeting of the Society next Friday night for the purpose of receiving the Vigilance Committee's report and take action thereon. Carried. . . . Messrs. F. Wilson[1] and Fraser[2] asked the Society to extend the indulgence granted them on their Society dues until the first of Jan'y. Motion to grant their requests was made and carried. . . .

₁ Henry F. Wilson, '77.
₂ Abel M. Fraser, '76.

Called Meeting of the Eumenean Society   Decr 19th 1873
House met at the usual hour. Roll called and Messrs Britt, S. Eagleton, Greer, Titcomb, H. Whaling and Williamson noted absent. The Vigilance Committee reported as follows "We the Vigilance Committee of the Eumenean Society, having investigated Mr Norris's case, find his conduct worthy of the notice of the Society, in that being cognizant of the intemperance of Mr Latimer he failed to report the same" Signed J. E. Fogartie, J. S. Williamson, C. B. McKeown, and A. B. Coit.[1]

The following motion was then made "Whereas there is a misunderstanding of the constitution moved that we drop the whole matter." Motion was carried. Mr Norris asked the Society to lend him twenty dollars ($20.00) until the first of April. Motion made and carried to grant his request. . . .

[1] The undergraduates heretofore not identified were Marion C. Britt, '74, Baxter D. D. Greer, '74, James E. Fogartie, '74, and Albert B. Coit, '75.

From a Wilson Notebook

[c. Jan. 1, 1874]

Correspondants. No. of letters sent to each & rec'd.

		Sent	Received.
1	Father	11111111	1111111
2	Mother.	1111111	1111111
3	Annie.	111	11
4	Marion.	11	11
5	Hattie.[1]	1	
6	Preston.	11	1
7.	Browne.[2]	1	1
8	Josie.[3]	11	1

Ocasional correspondants.

1.	Jessie Bones.[4]		
2.	Douglas McKay.	11	1
3.	Samuel Simonton.		
4.	Fitz W. McMaster.[5]		
5.	Thomas McConnell.[6]		

6. James Taylor.[7]
7. Dr. George Howe, Jr.[8]   1   1
8. Robert D. Perry.[9]
9 Mrs. James W. Bones[10]
10. Mr. Thomas Woodrow, Jr.[11]

WWhw entry in notebook described at Sept. 29, 1873.
[1] Harriet Augusta Woodrow, WW's first cousin, daughter of Thomas, Jr., and Helen Sill Woodrow, of Chillicothe, Ohio.
[2] Probably D. L. Browne of New York City, a practitioner of Graham shorthand.
[3] Joseph R. Wilson, Jr.
[4] Jessie Woodrow Bones, WW's first cousin, daughter of James W. Bones, commission merchant of Rome, Ga.
[5] Fitzwilliam McMaster of Columbia, S. C.
[6] Probably a friend from Columbia.
[7] A friend from Columbia, nicknamed "Judge."
[8] George Howe, Jr., M.D., WW's brother-in-law, husband of Annie Wilson Howe; a physician in Columbia, S. C.
[9] Probably a friend from Columbia, S. C.
[10] Marion Woodrow Bones, maternal aunt of WW.
[11] WW's maternal uncle.

From the Minutes of the Eumenean Society

Regular meeting of the Eumenean Society   Jan. 3rd 1874
House was called to order by the Vice Pres. at the usual hour. . . .
The following appointments were made for two weeks hence

Composition	Select Speaking	Original
Leckie	Looney	Wilson T.
Frierson[1]	Rice	Titcomb
Smith	Simpson W.	Wilson S.
Brearley[2]	Stewart	Wilson F.
Baird	Moore	Williamson . . .

[1] David E. Frierson, '76.
[2] William Brearley, '74.

Regular Debate   January 16th 1874
House convened at the usual hour. . . . The following question was then debated: "Is slavery justifiable?" The Com. decided in favor of the Aff. House, Neg. . . . The following question was then chosen: "Ought Regulus to have returned to Carthage"? . . .

Regular Meeting of the Eumenean Society   Jan'y 31st 1874
House was called to order at the usual hour. Scripture having been read, divine blessing was asked by Mr L. Simpson. . . . The following fines were imposed: Mr Bryan unbecoming position (10¢). Looney same offense (10¢). Messrs Baird & Eagleton talking (10¢) each. Mov[ed] & car[ried] that Messrs Baird & Eagleton

be excused on plea of not talking. Mr Smith talking (10¢). Mov.
& car. that Mr. Bain[1] be allowed to speak. T. Wilson talking (10¢).
Williamson not addressing Prest (10) Bryan, Fraser and Caldwell
not retur[n]ing books (10¢) each. Mr Leckie not returning books
(2) (20¢)

The following Appointments two weeks hence

Comps	Select	Orign
Coit	Eagleton H.	Bryant
Craig	Wilson F.	Caldwell
Baird	Wilson S.	Dixon T.
Looney	Leckie	Bryan
Wilson T.	Sullivan[3]	Rice
Seabrooke[2]	Brearley	Davis P.[4]
		Moore W. R.

B. H. Rice   Rec. Sec.

[1] A visitor, not a student at Davidson.
[2] Josiah M. Seabrook, '77.
[3] James M. Sullivan, '77.
[4] Rufus P. Davis, '74.

Regular Debate   Feby 6th 1874

House convened at the usual hour. . . . The following question
was debated, "Do temperance Societies respecting the use of in-
toxicating liquors produce more good than evil?" After the discussion of which the Com. & House decided in favor of the Aff.

The following question was then chosen for two weeks hence,
"Should our government force poor children to attend the free
schools?"

Aff.	Neg.
Sullivan	Stewart
Wilson T.	Wilson F.
Titcomb	Wilson S.
Moore W. R.	Williamson

B. H. Rice   Rec. Sec.

Regular Debate   Feby. 20th 1874

House assembled at the usual hour. . . . Messrs Brooke, Fraser &
Leckie were appointed to decide on the merits of the discussion.
"Should Government force the education of poor children," was
then discussed. The Committee decided in favor of the Neg, House
Aff. . . .

Called Meeting   Feby. 24th 1874

House having been called to order, roll was called the following
absent: Messrs Davis R., Looney, Mebane, Moore R. The Presd

then stated to the House that Prof. Blake was present and would offer some suggestions relative to the best method of improving the grassplots. Prof. Blake then in a tone of high commendation on the morals of the Society said he deplored our lack of energy in a physical point of view and called the attention of the Society to their lethargy in reference to this point and urged them in a more uniform and earnest manner than heretofore to devote themselves to the improvement of the external as well as internal condition of the Society. He also suggested the efficacy of a committee of three to be appointed to supervise the improvement of the grounds, Library & whatever else pertains to the interest of the Society, invested with authority to note all delinquents of those whom the Society have appointed to perform any duty. It was then moved and carried that the thanks of the House be returned to Prof Blake for his advice. Moved & carried that a committee of three be appointed to confer with Prof. Blake and to propose such plans to the Society as they deem proper. Committee Messrs Fogartie, Davis P. and Mebane.

B. H. Rice   R. Secretary

Called Meeting   March 2nd 1874

House assembled & roll was called. . . . Mr Fogartie asked the House to extend his dues for six weeks which they did, also Mr T. Wilson's dues, for one month.

B. H. Rice   Rec. Sec.

Regular Meeting   March 14th 1874

House assembled at the usual hour. . . . After regular exercises General business was called for. Mr. Dixon proposed to the Society to purchase a book—"Home life in the Bible" stating as one reason for so doing that a young lady was agent for it whose photograph was in his possession and might be seen by any members of the Society desiring to see it. Motion made, second & carried to turn this business, in regard to purchasing the book over to the Exec. Com. The name of Rev. Dr. Woodrow,[1] Columbia, S. C., was proposed for honorary membership. Motion made and carried to elect the gentleman. . . . The Pres. appointed the following Committees.

Query Com.	Vigilance Com.	Light Com.	Stove Com.
Mebane.	Frierson.	Moore S.[2]	Wilson T.
Rice. and	Frazer.	Dixon.	Sharpe.
Bryan.	Stewart.	Caldwell.	Sullivan.
	Seabrook.		
	Titcomb.		

Assistant Librarian—F. Wilson

Appointments for to day two weeks

Composition	Select	Origonal
Bryant.	Coit.	H. Eagleton.
Caldwell.	Craig.	H. Wilson.
Dixon.	Baird.	S. Wilson.
Rice.	Looney.	Moore, R.[3]
P. Davis.	T. Wilson.	Sullivan.
W. R. Moore.	Seabrook.	Brearley.
S. Wilson		Leckie.

The House then adjourned.

R. M. Davis   Rec. Sec. Eu. Soc.

[1] James Woodrow, uncle of WW, born Carlisle, England, May 30, 1828, son of the Rev. Thomas Woodrow and Marion Williamson Woodrow. A.B., Jefferson (now Washington and Jefferson) College, 1849; student of Agassiz at Harvard, 1853; A.M. and Ph.D., Heidelberg University, 1856. Taught in Alabama, 1850-53. Married Melie, or Felie, S. Baker, Aug. 4, 1857; ordained by Hopewell (S. C.) Presbytery, 1859. Professor, Oglethorpe University, 1853-61; Perkins Professor of Natural Science in Connection with Revelation, Columbia Theological Seminary, 1861-86. Chief, Confederate Chemical Laboratory, Columbia, S. C. Treasurer, Committee on Foreign Missions, Presbyterian Church, U. S., 1861-72. Editor and publisher, Columbia *Southern Presbyterian*, 1861-85 and 1865-93, respectively. Professor, South Carolina College (now the University of South Carolina), 1869-72 and 1880-91; president, 1891-97. President, Central National Bank, Columbia, S. C., 1888-91, 1897-1901. Died Columbia, S. C., Jan. 17, 1907. D.D., Hampden-Sidney; LL.D., Davidson; honorary M.D., University of Georgia; Doctor of Canon and Civil Law, Washington and Jefferson. Moderator, Synod of Georgia, Presbyterian Church, U. S., 1879, and of the Synod of South Carolina, same denomination, 1901.

[2] William S. Moore, '77.

[3] There were only two Moores in college, W.R., and W.S.

Regular Debate.   March 27th 1874

The house assembled at the usual hour. . . . There being no further special business requiring the attention of the house, Messers McKeown, T. Wilson and Craig were appointed to decide on the merits of the discussion and the following debate was then entered upon.

"Is a Mob ever justifiable in taking the life of a king who is a tyrant and usurper?" After the discussion an opportunity was given for explanations. The committee rendered their decision and the debators handed in their questions. The question was then laid open to the house for discussion. After some discussion on part of the house the decission of the house was called for.

The com. decided in favor of the Neg. and the house in favor of the Aff. . . .

Regular Meting   March 28th 1874

House assembled at the usual hour. . . . Scriptures were read and prayer offered by Mr. T. Wilson. . . . Excuses for absentees called for. The following fines were ordered by the Pres. Bryant failing to perform duty (50¢). For books not returned at the proper time, Greer (20¢). T. Wilson (10¢). S. Wilson (20¢) Craig (10¢). T. Wilson improper conduct in the hall (20¢). . . .

From a Wilson Notebook

[c. April 5, 1874]

Naval.

Her Britannic Majestys Squadron "Flying Squadron."

Commander-in-chief—Vice-Admiral Lord Thomas W. Wilson, Duke of Eagleton, vice-admiral of the red. Second-in-command— Rear-Admiral Sir Richard Bluewater, Bart., rear-admiral of the red.

Six vessels:

1. Her Majesty's Ship "Renown," senior flag ship, 4,000 tons, 2,000 horse-power, 26 guns; on the main deck 12 400-pounders, on the spar deck 12 62 pounders, and two pivot guns, one a 600 pounder, and the other a 300 pounder, 800 men, including 75 marines. 40 officers. Captain James T. Graham.

2. Her Majesty's Ship "Wanderer," 4,000 tons, 1,900 horse-power, 26 guns: on the gun deck 12 400 pounders, on the spar deck 12 62 pounders and two pivot guns, one a 600 pounder, and the other a 300 pounder, 700 men, including 50 marines. 40 officers. Captain Samuel A. Whitfield.

3. H. M. S. "Agamemnon," 3,500 tons, 26 guns, 1,750 horse-power. On the gun deck 12 300 pounders, on the spar deck 12 62-pounders, and 2 400-pounders, on pivots. Captain George F. Collingwood. 550 men, 30 marines. 30 officers.

4. H. M. S. "Albatross," junior flag-ship, 3,000 tons, 1,500 horse-power, 10 guns: on the main deck 6 400-pounders, and on the spar deck 2 62-pounders and 2 500-pounders on pivots 550 men 50 marines. 30 officers. Captain Alexander Sprunt, Jr.

5. H. M. S. "Cambria," 3,000 tons, 1,500 horse-power, 10 guns: on the main deck 6 400-pounders, and on the spar-deck 2 62-pounders, and 2 500-pounders on pivots. 500 men, 30 marines. 25 officers. Captain Albert C. Howard.

6. H. M. S. "Scotia," 3,000 tons, 1,500 horse-power, 10 guns: on the main deck 6 400-pounders, on the spar-deck 2 62-pounders and 2 500-pounders on pivots. 500 men, 30 marines. 25 officers. Captain Richard G. Douglas.

7. H. M. D. S. "Alert," 400 tons, 150 horse-power, 50 men. 6 officers. Lieutenant James S. Smart, commander.

List of officers.

Commander-in-chief—Lord Thomas W. Wilson, Duke of Eagleton, Admiral of the blue.

Second-in-Command—Sir Richard Bluewater, Bart. K. B. Rear-Admiral of the red.

Aid to the Commander-in-chief—Sir Richard B. Collingwood, Bart.

Captain—James T. Graham, H. M. S. "Renown."

H. M. S. Renown, flag-ship of H. M. Flying Squadron

["]This new, but already celebrated, man-of-war was built at the Royal Navy Yard at Portsmouth in 1870-1871, together with her consorts, Wanderer, Enchantress, Dauntless, Invincible, Matchless, Druid, Thunderer, and Carnatic, and the little despatch vessel Woolwich, according to plans drawn by her celebrated commander Lord Wilson. Since their launching these vessels have been pronounced by all the best judges to be the best vessels in the Royal Navy, which is high praise indeed. As all these vessels are alike in every particular, except size and armament, a description of the Renown will be a description of them all: This graceful and beautiful vessel, now employed, as indeed she has been ever since she was built, as the flagship of Lord Wilson, Duke of Arlington, Commander-in-chief of H. M. Flying Squadron, is one of the most curious and yet one of the most beautiful vessels in the Royal Navy. She is an excellent type of the now class of vessels that is being introduced into the Navy and particularly worthy of notice as the fastest man-of-war ever built. Her capacity is about 4,500 tons and her original dimensions were 325 feet length, 55 feet width, and 39 feet depth. A peculiar feature in her model is the rising of her keel for 60 feet forward, gradually curving into the arc of a circle as it blends with the stem. The arch form thus given to her forefoot secures a great increase of strength over that attainable with the prevailing angular form, while, at the same time, her freedom of movement is materially added to by the superior adaptation of this figure to meet the resistance of the water. Instead of the round bluff swell common to other classes of ships, which gives to their bows the shape of a duck's breast, her lines are concave forward and aft up to a few feet above the load displacement line, but those above this gradually become convex except in the bow in which the angular form is preserved entire. Ease and grace, however, are imparted to this part of the ship by the rise of her sheer, which is nicely graduated throughout her length, as are all her lines and mouldings to correspond with it. Her stem is semi-eliptical in form. Her decks are 3 separated by 10 ft. spaces. On her spar deck she carries 6 guns, on the broadside 4 100 pound rifles, muzzle-loaders, and on pivots 2 600 pound-rifles, breachloaders. On the gun deck she carries 14 guns 400 pounders, muzzleloaders, making her one of the most heavily armed vessels in the Navy. On the spar deck she carries 4 large cutters, each of 20 tons, 30 ft. long, 10½ ft. wide, and 5 feet deep, fitted with sails and all the other modern appliances for warfare. She has also 2 quarter boats of 26 ft. length, a barge of 40 ft. length, and a captain's gig of 22 ft. All the heavy work of the ship, such as taking in stores, setting up rigging, working the fire engine[,] hoisting the top-sails, and working the pumps can be done by steam. She also has an ingenious machine for distilling fresh water from salt water. Her timbers were carefully selected of the best quality; her keel is of rock maple in two tiers, which combined are side 16 inches and mould 32; and her frame is of iron and seasoned teak. Her masts are three in number, built of hard pine, the parts dowelled together and hooped over all with iron. Her bowsprit is built and hooped in the same manner. The main yard is 120 ft. long. A spare set of her heavy spars is stowed on the upper deck below the spar deck, and an oblong opening on each side of the ship through the latter admits their passage. A single suit of her sails covers 16,000 sq. yds. They are of an improved cut, designed to secure the most perfect cut, and most of their sewing was effected by machine sewing. She has 4 anchors, the best bower weighing 8,500 pounds, the working bower 6,500 pounds, the small bower, or stream anchor, 2,500, and the kedge 1,500 lbs. Her bower chains are each 120 fathoms long, and of 1¼ inch iron. The 2 prominent features of this vessel and her consorts are the shape of the bow and the increased length of the vessel. As already described in the account of the Renown in place of the convex forms noticed in the older vessels in tracing the lines from the stem aft along and below the water, is now substituted a concave surface giving to the bows the shape of an elongated wedge slightly hollowed on the face, by which the waters are more easily parted and thrown aside as the ship makes her way through them. This wedge shape is extended even to beyond the centre of the ship, so that the broader part, instead of being, as formerly, one third of the distance from the bows, is now about the same propational distance from the stern. Above the water-line the same proportions are retained. The Renown is, beyond a doubt, the fastest vessel in the Royal Navy, and, it is almost certain the fastest vessel in the *world*. She can, without straining her engines, in moderately calm weather, attain the high speed of 20 knots per hour, which is the highest rate of speed ever attained by steamers or any other vessels ever built in this country or elsewhere. Since she was built her planer and commander, Lord Wilson, has realized all his hopes as regards her performance &c. &c &c." London Times, April 5th 1874.

WWhw memoranda in notebook described at Sept. 29, 1873. The second entry, "H. M. S. Renown," is on loose sheets tucked into this notebook.

From the Minutes of the Eumenean Society

Regular Meeting   April 11th 1874

The house assembled at the usual hour. . . . The following appointments were made for to day two weeks on

Composition	Select Speak.	Origonal Speak.
H. Eagleton.	Dixon.	Seabrook.
F. Wilson.	Rice.	T. Wilson.
R. Moore.	P. Davis.	Looney.
Sullivan.	S. Wilson.	Craig.
Brearley	Britt.	Baird
Leckie.	R. Davis.	Coit
Robinson.[1]	Norris.	– finis –

House then adjourned

R. M. Davis   Rec. Sec.

[1] Charles W. Robinson, '74.

Regular Meeting   April 25th 1874

House assembled at the usual hour: roll called and the following gentlemen were noted as absent. Messers. Brearley, Coit, P. Davis, Greer, Rice, and S. Wilson.

Scriptures were read and prayer offered by Mr. Mebane. Minutes of the last meeting were read and special business called for. The house excused Mr. H. Eagleton from further attendance on plea of sickness. Moved and carried that the house now proceed to the election of three members to draw up a resolution defining the duties of the Vig. Com.

The house then proceeded to the election, which resulted in the election of Messers. Britt, Robinson, and Mebane.

On motion the newly elected com. were allowed to retire to attend to the business. Mr. Moore was appointed to act as review. The house then proceeded to the regular exercises of the morning. Mr

Reedy was excused by the house from further attendance on plea of sickness.

The chairman of the com. elected to draw up a resolution defining the duties of the Vig. Com. offered some recommendations, which required the immediate action of the Society. Motion made that the recommendations of the Chairman of the com. be received, namely, that two more members be added to that com. & that they be allowed to prepare a revision of the Constitution & be excused from attendance on Society until the work be completed. The motion was carried. The house then proceeded to the election of these two additional members to the Com. which resulted in the election of Messers Williamson and S. Wilson. . . .

At the close of the regular exercises general business was called for. On motion the house authorized the Ex. Com. to purchase a book corresponding to our honorary member book in which to enscribe the names of our Alumni and that one member be appointed to enscribe those names. The motion was carried and Mr. Thomas Wilson was appointed to do the work. . . .

From a Wilson Notebook

[c. May 1, 1874]

Nines of Davidson College, N. C.

Junior Nine.		Freshman Nine.	
Burwell,[1]	Catcher	Eagleton, H.	Third Base.
Baird,	Pitcher	" S.	Left Field.
Irwin	First Base	Glenn, C.	Right Field.
Horner	Second Base	Houston,	Centre Field.
Rice,	Third Base	Lapsley,	First Base.
Glenn, R.	Left Field.	Looney	Pitcher
Walker,	Centre Field.	Phillips	Catcher.
Palmer,	Right Field.	Rumple,	Short Stop.
A. Sprunt[2]	Short Stop	Wilson,	Second Base.
Horner, Captain.		Looney, Captain.	

WWhw entry in notebook described at Sept. 29, 1873.

[1] Undergraduates not previously identified were Richard S. Burwell, '75, Charles M. Glenn, '77, Robert B. Glenn, '75, Jerome C. Horner, '75, Robert L. Houston, '77, John R. Irwin, '75, Thomas W. Palmer, '75, William B. Phillips, '77, William R. Walker, '75, and Watson W. Rumple, '77.

[2] Alexander Sprunt, Jr., of Wilmington, N.C., A. B. Davidson, '75; Union Theological Seminary in Virginia, 1878; ordained 1878; Moderator, General Assembly, Presbyterian Church, U. S., 1923.

From the Minutes of the Eumenean Society

Called Meeting of the Eumenean Soc.
Friday evening May 1st 1874.

House assembled at six o'clock. President stated that the meeting was called by the request of the members and asked some one to state the object of the meeting. It was stated that Gov. [Zebulon B.] Vance was to deliver a lecture this evening at the request of the students, and motion made that the regular debate for to night be postponed till next Friday in honor of the Gov. The motion was carried. There being no further business requiring the attention of the house the meeting adjourned.

R. M. Davis   Rec. Sect.   Eu. Soc.

Regular Debate   May 8th 1874.

House assembled at the usual hour. . . . Scriptures were read, and prayer offered by Mr. Smith.

Minutes of last debate were read and special business called for. On motion our Exc. Com. were directed to confer with the Cor. Com. of the Phi. Society[1] in regard to taking a share in a grass mower to be purchased by the two Societies, and if the other Society does not consent, to purchase one for ourselves. The Chr. of our Exc. Com. proposed to the Society to purchase a large picture of Gen. R. E. Lee. On motion the Com. were directed to purchase the picture. Motion made and carried to appoint a Com. of three to make out a list of books to be purchased by the Exc. Com. to the amount of such a sum as the com. should see fit to expend. App. on that Com. Messers. Mebane, Britt and Bryan.

There being no further special business requiring the attention of the house, the regular exercises of the evening were then entered upon. Messers. Brooke, Sullivan and Dixon were appointed as a com. to decide on the merits of the debate. Messers Smith and Craig were appointed to fill vacancies on the Affirmative caused by the absence of Messers S. Wilson and Brearley. Messers Baird and Fraser to fill vacancies on the Negative caused by the absence of Messers. Titcomb and Reedy.

Mr. McKeown was excused from further attendance on plea of sickness.

At the close of the regular exercises an opportunity was given for necessary explainations; the Com. rendered in their decission and the debators handed in their questions.

The question was then laid open to the house for discussion. After some discussion from the house on the part of Messers. Hensell and F. Wilson in support of the Affirmative. The decission of the house was called for. The Com. and house both decided in favor of the Aff.

The following fines were ordered by the Pres Mr. Reedy for not returning to the hall (25¢) Mr Baird for quoting Scripture (10¢) Mr. Bryan for talking (10¢) Messers Looney and S. Moore for unbecoming position 10¢ each. Mr. Greer for spitting out the window (10¢). The following question was app. for to night two weeks. "Is the co-education of the sexes ever beneficial?" To discuss which were app. on the

Affirmative	Negative	The house then adjourned.
T. Wilson	Seabrook	
Stewart	S. Wilson	
Fraser	Craig	
Norris	Mebane	

R. M. Davis Rec. Sec Eu. Soc.

1 The Philanthropic Society, the other literary and debating society at Davidson College.

Regular Meeting   May 9th 1874.

House assembled at the usual hour. . . . At the close of the regular exercises general business was called for—none. Report of officers called for. Librarian made his report. The Chairman of the Com. appointed to conpy [copy] off into the new constitution, the constitution, resolutions and other contents of the old constitution book, reported that they had completed the work and also stated that Mr. Thomas Wilson had given them valuable assistance in the work and proposed that the Society return thanks to Mr. Wilson for his assistance. Motion made and carried to return thanks to Mr. Wilson for his assistance in that work.[1] Motion made and carried to return thanks to the Com. also for their works and that they be discharged. Resolutions called for—none. The following fines were ordered by the Pres. Messers. Looney and Sullivan for not returning to the hall (25¢) each. Messers. Baird and P. Davis for not returning books at propper time (10¢) each. The following appointments were made for to day two weeks. On

Composition	Select Speaking	Orig. Speaking
Seabrook.	H. Eagleton	Dixon
T. Wilson	P. Davis	Rice
Looney	R. Moore	F. Wilson
Craig.	Sullivan	Britt

Baird	Brearley	R. Davis
Coit.	Leckie	Norris
	Robinson	

House then adjourned.

R. M. Davis   Rec. Sec.   Eu. Soc.

[1] WW copied the entire constitution—not printed here—into a new book in a youthful, ornate hand. The document is in NcDaD.

From Janet Woodrow Wilson

My darling Boy,   Columbia, S. C., May 20th 1874

I am so anxious about that cold of yours. How did you take it? Surely you have not laid aside your winter-clothing? Another danger is in sitting without fire these cool nights. Do be careful, my dear boy, for my sake. You seem depressed—but that is because you are not well. You need not imagine that you are not a favorite. *Everybody* here likes and admires you. I could not begin to tell you the kind and flattering things that are said about you, by everybody that knows you. Yes, you will have no lack of friends in Wilmington[1]—of the warmest sort. There seem to be an unusual number of young people about your age there—and of a superior kind—and they are prepared to take an unusual interest in you particularly. Why my darling, nobody could *help* loving you, if they were to try!

I have a bad head-ache this morning dear—and wont attempt to write you a letter. My chief object in writing is to tell you that I love my absent boy—oh *so* dearly—and to enclose $5.00. If that is not enough be sure and let me know, dear.

Josie was delighted at the receipt of your letter last night. He joins me in warmest love to dearest brother

May God bless you, my sweet boy.   Your own   Mother.

ALS (WP, DLC) with env. addressed to WW at Davidson College, N. C. Enc.: poem in hand of JWW across face of which WWhw notation: "Rec'd May 22nd/74."

[1] JRW just resigned his professorship at the Columbia Theological Seminary (see n. 2 at WW to Ellen Axson, Oct. 12, 1884, Vol. 3) and received a call from the First Presbyterian Church in Wilmington, N. C. The Fayetteville *North Carolina Presbyterian*, June 3, 1874, announced that JRW had just accepted the call. He preached his first sermon in Wilmington on June 14, 1874.

From the Minutes of the Eumenean Society

Regular Debate   May 22nd 1874.

House assembled at the usual hour; roll called and the following gentlemen were noted as absent. Messers. Brearley, Coit, Fraser, Lapsley, Leckie, Rice, Sharpe, Simpson, F. Wilson, T. Wilson.

Scriptures were read and prayer offered by Mr. Norris. Minutes of last debate were read and special business called for. On motion Messers. T. Wilson and Reedy were excused from farther attendance on plea of sickness. . . . Messers Greer and Brooke were appointed to fill vacancies on the Aff. occasioned by the absense of Messers T. Wilson and Fraser. Messers Sullivan and Robinson to fill vacancies on the Neg. occasioned by the absence of Messers S. Wilson and Mebane. . . .

Regular Meeting   May 23rd 1874.

House assembled at the usual hour. . . . Scripture were read, and prayer offered by Mr. Mebane. Minutes of last meeting were read and special business called for. This being the regular time for the election of Society officers, a motion was made to postpone the exercises of the morning till next next [sic] meeting. The motion was carried. On motion the house then proceeded to the election of the officers for next term. The ballot resulted in the election of Mr. Mebane, President, Mr. Williamson Vice Pres. Mr. F. Wilson Rec. Sec. Mr. Norris Reviewer Mr. Stewart Librarian. Mr. T. Wilson Cors. Sec. . . . The appointments for to day two weeks same as the app. for to day on

Composition	Select. Spk.	Orig. Spk.
Seabrook	H. Eagleton.	Dixon
T. Wilson.	P. Davis.	Rice
Looney.	R. Moore.	F. Wilson
Craig.	Sullivan	Britt
Baird	Brearley	R. Davis
Coit.	Leckie	Norris
	Robinson	

House then adjourned.   R. M. Davis   Rec. Sec.

From a Wilson Notebook

[c. May 23, 1874]

Records of Corresponding Secy. Eumenean Society 1874-5.

Elected	Answered	Residence	When Elected
1 Alex. Martin, D.D.[1]	Alex Martin.	Danville, Virginia.	1874
2 Hon. John W. Burton		Murphreesboro, Tenn.	1874
Rev. Flyn Dixon[2]	Rev. Flyn Dixon		

WWhw entry in notebook described at Sept. 29, 1873.
1 Pastor of Danville, Va., Presbyterian Church.
2 The Rev. A. Flinn Dickson, pastor of Purity Presbyterian Church, Chester, S.C.

From the Minutes of the Eumenean Society

Reg. Debate   May 29th 1874.

House assembled at the usual hour. . . . Motion made and carried to excuse Messers T. Wilson and Reedy from farther attendance on plea of sickness. . . . The following question was chosen for to night two weeks. "Is the tendency of the fassions immoral"?

To discuss which were appointed on

Affirmative	Negative
S. Moore	Stewart
Lapsley	F. Wilson
Baird	Bryan
Williamson	Coit

The house then adjourned   R. M. Davis   Rec. Sec.

Three Items from a Wilson Notebook

[c. June 1, 1874]

Adresses of Ponography

Adresses of Ponographic men to whom letters should be addressed by Ponographic students—:

Andrew J. Graham, Ponetic Depot, New York. Joseph F. Snipes, Care Frank Leslie, 537 Pearl St. New York.

Books to be sent for to the first named adress: Ponographic Dictionary $4.40; First Ponographic Reader $1.58; Second Ponographic Reader $1.97; Total $7.85.

Ponographic Stationary to be sent for to the same address: Reporting Cover .54 cts.; Box of Phonographic pens $1.62. Grand Total $10.01.

Additional addresses.

D. L. Browne, 563 Broadway, New York, New York.

List of Books and other things to carry home:

Greek Lexicon, Latin Lexicon, Hadley, Dr. Phillips Lectures on Math. Blank Book, Scrap Book, Singing Book, Album, Phonography, Bingham's Latin Grammar, Xenophons Anabasis, and Memorabilia, Robinson's Algebra, Harkness First Greek Book, Herodotus, Towne's Algebra, Goodwin's Greek Grammar, Arnold's Greek Prose, Gildersleeve's Grammar and Ex Book, Trench, Chauvenet, Taylor's General History.

Important Memoranda.

Write home about going to the Bryant and Stratton business college after leaving here in 1879, and ask them what they think about it. *Beg hard.*

WWhw memoranda in notebook described at Sept. 29, 1873.

From the Minutes of the Eumenean Society

Regular Debate   June 5th 1874.
House assembled at the usual hour. . . . Messers Brooke, F. Wilson and T. Wilson were app. to decite on the merits of the debate. Messers Bishop and Seabrook were app. to fill vacancies on the Negative, occasioned by the absence of Messers. Looney and Hensell.

At the close of the debate an opportunity was given for necessary explainations: the com. rendered in their decission, and the debators handed their questions. The question was then laid open to the house for discussion. After some discussion from the house on part of Mr. Smith in support of the Aff. and Mr. Sullivan in support of the Negative. The decission of the house was then called for. The Com. and house both decided in favor of the Negative.

The following question was chosen for tonight two weeks. Which has exercised the greatest influence on the history of the world, the judgement or the passions. . . .

A Memorandum
[c. June 18, 1874]
Stood Finals on Algebra June 18th 1874 under Dr Phillips

WWhw memorandum in notebook described at Sept. 1, 1873.

From the Minutes of the Eumenean Society

Regular Debate   June 19th [1874]
House assembled at the usulal hour: roll called, and Messers Brearley, Britt, P. Davis, R. Davis, S. Eagleton, Greer, McKeown, R. Moore, Reedy, Rice, Robinson, were noted as absent. A passage from the bible read, and prayer offered by Mr Fogartie. Special business called for,—Motion made and carried to appoint a committee of eleven to attend to fixing up the Hall save the curtains—comt. Messrs. Noris, Bryan, Craig, R. Davis, Baird, Hensell, Lapsley, Leckie, Looney, McKeown, T. Wilson, S. Moore. . . .

From a Wilson Notebook

[c. July 1, 1874]

"The Royal United Kingdom Yacht Club"

Vessels

Name	tonnage	owner	Nationality
1. Eclipse,	280,	Lord Thomas W. Wilson,	English
2. Foam,	280	"　　W. B. Hutchinson,	"
3. Albatross,	280	"　　L. D. Alexander,	"
4. Osprey,	280	"　　C. R. Shields,	Irish
5. Sea Bird,	280	"　　T. W. Wilson,	English
6. Circe,	275	Sir J. Warren,	"
7 Dauntless,	275	Mr. S. W. Beach,	Scotch
8 Renown,	270	"　　H. Harrington,	"
9 Gazelle,	269	Lord P. C. McCarthy,	Irish
10 Aurora,	268	Mr. A. C. O'Brien,	"
11 Beatrice,	265	"　　C. W. Fletcher	English
12. Enterprize,	260	"　　J. Mc. Campbell,	Scotch
13. Independent	260	Sir J. Wm Leckie,	Irish
14 Imogen,	260	"　　C. Cunningham,	English
15 Kestrel	260	"　　F. B. Clarence,	"
16 Magic	250	Mr. L. C. Evans,	"
17 Naiad	250	"　　Alex Sprunt,	Scotch
18 Orion	250	"　　James　"	"
19 Palmer,	250	Mr. H. Brown,	English
20 Restless,	250	Sir H. P. Hamilton,	"
21 Victoria,	220	Mr. H. L. Harrison,	"
22 Witch,	220	"　　R. T. Liston,	"
23 Hibernia,	220	"　　H. C. Malloy,	Irish
24 Alert,	220	"　　P. D.　"	"
25 Scotia,	220	"　　H. R. McKenzie,	Scotch
26 Lorne,	220	"　　T. Woodrow,	Scotch
27 Clyde,	220	"　　V. P. McIver,	"
28 Ocean Sprite,	220	"　　E. P. Robinson,	English
29 Genevieve,	220	"　　I. E. Fraser,	Scotch
30 Perth,	220	Lord H. M. Russell,	English

Total, 30 vessels, including 15 English, 9 Scotch, and 6 Irish.

Officers:

Commodore: Lord Thomas W. Wilson, Duke of Carlton, Admiral of the white, Royal Navy, &c. &c.

Vice Commodore: Captain T. Woodrow, Royal Navy.

Rear Commodore: H. C. Malloy.

Secretary: Lord W. B. Hutchinson, Earl of Arlington.
Treasurer: R. T. Liston.

Rules and Regulations[1]

1. The name of this organization shall be the "Royal United Kingdom Yacht Club" of Great Britain and Ireland
2. The officers of this Club shall be a Commodore, Vice Commodore, Rear Commodore, Secretary, and Treasurer, who shall be elected every 4 years.

    I.   The Commodore shall have the same authority over the fleet of this Club as that possessed by Admirals over the fleets of the Royal Navy which they command. He shall preside over all the meetings of the Club, and no bill or resolution of any kind can pass into a law of the Club without his approval and signature. His veto makes a bill null and void, even if adopted unanimously by the Members.

    II. The Vice Commodore commands the centre division of the fleet and takes the place and assumes the duties of the Commodore on all occasions when that officer is absent from duty and when that officer may please to invest him with the command.

    III. The Rear Commodore shall command the rear division of the fleet, and command, in the absence of the Vice Commodore, all the vessels of both the centre and rear divisions assuming, also, all the duties of that officer. If both Commodore and Vice Commodore should be absent he shall be chief officer.

    IV. The Secretary shall keep a record of all the proceedings of the Club, a list of the vessels composing its fleet, giving their tonnage, owner and builder, together with any peculiarity of their construction. He shall also conduct all the official correspondence of the Club.

    V.   The treasurer shall keep all the funds of the Club, of the condition of which he shall give an annual report in the Grand Annual Meeting of the Club.
3. To become a law any bill or resolution must pass the House by a 2/3 vote and receive the signature of the Commodore.
4. The Grand Annual Meeting of the Club shall take place on the first Monday of every June. All the Members are required to be present at this meeting. Absence from this meeting without sufficient excuse shall involve the fine of £5 for each and every absence. When an excuse for absence from this meeting is offered it shall be judged sufficient or insufficient by vote of the house. All other excuses are pronounced valid or otherwise by the Commodore.

5. All the vessels belonging to this Club shall be schooner rigged and over 200 tons burden.

6. The fee for entrance to the Membership of this Club shall be £100 for every member and £900 for every vessel.

7. No one shall be received into the membership of this Club except by a 4/5 vote of the House, and no one is eligible for membership unless he be over 21 years of age.

8. There shall be 10 Annual Regattas every year in the months of June and July which shall be known by the names: The Carlton Annual Regatta, for which Lord Wilson pledges himself to offer 3 prizes, the first to be of gold, the second of silver and the third of wood, these prizes to be of whatever design Lord Wilson will please. The yachts of Lord Wilson will not, of course, enter for these prizes. The Arlington Regatta, for which Lord Hutchinson will offer 2 silver prizes. The Irish Regatta, for which the Irish members of the Club will offer 4 prizes, 2 of gold and 2 of silver. The Scotch Regatta, for which the Scotch members will offer 1 gold and 2 silver prizes. The English Regatta for which the English members will offer 4 silver prizes. The British Reggatta for which the Club will offer 1 gold prize. The Liverpool, London, and Plymouth Annual Regattas for which the Club offers one gold Prize each. They will be sailed on the Mersey, Thames; and Plymouth Harbor respectively. Last, on the first Wednesday of every July, the Grand Annual Regatta of the Royal United Kingdom Yacht Club for which the flag of Championship is offered by the Club.

WWhw entry in notebook described at Aug. 1, 1873.

[1] This constitution, fanciful though it was, appears to have been the first of WW's many frames of government running straight down to the Covenant of the League of Nations. It reveals his passion, even at an early age, for constitutional order.

Ray Stannard Baker, *Woodrow Wilson: Life and Letters*, I, 29, 45, says that WW while a boy in Augusta, Georgia, some years earlier organized the Lightfoot Club "for various secret, mysterious, and adventurous purposes," including baseball, and wrote a "kind of constitution" for the club. William Bayard Hale, *Woodrow Wilson: The Story of His Life*, p. 33, from which Baker drew much of his information about WW's early life, describes the Lightfoot Club but does not mention a constitution. No copy of it has ever been found, but see the document printed on p. 6, which indicates that the Lightfoot Club was only a baseball club.

As has been noted at May 9, 1874, note 1, WW copied out the new constitution of the Eumenean Society at Davidson College into a constitution book in 1874. All evidence indicates that he had had no hand in drafting it.

WW's next constitution, following that drafted for the Royal United Kingdom Yacht Club, was the one that he wrote for the Liberal Debating Club at Princeton in 1877. It is printed at Feb. 1, 1877. The next (and last to be printed in this volume) was a new constitution for the Jefferson Society at the University of Virginia, which WW helped to draft in 1880. It is printed at Dec. 4, 1880.

From a Wilson Notebook

[c. July 17, 1874]

Phonography By Thomas W Wilson from Graham's Hand
Book of Standard or American Phonography

Comprizing 25 lessons in the Corresponding Style of Phonography taking up 112 pages. Also full exemplification of the Reporting Style, together with full lists of word signs and contractions and a partial list of words in the Reporting Style. Also very copious exercises, both reading and writing, taking up about 58 pages. The best book on Phonography ever printed. I regard this book as a perfect gem and would not part with it or the knoledge I have gained from it for anything.

Thomas W. Wilson.

WWhw entry in notebook described at Sept. 29, 1873.

Four Letters from Andrew Jackson Graham

Dear Sir: 8/8/74
In my alphabetically-arranged accounts I find your name, and account of Hand-Book which I sent you in 1873 on order & remittance from Mr. Snipes; nothing later; so that your remittance of July 22 cd not have been recd. Hope you sent in some safe way.

Yours truly   A. J. Graham

APS (WP, DLC).

By Cash   8/15/74
First Reader   1.58
Reader can not be sent for some time, as both First and Second Reader are out now. The latter will be ready again in two or three weeks; the former has to be re-engraved, & cannot be ready again before middle of Nov.   Yours truly   A. J. Graham
Several thieves have recently been arrested in our Post Office. One is under $75,000 bail.

APS (WP, DLC).

Friend Wilson: 8/28/74
I have just entered your order for the 2nd reader. I hope it will soon be ready. You speak [of] mistakes made by yourself. You did not make many, but if you would apply the 1st Reader money toward the purchase of the phonographic dictionary, $4.40, it would

be a good thing for you, as by referring to that whenever you doubt as to the outline of a word, you would avoid mistakes. . . .[1]

Yours truly   Andrew J. Graham

No. 4

Transcript of shPS (WP, DLC).
[1] In the remaining sentence Graham corrected Wilson's writing of "Second," "Reader," and "Order."

Dear Sir: 9/7/74
I have received and entered your subscription for the Student's Journal. But as the Journal is behind on account of my sickness and other divers causes, waiting for the August number will be a trial of your patience I fear.

The Second Reader has not come in yet, though the binders promised them last Saturday. It must be along soon; and as soon as ready a copy will be sent to your address at Wilmington, North Carolina. Do you know Mr. M. L. Little, Newton, North Carolina? He is a phonographer, who has taught phonography some in his region. Do you have a prospect of getting employment in the South? Or perhaps you are not seeking to become a professional phonographer. One of my pupils has just got a situation in a railroad office at $1,800.00; and another has recently written that he will receive $5,000.00 for his report in one case! Another pupil in Buffalo has written that he has all he can do.

Yours truly,   Andrew J. Graham

No. 1

Transcript of shPS (WP, DLC). All four letters pasted in scrapbook described on p. 5.

From a Wilson Notebook

End of Corresponding Style   9/9/74
For Specimens of Reporting Style see Page 60.

When the Corresponding style was finished I had the Hand Book and Dictionary and had sent on for the 2 Readers. Ordered the Hand Book from Mr. J. F. Snipes, Stenographer; Father sent me the Dictionary; and I ordered the Readers from Mr. Graham direct. Commenced the Corresponding Style on July 17th 1874 and finished it on Sept. 9th 1874.

(Signed)   Thos. W. Wilson

WWhw memorandum in notebook described at Sept. 29, 1873.

Three Letters from Andrew Jackson Graham

Friend Wilson: 9/14/74

The 2nd reader was sent yesterday addressed "Wilmington, N. C." I rec'd your order for the Journal also to be addressed to Wilmington. I have no entry however on the subscription book of "care of Rev. Dr. J. R. Wilson." Need it be added? Perhaps I may not have written to you in response to your orders for I dispense with writing, some days, whenever I possibly can.

Yours truly, Andrew J. Graham

No. 2

Dear Sir: 9/16/74

I have entered your remittance, 63 cents; but I cannot send you Volume I of the Visitor: It has been out of print sometime—and some of the plates have been destroyed. It would be interesting but not specially valuable to you. I have some copies on hand of No. 4 of that Volume containing the Phonographic Numerals. I think you are getting on very nicely with the phonography; and with the Second Reader which I sent you recently, I presume you will soon have a good knowledge of the reporting style. You should have the dictionary to refer to whenever you are in doubt as to the best outline. Yours truly, Andrew J. Graham

No. 3

Dear Sir: 9/25/74

I have just entered your order for the reporting cover, which will be sent today. You mentioned that your father obtained a dictionary at my place. You will confer a great favor by asking your father to specify the date if possible, or as near as he can when he got it; for I presume that my unfaithful clerk has not put it down. The appearances are that, taking advantage of my sickness and enforced absence from my office, he has appropriated sales and books to the amount of several hundred dollars. I have a number of cases of known appropriation, but I want to make the matter so clear that he will feel obliged to confess, for I desire simply to have him reimburse me, and not to imprison him. Early attention to this will be a special favor.

Yours truly, Andrew J. Graham

Let your father also state the price he paid. I presume it was $4.
No. 5

Transcripts of shPS (WP, DLC). All three items pasted in scrapbook described on p. 5.

From the Minutes of the Eumenean Society

Regular Meeting Eu. Soc.   Oct 3rd 1874

House assembled at the usual hour. Roll called and Messrs. Baird, Bishop, Fraser, and Leckie were absent. Divine blessings invoked by Mr Simpson. Minutes of the last meeting read and Special business called for. Motion was passed to proceed to the election of two of the Officers of Society, which vacances were occasioned by the non returning of those Gent. The ballot resulted in the election of Mr. Coit as Reviewer and Mr. Brooke as Cor. Sec. .... Motion was carried to return the thanks of Society to Mr. T. W. Wilson for his services in copying off the names of our Alumni into the new book. . . .

From Andrew Jackson Graham

Dear Sir: 10/8/74

I am not troubled by small orders except by the thought sometimes that it must be very vexatious to send for an article that is out of print. . . .

Do not rest satisfied with writing an exercise or a page in the 2nd reader once or twice, write from reading after a time fifty to one hundred times. Such practice does more to familiarize and to accustom the hand to tracing the characters easily and quickly than any other practice.   Yours very truly,   Andrew J. Graham

Transcript of shPS (WP, DLC). Pasted in scrapbook described on p. 5.

A Notation

[Dec. 10, 1874]

Recommenced in Wilmington, North Carolina, 12/10/74 in preparation for Princeton College New Jersey. Thomas W. Wilson.

Transcript of WWsh note, p. 11, Thomas Kerchever Arnold, *A Practical Introduction to Greek Prose Composition*, revised and corrected by Rev. J. A. Spencer (New York, 1876). (WW Library, DLC).

To Andrew Jackson Graham

From THOMAS W. WILSON.— [Wilmington, N.C., c. Jan. 1875]

I received the Numbers of Volume V. *Visitor*, which you sent me. I cannot express to you how very fond I am becoming of your system. I have just finished committing to memory the lists of reporting word-signs, and find them very easy to learn because they are so naturally formed. The more I learn of Standard Phonography the more I admire it. When do you think you will have finished your phonographic edition of the New Testament?

[*Ans.*—I think that work will have to be long deferred. Ed.]

Printed letter in *The Students Journal*, IV (Jan. 1875), 14. Last sentence in brackets is Graham's; brackets are his also.

From Two Wilson Notebooks   2/11/75

I have Graham's Hand Book, (First) (and) Second Reader, Dictionary, Volume 5th of the Visitor, Note Book &c, &c, &c, &c, &c.
                                (Signed)   Thomas W. Wilson

WWhw entry in notebook described at Jan. 5, 1873.

My Phonographic Library:

		Cost
1	Hand Book	$2.20
2	First Reader	1.58
3	Second Reader	1.87
4	Dictionary.	4.40
7	Volume Four of the Visitor	
8	Volume Five of the Visitor	2.87

                                                Total

WWhw entry in notebook described at Aug. 1, 1873.

Notebook

                                [April 1,1875-Nov. 23, 1876]
Inscribed on cover (WWhw):
  "Vol. One T. W. Wilson Diary 1876–June 3rd", and on flyleaf
  (WWhw): "Thomas W. Wilson Wilmington, N. C. 4/1/75"
Contents (in WWsh unless otherwise noted):
  (a) Essays on geology "Taken From the 'Standard Phonographic Visitor,' Volume Fifth. Andrew J. Graham," copied c. April 1-10, 1875.
  (b) Exercises in phonography described by WW as follows: "The Following Lessons on Phonography are from the pen of Mr. J. F. Snipes, Stenographic Law and News Reporter, New York City. They appeared in Frank Leslie's Boys and Girls Weekly from which I copy them, putting them in Chapters." Copied c. April 11-24, 1875.
  (c) Various items from Graham's *Second Reader*, including "Specimens of Law Reporting," "On the Distinction of Words," "Study of Words," "Ancient and Modern Philosophy," "Logic," "Geology," "Evi-

dence of the Circulation of the Blood," "Religion and Science," "Our Friends in Heaven," "Creation," "The Age of the Human Race," "The Infallibility of the Church," "Audi Alteram Partem," "The American Bible Society," "Politics: Speech of Mr. Gaulden of Georgia," "No Law for Slavery," "Law Reporting," "Charge to the Jury," "Alexander Von Humboldt," and "Progress in the East."

(d) "My Journal" (WWsh), diary, June 3-Nov. 23, 1876, for transcripts of which see below by dates.

(e) "The Union" (loose material, WWsh), for transcript of which see at Nov. 15, 1876.

(f) "The Ideal Statesman" (WWhw), signed "Atticus," for which see at Jan. 30, 1877.

(WP, DLC).

To Andrew Jackson Graham

Dear Sir: [Wilmington, N. C., c. April 24] 1875
I have just received the numbers of the [Student's] Journal for October November and December and have enjoyed their perusal very much indeed. I always look forward with pleasure to the receipt of a copy of the Journal. I always make it a practice to copy out into the Reporting Style all the articles that interest me. I am spending all the time I have to spare and more too I am afraid on the study of phonography and am now pretty deep in the Reporting Style. The more insight I get into your system the more I admire and enjoy it. I have not had any opportunity of examining any other system but being fully convinced that your system is adequate in every particular for the most rapid reporting and being delighted with your splendid series of textbooks I care not to see the other systems. I do not think that there could be a better system than yours. I wish to ask you what would be your terms for teaching one to report who can already write the Corresponding Style with considerable ease when he may be said to know the Corresponding Style. Such a one could learn to report in about two months could he not? I am studying for entering Princeton College where I expect to be next session and I may have a good opportunity of taking lessons from you during the summer vacation. I think that I have a thorough knowledge of the Corresponding Style together with some knowledge of the Reporting Style. What would be your terms to perfect my knowledge of the Reporting Style and make me able to report easily? I expect that phonography will be of great use to me in college but being young I have a great deal yet to learn about the art of putting a man's

words on paper as quickly as he can get rid of them. Enclosed find return postage.

                    Thomas W. Wilson
                    Your friend in science

Transcript of WWsh copy in notebook described at Aug. 1, 1873; there is an earlier draft in WP, DLC.

To Andrew Jackson Graham

No. 9 in short[hand]:[1]

Friend Wilson: [April 30, 1875]

   I am sorry to say that the state of my health is such that it does not answer for me to take any more pupils beyond those already studying with me. You are going on very nicely. Study the Second Reader carefully for the Reporting Style, and make good use of the Dictionary, and I will be sure that you will become a first-rate reporter.

                    Yours truly,   Andrew J. Graham

Transcript of WWsh copy in notebook described at Aug. 1, 1873.
   [1] Transcript of WWsh addition.

From John William Leckie

Dear Tom,   Davidson College, May 7th '75

   I may have made the remark before but I'll repeat it, you're a bully correspondent. With which classical quotation, my feelings been relieved and my letter started I will proceed, in so far as I may be able, to answer your voluminous epistle of two weeks ago.

   In the first place you're a miserable victim! You are nothing but a miserable moth fluttering around the flame of beauty and the first thing you know you will get your wings scorched (original? and very fine sentiment). You'd better drop it, me boy, like a hot potatoe. But what would you think if I were to tell you that I, myself, 1st personal Pronoun, Singular Number, was at last making up my mind to storm the outposts of that bugbear "society". That I was going to hitch my suspenders up tight, roll up my sleeves, set my teeth and charge it like the Light Brigade at Balaklava; or, to change my simile to an element more congenial to you, bear down on it, like a ship of war, carrying devastation in my path. In sober earnest, though, I have been thinking lately of what I knew all along: that if I am ever to be a preacher, I must be a little different from a fool or a ninny in Society, and that no attainments I could make in other directions could make up for the want of this. So

I am going to make another desperate effort though I shudder when I contemplate it, and think how green I am on what everyone else knows. . . .

Have you ever come across any of Ruskin's writings? I got ahold of some of his Lectures out of the Phi. library and I am delighted with them both for the originality of his thoughts and the beauty of the language. Your advice about the Phonography I think I will take. I intended to take it long ago. But I will try and do it in earnest in the summer.

About "that business matter" I concluded to let it drop as Amos said nothing more about it.

As to the last part of your letter I need not tell you how glad I am to hear any such good news, though I am painfully sensible that I am not as glad as I ought to be, if I were more in harmony with what God requires, and recognized as I ought the value of one soul. When I think that Jesus died (and what do those two words not contain?) for the price of one soul and then think of 51 of those precious souls being saved from death it shows a hard and very insensible heart that I am not more rejoiced than I am. Oh that God would give us hearts of flesh!

Your Friend,   J. W. Leckie.

ALS (WP, DLC) with WWhw notation on env.: "Letter from Leckie, Ans".

Two Letters from Andrew Jackson Graham

No. 10 in short[hand]: Addressed to Columbia[1]

Friend Wilson: 5/18/75

The publisher informs me that the Xenophon was sent to Columbia, South Carolina. I write this thinking that I have made an error in giving your address. I see that you have been in Columbia, South Carolina, but I find your later orders have been from Wilmington, North Carolina.

Yours truly,   Andrew J. Graham

No. 11 in short[hand]: Addressed Wilmington[1]

Friend Wilson: 5/18/75

As the Xenophon was sent by the publisher to Columbia, South Carolina, where I have just written you I write to this address lest by some error in the address the book should be lost.

Yours truly,   Andrew J. Graham

I could not find the book at once. 5/18/75
Note: I received the book all right—T. W. W.[1]

Transcripts of WWsh copies in notebook described at Aug. 1, 1873. The shPS
originals, partly mutilated, are pasted in scrapbook described on p. 5.
[1] Transcripts of WWsh additions.

Draft of a Letter to John William Leckie

Answer   [Wilmington, N. C., May 28, 1875]
I expect that you will not think me a good correspondent long
if I delay so long again in answering your epistle. I do not think
that I will get my wings scorched yet awhile; infrequency of my
visits to fair sex. Glad to hear that you have at last decided to go
into society. *My study arrangements now with Mr. Calhoun.*[1]
Senior monitors Whitehead[2] and Mebane. Junior Rose and Mc-
Gehee. Sophomore [*] Moore [,] Leckie. The two brothers left behind poor fellows. How does Frank Wilson stand? I suppose that
he is verbose with his speech? How does dear old Seabrook stand
in class. Stormy in Columbia. Ruskin's writings. I think I will read
some of them when I get time. Glad that you are going to study
Phonography. My advice about it. Study according to the Hand-
Book. My delight in Phonography increases all the time. Beautiful
study. ⟨Am preparing for Princeton, I hope that I will get in.⟩
Phonography will be of great use to me in college. Expect to be a
good reporter by the end of next summer. Father begins General
Assembly.[3] Copy of letter in Phonography. *Thomas W. Wilson.*

Transcript of WWshLS (draft) on blank page of J. W. Leckie to WW, May 7, 1875
(WP, DLC).
[1] Probably J. C. Calhoun, a teacher, of Wilmington, N.C.
[2] Davidson students not previously identified were John Whitehead, '75, Duncan Rose, '76, and Thomas McGehee, '76.
[3] The General Assembly of the southern Presbyterian Church met in St. Louis,
May 20-31, 1875.

From Marion Wilson Kennedy

My very dear brother:—   Kingstree, [S. C.] June 14th '75.
I was very glad to get your letter; after so long a silence on your
part, I was beginning to fear you had given up writing to me altogether. So you are very busy these times, getting to be a great student. I am very glad to know it. You must not neglect us altogether,
though, in your devotion to your studies. I can't consent to that
at all, my brother. You might get into such bad habits in that respect this summer, that you would just not write to us at all after

you get to Princeton, and that would be simply outrageous. . . .
Now, do tell us all about your plans, as far as you have made any.
What class do you intend entering at Princeton? How do you like
the prospect, now that it is right near at hand? Do tell us all you
can think of that you have found out about the College to which
you are going and its surroundings. We will be interested in it all.
I feel so stupid today that really I can't write any sort of a letter
that is at all worthy the name of one, as you can easily see. But
I want you to write again soon, very soon, and there is no telling
how long it may be before I feel like writing again. I am getting so
lazy about it of late, like most of the Wilson and Kennedy[1] name.
Have you heard from Auntie and uncle James Bones[2] lately? We
have not heard for some time. Were very sorry to hear how badly
uncle James Woodrow was feeling after the Assembly. Heard that
he had lost his voice almost entirely, by the time he got as far as
Marietta on his way home, besides being very feeble in other
ways. . . .

Your affectionate sister,   Marion W. Kennedy.

ALS (WP, DLC) with WWhw notation on env.: "Rec'd 6/18/75."
  [1] Her husband was Anderson Ross Kennedy, born Pickens District, S.C., Nov.
29, 1842. A.B., Davidson College, 1868; was graduated from Columbia Theological Seminary, 1872. Married Marion Wilson, Oct. 29, 1872. Licensed by Harmony
(S. C.) Presbytery, Presbyterian Church, U. S., 1871; ordained by same, April 1873.
Pastor, Indiantown, S. C., Presbyterian Church, 1873-75; without charge, Batesville, Ark., 1876; stated supply, Cotton Plant, Ark., 1878-1881; pastor, Maysville,
Ky., 1881-82; pastor, Second Church, Little Rock, Ark., 1882-88; pastor, Batesville,
Ark., 1888-90. Died Batesville, May 19, 1890. Moderator, Synod of Arkansas, Pres-
byterian Church, U. S., 1883; Stated Clerk, Arkansas Presbytery, 1883-89; Stated
Clerk, Synod of Arkansas, 1886-89.
  [2] Marion Woodrow Bones and her husband, James W. Bones.

From Douglas McKay

Dear Tom   Columbia S. C. June 25/75
      Your esteemed letter of the 10th came to hand and was esteemed
greatly on account of the promptness in answering, what was a
very tardy letter from me. Your returning good for evil qualities,
are well known and fully appreciated by me and were it not for
fear of imposing on you[r] good nature, my laziness would often
tempt me to take advantage of them more frequently. I assure you
I think of my duty with regard to prompt correspondence, and
attendance upon minor matters, every day: and I know full well
the affect they have in forming ones character in after years, and
yet I fail to accomplish any thing by reflection. Never mind Tom
you just wait till you and me get to be members of the U S Senate
and then we'll teach the young Ideas how to shoot, and tell them,

what are the fruits of an honorable ambition and all those good things, as we never have been taught. And if we never reach that high estate of honor, it will all be the Same in a hundred years hence. Wont it. . . .

Yours Sincerely   D McKay

ALS (WP, DLC) with WWhw notation on env.: "Ans 7/3/75," followed by his signature, Thomas Woodrow Wilson, in Graham shorthand.

From John Rennie Blake to Whom It May Concern

Davidson College N. C.   June 25th 1875

This is to certify that Mr Thos. W. Wilson passed through the Freshman Class, of 1873-74, in this institution—that during his connection with the College, his conduct as a student, & his bearing as a gentleman, commanded for him the esteem & confidence of the Faculty & that we now commend him to those with whom he may, by any providence, be thrown.[1]

J. R. Blake   Chm of Faculty

ALS (WP, DLC).
[1] WW's grades for the first semester were logic and rhetoric, 95; Greek, 87; mathematics, 74; composition, 96; and declamation, 92. His grades for the second semester were English, 97; Greek, 88; Latin, 94; mathematics, 88; composition, 95; and declamation, 92. From Walter L. Lingle, "Woodrow Wilson at Davidson College," *Davidson College Bulletin*, XXXII (Dec. 15, 1922). This is the only known reliable source since the records were destroyed when Old Chambers burned.

From Annie Wilson Howe

My dearest brother—   Columbia July 1st 1875

It is nearly two weeks since I wrote my last letter home. I am sorry, but I really *could not* write sooner. I have not heard from any of you since I wrote either, so we are in the same box you see. I am glad you are studying so hard—but you must not make yourself sick at it this hot weather. . . .

Yes, I think your plans for the summer are *very* pleasant. I was only disappointed that I did not come in for a share[.] I was in hopes you would at least *pass through* Columbia. I must possess my soul in patience for a while longer though, I see. When will father start and when will you all go to meet him? I suppose Wilmington is somewhat deserted by this time? What about the new parsonage?[1] . . .   Your loving sister, Annie

ALS (WP, DLC) with WWhw notations on env.: "Rec'd 7/3/75" and "Ans 7/5/75."
[1] The newly remodeled parsonage at Fourth and Orange Streets to which the Wilsons had just moved. The first Presbyterian Church was at Third and Orange

Streets. Before moving to the manse, the Wilsons resided at the house of C. H. Robinson, commission merchant, at Front and Nun Streets. See Louis T. Moore, *Stories Old and New of the Cape Fear Region* (Wilmington, N. C., 1956), p. 229.

From Marion Wilson Kennedy

My very dear brother:—   Kingstree, [S. C.] July 3rd '75.
    Your note came to hand safely last Sabbath, with the Express receipt. I do not know but that I felt more sorry than glad to have such sure *proof* of dishonesty somewhere on the route that package came from Kingstree, for it came the only way we can hope to get things at all promptly. . . . We were glad to hear at last what your plans for the summer were, as far as you told them; but do you know you did not tell anything about father's part of the programme? We gathered from some remark you made, about joining father in the north in the fall, that he was probably going to start on his travels earlier in the season than the rest of you,—but further than that, we are still entirely in the dark as to his movements. Tell father please to excuse that slip of my pen. I intended to write *her* instead of *his*. I remember well her (his) dislike of the masculine pronoun. *Why* I could never exactly understand. Do you hear how George[1] is getting on in Columbia, these days? I wish we could hear from Annie more frequently. It makes her seem so far off to have heard from her only once since she left Wilmington. I do not feel at all like complaining of the dear child's silence, for I know she thinks she can't possibly find time to write to me, but I do what sometimes amounts to very nearly the same thing, I get so anxious to hear from her. How was she when you last heard from her? I am sure she writes often home, and you must try and remember to tell us about her and hers when you write to us, Woodrow. That is so much prettier than Thomas; why don't you think so? . . .   Your loving sister Marion.

ALS (WP, DLC) with WWhw notations on env.: "Rec'd. 7/6/75" and "Ans."
  [1] George Howe, Jr., M.D.

From John William Leckie

Dear Tom,   Columbia, S. C. July 4th [1875]
    You know that we fellows get pretty busy & particularly lazy as examinations approach so that is my only excuse for leaving yours of May 28th unanswered till now.
    I went round to see Douglas[1] yesterday and he showed me a

letter from you or rather read me part of one from you in which you wanted to hear about Commencement and Examinations and all that sort of thing so I will report them to you as well as I can in long hand. . . .

As to short hand. I am still desirous of learning it and as soon as I am able will get a book and commence the study in earnest. You may think I am very slow about it as I am, but it is not for want of inclination but from not having got the book yet. I am very much obliged for your kind offer of assistance made through your letter to Doug. and I feel the worth that it will be to me as I believe correspondence is of very material aid in learning the art. I was much struck with the saving in *space*, shown in your last letter to me, made by this useful study as well as that in time which I have heard so much of already. Will you tell me what the mark / means which occurs so friequently on the page? Is it the sign of a stop in the sentence and if so is it a full stop or what is its value? . . .

Your loving friend   J. W. Leckie.

ALS (WP, DLC) with WWhw notation on env.: "Ans."; also on env.: WWsh draft of letter to J. W. Leckie, c. July 4, 1875, printed below.

1 Douglas McKay.

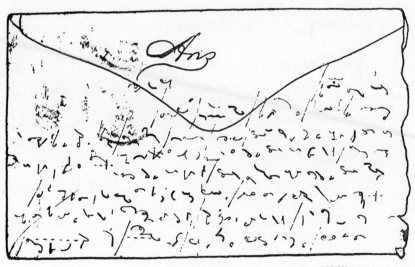

Wilson's Shorthand Draft of a Letter to John William Leckie, c. July 4, 1875

Draft of a Letter to John William Leckie

[Wilmington, N. C., c. July 4, 1875]

Notes on the examinations. What I think of the new plan of examinations. His [Leckie's] average on examination. Josh. Frank Wilson. Duffie.[1] Chapel Hill and Dr. Phillips.[2] Phonography[,] my advice about it. It will be hard to learn but worth the trouble. Do not expect to learn it in this one vacation but remember and practice what you learned during the next term at Davidson and you will probably be able to learn the rest next summer. The great mistake that I made was that I had to commence over again every time because I did not stick to what I learned. Shall be very glad to correspond on the subject of phonography and help you in every way possible by correspondence. Do not hesitate to write to me on the subject when I am at Princeton as I shall take time to write to you about once a week if possible. It will be a pleasure to me to correspond on the subject as I like nothing so well as writing and talking[.] After you commence the study I will tell you what I think is the best mode of correspondence. Meaning of sign. In my writing. Punctuation in phonography. Beautiful phonography. The steeple on the church; ridiculous to put such another one on the church; great mistake. His [Leckie's] father joining the church. Very glad to hear of it. Miscellaneous. Plumer Bryan's *grades*(?).

Thomas W. Wilson

Transcript of WWshLS (draft) on envelope of J. W, Leckie to WW, c. July 4, 1875 (WP, DLC).

[1] These were probably Josiah M Glenbrook, and certainly H. Franklin Wilson. Duffie was probably a friend in Columbia, S.C.

[2] Dr. Charles Phillips was returning to his former position at the University of North Carolina, which had just re-opened after being closed during Reconstruction.

From a Wilson Notebook

Memmoranda   [July 13-31, 1875]

7/13/75	Sent to Messrs Willmer and Rogers for a copy of The Illustrated London News for June 26/75; also for in-
(Rec'd)	formation as to the price of subscription
7/15/75	Ordered from J. A. Springer 2 loads sawed wood $2.70
7/14/75	Ordered from Alex.Sprunt & Son 1 case Ale—$18.00 Paid
7/31/75	Ordered from J. A. Springer 2 loads sawed oak $2.70
7/31/75	Ordered from J. M. Hardwick 1 tongue
7/31/75	Bought of Peck, Hardware, 1 lb. nails 10¢

Act with J. A. Springer for July $5.40

WWhw list in notebook described at Aug. 1, 1873.

From John Dooley[1]

Dear Tom,　　　　　　　　　Columbia, S. C. July 22nd, 1875

You take the breath out of a fellow, you answer so promptly. Why I hardly thought you had got my letter when back came your answer, and a big one it was, so I will have to try and let you have one proportionately large though it will be no small job under the present heated state of the weather. . . .

I see it is only necessary to say "Shorthand["] to you and you prick up your ears like the war horse at the sound of the trumpet. Your suggestions, as coming from one who has been over the road will be invaluable to me when I begin, which I suppose you are beginning to suppose will be never, but there is no danger of my letting the first available chance for getting the book slip, and when I get it, of failing to pursue the study. My old woman, Bohbäck, uses Pitman's and tries to cram it down my throat but I am faithful to Graham. Do you go much on the musical line lately? Remember me to Sprount[2] and believe me

　　　　　　Yours truly,　John Dooley alias P. A. T.

ALS (WP, DLC) with WWhw notations on env.: "Rec'd 7/26/75" and "Ans."
　1 A friend of WW's in Columbia.
　2 Alexander Sprunt, Jr.

From Joseph Ruggles Wilson

My dear Son—　　　　　　(near) New London, [Conn.]
　　　　　　　　　　　　Wednesday [Aug. 11, 1875]

I was truly glad to have yr letter. It contained my first, and, up to this time is, my only news from dear home. I could have wished it had been fuller and more detailed as to each of you and your welfare. It is probable that we will start to-morrow upon our fishing trip—to be gone two or three days. . . .

My health is quite good. I do hope that yr. & Josie's cough will not detain you all at home later than last week in August. You had better keep all letters at home—yourself writing to explain to correspondents—unless the contents I must know at once. I need not say that my love for you all is unbounded. Special love to darling mother.　　　　　　Your affexon　J. R. Wilson

ALS (WP, DLC) with WWhw notations on env.: "8/14/75," "Ans.," and miscellaneous figures in WWhw.

Notebook

[c. Sept. 7, 1875-May 4, 1884]

Inscribed on cover (WWhw):

"*Private*," and on flyleaf (WWhw): "Thos. W. Wilson '79 2/13/77 Private."

Contents:

(a) WWsh *vita*, printed at Sept. 7, 1875.

(b) WWsh "Diary," March 20, 1877, intermittently to Oct. 21, 1877, and Sept. 26 and 29, 1878, for transcripts of which see below by dates.

(c) WWhw list, "English Prose Writers."

(d) WWhw outlines of and notes for "Government by Debate," described and printed in part in editorial note, "Government by Debate," Vol. 2.

(e) WWhw list, "My Reading:—(*Principal* Works.)," 1876-79, printed on pp. 442-43.

(f) WWhw list, "*For Library*."

(g) WWhw quotations under title "*Extracts*," selected from *Eclectic Magazine*, Macaulay, Burke, and John Morley's *Burke*.

(h) WWsh draft of letter to John D. Green, to be printed in Volume 2 at Aug. 5, 1882.

(i) Nine miscellaneous loose items, including book list and four illustrations clipped from periodicals.

(WP, DLC)

Wilson's Shorthand Vita

[c. Sept. 7, 1875]

Autobiographical Outline by Thomas W. Wilson:—

Thomas W. Wilson

Born at Staunton, Virginia, 28th December, 1856.

Moved to Augusta, Georgia, [blank]

Removed from Augusta to Columbia, South Carolina, on the [blank]

Entered Freshman class of Davidson College, North Carolina on the [blank] September, 1873, and remained there until the [blank] June, 1874.

Removed from Columbia, South Carolina, to Wilmington, North Carolina, on the [blank] 1874.

Entered the Freshman class of Princeton College on the [blank] September, 1875 (class of 1879).

Transcript of WWsh memorandum in notebook described at Sept. 7, 1875.

Two Items from a Wilson Notebook

[Sept. 7-Dec. 18, 1875]

Expenses at Princeton College, N. Jersey
in a/c with Thomas W. Wilson

September 1875

9/7/75	Pkg. of Chlorate of Potash	.10
	One Blacking brush and box of blacking	.75
	One Box 500 matches	.15
9/8/75	Mending of Watch	1.00
	Hair cutting	.20
	One pkg. of paper	1.00
	One blk watch chain	1.90
9/9/75	Three pairs!! (pears)	.10
	Ray's Higher Algebra.	
9/10/75	Demosthenes Olynthiacs	1.40
	Herodotus, Thucydides	.90
9/11/75	Allen and Greenough's Latin Grammar	1.40
	National Fifth Reader	1.00
9/75	Pencil	.10
	Laundry List	.15
	Blank Book	.50
9/13/75	Washerwoman for Bag	.50
9/13/75	2 pears	.5
	Note Book	.25
9/17/75	Mrs. Wright for Board[1]	10.00

"Pay every two weeks"

"	Treasury for Public Rooms & Wash.	17.00
9/18/75	Shaving	.10
"	Mending vest	.15
"	Buying Barge for Crew (Subscription)	2.00
9/20/75	Pocket Memorandum Book	.50
"	Over-shoes	1.00
9/21/75	For cleaning Winter coat	.50
9/22/75	Nitric Acid	.10
"	Soda Water	.10
"	Mrs. Wright for board for 3 weeks	$30.00
9/23/75	Thermometer	.75
"	Brads	.12
"	New York Times	.6
9/24/75	Gymnasium pants	3.50
9/25/75	" slippers	2.25
9/25/75	Soap	.10
9/27/75	Entering Ball Ground	.25
9/30/75	For peaches and candy	16
9/75	Key to Rays Algebra	75
10/1/75	Gymnasium Shirt	1 75
11/5/75	For board and rent	$40.00
12/6/75	Subscription for boat	2.00

12/7/75	Mending pants	25
12/7/75	Chlorate of Potash	10
12/7/75	Apples	10
12/11/75	For board and rent, Nov.	40.00
12/11/75	To Bill in boling alley	13
12/15/75	Inkstand	75
12/15/75	Mending coat	20
12/15/75	Phonographic Magazine	20
12/16/75	Pens and pencil	15
12/16/75	Apples	5
12/18/75	Board, rent & coal to Dec. 22nd	39.00

WWhw entries in notebook described at Aug. 1, 1873. The list for the dates, Sept. 7-13, 1875, is a revision of a WWhw list appearing on the preceding page of this notebook.

1 WW roomed and boarded at Mrs. Wright's house, which then stood at the southeastern corner of Washington Road and Nassau Street, during his freshman year. He boarded at Mrs. Wright's during his sophomore year until about February 1877, when he moved to Witherspoon Hall. See WWsh diary for June 14, 1876.

Clothes brought to college with me: Princeton, N. J. 9/7/75

Ten (10) new shirts	marked	T. W. *Wilson*		
One (1) old shirt	"	"	"	"
1/2 Doz new cuffs	"	"	"	"
1/2 " " collars	"	"	"	"
Eleven old "	"	"	"	"
1/2 Doz pair old cuffs	"	"	"	"
1/2 " " new socks	"	"	"	"
One (1) Doz Hnkfs	"	T. W.	W.	
Two (2) Night Shirts	"	"	"	Wilson
Three pair summer drawers		"	"	"
" " " flannels		"	"	"
One (1) New summer vest marked		"	"	"

WWhw list in notebook described at Aug. 1, 1873.

Pocket Notebook

[Sept. 20, 1875-July 12, 1876]

Inscribed (WWhw):

"Thomas W. Wilson, Wilmington, N. Carolina, 9/20/75."

Contents:

(a) WWsh copies of various articles, many of which WW later transferred to his *Index Rerum* (printed at Feb. 22, 1876), among them being: "Thoughts," "British Navy (1870)," "The British Navy (1871)," "Standing Armies," "Americanisms," "British Empire," notes from Macaulay, "English Composition," "What to Read," "Hints to Writers & Speakers," "Salaries," "How to break one's-self of Bad Habits," "Manner of holding the Pen," selections from Bacon and Swift, "Of Goodness & Goodness of Nature," selections from Longfellow, Pope, Horace (in Greek), Aeschylus (in Greek), Tacitus (in Latin), Herbert, Burke, and Chaucer.

(b) WWsh exercises.

(c) Undated clothing list (WWhw).

(d) "Reading for Freshman and Sophomore years in College" and "Subjects for Essays (WWhw), printed at Jan. 1, 1876.

(e) Notes and diary-like entries by Joseph R. Wilson, Jr.

(f) Essay entitled "Orators" (WWsh), being mainly a copy of Webster's eulogy on Calhoun.

(g) List of certain authors and their works (WWhw).

(h) Expenses on trip from Princeton to Wilmington, June 26-28, 1876 (WWhw), incorporated by WW into list printed at Jan. 10, 1876.

(i) Diary (WWsh) for June 29-July 6, and July 8-12, 1876, incorporated in revised form by WW into Diary in Notebook described at April 1, 1875, item (d).

Woodrow Wilson Birthplace Foundation, Staunton, Va.

From the Minutes of the American Whig Society[1]

Whig Hall. Sept 24th 1875.

... Resolutions for the admission of new members being next in order, the following came up;—

Whereas David Steward of Md.[2] desires to become a member of Whig Hall, therefore resolved that he be admitted.

c-d R. Johnson[3]. . . .

Whereas &c S. [sic] W. Wilson of N. C.

c-d Richardson.[4]

Hw entry, bound ledger book (NjP).

1 The American Whig Society, founded in 1769, was one of the two literary and debating societies at the College of New Jersey. In WW's day it was divided into two houses—a Senate, composed of graduate members, which met annually at commencement, and a House of Undergraduates. Whig and its sister organization, the Cliosophic Society, founded in 1770, had their origins in clubs organized no later than 1765. They were still the centers of undergraduate life in the 1870's, but the proliferation of voluntary clubs and new undergraduate concerns was beginning to signal the onset of decline. Whig, sometimes in collaboration with Clio, sponsored many undergraduate literary and debating competitions. For ordinary hall debates, undergraduates were divided alphabetically into divisions.

WW's varied activities in the American Whig Society, and their importance to him, are illustrated by the extracts from the Society's minutes printed in this volume. They comprise almost every passage in which he was mentioned. Whig was the main center of WW's extracurricular life during his first two years at Princeton. Other activities in his upperclass years tended to diminish but not to end his participation in Whig affairs.

2 David Stewart, '78.

3 Robert W. Johnson, '76.

4 John E. Richardson, '77.

EDITORIAL NOTE

WILSON'S CLASSROOM NOTEBOOKS

Wilson's classroom notes have already been described in the note on his use of shorthand, pp. 12-16. What follows in this volume is a description of each classroom notebook, from which a clear picture of the subject matter to which Wilson and other students were being exposed may be seen.

The editors have had varying portions of the shorthand passages in these notebooks transcribed. The transcripts of lecture notes printed in this volume have been included for their significance and representative quality. Analysis suggests that Princeton undergraduates were generally being fed mediocre intellectual fare. Other evidence in this volume confirms the conclusion that Wilson, and undergraduates like him, were largely self-educated.

Classroom Notebook

[Oct. 16, 1875-June 21, 1877]

Inscribed (WWhw):
"Thomas W. Wilson Class of '79," containing
(a) WWsh lecture notes, with some WWhw headings and interpolations, taken in Professor Theodore W. Hunt's[1] freshman and sophomore English courses, Oct. 16, 1875-May 27, 1876, and Sept. 19, 1876-May 15, 1877. This was a two-year course in grammar, rhetoric, composition, and poetry. See *Catalogue of the College of New Jersey for the Academical Year 1875-'76* [Princeton, 1875], p. 18, and the same for 1876-77 [Princeton, 1876], p. 20. Some of the lecture topics were general principles of rhetoric and oratory, rhetorical processes, laws of rhetoric, figurative language, rhetorical figures (metaphors, allegories, hyperboles), kinds and qualities of style, including force and wit and humor, origin of language, study of language, the place of Anglo-Saxon in the family of languages, etymology, the principle of life in language, relation of thought to expression, forms of discourse, and argumentative discourse. Notes for three of Professor Hunt's lectures are on verso pages running from back to front, followed by
(b) Undated WWsh lecture notes, with some WWhw headings and interpolations and drawings, probably taken in Professor George Macloskie's[2] course on natural history during the third term of the academic year 1876-77, April 18-June 21, 1877. WW's notes cover that portion of the course that was a brief survey of the science of chemistry. In addition there are two small loose pages of WWsh and WWhw notes on chemistry.

(WP, DLC).
[1] The Rev. Theodore W. Hunt, Adjunct Professor of Rhetoric and English Language.
[2] The Rev. George Macloskie, Professor of Natural History.

From the Minutes of the American Whig Society

Whig Hall, Oct. 29, 1875

. . . Second Session
The literary exercises being next in order, the 9th Division Composed.

Saturday Oct. 16/75

1. Place given to the Subject
2. Cause of its Decline
3. History of Opinion — Objections
4. True Definition.

(1) [shorthand]

(2) [shorthand]

(3) [shorthand]

[shorthand notes continue]

Wilson's First Classroom Shorthand Notes at Princeton, Taken in Professor Hunt's Freshman Course in English

Performed.

R. Walker[1]   Subject   "Scandinavian Mythology"
T. Wilson   "Rome was not built in a day."
Yourt[2]   "Alfred the Great" . . .

[1] Richard W. Walker, Jr., '77.
[2] William R. Yourt, '77.

To Andrew Jackson Graham

From Thomas W. Wilson.—   [c. Nov. 1, 1875]

I am especially pleased with the Reporter's List, commenced in the July Number of the Journal. If continued it will prove very valuable indeed.

Printed in *The Student's Journal*, IV (Nov. 1875), 8.

From Two Wilson Notebooks

[c. Jan. 1, 1876]

Reading for Freshman and Sophomore years in College:

(1) Milton—Paradise Lost.
(3) History of the U. S.
    Philosophies of Locke, Hume, Hamilton and Kant.
    Cicero de Officiis: Chap. De Contentione Honeste et Utilis.
    Philosophies of Plato, Aristotle and Descartes.
(2) Diaries of Pepys and Evelyn.
Locke's Philosophical works:
Hume's Philosophical works: "Essays," "Treatise on the Human Mind," "Natural History of Religion."
Hamilton's Philosophical works:
Kant's Philosophical works:
Plato's Philosophical works:
Aristotle's Philosophical works: "Organon" or "Logic," "Rhetoric," "Poetics," "Ethics," "Politics," "History of Animals," "Physics," "Metaphysics," "Psychology," and "Meteorology."
Descartes Philosophical works:
    "Discours de la méthode"
    "Meditationes de Prima Philosophia," "Principia Philosophiae."

Subjects for Essays:

1. George Eliot's Novels.   4. Geothe and Rousseau.
2. Wordsworth and Byron.   5. M. Guizot.
3. English in the Curriculum.   6. History and its Uses.

7. Shelly and Byron
8. Sarcasm as an Element of Literary Criticism.
9. Compulsory Education.
10. Mental Needs of To-Day.
11. Thackeray and Dickens.
12. Moral Value of Knowledge.
13. The Danger of Talent.
14. Arbitration, a Substitute for War.
15. The Skepticism of Science.
16. Power of the Individual.
17. Early English Dramatists.
18. Corruption as an Element of Progress.
19. Chaucer.
20. Philosophic Reaction.
21. Lucretius.
22. Expediency.
23. The Will and the Noble in Man.
24. Thiers.
25. Clowns of Shakspeare.
26. Cavour.
27. Social Responsibility.
28. Humor and Pathos of Chas. Dickens.
29. The Comus.
30. Use and Abuse of Political Parties.
31. Independence in Politics.
32. Evolution vs. Religion.
33. Genius and Success.
34. Julius Ceasar. (The Play)
35. King Lear.
36. The Force of an Idea.
37. Failure an Element of Success.
38. Oliver Goldsmith.
39. The Power of Friendship.
40. The Force of Virtue.
41. Othelo.
42. Iago.
43. Means of gaining Truth.
44. Abuse of Public Men.
45. *The True Statesman.*
46. Fallow Land.
47. Power of Association.
48. Our Duty to our Age.
49. The Eloquence of Desolation.
50. Literature as a Companion.
51. Sources of Literature.
52. Character of Eloquence.
53. *The Union.*
54. America's Orators.
55. England's Orators.
56. Power of Principle.
57. Humility.
58. Public Opinion.
59. Japanese Empire.
60. Progress—Its Means and its Ends.
61. The True End (in education).[1]
62. Romanism.
63. Reconstruction of the South.
64. Self-Worship.
65. Practical Thought.
66. Advance of "
67. The Present Age.
68. Adversity's Test.
69. Work.
70. Improving by good Example.
71. Industry Essentially Social.
72. Art and Nature.
73. Decision of Character.
74. *Resolution and Independence.*
75. Knowledge as Power.
76. The Difference of Wits.
77. The Athenian Orators.
78. Let Winter Come!
79. Happiness?
80. Imitation in Art.
81. The Beautiful and the Useful.
82. Defence of Enthusiasm.
83. Generosity and Justice.
84. Resolution of Youth.
85. Popular Favor.
86. Morbid Literature.
87. Satire, an Element in Moral Reform.
88. The Progress of English Literature.
89. The Wits of Queen Anne's Reign.

90. Errors of Learning.
91. National Honor.
92. Means of Success.
93. Intellect and Feeling.
94. Identity of Distant and Different Eras.
95. Necessity of Progress.
96. Preparation the Index of Achievement.
97. Power of Concentration.
98. Distinterested Benevolence.
99. Change an Essential Element in Progress.
100. True Literary Inspiration.
101. True Love of Liberty—Its Meaning.
102. The Reformers in Literature.
103. The Choice of a Profession.
104. Brains and Brass.

WWhw entries in notebook described at Sept. 20, 1875. It is very likely that the essay subjects were suggested by Prof. Hunt. WW underlined topics that he chose for essays and speeches.
1 WWsh transcribed.

[Jan. 10-June 28, 1876]

January 1876 (Expenses)

(Cash on hand 1/10/76 $20.00

1/10/76	For state-room & meals on steamer	3.00
1/11/76	Baggage transfer	.50
1/11/76	Balto. cab	1.50
1/11/76	Hotel Bill (Carrollton)	4.00
1/11/76	Berger Entertainment	1.00
1/11/76	Handkerchief	25
1/11/76	Cane	75
1/11/76	Telegraph	38
1/12/76	Waiter of the Carrollton	25
1/12/76	Ticket for Princeton	4.95
1/12/76	Cake, Papers &c	.50
1/12/76	Delivery of Baggage (John)	25
1/12/76	Telegraph	.50
1/13/76	Apples (from John)	5
1/13/76	For being shaved	10
1/17/76	Otto's French Grammar	1.58
1/17/76	Caramels	15
1/17/76	Matches	15
1/18/76	Drew from bank (draft on N. Y.)	50.00

(Cash on hand 1/18/76 $50.00

1/19/76	Rawlinson's Ancient History	2.25
"	Umbrella	4.00
1/20/76	For a shave	10
"	To College Bill (Second term 1876)	21.50
1/22/76	Worcester's Pocket Dictionary	.75
"	Drawing Paper and Ruler	.60
1/24/76	" " " Pencils	.28
1/25/76	Expenses (Hall)1	3.00
1/26/76	Billiards	.90
1/31/76	For singing lessons (Prof Perkins)2	1.00

"	Mending of Pants	25
2/1/76	Rec'd $50.00 (Draft on N. Y.).	
2/4/76	For board to 2/2/76	30.00
2/5/76	For sleighing	5.00
2/7/76	For Hat	3.50
"	Hair-cutting	.20
"	Medicine & Mucilage	1.00
2/9/76	Shaving	10
2/12/76	Chrolate [chlorate] of Potash Troches	25
2/13/76	Chlorate of Potash	10
2/1/76	Ottos French Grammar (2nd hand)	1.30
2/17/76	Blank Book (for Index Rerum)	1.30
"	Shaving	.10
2/18/76	Mucilage	.25
2/21/76	Oil	25
2/25/76	Pair shoes	8.00
2/26/76	Excursion ticket to New York	2.00
"	'Bus fare	10
2/27/76	For stamp	.3
"	Boot Black	5
2/28/76	Newspapers	.15
"	Fare from Metropolitan to depot	.75
"	Ferry fare	.3
"	Cravats (2)	2.25
2/29/76	Expenses (Hall)[1]	1.25
"	Caramels	.10
3/2/76	Rec'd $50.00 (D. on N. Y.)	
"	Shaving	.10
3/6/76	For board & rent to 3/8/76	50.00
3/8/76	Shaving & India-rubber	20
3/8/76	Caramels	.15
3/9/76, 3/10/76 & 3/11/76, Three Tribunes		.15
3/11/76	Mending of Watch	1.00
3/12/76	Church Colection	.10
3/14/76	Shave and Hair cut	.30
3/15/76	Rubber	10
3/18/76	Box of Blacking	.25
3/25/76	Ticket to Glee Club Concert	.50
"	Paper	.15
4/1/76	Fencing Materials	10.00
"	Paper	.30
"	Shave	.10
4/7/76	Base Ball	1.25
"	Lamp wick	.5
"	Watch Key	5
4/10/76	Express	.40
4/11/76	Expenses (Hall)[1]	.25
"	Bank charges on Draft	.10
"	Matches	.15
"	Sharpening razor	.20
4/12/76	Extracts (100) No. 1 (Speeches)	.30

4/13/76	Envelopes	.85
"	Pectoral	.90
"	Bottle of ink	.25
"	Board to 4/12/76	50.00
4/14/76	Sodas	.20
4/17/76	Barber	.50
"	Writing Paper	.50
"	Pencil	.10
4/19/76	Cod Liver Oil	1.00
"	N.Y. Tribune,	.5
4/20/76	"	.5
4/21/76	"	.5
4/22/76	"	.5
"	Pens and Pen-Holder	.10
4/24/76	N. Y. Tribune,	.5
4/25/76	"	.5
4/26/76	"	.5
"	Shave	.10
April		
27	Court Plaster	.10
"	To Junction and back	.20
"	N. Y. Tribune	.5
28	"	.5
29	"	.5
"	Cough Mixture	.50
May		
3	Ticket to Gymnastic Contest	.75
"	Col. Draft on New York	.10
"	Rec'd " " " for $75.00	
5(4)	U. B. B.[3] suits	.50
13	Athletic games	.25
15	Cicero's Tusculan Disputations	1.13
16	Oil	.25
17	Match Game (Yale) 12 [to] 9	.50
18	Board to 5/17/76	50.00
"	Match Game	.25
20	" "	.50
"	Score Card	.5
22	Cough Mixture	.50
27	Match Game	.25
31	Lamp Chimney	.10
June		
10	Base Ball	.10
"	Hat	3.25
"	Express on pkg of clothes	.75
"	Cleaning of coat	.50
13	College Bill for 3rd term	13.00
"	J. O.[4] Invitations	.80
"	Stretching shoe	.10
15	Match Game	.25
"	Ice Cream (for 2)	.30

16	Princetonian[5] and Tribune	.20
17	Shave and hair cut	.30
19	Board to 6/21/76	50.00
"	N. Y. Times	.5
"	Board to 6/21/76	.20
23	Fire Works for spree	.20
24	Collecting Draft on N. Y.	10
24	Ticket to Glee Club Concert	.75
"	Athletic Games	.50
"	Sodas	.20
"	Expenses (Hall)[1]	.25
"	Board &c to 6/26/76	20.00
"	Packing Box	.40
"	"Lit"[6]	.50
26	Baggage Transfer (Ben.)	.50
"	Princeton to Baltimore	4.60
"	Baggage Transfer to boat	.25
"	Ticket to Wilmington	17.00
"	Meal and state-room	2.00
"	Shave (on boat)	.25
27	Boot-shine (on boat)	.10
"	Oranges	.25
"	Papers	.10
"	Dinner	1.00
"	Carriage	.50
"	Baggage Transfer (Wilmington)	.25
28	Express on pkg.	1.10

WWhw entries in notebook described at Aug. 1, 1873.

[1] WWsh. These "expenses" appear to be for dues and fines paid to the American Whig Society, often referred to as "Hall."

[2] Apparently a local music teacher; not on Princeton faculty.

[3] University Base Ball Association.

[4] The Junior Oratorical Contest, an annual contest in which representatives of Whig and Clio participated. See WW's Diary for this date.

[5] *The Princetonian*, an undergraduate weekly journal, the first issue of which was published on June 14, 1876.

[6] *The Nassau Literary Magazine*, founded in 1845, published by the senior class.

EDITORIAL NOTE

WILSON'S COMMONPLACE BOOK: "INDEX RERUM"

WILSON'S decision to keep an *index rerum*, made in late 1875 or early 1876, was probably prompted by the reading of an article by Andrew J. Graham in *The Student's Journal*, III (Sept. 1874), 8. Graham described an *index rerum* as a "methodically arranged commonplace book" and mentioned one type originated by the Rev. John Todd and entitled *Index Rerum or Index of Subjects*. It was first published in 1833; a second edition appeared in 1835 and was reprinted in 1861. Todd's work—a large book of blank, lined pages—differed from the well-known commonplace books in two particulars. Selections were usually copied in full in a commonplace book. In place of these, Todd suggested listing only citations or references to the sources of the selections, and arranging these references alphabetically under the initial letter and the first vowel in the subject heading under which the selection would fall. Todd's book was apparently used by many persons; he had earlier published a highly popular *Student's Manual* which was in use at Princeton during Wilson's student days and in which an *index rerum* was described, and it may be that Wilson was aware of Todd's volumes. In beginning his *Index Rerum,* Wilson seems to have followed Graham's recommendation to start with an "Indexed Ledger" or "blank book with ledger rulings," for it was just such a book that he purchased. In the list of expenses just printed is the entry "2/17/76 Blank Book (for Index Rerum) 1.30." In arranging his book, it is evident that Wilson followed some of Todd's suggestions, as well as Graham's, together with the commonplace method of entering passages in full. His extensive use of shorthand lent a typically personal and unique quality to the document.

Wilson, during the month following the purchase of his indexed ledger, began transferring into this book a number of quotations that he had copied earlier into his pocket notebook described at September 20, 1875. In one sense, the entries that appear in the pocket notebook are the real beginning of his *Index Rerum.* Wilson's practice of saving interesting and useful quotations and ideas may have antedated his attraction to the plan of arranging such selections in an indexed volume. In any case, he never completed the task of transferring these early selections into his *Index Rerum,* and from an approximate total of forty there remain in the pocket notebook more than a score that are not in the *Index Rerum.* Among them are items that bear the following headings: "Thoughts," "British Navy," "Americanisms," "Chief Ministers Under Charles II," "Act of Habeas Corpus," "Population," "Salaries," "Manner of Holding the Pen," and "Pope's Rule for the Use of Words." They also include long extracts from Francis Bacon's "Of Death," "Of Revenge," "Of Goodness and Goodness of Nature," and "Of Nobility", from Edward Bulwer-Lytton's *My Novel or Varietion in English Life*; brief extracts from the poetry of Geoffrey Chaucer, George Herbert, and Henry Wadsworth Longfellow; a number of quotations in Greek or Latin; and many brief references to authors and works.

Most of the entries in the *Index Rerum* seem to have been made during 1876. At the end of some passages, Wilson recorded the date on which he first copied the selection. The earliest of these is January 31, 1876; the latest is May 18, 1876. However, in his shorthand diary on July 18, 1876, and November 15, 1876, he mentioned writing up extracts for his *Index Rerum.* The entries were made over a relatively short period. Still they reveal something of the scope of Wilson's reading at an early age and complement references to reading made in his diary. Further, they shed light on the variety of ideas which intrigued Wilson as a youth and, in many cases, were to find reflection in his thoughts and actions as an adult.

In appearance, the *Index Rerum* is a large book, approximately 8½ by 13 inches, containing 288 pages with numbers and index letters in Wilson's handwriting. Most of the pages are blank. Of the one hundred and twenty-nine entries, Wilson used Graham shorthand for ninety-two. Some of these are entirely in shorthand; most, however, contain a sprinkling of longhand. On the other hand, nearly all the remaining thirty-four items are entirely in longhand; only a few contain any shorthand characters. Wilson wrote subject headings and the titles of individual selections in longhand, as he frequently did subheadings within a long shorthand passage. Aside from headings, Wilson seems to have shifted to longhand whenever he encountered words or phrases which were difficult to render into shorthand, or occasionally when he wrote proper names. Because the occurrence of occasional longhand words in shorthand passages seems to have no special significance, the editors have not felt it necessary to indicate these shifts within a passage. However, they have distinguished between passages entirely or largely in shorthand and those entirely or largely in longhand by making note of the latter with a dagger placed at the beginning of the passage.

In presenting the text of the *Index Rerum* the editors have sought to adhere as faithfully as possible to Wilson's text. All passages reproduced here are transcripts of his shorthand or appear as he wrote them in longhand. Selections, wherever possible, were checked against printed sources, but Wilson's changes or errors in copying have been retained. So, too, has Wilson's punctuation. Where this is not evident, as in much of the shorthand, the punctuation of the printed source was followed. Words underlined by Wilson have been italicized as have all foreign phrases, including the few which Wilson neglected to underline. A number of selections present problems that are dealt with and explained where they occur. A number of passages, written by Wilson on loose sheets, do not appear in alphabetical sequence; these have been placed at the end under the heading, "Unentered Items."

Wilson identified most selections at least by author; however, his citations are abbreviated at best. For the convenience of readers who may wish to put quoted passages in context or compare Wilson's renditions with the original, the editors offer a list of authors and works, insofar as they have been identified, in which the quotations in the *Index Rerum* may be found. It is virtually impossible in most cases to determine which edition of a work Wilson used; indeed, frequently he drew his selections from anthologies or from other intermediate sources. Therefore, with few exceptions, only the author and title of the work are given. Most of them are well known and are available in a number of current editions.

"Aristotle," *American Cyclopaedia* (16 vols., New York, D. Appleton & Co., 1873-1876), I, 705-707; "British Empire," *ibid.*, pp. 296-97; "Edmund Burke," *ibid.*, pp. 455-57. This is probably the edition used by Wilson.

Louis E. M. Bautain, *The Art of Extempore Speaking.*

Henry Lord Brougham, "Lord Chatham," "Mr. Burke," "Mr. Fox," *Historical Sketches of Statesmen Who Flourished in the Time of George III.*

Edmund Burke to M. Dupont, October 1789, *Correspondence of the Right Honourable Edmund Burke.*

Edmund Burke, "Speech on Moving Resolutions For Conciliation With America, March 22, 1775"; "Speech at the Guildhall in Bristol Previous to the Late Election Upon Certain Points Relative to His Parliamentary Conduct, 1780"; "Speech to the Electors of Bristol, November 3, 1774."

Lord Byron, *Childe Harold's Pilgrimage, Canto the Third.*

John C. Calhoun, "Speech on the Slavery Question, March 4, 1850."

Thomas Carlyle, "Burns," *Critical and Miscellaneous Essays*; "Summary, Lecture V: The Hero As Man of Letters," *Heroes and Hero Worship*; "Summary, Lecture VI: The Hero As King," *ibid.*

Pisistratus Caxton [Edward Lord Bulwer-Lytton], *My Novel or Varieties in English Life.*

Arthur Hugh Clough, "Say Not the Struggle Naught Availeth."

John Courtenay, *A Poetical Review of the Literary and Moral Character of the Late Samuel Johnson.*

Abraham Cowley, "Anacreontiques, II: Drinking."

William Cowper, "Winter Walk At Noon."

George Farquhar, *The Beaux Stratagem, Sir Harry Wildair.*

Oliver Goldsmith, "An Enquiry Into the Present State of Polite Learning in Europe: Introduction, Of Rewarding Genius in England, Of the Marks of Literary Decay in France and England"; "A Reverie"; "The Characteristics of Greatness"; "Happiness in a Great Measure Dependent on Constitution"; "Of Eloquence"; "On Education"; "On Justice and Generosity"; "On the Cultivation of Taste"; "On the Use of Language."

William Hazlitt, "Lecture IV: On Wycherly, Congreve, Vanbrugh, and Farquhar"; "On the Living Poets"; "On Shakespeare and Milton"; "On Dryden and Pope"; "On Thomson and Cowper"; "On Burns and the Old English Ballads."

J. B. Holbrook, unidentified selection.

Andrew Jackson, "Second Inaugural Address, March 4, 1833.'"

Francis Jeffrey, "Review of Archibald Alison, *Essays on the Nature and Principles of Taste,*" *Contributions to the Edinburgh Review*; "Review of the *Complete Works, in Philosophy, Politics, and Morals, of the Late Dr. Benjamin Franklin,*" *ibid.*; "Review of the Works of Jonathan Swift," *ibid.*

Thomas B. Macaulay, *History of England,* Vols. I and VI.

Thomas B. Macaulay on his memory, quoted in George Otto Trevelyan, *Life and Letters of Lord Macaulay*; T. B. Macaulay to a Friend in Leeds, August 3, 1832, *ibid.*, T. B. Macaulay to Macvey Napier, November 26, 1836, *ibid.*

Thomas B. Macaulay, "The Life and Writings of Addison," *Critical and Miscellaneous Essays.*

John Milton, *Paradise Lost,* Book VI & Book VIII.

"Standing Armies," New York *Sun*, December 28, 1875.

"Official Salaries in America," *Pall Mall Gazette*, April 5, 1876.

Alexander Pope, "Epistle to Mr. Jervas," "An Essay on Criticism."

William Shakespeare, *Richard III, Troilus and Cressida, Two Gentlemen of Verona.*

William Smith, *History of Greece.*

Edmund Spenser, "Oak and Briar."

Charles Hadley Spurgeon, unidentified selection.

Sir John Suckling, "Song."

"Hints to Writers and Speakers," *The Visitor*, IV (Nov. 29, 1869), 261-62; "How to Break Oneself of Bad Habits," *ibid.*, (Feb. 28, 1870), 419.

B. C. Walpole, *Recollections of the Life of the Late Right Honourable Charles James Fox* (New York, E. Sargeant, 1807), pp. 15 ff. This is probably the edition Wilson referred to; no other seems to have appeared.

Daniel Webster, "Second Speech on Foot's Resolution, January 26, 1830"; "Second Speech on the Sub-Treasury, March 12, 1838."

Richard Whately, *Bacon's Essays: With Annotations.*

Wilson's Commonplace Book: "Index Rerum"

[Feb. 22, 1876-c. Nov. 15, 1876]

T. W. Wilson Standard Phonographer

America, Burke on March 22, 1775   Ae

Mr. Speaker, I cannot prevail on myself to hurry over this great consideration. It is good for us to be here. We stand where we have an immense view of what is, and what is past. Clouds indeed, and darkness, rest upon the future. Let us, however, before we descend from this noble eminence, reflect that this growth of our national prosperity has happened within the short period of the life of man. It has happened within sixty-eight years. There are those alive whose memories might touch the two extremities. For instance, my Lord Bathurst might remember all the stages of the progress. He was in 1704 of an age at least to be made to comprehend such things. He was then old enough *acta parentum jam legere, et quae sit poterit cognoscere virtus.* Suppose, Sir, that the angel of this auspicious youth, foreseeing the many virtues which made him one of the most amiable, as he is one of the most fortunate men of his age, had opened to him in vision, that, when, in the fourth generation, the third prince of the house of Brunswick had sat twelve years on the throne of that nation which (by the happy issue of moderate and healing counsels) was to be made Great Britain, he should see his son, Lord Chancellor of England, turn back the current of hereditary dignity to its fountain, and raise him to an higher rank of peerage, whilst he enriched the family with a new one—if, amidst these bright and happy scenes of domestic honour and prosperity, that angel should have drawn up the curtain, and unfolded the rising glories of his country, and whilst he was gazing with admiration on the then commercial grandeur of England, the genius should point out to him a little speck, scarce visible in the mass of the national interest, a small seminal principle, rather than a formed body, and should tell him—"Young man, there is America—which at this day serves for little more than to amuse you with stories of savage men and uncouth manners, yet shall, before you taste of death, show itself equal to the whole of that commerce which now attracts the envy of the world. Whatever England has been growing to by a progressive increase of government improvement, brought in by varieties of people, by succession of civilizing conquests and civilizing settlements in a series of seventeen hundred years, you shall see as much added to her by America in the course of a single life!" If this state of his country had been foretold to him, would it not require all the sanguine credulity of youth, and all the fervid glow of enthusiasm, to make him believe it? Fortunate man, he has lived to see it! Fortunate indeed, if he shall live to see nothing that shall vary the prospect, and cloud the setting of his day!

Angels, battle of
    "From their foundations *loos'ning* to and fro,
    They plucked the seated Hills, with all
        their load,
    Rocks, Waters, Woods; and by the shaggie tops
    Up lifting bore them in their hands."

Addison's Essays   Ai
    See Addison's Essays Numbers 26, 329, 69, 317, 159, 343, 517:
2 Visits to the Abbey; the Visit to the Exchange; the Journal of the Retired Citizen; the Vision of Mirzah; the Transmigrations of Pug the Monkey; the Death of Sir Roger De Coverly.

Aristotle (The Philosophy of) From the American Cyclopedia.
    "No other philosopher has exerted so large an influence on so many centuries, and on the ideas of so many nations, as Aristotle. His merits as a metaphysical thinker may perhaps be variously estimated, but his performances in natural science, which he first created, and his method of philosophy, constitute his greatness. He was the first careful observer, dissector, and describer of animals. He first divided the animal kingdom into classes; described a great many animals before unknown to the scientific world; came near discovering the circulation of the blood; discriminated be-

tween the several faculties, the nourishing, feeling, concupiscent, moving, and reasoning powers of animal organism, and attempted to explain the origin of these powers within the body; and built his moral and political philosophy on the peculiarities of human organization. His philosophical method consists in the principle that all our thinking must be founded on the observation of facts. Logic is the fundamental science, and the principles which he laid down for it have never been superseded. It is acknowledged by Kant and (Hegel), the two most profound thinkers of Germany, that from the time of Aristotle to their own age logic had made no progress. He invented the categories, or fundamental forms of thought, universal expressions for the ever-changing relations of things, and limited their number to ten; and he devised the so-called 'syllogistics,' or science of forming correct conclusions. He likewise became the father of modern psychology, showing how the mind creates its speculative methods and general notions; and that though we cannot prove their correspondence with the reality, because there is no direct proof for things which transcend our senses and observation, yet we are always compelled to recur to these general notions and take them for indispensable forms of thinking, if we will think at all. Every science must, according to Aristotle, have a fundamental principle, which need not and cannot be logically proved, because it is in itself certain, and accepted as manifest truth. Aristotle first discriminated between the substance of things and their accidental peculiarities, and created the philosophical notions of 'matter' and of 'form.' He also established the philosophical notions of 'space' and 'time,' and showed their connection with matter, while he first furnished the world with what is called the cosmological argument for the existence of God. He states it thus: Although every single movement and existence in the world has a finite cause and every such finite cause another finite cause back of it, yet back of this infinite series of finite causes there must be an infinite immaterial being, a first something, unmoved, all-moving, pure energy, absolute reason, God. In psychology and anthropology, Aristotle is the author of the theory of different powers of the soul, of distinct feeling, willing, reasoning, and moving powers or faculties. The reasoning power is regarded by Aristotle not as a product of the body, but as bestowed on it from outside, and as perfect only in its separation from the body by death. Proceeding from the principle that whatever is to be the goal and highest good to humanity must not depend on casualties and ever-changing minor circumstances, but must be certain in itself, and impart to every other good its value, he maintains that the εὐδαιμόνια, or highest possible pleasure which is conceivable for man, is derived only from the perfect satisfaction of those faculties which distinguish him from the beasts, that is, of the reasoning powers.——his philosophy began to be better understood; and his philosophy has been further developed by Bacon, Descartes, Spinoza, and Kant.——It is not so much by his philosophical system that Aristotle has wielded his enormous influence, especially as this is only now beginning to be fully understood and justly appreciated, as by his logical inventions, and his method of philosophy in general."

Authors: Au

Addison, Aeschylus, Aristophanes, Aristotle.
Bacon, Burke, Burnet, Burns.
Caesar, Canning, Carlyle, Clarendon.
Dante, Demosthenes.
Euripedes.
Fielding, Froude.
Gibbon, Goethe, Goldsmith, Grandison.
Homer, Horace, Hume.
Johnson.
Lessing, Lucan, Lucian.
Macaulay, Mill, Milton, Müller, Montaigne.
Niebuhr.
Pascal, Pindar, Plato, Plautus, Pliny, Plutarch, Pope.
Quintilian.
Seneca, Schiller, Shakspeare, Sophocles, Swift, Spenser.
Tacitus, Terence, Thucydides.
Virgil, Voltaire.
Young. 5/18/76

Bad Habits, How to break one'self of, Ba

Understand clearly the reasons, and all the reasons, why the habit is injurious. Study the subject till there is no lingering doubt in your mind. Avoid the persons, the places, and the thoughts that lead to the temptation. Frequent the places, associate with the persons, indulge in the thoughts that lead away from temptation. Keep busy; idleness is the strength of bad habits. Do not give up the struggle when you have broken your resolution once, twice, ten times, a thousand times. That only shows how much need there is for you to strive. When you have broken your resolution, just think the matter over, and endeavor to understand why it was you failed, so that you may be on your guard against a recurrence of the same circumstances. Do not think it a little or an easy thing that you have undertaken. It is folly to expect to break off a bad habit in a day which may have been gathering strength in you for years.

Beauty   Be
"In our opinion, then, our sense of beauty depends entirely on our previous experience of simpler pleasures or emotions, and consists in the *suggestion* of agreeable or interesting sensations with which we had formerly been made familiar by the direct and intelligible agency of our common sensibilities; and that vast variety of objects, to which we give the common name of beautiful, become entitled to that appellation, merely because they all possess the power of recalling or reflecting those sensations of which they have been the accompaniments, or with which they have been associated in our imagination by any other more casual bond of connection. According to this view of the matter, therefore, beauty is not an inherent property or quality of objects at all, but the results of the accidental relations in which they may stand to our experience of pleasures or emotions; and does not depend upon any particular configuration of parts, proportions, or colours, in external things, nor upon the unity, coherence, or simplicity of intellectual creations—but merely upon the associations which, in the case of every individual, may enable these inherent, and otherwise indifferent qualities, to suggest or recall to the mind emotions of a pleasurable or interesting description. It follows, therefore, that no object is beautiful in itself, nor could appear so antecedent to our experience of direct pleasures or emotions; and that, as an infinite variety of objects may thus reflect interesting ideas, so all of them may acquire the title of beautiful, although utterly diverse and disparate in their nature, and possessing nothing in common but this accidental power of reminding us of other emotions." Jeffrey

British Empire.   Bi
In Europe: The United Kingdom of Great Britain and Ireland, with the adjacent islands in the British seas, including the Shetlands, Orkneys, Hebrides, Scillies, Man, the Channel islands, and the Isle of Wight; area 121,115 sq. m.; pop. in 1871, 31,817,108. Wales was incorporated into the kingdom of England in the reign of Edward I. Scotland, whose sovereign became king of England in 1603, long continued distinct for administrative and legislative purposes. It was fully joined to England by the act of union in 1707, by which the Scottish legislature was dissolved, and the Scotch were admitted to representation in the British houses of

lords and commons. The Scotch still maintain their own peculiar laws, customs, and national church. Ireland was nominally annexed to the crown of England in 1172; but for centuries it resisted the invader, and can scarcely be said to have been subjugated until it was reduced by Cromwell. It was governed by its own parliament till 1800, when by an act of union it was united to England, and, like Scotland, admitted to the rights of representation both by peers and commoners in the British parliament. Its laws are essentially the same as those of England, though passed specially for Ireland. The Anglican church was imposed upon Ireland as a state church, with all the endowments of the ancient Catholic church, although less than one eighth of the population are members of its communion; but it was finally disestablished in 1871. Heligoland, a small island in the German ocean, inhabited chiefly by fishermen, taken from the Danes in 1807; area, 0.21 sq. m.; pop. in 1860, 2,172. Gibraltar, taken from the Spaniards in 1704, consisting of a lofty steep rock, bristling with guns, and regularly fortified, and a small space of sloping ground on which stands its town; area, 2 sq. m.; pop. in 1871, 18,695. Malta, a strongly fortified naval and military station, with its dependency Gozo, taken from the French in 1800; area of both, 143 sq. m.; pop. in 1866, 139,502.

In Asia: British India is divided into British possessions and native states more or less under the control of the British government. Since Aug. 2, 1858, all the territories heretofore under the government of the East India company have been vested in the crown, in the name of which all authority is exercised. The executive authority is vested in a governor general, who acts under the orders of the secretary of state for India, and also appoints various lieutenant governors and commissioners for the several presidencies and provinces. The provinces of Hyderabad, Mysore, & Coorg (47,-661 sq. m.; pop. 6,389,792) are under the direct administration of the governor general. The remainder is under the following functionaries: lieutenant governor of Bengal, 239,591 sq. m., pop. 30,086,898; lieutenant governor of the Punjaub, 102,001 sq. m., pop. 17,596,752; chief commissioner of Oude, 24,060 sq. m.; pop. 11,220,747; chief commissioner of Central Provinces, 84,162; 7,985,411; chief commissioner of British Burmah, 98,881; 2,463,-484; governor of Madras, 141,746; 26,539,052; governor of Bombay, 87,639, 11,093,512; commissioner of Sinde, 54,403, 1,795,-594. Total area of British possessions in India, 963,929 sq. m., pop. 151,146,426. There are some sixty or seventy native chiefs and states under the control of the British government; area 646,147 sq. m., pop. 46,245,888. Besides India, the British possessions include in Asia the islands of Ceylon and Singapore, Hong Kong in China, and a few small settlements, with a total population of about 2,800,000; also Aden, a seaport at the mouth of the Red sea, pop. about 50,000.

In Africa: Cape Colony, extending from the Cape of Good Hope to the Orange river, taken from the Dutch in 1806; 200,610 sq. m., pop. 566,158. Port Natal, N. E. of Cape Colony, settled in 1838; 17,801 sq. m., pop. 269,362. Sierra Leone, settled in 1787, as a colony for slaves who had been released from their captors; 468 sq. m., pop. 55,374. Gambia, N. of Sierra Leone, settled in 1631; 21 sq. m., pop. in 1851, 6,939. The Gold Coast Settlements, comprising several forts and trading posts, of which Cape Coast Castle is the chief; 16,629 sq. m., pop. estimated at 400,000. Mauritius, and several small islands adjacent, lying in the Indian ocean, taken from the French in 1810; 708 sq. m., pop. 322,924. St. Helena, an island in the Atlantic, ceded by the Dutch in 1651; 47 sq. m., pop. 6,860. Ascension, an almost uninhabited rock N. of St. Helena.

In America: Dominion of Canada, comprising the former territorial divisions of Canada, New Brunswick, Nova Scotia, Hudson Bay territory, British Columbia, and Vancouver island; 3,481,779 sq. m., pop. 3,684,000. Newfoundland; 40,200 sq. m., pop. 146,-536. Prince Edward Island; 2,173 sq. m., pop. 94,021. The Bermudas, in the Atlantic ocean, off the coast of the United States; 24 sq. m., pop. 11,796. West India Islands; 12,636 sq. m., pop. 1,028,-708. British Honduras; 13,500 sq. m., pop. 25,635. British Guiana, taken from the French in 1803; 99,925 sq. m., pop. 122,812. Falkland Islands, in the Atlantic, off the S. E. coast of South America; 4,741 sq. m., pop. 686.

In Australasia: Australia, 2,973,127 sq. m., pop. in 1871, 1,561,027, comprising the following colonies: New South Wales, organized in 1788, 323,437 sq. m., pop. 501,611; Western Australia, organized in 1829; South Australia, organized in 1836, 383,328 sq. m., pop. 188,995; Victoria, organized in 1851, 86,831 sq. m., pop. 729,868; Queensland, organized in 1859, 678,000 sq. m., pop. 115,567; Northern territory, not yet organized, 523,531 sq. m., pop. 201. Tasmania, formerly Van Diemen's Land, settled in 1803; 26,215 sq. m., pop. 97,368. New Zealand, settled in 1839; 106,259 sq. m., pop. 294,028. Labuan, an island near Borneo; 50 sq. m., pop. 3,828. Sarawak, a protected state in the island of Borneo, established in 1844 by Sir James Brooke; 3,000 sq. m., pop. 50,000.

The following table gives approximately, the round numbers, the area and population of the British empire:

Countries	Area in square miles	Population
Europe	121,000	32,000,000
Asia	1,640,000	200,000,000
America	3,700,000	5,000,000
Africa	250,000	1,700,000
Australasia	3,100,000	2,000,000
Total	8,811,000	240,700,000

Boccaccio   Bo
  The most celebrated Italian novelist. Born in Paris in 1313.

Burke (Edmund)   Bu
  Born in Dublin 1730 or according to some authors 1728. His family was of Norman descent Burke having been originally the same name as Burgh his father Richard Burke was an attorney of the first rank in the profession in Dublin. Edmund was the second son out of a family of 14 or 15 children all of whom died young except three sons Garrett Edmund and Richard and a daughter named Julianne. He was accustomed while at college to spend three hours every day in the public library. It is related that when Richard Burke was found one day in a reefer shirt after his brother had made a great speech in the House of Commons and was asked the cause he replied: "I have been wondering how Ned contrived to monopolize all the talents of the family; but then I remembered when we were at play he was always at work". He entered the House of Commons January 14 1766 being returned from Wendover. Died July 9, 1797.

Taken from American Cyclopedia:
  Edmund Burke, an English statesman, born in Dublin, Jan. 1st, 1730, died at Beaconsfield, England, July 9, 1797. He was one of 14 or 15 children of Richard Burke, an attorney, descended from the Norman De Burghs who early settled in Ireland. His mother was of the ancient Irish family of Nagle, of Castletown Roche, county of Cork, and a grand-niece of Ellen Nagle, the wife of the eldest son of the poet Spenser. He entered Trinity college, Dublin, as a pensioner in 1744, Oliver Goldsmith being a fellow student. He took his bachelor's degree in 1748, and in 1750 went to London, where he had previously been entered as a law student of the Middle Temple. But he abandoned the law, and after an unsuccess-

ful application for the chair of logic in the University of Glasgow, devoted himself to literary labors. His father made ample allowance for his maintenance, and there seems to be no foundation for the report of his having been at that time without any resources excepting his pen. He contributed political articles to the periodical press, but his first separate production, "A Vindication of Natural Society," purporting to have been written by "a late noble writer," did not appear till 1756 and was ascribed to Bolingbroke, whose style was admirably imitated, although it was written with a brilliancy and fervor to which Bolingbroke never attained. The "Philosophical Inquiry into the Origin of our Ideas of the Sublime and Beautiful" (1756), written when Burke was in his 27th year, secured for him the regard of Johnson, Reynolds, and other eminent men, and placed him at the head of the aesthetical critics of his day. In 1757 he visited Bath for the improvement of his health, and lived in the house of his physician and remote kinsman, Dr. Christopher Nugent, whose daughter Jane Mary he married the same year. Speaking of her he long afterward said, "Every care vanished the moment I entered under my own roof." She bore him two sons, one of whom died in infancy, and the other, Richard, in 1794. After his return to London appeared "An Account of the European Settlements in America" (2 vols., London, 1757). Burke's autograph receipt for fifty guineas to Dodsley, the publisher of this work, is still extant, and internal evidence indicates him as the author, although doubts have been expressed on the subject, and it is not included in the common editions of his works. The abbé Raynal made use of it in his work on the American revolution, and Dugald Stewart and Prior praise it highly. He directed for many years the "Annual Register," established by Dodsley in 1759. Previous to this he had commenced for that publisher an "Essay toward an Abridgment of the English History" (London, 1757), bringing the narrative down to the time of King John. The reason for its discontinuance is not known. About this time Burke was introduced by the earl of Charlemont to William G. Hamilton, popularly known as Single-Speech Hamilton, secretary to Lord Halifax, the newly appointed lord lieutenant of Ireland. In 1761 he became Hamilton's private secretary, and in 1763 received a pension of £300. Hamilton had been instrumental in procuring this pension, and conceived that he had thereby bound the recipient to him for life. Burke therefore resigned the secretaryship and threw up the pension, which he had enjoyed only a year. Upon the fall of the Grenville administration in 1765, the marquis of Rockingham, the new prime minister, appointed Burke his private secretary, and he was soon afterward returned to parliament for Wendover, Buckinghamshire, a borough belonging to Lord Verney. The very day he took his seat, Jan. 14, 1766, he made remarks on the address of thanks to the throne in a strain of eloquence which attracted the attention of Pitt, afterward earl of Chatham. He speedily became the animating spirit of the Rockingham administration, and in the stormy debates relating to the American stamp act he was the most effective in urging moderate and conciliatory measures. Out of the house, as well as in it, his industry was indefatigable, while his knowledge of colonial affairs was exceedingly useful. On the dissolution of the Rockingham administration in July, 1766, Burke published anonymously "A Short Account of a late Short Administration," in which he vigorously defended the policy of the whigs. In the compromise cabinet which Lord Chatham undertook to form he was offered a place, which he declined, as he did a similar offer on the part of the duke of Grafton in 1767. The parliament was dissolved in 1768, when Burke was again returned for Wendover. About the same time he purchased for £20,000 a fine estate near Beaconsfield, Buckinghamshire; a part of the purchase money having been advanced, at first as a loan, and afterward as a gift, by the marquis of Rockingham. In 1769 Burke published his "Observations on a late Publication, entitled 'The Present State of the Nation,'" which later was ascribed to Mr. Grenville or to his former secretary, Mr. Knox, and in 1770 his celebrated "Thoughts on the Cause of the Present Discontents." In November, 1771, he was appointed agent of New York to represent the interests of that colony in England, for which he received a salary of £700. During the sessions of 1772-3 he distinguished himself by his masterly and elaborate reviews of the affairs of the East India company. Still more did he distinguish himself during the next session, 1774, on the state of the American colonies, then driven almost into insurrection by the course of the English government. His great speech on American taxation was delivered on April 19 of that year. On the dissolution of the parliament he was nominated for the city of Bristol, for which he was returned on Nov. 3, after a severe contest of 27 days. On March 22, 1775, he delivered another remarkable speech in behalf of the Americans, which he subsequently published. His zealous support of the colonies rendered him unpopular with his constituents, and he was compelled to defend himself in "Two Letters to Gentlemen of Bristol." All the while the questions of the Catholic disabilities and of the trade with Ireland occupied a large share of his attention. On Feb. 11, 1780, he introduced his celebrated bills for regulating the household, the army, navy, and pension pay offices, ordnance, the mint, the exchequer, &c. These he commended in a speech on "Economical Reform," which is almost without a parallel in the records of parliamentary eloquence. But his talents did not reconcile the electors of Bristol to his politics, and declining a reelection, he was returned for Malton, which borough he continued to represent during the remainder of his public career. The Rockingham party again coming into power in March, 1782, Burke became a privy councillor and paymaster general of the forces; but, not possessing an aristocratic family connection, he was not allowed a seat in the cabinet. No office in the gift of the government was more lucrative than that of paymaster; yet Burke's first act was to introduce a bill for its reorganization, which materially lessened his own emoluments. In that department alone he was said to have effected an annual saving of £47,000. On the death of the marquis of Rockingham, Burke retired for a time; but the ministry of the duke of Portland in 1783 restored him to his former place. In that year he began his labors on East Indian affairs, with his voluminous reports on the administration of justice in Bengal and other provinces; and for several years he was absorbed in the investigations and trials which arose out of the subject. During this time he conducted the impeachment of Warren Hastings for maladministration of the government of India. His great speech, shortly after the opening of the session of 1786, on presenting the articles of impeachment, is a masterpiece of eloquence. He regarded this impeachment as the crowning act, and destined to be the glory or shame, of his public life. It is now acknowledged to have been its crowning glory. When the French revolution broke out, Burke undertook to oppose its principles and influence. In 1790 appeared his "Reflections on the Revolution of France," a letter to a French gentleman, of which 30,000 copies were at once sold, and which was translated into French by Dupont. It was an eloquent production, and gave rise to many sharp controversies, leading to an open rupture with Fox, who had been associated with him in the impeachment of Hastings, and was now the whig leader in the house of commons. Their formal separation was an affecting scene. Fox paid a warm tribute to the character and genius of his old friend, now his opponent. Burke was henceforth isolated from his former political friends, but continued his activity, and published several books and pamphlets. He retired from the house of commons June 20, 1794. In the following August he was deeply affected by the death of Richard Burke, his only surviving son, but he still retained his cheerfulness and activity. In 1795 he received a pension of £1,200 from the civil list, and soon after another of £2,500 from the 4½ per cent. fund. In his retirement his pen was still busy, and in a "Letter to a Noble Lord," and "Two Letters on the Proposal for a Regicide Peace," he showed all his original power. Not long before his death he founded a school for the children of French emigrants. He retained his faculties to the last, and had Addison's essay on the immortality of the soul read to him on his deathbed. Mr. Fox, in proposing his interment in Westminster abbey, drew tears from almost every one present in the house of commons. Burke's genius has been extolled by Sir Robert Peel, Earl Russell, and other eminent men. Macaulay regarded him, in aptitude of comprehension and richness of imagination, as above every orator, ancient or modern; and Wilhelm von Schlegel in his "Lectures on Literature" awards him high praise for having been to England and to all Europe, and especially to Germany, a new light of political wisdom and moral experience. His conversational power was as remarkable as were his oratorical efforts and his written works. The authorship of the letters of Junius was at one time ascribed to Burke, and it was at all events believed that he knew who the author was, but he never made any disclosures on the subject.—Taken from American Cyclopaedia vol. 1873.

Burke's style

"But in all other styles, passages without end occur of the highest order—epigram—pathos—metaphor in profusion, chequered with more didactic and sober diction, nor are his purely figurative passages the finest even as figured writing; he is best when the metaphor is subdued, mixed as it were with plainer matter to flavour it, and used not by itself, and for its own sake, but giving point to a more useful instrument, made of more ordinary material; or at the most, flung off by the heat of the composition, like sparks from a working engine, not fire-works for mere display." —Brougham.

Cabal (Macaulay's H. E.)   Ca

Sir Thomas Clifford, Lord Arlington (Henry Bennett), Buckingham, Ashley, and Lauderdale. These names by a strange caprice spelled *Cabal.*

Chatham:

"It was the magnificence of his person, the haughty assumption of superiority, the scowl of his imperial brow, the ominous growl of his voice, 'like thunder heard remote,' and above all the evidence that these furnish of an imperious and overwhelming will, that abashed the proudest peers in the House of Lords and made his word perform the offices of his beliefs."

Clive (Robert)

Clive was born at the seat of his ancestors near Market-Drayton in Shropshire on the 29th of September 1725. He was the oldest son of Mr. Richard Clive. The Clives had been settled here in Shropshire since the 12th century. His mother was a Lady Manchester of the name of Gaskill, he died by his own hand on the 22 of November 1774 having just completed his 49th year.

Criticism

Hume says that criticism can never be of any avail until critics cite innumerable examples.

†Criticism (Pope)
"Whoever thinks a faultless piece to see
Thinks what ne'er was, nor is, nor e'er shall be."

"True wit is nature to advantage dressed,
What oft was thought, but ne'er so well expressed."

Criticism, Province of,

"The manner of being useful on the subject (decline of literature) would be, to point out the symptoms, to investigate the causes, and direct to the remedies of the approaching decay. This is a subject hitherto unattempted in criticism; perhaps it is the only subject in which criticism can be useful." Goldsmith's inquiry into present state of polite learning.

Cromwell's Army (Macaulay's H. E.)   Co

With reference to the disbanding of Cromwell's army Lord Macaulay says: "The troops were now to be disbanded. Fifty thousand men, accustomed to the profession of arms, were at once thrown on the world: and experience seemed to warrant the belief that this change would produce much misery and crime, that the discharged veterans would be seen begging in every street, or that they would be driven by hunger to pillage. But no such result followed. In a few months there remained not a trace indicating that the most formidable army in the world had just been absorbed into the mass of the community. The Royalists themselves confessed that, in every department of honest industry, the discarded warriors prospered beyond other men, that none were charged with any theft or robbery, that none was heard to ask an alms, and that, if a baker, a mason, or a waggoner attracted notice by his diligence and sobriety, he was in all probability one of Oliver's old soldiers."

Dante   Da
The most celebrated Italian poet born in Florence in May 1265.

Democracy: De
"It has frequently been observed that colonies are favorable to the development of democracy. Ancient customs and usages cannot be preserved in a colony as at home. Men are of necessity placed on a greater equality, since they have to share the same hardships, to overcome the same difficulties, and to face the same dangers. Hence it is difficult for a single man or for a class to maintain peculiar privileges, or exercise a permanent authority over the other colonists. Accordingly, we find that a democratical form of government was established in most of the Greek colonies at an earlier period than in the mother country, and that an aristocracy could rarely maintain its ground for any length of time." Smith's History of Greece.

Extract from "My Novel, or Varieties in English Life."   Ea
"Dr. Arnold said, from his experience of a school, that the difference between one man and another was not mere ability—it was energy. There is a great deal of truth in that saying."

Earnestness:
"Let a man but speak forth with genuine earnestness the thought, the emotion, the actual condition of his own heart; and other men, so strangely are we all knit together by the tie of sympathy, must and will give heed to him." Carlyle

Excellence: Ee
"To aim at excellence, our reputation, our friends, and our all must be ventured; by aiming only at mediocrity, we run no risk, and we do little service." Goldsmith on the Characteristics of Greatness.

English Composition   Ei
"Dreaded by teachers, hated by pupils, the useful necessary exercise of English composition has tabood the schoolroom. The consequence of which is that very few pupils acquire any facility of expression until they gain it from experience outside the schoolroom. Editors uniformly observe that ability to properly prepare a paper for the press is rare among adults; and the prospect is that it will be equally so among the next generation. Benjamin Franklin who began to be a poet and philosopher at a very early

age made his first grand display of genius in discovering and practically testing the true method of teaching composition. Franklin was the teacher, the pupil was Benjamin; the age of the teacher and pupil was respectively 11 years. The modus operandi was as follows: Franklin required Benjamin to read carefully a selection from the works of the perspicacious and elegant writer Joseph Addison; which being done, the youth was given several days in which to think over, remember, and forget. At the expiration of the allotted time he was required to reproduce on paper as much of the selection as he remembered in the best language he could command and with special attention to orthography, syntax, and punctuation. This being done, the teacher, Franklin, criticized all the errors in the last aforementioned particulars and returned the paper to Benjamin to be compared with the original. And then the boy toiled over improvements the teacher had prepared with so much care; he compared, sentence by sentence, the copy with the original. His own defects of style were thrown into bold relief; uncouth expressions were found to have taken the place of elegant homologues; the purity of Addison had lost much of its beauty by passing through the hands of Benjamin, but still neither pupil nor teacher was discouraged. Both loved the exercise. The pupil observed closely his faults and corrected them to the best of his ability; the teacher enjoyed the evident progress of his pupil as exhibited in succeeding efforts. Why should not this rational system of instruction in composition be adopted by teachers? The old method of requiring an original essay once a week or oftener is not successful for other reasons: it requires the expression of original thought by children who have no original thoughts worth expressing. It does not teach elegant composition there being no criteria by which to test the efforts. The method discovered by Franklin we know to be good. We have tried it with considerable success. The pupils think no more of writing a page of foolscap every day than of preparing an arithmetic lesson. But they are not compelled to cudgel their brains for insipid puerile ideas which on paper are just as silly to themselves as to adults. Neither do they deliberately copy the lesson; they write with nothing above the desk but paper and pencil." Professor J. B. Holbrook.

English and American Officials: from the Pall Mall Gazette, April 5/76

"The salaries of Cabinet Ministers in England are often inadequate to their expenditure while in office, though less conspicuously so than in America where the payments are lower and the cost of living greater. Yet no hint of corruption is ever brought against an English public man. There are two reasons which seem to explain this difference. One is the singular ostracism which is imposed either by their own will or by circumstances on the men of the highest character and greatest ability in the United States. It is a commonplace of American politics that no really eminent politician would stand any chance of being elected President. The composition of the Cabinet depends in a great measure on the President, and, as like loves like, an obscure First Magistrate naturally surrounds himself with obscure Ministers. With the great prizes in the race distributed on this principle, it is not wonderful that eminent politicians are rare. The best men in America for the most part prefer other careers. Now there are, speaking broadly, only two motives that lead a man to take up politics as his business—the hope of doing something for the State, and the hope of doing something for himself. Very obscure men may undoubtedly be actuated by the first of these motives, but a larger proportion of them than of abler men will be likely to be actuated by the second. Putting patriotism and all similar considerations aside, the ambition of a man of Mr. Calhoun's or Mr. Webster's mark will have immeasurably less to do with money than the ambition of a man of General Belknap's mark. The other reason which makes the temptations connected with inadequate salaries especially operative in America is the absence of men of great hereditary wealth, or of that hereditary position which takes the place of wealth. In every English Cabinet there are men to whom their official income is a matter of absolutely no moment, and others whose social estimation is determined by circumstances in which money plays a very small part. The constant presence of these elements generates a special public opinion, which is of great value as a safeguard against corruption in the poorer members of the particular society. A man who is suddenly introduced into "administration circles" at Washington finds his social position determined simply by his expenditure; and as his colleagues have for the most part no ostensible means of providing for their expenditure beyond their salaries, he easily jumps to the conclusion that what they do in the way of spending money he may do; and from that the transition is easy to the further inference that what they do in the way of making money he must do."—Copied 5/1/76 by Thomas W. Wilson, Standard Phonographer.

Eloquence: Eo

["]Convincing eloquence, however, is a gift more serviceable to its possessor than the most florid harangue or the most pathetic tones that can be imagined; and the man who is thoroughly convinced himself, who understands his subject, and the language he speaks in, will be more apt to silence opposition, than he who studies the force of his periods, and fills our ears with sounds, while our minds are destitute of conviction." Goldsmith on Education, in the Bee.

"He that is sensibly touched, sees things with a very different eye from the rest of mankind. All nature to him becomes an object of comparison and metaphor, without attending to it; he throws life into all, and inspires his audience with a part of his own enthusiasm. . . . A man even may be called eloquent, who transfers the passion or sentiment with which he is moved himself, into the breast of another; and this definition appears the more just, as it comprehends the graces of silence, and of action. An intimate persuasion of the truth to be proved, is the sentiment and passion to be transferred; and he who effects this, is truly possessed of the talent of eloquence." Goldsmith on Eloquence, in the Bee.

Education: Eu

"An educated man stands, as it were, in the midst of a boundless arsenal and magazine, filled with all the weapons and engines which man's skill has been able to devise from the earliest time; and he works, accordingly, with a strength borrowed from all past ages. How different is *his* state who stands on the outside of that storehouse, and feels that its gates must be stormed, or remain forever shut against him! His means are the commonest and rudest; the mere work done is no measure of his strength. A dwarf behind his steam-engine may remove mountains; but no dwarf will hew them down with a pickaxe; and he must be a Titan that hurls them abroad with his arms." Carlyle

Education:

"Regular education, we think, is unfavourable to vigour or originality of understanding. Like civilization, it makes society more intelligent and agreeable; but it levels the distinctions of nature. It strengthens and assists the feeble; but it deprives the strong of his triumph, and casts down the hopes of the aspiring. It accomplishes this, not only by training up the mind in an habitual veneration for authorities, but, by leading us to bestow a disproportionate degree of attention upon studies that are only valuable as keys or instruments for the understanding, they come at last to be regarded as ultimate objects of pursuit; and the means of education are absurdly mistaken for its end. How many powerful understandings have been lost in the Dialectics of Aristotle! And of how much good philosophy are we daily defrauded, by the preposterous error of taking a knowledge of prosody for useful learning! The mind of a man, who has escaped this training, will at least have fair play. Whatever other errors he may fall into, he will be safe at least from these infatuations: And if he thinks proper, after he grows up, to study Greek, it will probably be for some better purpose than to become critically acquainted with its dialects. His prejudices will be those of a man, and not of a schoolboy; and his speculations and conclusions will be independent of the maxims of tutors, and the oracles of literary patrons." Jeffrey

†Farewell: Fa

"To night is my departing night,
For here nae longer must I stay;
There's neither friend nor foe o'mine,
But wishes me away."

"What I have done thro' lack of wit,
I never, never can recall;
I hope y're a' my friends as yet,
Good night and joy be with you all."

Filicaja (Vincenzo) Fi
A celebrated Italian lyric poet and senator of Florence born in that city in 1642.

Charles J. Fox: Fo
Born in London on the 24 of January 1749. In May 1768 he was returned to Parliament for Midhurst though he had not yet attained the age of 20. He was the third son of the first Lord of Holland. He powerfully seconded Burke in the Impeachment of Warren Hastings in 1788. Died 13 of September 1806. See Recollections of Charles J. Fox by B. C. Walpole, 1806.

Granville (Leveson Gower) Earl, Ga
An English statesman and son of Marquis Stafford was born 1773. He was appointed Lord of the Treasury under Pitt in 1800 and was afterwards employed in important missions to Russia the Netherlands and France.

Gibbon (Edward) Gi
Was born at Putney in 1737. Became a member of Parliament and supported Lord North's administration. One of England's greatest historians. Died in London January 1794.

Goldsmith Go

For a most happy effort at letter writing by Oliver Goldsmith see letter addressed to Bryanton dated August 14/1758 to be found on pages 138-139 of Volume First Forster's Life of Goldsmith. In this charming letter he supposes a Chinese philosopher thus describing him at some future time. We quote—"Oliver Goldsmith flourished in the 18th and 19th centuries. He lived to be 103 years old . . . age may justly be styled the sun of . . . and the Confucius of Europe . . . learned world, were anonymous, and have probably been lost, because united with those of others. The first avowed piece the world has of his, is entitled an 'Essay on the Present State of Taste and Literature in Europe'—a work well worth its weight in diamonds. In this he profoundly explains what learning is, and what learning is not. In this he proves that blockheads are not men of wit, and yet that men of wit are actually blockheads."—The little letter is a gem of wit.

Heroism, a case of He

"An English transport, carrying passengers and troops, sprung a leak upon the Indian ocean. Held to their duty by a young ensign the 400 troops gave up the lifeboats to the passengers; and forming in rank and file on the deck, as the loaded boats sailed off to a safe distance, the passengers got the sound of the young ensign's voice as he shouted, standing face to face with death: 'Fire, my boys, a broad salute to Old England.' There came a volley of musketry and when the smoke cleared away not even a full spar stood where the vessel and her gallant freight had gone down."

Hints to writers and Speakers (page 251)[1]

[1] See Writers and Speakers, Hints to. (This and following footnotes by the editors.)

History: Its use Hi

"But history is the inexhaustible source from which he will derive his most useful knowledge respecting the progress of the human mind, the constitution of government, the rise and decline of empires, the revolution of arts, the variety of character, and the vicissitudes of fortune." Goldsmith on the Cultivation of Taste.

†Johnson's Latin Lines Jo

"And with like ease his vivid lines assume
The garb and dignity of ancient Rome.
Let college verse-men trite conceits express,
Trick'd out in splendid shreds of Virgil's dress;
From playful Ovid cull the tinsel phrase,

And vapid notions hitch in pilfer'd lays;
Then with mosaic art the piece combine,
And boast the glitter of each dulcet line:
Johnson adventured boldly to transfuse
His vigorous sense into the Latin muse;
A[s]pired to shine by unreflected light,
And with a Roman's ardour think and write." (Courtenay)

Justice: Ju
"Justice may be defined, that virtue which impels us to give to
every person what is his due. In this extended sense of the word, it
comprehends the practice of every virtue which reason prescribes,
or society would expect. Our duty to our Maker, to each other, and
to ourselves, are fully answered, if we give them what we owe
them. Thus justice, properly speaking, is the only virtue, and all the
rest have their origin in it." Goldsmith.

Language, Learning a: La
"My way of learning a language is always to begin with the Bible,
which I can read without a dictionary. After a few days passed
in this way, I am master of all the common particles, the common
rules of syntax, and a pretty large vocabulary. Then I fall on some
good classical work. It was in this way that I learned both Spanish
and Portuguese, and I shall try the same course with German."—
Macaulay.

Language, Use of.
"Men who know the world hold, and I think with some show
of reason, that he who best knows how to conceal his necessities and desires, is the most likely person to find redress, and that
the true unit of speech is not so much to express our wants as to
conceal them."—Goldsmith.

Leuthen, Battle of,   Le
Between Frederick the Great and Prince Charles of Loraine on
December 5, 1757. Prussians 40 thousand enemy 60,000.

Liberty: Li
"Abstract liberty, like other mere abstractions, is not to be
found."—Burke
"Permit me then to continue our conversation, and to tell you
what the freedom is that I love. It is not solitary, unconnected, individual, selfish liberty. It is social freedom. It is that state of things
in which the liberty of no man, and no body of men, is in condition
to trespass on the liberty of any person, or any description of per-

sons, in the society. This kind of liberty is, indeed, but another name for justice; ascertained by wise laws, and secured by well-constructed institutions. I am sure that liberty, so incorporated, and in a manner identified with justice, must be a gift dear to every man who is capable of conceiving what it is. But whenever a separation is made between liberty and justice, neither is, in my opinion, safe."—Burke.

Literary Community

"The consequences of living in a refined and literary society or community, are nearly of the same kind with those of a regular education. There are so many critics to be satisfied—so many qualifications to be established—so many rivals to encounter, and so much derision to be hazarded, that a young man is apt to be deterred from so perilous an enterprise, and led to seek for distinction in some safer line of exertion. He is discouraged by the fame and the perfection of certain models and favourites, who are always in the mouths of his judges, and, 'under them, his genius is rebuked,' and his originality repressed, till he sinks into a paltry copyist, or aims at distinction, by extravagance and affectation. In such a state of society, he feels that mediocrity has no chance of distinction; and what beginner can expect to rise at once into excellence? He imagines that mere good sense will attract no attention; and that the manner is of much more importance than the matter, in a candidate for public admiration. In his attention to the manner, the matter is apt to be neglected; and, in his solicitude to please those who require elegance of diction, brilliancy of wit, or harmony of periods, he is in some danger of forgetting that strength of reason, and accuracy of observation, by which he first proposed to recommend himself. His attention, when extended to so many collateral objects, is no longer vigorous or collected;—and the stream, divided into so many channels, ceases to flow either deep or strong; —he becomes an unsuccessful pretender to fine writing, or is satisfied with the frivolous praise of elegance or vivacity." Jeffrey

Macaulay, See pages 43, 35,[1]   Ma

Macaulay (T. B.) Baron was born at Rothley Temple in Leicestershire, October 25, 1800. His father, Zachary Macaulay, was a native of Scotland Highland descent; his mother Selina Mills, the daughter of a bookseller of Bristol was of Quaker family. His home education was religious and somewhat severe. Was admitted to the bar in 1826. Entered Parliament in 1830 as a representative of Calne. Was in India from 1835-8. Was made Secretary of War in the Milburn ministry. In 1846 he was made Postmaster General. Died December 28, '59.

¹ See Cromwell's Army.

†Man:

   "Homo sum; nihil humani, ā me alienum puto."—Terence

Memory, Macaulay's   Me

   " 'My accuracy as to facts, I owe to a cause which many men would not confess. It is due to my love of castle-building. The past is in my mind soon constructed into a romance.' He then went on to describe the way in which from his childhood his imagination had been filled by the study of history. 'With a person of my turn,' he said, 'the minute touches are of as great interest, and perhaps greater, than the most important events. Spending so much time as I do in solitude, my mind would have rusted by gazing vacantly at the shop windows. As it is, I am no sooner in the streets than I am in Greece, in Rome, in the midst of the French Revolution. Precision in dates, the day or hour in which a man was born or died, becomes absolutely necessary. A slight fact, a sentence, a word, are of importance in my romance. 'Pepy's Diary' formed almost inexhaustable food for my fancy. I seem to know every inch of Whitehall. I go in at Hans Holbein's gate, and come out through the matted gallery. The conversations which I compose between great people of the time are long, and sufficiently animated, in the style, if not with the merits, of Sir Walter Scott's. The old parts of London, which you are surprised at my knowing so well, those old gates and houses down by the river, have all played their part in my stories.' He spoke, too, of the manner in which he used to wander about Paris, weaving tales of the Revolution, and he thought that he owed his command of language to this habit." 5/18/76

Mathematical Writers

   "An algebraist, who can work wonders with letters, seldom condescends to be indebted to words; and thinks himself entitled to make his sentences obscure, provided his calculations be correct and distinct. A writer who has nothing but words to make use of, must make all the use he can of them: he cannot afford to neglect the only chance he has of being understood." Jeffrey.

Macchiavelli   Mi

   A famous Italian statesman diplomat and writer whose name abounds in anagrams and paradoxes from whose name has been derived a synonym of perfidious policy (machiavellism). Born at Florence 3 of May 1469.

†Oratory: Oa

An orator should be: *"vehemens ut procella excitatus ut torrens, incensus ut fulmen; tonat, fulgurat, et rapidis eloquentiae fluctibus cuneta proruit et proturbat."* Tullus.

†Ovid's Works: Oi

Fasti, Epistles, Art of Love, Art of Pleasing, Tristia, Metamorphosis (?)

Palmerston (Henry John Temple) Viscount, Pa

An eminent English Prime Minister born at Broadlands near Romsey, Hampshire on the 20th October 1784 he was the oldest son of Henry Temple and second Viscount of Palmerston and was descended from ancient family of which the famous Sir William Temple was a member. He succeeded Lord Aberdeen as Prime Minister in February 1855 and [was appointed ?] chief of the Whigs and Liberals. Resigned in February 1858. In 1859 he succeeded Lord Derby as the head of the Ministry [including ?] Russell, Foreign Secretary and Gladstone, Chancellor of the Exchequer. He continued to be Prime Minister until his death October 18/65.

Parliament, nature of:

"From a very different reason there has been no direct buying of votes within the memory of the present generation. The House of Commons is now supreme in the state, but is accountable to the nation. Even those members who are not chosen by large constituent bodies are kept in awe by public opinion. Everything is printed; everything is discussed; every material word uttered in debate is read by a million of people on the morrow. Within a few hours after an important division, the lists of the majority and the minority are scanned and analyzed by every town from Plymouth to Inverness. If a name be found where it ought not to be, the apostate is certain to be reminded in sharp language of the promises which he has broken, and of the professions which he has belied. At present, therefore, the best [way] in which a government can secure the support of a majority of the representative body is by gaining the confidence of the nation." Macaulay's History of England chapter 15 volume 5 (8 volume edition) page 340.

†Phrases

"Pleasure Stage Coach, Waggon of Industry, Vanity Whim, Fame Machine." Goldsmith.

Peel (Sir Robert)   Pe

A celebrated English statesman born near Bury 5th of February 1788 was an eldest son. Entered Parliament as a supporter of the Tory ministry in 1809. Became Prime Minister in December '34 but was compelled to resign in April '35. Again became Prime Minister in August '41. Resigned again June 29/46. Died July 1850 from injuries received by a fall from his horse on the 29th of June of the same year.

Pursuit of Truth:

"In every duty, in every science in which we would wish to arrive at perfection, we should propose for the object of our pursuit some certain station even beyond our abilities; some imaginary excellence, which may amuse and serve to animate our enquiry." Goldsmith on the Characteristics of Greatness.

Porson (Richard)   Po

A prominent Greek scholar and critic born in Norfolk England December 25 1759. He had a prodigious memory and great critical acumen and was remarkable for probity and love of truth. Died in London in September 1808. He was considered the greatest verbal critic of modern times. He could repeat several pages of a book after he had read them once.

Read, What to   Re

"Are you deficient in taste? Read the best English poets such as Thomson, Gray, Goldsmith, Pope, Cowper, Coleridge, Scott, Wordsworth. (2) Are you deficient in religion? Read Milton, Akenside, Burke, Shakespeare. (3) Are you deficient in pure reasoning? Read Chillingworth, Bacon, Locke. (4) Are you deficient in judgment and good sense in the common affairs of life? Read Franklin. (5) Are you deficient in sensibility? Read Goethe, and McKenzie. (6) Are you deficient in political knowledge? Read Montesquieu, the *Federalist*, Webster and Calhoun. (7) Are you deficient in patriotism read Adams and the life of Washington. (8) Are you deficient in conscience? Read some of President Edwards works." Visitor.

Representative, Duty of a, (Burke)

"I am sorry I cannot conclude without saying a word on a topic touched upon by my worthy colleague. I wish that topic had been passed by at a time when I have so little leisure to discuss it. But since he has thought proper to throw it out, I owed you a clear explanation of my poor sentiments on that subject.

"He tells you that 'the topic of instructions has occasioned much altercation and uneasiness in this city'; and he expresses himself (if I understand him rightly) in favor of the coercive authority of such instructions.

"Certainly, Gentlemen, it ought to be the happiness and glory of a representative to live in the strictest union, the closest correspondence, and the most unreserved communication with his constituents. Their wishes ought to have great weight with him; their opinions high respect; their business his immediate attention. It is his duty to sacrifice his repose, his pleasure, his satisfactions, to theirs, and above all, ever, and in all cases, to prefer their interest to his own.

"But his unbiased opinion, his mature judgment, his enlightened conscience, he ought not to sacrifice to you, to any man, or to any set of men living. These he does not derive from your pleasure, —no, nor from the law and the Constitution. They are a trust from Providence, for the abuse of which he is deeply answerable. Your representative owes you, not his industry only, but his judgment; and he betrays, instead of serving you, if he sacrifices it to your opinion.

"My worthy colleague says, his will ought to be subservient to yours. If that be all, the thing is innocent. If government were a matter of will on any side, yours, without question, ought to be superior. But government and legislation are matters of reason and judgment, and not of inclination; and what sort of reason is that in which the determination precedes the discussion, in which one set of men deliberate and another decide, and where those who form the conclusion are perhaps three hundred miles distant from those who hear the arguments?

"To deliver an opinion is the right of all men; that of constituents is a weighty and respectable opinion, which a representative ought always to rejoice to hear, and which he ought always most seriously to consider. But *authoritative* instructions; mandates issued, which the member is bound blindly and implicitly to obey, to vote, and to argue for, though contrary to the clearest conviction of his judgment and conscience,—these are things utterly unknown to the laws of the land, and which arise from a fundamental mistake of the whole order and tenor of our Constitution.

"Parliament is not a *congress* of ambassadors from different states and with hostile interests, which interests each must maintain, as an agent and advocate, against other agents and advocates; but Parliament is a deliberative assembly of one nation, with one interest, that of the whole—where no local purposes, no local prejudices, ought to guide, but the general good, resulting from the general reason of the whole. You choose a member, indeed; but when you have chosen him, he is not member of Bristol, but he is a member of Parliament. If the local constituent should have an interest or should form an hasty opinion evidently opposite to the real good of the rest of the community, the member for that place ought to be as far as any other from any endeavor to give it effect." On another occasion he told them (1780) "I did not obey your instructions. No. I conformed to the instructions of truth and Nature, and maintained your interest, against your opinions, with a constancy that became me. A representative worthy of you ought to be a person of stability. I am to look, indeed, to your opinions,— but to such opinions as you and I must look to five years hence. I was not to look at the flash of the day. I knew that you chose me, in my place, along with others, to be a pillar of the state, and not a weathercock on the top of the edifice, exalted for my levity and versatility, and of no use but to indicate the shiftings of every popular gale."

Duty of Representatives (Macaulay)

"I wish to add a few words touching a question which has lately been much canvassed: I mean the question of pledges. In this letter and in every letter which I have written to my friends at Leeds I have plainly declared my *opinions*. But I think it, at this juncture, my duty to declare that I will give *no pledges*. I will not bind myself to make or to support any particular motion. I will state as shortly as I can some of the reasons which have induced me to form this determination.

"The great beauty of the representative system is, that it unites the advantages of popular control with the advantages arising from a division of labor. Just as a physician understands medicine better than an ordinary man, just as a shoemaker makes shoes better than an ordinary man, so a person whose life is passed in transacting affairs of State becomes a better statesman than an ordinary man. In politics, as well as every other department of life, the public ought to have the means of checking those who serve it. If a man finds that he derives no benefit from the prescription of his physician, he calls in another. If his shoes do not fit him, he changes his shoemaker. But when he calls in a physician of whom he hears a good report, and whose general practice he believes to be judicious, it would be absurd in him to tie down that physician to order particular pills and particular draughts. While he continues to be the customer of a shoemaker, it would be absurd in him to sit by and mete every motion of that shoemaker's hand. And in the same manner, it would, I think, be absurd in him to require positive pledges, and to exact daily and hourly obedience, from his representative. My opinion is, that electors ought at first to choose cautiously; then to confide liberally; and, when the term for which they have selected their member has expired, to review his conduct equitably, and to pronounce on the whole taken together.

"If the people of Leeds think proper to repose in me that confidence which is necessary to the proper discharge of the duties of a representative, I hope that I shall not abuse it. If it be their pleasure to fetter their members by positive promises it is in their power to do so. I can only say that on such terms I cannot conscientiously serve them." 5/18/76

Russell (Lord John) afterwards Earl Russell   Ru
An eminent British Whig statesman born in London on the 18 of August 1792. He was third son of the sixth Duke of Bedford. His mother was a daughter of the Fourth Viscount Torrington. He was elected to Parliament for Tavistock in 1813. On the accession of the Whigs to power in 1830 Lord John was appointed Paymaster General and a member of a committee of four by which the celebrated Reform Bill was prepared. This bill became a law in 1832. Became Prime Minister in July 1846. In October 1865 he was called by public influence and royal summons to the office of Prime Minister vacated by Lord Palmerston. His principal colleagues were W. E. Gladstone as Chancellor of the Exchequer; Lord Clarendon, Secretary of Foreign Affairs, etc. Resigned June 18/66.

Standing Armies   Sa
"The number of men at present maintained in the standing armies of the civilized nations of the world is not less than 3 million. All these are snatched away from useful industries and admitted to idleness and vicious life while the laboring people are taxed for their support and for the costly armament they require. The annual grants of the naval and military objects of Europe is $596,963,300; the loss of labor involved by the withdrawal of so many men from product[ion] and industry costs $660,874,460; and the interest of the capital invested in military and naval establishments amounts to $152,200,000. This makes the total more than $1,4 hundred million taken every year from the people of

Christendom for the maintenance of the military establishment."
New York Sun 2/22/76[1]

[1] The date that WW made this entry. The extract was from the New York *Sun*, Dec. 28, 1875.

Passions, Strength of,

"A lad whose passions are not strong enough in youth to mislead him from that path of science which his instructors, and not his inclinations, have chalked out, by four or five years' perseverence probably obtains every advantage and honour his college can bestow. I forget whether the simile has been used before, but I would compare the man whose youth has been thus passed in the tranquility of dispassionate prudence, to liquors which never ferment, and consequently continue always muddy. Passions may raise a commotion in the youthful breast, but they disturb only to refine it. However this be, mean talents are often rewarded in colleges with an easy subsistence." Inquiry Into Present State of Polite Learning. Chapter X.

Sparta: Spartans, Perioeci, Helots=*villans*.

The latter were expected to wear peculiar dress—a leather cap and sheepskin and they were sometimes expected to make themselves drunk, as a warning to Spartan youth.

"Spectator"   Se

Established by Addison and Steele from March 1, 1711, to December 6, 1712.

Sheridan (Richard Brinsley Butler)

A celebrated Irish orator and dramatist born in Dublin 1751. Studied at Harrow where he was chiefly noted for his indolence and left school with a reputation of "inimitable dunce." In 1780 he represented Stafford in parliament where he soon became conspicuous as an orator and supporter of measures of Fox and the opposition. On the impeachment of Warren Hastings in 1787 he delivered his celebrated Begum speech which made an extraordinary sensation at the time. Died July 1816.

†Speaking

"So charming left his voice, that we, awhile
Still thought him speaking, still stood fixed to hear."[1]

"To a great speaker, it is always an advantage to follow a powerful adversary. The audience is prepared for attention, nay, even feels a craving for some answer." Brougham.

[1] WW apparently copied this from Henry Lord Brougham, who incorrectly quoted it in *Historical Sketches of Statesmen Who Flourished in the Time of George III* (2 vols., Philadelphia, 1842), I, 172.

Swift (Jonathan) Si

A celebrated humorist and satirist born in Dublin on the 30 of November 1667 was the son of Jonathan Swift an English attorney. Died in Dublin October 1745.

Soul, The, So

"If the soul be happily disposed, every thing becomes a subject of entertainment, and distress will almost want a name. Every occurrence passes in review like the figures of a procession; some may be awkward, others ill dressed; but none but a fool is for this enraged with the master of the ceremonies." Goldsmith.

Tasso. Ta

A celebrated Italian poet born at Sorrento the 11th of March 1544. His most celebrated poem was "Jerusalem Delivered."

Talleyrand (Charles Maurice) Prince of Benevento.

Commonly known as simply Talleyrand a celebrated French diplomat and wit born in Paris on the 13 of February 1754 was the oldest son of Charles Daniel Count of Tallyrand. An accident which occurred in his infancy made him lame for life. On account of this he was obliged to enter the clergy against his will. Was at one time a refugee to the United States. Became Minister of Foreign Affairs in 1799. Died in Paris in May 1838. Among his famous sayings is "Language is given to man to conceal his thoughts".

†Talent and Genius

"Talent, the sunshine on a cultivated soil,
Ripens the fruit by slow degrees for toil;
Genius, the sudden Iris of the skies,
On cloud itself reflects the wondrous dyes
And to the earth in tears and glory given,
Clasps in its airy arch the pomp of heaven."

Truth (Whately's Annotations on Bacon's Essay of Truth) Tu

In speaking of the attainment of the habit of always seeking for truth he says: "Many objections have been urged against the very effort to cultivate such a habit. One is, that we cannot be required to make Truth our main object, but *happiness*; that our ultimate end is not the mere knowledge of what is *true*, but the attainment of what is *good* to ourselves and to others. But this, when urged as an objection to the maxim, that Truth should be sought for its own sake, is evidently founded on a mistake as to its meaning. It is evident, in the first place, that it does not mean the pursuit of *all* truth on all subjects. It would be ridiculous for any single individual to aim at universal knowledge, or even at the knowledge of all that is within the reach of the human faculties and worthy of human study. The question is respecting the pursuit of truth in each subject on which each person desires *to make up his mind and form an opinion*. And secondly, the purport of the maxim that in these points truth should be our object, is, that not mere barren knowledge without practice—truth without any *ulterior* end, should be sought, but that truth should be sought and followed confidently, not in each instance, only so far as we *perceive* it to be expedient, and from motives of policy, but with a full conviction that in the end, it is always expedient, with a view to the attainment of ulterior objects (no permanent advantages being attainable by departing from it), and also, that, even if some end, otherwise advantageous, *could* be promoted by such a departure, that alone would constitute it an evil;—that truth, in short, is in itself, independently of its results, preferable to error; that honesty claims a preference to deceit, even without taking into account its being the best policy."—In another place he says: "When, however, we have made up our minds as to the importance of seeking for truth in every case with an unprejudiced mind, the greatest difficulty still remains; which arises from the confidence we are apt to feel that we have already done this, and have sought for truth with success. For every one must of course be convinced of the truth of his own opinion, if it be properly called *his* opinion; and yet the variety of men's opinions furnishes a proof how many must be mistaken. If any one, then, would guard against mistake, as far as his intellectual faculties will allow, he must make it the first question in each, 'Is this true?' It is not enough to believe what you maintain; you must maintain what you believe, and maintain it *because* you believe it; and that, on the most careful and impartial view of the evidence on both sides. For any one may bring himself to believe almost anything that he is inclined to believe, and thinks it becoming or expedient to maintain. Some persons, accordingly, who describe themselves—in one sense, correctly—as 'following the dictates of conscience,' are doing so only in the same sense in which a person who is driving a carriage may be said to be following his horses, which go in whatever direction he guides them. It is in a determination to 'obey the truth,' and follow wherever she may lead, that the genuine love of truth consists; and this can be realized in practice only by postponing all other questions to that which ought ever to come foremost—'What is the truth?' If this question be asked only in the second place, it is likely to receive a very different answer from what it would if it had been asked in the *first* place. The minds of most men are preoccupied by some feeling or other which influences the judgment (either on the side of truth or error, as it may happen) and enlists their learning and ability on the side, whatever it may be, which they are predisposed to adopt." 2/14/76

Thunders[t]orm among the mountains
"From peak to peak, the rattling crags among
Leaps the live thunder! Not from one lone cloud,
But every mountain now hath found a tongue,
And Jura answers, through her misty shroud,
Back to the joyous Alps, who call to her aloud. . . .

"How the lit lake shines, a phosphoric sea,
And the big rain comes dancing to the earth!
And now again 'tis black,—and now, the glee
Of the loud hills shakes with its mountain mirth,
As if they did rejoice o'er a young earthquake's birth."
Byron.

Union, The,   Ui
"Without union our independence and liberty would never have been achieved; without union they never can be maintained. The loss of liberty, of all good government, of peace, plenty, and happiness, must inevitably follow a dissolution of the Union. In supporting it, therefore, we support all that is dear to the freeman and the philanthropist." Andrew Jackson.

"Here, standing on the platform of the general Constitution—a platform broad enough and firm enough to uphold every interest of the whole country—I shall be found." Webster.

"I came into public life, Sir, in the service of the United States. On that broad altar, my earliest, and all my public vows, have been made. I propose to serve no other master. So far as depends on any agency of mine, they shall continue *united* States;—united in interest and in affection; united in every thing in regard to which the Constitution has decreed their union; united in war, for the common defence, the common renown, and the common glory; and united, compacted, knit firmly together in peace, for the common prosperity and happiness of ourselves and our children." Webster.

"When my eyes shall be turned to behold for the last time the sun in heaven, may I not see him shining on the broken dishonored fragments of a once glorious Union; on States dissevered, discordant, belligerent; on a land rent with civil feuds, or drenched, it may be, in fraternal blood! Let their last feeble and lingering glance rather behold the gorgeous ensign of the republic, now known and honored throughout the earth, still full high advanced, its arms and trophies streaming in their original lustre, not a stripe erased or polluted, nor a single star obscured—bearing for its motto, no such miserable interrogatory as—*What is all this worth?* —nor those other words of delusion and folly—*Liberty first and Union afterwards*—but everywhere, spread all over in characters of living light, blazing on all its ample folds, as they float over the sea and over the land, and in every wind under the whole heavens, that other sentiment, dear to every true American heart,—liberty and union, now and forever, one and inseparable." Webster.

"But the only reliable and certain evidence of devotion to the constitution is, to abstain, on the one hand, from violating it, and to repel, on the other, all attempts to violate it. It is only by faithfully performing these high duties that the constitution can be preserved, and with it the Union." Calhoun.

What to Read (Page 199)[1]   Wa

[1] See Read, What to.

Walpole (Sir Robert) Earl of Oxford
A celebrated English statesman born at Houghton on the 28th of August 1676 was a son of Robert Walpole Esquire *M. P.* Entered Parliament in 1700 as a supporter of the Whig party. Became Prime Minister in 1721. Had power for 20 years.

Writers and Speakers, Hints to   Wi
"William Cullen Bryant gave the following excellent advice to a young man who offered him an article for the Evening Post:

" 'My young friend, I observe that you have used several French expressions in your article. I think, if you will study the English language, that you will find it capable of expressing all the ideas you may have. I have always found it so, and in all that I have written I do not recall an instance where I was tempted to use a foreign word, but that, on searching, I found a better one in my own language.

" 'Be simple, unaffected; be honest in your speaking and writing. Never use a long word when a short one will do. Call a spade a spade, not a well-known, oblong instrument of manual industry; let a home be a home, not a residence; a place a place, not a locality, and so of the rest. Where a short word will do, you lose by using a long one. You lose in clearness; you lose in honest expression of your meaning, and in the estimation of all men who are competent to judge, you lose in reputation for ability.

" 'The only true way to shine even in this false world, is to be modest and unassuming. Falsehood may be a very thick crust, but in the course of time will find a place to break through. Elegance of language may not be in the power of all of us, but simplicity and straight-forwardness are.

" 'Write much as you would speak; speak as you think. If with your inferior speak no coarser than usual; if with your superior speak no finer. Be what you say, and within the rules of prudence. No one ever was a gainer by singularity of words or in pronunciation. The truly wise man will so speak that no one will observe how he speaks. A man may show great knowledge of Chemistry by carrying about bladders of strange gases to breathe, but he will enjoy better health, and find more time for business, who lives on common air.

" 'Sidney Smith once remarked: After you have written an article, take your pen and strike out half of the words, and you will be surprised to see how much stronger it is. Visitor.' "

Wits of Queen Anne's Reign

"Speaking generally of that generation of authors, it may be said that, as poets, they had no force or greatness of fancy—no pathos and no enthusiasm;—and, as philosophers, no comprehensiveness, depth, or originality. They are sagacious, no doubt, neat, clear, and reasonable; but for the most part cold, timid, and superficial. They never meddle with the great scenes of nature, or the great passions of man; but content themselves with just and sarcastic representations of city life, and of the paltry passions and meaner vices that are bred in that lower element. Their chief care is to avoid being ridiculous in the eyes of the witty, and above all to eschew the ridicule of excessive sensibility or enthusiasm— to be at once witty and rational themselves, with as good a grace as possible; but to give their countenance to no wisdom, no fancy, and no morality, which passes the standards current in good company. Their inspiration, accordingly, is little more than a spritely sort of good sense; and they have scarcely any invention but what is subservient to the purposes of derision and satire. Little gleams of pleasantry, and sparkles of wit, glitter through their compositions; but no glow of feeling—no blaze of imagination—no flashes of genius, ever irradiate their substance. They never pass beyond 'the visible diurnal sphere,' or deal in anything that can either lift us above our vulgar nature, or ennoble its reality. With these accomplishments, they may pass well enough for sensible and polite writers,—but scarcely for men of genius; and it is certainly far more surprising, that persons of this description should have maintained themselves, for near a century, at the head of the literature of a country that had previously produced a Shakespeare, a Spenser, a Bacon, and a Taylor, than that, towards the end of that long period, doubts should have arisen as to the legitimacy of the title by which they laid claim to that high station. Both parts of the phenomenon, however, we dare say, had causes which better expounders might explain to the satisfaction of all the world. We see them but imperfectly, and have room only for an imperfect sketch of what we see." Jeffrey.

Writing, Habit of,

"By a long habit of writing an author acquires a justness of thinking and a mastery of manner which holiday writers, even with ten times his genius[,] may vainly attempt to give." Goldsmith.

Writers, Characteristics of Good:

"Yet this is certain, that the writer who never deviates, who never hazards a new thought, or a new expression, though his friends may compliment him upon his sagacity, though criticism lifts her feeble voice in his praise, will seldom arrive at any degree of perfection. The way to acquire lasting esteem, is not by the fewness of a writer's faults, but the greatness of his beauties, and our noblest works are generally most replete with both." Goldsmith on Characteristics of Greatness.

†Wit:

"Some to whom heaven in wit has been profuse,
Want as much more, to turn it to its use." Pope.

Wit and Humor

"Wit raises human nature above its level; humour acts a contrary part, and equally depresses it." Goldsmith's Polite Learning.

"Thus then, the pleasure we receive from wit, turns on the admiration of another; that which we feel from humour, centres in the admiration of ourselves." Goldsmith's Polite Learning.

Write, How to,

"Let us, instead of writing finely, try to write naturally; not hunt after lofty expressions to deliver mean ideas, nor be for ever gaping, when we only mean to deliver a whisper." Goldsmith's Polite Learning.

Unentered Items on Loose Pages

†"The archers green glimmer under the waving branches; the print on the grass remains where they have just finished their noontide meal under the green-wood tree; and the echo of their buglehorn and twanging bows resounds through the tangled mazes of the forest, as the tall slim deer glances startled by."—*Hazlitt de Robin Hood and His Merie Men.*

Fame

"Genius is the heir of fame; but the hard condition on which the bright reversion must be earned is the loss of life. Fame is the recompense not of the living, but of the dead. The temple of fame stands upon the grave: the flame that burns upon its altars is kindled from the ashes of great men. Fame itself is immortal; but it is not begot till the breath of genius is extinguished. For fame is not popularity, the shout of the multitude, the idle buzz of fashion, the venal puff, the soothing flattery of favour or of friendship; but it is the spirit of a man surviving himself in the minds and thoughts of other men, undying and imperishable. It is the power which the intellect exercises over the intellect, and the lasting homage which is paid to it, as such, independently of time and circumstances, purified from partiality and evil-speaking. Fame is the sound which the stream of high thoughts, carried down to future ages, makes as it flows—deep, distant, murmuring evermore like the waters of the mighty ocean." *Hazlitt.*

"The love of fame, as it enters at times into his mind, is only another name for the love of excellence; or it is the ambition to attain the highest excellence, sanctioned by the highest authority— that of time." *Hazlitt.*

†Rabelais, Racine, Molière, Cervantes, Corneille.

†Mercutio, Touchstone. (?)

> †1. Why so pale and wan, fond lover?
>   Prythee why so pale?
> Will, when looking well can't move her,
>   Looking ill prevail?
> Prythee why so pale?
>
> 2. Why so dull and mute, young sinner?
>   Prythee why so mute?
> Will, when speaking well can't move her,
>   Saying nothing do't?
> Prythee why so mute?

3. Quit, quit for shame this will not move,
   This cannot take her;
   If of herself she will not love,
   Nothing can make her.
   The Devil take her.[1]

[1] The poem is "Song," by Sir John Suckling. WW wrote "Sucklings" in large letters across the first two stanzas.

†Drinking

"The thirsty earth soaks up the rain,
And drinks and gapes for drink again.
The plants suck in the earth, and are
With constant drinking fresh and fair.
The sea itself, which one would think
Should have but little need of drink,
Drinks twice ten thousand rivers up
So filled that they o'erflow the cup.
The busy sun (and one would guess
By's drunken fiery face no less)
Drinks up the sea and when he's done,
The moon and stars drink up the sun.
They drink and dance by their own light,
They drink and revel all the night.
Nothing in nature's sober found,
But an eternal health goes round.
Fill up the bowl then, fill it high,
Fill all the glasses there: for why
Should every creature drink but I;
Why, man of morals, tell me why?"—*Cowley*

"Of the four writers here classed together, we should perhaps have courted Congreve's acquaintance most, for his wit and the elegance of his manners; Wycherley's, for his sense and observation on human nature; Vanbrugh's, for his power of farcical description and telling a story; Farquhar's, for the pleasure of his society, and the love of good fellowship." *Hazlitt*

†"She had good nature about her mouth, the smile of beauty on her cheeks, sparkling wit in her forehead, and sprightly love in her eyes"—*Farquhar*

†"No man is the lord of anything,
 Till he communicate his parts to others
 Nor doth he of himself know them for aught,
 Till he behold them formed in the applause,

Where they've extended! which like an arch reverberates
The voice again, or like a gate of steel,
Fronting the sun, receives and renders back
Its figure and its heat." *Sps.*

†"Rouse thyself; and the weak wanton Cupid
Shall from your neck unloose his amorous fold,
And like a dew drop from the lion's mane
Be shook to air" *Sps.*

†"And so by many winding nooks it strays,
With willing sport to the wild ocean"—

†"Tis with our judgments, as our watches; none
Go just alike, yet each believes his own"—Pope

†"Still green with bays each ancient alter stands,
Above the reach of sacrilegious hands;
Secure from flames, from envy's fiercer rage,
Destructive war and all—involving age.
Hail, bards triumphant, born in happier days.
Immortal heirs of universal praise!
Whose honours with increase of ages grow,
As streams roll down, enlarging as they flow."
Pp.

†"But of the two less dangerous is the offence
To tire our patience than mislead our sense"
Pp.

†"Tis not enough no harshness gives offence;
The sound must seem to echo to the sense"
Pp.

†"Be silent always, when you doubt your sense
And speak, though sure, with *seeming* diffidence"
Pp.

†"Horace still charms with graceful negligence,
And without method talks us into sense."
Pp.

†"Soft, without weakness, without glaring gay"
Pp.

†"Alas! how little from the grave we claim!
Thou but preserv'est a face, and I a name" Pp.

Thomson: The Seasons; Castle of Indolence. Liberty

See Spenser's *"Oak and Briar"*

"The most indispensable part of the love of liberty has unfortunately hitherto been the hatred of tyranny. Spleen is the soul of patriotism and public good." Hazlitt

†"Knowledge and Wisdom, far from being one,
Have oft-times no connection. Knowledge dwells
In heads replete with thoughts of other men;
Wisdom in minds attentive to their own."   *Cowper*

Some to the fascination of a name
Surrender judgment, hood-wink'd. Some the style
Infatuates, and through labyrinths and wilds
Of error leads them by a tune entranc'd.
While sloth seduces more, too weak to bear
The insupportable fatigue of thought,
And swallowing, therefore, without pause or choice,
The total grist unsifted, husks and all. *Cowper*

See Farquhar's "Beaux' Stratagem."

"Authors after their death live in their words: players only in their reputations and the breath of common tradition. They that die leave the world no authoritative copy. Their once certain popularity is as short lived as it is dazzling and in a few years nothing is known of them but that they *were*." *Hazlitt*.

"Imagination is like a double-faced mirror, in part turned towards the outer world, and reflecting its objects, in part towards the light of ideas, tinging it with its hues, forming it into representations, and disposing it into pictures, while decomposing it as the prism does the solar ray."—Bautain.

†"What you conceive aright you express clearly;
And the words to say it in come easily."

"Leave consequences to God, but do right. Be genuine, real, sincere, true, be right, God-like. The world's maxim is, trim your sails, and you let circumstances judge, but if you would do any good in your generation you must be made of sterner stuff, and help mold times rather than be made by them. You must not yield to customs. Like the anvil, endure all blows, until the hammers break themselves. When misrepresented, use no crooked means to clear yourself. Difficulties do not last long. If in the course of duty you are tried by the distrust of friends, gird up your loins and say in your heart, 'I was not driven to virtue by the encouragement of friends, nor will I be repelled by their coldness.'

Finally, be just and fear naught; 'corruption wins not more than honesty'; truth lives and runs when falsehood dies and rots."— *Spurgeon*

†"Since I am crept in favor with myself,
I will maintain it with some little cost."—*Richard*

†"For, while the tired waves, vainly breaking,
Seem here no painful inch to gain,
Far back, through creeks and inlets making,
Comes silent, flooding in, the main."

Carlyle's Heroes and Hero-Worship

King: Cromwell, Napoleon.

The King the most important of Great Men; the summary *of all* the various figures of Heroism. To enthrone the Ablest Man, the true business of all Social procedure: the Ideal of Constitutions. Tolerable and intolerable approximations. Divine Rights and Diabolic Wrongs. The world's sad predicament; that of having its *Able-Man to seek*, and not knowing in what manner to proceed about it. The era of Modern Revolutionism dates from Luther. The French Revolution no mere act of General Insanity: Truth clad in hell-fire; the Trump of Doom to Plausibilities and empty Routine. The cry of Liberty and Equality at bottom the repudiation of sham Heroes. Hero-worship exists forever and everywhere; from divine adoration down to the common courtesies of man and man: the soul of Order, to which all things, Revolutions included, work. Some Cromwell or Napoleon the necessary finish of a *Sans-culottism*. The manner in which Kings were made, and Kingship itself first took rise. Puritanism a section of the universal war of Belief against Make-believe. Laud a weak ill-starred Pedant; in his spasmodic vehemence heeding no voice of prudence; no cry of pity. Universal necessity for true Forms: How to distinguish between True and False. The nakedest Reality preferable to any empty Semblance, however dignified. The work of the Puritans. The Skeptical 18th century, and its constitutional estimate of Cromwell and his associates. No wish to disparage such characters as Hampden, Eliot, Pym; a most constitutional, unblamable, dignified set of men. The rugged outcast Cromwell, the man of them all in whom one still finds human stuff. The One thing worth revolting for—Cromwell's hypocrisy, an impossible theory. His pious Life as a Farmer until 40 years of age. His public successes honest successes of a brave man. His participation in the King's death no ground of condemnation. His eye for facts no hypocrite's gift. His

Ironsides the embodiment of this insight of his. Know the men that may be trusted: Alas, this is yet, in these days, very far from us. Cromwell's hypochondria: His reputed confusion of speech: His habit of prayer. His speeches unpremeditated and full of meaning. His reticences; called lying and dissimulation: Not one falsehood proved against him. Foolish charge of 'ambition.' The great Empire of Silence: Noble silent men, scattered here and there, each in his department; silently thinking, silently hoping, silently working. 2 kinds of ambition; one wholly blamable, the other laudable, inevitable: How it actually was with Cromwell. Hume's Fanatic-Hypocrite theory. How indispensable everywhere a King is, in all movements of men. Cromwell, as King of Puritanism, of England. Constitutional palaver; Dismissal of the Rump Parliament. Cromwell's Parliaments and Protectorship: Parliaments having failed, there remained nothing for him but the way of Despotism. His closing days: His poor old Mother. It was not to men's judgments that he appealed; nor have men judged him very well—The French Revolution, the third act of Protestantism. Napoleon, infected with the quackeries of his age: Had a kind of sincerity,—an instinct towards the practical. His faith,—"The Tools to him that can handle them", the whole truth of Democracy. His heart-hatred of Anarchy. Finally, his quackeries got the upper hand: He would found a Dynasty: Believed wholly in the dupeability of Men. This Napoleonism was unjust, a falsehood, and could not last.

Man of Letters—Johnson, Rousseau, Burns.

The Hero as Man of Letters altogether a product of these new ages. A Heroic Soul in very strange guise. Literary men genuine and spurious. Fichte's Divine Idea of the World: His notion of the True Man of Letters. Goethe, the Pattern Literary Hero.—The disorganized condition of Literature, the summary of all other modern disorganizations. The Writer of a true Book our true modern Preacher. Miraculous influence of Books: the Hebrew Bible. Books are now our actual University, our Church, our Parliament. With Books, Democracy is inevitable. Thought the true *thaumaturgic* influence, by which man works all things whatever. Organization of the "Literary Guild"—Needful discipline; priceless lessons of Poverty. The Literary Priesthood and its importance to society. Chinese Literary Governors. Fallen into strange times; and strange things need to be speculated upon. An age of Scepticism: The very possibility of Heroism abnegated. Benthamism and eyeless Heroism. Scepticism, Spiritual Paralysis, Insincerity: Heroes gone-out; Quacks come-in. Our brave Chatham himself lived the strangest mimetic life all along. Violent remedial revulsions: Chartisms, French Revolutions: The Age of Scepticism passing away. Let each Man look to the mending of his own Life. Johnson one of our Great English Souls. His miserable Youth and Hypochondria: Stubborn Self-help. His loyal submission to what is really higher than himself. How he stood by the old Formulas: Not less original for that. Formulas; their use and abuse. Johnson's unconscious sincerity. His Twofold Gospel, a kind of Moral Prudence and clear Hatred of Cant. His writings sincere and full of substance. Architectural nobleness of his Dictionary. Boswell, with all his faults, a true hero-worshiper of a true Hero. Rousseau a morbid, excitable, spasmodic man; intense rather than strong. Had not the invaluable talent of Silence. His Face expressive of his character. His Egoism; Hungry for the praises of men. His books; Passionate appeals, which did once more struggle towards Reality; A Prophet to his Time; as he could, and as the Time could. Rosepink, and artificial bedizenment. Fretted, exasperated, till the heart of him went mad: he could be cooped, starving, into garrets; laughed at as a maniac; but he could not be hindered from setting the world on fire. Burns a genuine Hero in a withered, unbelieving, secondhand Century. The largest soul of all the British lands came among us in the shape of a hard-handed Scottish Peasant. His heroic Father and Mother, and their sore struggle through life. His rough untutored dialect: Affectionate joyousness. His writings a poor fragment of him. His conversational gifts: High duchesses and low ostlers alike fascinated by him. Resemblance between Burns and Mirabeau. Official Superiors; The greatest thinking-faculty in this land superciliously dispensed with. Hero-worship under strange conditions. The notablest phasis of Burns's history his visit to Edinburgh. For one man who can stand prosperity there are a hundred that will stand adversity. Literary Lionism.

WWsh and WWhw bound ledger book (WP, DLC).

To Annie Wilson Howe

My very dear sister: Princeton, N. J., 4/19/76
    At last I sit down to write you a few lines. I have no excuse for my neglect of you in the matter of letter writing except my inexcusable laziness in the matter, which I am afraid will lose me several good friends if I do not speedily mend. But you may rest assured that my neglect has not arisen from any want of love for you or because I do not often think of you, because I love you more than you would think and you are in my thoughts every day. As this

is holiday now I have a good deal of time on my hands, almost too much in fact. All the boys are away except those who, like me, live too far away from home to make it worth while to go during a two weeks' vacation. Several very nice Southern fellows are here, among others Sam. Melton.[1] He is very pleasant indeed. He asked me to give his regards to you when I wrote.

I am so glad that dear mother is going to stay with you while father is at the Gen. Assembly;[2] it will do her so much good, at the same time being such a pleasure to you.

I do hope that you, brother George and darling little Wilson[3] are quite well.

I am feeling quite unwell just now, as I am suffering from a severe cold and consequent return of my cough. I am greatly troubled about my cough, it seems determined never to leave me.

I intend writing to Judge Taylor this afternoon; I expect he is very much put out on account of my neglect of him.

I have been employing most of the last week in reading and have, consequently, not had such a dull time as I expected. I have contracted a great admiration for the writings of Macaulay and Addison of late and find a great deal of enjoyment in reading their works. I would give anything to become as great a writer as Macaulay. There is something very fascinating in his writings, even when he is treating of the most common place & and [sic] uninteresting things: uninteresting at least when described by any other pen.

Give my regards to all my Columbia friends and say that I have by no means forgotten them. Please excuse this extremely short and dull note; my brain and hand are both so unman[a]g[e]able from infrequent use that I have no control over them. I will write again very soon. Please write me very soon. Unbounded love to brother Geo. dear little Wilson and your own self from

Your loving brother   Thomas

ALS (WC, NjP).
    [1] Samuel D. Melton, '76, of Columbia, S. C.
    [2] General Assembly of the southern Presbyterian Church met in Savannah, Ga., May 18-27, 1876.
    [3] James Wilson Howe, son of Dr. and Mrs. George Howe, Jr.

EDITORIAL NOTE
WILSON'S SHORTHAND DIARY

THE main body of the Wilson Papers, when deposited in the Library of Congress in 1939, included a number of abortive Wilson diaries and journals, and scholars concluded that Woodrow Wilson lacked the determination and patience to keep an intimate record for a long period. What might have been an exception but in the end only confirmed the generalization was a shorthand diary that Wilson kept while an undergraduate at Princeton. It came to light only when Mrs. Wilson deposited it in the Wilson Papers in 1952. It was displayed four years later in the Woodrow Wilson Centennial Exhibit of the Library of Congress. Why it was kept hidden for so long from the view of scholars, even from that of Wilson's official biographer, Ray Stannard Baker, is something of a mystery. Perhaps it was one of those specially cherished documents related to Wilson's early years that were carefully preserved—first by himself and later by his mother and two wives—and then forgotten.

This diary consists of two main parts, and a third of a temporary nature which Wilson used as a basis for certain entries in the first part.[1] This first part, to which Wilson gave the heading "My Journal," is in a large ruled notebook 7¾" x 13". It covers the period June 3 to November 23, 1876, and consists of fifty-five pages of closely written shorthand in black ink that remains sharp and clear. The first page has an elaborate pencil drawing as a heading showing various Graham shorthand publications framed by Doric pillars. At the center of this illustration is a large shorthand outline for the words "My Journal." The second main part, which Wilson labeled "Diary," is in a smaller book with ruled pages 7⅞" x 10". It is also written in black ink, except for a few headings in red ink, and consists of six pages on which there are only fourteen entries, twelve for 1877 and two for 1878.

The work of transcribing and editing this diary stretched over a period of more than six years. Mr. Gehman began the transcription in the autumn of 1959 and completed a tentative transcript in January 1960. Then followed several conferences in 1960 and 1961 during which the editors worked through the diary with Mr. Gehman, concentrating on doubtful and undeciphered words, phrases, and names. In this manner it was possible to establish, for example, that the tentative readings "t-y-k-n-l," "r-n-s," "K-l-y," "Cleck," "Keystone Age," "Stony Brook," "sublime," "facing," and "devotions" finally became "Tyrconnel," "Reunion," "Clio," "Eclectic," "Augustan Age," "Stony Park," "blame," "for single," and "divisions." In addition, Marjorie Sirlouis in 1964 checked Mr. Gehman's transcript against photocopies of the original. She was able to transcribe nearly all remaining doubtful words and phrases.

The transcription of this shorthand diary now makes it possible to evaluate Wilson's most sustained effort at diary-keeping. We may safely call it one of the best contemporary records of student life at Princeton during the latter part of the nineteenth century. But its chief value is the revealing portrait that it gives of the youth who would become a President of the United States. Although the diary displays little of the agonizing soul-searching that might be expected in this kind of youthful record, it is more than conventionally introspective. It reveals detailed

[1] The WWsh sources for the transcripts printed in this volume are in the notebooks described, for the first part, at April 1, 1875, item (d); for the second, at Sept. 7, 1875, item (b); and for the third, at Sept. 20, 1875, item (i).

information about Wilson's attitudes toward his studies, fellow-students, and professors; the development of his historical and literary tastes, which led him far beyond the bounds of the prescribed reading assignments; his efforts to improve his style in writing and speaking; and his strong religious faith.

How does one account for the abrupt termination of a record kept without interruption for twenty-five weeks? Wilson gave his own explanation in a longhand postscript to the entry for November 23, 1876: "Discontinued for want of time to do it *Justice*." The explanation is entirely credible in light of Wilson's interests and more absorbing concerns at this time. His great ambition was to become a man of affairs, a leader of men. His life as a student was beginning to afford him a field of action for testing his abilities. When he wrote the postscript to his diary and during the three months that followed, he was engaged in a number of extracurricular activities: contributing to *The Princetonian*, preparing speeches and orations, and organizing and writing a constitution for the Liberal Debating Club. He did make later sporadic attempts to continue his diary, but they resulted merely in the addition of fourteen entries, some of which were made during a summer vacation.

Thus Wilson did not leave us an intimate record of his undergraduate life to match the monumental diary of Samuel Pepys, or one comparable in length to that of John Quincy Adams. Even so, his diary by its very form must be considered unusual. It belongs in that select category of shorthand diaries kept by persons who were or became prominent figures in American history, the earliest example of which is the diary of William Byrd of Westover. This use of shorthand by a diarist adds piquancy by suggesting that the author never intended this personal record for eyes other than his own. But Wilson, by consciously taking Pepys' diary as a model, as is revealed in his very first entry, also might have entertained the hope that his diary would some day be transcribed and published. In one entry he did write, after reading another diary that he had kept for a short time in 1873 (it has never been found), that he felt encouraged to "keep on with this diary in the hope that it may prove of great interest to me in after life." Insofar as the editors have been able to determine, however, he made no references to this shorthand diary after he discontinued it, either in letters, speeches, or conversations.

The editors have of course printed transcripts, arranged chronologically, of the entire diary. They wish to make it clear that the following version is neither a free one nor condensed or cut. They realize the dangers of error in transcribing such a document, and they present the following rendition in the hope that it does no violence to its author's intentions.

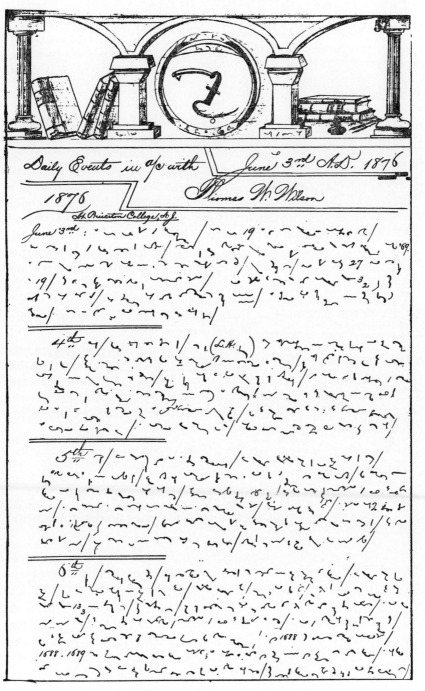

The First Page of Wilson's Shorthand Diary

From Wilson's Shorthand Diary: "My Journal"

Daily Events in a/c with THOMAS W. WILSON

Commenced June 3rd, A.D. 1876

1876

At Princeton College, N. J.

June 3rd: I now commence the diary which I have for some time contemplated. I am now 19 years old and am by the blessings of God in the enjoyment of excellent health. I have not employed the day to very much advantage having spent most of my time in loafing. My only reading today has been the life of Samuel Pepys prefixed to his diary and correspondence by Lord Richard Braybrooke in the edition of '69. I like Pepys am writing my diary in shorthand but here the resemblance between his diary and mine cease[s]. Pepys was a strange man. He commenced his diary when he was 27[;] I commence mine at the age of 19. I was led to read this diary from the frequent references to it in Lord Macaulay's History of England.

News was received that Harvard beat Yale in baseball by a score of three to two at which there was great rejoicing here in which I heartily joined. After the shameful way in which Yale treated us I will always be glad to hear of her defeat in *anything*.[1] On the strength of the good news Enos[2] treated to ice cream—there are different ways of showing appreciation of good news.

I am quite lonely tonight since McCarter[3] is away spending Sunday at home.

WWsh section in notebook described at April 1, 1875, item (d). All subsequent Diary passages through Nov. 23, 1876, are from this source.
[1] Yale defeated Princeton 12 to 9 on May 20, 1876.
[2] Alanson T. Enos, first-year School of Science
[3] Robert H. McCarter, born April 28, 1859. A.B., College of New Jersey, 1879; LL.B., Columbia Law School, 1882; LL.D., Princeton University, 1904. Admitted to bar, 1882, and practiced law in Newark, N. J. Attorney General of New Jersey, 1903-08. Died May 30, 1941.

[June] 4th Sunday. I have spent a quiet and somewhat tiresome day. Heard Dad (L. H. Atwater)[1] preach a spiritually uninteresting sermon—I may have thought it uninteresting because I did not pay very strict attention to it however. I think that he could have argued some points a lot better than he did even if he *is* a professor of logic—some of the offerings were very poor. He had such an extremely listless set of hearers however that he had no very great encouragement to do his best—perhaps few of our men heard all the sermon.

After dinner took a stroll in the woods with Enos[,] Pope[,][2] and

Woods[3] and had a right pleasant time. Rain in the evening laid the dust and made the atmosphere much more pleasant.

Four weeks from today we will have the baccalaureate sermon from Dr. McCosh[4]—my freshman year will then be over!

Tomorrow our boys start on their baseball trip—may they have success! Enos and I had quite a long conversation on different forms of government especially on the relative merits of a limited monarchy and republic such as this. I found that we both agreed very well on that point: that the limited monarchy is much the more preferable and is the only form of government which gives true liberty to the people. The English form of government is best by far after all. In this connection he gave me a long account of France and Frenchmen as seen by himself which was very interesting.

1 The Rev. Lyman H. Atwater, Professor of Logic and Moral and Political Science, College of New Jersey, nicknamed "Dad" by undergraduates. See WW's later comment at Feb. 7, 1878.

2 Paul Pope, a friend from Wilmington, who entered Princeton in 1875 on probation and was later expelled.

3 Hiram Woods, Jr., born Baltimore, Nov. 11, 1857. A.B., College of New Jersey, 1879; M.D., University of Maryland, 1882. Practiced in Baltimore, 1883-1929. Professor of Ophthalmology, University of Maryland Medical School, 1894-1919. Author of numerous articles in medical journals. Died Jan. 15, 1931.

4 The Rev. James McCosh, eleventh President of the College of New Jersey. Born Ayrshire, Scotland, April 1, 1811. M.A., University of Edinburgh, 1833. Licensed to preach by Church of Scotland, 1834. One of the founders of the Free Church of Scotland in 1843. Professor of Logic and Metaphysics, Queen's College, Belfast, 1852-68. Elected president, College of New Jersey, April 29, 1868; inaugurated, Oct. 27, 1868. One of the earliest apologists in the Church of the Darwinian theory of evolution. Author of numerous works on Christianity, philosophy, and psychology. Retired, 1888; died, Nov. 16, 1894.

[June] 5th Monday. Cooled by the rain of yesterday and last night[,] the day has been very pleasant indeed. Played baseball with the Bowery Boys[1] both at noon and after chapel and enjoyed it very much. Had a very "soft snap" today—no recitations at all. We have Latin under Condit[2] in Professor Duffield's[3] room and since Duff wished to use his room himself we could have no Latin. Then I got off from Greek this afternoon because tutor Marquand[4] did not get back from New York in time to hear us. I think the American plan of recitations at college make[s] us silly at any rate. Spent the evening in reading the tenth chapter of Macaulay's History of England which closes with the accession of William & Mary. The more I read Macaulay the more I am interested in him and his subject—the more I become fascinated by history. If all history were written thus I would read little else. The history of England in the time of Charles II and James II deserves a great deal of study as it is full of the record of events which teach some of the most important principles of government. This morning I read a little more in Pepys's diary but I find that I must read up the history of the times in order that I know a little more before I can appreciate it. Think I will commence Evelyn's diary tomorrow. No letter from my aunt—I am very anxious to hear as I have not heard for some time. I will have plenty of time to read tomorrow as I have two lessons already prepared for tomorrow's recitations.

[1] Undergraduates who boarded at Mrs. Wright's house called "(W) Right Bower."
[2] Isaac H. Condit, Tutor in Latin.
[3] The Rev. John T. Duffield, Dod Professor of Mathematics.
[4] Allan Marquand, Tutor in Greek.

[June] 6th Tuesday. A very pleasant day as far as the weather was concerned. As I had most of my lessons prepared I spent most of the day reading Macaulay—except that Pepys held my thought a little this afternoon. Played baseball both at noon and after chapel. At noon played a picked nine and suffered defeat—after chapel had practice with the nine. Bowery boys played very well I thought. Our captain, Enos[,] does well. About supper time news arrived from New Haven that we were beaten by Yale by a score of 13 to 3—Jim Woods[1] hurt. It was a bitter disappointment to me. Although I had scarcely expected our nine to beat the Yale fellows[,] still hope lived to the last and I was disappointed in spite of myself. The nine plays Amherst tomorrow I believe. Tried to forget my disappointment in the perusal of the 11th chapter of Macaulay's History of England which closes with the declaration of war with France. The next chapter will be full of interest as it contains an account of the state of Ireland and the troubles there. As far as I have followed William in his reign I think that he governed himself wisely and justly and overcame difficulties which no other man then living could have overcome. The Revolution of 1688 was certainly one of the most remarkable events in any annals of history. 1688 and 1689 are years which are now remembered and will long be remembered as the most eventful years in the history of the world; years in which a great and yet bloodless revolution was accomplished—a revolution which was one of the most important to liberty that has ever occurred.

The interest of these events is greatly enhanced to modern readers by the clear and splendid diction of Macaulay who makes the most stupid things alive with interest of romance.

There was a mass meeting of the students this afternoon to form an athletic association but I did not attend since such meetings only bore me.

[1] He was one C. Woods, not listed in the Princeton catalogues or alumni directories.

[June] 7th Wednesday. Weather very pleasant today. In the morning studied Greek and French. In the afternoon read Macaulay for about two hours—cutting French recitation—studied 9th proposition in Geometry.

Played a practice game with the Lit boys[1] at noon, and beat them by a score of 12 to 9. Played in a scrub game after chapel.

Read Macaulay all the evening, finishing the 12th chapter of the History. This chapter is one of the most interesting things in the English language. Parts of it almost fascinated me by their beauty. What a master of the English language Macaulay proved himself to be. The great interest of this chapter lies not only in the writing but also in the grave importance of the events described. It gives the most perfect view of the state of Ireland in 1688-9 that can be given in so short a space.

The intrigues and perfidy of Tyrconnel; the arming of the Irish and their fearful abuse of power; the danger and suffering of the English; James's arrival in Ireland; his calling parliament, and the perfidy of that parliament to the English; the resistance of the inhabitants of North Ireland at Enniskillen and Londonderry; and the final triumph of the English are all described with such clearness, energy and eloquence as to make the reader imagine himself transferred to the 17th century, urged by the many passions which then urged [?] men both good and wise in common with the most wicked, and taking an active part in these events which so greatly influenced the future of England and the English.

This eloquence and eminent ability to describe these events is chiefly due to Macaulay's vivid imagination, which made him imagine himself acting and working in the midst of the events which he described and which enabled him to impart some of his enthusiasm to his readers. Surely, he is the best historian England has ever produced.—

More bad news about the ball nine. They were beat today by Amherst with a score of 18 to 12. They had better come home! Some men seem to think that the failure of Princeton in games of this sort argues badly for the College, but I do not view it in this light at all. Failure in athletic sports does not detract from the excellence of the college.

Was again disappointed at receiving no letter from home. Have not read the newspapers today and am consequently profoundly ignorant of all that is going on in the world—except in Princeton, in our little college world.—

Thank God for health and strength through another day!

[1] Probably members of "Little But Soon," an undergraduate eating club.

[June] 8th Thursday. Done very little today. Studied Greek and reviewed in Latin, most of the morning—very dull work. At noon played baseball a little, and was miserably beaten. Studied review in Latin all the afternoon. After chapel played game of ball with the Sigma Nu's,[1] and beat them by a score of 18 to 11. This was the first game in [?] which our whole nine has played together. In the evening Enos and Pope were up so that I did very little.

Not having been able to get a copy of the 5th volume of Macaulay's History of England out of the library today I had to content myself with a portion of Pepys' Diary. Read in the beginning of it, about March 1660, about two months before the restoration of Charles II. Pepys is a very quaint old fellow in his modes of expressing himself, and very amusing indeed to me.

Received a short letter from father today at noon, enclosing a draft on New York for $50.00, which was of course very acceptable. Dear father always writes an extremely interesting letter. Three weeks from today I will be on my way home!

The blessings of another day are added to my load of gratitude to God.

[1] One of the miscellaneous voluntary organizations of '79 men.

[June] 9th Friday. *Cut* Latin at 8½ o'clock. Studied Plato's Crito from 9 to 11, and found it very enjoyable. Went to gym at XI O'clock and left the room in about 15 minutes. Read and slept most of the time from 2 to 4. Recitation on Crito at 4 o'clock. After recitation tutor Marquand read the end of Crito to us. I think that the Crito is one of the most masterly pieces of argument I ever had the good fortune to read—it is one of the few pieces of Greek that I ever read with any pleasure to myself. The re-perusal of it will be anything but a task.

Read a little of the 13th chapter of Macaulay's History of England, and a little in Pepys' Diary in the afternoon, but was too sleepy on account of the warm weather to enjoy either of them very much. I like old Pepys more and more as I get on in his Diary. It is certainly a most self-divulging book.

Attended both sessions of the Lit[1] but did not find them as interesting as usual. Held a most miserable debate. Several tolerable essays and one or two good speeches mostly comic. Got home about XI o'clock and went to bed rather tired.

Received a new suit of clothes, which are very acceptable indeed. They suit and fit me very well indeed.

Thank God for health and strength of another day!

This is the first day this week that I have not played baseball.

1 The American Whig Society.

[June] 10th Saturday. Read a little oratory this morning analyzing some sentences containing figures of different sorts. Very interesting work. Played the Lit boys at noon five innings and beat them by a score of 8 to 7. We would have beaten them much worse if we had all our players—we had two men with us that did play on the nine and that were not as good as the regular men. I pitched. Tried to read this afternoon but owing to the hot weather was too sleepy to do much of it. Went over to the Lit and read the papers for a little while—no news of any importance. Our Class nine beat the juniors of Germantown[1] today, by a score of 9 to 4—very good game indeed. Yesterday the University nine were beaten by the Bostons by a score of 14 to 7[2] which was doing very well indeed since the Bostons are considered among the best of the professional nines. Today they beat the Chelseas of Brooklyn by a score of [9 to 4]. They arrived here tonight poor fellows.

Spent most of the evening in reading Macaulay's History of England 13th chapter and have consequently been most highly entertained. No modern writer can compare with Macaulay as a historian in my opinion. I read very slowly but enjoy immensely as I go along. I sometimes wish that I could read a little faster but I do not know that it would be an advantage. Macaulay's outline of the history of the Highlands in this 13th chapter is certainly a most masterly piece of composition and has given me a better idea of the condition of the old Highlands than anything I ever read—not even excepting Scott's novels in relation to the Highlands.

Macaulay had such a clear conception of everything that he describes in his *History* and such mastery of language in which he expressed his thoughts that he presents all the events of history before one's eyes in the most vivid and yet concise way.

Received a most welcome letter from dear mother this morning and enjoyed it immensely of course.

God bless all that are dear to me and continue to bless them and me as He has in the past!

1 They were called the Germantown Juniors.
2 Actually, the score was 14 to 5.

[June] 11th Sunday. In the morning read a little in the Bible and went to the First [Presbyterian] Church and heard a sermon from Harris[1]—a sermon which I considered a very poor attempt. Spent most the time between dinner and 4 o'clock in reading an old diary which I kept for a little over a month in the early part of 1873. I find it very interesting reading indeed, which encourages me to keep on with this diary in the hope that it may prove of great interest to me in after life.

A record of the daily events at college will then be of the greatest interest to me no doubt. At 4 o'clock went with Pope to the Episcopal church, and heard—or rather didn't hear—a very dull sermon from the Rector, Mr. Baker.[2] I think the Episcopal service very stupid indeed—it is in my opinion a ridiculous way of worshiping God, and one which must give very little pleasure to God. A mere dull form. Went to church at the First Church again at night and heard a very good sermon from a minister of Hoboken. Dod[3] I think was his name. He preached on the text "Why halt ye between 2 opinions etc." His discourse was by no means a profound one but was such as to confer already grouped facts upon the attentive listener. Sunday, which ought to be one of my most interesting days, is one of my dullest. The reason for this is I suppose that I have nothing to read having provided myself with no Sunday reading. I shall certainly provide myself with such reading as is fit for Sunday before I return to college again. Two weeks from today will be the day for Jim's[4] baccalaureate sermon—then home! A good many pretty girls at church tonight, one of the prettiest who was with "Jeff" Davis.[5] This very warm weather makes it difficult for me to keep awake during service.

Thank God for health and strength of another day!

Wrote a letter to mother this afternoon—a very short one. Received back my essay from Professor Hunt yesterday with the comment "Your argument is ingenious and somewhat forcible. The diction and sentences are good" which I suppose he meant for praise. The essay was on "The past and present of American oratory."[6]

1 The Rev. William Harris, Treasurer of the College of New Jersey.
2 The Rev. Alfred B. Baker, rector of Trinity Episcopal Church, Princeton, N. J.
3 The Rev. Samuel B. Dod, Presbyterian evangelist from Hoboken, N. J.
4 President McCosh.
5 Probably John D. Davis, '79.
6 Not found.

[June] 12th Monday. Spent most of the morning in studying geometry and Greek (Xenophon's Memorabilia). Spent most of the rest of the day from 12 to 5 in reading Macaulay's History of England: the end of the 13th chapter and the beginning of the 14th since the weather made it more pleasant to stay indoors than go out. After chapel went to Hall library[1] and read a review of

"Green's Short History of the English People" in the London Quarterly[2]—not having read the book of which it is a review I cannot form an opinion of the justice of the reviewer's criticisms and remarks on Mr. Green's History.

After supper went down street and then came back to my room and spent most—in fact all—of the afternoon in the perusal of the 14th chapter of Macaulay's History. I become more and more interested as I advance in this remarkably fascinating work. It has for me all the interest of a novel.

The day has been rather dull, owing no doubt, to the gloominess of the weather. I have no reason to complain of any ill health, however—for which God be praised. As the time approaches for examinations I feel less and less like preparing for them.

I must not allow myself to become too much enamored of the history else I should altogether neglect my studies; which are of so much importance to me at this period of my life.

[1] The American Whig Society library.
[2] A scathing, unsigned review in the London *Quarterly Review*, cxli (April 1876), 285-323.

[June] 13th Tuesday. During morning studied Euclid and Xenophon's Memorabilia, with very little interest. Was from necessity kept from attending chapel and Latin recitations. Was kept from chapel on account of late breakfast and from Latin by natural causes.

At noon went to the Treasurer's Office and paid bill for third term—$13.00. Then went to the Library[1] and spent most of the noon hour there looking up references of various kinds. Spent most of the afternoon and evening in perusal of Macaulay's History, chapters 15 and 16 which have fascinated me very much. After chapel went to Hall and tried to read but found that I cannot settle down to it and so gave it up and spent most of the hour before supper in loafing around generally.

Did little else than get my ticket for Junior Oratory exercise and the invitations to same which cost me the sum of 80¢. I have not taken enough exercise today because the weather has been so unfavorable to outdoor exercise as well as indoor exercise.

I must be careful to take regular exercise, however, because my health depends upon that more than upon anything else in my opinion. I have not yet commenced to study for examinations, but must soon do so. I am allowing Macaulay to draw me away too much I am afraid. His description of the events of the early part of 1690 which I have been reading today are certainly masterful. But it is impossible to say which part of his great work is the most to be admired. I would that he lived to complete this wonderful history.

Well, another day has passed, and I am $13.80 poorer than I was when it dawned.

Thank God for the health and strength of another day.

Two weeks from tonight I will be free to go home!

1 The Chancellor Green Library, completed in 1873. The books were moved to it from Nassau Hall in 1874.

[June] 14th Wednesday. Had no French recitation at 8½ o'clock since Kargé[1] had an examination today. Spent from 8.45 to 10 studying geometry. From 10.45 to 12 I read Macaulay's History, chapter 16.

At noon went down to University baseball ground, expecting to see a game between our fellows and the Lafayette boys, but no game came off—for what reason I do not know.

At 12.30 went to the Treasurer's office to draw for room in the new dormitory—Witherspoon Hall.[2] I had very good luck indeed, and drew 5th choice. I chose No. 7 West Entry, which will I think be a very fine room indeed. Jack Farr[3] drew first choice, and had the room right above me—Handy,[4] who had third choice, the room next to Jack's. Hi Woods got 7th choice and took a room in the other end of the building—East Entry. I am very well satisfied with my room and have reason to be. My mind is now easy about a room. I feared that I would get a very poor chance. McCarter has got to room in North Reunion with Dennis, '79.[5]

Spent most of the afternoon in reading Macaulay and finished the 16th chapter a few minutes before chapel time. I have now read 5 of the 8 volumes. I can easily finish the rest of the History in the few weeks during the approaching vacations. I continue to become more and more fascinated with this more than interesting history. Oh that I could learn to write thus!

Pope passed his entrance examinations in Greek all right this afternoon, and starts for home tomorrow morning, at 9:45. I only wish that I could go home with him now.

Spent most of the evening in studying the First Book of Geometry for examination. Studied 35 propositions.

The first number of the new college paper—"The Princetonian" —made its appearance today. It promises to be a very lively and interesting journal. I shall patronize it as well as the "Lit."

McCarter and I had a short discussion on the English government this evening. These discussions are very interesting. He thinks that the English will soon turn out their sovereigns and establish some other kind of a ruler—I think otherwise.

[1] General Joseph Kargé, Woodhull Professor of Continental Languages and Literature.
[2] Completed early in 1877.
[3] John Farr, '79.
[4] Parker Handy, '79.
[5] Alfred L. Dennis, Jr., '79.

[June] 15th Thursday. Went to our last recitations as freshmen today, and gave three cheers after each of them. Spent most of the morning studying geometry and Plato's Crito[,] the latter of which is very interesting indeed. It is one of the few Latin [sic] books which I have read and admired at the same time. At noon went down to see the match between our nine and the Orange nine of this state. Our fellows beat them by a score of 14 to 7. Our men had the toss, and when they went to bat for the last time the score stood 8 to 7 in our favor. Our fellows then went to work and made six runs in one inning, and so doubled the Orange nine. Our men played beautifully. The Orange men played pretty well, though nothing remarkable about their playing.

Study review in Xenophon's Memorabilia for examinations all the afternoon and evening. Very stupid work. The book is not by any means stupid, but it is stupid to read any book when you know that you are obliged to read it.

I expect our examinations on Greek to be very hard indeed, since we have a new tute. Tomorrow is the day for examinations of the *entire* class—'80. Several innocents[1] arrived tonight and this afternoon, and were duly hazed by our fellows.

Poor '80 will have a very hard time next year. How nice it is to think that my freshman year is over. I have only been through two freshman classes now.

Thank God for health and strength to live and learn.

Caught ball a little with Woods this afternoon.

[1] Boys who came to Princeton to take entrance examinations.

[June] 16th Friday. Spent most of the day studying for English examination which comes tomorrow. No recitations. This was the day for examination of the '80 men. This morning a great many fellows of our class got around Dickinson Hall and watched for the new fellows. We got a good many of them into the writing room and Larkin[1] and Kerr[2] examined them. For a while they were thoroughly taken in but soon found out the joke and went to the right place. The plan was so hastily gotten up that it was poorly carried out. We frightened most of them most thoroughly. A good many of them were very much frightened.

Caught ball with Enos at noon. After chapel went to the Hall. No second session. Took a short walk after supper and went to post.

Studied English most of the evening. Dull work. Thank God for health and strength. This night one week we will be free—through all examinations.

News from the Republican convention this afternoon that Governor Hayes of Ohio has been nominated for President of the United States. A great surprise—everybody seemed to expect that Blaine would be nominated. This gives me some hopes that, since a man like Hayes who is comparatively unknown is nominated, the Republican ticket will be defeated and the Democratic ticket elected. I do most sincerely hope that the Democrats will nominate a good and prominent man like Tilden. The Democrats will be very likely to abuse power if they get it, however. Men are greedy fellows as a rule.

1 Francis Larkin, Jr., '79.
2 Alexander J. Kerr, '79.

[June] 17th Saturday. Spent from 9 to 12 in examination room. Had our first final examination on English. This was the first of the series of the finals for fresh year. The paper was long and quite hard. Got through pretty well, however.

At noon received a letter from dear father about many matters reproving me for my extravagance. The reproof was thoroughly merited. The letter made me very sad indeed. I answered it immediately after dinner. In the afternoon I went to see the barber and got shaved and my hair cut.

Spent about a half hour studying geometry for the examination on Monday next. Loafed around generally between five o'clock and supper time. Caught ball after supper until dark. Studied geometry from 8 to 10—very stupid work indeed. Father's letter has thrown a damper on my spirits today all the more because I felt that it was more or less merited as I have been very extravagant in a small way just as I wrote to him.

Thank God for health and strength and such parents as He has been good enough to give me—what could I do without them. About one week from today I will be at liberty to go to them.

Very stupid day.

[June] 18th Sunday. Did not go to chapel but slept until about 8-1/4 o'clock. After breakfast I walked about until church time as my room was not fixed up and I did not care to loaf on the front steps with the other fellows since it was Sunday and I felt in no very good humor. Heard a very good sermon in Chapel from Dr. Green[1] of the Seminary.

After dinner took a long walk with Enos about the country and did not get back until supper time—5½ o'clock. Did not go out after supper but after sitting for a while upon the front steps with Enos went to bed at about 8½ o'clock with the intention of getting up very early in the morning.

A week from today we have the baccalaureate sermon.

Thank God for health and strength.

[1] The Rev. William Henry Green, D.D., Professor of Oriental and Old Testament Literature, Princeton Theological Seminary.

[June] 19th Monday. Got up about 5 o'clock and studied geometry for examination until about 7:45 o'clock. Commenced study again about 9 o'clock and studied until one. Immediately after dinner at 1½ o'clock went over to examination on geometry. Had a very fair paper with 14 questions on it. I answered 8 of them correctly. I could have answered several more but owing to the short time allowed could not write out the proofs for more than 8[.] Got out about 5 o'clock just too late to attend chapel. After chapel strolled around and loafed. After supper took a short walk down towards the canal with Enos. Went over to the Hall about 8 o'clock and read the conclusion of the "Lady Candidate" in Blackwoods and got an article called "The American Republic," in the International Review.[1] The story had little point to it and the article did not amount to much, being simply a résumé of this country's history and general praising of it—comparing it favorably with every other country, and predicting its future advance and greatness. The old old story.

The American *Republic* will in my opinion never celebrate another Centennial. At least under its present Constitution and laws. Universal suffrage is at the foundation of every evil in this country.

I am, thank God, still free[,] happy and perfectly healthy. I cannot be too thankful for all God's mercies to me.

Paid my bill for board up to 6/21/76 this morning. On the 26th I leave for home!

[1] [Anon.], "The Lady Candidate," *Blackwood's Edinburgh Magazine*, cxix (May 1876), 560-76 (Pt. i); cxix (June 1876), 689-706 (Pt. ii); Franz Sigel, "The American Republic," the *International Review*, iii (July 1876), 462-78.

[June] 20th Tuesday. Did not go to morning chapel. A day of study. From 9 to 12 studied French for examination. At 12 went out and loafed. After dinner studied about half of an hour. Went into French examination at 3 o'clock. Very easy paper with only 9 questions. I did pretty well. Got out a little after 4 o'clock. Exercised [a] little later. In the evening studied the rest of Xenophon's Memorabilia for examination.

[June] 21st Wednesday. No examination today. Did not go to chapel either in the morning or evening. From 9 to 12 studied and read [a] little of Plato. Exercise at noon catching ball. Studied Roman history all afternoon, writing out a synopsis of the principal events. Exercised after chapel. After supper went to post and from thence to the Hall where I read until 8 o'clock. From 8 to 10 in the evening studied Roman history and Latin Grammar with McCarter. Eight hours of study today—my general average 3 hours per day when no examinations are on hand.

Thank God for health and strength. A week from today I will be home.

[June] 22nd Thursday. From 8½ o'clock to 11 in examination on Latin. Rather long but comparatively easy paper. Did pretty well. Didn't do much between 11 o'clock and dinner except loaf around generally. After dinner wrote a letter to dear father. At 3 o'clock went down to ball ground to see game between our nine and the New Haven professional nine.[1] Bad game. Score 3 to one in their favor. Our fellows played beautifully. The score was about as good as any amateur nine could make with such a nine as the New Haven which is one of the best in the country. Frank Dunning[2] got behind the bat. The New Haven men played splendidly. It was the best game I ever saw. Jim Denny[3] made a two-base hit. The game lasted from a little after 3 o'clock to 5.

Fellows changed seats in Chapel this afternoon. Played ball after chapel until supper time. Read in the Hall from 7 to 8. Read the first part of a very good story in Blackwood's called the Woman Hater.[4]

From 8-1/4 to 10½ studied Greek Grammar for tomorrow's examination which will be the last. During study had a short discussion with McCarter about Socrates and demons [dialogues?] which I think was nothing to his genius.

Tomorrow at noon my study for the term will be over. One week from this evening I expect to hear father lecture.

Thank God for health and strength.

1 Actually, this game was played on June 21, 1876.
2 Frank Dunning, '76.
3 James O. Denny, '77.
4 [Anon.], "A Woman-Hater," *Blackwood's Edinburgh Magazine*, CXIX (June 1876), 653-72 (Pt. I). This novel was serialized in 13 parts, concluding in *Blackwood's*, CXXI (June 1877), 649-79.

[June] 23rd Friday. From 9 to 11½ passed my last examination for this year—Greek. A very fair though rather hard paper. Didn't do very well. At noon went to see match [?] game between '77 and '76[.] '77 victorious. Spent most of the forenoon loafing. After chapel went to Hall. No second session. In the evening went to hear the first Lynde Debate.[1] The question was Has Our Country Advanced Morally in the Last Century. The debate was a success and excellent speeches were made on both sides. I am afraid however that Clio took the first prize. After the debate went on a general spree—the class celebration on becoming sophomores. Sent off a great many fireworks and shot cannon off three times. Went to bed very tired at about 12 o'clock.

1 The Lynde Debate, endowed by Charles R. Lynde and begun in 1876, was an annual extemporaneous debate held at commencement between three representatives chosen by the American Whig Society and three by the Cliosophic Society.

[June] 24th Saturday. Got up rather late. Spent most of the morning in packing in preparation for travel next week. Never knew that I had so many things until I commenced to pack them. After dinner I went to see the athletic games. They were not remarkably good but very pleasant. Handy McCosh took the general prize, beating Mann by one point. Dr. McCosh made a very nice little presentation speech.[1]

In the evening went to Glee club concert and enjoyed it hugely. Good singing is my delight. The club sang splendidly and the instrument club gave us some very good pieces. After packing a little more went to bed very tired.

1 In the Caledonian Games, an annual track and field meet for undergraduates, Andrew J. McCosh, '77, scored eleven points to ten scored by Joseph M. Mann, '76.

[June] 25th Sunday. Got up very late. Went to hear the baccalaureate sermon but after hearing the opening anthem thought better of it and left the church. Laid in shade on the campus with McCarter until after church. A great many pretty girls at the church but not nearly as many as we see every day in the sunny South.

Spent most of the evening in lying down in my room and finished packing. Went to last class prayer meeting for this year. After prayer meeting took a very short walk with Woods and then went to my room and did my final packing. Start for home tomorrow morning.

Thank God for health and strength and privileges of another Sabbath.

[June] 26th Monday. Got up at about 5 o'clock and finished preparations for departure. Told all the fellows goodbye, and got promise from McCarter that he would write me. Started for home on the 9:45 train. Had a long and rather weary day's journey to Baltimore. It was a very pleasant relief to get on the boat at Baltimore. Sat on the deck almost all the afternoon and enjoyed the delightful breeze. Read most of the articles in the last Lit during the evening and found them very sensible and some of them very fine. Stateroom very warm but I had a very good night's rest.

No pretty girls on board.

[June] 27th Tuesday. Arrived at Portsmouth at 5 o'clock in the morning, and immediately started for Wilmington. Splendid and very dry road, traveling in the dust. Arrived at home very dirty at 6 o'clock in the afternoon. A very hard day's travel.

My relief at getting home was immense. I cannot express my delight at seeing all that are dear to me again. Found that dear father has gone to Davidson Commencement, since he is one of the trustees.[1] He expects to be back again on Thursday. Found dear mother and Josie all alone, and very glad to see me. Spent most of the evening reading and talking with mother and Josie.

Went to bed happy and thankful to God for all His mercies.

---

[1] He had been elected a representative of Wilmington Presbytery.

At Wilmington, N.C.

[June] 28th Wednesday. This is Commencement day at College. Spent a very pleasant and rather dull day. Read most of the time that I was not loafing around trying to keep cool.

Went down street in the morning to the Presbyterian office[1] and the telegraph office on business and saw Mr. McLaurin[2] and Mr. McIntire.[3] The streets are very dull indeed no business worth speaking of going on. Stayed at home for the rest of the day.

During the day and evening read the 17th chapter of Macaulay's History of England and found it extremely interesting of course. What an immense quantity of material for historical novels might be found in the events which he records.

Tomorrow morning father comes home. Thank God for health and strength of another day.

1 JRW had assumed the editorship of the *North Carolina Presbyterian* on about June 28, 1876.
2 John McLaurin, business manager of the *North Carolina Presbyterian* and treasurer of Wilmington Presbytery.
3 Probably R. M. McIntire, dry goods merchant of Wilmington, N. C.

[June] 29th Thursday. Dear father arrived this morning from Davidson—and more than glad to see him. It rained during the day and cleared the atmosphere very much indeed, rendering the air much more pleasant. Stayed at home all the day since the weather prevented my going out. Read the 18th chapter of Macaulay's History, and found that I enjoy his writing more and more—he is wonderful. This chapter carries us up to the year 1692.

In the evening went to prayer meeting with father—mother was too unwell to venture out. Spent most of the evening playing mystery [?]¹ With father and mother. Suffered with a rather severe toothache during the evening.

1 This is the best possible transcript of the shorthand outlines. Hereafter the word will be printed without brackets. "Mystery," if such it was called, was a game of billiards, for future diary entries refer to three- and four-ball games. The Wilsons were obviously *au courant* since the new three-ball game had been introduced from France as recently as about 1870. Joseph R. Wilson, Jr., later told Ray Stannard Baker that his father set up a home-made billiard table in the basement of the Wilmington manse. Perhaps the family used "mystery" as a code name because of the daring nature of such recreation at the manse.

[June] 30th Friday. Went down street with father, and while down there bought a straw hat. In the afternoon we had considerable rain accompanied by thunder and lightning.

Mother was suffering during most of the day with some of her old pains.

Read the 19th chapter of Macaulay's History. Heard during the day of the nomination of Hendricks by the Democrats for the Vice-Presidency their ticket is now Tilden and Hendricks—I certainly hope that they may be elected. The simple fact that there is nothing against Hayes and Wheeler, the Republican candidates,— though they are obscure—will be very apt to make their election more sure I am afraid. This was the case of Lincoln's election. Tilden however means reform and the only platform of the Democrats is reform.

Spent most of the day in the house owing to bad weather. The storms which prevailed during most of the day rendered dear mother very nervous in her present weak condition. I pray that she may get well.

Did nothing in particular in the evening except write this journal which is a great release to me. I have been suffering during most of the evening with a very severe pain in my bowels. Played two games of mystery with father before going to bed.

[July] 1st Saturday. Went down street several times during the day. Read the sports of the day at Princeton for Monday and Tuesday in the New York Herald. Read most of the 20th chapter of Macaulay's History. Dear mother was confined to bed most of the day. Went to bed rather early. Thank God for health and strength.

[July] 2nd Monday. [Sunday] Went to church both morning and afternoon, and also to Sabbath school. Very few people at Sabbath *school*. Saw Alex Sprunt and Pope at Sabbath school. Alex Sprunt asked me to go to the Sound with him on the 4th—promised to go if possible. Had good talk with him about Davidson and Princeton —nice to meet old acquaintances. Both father's sermons today were excellent as usual. Met a good many friends who *expressed* themselves glad to see me. Did not read any during the day. A good many young ladies seem to have gone away before my arrival. Miss Annie Kidder[1] was in church both morning and afternoon and impressed me as a very nice lady from her looks at least.

1 See note at July 12, 1876.

[July] 3rd Monday. Went down street in the afternoon and bought a few things for Josie and mother. Alex Sprunt called to see them[.] He could not take me to the Sound tomorrow since his brother was sick and had broken up their arrangements. Alex very pleasant but not at all bright. In fact I have come to the conclusion that very few people are bright.

Finished the 20th, and read the 21st chapter of Macaulay's History. English history is certainly well worth reading specially when written as Macaulay wrote it.

Mother urged me to make some visits this week, but I cannot prevail upon myself to do so. I have become so unaccustomed to visit that it is hard for me to commence again. The girls hereabouts are as far as I have seen them so uninteresting. I shall try for my own sake however to make a few visits. I would much rather stay at home and read.

[July] 4th Tuesday. The one hundredth anniversary of American independence. One hundred years ago America conquered England in an unequal struggle and this year she glories over it. How much happier [?] she would be now if she had England's form of government instead of the miserable delusion of a republic. A republic too founded upon the notion of abstract liberty! I venture to say that this country will never celebrate another centennial as a republic. The English form of government is the only true one.

I passed a very quiet day. Did not go to the Sound as I expected but stayed at home and read most of the day. In the morning fixed Josie's boat for him and read a little. In the afternoon wrote a letter to sister Annie and wrote up this diary for several days. In the evening played mystery and read.

Finished the 21st chapter and read all but about 30 pages of the 22nd chapter of Macaulay's History. To bed about 11½ o'clock. Splendid illuminations throughout the North this evening.

Thank God for health and strength.

[July] 5th Wednesday. Spent very quiet day reading and loafing *around the house*. Father was called out to the Sound to see Mrs. Carr who is supposed to be at the point of death.

He went out about 11 o'clock in the morning and returned about 6 in the afternoon. Finished Macaulay's History and read a little in the "Arctic and Tropical World" by Dr. Hartwig,[1] which judging by the first chapter promises to be a very interesting book indeed. The style is pleasant and the matter interesting. Took a short walk to the post office in the evening after tea. Exercised at about 5 o'clock with my Indian clubs and took a bath. Played three games of mystery with father in the evening. Thank God for health and strength.

Received a letter from Hi Woods about commencement [?] affairs etc. The Harvard game was a fizzle ending in no game. Denny did not get the oratory fellowship—it was given Cunningham and William Allen Butler. Billy Smith received the first prize J. O.[;] Slemmons second[;] Rowland third[;] Dunning[2] fourth. What unexpected awards!

[1] George L. Hartwig, *The Polar and Tropical Worlds* (Springfield, Mass., 1871).
[2] The undergraduates named were William A. Butler, Jr., '76, Clarence Cunningham, '76, Collins Denny, '76, William F. Dunning, '77, Samuel J. Rowland, '77, William E. Slemmons, '77, and Wilton M. Smith, '77.

[July] 6th Thursday. In the morning went down street for one or two things. Read the second chapter of "Arctic and Tropical World" and find the book very interesting indeed. Wrote several articles in my Index Rerum. After dinner wrote to sister Marion. Read several articles in the American Cyclopedia. After tea went to prayer meeting after which walked down to the post office for the mail. Played two games of mystery with father.

Thank God for continued health and strength.

[July] 7th Friday. Read [a] little in the morning in the American Cyclopedia and put up a frame for one of mother's flowers. Wrote a letter to Hi Woods in answer to his of the 3rd instant. Loafed most of the evening and afternoon. Played two games of mystery with father in the evening. Intended to go to Sprunts[1] in the afternoon with father but was prevented by storm which came up about 5 o'clock.

Heard of the slaughter of General Custer's force by the Indians in which General Custer himself and five companies perished. It seems that he attacked about 4,000 Indians with about 400 men against the orders of a superior officer and perished in the act. He thought I suppose that he would make a name for himself.

[1] The family of Alexander Sprunt, Sr., a leading shipping and commercial merchant of Wilmington, N. C. Alexander, Jr., James, and William H. were his sons.

[July] 8th Saturday. Went down street with father and wrote letter to McCarter. Wrote up my journal for the 7th and wrote two cards about the present bad condition of the streets of this city one of which I sent to the Star and the other to the Journal. I don't suppose that they will be published but still it does no harm to try to do something. The city authorities have been shamefully negligent about this matter. This city as contrasted with the northern cities is filthy. Took a walk after tea and played two games of mystery with father and one with mother.

Read some of a novel entitled "The Heir Expectant"[1] which does not promise to be very good. Some of the characters however are striking and somewhat interesting.

[1] By Isabella Harwood (3 vols., London, 1870).

To the Editor

Mr. Editor:—　　　　　　　　　　　　　　　　　　　　　[*July 8, 1876*]

At this time of the year, as the hot weather comes upon us, it becomes the imperative duty of the city authorities to take every measure in their power to improve and preserve the health of the city. They have been shamefully negligent in this respect. Any one who has had occasion, as I have lately had, to visit the less frequented streets of this city, will see how shamefully they are neglected. Everywhere, weeds of the rankest and most unhealthy kind are allowed to grow, and filth of every description to accumulate. Every open gate reveals premises which are to say the least, disgraceful to the owners, and which make the present comparative health of the city a wonder to every reasoning man. Nor is this state of things confined to the outskirts of the city. Even the main streets are in a shameful condition and the pretended repairs which are from time to time made only render matters worse. At this season of the year it is impossible to attach too much importance to cleanliness, and I am confident that I represent the sense of the whole community when I urge the city authorities to do all in their power to remedy the present deplorable condition of the city. It is also the duty of every citizen to heartily co[-]operate with the authorities in this matter, as it is only thus that we can hope to make the city inhabitable during hot weather.

A CITIZEN.

Printed in the *Wilmington Journal*, July 14, 1876. The Wilmington *Morning Star* did not print this letter.

From Wilson's Shorthand Diary

[July] 9th Communion Sunday. Went to church in the morning and had all the communion service. A very interesting and enjoyable service. Read and rested most of the afternoon. Went to Sunday School and afternoon service. After tea went to Second Church with Alex Sprunt and Rufus Hicks. Both father's sermons were excellent—Mr. Payne's[1] was moderately good.

[1] The Rev. C. M. Payne, pastor of the Second Presbyterian Church of Wilmington.

[July] 10th Monday. During the morning read several articles in the American Cyclopedia. Articles on Calhoun[,] Clay[,] and the *English* Constitution. How far superior that Constitution is to ours! Spent most of the day very idly for which I ought to be very much ashamed. After tea walked down to the post office for the mail. Walked home with Mrs. McRae who walked to the door to bring father some ice cream from her home. Played three games of mystery with father.

Thank God for health and strength.

From Robert Harris McCarter

"Low Moor" Monmouth Beach [N. J.] July 10th, '76
My Dear "Phunny"

You don't know how glad I was to hear from you. My letters as yet have been like Angel's visits—few & far between, & you can imagine how acceptable a "word" from you was. . . .

I finished the first volume of Macaulay (Library Edition) last Saturday. It was decidedly the most interesting as well as instructive piece of reading that I have ever taken up. To say that I *enjoyed* it would not express it.

I am sorry to say, contrary to your expectations, I have not let *"poetry"* & its advance trouble me much as yet. I only jump at your suggestion about the matter too readily. I don't think that there is as much *need* of that extremely *fine* poetry at present, as there was formerly.

This is seen also in the decline of the *"Drama."*

I think the invention of the art of *"Printing"* is one of the main causes of this decline. The masses are much better educated. Poetry was formerly the only way in which they could be reached. News & ancient "traditions" were handed down not by written or printed records but by ballads & Lyric poems. This is just an idea of mine & is as short & *poor* as the time & attention I have given to the subject. If you would *give me* some of your thoughts *"pro &* *con*["] you would oblige me exceedingly. No room for more. Believe me as ever   Robert Harris McCarter

ALS (WP, DLC) with WWhw notation on env.: "Ans."

From Wilson's Shorthand Diary

[July] 11th Tuesday. Got up at six o'clock and went to market. Carried[1] Josie with me. Passed most of the day in reading [* *], which so far as I have read has proved a very interesting work. The characters are somewhat original and pleasing but some of them are rather unnatural. In the afternoon took a short walk with Paul Pope. Went down for the mail immediately after tea. After playing mystery with father until about 10 o'clock I read a little more.

Thank God for continued health and strength.

1 That is, escorted.

[July] 12th Wednesday. Went to market in the morning. Spent most of the day in reading [* *]. Very interesting—more and more so. After tea took a ride in the street cars with Josie; at night [?] walked, and went to the post office. Mr. Kidder and his daughter Annie[1] called in the evening. After that again played three games of mystery with father. Read a letter from sister Annie in which she promised to come over. How glad we will be to see her!

Thank God for continued health and strength.

1 Edward Kidder, merchant and mill owner, of Wilmington, shared his house on Third Street (see WW's diary for Aug. 10, 1876) with his sons, George W. and Gilbert P. as well as with Frederick, a clerk. It is not possible to identify Annie's father from among these four Kidders.

[July] 13th Thursday. Got up at six o'clock and went to market. Finished [* *]. I was much disappointed in it[.] It did not prove as good a book or as interesting as the beginning of it promised.

Talked over my article on "The Past and Present of American Oratory" with father which did me much good. Discussed with him also the elements of greatness—of great men.

Wrote up my diary[,] an account of the general use of my minutes. Wrote two or three business letters about [General] Assembly business. Went to prayer meeting in the evening. After prayer meeting walked down to the post office; and played three games of mystery with father. I have determined not to read any more novels; at present at least. Most novels certainly do more harm than good. They have a tendency to make me gloomy.

Thank God for health and strength.

[July] 14th Friday. Got up at six o'clock and went to market. During the morning read life of Gibbon in preparation for the reading of his History of the Decline and Fall of the Roman Empire, which I intend to commence tomorrow. Read review from the Cornhill magazine on the "Life and Letters of Lord Macaulay," which was perfectly ridiculous.[1] The writer, who seems to be a perfect ass[,] accuses Macaulay of being superficial—but his arguments are too sublimely ridiculous to be repeated here.

In the afternoon worked in the garden a little. After tea went to the post office and played four games of mystery with father.

Thank God for health and strength.

1 [Anon.], "Hours in a Library. No. XII.—Macaulay," The Cornhill Magazine, XXXIII (May 1876), 563-81.

[July] 15th Saturday. Got up at six o'clock and went to market. Read first chapter of Gibbons History of the Decline and Fall of the Roman Empire. Found it very interesting indeed. This chapter describes the state of the Empire just before its power began to wane. Gibbon here describes also the military condition of the Empire together with the manner of disciplining the soldiers; the divisions of the Empire, etc. His writing is very pleasant though rather cut and dried. Wrote up my diary[,] an account of the use of my minutes. In the afternoon tried to take a nap but failed on account of the mosquitoes and heat. Father read to me part of Macaulay's Essay on Milton and we then had a talk about poetry and the advance of civilization—I rather think that civilization tends to the deterioration of poetry. Civilization brings man out of that condition in which poetry seems natural to him. It removes compassion from the breast and narrows the sphere of religion and thus makes the human mind deal more with principles and less with particular events. Thus children are the most apt to be poetical in the sense that they have religion. To be a poet[,] says Macaulay[,] a man must become as a little child. Shakespere's ignorance no doubt helped rather than impeded his poetical spirit. To read Plutarch's lives and the rich funds of incident which he there found made the scenes presented to his mind appear as real to the imaginative mind and thus prepared the way for his wonderful abilities which endeavored to make the events which he saw so clearly, as clear to the minds of the readers as to his own.

The men described in Plutarch's masterful sketches stood before him as live characters in the spirit of his religion. In religion he was a little child.

—Went down street on business[.] After tea walked down to the post office and played three games of mystery with father. Thank God for health and strength.

[July] 16th Sabbath. Got up rather late. Went to church and heard an excellent sermon from dear father. Spent the rest of the day in the house trying to keep cool. In the evening took a short walk and went to Second church where I heard a sermon from Mr. Payne on the text "I know thy works," from Revelation. The sermon was poor. Walked back most of the way with Alec Sprunt. Retired early.

[July] 17th Monday. Got up at six o'clock and went to market. Spent the morning in reading. Made two frames for mother's flowers. Read the second chapter of the Decline and Fall of the Roman Empire. The interest increases as I advance. What an interesting lesson the history of the great Empire teaches. In the afternoon wrote a letter to McCarter[,] four pages of which were on the subject of poetry. I am afraid that I bore him with my lengthy dissertation. Went to the post office to mail my letter and called at the Sprunts. Willie was out on the front porch and seemed to be getting quite well again. Alec was not at home.

After getting back helped father a little in preparing for making a fence in the back yard. After tea sat on the porch with dear mother and little Josie for a little while and then went upstairs and played three games of mystery with father. Thank God for health and strength.

[July] 18th Tuesday. Got up early and went to market. Read a little and wrote up my diary an account of the use of my minutes together with an article in my Index Rerum on the philosophy of Aristotle. Read some articles in the Eclectic magazine, and looked over some engravings of the Eclectic collection. In the afternoon read a little on Macaulay's essay on Mill's theory of government. Took a very short nap. About five o'clock went down and made a call on Paul Pope and had a short walk with him. He tells me that Edward Latimer intends to go to Princeton next term. He is going to try to enter the junior class I believe.

Came home about six o'clock and helped father with the fence in the back yard. After tea helped mother water her flowers and went to the post office for the mail—very strange that my report did not come from College. I must try to be less finicky [?] about it. Played three games of mystery with father.—Have done much less reading today than usual.

Thank God for health and strength.

[July] 19th Wednesday. Got up at about six o'clock and went to market. Read the morning papers and the North Carolina Presbyterian which is now made very interesting by father's able articles. His becoming editor has saved the paper.

Read Macaulay's essay on Mill's theory of government—a very able and extremely interesting article. He certainly shows Mill off to a great disadvantage. How absurd Mill's theory of government was[,] to be sure. He made his theory more absurd because he was constantly saying things which are altogether inconsistent with it and with each other. He advances an argument and then himself refutes it. The trouble was that since he was a man of ability his own common sense showed him that he was in the wrong and this common sense was constantly leaking out inadvertently—

Finished fence in back yard. After dinner cut out some engravings from the Eclectic for pasting in my scrapbook. Most of the engravings which I cut out were from collection about the date

1860 and are by that great engraver John Sartain. They will make a very interesting collection. I think that I shall get a new scrapbook for the purpose.[1] Read an article on Macaulay and certain things in number of the Eclectic for 1860.

At about 3½ o'clock went out to the poor house with father in the buggy. Father there gave these poor people a simple and interesting talk on the 23rd Psalm. He gave out a hymn which was raised by an old Negro—the tune was at least original. It is heartrending to see some of these poor creatures. I suppose however that it is good to know that there [are] such people on earth. How happy we who are not [in] such bad condition should be.

Helped father a little with another fence. After tea helped dear mother water her plot[;] went to the post office for the mail and played three games of mystery with father.

Settled upon Twiwood as my nom de plume.[2]

Thank God for health and Strength.

[1] WW did get a "new scrapbook" (WP, DLC), more accurately called an album, which he filled with fifty-seven engravings from the *Eclectic Magazine of Foreign Literature, Science, and Art.* All but five of these are clearly identified as engraved by Sartain, an American artist who lived in Philadelphia. Most of the engravings which WW inserted in his album are portraits of rulers, dukes, lords, statesmen, diplomatists, historians, and poets; but he also chose imaginary scenes based on history and literature. Among the European figures represented are Queen Elizabeth, Napoleon III, Garibaldi, Lord John Russell, Gladstone, Macaulay, and Elizabeth Barrett Browning. Among the Americans represented are Jackson, Calhoun, Webster, Clay, Edward Everett, Irving, and Longfellow. Among the dramatic scenes depicted are "Marie Antoinette Going to Execution," "Napoleon Inducing Pope Pius VII to Sign the Concordat," "Shakespeare Brought before Sir Thomas Lucy for Deer Shooting," "Sir Walter Scott and His Literary Friends at Abbottsford," and "Commencement Day, Yale College, July 26th 1860." Also in this album is a quantity of loose engravings consisting mostly of illustrations clipped from periodicals, a few of which are from the *Eclectic Magazine.*

[2] WW, insofar as is known, used this pen name only in signing six religious essays in the Wilmington *North Carolina Presbyterian* which are printed beginning at Aug. 11, 1876, and ending at Dec. 20, 1876.

[July] 20th Thursday. Josie's birthday. Got up at about six o'clock and went to market. Must get up earlier tomorrow morning as exercise too late. Dear mother was too unwell to get up this morning. Read Macaulay's Essays on Bentham's Defense of Mill and on the Utilitarian Theory of Government—both very fine specimens of reason[,] in my opinion[,] though of course such profound (?) critics as the one in the last number of the Eclectic magazine[,] differing from me in political views[,] charge him with being superficial in all his reasons.

Drew a little with Josie—commencing a large ship—Man of War. It delights the dear little fellow so for me to draw with him. After dinner looked over Scribner's Magazine for August and read some

little stories to Josie out of "St. Nicholas." The stories in this little
paper are excellent—interesting both to young and old. Went down
to make a call on John Bellamy[1] and found him out. Went to the
barbers and got shaved.

Commenced Macaulay's essay on Machiavelli which promises
to be extremely interesting as most of his articles are.

After tea went to prayer meeting with father—mother still confined to her room but feeling a little better. Father gave us one of
his usual happy addresses. After prayer meeting went to the post
office to mail some letters and get the mail. Played three games
of mystery with father. Thank God for health and strength.

—Heard today the result of the University boat race at Saratoga.
Cornell first[,] Harvard second[,] Columbia third[,] Union fourth[,]
Wesleyan fifth[,] Princeton *last*. I think that Princeton better sell
out all our boats and give up rowing entirely. She has had nothing
but defeat in it as yet.

1 John D. Bellamy, born Wilmington, N. C., March 24, 1854. A.B., Davidson
College, 1873; studied law, University of Virginia, 1873-75, admitted to bar, 1875,
and practiced in Wilmington. Member of North Carolina Senate, 1900-02; Democratic member United States House of Representatives, 1899-1903. Died Sept. 25,
1942.

[July] 21st Friday. Overslept myself and did not go to market.
Read Macaulay's essay on Machiavelli and found it both instructive and interesting. I think that Macaulay fully succeeds in ex-
onerating Machiavelli from much of the blame which is usually
put upon him.

Wrote up my diary from copy[,] an account of the use of my
minutes. Wrote a letter to sister Annie. Read most of Edward
Everett's oration on Daniel Webster out loud for the practice of
my voice. I have done so little reading out loud that I need a great
deal of practice. Everett's style is so peculiar that it is very difficult
to read but it is all the more practice.

Helped father take down the swing in the back yard and pull
away the lumber which was scattered about the yard. After tea
went to the post office for the mail. On the way down met Pope
and he walked to the post office with me. We discussed Princeton's
failure to do anything in the race. It seems that he has received a
letter from Van Dyke[1] saying that he has no conditions. Good news
for him. I find him a very pleasant fellow. Played three games of
mystery with father. Read the second part of the novel entitled the
"Woman Hater" in Blackwoods.[2] The writing is lovely and unusual
but I am not sure that it pleases me altogether. It is rather too
abrupt and the attempts at wit are rather abortive at times. I can-

not yet tell exactly how the story will come out but it promises nothing very fine in the way of a conclusion.

Thank God for health and strength.

¹ Henry Nevius Van Dyke, A.B., College of New Jersey, 1872. Registrar, same institution, 1873-1910. Also served as tutor in mathematics and instructor in classics and mathematics. Not to be confused with Henry Jackson van Dyke, Jr., of the Class of 1873, mentioned on p. 191, for whom a biographical note will appear in a later volume.

² *Blackwood's* for July 1876, pp. 1-20. See WW's Diary for June 22, 1876, note 4.

[July] 22nd Saturday. Owing to my oversleeping myself and the bad weather did not go to market. Finished Edward Everett's oration on Daniel Webster. Commenced Macaulay's article on Hallam's Constitutional History[.] It promises well in the way of interest.

Played three games of mystery with father at about 11:45 contrary to our usual custom. Wrote up my diary for the 21st. The plan which I now pursue with reference to my journal is to write at night the events and ideas of the day on a slip of paper such as I always keep in my pocket-book and then on the following day to copy it in my regular diary. This plan works very well indeed so far. Being sleepy at night just before retiring the trouble of getting out my diary and writing it up in ink would very probably lead me to neglect it and not write it up until the next day when I would be very apt to have forgot the events of the day before. With my present plan it is little or no trouble to put down the occurrences of the day.

The rain which commenced yesterday continues today. It was very much needed and will indeed be very welcome to all the farms of the neighborhood. The crops and land were suffering very much from want of rain, in this vicinity at least.

Studied Phonography a little from the Dictionary and Hand-Book.

Graham's is certainly a splendid system of shorthand. None can be superior.

Loafed around and read some little pieces from the papers. Read some short articles in Scribner's Magazine. Went down street and bought some shoes—like quarter gaiters. Helped father take down the old fences in the back yard—glad to get rid of them. Helped father prepare a little piece for his paper. After tea went to the post office for the mail. Played four games of mystery with father—three three-ball games and one four-ball. Wrote my diary for the day.

Thank God for health and strength.

[July] 23rd Sabbath. Went to church in the morning and heard an excellent sermon for the last time this season from father on the text "Wilt thou be [made] whole?" John 6:5 [5:6]. Dear mother was too unwell to venture out. Stayed in the house the rest of the day and in the evening. In the evening we had quite a severe storm [of] rain accompanied by thunder and lightning.

Received a letter from sister Annie saying that she will perhaps be over about the second week in August. I hope however that she will come sooner than that.

Thank God for health and strength.

[July] 24th Monday. Did not go to market. Weather very inclement. Wrote a letter to "Judge" Taylor and one to cousin Jessie Bones. Helped John [?] fix carpet—beat it etc. Made a wooden sword for Josie since the dear little fellow wanted one to parade with. Wrote up my diary for the 22 and 23 July.

Went down street to order a carriage to take father to the depot tomorrow morning when he starts for the North on his usual summer trip. Played three games of mystery with father before tea and one afterwards. During the evening several people called to bid father goodbye. Helped mother a little with father's packing—brought down trunk for her[,] dusted off father's clothes and handed her the things since she was feeling very unwell.

From Robert Harris McCarter

My Dear Wilson—   Monmouth Beach [N. J.] July 24th '76
    . . . Your remarks about the subject "at issue" were in my judgement admirable & I assure you it will take a brain far more fertile than mine to confute any of the arguments brought out there. I am glad moreover that they are arguments for *my* side of the question. I have as yet given the subject little or no consideration but with the help of some reading (Macaulay etc.) I hope soon to begin. You know how prone one is when one has *nothing* to do to take up *any thing* which seems like *work*. I think that one proof of the decline is the entire or almost entire absence of originality of subjects & thought presented in the poems of today (what figure?) (as for me I have forgotten all about metonymy, syne[c]-doche etc, long ago. How is it with you[?]) But excuse this degression[.] I came across this the other day.

    "Poetry & Philosophy endure through all time but change their form from age to age."

Did the writer mean to say that the *Essence* of poetry remains the same at all times but that only the *form* is subject to change? Opinion differs as to the position which the greatest poets occupy. You know that *"our favorite"* Macaulay put "William" ahead of Homer while the latter is considered by far superior to the author of *Julius Caesar* by many. But I consider this of small comfort

I hope by May next to have done some reading and thinking and to express my poems to you.

Dont think that your last *bored* me. Far otherwise[.] Go it again[.] Hoping etc I remain as ever   Yours

Robt Harris McCarter

ALS (WP, DLC) with WWhw notation on env.: "Ans" and WW signature in Graham shorthand.

From Wilson's Shorthand Diary

[July] 25th Tuesday. Got up at about six o'clock. Had early breakfast and father left for the North at seven o'clock. Spent the morning helping mother fix in the new wing of the house. Went down street to the bank and for several articles for mother. Helped mother with the new carpeting of the wing. After dinner cut the oilcloth for the bay window. Went down street twice both times on business. Carried some copy to the printer's office.

Read part of a novel entitled "Flesh and Spirit"[1] by the author of The Odd Trump to mother while she sewed the carpet—so much for my resolution not [to] read any more novels.

Thank God for health and strength.

[1] George J. A. Coulson, *Flesh & Spirit* (New York, 1876).

[July] 26th Wednesday. Spent the day helping mother carpet the two new rooms which have recently been added to the house. During the intervals of work while mother was sewing different pieces of the carpet together I read some more to her from Flesh and Spirit. In the evening read until a little after 11 o'clock almost finishing the book. Went down street three times on business.

[July] 27th Thursday. Helped mother all day in the new house. Carried down almost all the furniture for the new rooms and varnished 2 wardrobes[,] 2 bureaus and a bedstead. Varnish improves them very much indeed—makes them look as well as new. They are such fine pieces of furniture that all that they needed was a good coat of varnish.

Went down street and made some purchases for mother and went to the Presbyterian office. In the evening went to prayer meeting—missed father's discourse very much. The meeting was led by Mr. McLaurin. After prayer meeting I went to the post office. After returning from the post office finished Flesh and Spirit. Both mother and I are very much disappointed with the story. It depicts some phases of American character excellently but the plot is miserable in my opinion. The author is evidently in sympathy with the South which makes me like him more than I otherwise would. The beginning of the book pleased me—the end did not. No more novels please!

[July] 28th Friday. Got up rather late. Feeling quite badly all day with a strange swimming in my head which troubles me very much. Hope however that it will be all right tomorrow.

In the morning carried down some more furniture into the new rooms and helped mother in various ways. After dinner did nothing in particular because of my swimming head.

Read good deal of Bautain's Art of Extempore Speaking. It is an excellent book and I enjoyed it more than I have enjoyed any book in some time. The style is extremely pleasing and every page contains advice which every speaker would do well to follow to the letter. Played a little on the organ and sang the tenor to some pieces. After tea went to the post office for the mail thinking that the walk might do me some good—but it did not.

In the evening read some more of the Bautain's work—more and more pleased with it.

Thank God for health and strength which he has granted me so far in my life.

[July] 29th Saturday. Woke this morning with the same swimming in my head and with a slight headache. My head became better during the day however. Went down street and made some purchases for mother, and went to the Presbyterian office where I sat for a little while. Read some more of Mr. Bautain's work during the day. He apologizes in one place for giving some practical directions—why[,] these are just what is needed. Metaphysical treatises are all very well but they cannot very well be acted upon[.] A discourse upon our extempore speaking should certainly be something which can be acted upon. The more practical suggestions the better. Some of Bautain's thoughts are admirable and well worth being weighed by everyone.

Wrote a long letter to McCarter boring him no doubt by the length of my discourse on poetry. This subject interests me very much. Fixed nets and beds in the new room. Slept there tonight for the first time. After tea went to the post office for the mail and received a letter from Woods together with the extra copy of the Princetonian which he sent me. Spent the rest of the evening with Bautain. Thank God for health and strength.

[July] 30th Sabbath. Owing to father's absence there was no service in the church today—went to prayer meeting in the lecture room. Mr. Worth[1] led. There was no one to lead singing[.] We had only two passages read from the Bible and two prayers. Spent the day quietly at home. It rained most of the day. In the afternoon wrote letter to sister Annie, and postal card to Doug McKay. Read a little in [*] papers.

In the evening went to second church and heard a sermon from Mr. Payne. The sermon was as good as usual—that is, poor. There was quite a large congregation.

Thank God for health and strength.

[1] Probably David Worth, merchant of Wilmington and an elder in the First Presbyterian Church.

[July] 31st Monday. Got up about 8 o'clock. Went down street on business and to the Presbyterian office. Saw Alec Sprunt down street and walked about with him a little. Helped mother take up carpet *and arrange for the arrangement* of the rest of the house. Spent an hour or two with Bautain[.] Helped mother put down the carpet in side room.

Spent the evening with Bautain finishing his treatise on extempore speaking.

Thank God for health and strength.

[August] 1st Tuesday. Got up at about 8 o'clock with a severe headache which however wore off pretty much during the day. In the morning helped mother put down the carpet in the sitting room.

Read the changes affixed to Bautain's work by a member of the New York bar—that is, I glanced over them. They are good enough in their place but are very commonplace. They gave me no information.

Read Shakespeare's "Othello." I read it with some pleasure though I cannot agree with Macaulay in assigning to it first place in the writings of the great dramatist. The character of Iago is extremely well-drawn but there is no piece of his which had not some well-drawn character. It is in one sense a master piece of drawing but fails to satisfy me. The pleasure of its perusal is somewhat marred by the many improper passages which occur in the course of the play. "The Merchant of Venice" is much more to my taste.

After dinner read The Merry Wives of Windsor—an excellent play. Excellent in more respects than one. The character of Sir John Falstaff is splendid and in his sayings one sees the origin of many jokes which are now given out of company as original and new—how Shakespeare would be amused! Although all of Shakespeare's expressions are not such as would be very appropriate for utterance in the parlor still the moral of the play is always good however foul may have been the course it has developed. "Will" was the genius. I think I shall read "King Lear" next.

During the fixing of the house I have no time to read anything longer than a play of Shakespeare during the day. After the house is in order I shall again visit Rome with Gibbon.

Thank God for health and strength.

[August] 2nd Wednesday. Got up rather late. Helped mother put down the carpet in the spare room and varnished three pieces of furniture. After dinner did a little arrangement in the sitting room with the books etc. Wrote a letter to father and sent him the North Carolina Presbyterian for this week. Went to the post office and mailed letters.

Began Shakespere's "King Lear" but was unable to finish it as Mr. McLaurin came in and prevented any further reading on my part. After tea called on the McKoys[1] and spent a very pleasant evening.

Thank God for Health and strength.

[1] William B. McKoy, B.S., Princeton, '76; and Robert H. McKoy, B.S., Princeton, '76.

From Robert Harris McCarter

My Dear Wilson: Monmouth Beach [N. J.] 8/2/76

I received yours of the 29th "ultimo" today & was not disappointed as to the *treat* I expected on receipt of the letter. I am glad to see that you have determined to "stand up" for our "Alma Mater" through "*thick & thin.*" . . .

I am deep in Macaulay & am as much interested as ever. Unfortunately I have not been able to get, as yet, the books referring to the "subject at issue."

You say we must prove that, even if we allow that poetry has declined, *Civilization* & not some other motive cause has been the cause of this decline. I grant this but if we allow that it has declined I don't think we will have much trouble to find that civilization & its effects are the causes of this. As you said in your last, you gave some hints in one of your previous letters that prove this point.

Do you remember this passage?

"It is indeed only by reading that men can become profoundly acquainted with any science. But the arts of *Poetry* & Rhetoric may be carried near to absolute perfection & may exercise a mighty influence on the public mind in an age in which *books* are wholly or almost entirely unknown."

The Author (Macaulay) then goes on to say that in the Highlands (of Scotland) banquets were held in which men who did not know their letters some times "poured forth rhapsodies," some passages of which would rival the finest selections of the works of Dryden or Otway. What does this show? One thing at least: A High or even Meagre state of civilization is not necessary for the production of poetry.

If when selecting *Homer* as a proof, our opponents tell us not to make use of so isolated a reference, we can bring up the history of any *nation* of the World & prove that the best poetry that has been produced in that Country was brought forth in a time in which the civilization of that Country was very low; or at least at a time in which the civilization was in a worse state than it has been or will be at some other time. If this is true we must allow, since civilization never reaches such a pitch as at present, that as a natural consequence *poetry is* & *must be,* by some undefinable law, on the decline. What then is the cause of the Decline? Should not an enlargement upon the idea conveyed in the "hints" before referred to, prove that civilization & its accompanying improvements are the main instruments of this downfall?

If you know of some books that will assist me in this work you would do me a great favor by mentioning them.

I am as much in love with *the subject* as I was once—way back in my infancy—in love with a little *girl* with bright eyes & curls.

Marquand treated me a little better than you. He gave me 95. "That rascal" Kargé pulled me down. He gave me, 87. I told you I *flunked* (spelt right?) in that examination. My term grade was 90.2 but as my first term was low, my yearly average was made to suffer so I got, 87 for my *grade* & 37th in class[.] A slight improvement on 53rd.

I agree with your explanation of the meaning of the Extract I
sent you. Hoping you are not *"Awearied"* & with hopes of hearing
from you soon I remain as ever Yours   Robt Harris McCarter

ALS (WP, DLC) with WWhw notations on env.: "Received [WWsh] 8/6/76;
Thomas Woodrow Wilson [WWsh] Ans."

From Wilson's Shorthand Diary

[August] 3rd Thursday. Did very little work during the day as
the house is almost entirely fixed now. Read Shakespere's "King
Lear" and commenced his "Much Ado About Nothing". I think that
his King Lear is one of the finest pieces I ever read. This is in my
estimation Shakespere's best effort. I have read very few things
that have impressed me as this has done. The grief and distraction
of the old King is sublime. I am inclined to think however that
pieces of this kind are somewhat marred by a last scene in which
so many persons die.

This leaves an impression somewhat like this: We have come
to the last scene; given a certain number of persons to be disposed
of in this scene: therefore the dramatist must rack his brain for
some speedy method of getting rid of them. They might at least
be killed more gradually.

Alec Sprunt called in the afternoon and asked me to go to the
Sound with him tomorrow morning to spend the day. After his
call I went around to see the McKoy boys on business: about getting up a dinner for Princeton graduates some time during the
coming week. Found Will McKoy out and so I walked down to John
Bellamy's office with Bob [McKoy] and spent the rest of the afternoon there talking with the "great young lawyer" as [he] would
feign call himself. Commenced a letter to Woods but did not finish
it.

Went to prayer meeting in the evening. The meeting was led by
Mr. Worth who made it rather too tedious. After prayer meeting
Mr. and Mrs. Robinson called and stayed a little while.

Thank God for health and strength.

[August] 4th Friday. Got up a little after six o'clock[.] Ate breakfast and went to Alex Sprunt's house to start for the Sound. Spent
a very pleasant day at the Sound. Got back home about 8½ o'clock.
About 9 o'clock went around to the McKoy's to make arrangements
about the dinner we intend to have for Princeton graduates in this
state. Stayed until about 11 o'clock.

After my call there went to the post office for the mail. Thank
God for health and strength.

[August] 5th Saturday. Finished my letter to Woods. Sent for 23 copies of the minutes. Cast up my general estimate account[.] Read "Much Ado About Nothing." It is an excellent play and one in which "Will" shows extreme wit and good sense. King [Lear] is I think the finest of his pieces but I am in love with all of them. There is no place in any one of his pieces in which the play drags for one moment—there is life in every minute of them. I have now read "King Lear," "Julius Caesar," "Othello," "Merry Wives of Windsor," and "Much Ado About Nothing." I also read "Romeo and Juliet" some time ago.

Of these King Lear [is] sublime; certain passages of Othello are truly fine though I cannot agree with Macaulay when assigning to this piece the first place among Shakespere's productions. Julius Caesar is unusually full of life and abounds in some of the finest passages in the English language; Merry Wives of Windsor fully fulfills its office and is in its way a masterpiece; Much Ado About Nothing abounds in wit of the most pleasing kind but is not remarkable even as a play when compared with some other of Shakespere's works. Romeo and Juliet I think not scholarly. It does not lack some of the old Shakespere's fire but is in my opinion one of his poorest pieces.

Read Macaulay's sketch of the life of Sam Johnson prefaced to the works of that great man. A masterly sketch. Read Sam Johnson's remarks on the Life of Cowley. The account of his life is rather meager the materials which have been left being very few, and his biographer (Sprat) having been influenced by the events of the time and as well [by] some of the most important events of Cowley's life. Strange to say I did not altogether like Johnson's style —this may be however because it is new to me and it takes some time for me to get accustomed to it.

After tea I walked to the post office for the mail.

Thank God for health and strength.

[August] 6th Sabbath. Got up rather late. Went to prayer meeting in the morning. The meeting was led by Mr. Chadbourn[1] who read us a short discourse from a book of sermons. The meeting was very pleasant. Spent the rest of the day in the house[.] Slept from three to six o'clock in the afternoon.

After tea Alec Sprunt and Mr. Calhoun called to tell us goodbye. Did not go to church in the evening. Spent the evening talking with mother. Thank God for health and strength.

[1] Probably George Chadbourn of Wilmington, president of the executive committee of the North Carolina Presbyterian Publishing Co.

[August] 7th Monday. Put up 50 copies of the minutes in the morning, and cast up assembly accounts. Wrote a letter concerning the minutes, etc. to Rev. Dr. Stillman[1] of Alabama. Got out my copy of the "Half Hours with the Best Authors" by Charles Knight and enjoyed several hours of pleasant reading during the afternoon and evening spending my time with Addison[,] Jeffrey[,] Guizot[,] Ir[v]in[g] and other distinguished men. The selections in these volumes are admirable.[2] This afternoon I for the first time made acquaintance of Sir Roger de Coverley—how much I have missed by not knowing him before. I shall endeavor to become more familiar with such a fine character. Some of Addison's wit is irresistibly fine—so to speak. Thank God for health and strength and mind that can appreciate such reading.

[1] The Rev. C. A. Stillman, D.D., founder and first president of the Institute for Training Colored Ministers, afterward Stillman College, at Tuscaloosa, Ala. Moderator of the General Assembly of the Presbyterian Church, U.S., 1877.
[2] Charles Knight, ed., *Half-Hours with the Best Authors*, was a six-volume anthology of widely selected articles, stories, essays, poems, extracts, etc. The following samples of WW's marginal comments reveal how avidly he read these volumes.

EDITORIAL NOTE
WILSON'S MARGINAL NOTES

The following are first samples of Wilson's marginal comments on reading. Insofar as the documents show, he began the practice of recording comments, both in shorthand and longhand, on the pages of magazines and books while studying Graham shorthand during the summer of 1874, making what seem to have been his first marginal notes on A. J. Graham's *Hand-Book of Standard or American Phonography*. He continued this practice in varying forms throughout his life, but the greater portion of his comments on books falls between 1876 and 1902. All told, out of approximately 8,000 volumes in the Wilson Library in the Library of Congress, Wilson made more or less significant marginal comments on 150 volumes, excluding marginalia consisting merely of linear marks and inscriptions. All marginal notes printed in this and subsequent volumes are to be found in the magazine materials in the Wilson Papers and in books in the Wilson Library, unless otherwise noted.

Wilson's marginal notes were of various types. There was the substantial comment, written often at the end of a speech, chapter, or book. An example of this type is Wilson's comment on John Bright's strictures against the Confederacy, printed on pp. 664-65. More frequent were the shorter marginalia that were well-conceived and thought-out, even though they reflected spontaneous reactions. Examples of these are the marginal notes on Albert Stickney's *A True Republic*, *The Federalist Papers*, and John R. Green's multivolume *History of the English People*, scattered throughout this volume and the next. A third type was the brief, impulsive reaction to a noble passage,

well-turned phrase, or something with which Wilson strongly dis-
agreed. There are numerous examples of this type, particularly among
the marginalia in Charles Knight (ed.), *Half-Hours with the Best Authors*, in the following pages. Wilson frequently used marginal notes
to summarize the contents of books; some of these were loose pages
tipped into volumes. He did this as a student preparing for examinations and as a scholar and teacher while drafting articles, books, and
lectures. For example, see his comments on James McCosh, *History of
Philosophy: Notes Taken in the Lecture Room*, printed at Sept. 11,
1878.

Marginal notes in this and future volumes are representative of a
much larger body of comments and have been selected to illustrate not
only the various types but also to shed further light on the breadth
and depth of Wilson's reading.

Marginal Notes

Charles Knight, ed., *Half-Hours with
the Best Authors* (6 vols., New York,
[18–?]).

Vol. I, 35: "The Sack of Magdeburg,"
from Walter Harte's biography of Gus-
tavus Adolphus.

Upon entering my house, we found it
filled with a multitude of plunderers,
whom the officer, who was a colonel,
ordered away. He then said he would
take up his lodging with us, and having
posted two soldiers for a guard to us,
left us with a promise to return forth-
with. We gave, with great cheerfulness,
a good breakfast to our sentinels, who
complimented us on the lucky fortune
of falling into their colonel's hands; at
the same time representing to us that
their fellow-soldiers made a considerable
booty while they continued inactive
merely as a safeguard to us, and therefore beseeching us to render them an
equivalent to a certain degree.

Transcripts of WW Short-
hand Comments

[c. Aug. 7, 1876]

Much of this account cor-
responds exactly with the
facts concerning the burning and sacking of Colum-
bia[,] South Carolina. All
such scenes are more or
less alike.

Vol. I, 56: "Sermon upon the Government of the Tongue," from Joseph Butler's *Sermons*.

People who are given to scandal and
detraction, may indeed make an ill use
of this observation; but truths which
are of service towards regulating our
conduct, are not to be disowned, or even
concealed, because a bad use may be
made of them. But this would be effectually prevented, if these two things

Still when we speak
good of anyone which is
not true we violate truth
and thus err.

were attended to; *First,* That though it is equally of bad consequence to society that men should have either good or ill characters which they do not deserve, yet when you say somewhat good of a man which he does not deserve, there is no wrong done him in particular; whereas when you say evil of a man which he does not deserve, here is a direct formal injury, a real piece of injustice, done him.

Vol. I, 180: Biographical note prefacing George Herbert's poem, "Sunday."

George Herbert, the fifth brother of Lord Herbert of Cherbury, was born in 1593; died in 1632. His character as a minister was full of Christian graces. He belonged to the same class of clergymen as Hooker;—devoted to pastoral duties,—enthusiastic in his reverence for the offices of the Church. His religious poetry used to be neglected for its quaintness; but the present age has restored it to its proper rank amongst the writers who have left us gems which antiquity cannot rust.

Gems cannot rust. The proper expression would have been Gems whose brilliance antiquity cannot dim.

Vol. I, 192-200: Selection from "Before the Gate," scene from Dr. Anster's Translation of Goethe's *Faustus.*

One of the most extraordinary pieces I ever read— what power is here!

Vol. I, 235-44: Isaac Barrow's sermon on "The Industry of a Gentleman."

Every gentleman would do well to read this excellent piece.

Vol. I, 272-86: Selections from Act I, Scene I; Act III, Scene I; Act IV, Scene II; and Act V, Scene V of John Webster's *Duchess of Malfi.*

A noble writer. I must read more of him.

Vol. I, 308: Robert Hall's sermon, "The Advantage of Knowledge to the Lower Classes."

Sound religious instruction is a perpetual counterpoise to the force of depravity. "The law of the Lord is perfect, converting the soul; the testimony of the Lord is sure, making wise the simple; the commandment of the Lord is pure, enlightening the eyes; the fear of the Lord is clean, enduring forever; the judgments of

I have always thought this a noble passage.[1]

[1] At the end of this sermon on religious knowledge WW wrote in shorthand: "A noble setting forth of truth."

the Lord are true and righteous altogether."

Vol. II, 202: Opening scene of Thomas
Dekker's *Old Fortunatus*.

> Fort. Oh, whither am I wrapt beyond
>   myself?
> More violent conflicts fight in every
>   thought,
> Than his, whose fatal choice Troy's
>   downfall wrought.
> Shall I contract myself to wisdom's love?
> Then I lose riches; and a wise man, poor,
> Is like a sacred book that's never read,
> To himself he lives, and to all else seems
>   dead;
> This age thinks better of a gilded fool,
> Than of a threadbare saint in wisdom's
>   school.
> I will be strong; then I refuse long life;
> And though mine arm should conquer
>   twenty worlds,
> There's a lean fellow beats all conquerors;
> The greatest strength expires with loss of
>   breath,
> The mightiest (in one minute) stoop to
>   death.
> Then take long life, or health; should I
>   do so,
> I might grow ugly; and that tedious scroll
> Of months and years much misery may
>   enroll

Vol. II, 197-203: Opening scene of
Thomas Dekker's *Old Fortunatus*.

Vol. III, 67: Selection from Hartley Coleridge, *Biographia Borealis, in the life of
Dr. John Fothergill*.

We doubt, indeed, whether any new
translation, however learned, exact, or
truly orthodox, will ever appear to English Christians to be the real Bible. The
language of the authorized version is the
perfection of English, and it can never be
written again, for the language of prose
is one of the few things in which the English have really degenerated. Our tongue
has lost its holiness.

This old man's struggle is well portrayed and ends in the way all such struggles end. When one stoops to argue with himself his desires get the better of him and the false argument is out of place in such case.

If all Dekker's writings were like this he might compare with Shakespeare not unfavorably. This is one of the finest scenes in some respects that I ever had the pleasure of reading.

Do not agree with him.

Vol. III, 110: Knight's comment on habits of Robert Burns, prefacing a selection from "The Cotter's Saturday Night."

It has been a reproach to the contemporaries of Burns that they were unworthy of his genius—that they offered him the unsubstantial incense of flattery, and left him to starve. The reproach appears to us signally unjust. It is difficult to imagine how, with the unfortunate habits which Burns had acquired, and with his high-spirited but repulsive independence, his fate could have been other than it was. With such examples of the unhappiness of genius, we still cannot regret that there are no asylums where poets may be watched over like caged nightingales.

They might at least have been the means of procuring for him a more genial position than the excise.

Vol. III, 111-116: Robert Burns, *The Cotter's Saturday Night.*

Most beautiful and masterly description. Such pieces as this would soon take away my distaste for poetry.

Vol. III, 145-47: John Dryden's essay on the character of Polybius, the historian.

Not but that there may be a necessity of saving a nation by going beyond the letter of the law, or even sometimes by superseding it; but then that necessity must not be artificial,—it must be visible, it must be strong enough, to make the remedy not only pardoned, but desired, to the major part of the people; not for the interest only of some few men, but for the public safety; for, otherwise, one infringement of a law draws after it the practice of subverting all the liberties of a nation, which are only intrusted with any government, but can never be given up to it. . . .

The best way to distinguish betwixt a pretended necessity and a true, is to observe if the remedy be rarely applied, or frequently; in times of peace, or times of war and public distractions, which are the most usual causes of sudden necessities. From hence Casaubon infers, that this our author, who preaches virtue and probity and plain dealing, ought to be studied principally by kings and ministers of state; and that youth, which are bred up to succeed in the management of business, should read him carefully, and imbibe him thoroughly, detesting the

The Republican party affords a signal instance of the evil of neglecting this principle.

Dryden was born only four years after Machiavel's death[2] so that Machiavel's works must have been widely known very shortly after his death[.] Considering the age and the comparative slowness with which books became known this was remarkable. Dryden seems to maxims that are given by Machiavel and others, which are only the instruments of tyranny. Furthermore, (continues he,) the study of truth is perpetually joined with the love of virtue; for there is no virtue which derives not its original from truth; as, on the contrary, there is no vice that has not its beginning from a lie. Truth is the foundation of all knowledge, and the cement of all societies; and this is one of the most shining qualities in our author.

I was so strongly persuaded of this myself, in the perusal of the present history, that I confess, amongst all the ancients, I never found any one who had the air of it so much; and, amongst the moderns, none but Philip de Commines. They had this common to them, that they both changed their masters. But Polybius changed not his side, as Philip did; he was not bought off to another party, but pursued the true interest of his country, even when he served the Romans. Yet since truth, as one of the philosophers has told me, lies in the bottom of a well, so it is difficult to draw it up; much pains, much diligence, much judgment is necessary to hand it us; even cost is oftentimes required; and Polybius was wanting in none of these. . . .

"I believe" (says Polybius) "that nature herself has constituted truth as the supreme deity which is to be adored by mankind, and that she has given it greater force than any of the rest: for being opposed as she is on all sides, and appearances of truth so often passing for the thing itself in behalf of plausible falsehoods, yet by her wonderful operation she insinuates herself into the minds of men; sometimes exerting her strength immediately, and sometimes lying hid in darkness for a length of time; but at last she struggles through it, and appears triumphant over falsehood." This sincerity Polybius preferred to all his friends, and even to his father. "In all other offices of life" (says he), "I praise a lover of his friends, and of his native country; but in writing history, I am obliged to divest myself of all other obligations, and sacrifice them all to truth."

think that it was remarkable for man to serve his God faithfully under the Romans.

2 WW's statement is in error by exactly one hundred years, a slip in his shorthand or in his memory for dates.

Would that these were the sentiments of all historians.

Vol. III, 264-270: From Act I, Scene I, Richard Brinsley Sheridan's "The Critic."

An excellent piece of satire. Sir Fretful Plagiary's counterpart is found everywhere and in every form.

Vol. III, 399: William Wordsworth's essay, "What Is a Poet?"

What then does the poet? He considers man and the objects that surround him as acting and reacting upon each other, so as to produce an infinite complexity of pain and pleasure; he considers man in his own nature and in his ordinary life as contemplating this with a certain quantity of immediate knowledge, with certain convictions, intuitions, and deductions, which by habit become of the nature of intuitions; he considers him as looking upon this complex scene of ideas and sensations, and finding everywhere objects that immediately excite in him sympathies which, from the necessities of his nature, are accompanied by an overbalance of enjoyment.

For all this the poet needs a large amount of religion.

Vol. IV, 25: Selection from John Milton, *Areopagitica, A Speech for the Liberty of Unlicensed Printing.*

Fool! he sees not the firm root, out of which we all grow, though into branches; nor will he beware until he see our small divided maniples cutting through at every angle of his ill-united and unwieldy brigade.

Further mastery of mighty phrase!

Vol. IV, 190-91: "The Progress of English Literature," an extract from Francis Jeffrey's review of *The Works of Jonathan Swift, Edinburgh Review*, xxvii (Sept. 1816), 1-58.

[Jeffrey depicts the decay of the literary reputations of Pope, Swift, and Addison.]

The more pity since some of their other characters are worthy of study as models of congenial good humor.

Vol. VI, 337: "Dr. Johnson's Dinner Talk," a selection from Boswell's *Life of Johnson.*

JOHNSON. "Luxury, so far it reaches the poor, will do good to the race of people; it will strengthen and multiply them. Sir, no nation was ever hurt by luxury; for, as I said before, it can reach but to a very few. I admit that the great increase of commerce and manufactures hurts the military spirit of a people; because it produces a competition for something else than martial honors—a competition for riches."

Didn't luxury hurt Rome? It is the fact that luxury can reach that phase which will speed a nation if it be falling.

From Wilson's Shorthand Diary

[August] 8th Tuesday. Spent most of the day reading some delightful tracts from the best authors in "Half Hours"—a most excellent book. Finished Addison's description of the character of Sir Roger de Coverley and am much pleased with that gentleman. After tea went to the post office and found nothing in box but the New York Sun. Thank God for health and strength.

[August] 9th Wednesday. Spent most of the day helping mother put down the carpets in the halls and on the staircases. After tea walked to the post office for the mail and received a New York Tribune and the New York Sun. On coming back home found Mr. John Sprunt[1] there and had a very pleasant talk with him. He is a very pleasant gentleman and remarkably well informed. After he left read the characters of Washington and Napoleon in "Half Hours." In the morning I wrote piece on *Work-Day Religion* for the North Carolina Presbyterian.[2] After Mr. Sprunt had gone mother read my piece over and made some suggestions upon it. Her suggestions were excellent. Thank God for health and strength.

[1] James?
[2] Printed at Aug. 11, 1876.

[August] 10th Thursday. Got up rather late. In the morning helped mother move three roots in the garden and put down the carpet in the lower hall. Went to the Presbyterian office and corrected some copy. Went to the bank for some money. Sent for two copies of the minutes. Wrote my diary for the 8th and 9th of this month. Did little but read in the afternoon.

During the afternoon we had a severe thunderstorm which did considerable damage in some parts of the city. After tea the rain ceased and I went to the Grand Democratic Ratification Meeting which was held on Third Street just before Mr. Kidder's residence. Heard a most excellent speech from Judge Fowle of Raleigh. He spoke two hours and I did not tire of his speech at all. His argument was strong and logical and he certainly showed up the radical party in the most unattractive light. He was introduced by Mr. George Davis[1] in a few eloquent remarks which just gave us enough of Mr. Davis to make us want more. The meeting was a success. Thank God for health and strength.

[1] A lawyer, of Wilmington.

From Hiram Woods, Jr.

Dear Tommy,   Baltimore, 8/10/'76.

I received your letter last Tuesday, and hasten to reply to it. I had the satisfaction of receiving my report on the afternoon of July 28th, having mailed your letter on the morning of that day. . . . If you ain't satisfied with 26th, what do you want? Allow me to congratulate you on your elevation. . . .[1]

Sincerely Yours,   Hiram Woods, Jr.

ALS (WP, DLC). WWhw notation on env.: "Received (WWsh) 8/14/76."

[1] Woods' tone is understandable, for not only was WW's class rank of 26th an "elevation" above his rank of 28th for the first term, but it outclassed Mc-Carter's 37th, reported in his recent letter to WW, and Woods' own 47th. Registrar's grade book for 1875-76, untitled (NjP).

From Wilson's Shorthand Diary

[August] 11th Friday. A rain during the day. Spent most of the day reading, as it was too wet to venture out-of-doors. After dinner I went down to the Presbyterian office on pressing business. Spent most of the day over *Half Hours* and am more and more delighted with the selections which Mr. Knight there gives me. This is a most excellent series of books.

Received telegram from brother saying Sister Annie will be here tomorrow morning.

Sent for one copy of the minutes and cast up my assembly accounts. Wrote a letter to father and sent it off. Fixed up my article for the paper and sent it to the office. This will be my first appearance in print and a most ridiculous appearance it is. My article on Work-Day Religion will never be very widely known, I am thinking. Thank God for health and strength.

A Religious Essay

[*Aug. 11, 1876*]

Work-Day Religion.

"The greatest lack in the church to-day is not of members, but of workers. As it has been said that 'the world needs not more men, but more man', so it may be said that the church needs not more servants but more service. It is a rare churchfold where one in ten of the entire membership is active in the work of the church. If one member more in every ten could be brought into activity, the whole world would feel the influence and respond to the labors of the new Christian workers."—*Exchange*.

The explanation of this scarcity of laborers in the Gospel cause is to be found in the view now commonly taken as to religion. The too general view seems to be that it is only a thing to be donned on certain occasions: a thing for Sunday wear.

The majority of christian people rejoice if, when listening to a sermon from their pastor, the way of salvation seems plain° and pleasant to them and they take comfort in the words of grace and peace. They are perhaps most of them faithful attendants upon the weekly prayer meetings also, and in these meetings their hearts swell with gratitude and love to God when they hear the glad gospel tidings. But here they rest content, thinking all done that is required of them. As they leave the house of God all the warmth of feeling which so delighted them while listening to the Word of God wears off, and they content themselves with the thought that upon the next Sabbath, on the next occasion of meeting for prayer, their faith will be renewed and their enjoyment of religion come back to them. In the meantime they never allow a thought of engaging in active work for the Lord to enter their world-absorbed minds, they become cold in their prayers, and never allow any one to imagine from their conversation, or the manner of their daily life, that they rejoice in the hope of everlasting life. This class numbers in it more professing christians than we are willing to suppose. The constant, sturdy workers are alas! the exceptions, not the rule. "One in ten of the entire membership" is truly an unusually large proportion.

Most of these lax members of whom we have been speaking, no doubt think that their chance of salvation is as good as that of any of their fellow members in the church, and are content to await the final judgment with serene confidence. Is this confidence justified? Christ's injunction was and is "Be ye holy even as I am holy." His holiness shone forth in every act of his life, in every word that proceeded from his mouth. He did not wait for Sabbath or the weekly appointments for prayer and thanksgiving, but every day and hour was spent in the service of His Father. Surely this is the way in which he would have us live! There should be no misunderstanding as to my meaning here. I do not mean that we should go about with long faces and puritanical looks, gestures, and false professions of love for God which we do not at the moment really feel in our hearts. This is not the way in which Christ was holy. We should not tire every one with untimely quotations from the Bible, or long discourses upon topics which concern none but Theologians. This was not the character of Christ's holiness. All His teachings lead us to be cheerful and unobtrusive, though constant, in our piety. It is our duty to be "diligent in business, fervent in spirit, serving the Lord."

The duties of our every-day life should be cheerfully and faithfully performed. The most humble and insignificant services of the household and the business office, should be attended to with the feeling that we are serving God in the conscientious discharge of them, and that by being diligent, honest, and cheerful in our every act, and by keeping our duty to our Creator and Savior before our eyes at all times, we are moulding ourselves more and more after the perfect image of Christ.

We should be fervent in spirit in the sense that we should be ardent and warm in the performance of every good act; that we should view life not as a mere time of enjoyment, but as a period allowed us for growth in Christian graces, and thus fit ourselves for the perfect enjoyment of eternity.

Life is a work-day. In this rendering an account of the talents which have been granted to us we will find that true enjoyment which the world knows not. With all this diligence and earnestness we should perform every act as an act of which we shall some day be made to render a strict account, as an act done either in the service of God or in that of the Devil; as an act which should be performed not merely for our own pleasure, except in so much as we delight in doing right.

"Whether, therefore, ye eat or drink, or whatsoever ye do, do all to the glory of God" are the words which should serve as our motto.

The Christian character is not one to be assumed only upon the Sabbath or other stated occasions, but is a character which is perfected only by that work-day religion—a religion pervading every act—which is carried with us into every walk of life and made our one stay and hope. The armor of God is not for a parade one day every week, but for constant use in warding off the attacks of the evil one, and thus for the securing of perfect safety.

"Be not weary in well doing."　Twiwood.

Printed in the Wilmington *North Carolina Presbyterian*, Aug. 16, 1876.

From Wilson's Shorthand Diary

[August] 12th Saturday. Got up about five o'clock. About six and one-half o'clock went to the depot to meet Sister Annie and little Wilson. They arrived all safe but very tired indeed. Sister Annie is looking much better than she was last Christmas which was the last time I saw her. Little Wilson—dear little fellow—is very shy now but his shyness will wear off in a very short time no doubt.

I sent for five copies of the minutes and cast up the assembly accounts.

Wrote a short letter to Dr. Stillman concerning his report before the last June assembly. My duties as stated clerk in father's absence lead to a good many vexations but I rather like the work than otherwise. Wrote two postal cards on assembly business. Went to the post office to mail the minutes[,] purchase stamps, etc. After tea walked to the post office for the mail and made one or two small purchases for mother. Read a little in *Half Hours*. The extracts in these volumes are excellent—but I have said this before!

Thank God for health and strength.

[August] 13th Sabbath. Went to church in the morning, at our Church, and heard the Reverend Mr. Summey[1] preach one of the most ridiculous sermons I have ever heard in my life. It was a characteristic sermon for a young preacher. His discourse was, however, sublime and profound as compared with the one I heard in the evening in the Second Church from one Mr. Black.[2]

Slept two or three hours in the afternoon. Thank God for health and strength.

[1] Probably the Rev. George Summey, age twenty-three, pastor of the Madison Avenue Presbyterian Church, Covington, Ky. He was originally from North Carolina and was apparently filling in for JRW.

[2] Probably James S. Black, licensed by Wilmington Presbytery on April 17, 1875, ordained in 1877.

[August] 14th Monday. In the morning went down street on business. Spent most of the day writing and reading. Went to the post office after tea. Wrote a long letter to McCarter giving him a long argument to prove that civilization tends to cause the decline of poetry. I think that I proved my point. Sent for two copies of the minutes.

Read a masterly piece on the progress of English literature by Jeffrey.[1] I seldom enjoyed anything as I did this.

Thank God for health and strength.

1 In *Half-Hours.*

[August] 15th Tuesday. Sent for three copies of the minutes and cast up assembly accounts. Wrote a letter to father. Went down street on some business for mother. Went to the Presbyterian office. Received a copy of this week's paper (North Carolina Presbyterian) with my article on *Work-Day Religion* in it—a lame article. Did very little reading today. I have done so much reading of late that I have tired myself out to a great extent. Read Gibbon's sketch of the rise and fall of Rienzi in *Half Hours*. Thank God for health and strength.

[August] 16th Wednesday. Went down to the Presbyterian office[.] Read the papers and transacted my business with McLaurin. Read the rough draft of the article for next week's paper. I call this piece the Christian Army and make a lame effort to describe Christian warfare.[1] A rather pretentious article I am afraid. Took a walk in the afternoon. Went to the post office after tea. Read [a] little in *Half Hours*. Read Jeffrey's article on the progress of English literature again—a masterly production.

Thank God for health and strength.

1 Printed at Aug. 17, 1876.

[August] 17th Thursday. Wrote my piece on Christ's Army as I have determined to call it. The new edition is not much improved. Went to the Presbyterian office on business. Did little during the day but read and loaf. Went down street in the afternoon and made some purchases for mother and myself. In the evening went to prayer meeting with mother and Josie—Sister Annie was not able to leave the baby long enough to go to church. She is almost too anxious a mother. The meeting was a very pleasant one. After prayer meeting walked to the post office. Copied my piece for the paper before going to bed.

Thank God for health and strength.

A Religious Essay   [*Aug. 17, 1876*]

Christ's Army.

One of the favorite figures with sacred writers in their references to the inhabitants of this world is that of representing mankind as divided into two great armies. The field of battle is the world. From the abodes of righteousness advances the host of God's people under the leadership of Christ. Immediately behind the great Captain of Salvation come the veteran regiments of the soldiers of the cross with steady tread, their feet shod with the preparation of the Gospel of Peace, girt about with truth, their breast-plates of righteousness glittering beneath the bright rays of their Master's love, each one grasping the sword of the Spirit. Later come the younger troops all eager for the fray. From the opposite side of the field, advancing from the tents of wickedness, come the hosts of sin led by the Prince of Lies himself, riding upon death's horse. Behind him a mighty army marshalled by fiends under the dark banners of iniquity. The object of the warfare on the part of the first is to gain glory for their Great Leader as well as the best good of the conquered by persuading them to leave the ranks of the evil one and enlist under their great Redeemer; that of the other to entice as many as will listen to them to go with them by the alluring paths of worldliness to everlasting destruction. The foes meet upon the great battle field of every-day life. With one sweeping charge the Christian band falls upon the overwhelming numbers of the Prince of Darkness and are met with a cloud of fiery darts from the hands of the Evil One. The battle waxes fierce. Some of the Christian leaders faithfully and eagerly press onward, rallying their broken ranks more vigorously upon every repulse. Others stand with folded arms, only now and then languidly issuing an order or encouraging their followers, and ever incurring the displeasure of their gracious Master by failing to carry out his orders or properly marshall and encourage his forces. The followers of the former, fight manfully, with only here and there a laggard or coward; those of the latter partake of the spirit of their leaders and do little towards gaining the battle. The hosts of sin, ever and anon charging, break through the weak portions of the opposing battalions, and then again quail before the uplifted swords of the Spirit. Here, the plumes streaming from the glistening helmets of salvation are seen among the retreating brigades of sin; there, Satan leads his followers to victory over the dead bodies of many a soldier of the Cross. Thus the battle of life progresses and the army of Saints ever gains ground under divine generalship; now slowly, now rapidly, driving before them with irresistable force the broken ranks of the enemy.

Surely in this great contest there is a part for every one, and each one will be made to render a strict account of his conduct on the day of battle. Will any one hesitate as to the part he shall take in this conflict? Will any one dare to enlist under the banners of the Prince of Lies, under whose dark folds he only marches to the darkness of hell? For there is no middle course, no neutrality. Each and every one must enlist either with the followers of Christ or those of Satan. How much more glorious to fight for the divine Prince of Peace, under whose glorious standards, whose shining folds are inscribed with *Love to God*, he will advance to sure victory and an everlasting reward! All professing Christians are, no doubt, more or less enthused by such thoughts as these, and hope that they can feel themselves soldiers in Christ's great army; but they do not *know* that they are such. Why should they not know? If they would be assured of the fact that their names are in the great Roll Book, let them fight for Christ. Ah! but how do this? As you would fight for any other cause. You know your enemies. They are evil thoughts, evil desires, evil associations. To avoid evil thoughts altogether is, of course, impossible. But whenever one of these subtle warriors of evil attacks you, do not fear to test your breastplate; wield with power the sword of the Spirit and with skill the shield of faith. Overcome evil desires, those powerful and ever present enemies, by constant watchfulness and with the strong weapon of prayer, and by cultivating those heavenly desires which are sure to root out the evil one. Avoid evil associations, evil companions. No one can make a good soldier who keeps company with the emissaries and friends of the enemy. These companions can be avoided by avoiding the places where they are to be found and seeking the more congenial and pleasant company of the good and upright, whose companionship will strengthen you in the struggle by making you feel that you are not alone in it. In every minor thing watch yourself and let no fiery dart enter your soul. One who thus faithfully does his duty and purifies himself in the smallest things has little to fear from the foe, and, if he withal leads others by his example and precept to do likewise, and fears not to warn the enemies of the Cross to turn from the error of their ways, he may rest assured that his name is enrolled among the soldiers of the Cross.   Twiwood.

Printed in the Wilmington *North Carolina Presbyterian*, Aug. 23, 1876.

From Wilson's Shorthand Diary

[August] 18th Friday. Went down street twice during the day on business and pleasure. Wrote a piece for the paper on the Bible as a book of poetry[,] history[,] philosophy[,] law and morals.[1] In the limited space allowed by such a paper one can do little justice to a subject of any interest. Wrote short note to father. In the afternoon while down street went up to John Bellamy's office and sat a while with him and Bob McKoy. Bellamy is an insufferably conceited man (or fool) in my opinion. In the evening walked to the post office for the mail and after returning read some excellent pieces in *Half Hours*. Thank God for health and strength.

[1] Printed at Aug. 25, 1876.

From Robert Harris McCarter

My Dear Wilson:—   Monmouth Beach [N. J.] Aug. 18th 1876

We read in Plutarch that the enemies & slanderers of Demosthenes were accustomed to give vent to their spleen by saying that his orations "*smelt* of the lamp."

I fear that what I will say today will "*smell*" of *Macaulay*. He gives some very valuable hints in his essays on *Milton* & *Dryden*. Both of which I consider masterpieces—worthy of the author.

That imagination & passion are the principal ingredients of poetry, it seems to me, to be undeniable.

That as civilization advances this scope for the imagination & passion decreases seems to be just as undeniable.

Let me give you some extracts[:] "Nations like individuals first perceive & then abstract. They advance from particular images to general terms. Hence the vocabulary of an enlightened people is philosophical, that of a *half-civilized* society is *poetical*."

"In proportion as men know more & think more, they look less at individuals & more at classes. They therefore make better *theories* & *worse poems*"

"Information & experience are therefore necessary, not for the purpose of strengthening the *imagination* which is *never so strong* as in people *incapable* of *reasoning*—savages, children, madmen & dreamers; but for the purpose of enabling the artist to communicate his conceptions to others."

Macaulay very prettily compares the illusion which poetry makes on the mind to the illusion a magic lantern makes on the eyes. And as the magic lantern shows to the best advantage in a *dark room*, so poetry makes the best effect in *dark ages*.

As learning advances[,] the science of Criticism—together with all other sciences—also advances. It is just this science of criticism that is the ruin of true poetry. Thus "the *imaginative* School of poetry fades into the *critical* school[.]" As soon as this critical age arrives we must bid our adieus to real poetry. True there may be attempts at poetry, but the attention of the artist is on any thing but the right thing.

We should admire a *poem* published in an advanced age for the poet has been laboring under the most difficult & trying circumstances to produce that poem. A *Critical* poet can no more create a *new* piece than a physician can make a new body out of the pieces of flesh he has after dissecting.

So much for this time. . . .

Hoping to hear from you soon

                    I remain   As ever yours   Robt Harris McCarter

ALS (WP, DLC). Probably an answer to WW's letter of Aug. 14, 1876, arguing that poetry declines as civilization advances. See WWsh diary, Aug. 14, 1876.

From Wilson's Shorthand Diary

[August] 19th Saturday. Spent the day at Smithville. Thank God for health and strength.

[August] 20th Saturday. [Sunday] Spent the day in the house reading etc. In the evening heard Mr. Payne preach in our Church. A poor sermon. Thank God for health and strength.

[August] 21st Monday. Got up quite early and went to the Sound with the McKoys to spend a few days. Spent a very pleasant day on the water and loafing around. This is the right thing to rest my body and mind. May God take care of and bless the dear ones at home in my absence. Thank God for health and strength.

[August] 22nd Tuesday. Spent a very pleasant day on the water pulling around, hauling a seine etc. Read part of an article in Blackwood's[1] magazine entitled Domestic Yachting.

Thank God for health and strength.

1 [Anon.], "Domestic Yachting," *Blackwood's Edinburgh Magazine*, cxx (Aug. 1876), 143-71.

[August] 23rd Wednesday. Went out fishing early in the morning but caught nothing. About eight o'clock four ladies came out to spend the day which deprived the day of much of its pleasure as we could not dress and act just as we pleased. Took a walk over to the old battery with the ladies. After tea and the ladies departure took row in dark and had a very pleasant time. Wanted to go home today but was prevented. Will go Friday morning in spite of everything. By staying here I am neglecting my duties at home. Will McKoy went to town with the ladies.

Thank God for health and strength.

[August] 24th Thursday. Raining and cloudy. Went out rowing about eleven o'clock when the rain ceased. Spent most of the day reading Blackwood['s] and lolling around. About nine o'clock in the evening Will McKoy came back from town with a young Episcopalian minister by the name of Drane[1] who turned out to be a very pleasant gentleman.

Thank God for health and strength.

[1] The Rev. Robert B. Drane of Wilmington, N. C.

[August] 25th Friday. Went out fishing and stayed out from eleven o'clock until about two. I did not fish as I despise the sport but sat in the boat and pulled on oar. I enjoyed the trip very much. In the afternoon set off for town. Got home again about six and a half o'clock and was very glad indeed to do so though I have had a very enjoyable time at the Sound. Spent the evening writing after returning from the post office. Copied my article on the Bible.

Thank God for my safe return home and for health and strength.

A Religious Essay

[Aug. 25, 1876]

The Bible

The Bible is so commonly known and so universally spread through this christian country that few people appreciate the treasure they see every day in their libraries. Let anyone turn over its pages carefully and scan its contents with a critical eye. It is a treasury of poetry, history, philosophy, laws and morals which will never be equalled. Not in the whole range of literature can be found more sublime poetry than the Bible affords. With a verse peculiar to itself, its flowing periods are eminently pleasant to the ear. Here in the old Hebrew poems of David we find the nature, in all her manifold beauty, all this beauty represented as only contributing to the glory of its great Maker. Here are to be found the truest descriptions of the human passions, and in the free flow of his luxuriant imagination Israel's ancient bard pours forth the grandest images. As poems the poetical books of Scripture undoubtedly stand in the first rank, perfect in their style and kind. As a history the Bible is one of the most valuable of ancient records, though it gives and professes to give, little information as to the history of the period. Into these sacred pages the historian can dip without fear of finding anything but truth. Only giving such fragments of history as will serve for purposes of illustration, these fragments are yet of great value and complete in themselves.

As a philosophical work this wonderful book is unsurpassed. In its teeming pages is developed a system of mental and moral philosophy than which none has ever been more simple and yet more profound, more plain, or more logical. No philosopher ancient or modern has ever been able to conceive of motives more powerful than are here set forth. Here is found the key to every man's character, for which philosophers have so long and so vainly sought. Here is found the philosopher's stone in a setting of the jems of divine inspiration and truth. Here each and everyone can find a mirror in which he can see his own character most faithfully portrayed. From the laws of the old and new Testaments every civilized nation has taken the foundation of its laws. At no time can any nation be prosperous whose laws are not founded upon these eternal principles of right and wrong, of justice and injustice, of civil and religious liberty. Above all, in these pages may be found the most perfect rule of life the mind can conceive. Dimly through the old, and brilliantly through the new Testament, shines the principle of love to God as the foundation and cause of men's duties to God, to each other, and to their own souls. One who forms his every-day life after the perfect model of Christ's life will himself be a model which no man can afford to despise, besides thereby gaining for himself an assurance of everlasting life.

The radical error among modern christians is neglect of the Word of God. We are too apt to seek for religious information and instruction from other sources. Christian people are too much in the habit of seeking for instruction or improvement from lesser streams of knowledge, in preference to going to the eternal fountain head which is ever at hand. This is a great mistake. Though a man read this precious volume continuously for a life time he cannot exhaust one-half of its treasures. With every perusal new rays of light burst upon the soul and give a new charm even to those portions with which he is most familiar. Let us value more this old and yet ever new volume. "Search the Scriptures, for in them ye think ye have eternal life."   Twiwood

Printed in the Wilmington *North Carolina Presbyterian*, Aug. 30, 1876.

From Wilson's Shorthand Diary

[August] 26th Saturday. Went down street in the morning but stayed at home most of the day and read. Read an excellent article in the International Review on Macaulay.¹ It was out of the usual run of such articles and contained some excellent thoughts. Went down street twice during the day on business. Read review of different magazines received for the "Editor's Book Table" of the North Carolina Presbyterian. Read some scenes from old John Webster's "Duchess of Malfi" and found them very good indeed[.]² Possesses no little fire and shows in no small degree the signs of genius. Webster exactly expressed my sentiments when he said that "Detraction is the sworn friend to ignorance." Thank God for health and strength.

¹ Edward A. Freeman, "Lord Macaulay," the *International Review,* III (Sept. 1876), 689-96.
² In *Half-Hours.*

[August] 27th Sabbath. Spent the day in the house as there was no service in the church in the morning. Mr. Payne of the Second Church preached in our church in the evening in his usual solemn style[.] I thought his sermon somewhat better than usual. He made some gross history errors saying among other things that the Roman soldiery was based on the scum of the provinces whereas history shows that it was based on the *cream of the provinces.*

Read during the day Milman's account of St. Paul's visit to Athens which I thought very fine.¹ Read some religious articles from *Half Hours* and found them excellent.

Thank God for health and strength.

¹ In *Half-Hours.*

[August] 28th Monday. Helped mother put the study in order and carried piles of paper upstairs. Read the "Page's Scenes" in the Philaster by Fletcher and Beaumont. In the evening read Jeffrey's account of the war in La Vendée.¹ Went to the post office.

Thank God for health and strength.

¹ Both in *Half-Hours.*

[August] 29th Tuesday. Spent the day reading. Read Campbell's "Koran" with approval.¹ Finished Jeffrey's account of the war in La Vendée. Very interesting and finely written English. Went down in the afternoon to the post office. Received a message from father praising my first article in the paper very highly indeed.

Thank God for health and strength.

1 In *Half-Hours.*

[August] 30th Wednesday. At home most of the day. Read part of an article on the political career of Mr. Disraeli the present Earl of Beaconsfield.[1] This article which is in the British Quarterly is very hard on the new Earl showing him to be an inconsistent sentimentalist with no fixed principles at all. Wrote a letter to father. Spent evening putting engravings in my scrapbook. Thank God for health and strength.

1 [Anon.], "Political Career of Mr. Disraeli," *British Quarterly Review*, LXIV (July 1876), 67-82.

[August] 31st Thursday. Finished the article on Mr. Disraeli's political career but will not pronounce upon that gentleman's character until I read the other side of the question. I have never been impressed with [the] idea that he was a great man however. Went to the Presbyterian office on business. Fixed some more engravings in my scrapbook. It is now only four days before I must start for college! I wish that my vacation were only beginning. Went to the post office after tea. There was a storm during the evening which seemed very acceptable to the dry earth and did a great deal to cool the atmosphere. Read part of an article in the London Quarterly Review on John Wilson Croker, defending him and undertaking to prove him an upright and talented statesman.[1] Macaulay's denunciation of Croker was certainly too vicious, so much so as to be undignified and ridiculous—unworthy of Macaulay's pen. Thank God for health and strength.

1 [Anon.], "John Wilson Croker," London *Quarterly Review*, CXLII (July 1876), 83-126.

[September] 1st Friday. Finished London Quarterly Review of John Wilson Croker's life and thought it dignified and just. Wrote an article for the Presbyterian on "Christian Statesman." It is a poor article but will do I suppose. Went to the post office after tea. In the evening wrote analysis of an article on criticism which I intend writing for use at college. Thank God for health and strength.

A Religious Essay   [*Sept. 1, 1876*]

A Christian Statesman.

There is a growing tendency to confine religion to certain walks of life. To the minister of the Gospel, it is of course considered essential; he must be pure in all his dealings, and his life must be a model of Christian consistency; his conversation must be free from all vanity, and he must in all things set his people a godly example. As the conditions and occupations of life differ more and more from those of the minister, and men's duties diverge more and more from the duties of a pastor, less and less of religion is generally considered necessary. Religion is thought out of place in the business office; it is thought wonderful for a soldier to be a true Christian; a lawyer is too often justified in a lie; and we would be tempted to smile at hearing of a praying statesman. This belief is in direct opposition to the Scripture views of religion. In the Bible a saving faith in Christ is represented as an ornament and help to the business man; an unfailing aid to the soldier who is fighting in a just cause; the true dignity and motive of the lawyer, causing him to uphold truth and justice, and always to strive to deal out the law with an equal hand; and above all, as the first requisite for a statesman, upon whom rests so heavy a responsibility, both to God and man. This last phase of the subject, is the one we wish to present to thoughtful minds by a very brief statement of the principles bearing upon it.

Although there are principles of duty to his party and to the cause he has espoused, still no statesman should allow party feeling to bias his opinions on any point which involves truth or falsehood, justice or injustice. He should search for truth with the full determination to find it, and in that search he should most earnestly seek aid from God, who will surely hold him responsible for the course he pursues. When he has arrived at what he is convinced is the truth, he should uphold that truth, both by word and deed, irrespective of party. In no case should he allow expediency or policy to influence him in the least, if the support of the measures which seem expedient or politic, involves a support of untruth or injustice. And let no statesman think that by silence or refraining from acting on any subject or question, he can escape responsibility. When he does not actively advocate truth, he advocates error. Those who are not for truth are against it. There is here no neutrality.

On the other hand, when the statesman has become convinced that he has arrived at the truth, and has before his mind the true view of his subject, he should be tolerant. He should have a becoming sense of his own weakness and liability to err, and, while supporting with the utmost vigor what he considers to be the truth, he should treat his opponents with due forbearance, and should avoid all personal attacks, which show a want of real argument, and which will only engender useless and unchristian enmity.

In short, let his faith be in Christ his Saviour, let his truth be truth which is in accordance with the Bible's standard, and let his whole conversation and life be such as becomes a Christian, and, therefore, a gentleman.   Twiwood.

Printed in the Wilmington *North Carolina Presbyterian*, Sept. 6, 1876.

From Wilson's Shorthand Diary

[September] 2nd Saturday. Helped mother put down carpet in the study. Collected some small things for packing on Monday. Sent for copy of the minutes. Went down street on business for mother. Went to Presbyterian office. Read extracts from the dramas of the best modern dramatic poets in *Half Hours* and enjoyed them very much as I do all drama—all drama worth reading. Only two days before I must be off for college. May God bless and protect the dear ones at home in my absence! Thank God for health and strength.

[September] 3rd Sabbath. Went to Prayer Meeting in morning and heard Mr. Worth read "A Short Discourse." Slept most of the afternoon. Thank God for health and strength.

[September] 4th Monday. Spent the day packing and got ready for going away to Centennial and college. Went down street several times during the day to make several purchases and various preparations for my departure. Thank God for health and strength.

[September] 5th Tuesday. Traveled all day. It was harder even than ever to part with dear mother and sister and little Josie and especially dear little Wilson. How I am blessed in my home! Reached Portsmouth about 7½ o'clock in the evening and went on board the Baltimore boat which was crowded to overflowing. All the state rooms were engaged and I had to sleep on the floor with numerous others. Slept very little and spent a very uncomfortable night. Thank God for health and strength.

[September] 6th Wednesday. Reached Baltimore about 7½ o'clock in the morning and went around to the depot of the P. W. & B. R. R. Co[.] Got breakfast at restaurant in the depot building and started for Philadelphia about 9 o'clock in crowded train of 13 cars. Reached Philadelphia about one and found father at the Girard House where he was waiting for firemen's procession to pass. The procession passed somewhat after my arrival and took an hour and a quarter to pass. It was long and monotonous. In evening we went to several places of amusement with the Reverend Mr. Young[1] of Nashville, Tennessee[,] but found all of them very much crowded and finally brought up at "Professor Wyman's" where we saw some amazing performances by figures governed by wires. Thank God for health and strength.

[1] The Rev. John S. Young, pastor of Second Presbyterian Church in Nashville.

Philadelphia, Pa.

[September] 7th Thursday. Spent the day at Centennial grounds. Went through the main buildings Machinery Hall, the Art Building and had a short survey of the Government Building. The exhibition of the articles in all departments is extensive and most tasteful and elegant. What an immense amount of brain work one sees in such a place as Machinery Hall! The machinery in this building is as it were the cause of all the exhibits in other buildings. Here is to be found the machinery by which all the other articles were made. In the Art Building we found some beautiful sculpture and painting though most of it was rather second rate in my judgment. By far the best display of arts in this building was that of England. Returned to town about 4½ o'clock tired and satisfied with the *day's works*. In evening went to hear a performance of a company of minstrels and found the performance chaste and highly amusing. Nothing relieves the mind so much as a performance of this kind. Yet a constant attendance at such places would be purgatory to me. Thank God for health and strength both of body and mind.

[September] 8th Friday. Went out to the Centennial grounds at about 8½ o'clock and stayed there until one o'clock, when we bade the exhibition goodbye. Visited Agricultural Hall and revisited the Government Building examining the lighthouses etc. One of the things which interested me most of all was a machine for making stamped envelopes which is certainly very wonderful. After leaving the grounds we went to an exhibition of the "The Siege of Paris" just outside the ground and found it very interesting indeed.

Went into town and bought some furniture for my college room. Went to Wanamaker's clothing house and supplied myself with winter clothes. In the evening took a long stroll with father. We obtained our tickets for Princeton and engaged the baggage wagon to call for our trunks.

[September] 9th Saturday. Spent the morning idly. Started for Princeton about 1:50 p.m. and reached there all right at 3:10 p.m. Put up at the University Hotel and found the conditions there as good as could be desired. Engaged board at Mrs. Wright's. In the evening Drs. Aiken[1] and Hodge (C. Wistar)[2] called on father and were both, Dr. Aiken especially, very pleasant indeed. Thank God for health and strength.

[1] The Rev. Charles Augustus Aiken, D.D., Archibald Alexander Professor of Christian Ethics and Apologetics, Princeton Theological Seminary.
[2] The Rev. Caspar Wistar Hodge, D.D., Professor of New Testament Literature and Biblical Greek, Princeton Theological Seminary.

[September] 10th Sabbath. A cloudy day. In the morning went with father to the Seminary Chapel and heard an excellent discourse from the Reverend Dr. Hodge, Sr.,[1] the great theologian. After the service father stopped to speak to Dr. Hodge who was his instructor when in Seminary here many years ago. Dr. Hodge has been professor here for about fifty-six years. He seemed very glad to see father and said that he was sorry that he had not known that father was here sooner as he would have liked to have had him preach. Upon arrival at the hotel we met Dr. McCosh in the hall. He was very cordial for *him* and had quite a talk with father etc etc. At dinner Mr. Van Dyke of the Seminary[2] and the son of Dr. Van Dyke of Nebraska [sic],[3] who is a great friend of father's sat with us. In the afternoon both father and I stayed at home since we both suffer from an affliction of the bowels consequent upon the sudden change in the water. Father preached in the evening in the First Church and was most heartily thanked and congratulated by all the professors. I slept at Mrs. Wright's.

[1] The Rev. Charles Hodge, D.D., Charles Hodge Professor of Exegetical, Didactic, and Polemic Theology, Princeton Theological Seminary, the preeminent nineteenth-century American Presbyterian theologian.
[2] Henry J. van Dyke, Jr., a senior at the Seminary.
[3] Henry J. van Dyke, D.D., pastor, Clinton Street Presbyterian Church, Brooklyn, N. Y., a director of Princeton Theological Seminary.

[September] 11th Monday. Immediately after breakfast I went to the hotel to see father before his early start. We met Professor Cameron[1] in the hall of the hotel and father had quite a discussion

with the *jackass* on the southern question. He is one of the kind of
men that have rent the country and are the curse of the South. He
is one of those who says that he was born in the South and knows
all about it when they know less than a two year old baby. Such
men are a scandal to leaders, as Macaulay said of Croker. Father
left on the 9:45 train. I accompanied him to the Junction. It was
chilly and rained all day. Went about the streets a good deal during the day on various tours of business. Unpacked my trunks.
Spent the evening writing up my diary from my "diary slips."
Thank God for health and strength.

[1] Henry Clay Cameron, Professor of Greek Language and Literature, College of
New Jersey.

[September] 12th Tuesday. Had my furniture brought up from
the depot in the morning and fixed up my room in ship-shape.
Immediately after dinner wrote my diary. Met several very nice
freshmen today, amongst others a Mr. Nicoll,[1] a brother of our
boat captain. Spent most of the day fixing my room. Went down
to the train several times to see if anyone whom I knew was on
board and met several of our class just coming back. Pope came
back from New York in the afternoon. I was very glad to see him
as I think him a very nice fellow. His room being right next to
mine it is well that he is as nice as he is. Spent the evening talking
with Pope and two freshmen—Banks[2] and Chapman.[3] Banks seems
to be a pretty nice fellow, I did not like Chapman as well. Thank
God for health and strength.

[1] Edward H. Nicoll, '80.
[2] William B. Banks, '80.
[3] Harry E. Chapman, '80.

[September] 13th Wednesday. Spent the day loafing around with
Pope. Went down to the train several times and saw a great many
of our fellows as well as a great many freshmen. In the morning
read in *Half Hours* "The Duel" an extract from Charles Dickens'
"Nicholas Nickelby" and enjoyed it very much indeed. Dickens had
real power as a writer. In the afternoon went to *Jim's* lecture opening the college and had a quite gay time stomping at the freshmen
as they came in. Good many of my class arrived immediately after
the lecture. McCarter did not put in an appearance, strange to say.
Among friends Jim Reed[,][1] Jack Farr, Dennis and *many others*
arrived. Walked down to the mail after tea and over to University
Hotel and saw a great many fellows just arrived. Jimmy says that

166 applications for admission have been received so far. Our class will probably receive about 20 new members. Thank God for health and strength.

1 James M. Reed, Jr., '78.

Classroom Notebook

[c. Sept. 13-Dec. 20, 1876]

Inscribed on cover (WWhw):
 "Soph. Year   First Term,   Mathematics   T. W. Wilson."
Incomplete notes of first term of Professor Duffield's sophomore mathematics course.

(WP, DLC)

From Wilson's Shorthand Diary

[September] 14th Thursday. Very little of interest today. Heard lecture from Professor Packard[1] on the Augustan Age which interested me very much indeed. Took pretty full notes on this lecture. McCarter arrived in the evening. I was truly glad to see him once more. I am afraid though that he is in a very bad crowd this year. He is I think in the *hazing* crowd and will be shipped if [he] don't take care.

Thank God for health and strength.

1 William A. Packard, Professor of Latin and the Science of Language.

[September] 15th Friday. Heard another excellent lecture from Professor Packard on the Augustan Age and Horace's connection with it in common with the other poets of the day. Took pretty full notes on him. Made two recitations to Cameron on *Demosthenes De Corona* which recitations he made very stupid as usual. I am very glad however that we have De Corona. It is a work that everyone should read as one of the greatest speeches ever made. As a lawyer I will especially enjoy it. As far as I have read it is an excellent thing. It has been called "the greatest speech of the greatest orator of the world."[1] Enos arrived today and I was extremely glad to see him. He is a thoroughly nice fellow. He is a man that is in earnest in everything which he does; one who views life not as a time for pleasure (*we may be sure*) but as a time for earnest work and endeavor. Thank God for health and strength.

1 WW translated part of this speech into English. See the two-page item in WP, DLC, "Demosthenes—On the Crown."

From Janet Woodrow Wilson

My darling Son,   Wilmington, N. C. Friday morning
                                          [Sept. 15, 1876]

. . .We received your most welcome letter yesterday. I was sorry that your dear father could not stay with you longer, dear, but I need not try to tell you how glad I was to see his face again. I think he is looking remarkably well, dont you? I do hope he will be well and strong this winter. How are you now, dear? I hope you are going to be comfortable in your present room. It will be so nice to have your own new furniture at once. I will send your pictures next week. Do you want your carpet? I may have to send some of your bed-clothes just to pack the pictures in—but you can leave them in the box till they are wanted. Have you received your furniture all right? What a bargain it was to be sure! I could scarcely believe your father was in earnest when he told me the price. I want you to describe it to me please dear. You know papa is not very good at recollecting such things. . . .

                                          Your own   Mother.

ALS (WP, DLC) with WWhw notations on env.: "Received [WWsh] 9/18/76; Ans." Enc.: Marion Wilson Kennedy to WW, Sept. 7, 1876.

From Wilson's Shorthand Diary

[September] 16th Saturday. In the morning cut Kargé recitation on French. Spent most of the day and the night with Enos who was trying to persuade me to come and room with him. I cannot do this[,] however, I think. He was one of the most homesick fellows I ever saw. He is a good fellow of deep affections. Spent the night with him to keep him company in his loneliness. Thank God for health and strength.

[September] 17th Sabbath. Spent the day and night with Enos at his earnest request. It stormed hard all day but cleared up during the night. Heard Jim preach in the morning, and in his sermon was very good. His delivery spoils his addresses, however. No other service during the day except prayer meeting of different classes in the evening. I attended our class prayer meeting in the Chapel in the evening and enjoyed it very much indeed. Andy Chambers[1] made an earnest address[,] which was excellent. The meeting was led by Jack Davis our second man. Read an article in Dr. Macmillan's[2] on the relations of natural and spiritual things during the afternoon and found it both interesting and instructive. Thank God for health and strength.

1 Andrew A. Chambers, '79.
2 Probably (anon.), "Natural Religion," Pt. VII, *Macmillan's Magazine*, xxxiv (June 1876), 156-67. This work appeared in ten parts, from Feb. 1875 through Jan. 1878.

[September] 18th Monday. Went into Cameron twice during the day for recitations on Demosthenes De Corona which would be very interesting with anybody but Cameron. He called me up in afternoon recitation and I made quite a good recitation *of course*.[1]

At noon went out on the campus and watched the university baseball nine practice. Went to college library and got a copy of Jeffrey's Essays.[2] Wrote a letter to dear mother. Took a walk after Chapel with Hi Woods. Received letters from mother and Sister Marion. In the evening read a little of Horace's First Satire and spent most of the evening reading Jeffrey's essay on the beautiful which is one of the most just and clear articles it was ever my pleasure to read. His ideas which are good ones are most forcibly expressed. Spent the night with Enos at his earnest request.

Thank God for health and strength.

1 Here follows the Graham shorthand symbol for merriment.
2 WW refers to Francis Jeffrey, *Contributions to the Edinburgh Review*, probably the one-volume edition published in New York in 1873. All the Jeffrey "essays" mentioned by WW appeared in this volume. For example, the "essay on the beautiful" that WW praised in this entry was Jeffrey's review of Archibald Alison, *Essays on the Nature and Principles of Taste*.

[September] 19th Tuesday. Went into recitations with Packard[,] Hunt and Duffield in all of which I learned something which is more than I can say of all my recitations. In Cam[eron's] I learned nothing. Duff is splendid. In the evening and at odd intervals during the day read Jeffrey's article on the beautiful which I finished and pronounce excellent and most conclusive. No one can help following him with pleasure in his clear reasoning and agree with him in his most just conclusions. That the theory which he advocates in so masterly a manner is the correct one I have no doubt whatever as it is the only one which bears close scrutiny or bears the ordeal of being carried out to the fullest extent in every direction. One can follow its lead with confidence Jeffrey's illustrations are peculiarly apt. The art of illustration is the first which anyone who wishes to become [an] author should cultivate. In the evening there were two cane sprees in front of the post office.[1] In the first the '80 man was victorious[;] in the second our man took the cane. My despondency was something sublime immediately after the first spree. The '80 were wild with their victory. Went up to Enos' room for a few minutes and then went up to McCarter's room and sat about half hour. Wrote up my diary, took a bath and went to bed. Thank God for health and strength. Later: There was a third cane spree between Comstock[1] of our class and '80's champion, Nicoll, in which Comstock was victorious getting the cane in fine style. I feel better.

[1] The freshman winner was F. T. Bryan, '80. The sophomore winners were H. Irving Van Hoesen, '79 and George C. Comstock, '79. See Parke H. Davis, "The History of the Cane-Spree," *Princeton Alumni Weekly*, xi (March 8, 1911), 348-51. See also the note on the cane spree at Oct. 27, 1876.

[September] 20th Wednesday. Went into mathematics twice and found Dr. Duffield a splendid teacher—was plain that no one could have any excuse for not understanding him and yet so fine a master of the subject. Read Jeffrey's article on Benjamin Franklin during the day and admired it much. It is written in his usual clear and happy style and its criticisms are eminently just and even sometimes profound. In the evening studied Horace for about an hour, and then read part of Jeffrey's article on the life and works of Jonathan Swift which well repaid me for the reading. Jeffrey's review of the progress of English literature given at the commencement of this essay considering the small space in which it is given is wonderfully good, and certainly gives the true explanation [of the] changes and alternate progress and retrogression of letters in England. His estimate of the authors in Queen Anne's reign is replete with good sense and clear judgment and is in my opinion a perfectly just evaluation of the abilities of such writers as Addison Pope and Swift. Their defect, he says, was a want of Renaissance sensibility and enthusiasm, and their great merit great good sense[,] clear judgment and mastery of the lower kind of sarcasm. They were inimitable in the style in which they wrote. They perfect an imperfect sort of writing. Thank God for health and strength. Took a long walk down to Stony Brook with Woods after chapel in the afternoon.

[September] 21st Thursday. I went into recitation on Latin twice and into lecture on natural history. I enjoyed the latter very much indeed. It is a relief to have natural history after such an eternal round of Latin[,] Greek and mathematics. Studied pretty much all day. During the day ruled my Index Rerum. In the evening studied Smith's History of Greece: the changes in the geography of the country and the mythical period. I find it very interesting as all histories [are] to me. After studying the history read some more of

Jeffrey's essay on Swift and became deeply interested. Did not have time to finish it. Thank God for health and strength.

[September] 22nd Friday. Went into recitation[,] Cam twice— once Grecian history and once a recitation on Demosthenes De Corona. In the afternoon had a lecture from Packard on the facts to be collected from the writings of Horace concerning his life. A very interesting lecture. Spent the afternoon reading. Finished Jeffrey's article on Swift and pronounce it splendid. His judgments are clear[,] his reason is exact and conclusive[,] his style fascinating[,] and his genius decided. In the evening went to hall and spent a very pleasant evening indeed. Came to my room about twelve o'clock and went to bed very willingly. Thank God for health and strength.

[September] 23rd Saturday. Went into French recitation to Kargé and had quite an amusing time of it. At noon I went into Hall library. Heard that the freshmen would have to do their cane-spree with us this evening if it be not pouring [?] rain. I have two bets each for soda water that our class keeps the most canes. Spent the evening and afternoon reading. Read Macaulay's essay on the Disabilities of the Jews; better part of his essay on Boswell's addition to literature in the shape of the life of Johnson and edited by one Croker. I have before expressed my opinion of the way in which Macaulay censures Croker in this essay. He certainly used unwarrantably strong language. Read also his essay on the Pilgrim's Progress. His style is certainly inimitable—but it has been enlarged upon too often to need any remark from me. I read him yesterday principally for purposes of criticism as Professor Hunt requires a composition from us on the use of figured language in the essays of Macaulay. He has given us the privilege of writing upon either Macaulay, Addison, George Eliot, Shakespeare, or [blank]. I chose Macaulay because I was most familiar with his writings. Spent from half after four until five exercising in the gymnasium. In the evening about nine o'clock had short cane spree with one of the freshmen rooming here at Wright's in which I was victorious. Little praise to me though because he was shorter than I. I only fought on his proposition however. Although I did not make much progress in my reading for my essay—that is[,] it is a very difficult task to criticize Macaulay's use of figured language in any one of his essays within the limit of six pages to which Professor Hunt has limited us. He is not happy in his choice of subjects or in his rules regarding the writing of the essays.

I will write only upon the general characteristics of his use of figures and can thus do something, though very little, in six pages. Our professor will have to be satisfied with general statements on my part and no particular judgments or criticisms. Indeed it has been very hard to think that young men such as we have critical judgment enough to criticize such great writers as he has given us a choice from. The very name of the author is apt to awe us. I myself though have little reverence for the author—no great *name* appalls me, though *great writing* does when I think how hopeless the task of trying to write as well as the great author I may read has done. But one can but *try*. "Genius is divine *perseverance*." Divine *patience* I believe he originally used, perseverance is better in my opinion. Genius I cannot claim nor even extra brightness but perseverance *all* can have. Before going to bed I prayed out loud and found that I enjoyed my prayer much more than usual. This is a lesson to me. I would advise everyone to pray out loud. One feels more as if he was praying to God and talking with Him when his tones are audible. I prayed last night as I have seldom done in the last few months. Oh that God would give me more of His Holy Spirit and make me something more than the cold Christian I have been of late! I bless His holy name for the health and strength of all my past life. During all my life I have had nothing but blessings from His hand but He has had nothing but a slight cold love from me. I shall henceforth endeavor to make Him some slightly better return for His many mercies.

[September] 24th Sabbath. There was no morning Chapel today and the natural consequence was that I overslept myself this morning. Heard a sermon from Dud Atwater in Chapel which put almost everybody to sleep. It was one of the driest efforts I ever heard. The sermon took up about three-quarters of an hour. If he were only speaking a little faster he could preach such a sermon as he did this morning in half an hour. He talked like an enemy of commentary and showed himself a very *common-tator*. But I have determined never to pun again. Addison cured me of it. It is a bad habit. Immediately after Chapel service took a short walk with Woods around the small triangle.[1] After dinner wrote up my diary. While waiting for the church bell I read a slight piece on *Christian Charity* by Bishop Sumner, late bishop of Chester.[2] He seems to have the true idea of Christian charity. His article is practical and sensible in an eminent degree. Wrote a letter to

Sister Marion and dear mother also[.] Had a beautiful postal from home. Went to class prayer meeting at 7:40 in the evening. The prayer meeting was not as interesting as usual as a very few spoke at all. Only Seeley[3] who led the meeting and Davis and Chambers made any remarks. Seeley's remarks did not amount to much, Davis' were very good and Chambers always has something interesting to say and some valuable lesson to impart. He is every inch a speaker—the tones of his voice show training—all his emphasis suggests a truth and his words are well chosen. After prayer meeting finished my letter to dear mother and went to the post office and mailed both my letters. The day has been rainy and the weather very disagreeable indeed. It does not rain hard—a good hard rain would be much preferable to the drizz[ling] driv[ing] mist which now prevails. I heard this evening in prayer meeting that Henry[4] of our class is very sick with typhoid fever. I hope he may speedily recover. Read a short sketch of St. Paul's Character from the pen of one *Cave*.[5] A very good sketch though nothing particularly good showed itself in it. Noted down a few thoughts for an article for the Presbyterian on the duties of sons to their parents[6] but my thoughts come hard this evening and I have no pleasure in *thinking* so I must not think any more. No one ought to try to write when it requires such an immense effort as it does from me this evening. My heart feels full and yet my thoughts will not clothe themselves in any suitable words and will not even put themselves into tangible form. Striving thus to express my thoughts which will not come and yet on the subject of which I am full is one of the most painful things I know of. I will wait until another day. A good sleep will do more towards clearing my mind than anything else at present. Thank God for health and strength.

1 The large and small triangles were walks much used by undergraduates well into the 1920's. Both start at the junction of Mercer and Stockton Streets, these being the V of the triangles. The base of the small triangle is Lover's Lane. The base of the large triangle is Quaker Road along Stony Brook, the route WW took with Woods on Sept. 20, 1876.

2 In *Half-Hours*.

3 William B. Seeley, '79.

4 Thomas Henry, '79.

5 William Cave, Canon of Windsor, distinguished divine and prolific author. The selection is from his *Lives of the Apostles*, which WW probably read in *Half-Hours*, III, 380-87.

6 Printed at Oct. 8, 1876.

[September] 25th Monday. Went into Greek Testament and Greek recitation with Cameron twice by both of which I was much bored. Studied Greek during the morning. Immediately after dinner having nothing else to do and feeling very little like reading or any kind of confining work I loafed around generally—went through the new building,[1] made a short visit to Woods, caught ball with him for some time before recitation and then was bored by Cam for an hour. Spent the evening after coming back from the post pretty much in a simple way—watching the freshmen who board here have a small cane-spree and trying tests of strength with them. Accomplished very little studying during the day and no reading at all. About eleven o'clock heard the fellows shout up on the campus and went up to see what was the matter. Found that there had been three cane-sprees in two of which '80 was victorious and in the other of which one of our fellows took the cane away from one of the '80's strongest men. These sprees made the number of canes taken by the two classes just even. They will not be even after the June cane-spree however. Thank God for health and strength.

[1] Witherspoon Hall.

From Janet Woodrow Wilson

My precious boy   Wilmington, N. C., Sep. 25th '76
    . . . I am glad that you are going to try and write something for the paper [*North Carolina Presbyterian*] dear. Do you know your pieces have been greatly admired? It seems that it is known that you wrote them.[1] You should feel very much encouraged I think. But you must not write, if in so doing you are obliged to take some of your time for out-door recreation. . . .
    I am so very glad, dear, that you are finding your time at college pleasant. I was sure you would as soon as you got a taste of sure enough study—which you never had a chance to have before. I am *so glad* that you love to study now, my dear, dear son—for now I know your future will be all right. . . .
    Your father preached two glorious sermons yesterday. Had a good congregation in the morning, as some second church people were present as well as some Methodists. At night he preached at the second church, which was *packed*. He preached without manuscript—and was at his very best—some passages were grandly eloquent. I wish you could have heard him.
    Good bye my precious one. Your dear father joins me in fondest love to our precious boy. Sister & Josie send ever so much love.

Baby[2] hasn't forgotten "Unca." He call[s] your father "Arder" and graciously allows him to carry him down to meals.

Your own   Mother

ALS (WP, DLC) with WWhw notations on env.: "Received" [WWsh] "9/28/76"; "Ans."
    1 She refers to "Work-Day Religion," "Christ's Army," "The Bible," and "A Christian Statesman," printed at Aug. 11, Aug. 17, Aug. 25, and Sept. 1, 1876, respectively, for which WW used the pen name "Twiwood."
    2 J. Wilson Howe.

From Wilson's Shorthand Diary

[September] 26th Tuesday. Went into French recitation once and into recitation on mathematics once. Cut second recitation on French. Did very little during the morning as Woods came up and stayed for some time. At noon went over to the Hall and got the first volume of Brougham's Historical Sketches of Statesmen who flourished in the time of George III. In the afternoon studied a little on mathematics, wrote letter to father, read one or two pieces from Goldsmith's "Bee" and talked with Woods who came [*] up again to borrow a book in which he had become interested in his morning visit. Went to the gymnasium immediately after Chapel and exercised for about half an hour. During the evening I read Lord Brougham's sketches of the characteristics of George III and Chatham. How bitter Brougham is in some of his passages. He seems to despise the present generation—that is the generation that was *then* present. His statements are sometimes contradictory it seems to me but still his style is on the whole interesting and somewhat forcible—and shows a mind of decided character and well formed opinions but extremely bitter and scornful. He strikes one as a man who has had some disappointments and therefore practically enemy to all mankind. I will read some of his writings before I pronounce any opinion on him however. There are so many things which I would like to read right away that I scarcely know what to read first. Thank God for health and strength.

[September] 27th Wednesday. Very little of interest today. Studied mathematics twice and had two recitations in it. At night the long looked for cane-spree came off. As I was not feeling very well I did not enter it. The fighting was very lively and many fights were very fine in their displays of strength and skill. Some of the freshmen fought remarkably well and did themselves credit.

The respective number of canes taken by the two classes is variously estimated but the real number seems to be about 44 for '79 and about 29 for '80. We therefore beat the freshmen pretty badly notwithstanding their plucky fighting. After the thing was over I was sorry that I had not gone in. Some of our best men could find no one who would take them. The juniors were very careful not to have any of their protégés on our best men. Thank God for health and strength.

[September] 28th Thursday Latin[,] natural history[,] and Latin was the routine today. I like natural history very much. In fact I like it more than I thought that I would. Read good deal during the day. Thank God for health and strength.

[September] 29th Friday. Two recitations with Cam! Made recitations in Latin. In the evening went to dear old Whig Hall and spent a delightful evening. Thank God for health and strength.

[September] 30th Saturday. Went into French recitation and had quite a fine time with Kargé. Spent the afternoon in my room with a crowd of freshmen who bored me very much indeed. I intended to spend the evening writing my essay but these young rascals kept me from doing so by their long stay. Took some exercise in the gymnasium just before supper and felt better after it. Spent the evening writing my essay and finished about four pages of it. Thank God for health and strength during the past month. May He continue His goodness to me in the future as in the past.

[October] 1st Sabbath. Communion Sabbath. Went [to] church in the morning and took communion. Heard very good sensible sermon. Did not catch the name of the minister.[1] Spent the afternoon rather profitlessly in Woods' room with some seniors and two of our class. Went to Chapel in the afternoon. After tea went to class prayer meeting and there said a few words for the first time since I have been here. After prayer meeting went to church and heard a sermon addressed to the young men by Harris the treasurer of the college. Thank God for having let me spend another communion Sabbath and for having let me somewhat feel of the love for Him and consecration to His service.

[1] The Princeton weekly, the *Princeton Press,* carried a notice only of the evening service in the First Church for Oct. 1, 1876.

[October] 2nd Monday. Went into recitation in Greek Testament and into two recitations on Greek (Demosthenes De Corona). Was called upon to recite in Greek Testament and in Demosthenes. Worked on my essay at odd intervals during the day. At noon went to the baseball grounds to see the university nine practice. Spent about ¾ of an hour in the library in the afternoon looking over books. In the evening studied French for about an hour and a half, finishing my essay and commenced Boswell's Life of Johnson. What a conceited jack Boswell is! I have only got as far as the introduction. If all the rest of his composition is as conceited as the introduction it will be insufferable. The freshmen had their prep school affair this evening. Exercised in the gymnasium a little this afternoon. Without exercise of this kind I feel utterly unable to do work of any kind. Thank God for health and strength.

[October] 3rd Tuesday. Went into recitation on French[,] English and mathematics. Read exercise in French and was not called upon in either English or mathematics. Copied up my notes on mathematics this morning. This noon went down and watched the University nine practice. They did very well indeed. They play a game soon I believe. This evening I wrote a letter to dear mother and read part of Macaulay's Essay on Southey's Colloquies. About 9½ o'clock heard some shouting up on the campus and [went] to see what was the matter. Arrived in time to find that it was caused by nothing at all. Thank God for health and strength.

[October] 4th Wednesday. Two recitations in mathematics in one of which I was called up and made quite a tear. It is easy to make a tear in Jim or Duff. Copied up my notes on mathematics. At noon went to the gymnasium and exercised for about ¾ of an hour. Studied and wrote up notes during the afternoon. Spent the evening reading Macaulay's essay on Southey's Colloquies on Society and enjoyed it very much indeed. Re-wrote my essay on Macaulay's use of figured language. Thank God for health and strength.

[October] 5th Thursday. Suffering from a severe toothache and consequent pain in the head I did not go to recitations today but only attended lecture on natural history. Spent this morning copying my essay on Macaulay's use of figured language. I am glad to be done with it. The subject is not one to suggest many thoughts and the discussion of it I find to be somewhat of a labor. Spent this afternoon reading Boswell's Life of Johnson and read the same this evening. What a conceited jack Boswell is to be sure. Some of his opinions are the most ridiculous conceivable. His admiration of Johnson is a complete [?] admiration and does not recommend to his readers. But I feel that he has produced a good biography. I have not become extremely interested in it however as I have not advanced in the work further than the account of Johnson's early life and these accounts are disconnected and somewhat uninteresting as very few of them can be relied upon. One derives interest from the account of the facts which he is constantly led to doubt. I have been feeling badly all day with a dull swimm[ing] feel[ing] about my head which troubles me some. I enjoyed my exercise in the gymnasium this afternoon however and thought [it] did me good. Last evening I was feeling particularly bright and wrote my essay with ease and pleasure. I am troubled at not receiving my usual letter from home this week. I hope that none of the dear ones there are unwell. I received North Carolina Presbyterian with two vigorous articles from dear father's pen. Thank God for health and strength.

[October] 6th Friday. Recitations on Greek History, Demosthenes De Corona and Horace today. Did little but study during the day and did very little of that. This afternoon and evening read a portion of Brougham's sketch of Burke's character. It is a very well written piece, but I will not pronounce upon its merits as a piece of criticism until I know more of the subject with which it deals. Knowing little of the French Revolution and the history of the latter part of the 18 century I cannot say whether Burke's actions at that time were consistent or not. Spent a very pleasant evening in Hall. Thank God for health and strength.

[October] 7th Saturday. Recitation on French. This afternoon recopied part of my essay on Macaulay's use of figured language to improve a part which was very imperfect. Spent about an hour and half in gymnasium exercising. Just before dinner I went over the new building with Jack Farr and Vanuxem.[1] The building is progressing very nicely and promises well to be shortly finished. Spent the evening reading Boswell's Life of Johnson and Brougham's sketch of Fox's character and career. Brougham's style is certainly a very happy one and his judgments as far as I can judge without a minute knowledge of the facts and persons of whom he speaks are very just. Thank God for health and strength.

1 Louis C. Vanuxem, '79.

[October] 8th Sabbath. Got up about 8:45 and ate a late breakfast—not alone however. Went to church this morning and heard a sermon from Cam. He preached in his usual dull style. All this afternoon from 2½ o'clock to a little after four I spent in writing off and copying an article for the North Carolina Presbyterian on the duties of sons to their parents. I found some difficulty in writing and did not at length fully satisfy myself but the article is as good as I generally write—that is very ordinary. About four o'clock this afternoon I went up to Woods' room and found him asleep on his bed—the lazy rascal! Found Prentiss[1] up there reading. Took up Bickersteth's "Yesterday, Today and Forever," and read it until Chapel time.[2] At 5 o'clock went to Chapel and heard a short discourse from some strange minister whose name I have heard several times but always forget. This evening went to class prayer meeting, where I heard some very good remarks by Reid[3] and Billy Elsing.[4] Went to church afterwards and heard a very good sermon from Dr. Murray.[5] He is an earnest and good man, an excellent professor of English literature. I shall enjoy his course hugely next year. Thank God for health and strength.

[1] George L. Prentiss, '79.
[2] Edward H. Bickersteth, *Yesterday, To-day and For Ever: A Poem, in Twelve Books* (New York, 1869).
[3] David C. Reid, '79.
[4] William T. Elsing, '79.
[5] The Rev. James O. Murray, Holmes Professor of Belles Lettres and English Language and Literature, College of New Jersey.

A Religious Essay

[*Oct. 8, 1876*]

One Duty of a Son to His Parents.

As a young man speaking to young men, I would say a few earnest words to sons as to one at least, of the duties they owe their parents. We all desire to be regarded as gentlemen, and yet do we always act like gentlemen at home? We all desire to be loved, and yet do we strive to make ourselves lovely at home? He only is a gentleman who is such everywhere, and under all circumstances.— Leaving out for the present all consideration of how the Bible commands us to bear ourselves towards our parents, and the promises it makes to such as honor them, let us look for a moment at this duty from a somewhat lower point of view. A gentleman ought certainly to possess civil manners as distinguished from those of the vulgar or clownish. Does *he* possess such manners, who, when in general company is affable, treating all around him as a gentleman should, yet the moment he enters his own home, throws off all restraint, and is guilty of an opposite conduct. Any young man of spirit would feel disposed to knock another down who dared in his presence to insinuate that his father was anything other than a gentleman. And yet many who would bitterly resent an insinuation against their fathers, permit themselves to speak of these same fathers as "*the old man*," "*the governer*," &c.—regard lightly their commands or advice—and treat them as they dare not presume to treat any other gentleman. They seem to think that near relationship exempts them from the duty of politeness to their parents, and gives them an excuse for acting towards them as they would allow no others to do. What can be more unworthy? As if owing everything to one's parents—position in society, education, existence itself—were a reason for conducting himself as he would not think of doing to his most trivial acquaintance! If it is your habit upon entering your home to take unhesitating possession of the best place at the fireside, and while you exact from those in the home-circle every attention and courtesy, it never occurs to you that you are under any obligation to contribute to the comfort of those from whom you receive so much, you cannot believe yourself to be truly a gentleman. The same politeness and consideration are surely due to your father as are due to any gentleman whom you may meet in the drawing-room, or in the intercourse of business. If any stranger were to do for you what he does, would you treat that stranger as you feel meanly privileged to treat your father? Your mother, who brought you forth, nourished you in your helplessness, loves you as only a mother can—who will trust you when all others forsake you, and is ready to give her all to make you happy—are you to do nothing for her? Would you treat her with *less* courtesy than you extend to those who have done nothing for you, and are nothing to you? Surely you do not reflect whose loving glance it is that you slight, or whose tender care it is that you ignore! We none of us realize how much we owe to our parents—how every impolite word which we speak to them will recur to us after they have been taken from us, with a pang whose bitterness we will scarcely be able to bear. I only speak what I feel from the depths of my heart when I say that I could not respect myself if I put on the gentleman in society, and were careless of my manners at home. I could never for one moment trust that I am a Christian if I should be impertinent to my parents, or wittingly do anything to pain those to whom I owe everything in the world, and to whom I am everything.

A Son

Printed in the Wilmington *North Carolina Presbyterian*, Dec. 27, 1876.

From Wilson's Shorthand Diary

[October] 9th Monday. Recitation in Greek Testament and one recitation in Greek (Demosthenes De Corona) followed by another in the same this afternoon. This morning Woods was up in my room. This afternoon I read some in John Forster's Life of Oliver Goldsmith and enjoyed it very much. It is my curse that I cannot keep at any one book long at one time[.] Although I had Boswell's Life of Johnson on hand I today went to the library and got out Forster's Life of Oliver Goldsmith and commenced to read it. I have now two biographies on hand. After tea went up to Woods' room to get a book I had left up there, stayed a little while and had a very pleasant talk. This evening studied French a little and read some more of the life of Goldsmith. I find Forster's style quite pleasant though at times very disjointed and even obscure. I am trying to finish this work before I get out and commence any other. I don't know whether it is a good plan to have two biographies on hand at once or not—I will try the experiment however. Thank God for health and strength.

[October] 10th Tuesday. Recitations on French, English, and mathematics. Studied in desultory way during the day. At noon saw match game of football between '79 and '77 in which we won three goals to their none. This afternoon studied mathematics and copied notes on Duff's last lecture. After chapel went to gymnasium and exercised for about ¾ of an hour. This evening I wrote a letter to dear mother and sent it off with my article for the paper. Spent the rest of the evening reading Forster's Life of Goldsmith in which I am becoming very much interested. Goldsmith was an altogether original character. Today the Indiana elections took place. I am eager to see the returns. They will probably come in slowly however and we will not hear the full accounts until day after tomorrow—if then. My sincere hope is that Indiana will go Democratic. If Indiana goes Democratic and her good example be followed by Ohio and New York there will be little doubt of Tilden's election in November. There are numerous bets on the issue of the Indiana elections—may those supporting the Democrats win! Thank God for health and strength.

[October] 11th Wednesday. Two recitations on mathematics. Studied mathematics almost all day today and copied up my notes on it. At noon went to the gymnasium and exercised a little. Took a short walk with Woods this afternoon immediately after Chapel. This evening read my lesson in Horace for tomorrow's recitation and read Forster's Life of Goldsmith which is a most interesting book though Forster's style seems miserably obscure at times. It is difficult for me to discover what he is talking about at times. This may be owing to the man's dullness however. Goldsmith's character is worthy of study. Great excitement has prevailed today over the Indiana and Ohio elections but no reports that can be relied upon have as yet arrived. The Democratic papers this morning confidently claim a heavy Democratic majority in both Indiana and Ohio as well as in West Virginia, and the Republican papers as confidently claim a large Republican majority. We cannot know certainly until tomorrow afternoon—if then. I have little hopes that Ohio will go Democratic though I have strong hopes that Indiana will be sensible enough to do so. If we lose Indiana I am afraid that our chances are *slim* at least. If the Republicans carry Indiana there will be strong probability of that weak instrument of the corrupt Republicans, Hayes, being elected. I will wait and hope. The weather has been quite cold today—enough so to make an overcoat very comfortable. Thank God for health and strength.

[October] 12th Thursday. Two recitations on Latin today and lecture on natural history. Spent most of this morning studying at my Latin (Horace). This afternoon after dinner I sat down for a good long reading in Forster's Life of Goldsmith. But about 2:45 o'clock I heard the cry of Fire! up in the direction of the college and ran up to see what the matter was. Found that the cry was caused by fire over at the other end of town, in an old barn. After the barn was almost entirely burned up the "snobs"[1] arrived with a fire engine and the fellows immediately surrounded them and commenced making fun of their late arrival and of them generally. Jack Stewart[2] of our class shouted at one of them while standing quite near me to "pull down his vest" which so exasperated the fellow that he went for Jack and knocked him down. Upon this quite a fight ensued in which the snobs got rather the worst of it though most of the students ran off and behaved themselves in a most shameful manner. I escaped without any bruises as I did not go into the fight but merely stood on the defensive. This evening the snobs collected in force and tried to renew the fight but our fellows were sensible enough not to degrade themselves by accepting any challenge of this sort. We will have to kill some of these snobs yet before they will learn prudence. This evening I spent reading Smith's Greek History and Forster's Life of Goldsmith. I like Dr. Smith's style very much and think his history a most excellent one for its length. His style seems lucid and happy. This evening's reports of the elections in Indiana[,] Ohio and West Virginia give the Democrats Indiana and West Virginia and make Ohio doubtful though probably Republican. This is good news and makes me feel much better. I begin to have some hope of the Tilden election now though his prospects are not extremely bright. Copied my recent notes, etc. into my Index Rerum. Thank God for health and strength.

1 A volunteer fire company manned by "townies," or "snobs," traditionally harassed by students in the rivalry of town and gown. Harold Godwin, *A History of the Class of '79, Princeton College* (n.p., n.d.), p. 28, says that this episode occurred on Oct. 11.

2 John A. Stewart, Jr., '79.

[October] 13th Friday. Recitation on Greek History (Smith's)[,] Demosthenes De Corona and Horace today. Did very little reading today. The lesson in history this morning was very interesting indeed. It describes the condition of the Spartans at the time of Lycurgus. What an interesting story might be founded upon the state of the Spartan society at this time. At noon returned a book to the library and exercised at the gymnasium. This afternoon studied Horace and shaved. After Chapel and this evening I spent in Hall. Between supper and hall time I was up at Enos' room a little while and had a very pleasant talk with him. I heard who are on the freshmen crew today. The coach consists of Mister Smiley, a large man[,] and will from all accounts make a gay crew. Vanuxem and I walked down to the canal last Wednesday to see the fellows row. The freshmen were not out but our crew were and consisted of Katzenbach,[1] Wylly,[2] Dodge,[3] Larkin, Savage[4] and Gilman.[5] They rowed pretty well considering the short time they have been in training. While we were at the canal there was a mass meeting of the Democrats in college held in the English room and Williamson of '77[6] and McDonald of '78[7] received the nominations for president and vice-president of the college. Thank God for health and strength.

1 Peter Katzenbach, Jr., '79.
2 Albert Wylly, '79.

3 William Earl Dodge, '79, or his brother, Cleveland H. Dodge, '79. W. Earl Dodge died in 1884. Cleveland H. Dodge, born Jan. 26, 1860, was later vice president of the Phelps Dodge Corporation; member of the Board of Trustees of Princeton University; president of the Board of Trustees of Robert College; treasurer of the American Commission for Near East Relief, 1917; and a prominent philanthropist. He died on June 24, 1926.

4 Albert L. Savage, '79.

5 Frank P. Gilman, '79.

6 James F. Williamson, '77.

7 Henry M. McDonald, '78, or William W. McDonald, '78.

[October] 14th Saturday. No recitations today. Spent this morning doing little or nothing. Woods was in my room for some time and we had quite an interesting talk on politics etc. The returns this morning give a Democratic majority in Indiana of from 6,000 to 8,000 and about 12,000 in West Virginia. Hurrah for Tilden and Hendricks! If those states only behave themselves this well next month victory is ours! This afternoon went up to Enos' room and stayed couple of hours reading Forster's Life of Goldsmith which I am beginning to think a bore since it is very poorly written indeed. I will try to finish however as it contains the fullest account of Goldsmith's times to be obtained in any life of that great man. I think of writing an essay on the literature of the 18th century and to do this well will require a fair knowledge of all the writers of that eventful century. I must study pretty regularly for a few weeks. It is study in which I delight however. About 4 o'clock went to the gym and exercised for about three-quarters of an hour. Took a short walk by myself around the small triangle before supper. This evening went over to Hall for a little while and then to my room and read Brougham's sketches of Fox and Pitt which I enjoy much. That offers me subjects for a speech I intend to write and about decided upon "The True Statesman" or something to that effect.[1] Wrote out five or six heads upon this subject. I think it a very suggestive one and one on which I shall delight to write. This morning the preliminary contest in oratory of the candidates for the intercollegiate contest[2] took place and some very excellent speeches were delivered. It has not yet been announced who was the successful candidate. The gymnastic games came off today but I did not attend as I have been too often bored by such games already. Thank God for health and strength.

1 WW later changed the title to "The Ideal Statesman." Printed at Jan. 30, 1877.

2 This was an annual literary and debating competition under the auspices of the Inter-Collegiate Literary Association, or I. L. A., organized in 1874, in which Princeton participated without notable success, much to WW's chagrin. The other member institutions included Cornell University, College of the City of New York, Lafayette College, New York University, Rutgers University, St. John's College, Northwestern University, Syracuse University, Wesleyan University, and Williams College.

[October] 15th Sabbath. Went to Chapel this morning and heard a sermon from Dr. Shields.[1] His sermon was rather sloppy but interesting nevertheless. Spent most of this afternoon writing. Wrote article "Positivism"[2] for the North Carolina Presbyterian. I found some difficulty in writing today but the article suits me pretty well. Went up to Woods' room and stayed about an hour before afternoon Chapel. Immediately after tea after sitting for a while I went to prayer meeting where I made a few remarks upon Christian progress.[3] I find very little trouble in speaking now and do not feel as awkward upon first rising as I used to. After prayer meeting I went to church and heard a sermon from Dr. McCorkle[4] who was pastor of Second Church last year. Immediately after church this morning I took a walk by myself around the little triangle. Thank God for health and strength.

[1] The Rev. Charles W. Shields, Professor of History and of the Harmony of Science and Revealed Religion, College of New Jersey.
[2] See next document.
[3] WW may have later embodied these remarks in an article entitled "Christian Progress," printed at Dec. 20, 1876.
[4] The Rev. William A. McCorkle, D.D.

A Religious Essay

[Oct. 15, 1876]

The Positive in Religion.

Decision of character has always been most justly admired. A man is universally praised for being earnest in whatsoever undertaking he engages, and we are even sometimes attracted to the character of one who is determined in the pursuit of evil, who seems to be wrapped up in his wicked calling. We find ourselves instinctively admiring the bandit or highwayman who dies courageously and who not only does not give any sign of repentance, but even maintains his innocence to the last. Up to modern times the Christian who was a Christian "not in word only but in deed and in truth" was much admired. In this age of ours there is a growing tendency to depreciate all *positivism* in religion. Men say that the harsh tenets and severe doctrines of our fathers should now be replaced by more loving principles and milder teachings—that we should be allowed to put our own interpretations upon the teachings of the Bible, and simply to follow the dictates each of his own conscience. Men are apt to style this so-called "harsh" Christianity of our fathers and of the early saints of the church *puritanism*, whereas it was the true Christianity in which alone safety rests and salvation is sure; the Christianity of which puritanism was the *mockery*. No one can conceive of a more lovely and gentle character than that of Christ, and yet no one ever enforced God's commands—the commands which are now called harsh—with more vigor. We are not misinterpreting the commands of the God of Love when we say that his every command is to be obeyed in every particular, and that his severest commands are not inconsistent with his attribute of love. In every instance of disobedience which the Bible has given for our warning and instruction, the offender has been punished for not obeying God's commands *to the very letter*, even when his pretexts and excuses were more plausible and just than those of modern free-thinkers. Nothing is more injurious than the efforts of some men to prove that the service of Mammon is perfectly consistent with the service of God, and that, when God says "ye cannot serve God and Mammon," he means that you can. The key to the whole gospel lies in this promise: "Who will render unto every man according to his deeds: to them who by patient continuance in well doing seek for glory and honor and immortality, eternal life." Can we think that we are conforming ourselves to the image of Christ while we are endeavoring to conform ourselves more and more to the image of the world? Can we think that we are continuing patient in well doing when we are making the actions of the world the criterion by which to judge of the propriety of our daily walk and conversation as Christians? No; he is not a Christian who is one outwardly, but he is a Christian who is one inwardly, whose praise is of God and not of man. Nor is this view of religion by any means a gloomy one. By carrying sour faces, throwing out texts of Scripture upon all occasions appropriate or inappropriate, by making religion thus an offensive thing, we offend God. A gloomy and despondent Christian is as strange a sight as a criminal mourning over a pardon, and is just about as sincere. When positivism again characterises religion we are safe, and then only.   Twiwood.

Printed in the Wilmington *North Carolina Presbyterian*, Oct. 25, 1876.

From Wilson's Shorthand Diary

[October] 16th Monday. Recitation on Greek Testament and one in the morning on Demosthenes De Corona followed by one on the same in the evening. Read Forster's Life of Goldsmith to where he describes Goldsmith as undertaking the Bee and I then set to work to read the Bee and thus spent all the rest of the time reading it. Goldsmith's style is certainly most fascinating. How much more grandly simple than that of Addison! I have enjoyed today's reading most thoroughly. How large stores of literature are yet to be searched by me! This noon I exercised in the gym. Spent most of the afternoon reading. The Democrats are now jubilant over our victories in Indiana and West Virginia. The Republicans today nominated for president and vice-president in college Slemmons and Williams.[1] I hope that they will be defeated by our candidates, Williamson and McDonald. Spent the evening reading after returning from the class prayer meeting. Studied French for about an hour. Pope arrived from Philadelphia about 10½ o'clock this evening. Thank God for health and strength.

[1] Charles L. Williams, '78, or Charles S. Williams, '78.

[October] 17th Tuesday. Recitations on French, English and mathematics. Spent most of this morning studying Hart's rhetoric which is an immensely stupid book. Some of his ideas are extremely crude. This noon I went to the college library and took out a volume of Addison's Spectator which I intend to read in connection with Goldsmith's Bee for purposes of comparison. I think Goldsmith superior to Addison in wit and in various excellencies as far as my observation has gone. Spent the afternoon studying mathematics and copying notes on them. Vanuxem came over and we studied mathematics together for a while. After Chapel took walk down toward the prep school[1] with Woods. He is a very nice fellow. The weather has been tolerably cold today. Last Sabbath there was snow on the ground—the first snow of the season. The winter promises to be extremely cold as it is a very rare occurrence for snow to fall in October. A thick suit is very comfortable even now. This evening wrote letter to dear father and read some twenty or thirty pages of Goldsmith's Bee. I enjoy it very much indeed. His remarks on education are good and his ideas of eloquence exactly tally with mine and are therefore much admired by me. He has certainly arrived at the true idea of eloquence. He himself grows eloquent from his earnestness. He never utters a word but I follow his—this is most convenient. Addison's wit is like a smooth sea which pleases with its placidity while Goldsmith's wit, like the sea troubled by the winds[,] pleases with its rough earnestness and strength. The former follows along with the even flow of common sense and the other with the rough force of genius. After I become familiar with the writers of the 18th century, which I am fast becoming, I will write a short essay on the literature of that period which was so productive of great writers. Thank God for health and strength.

[1] This was the Preparatory School of the College of New Jersey, for information about which, see *Catalogue of the College of New Jersey for the Academical Year*

1876-'77 (Princeton, 1876), pp. 53-55. The Preparatory School was located at the northeastern corner of Nassau Street and Snowden Lane.

[October] 18th Wednesday. Spent this morning copying up notes on mathematics and studying for recitation. Two recitations on mathematics in neither of which was I called up. Advertisements were up that there would be a match game of baseball at noon today between the University nine and the Olympics of Paterson New Jersey but the Olympics did not put in an appearance and so I did away with my exercise at the gym for nothing at all but saw the University nine practice a little. Spent the afternoon studying mathematics. Immediately after chapel went to gym and exercised for a little while to loosen my muscles. This evening studied my Latin (Horace) for tomorrow morning after coming back from a short reading at the Hall. Read Goldsmith's Bee for about an hour and a half and enjoyed it much. Finished the Bee and pronounce it equal to if not superior to Addison's Spectator as far as it goes. Goldsmith's piece on the Augustan Age of England rather disappointed me not by any means coming up to my expectations. Thank God for health and strength.

[October] 19th Thursday. Recitation on Horace and lecture on natural history. Was called up in Horace and made a tolerably good recitation. This morning studied my Horace a little and read a little in Goldsmith's "Inquiry into the Present State of Polite Learning in Europe." I find this work very interesting indeed though I think Goldsmith mistaken in several instances. Most of his remarks are very sensible and just. This noon I walked down to the canal with McCarter and Farr and saw the different crews row. Four of our crew were out in the shell and rowed remarkably well. '78 will probably carry off the cup in the bumping races of next week. Spent the afternoon reading Goldsmith. This evening finished Goldsmith's "Inquiry" and am much pleased with it. Read also his essay on love for belles-lettres. Tomorrow has been given us as a holiday. Thank God for health and strength.

[October] 20th Friday. As today was the day for the unveiling of the Witherspoon monument in Philadelphia the students were granted a holiday to go to see the ceremonies. I did not go as I have seen enough of Philadelphia lately. Spent the day reading. Read Goldsmith's essays on the cultivation of taste, the origin of poetry as distinguished from other writing, use of the metaphor, use of the hyperbole, versification and found them exceedingly interesting. His style is delightful—so easy as to be a perfect clear medium. This evening read his essays on the clubs[,] on London, a wow-wow, etc and was very much entertained. This afternoon I took a walk around the small triangle with Pope and felt much better after it. I have enjoyed the day much in company with simple, charming Goldsmith. Thank God for health and strength.

[October] 21st Saturday. Recitation on French this morning at eleven o'clock—the only recitation of the day. Spent this morning studying French. This noon took a shave and was much relieved in consequence. Immediately after dinner lay down on my bed and went sound asleep and slept until about 4½ o'clock. After waking up went down to gym and exercised for about an hour which thoroughly woke me up and made me feel much better. After tea went to the post office with Pope and walked over to Lit room and got my Princetonian of this week. Spent this evening reading the Princetonian and writing an analysis of a few thoughts for a speech on independence of thought.[1] My thoughts flowed rather slowly as usual. I take some pleasure in that however and do not mind waiting a decent length of time for thoughts to come. Thank God for health and strength. Received a letter from dear mother and one from Woods who has gone home for a short holiday.

[1] Not found. Possibly later worked into WW speech in the sophomore contest in Whig, "The Ideal Statesman," delivered on Jan. 30, 1877.

[October] 22nd Sabbath. Got up about nine o'clock. Went to chapel and heard a sleepy sermon from [Professor] Packard. This afternoon wrote a letter to Sister Marion. Chapel at 5 o'clock and supper half an hour afterwards. After tea went to class prayer meeting which I enjoyed very much. While there made a few remarks upon our duties in everyday life. Now that I have begun speaking in these meetings I find no difficulty at all in making up my mind to speak but even find it hard to keep my seat. After prayer meeting went to First Church and heard a sermon by Dr. Gosman.[1] The sermon was by no means remarkable in its character. Thank God for health and strength.

[1] The Rev. Abraham Gosman, D.D., pastor, Lawrenceville, N. J., Presbyterian Church.

[October] 23rd Monday. Recitation on Greek Testament and two recitations on Demosthenes De Corona. This morning I wrote a letter to Cousin Jessie Bones and mailed it with one to Sister Marion which I wrote yesterday. This noon exercised at the gym.

This afternoon I spent in writing—finishing my speech on independence of thought. It is a very poor effort but will have to do. It seems to me that every piece I write is worse than any I have written before. I hope that this is not the case. This afternoon after chapel took a short walk by myself. Went to class prayer meeting at 6:40. Spent this evening writing and loafing. Thank God for health and strength.

[October] 24th Tuesday. Recitations on French, English, and mathematics. Spent this morning studying. This noon I went down to the canal to see the crews row. Tomorrow the fall races come off. There are poor prospects for fun as very few crews seem inclined to enter. Spent this afternoon studying mathematics. After chapel took a short walk with Woods who has just come back from a short visit home. This evening wrote letter to dear mother and tried to memorize my speech but the freshmen next door kept up such a racket that I could do no studying at all. We have the freshest crowd in this house I ever saw. I am disgusted with my speech and doubt whether I will speak it after all. Thank God for health and strength.

[October] 25th Wednesday. 2 recitations on mathematics. Spent this morning studying mathematics. This noon the fall races between class crews came off. The first race was between class crews of 78 and 80, in which '78 was easy winner. The second race was between class crews of 77 and '79, in which 79 was the winner. '77 steered miserably all the way running into the bank several times. I ran some way with the crews. Took dinner about two o'clock. Tomorrow races come off between 78 and 79 and between 77 and 80. The race between 78 and 79 will be well worth seeing I expect. These bumping races are quite exciting. This evening read Horace and rewrote my speech. I am disgusted with it. Thank God for health and strength.

[October] 26th Thursday. Recitations on Latin and one lecture on natural history. Spent this morning studying. At twelve o'clock went down to the canal to see boat race between 78 and 79. 79 was defeated after a very pretty race. Katzenbach rowed over the course alone for single scull-race-cup. Spent this afternoon learning my speech. After chapel sat up in Woods' room for some time. This evening went over to Hall for a little while, went down to the gym to see the ceremony of presentation of cup to 78. Spent this evening studying my speech and finished memorizing it pretty thoroughly. Large Republican meeting tonight. Thank God for health and strength.

[October] 27th Friday. Recitations on Greek history[,] Demosthenes De Corona and Horace. Spent most of this morning and afternoon studying for recitation besides learning some of my speech. Several chapel disorder marks incurred by our class this afternoon in chapel caused by some freshmen bringing canes into chapel before the time allowed by our late proclamation. After chapel our fellows went for the freshmen and took their canes away from them amidst much fighting among all the classes. There was a general row in which we all joined.[1] Spent this evening in Whig Hall. I generally come away from Hall discouraged since I there hear men of whose abilities I have a very poor opinion make fine efforts. I have come to the conclusion that my friends have no doubt come to long ago and that is that my mind is a very ordinary one indeed. I am nothing as far as intellect goes. But I can plod and work. Thank God for health and strength.

[1] The "general row" was not a proper part of the "cane spree," as that indigenous species of underclass rivalry was evolving in the Princeton of WW's day. College men in that day generally carried canes. The sophomores' effort to keep freshmen from carrying canes arose in the 1860's at Princeton and for some years manifested itself as a sort of general mayhem. In 1869 sophomores issued the first proclamation forbidding freshmen to carry canes before a fixed date. Defiance produced combat, both individual and general. In 1871 individual champions were chosen, matched in weight and skill, and coached by upperclassmen in what developed into an intricate kind of wrestling. One match in 1873 lasted two hours. Throughout the '70's, despite efforts to confine the rivalry to individual matches, the general rushes persisted.

The incidents to which WW refers followed by a month the first formal individual matches, and by two weeks the campus posting of a proclamation by freshmen, an unheard-of insolence. They drew from *The Princetonian* the question whether more than one sophomore "has a *right* to attack a Freshman who has the pluck or 'cheek' . . . to carry a cane before the issuing of the Soph. Proclamation." The paper protested against upperclassmen engaging "promiscuously . . . in the rushes." In WW's freshman autumn the sophomores took away seventy canes to twenty taken by his class. WW's diary for Sept. 19, 1876, records that two of the three formal matches were won by WW's sophomore classmates, one by a freshman. A century after the first cane sprees, the custom had degenerated into an amicable underclass beer-party.

See Parke H. Davis, "The History of the Cane-Spree," pp. 348-51. Also *The Princetonian* for Oct. 19, 1876, p. 11; Nov. 2, 1876, p. 1; June 13, 1878, pp. 41-42. WW, the editors believe, wrote none of these. The accounts of cane sprees in *A History of the Class of '79*, pp. 10, 27, offer details of the proclamations, confirm WW's diary entries, and make, of course, larger claims of '79 victories than does the article just cited.

[October] 28th Saturday. Recitation on French this morning. Spent this afternoon studying my speech and loafing in Woods room. Spent this evening studying my speech and read[ing] Addison and Irving[']s works. I find Irving very interesting indeed. A lazy and poorly spent day. Thank God for health and strength.

[October] 29th Sabbath. Rose late. In chapel this morning I heard a very interesting discourse from a missionary from India.[1] He discussed and explained very fully the Hindu system of theology or rather philosophy and as anyone who describes a system of philosophy can always claim my attention[,] I was a very earnest listener this morning. I have seldom been so much interested in any missionary discourse. Spent most of the afternoon reading. This evening I led the class prayer meeting reading a passage and making a few remarks. We had quite an interesting meeting. After prayer meeting went to Second Church (1 Church) [sic] and heard a most eloquent sermon from a Canadian minister.[2] His theme was the suffering of Christ. I never heard a man who had such a wonderful command of words as this one—his flow of appropriate beautiful and picturesque words was simply overwhelming almost making my head swim. This has been a most interesting day to me. Thank God for health and strength.

[1] The Rev. Samuel H. Kellogg, Presbyterian missionary at Allahabad Mission, India.
[2] The Rev. William Stephenson, D.D., who preached in the First Presbyterian Church, not the Second.

[October] 30th Monday. Recitations on Greek Testament and Demosthenes De Corona. Spent this morning studying. Spent this noon walking over the new building and exercising at the gym. Spent this afternoon copying notes on mathematics. This evening I went to Hall and read for a while after class prayer meeting then came to my room and spent the rest of the evening over Washington Irving's Sketch Book which I find a most pleasing companion. His style is flowing and pleasant. His thoughts though clothed in the most popular form are sometimes profound. A quiet pleasant day. Thank God for health and strength.

[October] 31st Tuesday. Recitations on French[,] English and mathematics. Spent the morning studying. Spent the noon loafing around going to Hall etc. Got Shakespeare's King Lear from Hall. I think of writing a criticism or rather essay on this grand production though I hardly feel equal to so great a task. As others have surpassed themselves in criticisms of this play I may be inspired in like manner. I certainly do not lack enthusiasm. King [Lear] is Shakespeare's greatest production. Spent the afternoon studying mathematics. Wrote a letter to dear mother and sent it off. Spent the evening up in Woods room and wandered around with him in the lovely moonlight. Had a talk on politics with Slemmons, the Republican candidate for president in college elections. I find him a very sensible fellow indeed although I cannot approve of his political views. I begin to be pretty sure of Tilden's election. Thank God for health and strength.

[November] 1st Wednesday. Two recitations on mathematics. Spent this morning studying mathematics. This noon I caught ball with Woods and Prentiss of our class. Spent this afternoon studying mathematics and reading King Lear—or rather introduction to it by Hudson.[1] Spent this evening reading Horace['s] epistles and King Lear. I think that I can say a few words upon this play if I can follow out the train of thought that has suggested itself to me. There are many things to be said on so grand a subject. Wednesdays are always tiresome days to me because they are *mathematics* days. Thank God for health and strength.

[1] Henry N. Hudson, ed. of the works of Shakespeare (1851-56) and author of *Lectures on Shakespeare*, 2nd ed. (New York, 1848).

[November] 2nd Thursday. Two recitations on Latin and lecture on natural history. Spent this morning studying Latin. Spent the afternoon in Hall. Read an excellent article in the North American Review on the "Southern Question."[1] It is an ably written piece. This noon watched match game [of] football between classes 78 and '80—three straight goals for '78. Loafed all evening most of the time up in Woods room. I spoke my piece. I felt so restless this evening that I could do no work of any kind. Thank God for health and strength.

[1] William Henry Trescot, "The Southern Question," *North American Review*, cxxiii (Oct. 1876), 249-80.

[November] 3rd Friday. Recitations on Greek history[,] Demosthenes De Corona and Horace. At noon went to gym and exercised for some time. After chapel and at 7½ o'clock went to Hall [;] enjoyed two very pleasant sessions. Thank God for health and strength.

From Joseph Ruggles Wilson

My darling son—   Wilmington [N. C.] Nov. 3   76
    I am goose enough to send you the money you order!
    Annie leaves this evening for Columbia. I am glad on yr. dear Mother's account, who, without acknowledging it, is quite worn out. The two babes[1] are in statu quo ab initio—except that the latest arrival is steadily growing, as is evinced in several ways especially

by his increasing ability to lift his voice high and higher when attacked by that angel—from below—the Colic!

I am greatly pleased with yr letters, dear Thomas. Please, though, tell us more about yr studies, companions, recreations [?]. May God's love abound in yr. heart.   J. R. Wilson

ALS (WP, DLC).

  [1] J. Wilson Howe and a recent arrival, George, born Oct. 3, 1876.

From Wilson's Shorthand Diary

[November] 4th Saturday. Spent the morning rather idly. At eleven o'clock I went to chapel to hear the first divisions of the "Chapel Stage" and there heard some very indifferent speeches.[1] Some of the speeches were worth notice but the majority were very ordinary. Tommy McKoy[2] made a fine speech on Robert E. Lee in which I followed him very closely of course because Lee is one of my favorites. He was a noble man and most able general. In the afternoon rode out to Lawrenceville to see the freshmen play football with the boys of the fine school there. '80 was victorious winning three goals to their *two*. Spent the evening trying to write an essay but could make no progress. Thank God for health and strength.

  [1] "Chapel Stage" was an oratorical exercise, the participants in which were members of the senior class divided into sections, one for each Saturday morning.
  [2] Thomas H. McKoy, '77, of Clinton, N. C.

[November] 5th Sabbath. Got up rather late this morning as there is now no morning chapel. Went to chapel at eleven o'clock and heard a dull sermon from *Harris*. He is an exceptionally dull preacher however. Spent this afternoon reading the North Carolina Presbyterian. Went to chapel at five o'clock and heard Jim give a short biographical sketch of the late Dr. Jacobus.[1] This evening went to class prayer meeting and there spent very profitable half an hour. After prayer meeting went to First Church and there heard one of the strangest efforts at preaching that it has ever been my fortune to listen to. The preacher[2] at the end of the sermon described a book of his own and its contents and advised us to read it, told us which of its various parts he considered the best etc. and altogether made a fool of himself. The discourse was *highly* entertaining toward the close however. Thank God for health and strength.

  [1] The Rev. Melancthon W. Jacobus, D.D., class of 1834; Professor, Allegheny Seminary, 1851-76; Moderator, General Assembly (Old School), 1869. He had died on Oct. 28, 1876.

2 The preacher was the Rev. Matthew R. Miller, D.D., pastor of Olivet Presbyterian Church, Louisville, Ky.; his subject, "The Permanent and Immutable in the Jews' Religion."

[November] 6th Monday. Recitations on Greek Testament and Demosthenes Corona. Spent this morning and afternoon studying Demosthenes and writing a little of my essay. I have chosen as my subject "The Working Class of the Day [and] Personal Happiness"[1] as the most suggestive of the five subjects which Professor Hunt gives for consideration. He certainly has a talent for choosing poor subjects. I think that I can make something out of this subject however by a little stretching. I must try to get time enough some time soon to commence an essay on Shakespeare's King Lear. I think that I will write one on this subject for the next "Lit." I wonder if one from my pen would stand any chance of getting a prize? I am afraid not. After Chapel we had our college voting[.] I have not yet learned the result but it is pretty certain that the Republicans have the majority in this election. This evening there was a large fire around the cannon and speeches from Republican and Democratic orators. I stayed and listened to some of the speeches but as the speakers were all very stupid I soon tired and left to study a little French and read some before going to bed. Read a little in Dante's Inferno. Tomorrow the nation makes its choice between Samuel J. Tilden and R. B. Hayes—I most sincerely hope that it will be sensible enough to elect Tilden as I think that the salvation of the country from frauds and the reviving of trade depends upon his election. We will not know the results positively for some days. Many a bet will be gained and lost on this election. The pools sold in New York today $175 for Tilden for the State of New York and $100 for Hayes and at some pools $200 for Tilden to $100 for Hayes. The election depends almost entirely upon New York's vote and her thirty-five electoral votes will be almost certain to give victory to the side on which they are cast. The selling of pools at 2 to one looks encouraging as pools selling in this way seldom lie. Thank God for health and strength.

1 Not found.

[November] 7th Tuesday. Election day. Recitations on French, English and mathematics. Spent this morning between recitations reading a little in Dante's Inferno and thus passed the time very pleasantly. Spent this afternoon between dinner and recitations studying mathematics. Went up to Woods' room to see if he had done an example which I was unable to obtain. This noon I exercised at the gym. After chapel as it was raining and walking unpleasant I came to my room and wrote letter to dear father. How I love the dear ones at home! Walked to the post office and mailed my letter. Spent all this evening reading Dante's Inferno and finished about half of it only as I am a very slow reader. I have been reading Longfellow's translation of this great work. I am unable to pronounce as to the merits of the translation as I am unacquainted with the original. As to the merits of the work I have nothing to say as my commendations would add little to Dante's most deserved praise—I will only say that I have seldom been so much impressed as I have been by this masterly production. I wonder how elections have gone today! I heard a rumor this evening that New York's had gone for Tilden by a majority of 75,-000[.] If this be so the state's certain[ly] *his* and he is doubtless our next president. I only hope that this report is true! A great deal depends upon the choice which the nation has this day made. Thank God for health and strength.

[November] 8th Wednesday. Two recitations on mathematics. Spent most of the day studying mathematics. Last evening and all day today the returns have come in heavy for Tilden. From today's outlook we might judge that Tilden was elected. I sincerely hope that it may be so. This evening we Democrats had a large bonfire around the cannon on the campus and fine speeches in honor of Tilden's supposed election. The bonfire and jollification was appointed to take place at 7½ o'clock but about that time reports arrived that Hayes had carried the Union by a majority of four votes in the electoral college. This report made the Republicans jubilant and they immediately got up a procession and tried in every way to demoralize us—jeering at our fire etc. But later in the evening most encouraging reports were received and with confidence once more restored we proceeded with our Democratic demonstration. Our bonfire was a perfect success and the speeches from Wardlaw, Williamson, Johns[1] and other Democratic speakers were some of the best that it has been my good fortune to hear. Wardlaw certainly excels in speaking. In consequence of the excitement which was something overwhelming I did no studying in the evening and went to bed at about 11 o'clock tired out with shouting and excitement. Thank God for health and strength.

[1] John B. Wardlaw, '77 and George S. Johns, '80, hitherto unidentified. H. Godwin, in his *History of the Class of '79*, pp. 31-33, recalls the procession of students to the houses of faculty members and a pro-Republican speech by Professor Cameron from an upper window, not reverently received. WW's silence on this part of the festivities suggests that he did not listen to the Republicans.

From Janet Woodrow Wilson

My darling Boy,   Wilmington N. C. Nov. 8th '76.

I have no letter-paper this morning—but you will not object to fools-cap I am sure.

Well—the election is over—but it will be some time, I suppose before we are certain of the result. This morning, the impression seems to be that we have probably carried the day—both as to Governor and President. That is too good to be true, I think. If I did not know what a prudent good boy you are, dear, I would be anxious about you during these days of excitement. It is a source of great comfort that you are able to be so prudent & forbearing in your intercourse with those infatuated people who are your associates in college. You can well afford to be indulgent in your treatment of their offensive sayings if we are really victorious— and if not—why you cannot afford to put yourself upon a level with them—in their ignorance and fanaticism. . . . Your loving Mother

ALS (WP, DLC)

From Wilson's Shorthand Diary

[November] 9th Thursday. A day of suspense in politics. In spite of the encouraging reports of last night reports today give Hayes a much better chance than he was supposed to have before. All day reports both private and official came in from parts of the state and country now saying that Hayes had certainly carried the country and now that Tilden was without doubt elected. I am in doubt as to which I shall believe. I am of course inclined to believe the Democratic reports before the Republican. Recitations on Horace and lecture on natural history. Spent the evening loafing around unexcited and listless near unable to settle down to anything. Thank God for continued health and strength.

[November] 10th Friday. Still another day of the most harrowing suspense about the size of the election. Conflicting reports pour in from all parts of the country. This evening['s] papers have given Tilden 184 out of a necessary 185 electoral votes and make him pretty sure of Florida which will give him 188 votes in the electoral college. The election is close beyond all precedent. Recitations in Greek history[,] Demosthenes De Corona and Horace. Did little reading today except a little in Shakespeare's King Lear. Oh for some decision one way or another in the election! This suspense is almost insupportable when I feel all the time that so much is at stake—the salvation of the country depends upon the success of the Democratic cause. The popular majority for Tilden overwhelming but the electoral vote very close. Surely this shows some wanting of good working in our institutions! Spent this evening most pleasantly in Whig Hall and in forgetful[ness] of the election returns and other disturbing questions. Thank God for health and strength.

[November] 11th Saturday. Another day of tiresome suspense as to the election. Recitation on French—first lesson in French history. Spent this morning studying French and looking over the morning papers. News encouraging. At 11 o'clock went to Chapel Stage and heard some pretty good speeches though some of them were very ordinary while still others were miserable. This afternoon I wrote an essay for Hunt for four hours steadily. In this time wrote and copied a five page essay on the "Characteristics of a Popular Writer."[1] I have seldom written an essay with so much ease and pleasure to myself. Professor Hunt limits to six pages— I wrote 5-¼. The evening papers give the State of South Carolina to Tilden from final returns and probably the State of Florida also. The Republicans begin "to weaken" and are all looking rather blue this evening. Tilden is in all probability elected though the election is very close indeed and on account of the frauds claimed it is possible that the decision of the matter will lie with Congress. This will be well for us as the Democrats will probably have a majority in the House of Representatives. Tilden's popular majority is about one-fourth of a million though he lacks one electoral vote. Spent most of this evening up in Springs" room— Spring[s] is from South Carolina[,] a very excellent and interesting young man and in '77. Read my essay to Woods which was a very egotistical thing to do. Thank God for health and strength.

1 Not found.
2 Richard A. Springs, Jr., '77.

[November] 12th Sabbath. Got up this morning about 9 o'clock. After breakfast took a walk by myself out to the prep school and back and then went to chapel. Spent this afternoon reading writing etc. Went up to Jack Stewart's room for about half an hour before afternoon chapel. After supper wrote a letter to my old friend Douglas McKay. Went to class prayer meeting. Jim was at the class prayer meeting and made us a few very appropriate remarks about personal responsibility which was the subject for this evening's meeting. After prayer meeting Woods came up to my room and stayed for a little while. Spent this evening rather listlessly as I did not feel in humor to read and had nothing else to do. What a grand thing it is to have a day of rest—a day free from all care and anxiety about recitations and the other cares of college life a day to oneself. This evening I have been trying to think of a subject for a speech. When one tries to think of a subject he is impressed with the fewness of good subjects. Thank God for health and strength.

[November] 13th Monday. Recitations on Greek Testament and Demosthenes De Corona. Spent this morning studying. At noon caught ball with Woods. This afternoon studied Greek for about ¼ of an hour[,] read some in the Lit[,] and wrote up notes on mathematics. The evening papers give the election to Tilden and almost all the Republicans are beginning to acknowledge that the Democrats have won the day. In the case of an election such as we have just had one realizes how large a country America is by the slow way in which returns come in. Hurrah for Tilden! This evening wrote French exercise and spent the rest of the evening trying to write speech. The effort was about as good as that of drawing an eyetooth. The thoughts just absolutely refuse to come. The subject I have settled upon is The Union.[1] I think that I can make something out of this. The subject is certainly a fruitful one. I have accomplished very little. Thank God for health and strength.

1 Printed at Nov. 15, 1876.

[November] 14th Tuesday. Recitations on French[,] English and mathematics. Spent the morning studying French and English. At noon loafed around generally. Spent the afternoon studying mathematics. After chapel copied up notes on mathematics for a few minutes, caught ball with Chapman etc. Spent the evening in the Hall. In senior prize speaking Wardlaw won the first prize and Richardson second. The decision was most just in my opinion. A very pleasant evening. Thank God for health and strength.

[November] 15th Wednesday. Two recitations on mathematics. Spent this morning studying mathematics. This noon spent hour at the gym exercising. Spent this afternoon studying mathematics and copying up notes on mathematics. This morning Vanuxem came over and studied with me: this afternoon I went over and studied with him. Spent the time between afternoon chapel and supper writing up extracts in my Index Rerum. This evening studied my lesson in Horace for tomorrow and then spent the rest of the evening writing my speech on The Union. I find writing very easy this evening. I finished my speech and am tolerably well pleased. I think that I can make some impression with it. I am afraid that I have used almost too many quotations from American statesman but altogether I think the speech will do. Thank God for health and strength.

Draft of a Speech

The Union   Nov. [15,] 1876

I am aware—that in treating this subject I am treading upon oft-trodden ground—ground often trodden by more worthy feet than mine. But I choose this hackneyed subject firmly as [blank] not thinking that I can throw any new light upon such a subject, but wishing to impress some important conclusions which follow from its consideration—conclusions which we are at present very prone to overlook.

No American can think of the Union and the principles upon which it is founded without a flush of pride and thrill of patriotism. We may not invent her virtues nor parade one's native land throwing off proud England's galling yoke.

The Constitution, the main-spring of the Union, has been the love and theme of our greatest statesmen in their youth, their guide and word in their old age. The Constitution founded by our fathers upon the sound principles of government, developed from the long experience of the mother country, and the lessons taught by the follies and wisdom of all Europe to save and kindle within the breasts of America's most honored sons, an enthusiasm which has ever struggled for utterance.

Hear noble Webster exclaim: "Here standing on the platform of the general Constitution—a platform broad enough and firm enough to uphold every interest of the whole country—I shall be found." "I came into public life in the service of the United States. On that broad altar my earliest and all my public vows have been made. I propose to serve no other master. So far as depends on any agency of mine they shall continue *united* States; united in interest and in affection; united in everything with regard to which the Constitution has decreed their union; united in war for the common defense, the common renown, the common glory; united, compacted, knit firmly together in peace for the common prosperity and happiness of ourselves and our children."[1]

The liberty which is the fundamental principle of that Union which has ever since its inception been the wonder and admiration of the civilized world, [is] preserved only by perfect accord between the states. When once the states are divided by sectional hatred, when once they begin to act separately and independently and thus clash with the common interest, when once they attempt to act without mutual love and trust to sanction and add power to all their acts, the Union trembles to its very foundations.

He alone manifests true patriotism who labors to smooth over all dissensions, to inspire sympathy and confidence between all parts of the country, and to instill into the minds of the people those principles which will lead them to act in their already truly grand capacity of a united brotherhood.

The fanatical partisans who enrage the people by their frantic wavings of the bloody shirt under the specious pretence of zeal for the Constitution by that very act prove themselves the Constitution's worst enemies. It was no doubt the fiendish acts of such men as these that led Calhoun to exclaim: "The only certain evidence of devotion to the Constitution is to abstain on the one hand from violating it and to repel on the other all attempts to violate it; it is only by faithful performance of these high duties that the Constitution can be preserved and with it the Union."[2]

Webster said "If we maintain those institutions of government and that political union—exceeding all praise as it exceeds all former examples of political associations—we may be sure of one thing that while our country furnishes materials for a thousand masters of historic art it will afford no topic for a Gibbon. It will have no decline and fall. It will go on prospering and to prosper."[3]

Jackson declared that "Without union our liberty and independence would never have been achieved; without union they can never be maintained. The loss of the liberty of all good government, peace, plenty and happiness must inevitably follow a dissolution of the Union. In supporting it, therefore, we must support everything that is dear to free men and the philanthropist."[4]

Having seen then the vital importance of that union which filled the great heart of Webster[,] called forth the impassioned words of Clay, won the earnest support of Carolina's favorite son[,] Calhoun[,] entreated the approval of [* *] and claimed the cooperation of Jackson we should be as those upon whom the fate of the Union in great measure depends, guard against the many and formidable evils which threaten it with dissolution.

Let us see, therefore, what the chief of these evils are. The Union is endangered by the traitors who have crept into favor in certain parts of the country by the miserable ambition of petty politicians and above all by the sad lack of great men to give direct counsels. Where shall we look for the explanation of this dearth of great minds[,] this blinding of guiding genius? The answer to this question is contained in the reply to another.

What caused the grand succession of noble men who directed our councils during the eventful years that elapsed between 1776 and 1855? They were brought forth by gradual and natural crises and the common love of country and warmth of patriotism which was the one great characteristic of that age.

A great political crisis is now present and the only thing our country requires to regain former prestige as a nation of mental and political giants is that in one mighty occasion have it close the lesions of all parts of the country to which the late war came so near being fatal.

Let us each one do everything in his power to promote that union of hearts for which the Southern people are so eager if their Northern brethren will only meet them half way, and North and South will soon be seen marching hand in hand in their great progress with the world and still grander make it "Liberty and union, now and forever, one and inseparable."

Transcript of WWsh in notebook described at April 1, 1875.
  1 From Webster's second speech on the Sub-Treasury in the Senate, March 12, 1838. Cf. *Writings and Speeches of Daniel Webster*, National Edn. (18 vols., Boston, 1903), VIII, 236-37.
  2 From Calhoun's speech in the Senate, March 4, 1850. Cf. *Works of John C. Calhoun*, R. K. Cralle, ed. (6 vols., New York, 1883), IV, 559-60.
  3 From Webster's speech "The Dignity and Importance of History," before the New York Historical Society, Feb. 3, 1852. Cf. *Writings and Speeches of Daniel Webster*, National Edn., XIII, 493.
  4 From Jackson's Second Inaugural, March 3, 1833. Cf. *A Compilation of the Messages and Papers of the Presidents*, 1789-1907, James D. Richardson, ed. (10 vols., Washington, 1908), III, 4.

From Janet Woodrow Wilson

My darling Son,   Wilmington N. C., Nov. 15th. [1876]
    I have been thinking more than usual, even, about you the last few days. The fear that you may be provoked beyond endurance, during these anxious days, by those Radical companions of yours, has crept into my heart. I know your self-control—or I would be miserable—but it is so hard to bear their ignorant thrusts quietly— and yet that is the only thing to be done—for ones own self respects sake. I trust you have been brave enough to disregard their insolence. Tommy dear dont talk about knocking any body down— no matter what they do or say—or rather dont *think* of doing such a thing. Such people are beneath your notice. Besides they dont mean anything personal—strange as it may seem.

Everything is quiet here—there is a feeling of intense anxiety as to the result of the election. No one doubts as to the fact that Tilden has been elected—but the anxiety is as to what the Government intends doing in the matter—with regard to those states completely in their power. There is no use talking about it though—we must wait patiently. . . .

God bless you my darling. Papa & Josie join me in fondest love to you.   Your own Mother.

ALS (WP, DLC) with WWhw notation on env.: "Ans 11/21/76."

From Wilson's Shorthand Diary

[November] 16th Thursday. Recitations on Horace and lecture on natural history. Spent the morning studying Latin. Was much bored by the natural history lecture. At noon I exercised at the gym. Spent the afternoon studying and reading. In the evening went to the Second Church to hear the first performance of the students lecture course. It was a reading from Mr. Vandenhoff.[1] He reads remarkably well. His performance was too short by half. After the reading spent the rest of the evening until about 11 o'clock up in Woods room. Came to my room and read over the Greek history. Thank God for health and strength.

1 George Vandenhoff, English actor, who gave a series of readings under the auspices of the Students' Lecture Association.

[November] 17th Friday. Recitations on Greek history[,] Demosthenes De Corona and Horace. Spent the morning studying. Nothing of much interest today. Spent a very pleasant evening in Hall. Thank God for health and strength.

[November] 18th Saturday. Spent the early part of the morning studying French. In French I was called up and made Prof. (Kargé) very mad indeed by laughing. He reproved me so severely for so doing that I refused to read any further which made him still more provoked. Went to Chapel Stage and heard several fine speeches. Between every third speech we had a selection from the college quartet. I enjoyed the singing much. Spent this afternoon studying my speech and exercising at the gym. Spent this evening finishing Dante's Inferno. A remarkable production[.] I have enjoyed it very much. Thank God for health and strength.

[November] 19th Sabbath. Rose late. Went to chapel and heard an excellent sermon from Dr. Murray on the text "Abhor that *which is evil.*" Spent the afternoon reading the North Carolina Presbyterian and taking a short nap. Went to afternoon chapel. Went to class prayer meeting in the evening. After doing a few trifling things went to bed. Thank God for health and strength.

[November] 20th Monday. A miserable stormy day. Recitations on Greek Testament, Demosthenes De Corona. Spent the morning studying and read some of Irving's delightful sketches from his "Sketchbook." At noon went to college library and took out Milton's *Paradise Lost* and "Lectures on Shakespeare" by H. N. Hudson. Studied a little in the afternoon on Demosthenes De Corona and spent the rest of the time before afternoon recitation in company with Irving and King Lear. Spent the evening reading King Lear. I can never tire of admiring Lear's sublime anguish; I can conceive of nothing more grand. Very pleasant evening. *"Will"* can never be surpassed either in tragedy or in comedy. Thank God for health and strength.

[November] 21st Tuesday. Recitations on French[,] English and mathematics. Spent this morning studying and talking with Woods. This noon I exercised at the gym. Spent this afternoon studying mathematics and reading King Lear. After chapel came to my room and wrote a letter to dear father. Spent this evening studying King Lear. I am now primed and ready to go off in the form of an essay on this magnificent play. Thank God for health and strength.

[November] 22nd Wednesday. Spent the morning studying mathematics and reading New York Herald. At noon I exercised at the gym. Spent the afternoon studying mathematics. After afternoon chapel took a walk with Woods. Spent the evening studying Horace and reading the New York Herald. Very interesting article in it on the constitutional questions involved in the decision of the presidential election. Thank God for health and strength.

[November] 23rd Thursday. Recitations on Horace and lecture on natural history. Spent this morning studying natural history. During the afternoon studied my Horace. Spent the noon hour attending to various business. Spent this evening reading Greek history and trying to make a choice of a subject for a speech which I will soon be under the necessity of writing. I find it hard to decide. I think something of writing on the subject

"Resolution and Independence."[1] I could very likely make something out of this. Thank God for health and strength. Discontinued for want of time to do it *Justice*.[2]

[1] Not found, if, indeed, it was ever written.
[2] It is impossible to tell when WW added this sentence, which is in WWhw. In any event, he discontinued his diary on this date and resumed it on March 20, 1877.

From Douglas McKay

Dear Tom   Columbia S C Nov 23/76
. . . During the past two months we have been in the midst of such intense political excitement that I have been entirely unfitted for anything except discussing the "Situation". Well Tom in the meantime you have not forgotten me, and I can sincerely say, I am glad of it. We have just finished one of the most active political campaigns ever entered into, by the people of this State, and I do hope and trust, that a better state of affairs will crown our efforts. I say "our efforts" for although I cast my maiden vote for Tilden & Hampton, I do not think I ever had such deep solicitude for the success of any cause, as I had for the success of our Democratic State Ticket. Wade Hampton is a man well calculated to arouse the dormant energies and enthusiasm of our people, for besides his unsullied war record, which endeared him very much to the older heads, he is a man, of whom it can truly be said, as of Bayard, "without fear and without reproach". . . .

I will not attempt to describe the enthusiasm which was displayed throughout the entire State, suffice it to say, that such demonstrations have never been known here before within the memory of the oldest inhabitant, and when I see the efforts that are being made to defraud us out of what we have gained, and gained honestly, it makes my blood boil, and causes me to think that so far as an honest and impartial administration of the laws is concerned, our great American Republic is a failure. And when I see so plainly that there is an endeavor to make the will of the people subservient to the wishes of a few unblushing scoundrels, such as some of those in power at Washington, I am the more persuaded that while the government of the Republic is beautiful in theory, its practical application fails entirely. I wish I had you here that I might tell you of some of the disgraceful frauds that have been enacted, and of some *that will be enacted*. They are enough to cause a blush of shame to come to the face of any American citizen, and cause us to look with scrupulous care, even among our judiciary, for an honest man. But I cannot go into detail, as these pages will not admit it. Suffice it to say, that the *entire* Democratic Ticket has been *fairly elected*, but I am convinced, that while we may get Hampton and a part of the State Ticket, that the Electoral vote will be counted for Hayes. The Democrats are very vigilant, and if things do turn out as we suspect they will, the corruption will most likely be made manifest, and we will fight them to "the last ditch." I tell you what it is Tom, I do not think that the people of this country will allow themselves to be cheated out of this Presidential Election, by such Returning Boards as those of South Carolina, or Louisiana, and I hardly think the present Administration will be willing to shoulder the infamy of electing their candidate by fraud. . . .

You speak of your College mates being divided into two parties, Republican & Democrat, and of your nearly getting into scrapes "with some of the fanatics." I can readily understand the heated discussions which are likely to ensue between some of the Southern & Northern boys, as there are many among the northern people who are bitterly prejudiced and intolerant, when the question of the Southerner and negro are involved. . . .

I am told that your old homestead here has been bought by Mr Gillspie. I am sorry that this is so, for while Mr G is a perfect gentleman and much respected here, I should rather have it so, that I might occasionally call there and be welcomed by the genial smile of your good father & spend an hour or two in pleasant conversation with you. . . .

Yours Sincerely   D. McKay

ALS (WP, DLC) with WWhw notation on env · "Ans."

From Janet Woodrow Wilson

My darling Boy—   Wilmington, N. C. Dec 1st [1876]
    . . . We received your most welcome letter this morning, darling, & I must confess I am greatly disappointed and distressed by the news with reference to your vacation. I have allowed myself to think that you would almost certainly come home—and have been laying all my plans with reference to your coming. I dont see how I can wait till Spring to see you. But I must not be less brave than my precious son. What are your reasons for not wishing to go to Baltimore, dear? Is it merely that you dont care to go—or is it something about *clothes*? Please

tell me all about it in your next. I am glad you enjoy the Libraries so much—that you are making such good use of them. You can never be unhappy or lonely, for long, with such resources at hand. Did your father ever tell you that he is getting that "American Cyclopedia" *for you*? He told me so the other day, and I was glad, for I know how much you think of it. I will put the volumes in some safer place as soon as I am strong enough. I am anxious that you should gradually collect a very *choice* Library. I believe most young men make the mistake of getting a number of books all at once, before they well know what they will need or enjoy, just that they may feel that they have a Library. And if they prove to be sure enough students, they regret having thrown away the money that they could spend to so much better advantage after a little while.

We are still in suspense as to political matters, but we have very little hope of any satisfactory settlement.[1] It is wonderful to see how quiet the people are about it. I am glad you have not allowed yourself to be provoked unduly—and indeed it is not worth while. After all there is a great deal about the Southern people that I dont like—only I like them decidedly better than I do the Northern. Hampton has behaved nobly, and I hope he may yet get the better of that rascal Chamberlaine.[2] But the only thing we can do, in any case, is to keep quiet & submit. The Northern people must fight it out among themselves this time, and I am thankful that it is so. Dont think of knocking anybody down, dear boy—no matter what they say. We must remember that they are ignorant—and I confess I have met with equal ignorance at the South with regard to the Yankees. I find the only way for me is to think as little as possible about politics, for there is nothing we can do. . . .

God bless you my darling boy. Papa & Josie join me in fondest love to you—Your own Mother.

You dont know how much comfort I take in the assurance of your good health. Take care of it I beg of you.

ALS (WP, DLC).
    [1] i.e. in the disputed returns for Tilden and Hayes.
    [2] Governor Daniel H. Chamberlain of South Carolina, who claimed victory over Wade Hampton in the gubernatorial election of 1876.

A Religious Essay   [Dec. 20, 1876]

Christian Progress

Addison, in his thoughtful essay on the immateriality of the soul, has made use of this beautiful figure: "The soul considered with its Creator, is like one of those mathematical lines that may draw nearer to another to all eternity without a possibility of touching it: and can there be a thought so transporting as to consider ourselves in these perpetual approaches to Him, who is not only the standard of perfection but of happiness." In this essay, which forms one of the most pleasing numbers of the *Spectator*, this genial writer seems to view the soul in its relations to its creator, rather in a philosophical light than in the light of revelation, and in its more specially religious bearings. He takes a pleasing glance at the possibilities and noble resources of the soul, and views it as something which was meant for, and is capable of almost infinite development in power and virtue. To a thoughtful reader, however, he suggests many a thought pregnant with deep meaning. He suggests that approximation to the divine character which is possible to every Christian who moulds his life after the perfect pattern with which our Lord has furnished us. But he does not seem to realize the difficulty which attends soul-progress. Turning to our Bibles we can study this subject by the aid of the light of inspired teachings. The Bible everywhere represents the Christian life as a progress,— a progress of the soul. But, although it always speaks of the Christian's journey as a pleasant one, since it is the only road in which true happiness can be found, it never describes it as a path strewn with flowers, but rather as one attended with and obstructed by many difficulties. In order to advance, the Christian must needs strain every muscle. This strain, though necessary at all times, is not, of necessity irksome, as God's all-powerful arm is ever around us, and the darkness which surrounds us is seldom so dense as to shut out the radiance of the Almighty's loving smiles. We can conceive of no more constant or eager striver after perfection than the apostle Paul, and yet even he said: "Brethren, I count not myself to have apprehended: but this one thing I do, forgetting those things which are behind, and reaching unto those things which are before, I press toward the mark for the prize of the high calling of God in Christ Jesus." All through his epistles he expresses this same distrust of himself, and gives vent to fears, lest his carnal mind should gain the mastery. In one place he says: "But I keep under my body, and bring it into subjection: lest that by any means, when I have preached to others, I myself should be a castaway." If this mighty soul, whose chief and only aim was to "walk worthy of the high vocation wherewith he was called," was troubled by such fears as these, what should be the feeling of the listless, half-souled follower of Christ! As the followers of this mighty Prince of Light we are ever under the stern necessity of fighting for our own safety, as well as the general advance of Christian doctrine. He who pretends to fight under the great banner of Love, should rejoice that there is no armor for his back, that to retreat is death, and should thus go forward with an eagerness and will which no slight cause can turn from their object. Twiwood.

Printed in the Wilmington *North Carolina Presbyterian*, Dec. 20, 1876.

From Janet Woodrow Wilson

My precious Son, Wilmington—N. C.—Thursday [Dec. 21, 1876]
. . . Have you seen Mrs Pope?[1] I confess I have been hoping that you would still come home through that source[2]—and I will not give up all hope till the last. I was so sorry to hear that you were not to go to Brooklyn in case you did not get home—that you had not been able to *reserve your chance*. I cannot help hoping that your friend has not made other arrangements—and may renew his invitation. In that case would you have funds enough? Answer frankly, please, dear.

Your father is very blue this week. I don't think he will ever be quite happy here. I knew beforehand that he would not—and then, you know, he is always blue when I am laid aside. This together with the fact that he has not much chance of seeing you, is quite enough to account for his "blues." Josie is quite unwell with a cold, but is better today. The dear little fellow is improving very much every way. . . .

We received your Postal this morning—and will look anxiously for your promised letter. I am rejoiced to hear that you are well—and very glad that your examinations are now over. When are you going to deliver your speech dear? You have said nothing about it for a long time. . . .

God bless you & make you happy. Your father & little brother send fondest love to you. Your own Mother.

ALS (WP, DLC).
[1] Mrs. A. Pope, wife of the general freight and passenger agent of the Wilmington and Weldon, Wilmington, Columbia, and Augusta, and Atlantic Coast Line Railroads. She had apparently been in Princeton visiting her son, Paul.
[2] That is, by a railroad pass obtained through Pope.

From Hiram Woods, Jr.

Dear Tommy,   Baltimore, Dec. 21, 1876.

. . . And now, although you are, no doubt, deep in Hazlett or some other fellow, I want to seize you from the danger of drinking too deeply of the "Piraean Springs," and bring you down to spending at least a part of your vacation like other mortals. To do this it will be necessary to get you out of Princeton. And so I now write to invite you to leave Princeton next Tuesday, Wednesday or any day best suited to yourself, come to Baltimore, and spend the rest of the vacation with me. . . .

Sincerely Yours,   Hiram Woods, Jr.

ALS (WP, DLC) with faint WWsh notes on env.

From Janet Woodrow Wilson

Wilmington, N. C. Saturday [Dec. 30, 1876]

My darling Tommy—

Your father thinks I had better send your ticket on to you at once—while you are still in Baltimore—so that you can arrange it in person before leaving. Mrs. Pope assured me that it would answer for any time.

I hope you are having a very happy time, my darling—and that you will make the most of it. Have you enough money to take you back to Princeton? If not, please let us know by return mail. . . .

Josie sends unbounded love to you God bless you, my precious son—and keep you safe & well.

Yours lovingly   Mother

ALS (WP, DLC)

Classroom Notebook

[Jan. 9-March 28, 1877]

Inscribed (WWhw): "Thos. W. Wilson, '79."

Contains WWsh lecture notes, with WWhw headings, taken in Prof. Duffield's sophomore mathematics course (navigation, surveying, and spherical trigonometry), Jan. 9-March 28, 1877.

(WP, DLC). This is a notebook made by folding pages 12″ x 9⅜″, making pages 6″ x 9⅜″.

From Marion Wilson Kennedy

Cotton Plant, Arkansas, January 14th 1877.

My dearest brother:—

I fully intended to help you through Christmas with one, at least, of my interesting epistles, but somehow could not find the time. Then mother wrote that Mr. Pope had sent you a "free pass" again, and we were in hopes you would get it in time to spend a few days at home, at any rate. Did you get home at all? We have not heard whether you did or not. . . .

With much love—and hoping to hear very soon from you,

ALS (WP, DLC).   Your sister   Marion.

From Janet Woodrow Wilson

Wilmington [N. C.] Wednesday [Jan. 17, 1877]—

My darling Son,

I wish I had written you last Wednesday, as I should have done—but I *always* make that mistake—in my endeavor to avoid fretting over the absence of the dear absentee. I have made a point of being *very busy* ever since you left—that I might not be unhappy about you. It was such a relief to receive your telegram, telling of your safe arrival in Princeton. I dare not tell you how we missed you, darling, after you left. I want to tell you how bravely dear little Josie behaved that morning. As soon as you had gone, he burst into an uncontrollable fit of crying—but when I discovered a handkerchief that I thought you had left, and I wanted him to run after you with it—he made a desperate effort to control himself, and ran after you. When he came back he said, "Mama, I did not let brother see that I was crying, for I smiled when I caught up with him." The little pet did not want to distress you by showing his distress.

I am very anxious to hear from you dear boy—how you are after your journey—how your cold is—and how you found things in P—. Dont forget to tell us about your journey. And I want you particularly to tell me how soon your money should be sent to avoid annoyance to you. Please repeat what you told me—very particularly, and I will see that it is attended to.

I wont write more today. Josie is writing you. Everybody enquires particularly about you. There is no news that I can hear of. Josie & Papa join me in fondest love to you, my own precious boy.

Your own Mother

ALS (WP, DLC) with WWhw notation on env.: "Ans."

From Joseph Ruggles Wilson

My beloved boy—   Wilmington, [N. C.] Jan 24 77.
    I enclose you my check for $100.00—all that I can now spare.
Place it in the Treasurer's hands as you suggested.
    We are all well. Our gladness was great at receiving the dis-
patch that informed us of your safe arrival at P. Your spunk in
walking that 3 miles deserves my commendation. That is the
way: conquer difficulties, let *them* not conquer. . . .
    My oldest brother—William[1]—of Des Moines, Iowa, died about
ten days ago—aged 67. He was a thorough Christian according to
his lights—and his end was most peaceful. . . .
    We all send love in greater abundance than ever if possible.
                    Your aff. father & friend, Joseph R Wilson

ALS (WP, DLC) with WWhw notation on env.: "Ans."
[1] William Duane Wilson.

To the Editor[1]

[Jan. 25, 1877]
    Mr. Editor:—Another intercollegiate oratorical contest is over,[2]
and Princeton has again been defeated. For three successive years
our orators have gone up to New York and come back without a
prize. We may congratulate ourselves as much as we please on
our success in other contests connected with the association,
the fact remains that in that department for competition in which
the association was primarily formed, we, as a College, have
failed.
    Our representatives have been the best from among us. They
have been the recipients of our first hall medals, and have distinguished themselves on J. O. stage. And yet, in competition with
other colleges, they have not been victors. The inference is
obvious. Either we do not possess the material from which to
make good orators, or the facilities for the development of that
material are not at hand. The character of our institution and
our very numbers forbid us harboring the first alternative. The
second is evidently the fact. Indeed it needs not the argument
from repeated failure abroad to convince us. Our experience and
observation as students have long impressed us with the fact
that very little attention is paid to oratory in Princeton College.
A conscientious endeavor to make the most of what elocutionary
course the curriculum furnishes, has but resulted in the conviction that, as far as local culture is concerned, Princeton, in her

advantages to the student, stands considerably behind some of our inferior Colleges. A few declamations in Freshman year, and several original speeches scattered along through the upper years, constitute our entire facilities in this line. This would doubtless be a sufficient drill if the aim of the College was simply to turn out good writers and thinkers, and make oratory of no importance.

But by the very act of sending representatives to compete with other Colleges in the exercise of Ciceronian art, we assume to ourselves a right to be heard as orators, and imply facilities here which warrant us in expecting success. These facilities we do not possess, and therefore, our participation in the New York contest bears on its face of ignorant pretension, or at least, of an unbounded confidence in native-born oratory. It is claimed by many that what the College proper lacks, the halls supply. In fact, it seems evident that the inactivity of the authorities as regards the extending of our elocutionary advantages can be traced to this dependence upon the halls. Just here the error lies. The work in Hall is the best of its kind. The weekly exercise as a means of practice to the speakers probably could not be better. But our halls do not pretend to, nor can they be *training* schools. They rather furnish the means of applying the principles taught by the elocutionist. They cannot take his place; so much is that the case that a proper benefit from the halls implies a certain amount of rudimentary work which only the competent instructor can give. What is needed (and I speak the sentiments of the College) is the establishment of a systematic course of instruction in vocal culture. A complete system of vocal training substituted as a part of the curriculum for the nominal course we now possess, would work wonders for Princeton, at home and abroad.

The reputation of the College as a participant in the annual exercises of the I. L. A. seems to demand something of the kind.

But what is of most account, the needs of the students who are endeavoring to get the best possible preparation for life's great work, proclaim the present insufficiency, and require something better.

Why shall a thorough course in elocution not be the next acquisition to the College? W.

Printed in *The Princetonian*, I (Jan. 25, 1877), 6-7.
¹ The style and contents of this letter all strongly indicate that it was WW's and are much more certain clues to authorship than the initial with which it was signed. It was most probably WW's first contribution to *The Princetonian* and the first of his long series of comments on the Inter-Collegiate Literary Association and Princeton's participation in its competition. A note on the edi-

torial handling of WW's contributions to *The Princetonian* appears at May 10, 1877.

[2] The reference is to the annual oratorical contest sponsored by the I. L. A.

From Joseph Ruggles Wilson

Dearest Son—   Wilmington, [N. C.] Tuesday [Jan.] 30th [1877]

We have just sent down to depot your box—with room fixings. Mother's health being not so good delayed it until now. It is a big store box. Mr. Pope thinks it will reach you (via N. York) on Saturday. It was altogether too heavy to send by Express. I enclose $5.00 to pay freight, &c.

We all love you most fondly darling. God bless you in your new quarters where I hope you will have many sweet hours of communion with Him.

In haste   Yours as always   Joseph R Wilson

ALS (WP, DLC) with WWhw notation at top of page: "Received Thursday February [WWsh] 1st/77"

From the Minutes of the American Whig Society

Whig Hall, Jan. 30. 1877

House met. Roll called.

To-night being the night of the Sophomore Contest the Clerk read Art. XXXIV of the By-Laws.

The Judges, Prof. Lindsay[1] and Messrs Wardlaw and B. Green[2] having arrived, speaking was immediately commenced.

The following gentlemen then spoke.

Mr. Talcott N. Y.,[3]	Heroes of History.
" Alexander N. Y.,[4]	Manfred's Soliloquies.
" Wilson N. C.	The Ideal Statesman.
" Kerr Ill.	Obedience to law.
" Stevens N. J.[5]	Loss of the Cumberlin
" Smith N. Y.[6]	Decision of Character.
" McCarter N. J.	William the Third.
" Sheldon N. J.[7]	The Misery caused by a Spirit of Persecution.
" Green Md.[8]	Our Bible and Our Liberties.
" Harlow N. Y.[9]	Theodore Parker.
" C. Dodge, N. Y.	The Diet of Worms
" Elsing, Ill.	An Enconium on Shakespeare.
" R. Blackwell, N. Y.[10]	Thoroughness . . .

The Judges having returned, rewarded the First Prize to Mr. Elsing of Ill. and the Second to Mr. Wilson of N. C. . . .

1 Edward D. Lindsey, Professor of Architecture and Applied Art.
2 Apparently W. Brenton Greene, a graduate student.
3 Charles Andrew Talcott, born June 10, 1857. A.B., College of New Jersey, 1879. Practiced law in Utica, N. Y. Mayor of Utica, 1902-06; member United States House of Representatives, 1911-15. Died Feb. 28, 1920.
4 Samuel Alexander, '79.
5 Edwin A. Stevens, '79.
6 Herbert B. Smith, '79.
7 Edward Wright Sheldon, born Dec. 17, 1858. A.B., College of New Jersey, 1879; LL.B., Columbia University, 1881. Prominent banker, corporation lawyer and director, and philanthropist. Trustee, Princeton University, Barnard College, and New York Public Library. Died, Feb. 14, 1934.
8 Edgar M. Green, '79.
9 Samuel A. Harlow, '79.
10 Robert W. Blackwell, '79.

A Speech

[Jan. 30, 1877]

The Ideal Statesman

Nothing in the metaphysical world is less understood than *Genius*. Philosophers have exhausted their ingenuity, scholars have spent their learning, and poets have poured out all their fancy in subtle distinctions between *Talent* and *Genius*. The epithet genius has been conferred indiscriminately upon those of extraordinary, those of mediocre, and those of meagre ability. But we need not trouble ourselves about the difference between a man of talents and a man of genius or the justice with which any man is dubbed a genius. These matters are of no real importance since none of us can gain either talents or genius by drawing a fine line of distinction between them. But we can profit by the experience of men of undoubted ability and capacity and can with advantage take to heart the lessons which their lives teach us. We can weigh the evidence of History and it is a fact of History which cannot be too often repeated that no man, whatever may have been his natural endowments of mind, has ever accomplished anything worthy of note except by untiring work and hard, though silent and, perhaps, unseen *work*. The popular idea that knowledge, experience, and facility, of action come naturally to some men is as false as it is natural. At every turn of life questions stare us in the face which demand instant attention and solution, and it is, therefore, of the greatest importance that we should discipline our minds so thoroughly that they can at once seize upon the most vital point of any subject and be so constantly on the alert that they shall always be ready to grapple thought with sinews hardened by exercise. Genius without discipline is a ship without rudder or sails—a mere inert mass. You see, then, the application of this principle: a highly cultivated mind is absolutely necessary for any great degree of success in any calling—outside of the merely mechanical occupations. And, moreover, I am persuaded that success in life is granted only to those who place perfection before them as their end and so live as constantly to approximate to the ideal. I wish to present to your minds the application of these principles to one of life's innumerable phases—No doubt many of us hope in future to have some hand in the government of our country:—we hope some day to become statesmen: and I may say that no worthier ambition could influence us. The work of governing a state and controlling the happiness of millions of fellow men is not one that should be lightly entered upon. I may even affirm that no other calling involves equal responsibility, since the efficiency of those in almost every other calling depends in great measure upon the wisdom of the legislator. Upon no (other) walk of life should we enter with more careful and sober thought and preparation. No sphere of action requires more thoughtful study or more profound learning. The governing of a great country is not a work to engage the idle moments of petty lawyers or make the fortunes of shallow-minded politicians. The amount of knowledge requisite for statesmanship is a[s] vast as it is necessary. In the Senate or the governers chair we wield an influence which should fill us with solicitude for our conduct and are burdened by a responsibility which should impress us with a deep sense of the magnitude and nobleness of our duties.

The True Statesman is a man of conspicuous business ability and a profound lawyer;—one who has all the principles of the law carefully arranged in a vigorous mind and to whom all the particulars as well as the broad principles of International law are as familiar as his alphabet. And not only should he have the law of his own country at his fingers' ends, but he should be intimately acquainted with all the more important legislative actions of every country on the globe. Daniel Webster, who may be said to have been the greatest statesman which this country has produced, is said to have been so thoroughly acquainted with the laws of all other countries that he could have legislated for them with the same ease and ability which he exhibited in his masterly guidance of the councils of his own country. He could, without further preparation, have made as able a premier of England as he was expounder and defender of our National Constitution. He was a most capable and astute lawyer. A statesman who is unacquainted with the law is as helpless as the soldier who is ignorant of the *use of arms*.

No *partizan* can be a statesman. By partizan I mean one who, while professing to adhere to principle, really adheres to nothing but party. One who sometimes, it may be, wisely, but at all times blindly, follows party leaders. A partizan follows his own convictions only so long as they coincide with the convictions of his party and with his own interests. To him Politics and State Craft are a game which is to be played fairly while it is in his own hands but in which threatened loss justifies any fraud or injustice. His cry is: "Party, right or wrong." But, unless a man rise above party and act from broad and fixed principles he cannot aspire to the exalted name of statesman. The statesman labors not for the advantage of his party, except in so far as that party is the exponent of sound principles, but he labors for the advancement of the interests of his party, for the advancement of liberty, law, and universal justice. No more can a statesman wilfully wreck the ship of state upon the rocks of party hate and prejudice than can a trustworthy helmsman steer his vessel to evident destruction. In fact one who possesses those traits of character which go to make up the statesman will himself be a party. Under his leadership patriots will advance to many a victory prouder than party victory—victories of principle and of right.

But, whatever advantages may accrue to the statesman from a profound knowledge of the law or complete freedom from the trammels of party prejudice, he will make little impression upon his generation if he be not endowed with some of Shakspeare's divine insight into human nature and some of Franklin's deep sympathy with all the efforts and strivings of the common mind. By these means alone can he retain that ascendency over his fellow men upon which his usefulness depends. *The proper study of the statesman is man.*

The true statesman leaves self out of every question. This is the test which the characters of so few public men can bear. Unselfishness is a rare gift and seems seldom to be united with great intellectual faculties. We find many unselfish men in our public service but how few the number that combine disinterestedness with that breadth of intellect which characterizes the statesman. History might almost lead us to conclude that selfishness is inseparable from great powers of mind. Hence we find that few have become great statesman. That all the acts of a statesman should be performed without a view to self-interest needs no proof. We have only to look at the results of selfishness to conclude that self-interest and the interest of the state must often clash with and counteract each other when brought in contact. The selfish statesman painfully reminds us of a blindfolded man endeavoring to run a race upon a course beset by pit-falls.

But a public man may be a sound lawyer, entirely free from partizanship and perfectly unselfish and still lack one of the most important, if not the most important, characteristic of a statesman. The legislator must be in advance of his age. Across the mind of the statesman flash ever and anon brilliant, though partial, intimations of future events. His prophetic finger points out the true way and he does the deeds of the present in the declining light of the past not only but in the rising dawn of the future as well. That something which is more than fore-sight and less than prophetic knowledge marks the statesman a peculiar being among his contemporaries. This quality was possessed by William of Orange in a marked, by Chatham in a high, and by Burke in a wonderful degree, and some of the speeches of Webster and Calhoun seem to us of this day like prophecies. Richelieu entered the future with wide-open eyes and was master of France; Lord North staggered blindly into it and fell. Charles the first saw the future and braved it; prejudice blinded James the second to it and he was overcome by its crowding events.

To set off his business talents, to defend his independence, to support his positions, and to paint in startling colors the future which dwells in his mind the statesman must possess an orator's soul, an orator's words, an orator's action. To nobleness of thought he must add nobleness of word and conduct.

We must conclude, then, that genius alone can compass statesmanship; and even genius seems always to fall short of perfection in this. Genius seldom graces this world with its presence and of all the geniuses that have flooded this earth with light none have become perfect statesmen.

I have painted the ideal statesman. I have placed before you a perfect type of statesmanship and what have we gained by the sight? You will say that we cannot become perfect and can, therefore, gain little by gazing upon perfection. But, although we cannot attain to perfection, we can live with that eagerness and devotion to principle which will enable us to become less and less imperfect, bringing us as near to the perfect as erring human nature can come. And let me again remind you that it is only by working with an energy which is almost superhuman and which looks to uninterested spectators like insanity that we can accomplish anything worth the achievement. Work is the keystone of a perfect life. Work and trust in God.   Atticus

WWhw copy in notebook described at April 1, 1875.

EDITORIAL NOTE
THE LIBERAL DEBATING CLUB

The Liberal Debating Club was a small private debating society organized by Wilson. He wrote its constitution, printed below, and, as the minutes scattered throughout following pages reveal, played the leading role in the club. It went out of existence with the graduation of Wilson's class. To show the importance of this organization to Wilson, the editors have included all its extant minutes in this volume.

The constitution of the LDC is the first clear revelation of Wilson's conviction that a parliamentary system on the British model provides the best vehicle for responsible leadership in a democracy. It is not insignificant that the structure of the government of the LDC clearly forecast the structure that Wilson would soon advocate in essays and books for the American government—that the President should be merely a presiding and administrative officer, and that his Secretary of State (and Cabinet) should stand or fall depending upon their ability to command a majority in Congress.

The constitution of the LDC also reflects Wilson's emphasis upon debate as the vehicle for political combat and survival in the clash of ideas, along with his conviction (later forcefully expressed in a speech at the University of Virginia, printed at June 30, 1880), that college men should grapple with the real issues of the day, not discuss hypothetical or obsolete questions.

A Constitution   [c. Feb. 1–c. March 15, 1877]

Constitution of the Liberal Debating Club

Article I

Sec. I   This society shall be known as the Liberal Debating Club and shall be founded upon the fundamental principles of *Justice, Morality* and *Friendship.*

Sec. II.   The members of this Club shall form a Brotherhood and shall be expected to assist and encourage each other in every possible way.

Article II

Sec. I.   The Liberal Debating Club shall consist of not less than four (4) and not more than eight (8) members and members can be admitted only by a unanimous vote.

Sec II   Four (4) members shall constitute a quorum for all business.

Article III

Sec. I. The government of this Club shall be vested in a *President* and *Secretary* of *State*.

Sec. II. The President shall be elected by a majority vote and his election shall take place by ballot.

Sec. III. The President shall be elected for a term of three (3) months.

Sec. IV It shall be the duty of the President to preside over all meetings of the Club, keep order therein, and perform other duties hereinafter set forth.

Sec. V. The Secretary of State shall be appointed by the President in accordance with rules hereinafter set forth and it shall be his duty to keep a record of all the proceedings of the Club and preserve in good order all the documents and papers of the Club.

Article IV

This Club shall be governed by the rules of Parliamentary Practice contained in Cushing's Manual, in so far as those rules are consistant with the provisions of this Constitution.

Article V

Sec. I The questions discussed by this Club shall be political questions of the present century.

Sec. II. These questions shall come before the Club in the form of *Bills* and shall pass through regular course as such.

Sec. III It shall be the duty of the Secretary of State, and the privilege of any member of the Club, to propose such questions as he may deem proper.

Sec, IV The Secretary of State shall be responsible to the Club for his opinions upon any question under consideration by the Club and, in case his opinions do not coincide with those of the majority of the members of the Club, it shall be his duty to resign and the duty of the President to appoint a Secretary of State whose opinions coincide with those of the majority of the members of the Club.

Sec. V. It shall be the duty of the Secretary of State to form and express an opinion on every question which comes before the Club and he shall remain in or be removed from his office according as his views coincide with or differ from those of his fellow members.

Sec. VI. Every member is expected to express his opinion on every *Bill* which comes before the Club.

Article VI

All bills shall be copied by the Secretary of State into a Record Book of the Club, provided for the purpose.

Article VII

The admission fee to this Club shall be $1.00 and the expenses of the Club shall be met by a sessional fee of 50¢ from each member.

Article VIII

The President shall be allowed to speak and vote on every question.

Article IX

The President shall, from time to time, appoint different members to write short essays stating in a plain manner the historical facts bearing upon questions under discussion by the Club.

Article X

All Bills shall be written out in legible form and, after action upon them, they shall be placed among the papers of the Secretary of State, to be copied into the Record Book of the Club.

Article XI

There shall be a meeting of the Club once every week, on Saturdays, when practicable, and when not practicable, on some other day of the week according to adjournment.

Article XII

No meeting of the Club shall be called to order after 9 o'clock P.M. or continue beyond 11 o'clock P.M.

Article XIII

The members of this Club are expected to keep its Constitution and all its transactions secret.

Article XIV

The Secretary of State shall act as the President's advisor in all matters of national or foreign policy.

Article XV

Sec. I. The President shall be, ex officio, Treasurer of the Club.

Sec. II. The Secretary of State shall dispose of the funds of the Club according to the orders of the Club and deposit an account of his expenditures with the President.

Sec. III The President shall always be ready to answer any questions as to the state of the Treasury.

Article XVI

No Bill shall pass through more than two (2) readings at any one meeting.

Article XVII

Sec. I. The mover of every Bill shall be entitled to the first speech thereon

Sec. II. The Sec. of State shall give one week's notice of every Bill which he intends to bring before the Club.

Sec. III Any member intending to bring a Bill before the Club shall give notice of such intention to the Secretary of State, whose duty it shall be to appoint a time for the introduction of said Bill.

Article XVIII

Upon the defeat of any Secretary of State the opposition shall file among the archives of the Club the arguments upon which they have based their opposition to said Secretary of State.

Article XIX

If there be an even number of members in this Club at any time, a tie vote upon any Bill shall be considered as sustaining the policy of the Secretary of State.

Article XX

No member shall decline to accept an appointment by the President either as Secretary of State or essayist.

Article XXI

Sec. I. It shall require a four-fifths' (4/5) vote to adopt any amendment or addition to this Constitution and said addition or amendment shall come before the Club in the form of a Bill and pass through regular course as such.

Sec. II It shall require a unanimous vote to suspend any provision of this Constitution.

Article XXII

All resolutions, other than Bills or simple motions, shall be written in a Resolution Book provided for the purpose and read to the Club by the President before they can be discussed or voted upon by the Club.

Article XXIII

Sec. I.   The proceedings of this Club shall be kept in a Record Book, an Argument Book, and a Book of Essays

Sec. II.   It shall be the duty of the Secretary of State to copy every Bill or resolution into the Record Book within one week after said Bill or resolution shall have been passed.

Sec. III.   It shall be the duty of every member appointed to write an essay to present said essay written in ink in an Essay Book provided for the purpose, said Essay Book to be kept by the Secretary of State among the other papers of the Club.

[Amendments][1]

Art V, Sec. I. Amended, Oct. 13, by adding the words: "or such literary matters as the club may see fit to discuss from time to time." T. W. Wilson, Pres. H. Woods, Jr., S. of S.

Art. VII   Amended Oct. 27, to read: "fee of 20¢ from each member," instead of "fee of 50¢" etc. T. W. Wilson, P. H. Woods, Jr. S. of S.

Charles Talcott N. Y., President
J. Edwin Webster Md. Sect. of State.[2]
Thomas W. Wilson, N. C.
Hiram Woods, Jr. Md.
Robt Harris McCarter N. J.

Edward W. Sheldon N. J.
William Thaddeus Elsing
Harold Godwin, N. Y.[3]
Charles W. Mitchell Md.[4]
M. G. Emery Jr. D.C.[5]

WWhw MS. in small notebook inscribed on inside cover, "Hiram Woods, Jr." (MdBJ).

[1] Not in WWhw. Signatures below by the members.

[2] J. Edwin Webster, born Sept. 24, 1857. A.B., College of New Jersey, 1879. Studied law at the University of Maryland; admitted to the bar, 1881. Practiced in Bel Air, Md. Died April 19, 1928.

[3] Harold Godwin, born May 21, 1858. A.B., College of New Jersey, 1879. Studied art and criticism in Paris, 1880-81. On staff of New York *Evening Post*, 1881-84; art critic, *New York Mail and Express*; art critic and, in 1890, managing editor, *New York Commercial Advertiser*; editor, *Current Literature* and *Short Stories*, 1890-1900. Died May 8, 1931.

[4] Charles Wellman Mitchell, born Feb. 4, 1859. A.B., College of New Jersey, 1879; M.D., University of Maryland, 1881. Studied at University of Prague, 1883, University of Vienna, 1883-84. Practiced in Baltimore. Professor of Pathology, Professor of Clinical Medicine, and Dean, University of Maryland Medical School, 1888-1900; Professor of Pediatrics, 1897-1914, and Professor of the Practice of Medicine, same institution, 1909-1912. Died Dec. 28, 1917.

[5] Matthew G. Emery, Jr., '79.

Three Letters from Janet Woodrow Wilson

My darling Boy,   Wilmington N. C. Feb 6th [1877]

We received yours of the 1st ins. yesterday morning—and the news[1] it contained filled our hearts with pride and gladness. Your dear father was *intensely* gratified—and no wonder—for the gift of oratory is a grand gift—as well as a very rare one. We are *very* thankful for your success, dearest son. There is no doubt that your talent in that direction will be of great advantage to you in your chosen profession—and you will now feel great encouragement to continue your efforts in that direction. I used to think, when you were persuaded sometimes to recite Shakespeare, in Columbia, that it would be your own fault if you were not an orator—for you have not only a fine memory, but the *acting talent*, if I may call it so, in such a degree that you can make yourself what you please in that line. I hope you will lay aside all *timidity*—and make the most of all your powers, my darling. . . . Your father desires me to send you the enclosed ten dollars—P. O. order—for any use you wish. . . .

Good bye, dear child   Your own Mother.

ALS (WP, DLC) with faint WWsh notations on env.
[1] That WW had won second prize in the American Whig Society's sophomore oratorical contest.

My darling Boy,   Wilmington N. C. Feb. 16th 77.

We have been a good deal annoyed at the long delay of your box upon its journey—and I put off writing from day to day, hoping to hear of its arrival. We received your notice of its arrival last night—which relieved us greatly. We are glad it gave you satisfaction dear. I confess I never thought about the pitcher &c—strange to say—but we could not very well have sent them I suppose. I enclose P. O. Order for $10.00. I think that will get everything you need for your washstand &c. Please tell me how everything looks about you, and if you are quite comfortable.[1] Are your rooms cheerful? I did not like to hear of your sleeping there without first having fire—even in warm weather. Have you cover enough for very cold weather. By the way if you have not money enough to get a cheap mattrass for under your bed, let me know. I think they use straw under beds in that country. You must have a comfortable bed certainly. I hope you have all the essentials for your grate before this. Perhaps you could get a mattrass from Mrs. Wright temporarily. . . . Yours lovingly,   Mother,

ALS (WP, DLC) with WWsh notation on env.
[1] A reference to WW's recent move to Witherspoon Hall.

My darling Son, Wilmington, N. C., Febry 28th '77.

We were so grieved to hear of your cold—and we will feel very anxious until we hear that it has quite left you. A cold taken in that way—from sleeping in an unseasoned room—is apt to be the most dangerous kind. I am very sorry now that you did not remain at Mrs. W's for the rest of the season—and just lock up your new room—and pay the rent for it. That would be far better than risking anything. But I hope to hear that you are well again my darling —do write particularly about how you are. I am so grateful to Mr. Woods for his attentions and kindness to my precious boy. Please give him my love and thanks. I hope we may see him here some day. I would like to know him. It is a great comfort to us to know that you have such a friend near you in case of your being sick.
. . .

Father & brother join me in fondest love to our absent darling. God bless and keep you Your own Mother.

ALS (WP, DLC).

From the Minutes of the American Whig Society

Whig Hall, March 2, '77

. . . Debate being next in order the IX Division debated the following:

Res'd:—That a man should be judged by his efforts rather than by his success

Aff.

Van Doren[1] to Weed[2] inclusive

Neg.

Wiggan " Wylly. "

Decided in the negative

Performed

Messrs Van Doren, Van Hoesen, Vanuxem, Vinton,[3] Voorhis,[4] Wiggan,[5] Wilds,[6] Williams, Wilson, Withington.[7]

[1] Peter A. V. Van Doren, '78.
[2] Charles L. Weed, '80.
[3] Cadwallader C. Vinton, '80.
[4] Ernest Voorhis, '80.
[5] Albert R. Wiggan, '80.
[6] John T. Wilds, '80.
[7] Irving P. Withington, '80.

From Janet Woodrow Wilson

My darling Son, Wilmington N. C. March 7 [1877].

I shall not be quite satisfied till I hear that you are *quite* rid of your cold. Please tell me particularly how it affects you now—and how it sickened you so seriously at first. Now dont forget to tell me all this, dear, please. . . .

It cannot be very long now before your father is relieved from the burden of the paper. The managers have concluded to offer it to *Mr. McLaurin*—as the best they can do under the circumstances. Your father thought of that plan some time ago—and thinks he can possibly make a paper suited to the tastes of the North Carolinians. I will be so glad when it is all arranged—for I fear that your father could not endure the strain upon him very much longer. I think that editing under favorable circumstances would be delightful to him—a paper with a large circulation among cultivated people, not only—but with access to a less meagre supply of exchanges, and means to procure necessary aid in giving variety, &c, &c. But under existing circumstances, it is not much else besides a burden. . . .

I am so glad that you are enjoying your new quarters. It must be delightful to be independent of Mrs Wrights whims—and free from the quarrels of her household. Where are you boarding, and how do you fare? I hope you are getting wholesome food? I will send you the Eclectic & Littells in a day or two. I have been busier than ever of late—as I have had a good deal to do in the way of planting &c in the garden. You will be pleased to see the improvement in the lot I am sure when you come home. God bless you my darling

Josie joins me in warmest love to you. Your father is not prepared to send the money today—so I enclose two-dollars for the present—pocket money. Your own Mother

ALS (WP, DLC) with WWhw notation: "Received [WWsh] ʒ'ⁱᵒʳʸ" and WWsh notation: "From mother to Thomas W. Wilson." Three sh outlines too faint to be transcribed following first notation. On verso of p. 2: WWhw pencil draft of Article XVIII of the constitution of the Liberal Debating Club.

From Joseph Ruggles Wilson

My darling boy— [Wilmington, N. C.] March 15 77

Your mother was unable to write you on yesterday by reason of illness. She has been in bed for the last 48 hours almost, and suffers a good deal although she is in no manner of danger. Such attacks she has had before, and well understands them. They require only quiet. I enclose you the remaining $55.00 and $10.00 additional for your own private use.

You will see by the paper of this week that I am at last out of that editorial entanglement—much to my joy as you may imagine.[1]

I cannot tell you, dearest son, how greatly we love you, and how longingly our thoughts travel to you every hour. May God abundantly bless and keep you. I trust that you are so living as to find His favor your chief happiness.   Your affc father   J R W

ALS (WP, DLC) with WWhw notation on env.: "Ans." On verso of letter: WWhw pencil draft of Article xv of the constitution of the Liberal Debating Club.
¹ JRW announced in the Wilmington *North Carolina Presbyterian*, March 14, 1877, that his editorial responsibility ceased with this issue, and that John Mc-Laurin was assuming editorial management.

From Wilson's Shorthand Diary

Diary   March, 1877 (From March 20th, 1877) To [blank]

20th Tuesday. This day I again take up my diary. I hope that this effort will prove more satisfactory than the spasmodic attempt at diary-keeping which I made last year from June to some time in September [November]. This is perhaps a more proper time for me to commence a journal of this sort than last year—not only because I am now a sophomore and can write with more dignity in consequence¹ but also because I now figure under the, to me, somewhat novel role of editor. I was yesterday elected by the class to be one of their two representatives on the Board of Editors of the PRINCETONIAN. McCarter filled this office during this year—Wilder² and I will fill it during the junior year—probably commencing our duties next term. This election together with the second prize for speaking which I succeeded in winning in Whig Hall, on the [30th] of Jan. last has given me somewhat of a reputation in college—whether this reputation is deserved or not is inconsequential. I will try my best to deserve it. I have not felt particularly well today. I was obliged to leave English recitation this morning on account of some trouble with my bowels and they have been irregular ever since causing me some little trouble and inconvenience. A good sleep tonight will probably relieve me greatly. I am a great believer in sleep as a remedy—in fact I believe in trying all natural remedies before resorting to any others. Thank God for health and strength.

WWsh entry in notebook described at Sept. 7, 1875, item (b). All subsequent diary entries are from this source.
¹ Here follows the Graham shorthand symbol for merriment.
² William Royal Wilder, born June 30, 1858. A.B., College of New Jersey, 1879; LL.B., Columbia University, 1882. Practiced law in New York City. Died April 19, 1925.

From the Minutes of the American Whig Society

. . . Literary Exercises.   Whig Hall. Mar 23rd '77.

Literary Exercises being then in order the IX Div. spoke.

Performed			*Failed*	
Mr	Vinton	Subj. "To[o] far"	Mr.	Van Hoesen
"	Waller[1]	" "Henry Clay."	"	Vanuxem
"	Webster	"	"	Voorhis
"	Weed		"	Wiggan
"	Wilds		"	Williams[3]
"	Wilson	"The Embodiment of Ideas."[2]	"	S. Wood[s][4]
"	Withington		"	Worl.[5]

Mr. H. Woods Subject. "Adversity the Test of Character."
" Wylly. . . .

[1] James B. Waller, Jr., '79.
[2] Not found. Submitted, unsuccessfully, under the title "Men and Ideas," for the prize offered by the *Nassau Literary Magazine* for the best undergraduate essay in each issue. See WWsh diary for May 27, 1877.
[3] Charles S. Williams, '78.
[4] Samuel S. Woods, '78.
[5] Edward E. Worl, '80.

From Joseph Ruggles Wilson

My dearest Son— [Wilmington, N. C.] Thursday March 27. [1877]

Your letters always give me great pleasure. The style in which they are written has been much improved within a year or less. The intelligence they convey is uniformily gratifying. And, all things considered, they are as long as necessity demands: although I often wish they were longer. Your cheerfulness is most gratifying to us all. There is no better gift than this, and none more deserving of cultivation. One of the principal uses of our wonderfully humane religion is to promote buoyancy of disposition, by freeing the soul from that which is alone worthy of the name, *Burden*: the sense of sin. I trust that your good spirits, darling boy, are due in great part to an easy conscience—to the smile of God. I am sure that you will rate at its true value the estimation into which you are rapidly growing among your fellow-students. Your dear mother and I rejoice in the evidences which go to show that your manly character and your superior talents are appreciated. But be not "puffed up." Let the esteem you have won be only as a stimulant to fresh exertion—regard it not as a final crown but only as an encouragement toward royalty in goodness and learning. You have so far justified our expectations—but not *more* than justified them —for we knew what you *could* do. And we as well know that what you have achieved is nothing to what you can accomplish. Modest energy spurred by Christian principle may properly lay claim to every rightful honor.

In one of your recent letters you ask my advice as to whether you should *read* a great deal (as you are doing) beyond that which your regular curriculum requires. It is certainly your duty to improve yourself in *all* ways but it as certainly [is] your *first* duty to conquer your text books. Having whipped these out, then give your mind full swing in gardens of poetry, in fields of history, in seas of philosophy, on mountain-tops of oratory. I do not care to have you prepare your class exercises in view of any possible class honors—but (1) for duty's sake (2) for the sake of mental discipline (3) for the foundation it is intended to lay on which to build unlimited knowledge. To learn *how* to learn is one great end of college studies: in other words to get the reins of that many-horsed chariot, the mind, fairly in the grasp of the will; so as to be able to turn and drive it where you please. Many young men come out of college with a good deal of knowledge, but without much training—with minds plugged but not hardened and suppled for lifting knowledge into *power*.

You ask, too, how best to prepare for a debate—whether by heads carefully arranged but with no body of memorized words to carry them—or by writing all and committing all. If one has a first-rate memory, he may adopt the latter method without fear and with great profit. The former method is, however, *intrinsically* preferable: it is truer, I mean, to nature[.] What is to be avoided, *always*, is a slip-shod performance[.] *Every* part of a speech ought to be most carefully and conscientiously prepared—and this can be done without writing it: by going over it again and again in thought so as to be sure that each point is well taken and each illustration is *to* the point. Experiment for yourself and you will soon find the way for *you*—for no two persons can follow one set of rules made by a third person. Pursue the bent of your own intelligence. But I must close. God bless you, sweet one. Your dear mother and Josie send more love than you can receive.

J R Wilson

ALS (WP, DLC).

From the Minutes of the Liberal Debating Club

Mar. 31st 1877.

Meeting called to order at 8-8 P.M. The debate being first in order, then came up. The quest. discussed was Resolved

That the Indians should not be driven out of the Black Hills. Was carried in the aff. The 2nd reading was then called for & carried The comittee appointed to draw up an order of business then made its report, which was adopted. The gent. from N. C.[1] then presented a bill for the 1st Sat. of next term. The meeting then adj. till 1st Sat of next term.

C[h]as. A Talcott, Pres

Hw entries in hand of the Secretary of State (WP, DLC).
1 WW.

J. E. Webster, Sec. of St.

April 5th 1877

The meeting called to order at 8-20. Then came discussion as to the eligibility of dif[ferent] gent. proposed for membership. On motion of gent. from Md,[1] it was carried, that Mr. McCarter be approached as to his willingness to become a member of the L. D. C. It was moved by gent from N. C. to allow any member to speak when there was no motion before the house, provided he preface his remarks by saying that he will make a motion before he sits down[.] It was then moved & carried to go into the comittee of the whole on the Indian quest. The gent. from N. C. took the chair and the Committee reported favorably to the house. A 3rd reading was then entered upon & the quest. finally carried. The reading of the Man[ual] then came up. By unanimous consent the gent. from N. C. sub[stituted] for his Mormon quest. the following[:] Whereas the Gov. of the U. S. in the 1st one hundred years of its existence has developed within itself elements of discord, which threaten its stability and tend to weaken its institutions & Whereas these elements of discord plainly spring from imperfections in the Executive department of the Gov. of the U. S. therefore be it Resolved[:]

I that the Ex. power of the U. S. shall be vested in a Pres, to be chosen for a term of six (6) years by the people, the members of whose cabinet shall form a Ministry, responsible to the House of Rep collectively, for the general conduct of the government and individually for the acts of each member. The Pres can be removed only on impeachment for & conviction of crime. Each executive act, to be valid, shall be counter-signed by the Minister of the department to which it relates. The Ministers shall be individually & collectively removed on impeachment by the House alone, without trial, for conduct disapproved of by the House.

II Resolved that the Legislative power of the U. S. shall be vested in a Pres. & Ministry & in a Senate & House of Rep to be constituted as heretofore, except that the Rep. shall be elected every seven (7) years, subject to an earlier termination of their office by causes herein provided for. The Pres. shall select his ministers from the members of either the Senate or the House of Rep. and shall through his ministry have the initiative in legislation in common with the members of either House & the right of debate on all matters pending therein.

III Resolved that whenever a majority of the members of the House of Rep. shall oppose any measure introduced or sustained by the administration, the Pres. shall either dismiss the members of his cabinet, & appoint other ministers from among the prominent members of the opposition; or, if he believes that the members of his Cabinet & not the House of Rep. reflect the will of the people, he shall with the consent of the Senate dissolve said House of Rep. & thereupon immediately order a new election of Rep to be held within 30 days after such adverse vote, such Rep to continue in office for seven (7) years from the period of such election or until the next dissolution of Congress.

IV Resolved that it shall not be necessary for any Senator or Rep. to reside in the state or district which he may be chosen to represent or to resign his seat if after being so chosen he shall be appointed to a Cabinet office; & no Senator holding a Cabinet office shall draw any other salary than that pertaining to his position in the Cabinet.[2]

A discussion of the preamble was then entered upon which was interrupted by a motion to adjourn.

Cas A Talcott Pres
J. E. Webster Sect of St.

[1] Three "gentlemen from Maryland" were members. This was probably Hiram Woods, Jr.

[2] There is a shorthand draft of this resolution on one of the loose pages in WW's *Index Rerum.* As the text of a transcript of this draft repeats, almost verbatim, the text of the resolution in Liberal Debating Club minutes, the transcript of the shorthand draft is not printed. The only difference between the shorthand draft and the text here printed concerned the election of the President. The shorthand draft set the term of the President at seven years, instead of six, and provided that he should be elected by the people "(or by Congress as might be preferred)."

From Janet Woodrow Wilson

My darling Son,   Wilmington [N.C.]—Wednesday [April 11, 1877]
   . . . I want to know what you think, dear, of my plan for the coming summer. Shortly after your return home from College, say in a week or two after your arrival, I propose that you, Josie, & I shall go to Rome [Georgia] to make a visit. I think you would enjoy it—as you would have your uncle James horse to ride—and from all accounts, you would find Jessie[1] a famous companion in your rides. You know she has a pony. In every way, it would be an improvement upon this dull place, where you have no young companions at all. The only drawback, which is a serious one, will be

your separation from your father—but he would have to go off part of the time anyway. He has quite given up any idea of going to Europe, I think.

I hope you are getting comfortably through with your examinations dear. I wish it were two years from now—and that I were anticipating joining you at commencement this Spring! Your father & little brother join me in fondest love to our precious absent one. God bless you my darling.   Your own Mother

ALS (WP, DLC) with WWhw notations on env.: "J. S. Mill"; "Prof. Cairnes."
¹ James Bones and his daughter Jessie, WW's first cousin.

From Douglas McKay

My Dear Tom   Columbia S C April 11/77
It was with great pleasure that I received your kind letter of Mar 18th. I am always gratified, at getting letters from any of my friends, but some how or other, I appreciate your correspondence, above almost any other, and I think the reason is, that I know I am not deserving your kind attention, inasmuch as I have treated you very shabbily at times, in not answering your letters more promptly. . . .

I was greatly gratified some time ago at hearing that you had won a prize at your college for Elocution, and not knowing exactly what effort was required, to accomplish this, I asked Sam Melton about it, and he told me that your feat must have been very praiseworthy, as you would have quite a number of competitors. You must accept my hearty congratulations for this achievement, and let me assure you that I trust it is only the beginning of higher honors to which you shall attain. . . . Yours Sincerely   D. McKay

ALS (WP, DLC) with WWhw notation on env.: "Ans."

From Joseph Ruggles Wilson

My precious son—   Wilmington, [N. C.], April 13 77
You will find enclosed my check for $20.00. You are of course to do as others do in the matter of these class expenses. I do not fear that you will go beyond and expend money uselessly, where only your own will is to be consulted. Your dear mother and I are very well pleased with your course in every particular. The stand you have taken amongst yr. fellow students is a source of pride to us—and we do not doubt that your manliness will continue to expand as your time lengthens. If you come out from college, darling son, with a character unimpaired and untainted our grati-

tude will know no bounds. I trust, therefore, that you are often in the attitude of prayer to Him who alone can keep you amid multiplied temptations. . . .

God bless you, sweet one

Your affectionate father   Joseph R Wilson

ALS (WP, DLC).

Classroom Notebook

[c. April 18, 1877-June 1878]

Inscribed (WWhw): "1877 Soph. Year–*Third Term.*"

Contains WWsh lecture notes, with WWhw headings, in sophomore mathematics course (analytical geometry) taken c. April 18, 1877-June 6, 1877; and a continuation of notes (undated) taken in Professor Cyrus F. Brackett's[1] physics course, which WW attended probably during his junior year, 1877-78.

(WP, DLC). This is a notebook made by folding pages 12″ x 9⅜″, making pages 6″ x 9⅜″.

[1] Cyrus Fogg Brackett, M.D., Henry Professor of Physics.

Two Letters from Janet Woodrow Wilson

My darling Son,   Wilmington N. C. April 26th '77

Your father says that since you had to spend the surplus of the money he sent upon a pair of shoes, he wished me to enclose five dollars in this—as he does not like you to be without some money—for your incidental wants. You must not fail to let us know, dear, when you are in want of anything. Have I told you about your cousin Frank Barr or not? Sometimes I get a little puzzled as to what I have written—in writing to your sisters and yourself, I am not always sure to which of you I have told certain things. . . .

Alex Sprunt is at home—looking very well—he always enquires with interest for you. Little Josie is quite well—& so am I. I have been interrupted in writing this, by company—and have been obliged to write very hastily. . . .   Your own Mother.

My precious Son,   Wilmington N. C. May 3rd 77

It was a week last Sunday since we received your last letter—and we are very anxious about you. What can be the matter? I trust it is only that you are very busy. But dearest boy, no matter *how* busy you may be, you must take time, *always*, to write to us—if it is only a Postal—to say that you are well. It may be that your letter has miscarried. You must remember, my darling, that our peace of mind depends upon our hearing frequently from you—

as to your welfare and happiness—so that it will be better for you to send a few lines more frequently—to allow for any chance miscarriage—that may occur. . . .

Papa & Josie join me in fondest love—   Your own Mother.

ALS (WP, DLC).

Editorial in *The Princetonian*

[May 10, 1877]

Princeton and the Next I. C. L. Contest.

While the attention of the College is so much occupied with athletic sports, the students overlook an association of which Princeton is a member, and in which, mainly, from the total lack of interest taken, she plays a very inferior part. I refer to the Inter-Collegiate Literary Association.

Although there have been flattering notices of the practical contest last winter, of the proceedings of the convention, of the formation of a Literary Association within the College, of a Board of Regents, and sundry other officers, probably one-half of the students scarcely comprehend the real condition of affairs and the miserable showing that Princeton is making in this association today.

The apathy is so great that no one seems to take even the trouble to inquire into the real state of the case, and yet, by our failures and mishaps in these contests, and from the lukewarm manner in which we enter into them, we are doing more to injure the College than could be accomplished by any number of defeats in base-ball and other athletic sports.

Looking back on our record since the first literary contest, I find the number of our victories to be—one first prize in Essays; one second prize in Mathematics, and the first prize in Mental Science last year.

True we did not send competitors in every branch, and last year we were only represented in Essays, Oratory and Mental Science. For the number of times we have entered, we have been fairly successful, but I feel assured no one will say that if the College had taken the interest it should have taken, we would have had representatives in every branch and a larger measure of success. Men have gone as individuals, working more for themselves than for the College, and wholly unsustained by any College enthusiasm. Ask any of our contestants whether they would not have labored to better advantage if satisfied that their fellow-students were prepared to cheer them on with sympathy and approving interest. They will certainly tell you it would have been very different, and we would not send a man to participate in a contest where scarcely a score of his fellow-students encouraged, even by their presence, his endeavors.

There must be something vitally wrong in such a state of affairs. We do not find the same apathy existing in our athletics or in other departments of College work. I am convinced that this feeling, or rather lack of feeling, arises either from ignorance of the real nature of the Association, or because there is a strong belief that we are engaged in a contest in which we have everything to lose and nothing to gain. Let us see whereon this last opinion rests.

The Association does not seem to have fulfilled the expectation of its founders. It is not a contest between the best Colleges of the land. With the exception of Cornell, Williams and Wesleyan, the Colleges represented are not those by whom any great influence has been exerted.

For our competitors in Mental Science, we had St. John's College, at Fordham, and the Northwestern University. We won the prize; far be it from me to disparage, for a moment, the ability of our representative, but I conscientiously believe it would have been a disgrace for us not to have done so. The argument might be advanced, that St. John's, being a Roman Catholic institution, pays special attention to Mental Science and the Schoolmen. This may be so, and yet the question arises, whether St. John's has obtained any reputation for its course in Mental Science. Have her graduates, by whose success or failure a College is judged, ever reached any distinction in that department of learning?

The Association cannot be in a very satisfactory state, if one can judge from the last contest. Scarcely any applause, a very poor audience, and a dead-and-alive performance, which dragged wearily along, till the audience hailed with joy the close of the proceedings. Princeton, although having two contestants, had scarcely fifteen men in the house, and but little interest was shown.

The Convention of College Presidents met the next morning. Circulars were sent to the Presidents of all the leading Colleges. To show the hearty manner in which they responded to the call, there were present, President Cattell, of Lafayette; President Crosby, of New York University; Dr. McCosh, and Father Grecheln, [Gockeln] of St. John's College, Fordham. This shows the interest taken by the College Presidents, and if, among the powers that be, such indifference exists, what can we expect to find among inferior mortals?

It is my firm belief that this "Association of Sporting Ethics," as the *Popular Science Monthly* terms it, cannot much longer continue in its present state. Be that as it may, as long as we are in it, let us try to kindle some enthusiasm, and not proceed further in this slip-shod manner, which cannot but work us harm. I understand that at Williams, the same apathy prevails, and the advisability of further participation is there discussed.

Of course these are individual views. I put these forth in the hope that some attention may be directed to this matter, which seems to me to be of vital importance to the College. If we cannot, in future, make greater efforts, or, at least, aid those who enter in our name, let us, if possible, withdraw from a contest in which, as matters now stand, we are doing ourselves positive injury.   T.

Printed in *The Princetonian*, II (May 10, 1877), 19-20. The editors believe that the editorial above and following articles and editorials from *The Princetonian* were WW's. All are unmistakably Wilsonian in style; all concern subjects in which he was keenly interested. In some cases WW may have rewritten items composed by other members of the Editorial Board or collaborated in writing them. The item above and following compositions have been selected to provide a broad representation of WW's interests and campus concerns. Many pieces deemed to have been of Wilsonian authorship have been omitted on grounds of insignificance or repetition.

The editors must add that there is no conclusive evidence that their selections are infallibly Wilson's. But nothing has been included that had not first been independently selected by each editor and then agreed upon by all as meeting the criteria stipulated above.

This editorial signals the beginning of WW's contributions to *The Princetonian* as a member of the editorial board. For his election to that body, see his Diary at March 20, 1877.

From Janet Woodrow Wilson

My precious Son,   Wilmington, N. C. May 10th 77

I have just read yours of last Tuesday. It seems to me you are not in quite as good spirits as usual—but I hope I am mistaken. The books you desired to be sent to you, were mailed yesterday morning. Your father carried them down to the office himself, to make sure that they were all right—and I hope they will reach you tomorrow evening. I will consult with your father about the clothes —and see what is best to be done. Last spring, I remember, you did not begin to wear your light clothing till after you got home—and as this season is still later, perhaps you could do better by waiting till you get home—or till you were passing through Philadelphia on your way home. What do you think? . . .

God bless you my darling. Papa is resting in the study—and Josie is out on his velocipede.   With fondest love   Your Mother.

P.S. Omitted. ALS (WP, DLC) with WWhw notations on env. "Ans."; "I borrowed one of your chairs."

From the Minutes of the Liberal Debating Club

May 12th 1877.

Meeting called to order at 8-35 PM. The admission of new members then came up, there being none the minutes were called for. The committee appointed to confer with Mr. McCarter then made its report. On motion of gent. from Md. we returned to the admission of new members & he nominated Mr. McC. who was unanimously elected[.] The manuel was then read by the gent from Md. The debate then came up & the quest. Whereas the U. S. &c &c was discussed and carried in the aff. The Pres. then appointed the Sec of St. to write an Essay for next meeting. The meeting was then adjourned.

Cas. A Talcott Pres
J E Webster Sect of St.

From Janet Woodrow Wilson

My precious Son,   Wilmington N. C., May 17th '77.

Somehow I have changed my day of writing you from Wednesday to Thursday—but as you preferred Wed. I will try to go back to it in future. There has been some change in the schedules of the R. Rs—& it is necessary to send letters to the P. O. at an earlier hour—but that can easily be managed. Your father left home for N. Orleans on Monday evening. I had a telegram from him this morning—announcing his safe arrival yesterday about noon—then a little later in the day I received a little shaky note which he had written on the train near Macon. He is well and will be pleasantly lodged in N. O. Write to him, dear, a few lines at least—it will give him so much happiness to hear from you there. He expects to be absent about three weeks—two Sabbaths. Just address your letter to him as Stated Clerk of Pres. Gen. Assembly, N. O. La. and it will be all right.[1]

I am beginning to let myself look forward to your coming home, my darling. I dare not let my thoughts stray in that direction too long beforehand, you know. After you come I want you to stay with your father as long as possible—but I suppose we will have to go to Rome some time in July. Your Auntie[2] has been extremely—critically—ill—but is now convalescing. Her disease was pleuro-pneumonia. I dont think you know that that is rather a weak point with your Aunt. She had a very severe attack of pneumonia in Canada—before we came to the U. States. Indeed that illness of hers had a good deal to do with your grandfathers decision to come to the States. He himself was not very strong in that direction—in that extreme climate

There is always *some* reason for my writing hurriedly, it seems. Today dear little Josie is sick in bed—he was in bed all day yesterday too—has dysentery—and you know he requires ever so much attention from me. I am, consequently, constantly up and down. I thought at first that by keeping him quiet in bed he would soon be all right—but as today is the third day—and as he is very feverish, I thought it safest to send for Dr. King[3]—who has prescribed for him today—and he is now much more comfortable. I found your bill, & enclose it in this. I hope you received the remittance safely? Cousin F. is staying with us—he is very anxious to see you, dear. I know you will love him. It is very pleasant to have him with us. Josie says tell you "that I am so glad to think that he is coming home next month—and that I love him so much—and that I will be so happy when he comes." Good bye, my darling. I love you with all my heart.   Your own Mother.

ALS (WP, DLC) With WWhw notation on env.: "Ans."
 [1] General Assembly met in New Orleans, May 17-26, 1877.
 [2] Mrs. Bones.
 [3] Dr. E. D. King lived, like the Wilsons, at this time on Fourth Street. A Dr. J. F. King had lived on Third Street in 1875-76.

From the Minutes of the Liberal Debating Club

May 19th 1877.

Meeting called to order at 8-10 PM. There being no prop[ositions] for the admission of new members, the minutes being called for were read. The gent from N. J.[1] then read the Manuel. The Sec of St. then read his Enony. The quest for debate was then read & discussed & decided in the neg. The gent. from N. C. proposed the following for next meeting Resolved that Prince Bismark was justifiable on both political & moral grounds in driving the Jesuits from Germany[.] The meeting then adj.

Cas A Talcott Pres
J E Webster Sec. of St.

 [1] Two "gentlemen from New Jersey"—Robert H. McCarter and Edward W. Sheldon—were now members of the Liberal Debating Club.

From Annie Wilson Howe

My darling Brother,   Columbia. May 20th/77.

. . . I have enjoyed the two numbers of the Princetonian which you have sent me very much. I felt as proud of the piece you wrote, in the first one, as if I had written it myself. I showed it to Dr. & Mrs. Howe[1] and they both praised it very highly. It does seem very funny to me to think of your writing anything of that sort or of *any* sort for the press. I can only think of you as the perfect boy you were when you got back from Davidson. How thankful you must be that you gave up Davidson for Princeton—*I* am I know. . . .

Your devoted sister Annie

ALS (WP, DLC) with WWhw and WWsh notation on env.: "Received [WWsh] 5/23/77" followed by WWsh "(Yale game)."
[1] Professor and Mrs. George Howe, Sr., her parents-in-law.

From Janet Woodrow Wilson

My dearest Son,   Wilmington, N. C. Wednesday. [May 23, 1877]
    . . . I see that Dr. Stillman is the Moderator of the Assembly. Your Uncle James W. was his unsuccessful rival for the position. I confess I am glad he was defeated—he has had too much success for his own good—and besides his voice unfits him for such a position. You will see from the papers that the next Assembly will meet in Knoxville. I am glad it is not to be in the far South. I am right anxious about your father being in N. O. during this hot weather. In his last letter he said his head was aching like five hundred—but that he hoped to be able shortly to reduce it to four hundred! . . .   Your own Mother.

ALS (WP, DLC).

To Joseph Ruggles Wilson

My dear father: Princeton, New Jersey 5/23/77
    It is a great comfort to have easy means of communicating with you while you are so far away, and, although you are, no doubt, very busy, I know that a letter from me is never unwelcome and will be all the more acceptable to you while you are away from home. Please give the General Assembly my respects and tell it that it cannot do better than listen to and heed the advice of its Stated Clerk. The said Stated Clerk has a very inconvenient way of seeing right to the heart of any matter which comes under his observation. The son of the said Stated Clerk is a queer fellow. He is entirely free from anything like his father's clear-sightedness and altogether his mind seems to be remarkably bright and empty. You could easily distinguish him in a crowd by his long nose, open mouth, and consequential manner. He is noted in college as a man who can make a remarkably good show with little

or no material. But, after all, he is a good enough sort of fellow and what he lacks in solidity he makes up in good intentions and spasmodic endeavors. He has a few queer ideas of his own and very few of them are his own. He writes sometimes but his style lacks clearness and his choice of words is far from good. Ideas are scarce in his compositions and what few there are go limping about in a cloud of wordy expressions and under a heavy weight of lost nouns and adjectives. Ideas are to his writings what oases are to the desert, except that his ideas are very seldom distinguishable from the waste which surrounds them. He attended a game between the Princeton and Yale base ball nines to-day on the Princeton grounds. He reports the game to have been an unusually beautiful one but that, much to his chagrin, Princeton was defeated by a score of six (6) to four (4). Last Saturday [May 19] Princeton was defeated by Harvard by a score of seven (7) to five (5) and these two (2) defeats following close upon one another have thrown him into a state of despondency about Princeton viewed from an athletic point of view. From what I have seen of him he is apt to allow himself to sympathise almost too heartily with everything that is afloat and, consequently, subjects his nervous system to frequent severe and, sometimes, rather unnecessary strains. Examinations are again close upon him, I believe, and, as he does not stand remarkably high in his class, he seems to look forward to them with some degree of anxiety. But perhaps the anxious look I have of late observed upon his rather unexpressive countenance is caused by dislike of the large amount of studying before him. He seems in fine health and sends love in large quantities to his father, the Stated Clerk.

Your loving son Thomas.

ALS (WP, DLC). There is evidence to suggest that this letter was not sent.

From Douglas McKay

My Dear Tom   Columbia S C May 23/77

Your charming letter of the 13th came to hand O K, and I cannot tell you how welcome it was. . . . You are a good fellow sometimes and I like to write to you whenever I can. But if I had you here now, I should he tempted to pull your ears, for accusing me of being in love, not that I think it a discreditable condition to be in, but because I have been trying for a long time to arrive at that blissful state, but have been unable to find any damsel who would reciprocate my feeling. . . . But my dear boy you need not be so

emphatic as to your not having been in love since you left Columbia—for that will not go down. Your Wilmington experience
is still fresh in my mind, and I fear you never told me how passionate that was. Oh Tom I've got you dead old fellow— . . .

   How I have filled up this letter with sentimental nonsense which
I know you will not enjoy; for a man engaging in writing editorials
for the "Princetonian" is not expected to dabble in such trash except as a matter of recreation. So you you [*sic*] will please excuse
this letter if there is nothing entertaining or instructive in it. . . .

Your Sincere friend D. McKay

Two Editorials in *The Princetonian*

[May 24, 1877]

   How few of us bring our judgments to bear upon our studies.
How many of us are parrot-like in our methods of acquiring knowledge. The great trouble is that few of us look upon our studies in
the proper light. Most of us have had instilled into us the idea that
all the studies of our College course are means by which our minds
are to be trained and strengthened. This idea, though true in itself,
too often leads us into error—the error of regarding mind culture
as an end rather than as a means. It is most necessary to have the
culture of our minds ever in view as an object, the accomplishment of which is both desirable and essential; but the mere desire
for a highly-cultured mind cannot induce enthusiasm in study;
and none but enthusiastic study tells upon our future career.
None but enthusiastic workers are successful workers. True success follows enthusiastic labor. Success has sometimes crowned
the labors of some unenthusiastic worker, but such success is but,
at best, a mean, still-born success. Enthusiasm, then, is necessary
to successful study. Mere desire for mind culture, or mere desire
for College honors, are not sufficiently powerful motives to bring
about enthusiasm in study, since he alone studies with enthusiasm
who earnestly applies himself to study with some noble end in
view. We do not mean to say that studying for class honors is
ignoble. When class honors are viewed in their proper light, as
means to an end, as the exponents of progress made, then they
are most worthy objects.

   What, then, can make us successful students by leading us to
be enthusiastic in study? Simply this: studying with our life's
work constantly in view, and viewing every hour's work as an

hour's preparation for our chosen profession. Nothing will so inspire one while laboring over some tough mathematical problem, as the thought that to conquer this problem is to prepare the mind for some future victory at the bar, some moment of brilliant presentation of the truth from the pulpit, or some successful cure of a stubborn disease. If we view all our studies in this light, we will cease to complain of the dearth of *practical* studies, since each study would then assume a practical character. Every time we overcome a difficulty in our studies we are rendered the more capable of overcoming the difficulties of life. Our minds are now in training for the great athletic struggles of our future life, and every time we neglect an opportunity of rendering our minds stronger, quicker and more skillful, we lessen our chances of future success.

❖

True Scholarship.

A comparison of American scholarship, as represented in our institutions of learning, with that of Germany and England, is very discouraging. It is true that every College can boast of hard students, but with the greater number of them the highest motive is grade, and far be it from us to honor with the title "scholar" the man who has no higher end in view than this.

While the mere student works with the spirit of a slave, the scholar seeks wisdom because he is inspired with a love for it, and to him no exertion seems too great to obtain it. He is genuine, not superficial. Instead of making a good recitation his highest motive, he is constantly training all his powers in the most perfect discipline; the judgment in selecting fields for exploration from the vast territories of knowledge which lie open to him; his industry and perseverance to assist in untiring efforts in gathering and storing away the precious truth, and his memory in holding them in constant readiness for future use.

When true scholarship offers so grand an opportunity for the exercise of our noblest faculties, we marvel that it should be so neglected. On the part of the student, misguided energy and an insufficiency of enthusiasm are at fault; but we must believe that to our collegiate system a large part of the blame can be attached. Nothing is so utterly destructive of true scholarship as what is technically called "cramming." To abolish the practicability of this operation should be the basis principle in the College regime.

But so far is this from being the case, that it would be impossible to devise a method better adapted to encourage and reward it than our present arrangement and style of examinations. Hay is much more likely to be made while the sun shines, if the shower is constantly impending, and the College work would be much more faithfully performed if the students knew not when they would be called to account.

But one great reason why scholars are so few and held in such low repute is, that the highest ambition with many men of excellent talent is to be able and polished writers. We are too prone to forget that knowledge is power, and that without a well-filled mind, our highest literary efforts can never be of much worth. They may even be tinctured with genius, and, without the restraining and correcting power of learning, be mere effusions. Then, too, the characteristics of mind which especially mark the scholar, are, to a large extent, the same with those which make the writer. Thus in both, the secret of success is the power of mental vision, of deep, thorough, condensed thought. Nothing so hampers the writer as a wandering mind. To comprehend his subject fully and justly, to hold it before his mind in all its shades and ramifications, and to reproduce it, requires the utmost concentration.

Further, the scholar who is versed in all literature is capable of drawing apt illustrations from science and art, and of leaving everywhere the impress of his own originality. If Princeton is to hold a high rank in literature, she must produce scholars; and if we are fired with an ambition for fame and for the glory of our *alma mater*, no pathway is nobler than true scholarship.

Printed in *The Princetonian*, II (May 24, 1877), 28, 30-31.

From the Minutes of the American Whig Society

Miscellaneous Business   Whig Hall, May 25th 1877.

Whereas, The present status of the Hall demands some immediate and decided action for perfecting the means for attaining the ends for which the Society was founded,

Therefore, Be it resolved, that a committee consisting of two members from the Senior, two from the Junior, and one from the Sophomore class in Hall, be appointed to take into consideration the present condition of the Society, and to recommend what seems to them the best means for perfecting its workings. c-d. Mc-Carter, Wilson, Gilman.

From the Minutes of the Liberal Debating Club

May 26th 1877

Meeting called to order at 8-20[.] At propositions for new members, the name of Mr Henderson '79[1] was proposed, & the proposition was laid on the table. The debate was next in order & the Jesuit quest. came up & the debate was opened by Mr McCarter in the Aff. after it was discussed it was moved by the gent. from N. C. to lay the quest of [on] the table, the meeting was then interrupted & adj

Cas. A. Talcott Pres
J. E. Webster Sec of St

[1] Robert Randolph Henderson, born Jan. 9, 1858. A.B. College of New Jersey, 1879; LL.B., University of Maryland, 1881. Practiced law in Cumberland, Md. Twice district attorney for Allegheny County; judge of Maryland courts, 1903-1921. Died Dec. 20, 1921.

From Wilson's Shorthand Diary

May 1877

[May] 27th Sabbath. My second attempt at diary-keeping has also proved *spasmodic* apparently. A diary is a very interesting thing to read but not a very interesting thing *to keep*. But when one is able to record his thoughts in shorthand he ought to be ashamed if he be not able to raise enough energy to keep a simple record of the daily events of his life. I will [make] one more effort to accomplish this seemingly difficult task. I have little to record this day except ever since my last entry I have done little that is of much credit to myself or my abilities. Editorial work goes easy so far. I have as yet found nothing but pleasure in it. During the last vacation I wrote two essays, one on "Men and Ideas," and one on heroism. I handed the one on "Men and Ideas" in for the "Lit" prize, and the one on heroism I handed in for the sophomore essay contest in Whig Hall. Success had spoiled me[.] I had an idea that because my speech in sophomore speaking had been very much praised I was a very fine writer and could take any prize for writing that I might try for. I see the consequence. Fred Campbell '77,[1] got the Lit prize, Kerr and McCarter won the sophomore prizes.[2] I grasped at two prizes and obtained neither. The essay on Men and Ideas was much better than the one on heroism, and if I had handed it in for the sophomore prize I would probably have stood a much better chance since the essay on heroism gained me honorable mention for writing the third best essay of those handed in (there were only five handed in).[3] But thinking that I could easily beat any competitor in the sophomore contest

I handed in an indifferent essay for that prize[.] I sent in my best for the Lit prize—the consequence I have noted above. Since my last entry Princeton has been defeated twice in baseball—once by Harvard and once by Yale and Princeton baseball stock is consequently very low. The men didn't train in the right way. I heard an excellent sermon this morning from Dr. Duffield—he is in my opinion an excellent preacher. His sermons always contain solid advice and they are all always eminently practical. I have now commenced to read Carlyle's French Revolution and am deeply interested in it. I have finished the first volume and am eagerly looking forward to enjoyment of the second if ever I gain sufficient time to peruse its exciting pages. Carlyle's style charms me above all things. There is a mellowness about his every word— an apparent deepness of vision—an aliveness of thought which is invigorating. His earnest Scotch character creeps out upon every page and he gains the sympathy and awakens the love of his reader. With a masterly ease he grasps the salient points of the great drama of the French Revolution and gives you the cream of the events—he interweaves the great event and its lessons—the great principles at work in that stupendous crisis and the contents of those principles. His grasp of the subject is masterly. If Carlyle had Macaulay's clearness of style there would be no limit to his power. Now that I am fairly into one of his books I will not be satisfied until I have read them all. Thank God for health and strength.

1 Frederick Campbell, '77.
2 The decision was announced in Whig Hall on May 25, 1877. See American Whig Society Minutes, May 25, 1877.
3 Not found.

From the Minutes of the Liberal Debating Club

June 2nd 1877.
Meeting called to order at 8-10 P.M The proposition for admission of new members being called for, the name of Mr. Henderson was proposed. The Pres. ruled it out of order to elect him, there not being a full number present. The gent from Md.[1] moved to lay it on the table till a special meeting. Mis. business being next in order, the Man[ual] was read by the gent from N. C. It was then moved by the gent from Md. that some action be taken in regard to the financial state of the society, & carried. The Pres moved that each member immediately pay 25¢ & was carried. The debate then came up and was decided in the aff. The gent. from N. C. the[n] proposed the following question Resolved that a Congress-

man should be elected for 6 years instead of 2. The debate was opened in the aff. by gent. from N C & was carried in the neg. The gent from Md. then proposed the following question for next meeting Resolved that the action of Spain was illegal in surrendering Tweed to the United States[.][2] The meeting then adjourned till 2nd Sat. of Junior Year   Cas A Talcott Pres

J E Webster Sec of St.

[1] Probably Hiram Woods, Jr.
[2] "Boss" William M. Tweed of New York City, who had fled to Spain to escape prosecution for fraud.

From Wilson's Shorthand Diary

[June] 3rd Sabbath. This is the anniversary of my last attempt at diary-keeping. I seem to have pretty common attacks of *diary fever*. My last diary was kept from June 3rd/76 to the latter part of October /76. I then made the mistake of recording every day's events whether they were worth record[ing] or not. Last year's events were perhaps more worth record[ing] than those of this year because last year I read more and had more to write about my reading and things of that kind. This year I will not feel obliged to record every day's events but only those best worth record[ing]. We had a very interesting meeting of the LDC last night. Talcott[,] Webster and Woods were present and we had an unusually pleasant time. We discussed the question whether it would be advisable to lengthen the term of office of Congressmen. I maintained to the best of my ability that a term of six years rather than one of two years would best serve the interests of the country. I was overcome by opinion rather than by argument from other members present. That my arguments were sound I am convinced as I have put considerable thought upon the subject. Today has been communion Sabbath and I feel that my relations with God have this day become more intimate. Thank God for renewed faith and for health and strength.

From Janet Woodrow Wilson

My darling Son,   Wilmington N. C. June 6th '77.

I suppose we may say now, that in *two* weeks more, you will be at home. I never knew weeks to pass so slowly as they are doing now. . . . I confess I am not at all reconciled to the idea of taking you away from your father—but he wishes us to go—indeed seems very anxious to get us off. I dont feel the least regret at the idea of leaving the Wilmingtonians, I assure you. The way they treat us during your father's absenses has made it impossible for me to regard the people with the slightest affection. They never come near me even when they know that Josie & I are all alone. . . .

Your own Mother

ALS (WP, DLC).

Three Editorials in *The Princetonian*

[June 7, 1877]

Writing of Fiction in Princeton.

We may well be proud of our array of statesmen and scholars, but it is a notable fact that our list of graduates contains few names of men who stand high in the ranks of fiction writers. While Yale boasts a Cooper and Bowdoin, a Hawthorne, Princeton is without a fiction writer whose fame can be mentioned as comparing with the fame which these novelists have attained.

The reasons for this are many, and their thorough discussion would require more space than can be given to this article. But there is one defect that can be remedied by the students, and of this we would speak. Our College papers offer an open field to the philosopher, the poet, the essayist, the literary critic, and the general critic or growler, but no corner is found throughout their many pages for the writer of prose fiction. Occasionally some one dreams a dream, the perusal of which is apt to send the reader himself to the land of dreams. *The Princetonian* has, indeed, opened its columns for one short piece of fiction, and for this it deserves praise, but its size and character do not admit of many pieces of this kind.

What we would suggest is, that the *Lit.* extend a hearty greeting to all worthy articles of fiction. Would it even be too much to open one of its prizes to competitors whose articles should be of this character?

We know that there are many who will raise the cry, "sentimentality, trash, dime novel literature," at this suggestion, perhaps, for the reason that their whole acquaintance with fiction has been confined to articles of this description. Let it be understood that we refer to something of an entirely different stamp. The better class of fiction is made up of character sketches, fancy sketches and mind studies; "chemical problems," as the *Atlantic* calls Hawthorne's works. Pieces of this character are the kind we advocate, and Princeton has men who would not meanly succeed in writing them. A well-written study of character contains far more thought than a great number of the so-called original pieces that fill our papers, many of which, although very good, are but the "revised and corrected" editions of the works of dead philosophers and critics. Let some encouragement be given in this College to men of an imaginative turn of mind, and perhaps it will be the breeze that will fan into a flame some hidden spark of genius, that will in after years illume with its glow the name of Nassau Hall.   R.

✧

The "Voice of the Alumni," in the last number of the *Lit.*, contains an eminently sensible and highly interesting article upon "Oratory in Princeton," from the pen of Mr. Henderson of '76.[1] We most heartily agree with Mr. H. in almost every particular. We had been thinking much upon Princeton's oratory, and Mr. H.'s piece came to hand at what was, to us, a peculiarly seasonable time. We wish to present a few thoughts which, though not original, are at least practical. We view oratory in an entirely wrong light in Princeton. We are apt to make the same mistake about oratory that so many of us make about other studies. We view oratory as an end, rather than as a means. Let us ask and answer two simple questions, and we will at once be upon surer ground. What is the object of oratory? Its object is persuasion and conviction—the control of other minds by a strange personal influence and power. What are the fields of labor open to us in our future life career as orators? The bar, the pulpit, the stump, the Senate chamber, the lecturer's platform. Keeping any one of these fields of labor in view, we can study intelligently. Even if, as Mr. H. hints, following a proper method of study and action should exclude us from all College prizes for oratory, we need not be at all discouraged. We wish the training, if we view our study and practice in the proper light, and the prizes are of secondary importance. Such prizes are only material indications of progress in a certain direction.

The first and great requisite in an orator is ability to express in easy, elegant language the thoughts and arguments which he wishes to present to his hearers. Without the developed power of facile expression he is powerless. The means of acquiring ease and force of expression are various. To the orator, constant practice in writing is essential to gaining elegance of expression. But constant practice in extempore debate is the great prerequisite to success in speaking; and for this reason we think the private debating society a most excellent institution. Our Halls are too large to give any of us such practice as is necessary, and work in private debating clubs is a necessary supplement to Hall work. No one can fail to see the advantage of frequent debate. The very act of putting one's thoughts into words renders expression more and more easy. This constant practice in speaking, together with continual practice in composition, makes the great orator.

And now we come to the chief and best means of training the orator—the imitation of classic models. The greatest and truest model for all orators is Demosthenes. One who has not studied deeply and constantly all the great speeches of the great Athenian, is not prepared to speak in public. You may smile at this statement, and say that such opinions are second-hand and out of date. If you think so, you lack, and ever will lack, the true spirit of eloquence. Some have studied the stirring orations of the great orator merely because compelled to do so for the purpose of acquiring some knowledge of the noble language which was Demosthenes' vehicle of thought—such smile at our praise of Demosthenes, and despise him as a model. We, none of us, study Demosthenes aright. In trying to catch the peculiar idiom, in looking upon his moving sentences as dull collections of words arranged to arbitrary rules, we fail to perceive the all-pervading eloquence with which every sentence is aglow. The orator must study Demosthenes to watch every turn of argument; for Demosthenes, more than any other orator of ancient or modern times, knew how to sway the human mind. He must watch every turn of expression, because Demosthenes, above all other orators, knew how to condense and give life to thought. He must study Demosthenes, not for the purpose of servilely imitating him, but in order that he may catch some of his spirit of eloquence. He must supplement his study of Demosthenes by a careful study of the great English orators. We may reject this method of training because it is old, but, before we decide to do so, let us reflect that, by just such methods of training as we have indicated above, the greatest orators of England gained their power, and that we must do likewise, if we would catch some of the true spirit of oratory, and bring back to the ears and hearts of the American people some of the old strains of eloquence which used to delight them. Only as the constant companions of Demosthenes, Cicero, Burke, Fox, Canning, and Webster, can we hope to become orators.   X.

1 William J. Henderson, '76.

❖

Intelligent Reading.

Probably every one has his own peculiar ideas as to the best methods of reading. There are some principles which may with safety be laid down for the guidance of every reader. Without the power of close attention reading is of little benefit. Reading should be done systematically, since desultory reading is worse than useless. These principles have become axiomatic. What I would now speak about, and lead others to reflect upon, is the means of retaining in memory what we read. It must be remembered that in reading, our object is not to remember everything that the author says, but to assimilate, if we do not reject, the ideas which he sets forth. Every book which is worth reading at all, is worth reading thoroughly, and the only true way of reading a work thoroughly, is that of concentrating our minds upon its contents, thinking long and deeply, under its guidance, upon the subjects of which it treats, and following out through all its ramifications the train of thought which it suggests. Our object in reading the work of some great historian, should not be to remember all the particulars of every event, or even every event which he chronicles, but it should be to catch the general course of events, and, above all, to grasp and retain the principles which characterize and are the causes of every turn of events.

The habit of note-taking is directly antagonistic to the interests of the reader. How can any one retain in mind any grand principle when he depends upon his note-book to recall it to his memory? How can any one ponder over and follow out a striking thought when he stops to put it down in cold black and white? One reason why modern scholars can not compare in attainments with ancient scholars, is because they are coming more and more to surround themselves with note-books, upon which they are wholly dependent. Their accuracy depends almost entirely upon their familiarity with the arrangements of their note-books. How can any orator be eloquent when he depends upon his notes for every thought? Imagine Demosthenes with notes in his hands! One reason why our orators are so inferior to those of Greece and Rome, is because they are hampered by notes, and, instead of having souls and tongues alive with knowledge and power, have committed all their knowledge to paper, and expended all their power upon wielding their pencils and arranging their ponderous masses of notes. Scholarship has declined because memory has grown weak; memory has grown weak for want of exercise. The way to become familiar with a subject is to read much and ponder more upon it, becoming thoroughly familiar with and leisurely digesting all that has been written upon it, and not to simply waste time by committing to paper and pigeon-holing every bit of information we may acquire upon it. It may be answered that there is a proper method of taking notes, that there are persons who may take copious notes upon the works which they are reading and yet not make the mistake of depending entirely upon their notes. Theoretically there may be some such person in existence; there is none such in real life. No being of such a character is possible as long as human nature is such as it is. Notes are pernicious, and contrary to nature. We should read every work with the same eagerness with which we peruse a novel—with that eagerness which alone can render reading effective, and then notes would be superfluous.   A.

Printed in *The Princetonian*, II (June 7, 1877), 40, 42-43, 44.

Pocket Notebook

                                                        [c. July 1, 1877-June 1882]

Inscribed on first page (WWhw):
    "Thomas W. Wilson," followed by WWsh signature, with "his mark" (WWsh) below.

Contents:
    (a) WWsh and WWhw bibliographical and reading notes.
    (b) WWsh outlines of speeches on "Independent Conviction," and on "Thomas Carlyle," printed at July 16, 1877.
    (c) WWsh outlines of essay "Prince Bismarck." Essay printed at Nov. 1, 1877.
    (d) WWsh quotations from Daniel Webster.
    (e) WWsh quotations from various writers.
    (f) WWsh and WWhw brief comments on various subjects, including WWsh copy of JRW on writing, from his letter of Jan. 10, 1878, printed at Jan. 14, 1878.
    (g) WWhw list of addresses of friends and business firms.
    (h) WWhw itemized personal expenses during May and June 1882, including those for trip to New York, to be printed at May 16, 1882, Vol. 2.
    (i) WWhw and WWsh note about "Elocution."

(WP, DLC).

From Joseph Ruggles Wilson

My dearest Son—   Wilmington [N. C.], July 7, 1877
    Your letter—so well written and so manly—came to hand this morning and afforded me sincere pleasure. It was my first news from you all, except that by telegram. The letter you say your mother wrote has never been received—by me at least. There is

some mistake touching it; and I feel deeply disappointed. I fear that it has fallen into other hands. . . .

Yr. appreciation of yr. amazing aunt[1]—that lusus naturae—is very just, I am afraid. It is not her *head* that is at fault; her *heart* is the chief offender,—and if it ached more her head would ache less. But then the (acre)acher-age of that organ is even less in extent than that of her brain. I am glad, though, that she did *not* call—for her presence & conversation would only have made yr. mother nervous. She had now better be regarded as a non-existent.

If you could inform me as to the precise day of yr. starting for Rome, I would be gratified. I will not know—as my information now stands—whether to direct another note to Columbia: or even whether you will receive this until it shall have been forwarded.

My health is on the upward go, I think. My solitude is my principal disease (by the way you spell disease twice as if it were de-cease; it is decease only when it terminates fatally!)

Love without measure to your dear mother, to dear Josie, and to the others all.   Your affectionate father   Joseph R W.

P. S. Since writing above, a package came from Lord & Taylor which I forward—just so—to Columbia. It ought to be there by the time you get this letter

ALS (WP, DLC).
[1] Perhaps Aunt Felie, Mrs. James Woodrow.

From Wilson's Shorthand Diary

July 1877   Rome, Geo. July 16th, 1877.
    16th Monday. I arrived here last Thursday, the 10th, with mother and Josie—or rather I arrived on the morning of the 13th being delayed 17 miles from here all the night of the 12th. I will in all probability spend the remainder of the summer here going on to college from here about the middle or early part of September. I have done little reading so far this summer and must now commence to do the reading and writing I had planned for this summer before leaving college. I have about finished Carlyle's French Revolution which I have enjoyed very much indeed. I have received a couple of letters from McCarter since leaving college and have enjoyed them much. I wrote to him today in answer to a long 11-page letter received from him last week. I wish I could find some agreeable way of hinting to him that his use of words is extremely loose and careless. He is getting into very bad habits from mere carelessness and thus threatening to ruin his diction. He is natu-

rally a gifted writer but still shows a considerable lack of cultivation. I also wrote a short note to sister Annie telling her of our safe
arrival. I will try to commence my speech, for the preliminary J.
O. contest, tomorrow. I have chosen the subject "Independent
Conviction";[1] I can say much upon this suggestive subject since it
is one which has long been engaging my thoughts and one of
whose careful consideration this country is much in need. I will
also soon commence an essay on that wonderful man Thomas
Carlyle.[2] Few have done Carlyle justice, few have viewed his mission and work in the right light. He has not been appreciated because his life work has not been comprehended. Had a very
pleasant ride in the afternoon with Jessie. Spent the evening reading Fox's speech on the "Westminster Scrutiny"—a masterly production. Thank God for health and strength.

[1] The manuscript has not been found, but see the transcript of WW's outline,
printed immediately following, and "Some Thoughts on the Present State of
Public Affairs," printed at Jan. 30, 1878, which seems to have been a substantial
revision of "Independent Conviction." WW finished this speech on July 20, 1877,
but did not deliver it in the preliminary Junior Oratory exercise in Whig Hall.
Instead, he delivered a speech on Bismarck, printed at Dec. 6, 1877.

[2] The manuscript has not been found, but see the transcript of WW's outline,
printed immediately following. WW read this essay in Whig Hall on Nov. 9, 1877.

Two Outlines of Speeches

[c. July 16, 1877]

Independent Conviction: Analysis—(Speech)

A: A short outline of the characteristics of the age:—

(a) Healthy tendencies: Diffusion and popularity of knowledge and the recognition of the fact that education is necessary
for the full development of character, etc.

(b) Evil tendencies—a superficial knowledge a mere schoolboy
knowledge of political economy in its highest sense. An age
when looseness of thought is mistaken for true independent
and original thought.

(c) These tendencies as exhibited in our own country.

(B) The present disorderly and chaotic condition of society traceable to lack of independent conviction. Definition of independent conviction: deep thought[,] proper investigation of causes
[of] loss of principles etc and dispassioned adoption of conclusions together with sustained action in compliance with these
principles and conclusions.

(C) The absence of this independent conviction in American
statesmanship. Causes for this absence:

(a) The spirit in which Americans enter public life.

(b) The lack of an over-all real independence of thought upon the great questions of the day.

(D) The proper functions of party:

(a) To embody convictions; not to embody prejudice.

(b) To give life and action to principles.

(c) To secure cooperative action.

(E) The relations of great men to party:

(a) As the natural leaders and formers of parties; Alexander Hamilton and Federalists.

(b) The hopes of this government's future welfare depend upon the drawing of new party lines consequent upon the rise in the future of statesmen such as this country has not seen for some time.

(c) The causes which can produce such statesmen.

(d) The true definition of great men—great statesmen—those who possess true independent conviction.

(F) Means of acquiring independent conviction:

(a) By diligent and careful study of history.

(b) By careful study of political economy in connection with history and development of government.

Thomas Carlyle   Analysis: (Speech)

Introduction:

(A) The characteristics and tendencies of the 18th century. His birth at the close of this century significant. A purifying element introduced.

(B) Glance at Carlyle's moral and intellectual character as traceable in his works.

(B') Carlyle's mission as exposer of frauds and shams of every kind. This fact of his character necessary to right appreciation of Carlyle's work.

(C) Carlyle as an historian

(a) On the subject matter (condensed wisdom). Its noble effect upon the era.

(b) Singular style. His style not in thorough keeping with his thought.

(D) The general grand effect of Carlyle's life and life work. An estimate of his place in the history of this century and worth to civilization. His place in political history.

Thoughts upon the above:

Matter: The strong prejudice which characterizes almost all of Carlyle's judgments of men and their characteristics necessary to his work as an exposer of shams since it generally happens that a man of unprejudiced judgment is too prone to silence and too apt to fail to paint vice in its true colors.

Carlyle a grim knight-errant meeting [*] fraud in all its forms and under whatever disguise.

Carlyle able at once to seize upon current central idea in historical events and to assess the effect of that idea upon the history of mankind.

The vigor of Carlyle's blame on the high crimes and his invective as well as the heartiness of his principles alike the evidence a large and truthful heart—a heart burning with shame at the world's double-facedness.

If Carlyle does dwell upon one of the characteristics of man and make those characteristics the man he always finds out with unerring skill and interest the fundamental characteristics of the character under consideration.

(Some have said that Carlyle dwells too much upon the particulars to the exclusion of some of the important events which find no place in his pages.)

These particulars upon which Carlyle so fondly dwells from the feathers which show the direction of the wind. He strains, seemingly by inspiration, upon those particulars which though trifles in themselves both render the picture more vivid and truly reflect the emotions of the national effort and the grand tendencies of the crises in the national history. As great waves are but the natural results of the irresistible movements of the mighty ocean and these movements are as truly indicated by the slight tossing of some speck upon his mighty bosom or by the aid of the spray. Thus also are great national movements as clearly indicated by trifling events as by grand convulsions. Great national movements are but grand manifest[ations] of each *individual's* definite desire, the summing up of each *individual's* earnest endeavor.

"As I stand on the brink of eternity no truth so fully meets my wants or so satisfies my intellect as that stated in the shorter catechism, 'The chief end of man is to glorify God.[']"

1826-32 Among the black morasses and granite hills of Dumfriesshire 15 miles from any town.

1827 Specimens of German experiments. 1832 went to London.

1823-4 Life of Schiller. 1831 Sartor Resartus. 1837 French Revolution.

1827 Miscellaneous. 1831 Characteristics

Transcripts of WWsh outlines in pocket notebook described at July 1, 1877.

From Wilson's Shorthand Diary

[July] 17 Tuesday. Wrote a little this morning upon the introduction to my speech. I am trying to compose and condense at the same time and find the task a somewhat difficult one though comparatively easy from previous practice. I find my subject a very interesting one. Finished Fox's speech on the "Westminster Scrutiny" and read his speech on the "Russian Armament." This speech must have been one of his most powerful productions as it allows full scope to his invective and full opportunity for the exercise of those faculties for which he was remarkable in debate. In the evening I took a long walk with Jessie to the summit of one of the highest hills in the neighborhood. I enjoyed the walk most thoroughly and the scenery was beautiful. Below us lay a broad valley stretching in all the beauty of its verdure between the two ranges of the Blue hills. Through the middle of the valley flowed a clear stream between 2 well shaded banks. Altogether the scene was one of peace and quiet beauty. I retired early as I was somewhat tired after our long walk. Thank God for health and strength.

[July] 18th Wednesday. A rather uninteresting day. Made some progress upon my speech and found writing today very satisfactory. Did very little reading only glancing over one or two of Sidney Smith's essays and part of the life of Alexander Stephens by *Cleveland*. Stephens is without doubt a remarkable even a wonderful man but I doubt if he is what this book represents him to be: the great statesman of the age and the most eloquent man of the day. His intellect is powerful but not marvelous. Stephens is a wonderfully powerful man but not a great man. I played croquet a good deal today and enjoyed it much more [than] on an ordinary day. I was cut out of my ride by the delay of supper in consequence of the long stay of the visitors. Thank God for health and strength.

From Robert Harris McCarter

My Dear Tommy—

Monmouth Beach [N. J.] Sea Bright P. O., 18th July '77

Your pleasant letter letter [sic] of the 16th inst. came to hand, and in the outset let me explain my position taken in my lest [last] letter. The proverb "There is nothing new under the sun" I regard & at the time of my last writing did regard as absurd. To say that in the regions of science, of art, of literature, nothing new has been discovered would be paradoxical. If I remember

rightly I was saying that students of our age have little or no originality of thought and said that to their writings we might *apply*
that proverb. Do not believe that I for an instance credit the proverb. Our point of disagreement in regard to the presence of originality of our writings seems to lie in our conception of what *originality* of *thought consists* & our ideas differ materially on the subject. If the originality expected in our speeches is what you define
it to be—then I give you your point. And if "*originality*" is thus used
why then Mr. Trench has omitted one word in his chapter on the
"Degeneracy of Words." Dr. Johnson went so far to say that none
of the writers of his brilliant age wrote anything that could claim
to be original, saying that if the musty books in the libraries were
read by the public, they would there find the same ideas expressed
differently—"*degested*" if you will—as those that *came* out in the
"*Rambler*," that had come out in the *Spectator*. Unlike you but like
myself he did not call the result of degestion of matter read, originality. However[,] the controversy rests on the the [*sic*] meaning
attached to originality.

I have almost decided to take the subject "Culture and Happiness" for my speech. It is a subject upon which I have thought a
good deal lately and you remember we had an essay to write on
almost the same subject. I remember you said to me that you
would like to talk with me on the subject after having heard my
essay. I inferred that you did not agree with some of my opinions
on the subject. I was not fortunate enough to have a discussion
& to gain your views. . . .

I have just enjoyed a short visit from Jack Farr. The summer is
going delightfully & by far too quickly. Before we know it we will
be back again at work. Junior year will be a radical change & I am
quite anxious to see how I will wrestle with Logic & Psychology.
If Mathematics are any test I shake for myself. Macaulays essays
have been instructing and amusing me for a few days. How he
does go for the "Utilitarian theory of government"! You I suppose
are still at Carlyle. You are traveling a pleasant road with a good
many sharp turns but no briers or pebbles to bother or hinder your
progress. . . .   As ever Yours   Robt. Harris McCarter

ALS (WP, DLC) with WWsh draft of reply to McCarter on env. and two pages
att.

Draft of a Letter to Robert Harris McCarter

[Rome, Ga., c. July 18, 1877]

Yours of the 18th instant came promptly to hand and was
read with pleasure. I would have written sooner in replying but I

have been out of town and had little or no time for writing of this kind.

I am glad that I misunderstood you with reference to the proverb. You expressed yourself as if you were a believer in the truth of its assertion. I had no time when I last wrote to elaborate my opinion upon *original* and I had no idea when writing the few sentences that I did write upon that subject that my thoughts would meet with anything but assent from you. But since you take issue with me as to fundamental principles I am nothing loath [to] canvass the subject with you. I am willing to take the abstract definition of original as I find it in the dictionary here. It is this: Original, the power of originating or producing new thoughts, or *intellectual combinations of thought.* I cannot remember the words in which I defined original in my last letter but I will answer by giving you another definition which imputes the idea which I had in my mind when jotting down the few thoughts upon this subject in my last. I would define original, then, to be the production by the mind of new or intellectual combinations of thought consequent upon the thorough digestion of information gained from extensive and careful reading and every kind of observation; and, as I said, none but men of powerful minds are capable of this digestion of information because none but well-trained minds can thus digest and none but minds characterized by a greater or less degree of power are susceptible of the training. The truth of this definition you deny, that is you deny that the result of the independent operation of a well-trained mind upon thoroughly digested materials is original thought. As well deny that a man who has made an entirely new instrument out of old and well-known materials and in accordance with universally recognized laws is an inventor. Without those materials and knowledge of those laws he could never have been

Transcript of WWshL (draft) (WP, DLC).

To Robert Bridges[1]

Dear Bob   Rome, Geo., 7/18/77.

I was both surprised and pleased to receive a note from you in shorthand.[2] I hasten to answer and write in a little more advanced style than you used because I am sure that you have advanced quite far into the study if you have continued as you commenced. You see I am far from home. I am enjoying myself here among the Georgia mountains. The country around here is beautiful. My uncle's family live here and I am very nicely placed. I have not

yet heard from Charles Talcott but live in hopes of seeing him fulfill his promise to write to me. Neither have I heard from Hiram,
the rascal. I have received two letters from McCarter,[3] however.
What did you think of the distribution of the prizes at college? I
was surprised at almost all of them. Hope that you can read this
and that you will soon write to me I remain as ever   Your sincere
friend,   T. W. Wilson
Address me care James Bones, Esq. Rome, Geo.

Transcript of WWshPS (Meyer Coll., DLC). Date, salutation, and postscript in
WWhw.
  [1] Robert Bridges, born July 13, 1858. A.B., College of New Jersey, 1879. Reporter,
Rochester *Democrat and Chronicle*, 1880-81; assistant news editor, New York
Evening Post, 1881-87; literary critic, *Life*, 1883-1900; assistant editor, *Scribner's
Magazine*, 1887-1914, editor, 1914-30. Poet and author. Litt.D., Princeton University, 1919. Died Sept. 2, 1941.
  [2] It is missing.
  [3] R. H. McCarter to WW, June 26 and July 9, 1877, ALS (WP, DLC).

From Wilson's Shorthand Diary

[July] 19th Thursday. Spent most of the day playing croquet[,]
riding etc. Made satisfactory progress on my speech and read the
introduction of Fox's speech on parliamentary reform—his great
effort in support of Mr. Gray's bill. Went with Jessie in buggy to
take the little dog Cliquot into the country and give him away. He
is a vicious little animal and was becoming a nuisance and then
Jessie expects another dog from Augusta in a day or 2. I see the
Atlanta papers regularly but they contain little of interest except
the reports of the Convention proceedings[1] and even these are certainly comparatively interesting. I suppose that it was wise to call
this Convention as the present situation is certainly a more miserable one than most states are cursed with. These men may possibly
succeed in bringing forth a more perfect instrument but I cannot
expect much wisdom from this collection of petty talkers. A few
eminent men are not enough to leaven the whole lump. Thank God
for health and strength.

  [1] The Georgia constitutional convention of 1877.

[July] 20th Friday. Josie's birthday. Wrote pretty steadily for
some time this morning and finished my speech: one of the most
miserable productions of which I was ever guilty. In the speech I
could not treat of independent conviction in a metaphysical way
nor could I wholly enumerate the innumerable beneficial effects
which follow whatever exists in the minds of the nation's leaders.
So I confined myself to the political point of view dwelling

upon this country's statesmanship and what hopes there were for its future welfare upon the drawing of new party lines consequent upon the rise of great statesmen, men of independent conviction. I do not hesitate to say that the ideas and principles set forth in this speech are both eminently true and of the utmost importance but I am afraid that they are stated neither forcibly nor clearly. Dear mother played a game of croquet with Jessie and me this afternoon. I took a ride with Jessie as usual. In the evening the child had some tableaux which proved unexpectedly very interesting indeed. Dear [*] and two of his little girls were here as spectators. Josie was in high glee and great spirits and was the life of the pretty exhibition. We were treated not only with tableaux but also with some tricks of legerdemain. The latter were performed by Josie with considerable difficulty. Thank God for health and strength.

From Charles Andrew Talcott

My dear Thomas,–   Utica [N. Y.] July 25 1877–

The first sentence in your letter was a crusher; it took me one week to fully comprehend its meaning, and it has taken me another, to find self-confidence enough to answer, in a rambling and incoherent manner, one whom I do not hesitate to pronounce the master of English diction! ! Your points in regard to Utica were well taken. The thick clouds of obscurity, which envelop Rome, Georgia, cannot be dispelled, so I must content myself with imagining it a delightful place, the defect of whose "lighthouse" equipment is supplied by the bright eyes of beautiful maidens. Vacation . . . is passing pleasantly away. I have been thinking a little about a preliminary J[unior] O[ratory]. My subject will probably be "Citizenship.["] Both the subjects, you spoke of having considered, seem to me to be excellent. "Independent Conviction" sounds better to my ears, because I think a biographical subject is apt to press a man into too narrow limits. . . .

Having managed to deface a good deal of paper I will close by asking [you] to write soon your opinion, of my J. O. subject, of the late riot,[1] and of Rome, Georgia.   Your Friend Charles Talcott

ALS (WP, DLC) with WWhw and WWsh notations on env.: "Received [WWsh] 8/7/77" and "Ans 8/14/77."

[1] A reference to riots of striking railroad workers in Martinsburg, West Virginia, and Pittsburgh.

Two Letters from Joseph Ruggles Wilson

[Wilmington, N. C.] Thursday [July 26, 1877]

My dearest Thomas—

I herewith return the draft of the speech[1] you sent to me for criticism. You will notice that I have ventured to suggest a number of corrections that will serve to make the movement of your sentences a little smoother and perhaps a little more vigorous. It is certainly well written, but has some marks of haste. Its sentiments are all good and true, deserving of thoughtful consideration. Your transitions, though, are abrupt. It is not always easy to perceive the exact tie of connection between thought and thought. Practise will correct this. There is no reason why you should not be a first-rate writer and a precise thinker. Like most young composers, you are apt to *generalize* too broadly—do not qualify with sufficient care. A *perfectly fair* statement of a case or a fact is extremely difficult, especially where we wish to *make a point*. Bold thinking is very desirable; but it loses its power so soon as it ceases to be without show of *caution*: for it then, by becoming too sweeping, *thins*. I am very anxious to have you reach a high standard of oratory; you can do so only by acquiring the habit of cautious (not timid or doubting) thinking: that sort of thinking which has mental eyes for looking all around and all through a subject; and which indulges in no statements for the support of which there is not good proof. That is, no genuine, or forceful, oratory is possible unless it have a foundation in truth, and in truth that all can be made to see. The true orator argues; he does not affirm nor dogmatize, unless his reputation is complete and his authority confessed. I am pleased, dear boy, with your progress towards the acquisition of oratorical efficiency. Be not content without an added step each day. Cultivate manner. In the last sense of the word the great orator is the great *actor*.

I am sorry that my letters are as irregular as your mother's have been. I rec'd hers of Tuesday a little while ago. Tell her I was so thankful to get it. Her letters are extremely valuable to me: they are so true as well as so kind and sympathetic. Your letters are also a help to me, dear old fellow. You must write me as to a *friend* as well as a father—the better & truer friend because a father. I am glad to have a friend in you, whose character I greatly esteem, and upon whose continued excellence in the future I look with confidence.

Give my love to that little rascal Josie—to that bigger rascaless, your mother—and you the weightiest rascal of the three, kiss them for me & have them kiss you for me. Love to all Bones

Your affectionate father   J. R. W.

ALS (WP, DLC) with WWhw notation on env.: "Ans." Also WWsh notation "Valuable in extreme." on env., Att.: JRW to WW, c. Aug. 10, 1877.
¹ It was almost surely "Independent Conviction."

My darling son: [Wilmington, N. C.] Friday [c. Aug. 10, 1877]
    I am very much pleased with the speech [on Carlyle] which I now return to yr hands. Its views are just. Its language is good. Its thoughts are evidently those of earnestness. If well spoken, it ought to produce an impression. I have made some corrections, as you will see, which it is likely your own judgment and taste will approve. You have one fault that generally characterizes young writers—of being too sweeping in your generalities. Try to correct this by cautious thinking and by qualifying adjectives. Truth ought always to be stated with well cut precision; it is then stated with *all* the force that rightfully belongs to it. Your estimate of Carlyle agrees with my own. I consider him both great and good. It is only to be regretted that his admiration of Christianity has not been attended by such a *love*—personal love I mean—for its divine founder as the friends of genuine piety could desire. Certainly Calvanism is not altogether to his taste:—although his later years *do* show some evidences of his having swung back towards his earlier training in this respect. His devotion to what he thinks the "True" is his splendid distinction. Imitate him, dear son, in this. The Lie is always the bad and the detestable. It is of the Devil its father. I am preparing to leave home for my summer vacation. I wish it were not going further from you all that this preparation is making. My heart longs for the dear ones upon whom its affections are set, with a longing that is sometimes almost intolerable. But, to do what is right is better than to follow mere inclination. Tell your dear mother that her letter of the 8th was received at the same time with yours. I will write to her once more before I leave. I am sure, dearest boy, that you show her all the love you feel, and that you feel as much as son ever felt for mother. She deserves the utmost of the affection and reverence and devotion of us all. There never was a truer wife or a better mother. I am so glad that she has in you a son of whom she feels that she has reason to be proud. Make her prouder still.

Give to Josie my fondest love. I need not send love to the sweet mother. Love also to All Bones.

Most affectionately   Your father & friend,   Joseph R Wilson

ALS (WP, DLC). Att. to JRW to WW, July 26, 1877.

From Hiram Woods, Jr.

Dear Tommy,   Saco, Maine, Aug. 14, 1877.

I received your letter at home some two weeks ago, but have been prevented from answering it by my preparations to come North. This trip of mine was rather a sudden thing. I left Baltimore in a Steamer for Boston last Monday (Aug. 6.). . . .

You spoke of Henderson in your last letter: We considered him, but did not vote on him on account of Bob's absence. I can't find much about Tweed. I think we had better select such questions for our debates as are capable of being worked up—that is—such as have had time to be recorded in History, or are of so recent occurrence as to be readily remembered. Your question—that long one—is about the kind I like. I am quite anxious to get back to College. . . . I want to see you very much, Tommy, and want you to make me a visit if you can on your way to College. We'll see the girls, and ride around generally. Ma told me to give you this invitation. I write you this now, so as to let you think about it, but will write to you more fully in regard to it when I get home. Write me soon, directing "245 Madison Ave."

Your Sincere Friend, Hiram Woods, Jr.

P.S. omitted. ALS (WP, DLC) with WWhw notation on env.: "Ans."

To Robert Bridges

Dear Bob: Rome, Geo. 8/20/77

I received your card dated August 11th in due time, and was very glad to see it.[1] Please tell me in your next if you have yet reached half lengths in your study of shorthand. I do not know according to what principles to write when I do not know with what principles you are familiar. I am glad that you found no trouble with my last epistle. If you will allow me to give you a little advice, I would caution you against confounding m with n and would advise you to make more use of the circle s (o) since it greatly shortens many forms. You are sometimes a dutchman in your writing without being aware of it, mistaking z for th. You seem to write with remarkable facility however. I received a letter from Hiram soon after I received your card. He says that he will certainly return to college. I am sincerely sorry to hear of his misfortune.[2] My stand in class was 30th and my marks were Math 92.5, Greek 91.8, Latin 96, English 95, French 92, [N]at [Natural History] 89. These marks are very good exponents of the amount of study I did on the several branches.

I am looking forward to the time when I can see you and all my friends once more, with great pleasure. Write soon again to

Your sincere friend   Thomas W. Wilson

Transcript of WWshPS (Meyer Coll., DLC).
  [1] It is missing.
  [2] Hiram Woods, Sr., had just failed in business.

Notes on President McCosh's Course on Psychology

[Sept. 12, 1877-June 20, 1878]

Additions:

1 Introductory Remarks: (a) In deduction we reason from cause to effect; in induction we reason from effect to causes. (b) Bacon's genius was not destructive but essentially constructive. (c) The only difference in the application of Bacon's method of reason when used in physical science and when employed in psychology is in the nature of the primary.

Analysis:

A Evidence of existence of Mind:

I Man has means of knowing the existence of mind as immediate as to man's knowing the existence of matter.

II It follows that we have a positive though limited knowledge of the mind even as we have a positive though limited knowledge of matter.

III. As matter cannot be resolved into mind so mind cannot be resolved into matter.

1. Because the 2 are made known to us by different organs.
2. Because one of them possessed of essentially different properties.

IV. The connection between mind and matter is a mystery.

B. Influence of Mind on Body:—

I Influence exerted upon the bodily organs by the will. Cerebrum the seat of will. Motion 108 feet per second.

II. Influence exerted upon the organs by attention being directed to them.

III. Influence upon the bodily frame exerted by motions.

IV. The influence of mental action in general upon the bodily frame.

C. Influence of Body on Mind:—

    1. Automatic of Reflex system. (Dr. M. Hall)

    2. Sensori-motor system (Sir Chas. Bell)

I. Dependence of the mind upon the senses. II. Dependence of the mind upon the brain. III. The train of thought or feeling affected by bodily states. Action and reaction in the mental sphere.

Connection between Body and Mind

Thalimi Optic Organ in which there is no sensation. An organ of sensation and yet no sensation. The nerve must get to it and thence to gray matter of the brain.

Corpora Sciata Centers of motion. The mind plays upon these organs and they can act automatically.

The two hemispheres of the brain correspond and yet it does not appear that they are the same. Speech is more particularly connected with the left hemisphere. They are virtually one and the same organ when they act and react upon each other. These hemispheres are the seat of all thought and without them there is no sensation. Sensation is an act of this main part of the brain.

Thought works chiefly through the gray layer. "Every sense has a center in these hemispheres of the brain" says Professor Ferrari who has most profoundly investigated this subject. Without mind there is no sensation nor action. Thus even hearing and seeing are operations of the mind.

Action and Reaction of Mind and Body.

Sight is the slowest motion, feeling next, sound last.

Centres of sensation in hemispheres. Every motion, every manifestation of force, is accompanied by change. Every action of the brain changes at least the position of the cells of the brain. This connection between mind and matter exists chiefly in actions of the brain affecting the gray layer of those and other portions of matter. Every mental state may have certain preliminary state corresponding to it. Others might be centers of each of the senses.

WWsh and WWhw notes on two loose sheets in *Notes on Psychology From Lectures Given by James McCosh* (Princeton, 1877). (WW Library, DLC).

From Janet Woodrow Wilson

My darling Son,   Rome Ga. Tuesday. Sep 18th '77.

   . . . I forgot to say that your father arrived here safely on Friday morning at 12 o'clock. You can imagine how overjoyed I was to

see him after our long separation. The joy of our re-union would
be perfect if we could only have the presence of our precious son.
Wonder if we will ever be so happy as to live together permanently,
my darling! Tommy dear, please write to your Auntie, as soon as
you can. It will gratify her—for she loves & admires you most sincerely. Jessie intended writing you before this, but has not accomplished it yet. Your father tells me that your memorandum was
filled—but he cannot tell me anything about the articles gotten—
so I will have to rely upon your giving me a description of your
clothing &c. I like to imagine how you look. How did you find your
rooms looking? Is there anything necessary to your comfort that
has been overlooked. Please, dear, tell me all about yourself & your
surroundings.

It seems that the nerve with which you submitted to your trial
at the dentists has been spoken of as something admirable. Your
Uncle James heard of it on the street. . . .   Your own Mother

ALS (WP, DLC) with WWhw notation on env.: "Ans."

From the Minutes of the American Whig Society

. . . Second Session. Whig Hall. Sept. 21st 1877.
. . . Messrs. Harlow, Sheldon, and Wilson were elected as historians of the past year. . . .

From the Minutes of the Liberal Debating Club

Sept 22nd 1877

Meeting called to order at 8-30[.] The prop[osition] for admission of new members being called for was ruled out of order there
not being a full house present. Mis. business being next in order
we proceeded to the election of a new Pres. There were two candidates Mr McC. & Mr Wilson, there was a tie vote on the 1st ballot.
On the 2nd ballot Mr. Wilson receiving a majority, was declared
elected & then took the chair. The debate then came up & the
question Resolved that the action of Spain was illegal in surrendering Tweed to the United States, was discussed & decided in the
Aff. The bill then passed its 2nd reading and it was [moved] & carried to go into the committee of the whole, The committee reported
the bill favorably to the house. The gent. from N Y[1] then proposed
the following for next meeting Resolved that the army of the U. S.
at present numbering 25,000 be increased by the addition of
15,000 men. The gent from Md moved that we do not have our

society in the B. B.[2] & was carried. The meeting then adj to meet
next Sat   T. W Wilson Pres.

J Edwin Webster Sec of St

[1] C. A. Talcott.
[2] *Bric à Brac*, the undergraduate yearbook.

From the Minutes of the American Whig Society

Whig Hall. September 28th 1877.

. . . Miscellaneous Business.

. . . Resolved, That a committee of five be appointed whose duty it shall be;—

II. To consider the advisability of making such alterations in the Constitutions and By-Laws as will discontinue the transcribing of the minutes and reports in the department of Records; and the abolition of the salary attached to the office of the Secy of Records.

I. To consider the advisability of making such alterations in the Constitution and By-Laws as will permit the use of the Sinking Fund for the renovation of the Hall.

And if these questions be favorably considered to report such changes as are necessary in the Constitution and By-Laws.

Lawrence,[1]   Dulles.[2]

Amended to strike out part II, which refers to the abolition of the salary of the Secy of Records. (Dickens.[3]) Accepted.

The resolution was then carried.

The election of the Book Committee resulted as follows,—

Slemmons, Bridges, Wilson, Kerr. . . .

[1] William W. Lawrence, '78.
[2] William Dulles, Jr., '78.
[3] Albert W. Dickens, '78.

From the Minutes of the Liberal Debating Club

Sep. 29, 1877

Meeting called to order at 8.10, a full house being present. Propositions for membership came up at this point, but were interrupted by the minutes being called for. On motion P[ropositions] for M[embers] were re-opened, when Mr. Henderson's name was proposed and lost. During the reading of Cushings Manual, which then followed, the club was interrupted by the entrance of a non-member. After this gentleman had left, the club proceeded with regular order of business and the reading of Cushing's Manual was completed. The third reading of bill discussed at last meeting was next in order. The bill was decided in the affirmative. The

Sec. of S. taking the negative view of the question, his office was declared vacant, and the present incumbent appointed to fill the position. The Club then proceeded to the 1st reading of Mr. Talcott's bill regarding the Army. The bill was decided in the neg. on its first reading. Mr. McCarter moved 2nd reading. C[arrie]d. The bill was again decided in the neg. Mr. McCarter now moved the Com. of Whole. Cd. Mr. McC. took the Chair, and the Com. of Wh. reported to the house that they had decided the question in the neg. At the request of Mr. Wilson the next meeting was assigned for discussion of the following question: Res—"That the treaty of Paris was not all that Civilization demanded of the signing powers." Club then adjourned to meet next Saturday evening.

T. W. Wilson Pres.
Hiram Woods, Jr. Sec. of S.

From Janet Woodrow Wilson

My darling Tommy—   Wilmington, N. C. [c. Oct. 3, 1877]

We received your sweet letter this evening. I dont think you realize how much pleasure your dear letters give us, darling. I am greatly surprised at your news with reference to Jimmie Woodrow[1] —and really pleased on the poor boy's account. I know he must be delighted. I am quite sure you will befriend him all you can. . . .

I must stop now my darling son. I will try to give you all the "bits of news" I can gather—for I *know* how pleasant it is to have them while absent from home. Papa & Josie join me in tenderest love to our absent dearest one.   Your own Mother

P.S. omitted. ALS (WP, DLC).
[1] James Wilson Woodrow, son of Thomas Woodrow, Jr., and brother of WW's cousin Hattie.

Editorial in *The Princetonian*

[October 4, 1877]

As the time for choosing an orator to represent us in the next Inter-Collegiate Oratorical Contest approaches, we are naturally led to speculate upon our chances of success in this department. Our association seems to have done everything in its power to enable the successful competitor in the preliminary contest, to acquit himself honorably upon the New York stage. It has voted him a handsome sum of money with which to engage the services of some competent instructor, in order that he may perfect his delivery as much as is practicable within so short a time as will be at his command between the time of his appointment and that of the contest. But this time will necessarily be short, and his improvement in delivery proportionately slight. Now, the fact that our representatives have to go elsewhere for competent instruction in oratory, seems to us strange and humiliating. While all other branches of instruction are here presided over by men of eminence and ability, and none need go blindly into any other department of study, we are still without efficient discipline and drill in elocution. We cannot too often give voice to the hope that the Board of Trustees will very soon add to the debt of gratitude which we owe them for the recent marked improvements in the means and modes of mental training, by securing the services of some eminent professor of declamation and voice-training. We know that there are among us many forceful writers and original thinkers, and we have every reason to believe, from frequent displays of oratorical powers upon chapel stage and elsewhere, that there is here much of such material as makes the orator. But to properly mould this material and develop our possibilities of oratorical ability into realities, systematic and intelligent training is all important. It is no discredit to the young orator that he cannot, unaided by experience, mature his vocal powers and impart the proper finish to his delivery. What we need and have long needed is a professor such as Hamilton already has. To the orator the proper control of his voice is almost everything. In gestures, in mere bodily action while speaking, our representatives upon the New York stage have been everything that could be reasonably desired, but in powers of voice-expression they have been sadly deficient. Not that they had naturally poor voices, but their voices had never been properly drilled and developed under a careful guide. While our present instructor is by no means lacking in ability as a speaker, our exercises under him are mere farces, for the simple reason that they are mere recitations, and are combined with no practical exercise of the voice. We do our best and are graded accordingly, without a word of practical advice. What we sorely need is an able instructor, himself a master of all the capabilities of the voice, to give to the training of those of our number who intend to be speakers, who are to make their way at the bar and in the pulpit, his undivided and unremitting attention. We do not need any one to give us rules for gesturing or bodily posture, for these are comparatively useless; but we do need some one to guide us in our efforts to train ourselves in the use of that sweetest of all instruments, the human voice.

One word more. We mean to give more of the truth in this matter. Our Professor of elocution, instead of giving his entire attention to students of the College, has classes in several preparatory schools and young ladies' seminaries. This is lamentably irregular. Shall we give the reason of this? Does he find over five hundred students a field too small for his energies? Is his instruction of such a kind that we, by declaiming before him, perhaps three times in four years, and receiving a criticism twenty words in length, may hope to acquire a practical and forcible delivery? It is quite time that "steps were taken" to fill this gap in a curriculum which is the pride of us all.

Printed in *The Princetonian*, II (Oct. 4, 1877), 76.

From the Minutes of the American Whig Society

Whig Hall, Oct. 5th 1877.

Your Committee appointed to consider the advisability of making such alterations in the Constitution as will permit the use of the Sinking Fund for the renovation of the Hall would report as follows:—

In the present instance no alteration in the Constitution need be made. Your Committee would recommend that a meeting of the Senate be called for the purpose of considering a resolution to appropriate the money in the sinking fund for the immediate renovation of Hall: and further that the present committee be authorized to call such meeting and advertise it as provided for in the Constitution and to prepare the necessary resolution for the Senate's consideration. This resolution would be to the effect that the section in the Constitution, prohibiting the use of the sinking fund for other purposes than enlarging or rebuilding, be suspended in the present instance so as to allow the use of the sinking fund for these repairs.

There is no necessity for enlarging on the absolute need of this step. It is to be hoped that every member will advance this project as much as possible, by talking it up with graduate members and by lending his own active interest.

Respectfully submitted, Dulles   Wilson, Lieb,[1] Bridges Lawrence chm

[1] David M. Lieb, '78.

From the Minutes of the Liberal Debating Club

Oct. 6, 1877.

House called to order at 8.40, Mr. McCarter being absent. There being no P[ropositions] for M[embers] the minutes were read. Mis business being then in order, Mr. Woods made the following motion which was carried: Res–"That the Sec. of S. obtain from Mr. Talcott the funds he now holds for the Society, and that with it he purchase a minute book. This book, with the minutes, he shall hand to the late S. of S., who shall copy the minutes up to the expiration of his term of office." Mr. Webster then read from Cushing's Manual, after which the Pres. appointed Mr. Talcott to write an essay stating the facts in relation to the treaty of Paris, to be read at next meeting. The third reading of the bill presented by Mr. Talcott then came up, and was decided in the neg. Mr. Wilson's bill in regard to the treaty of Paris was then carried on its first reading. On motion of Mr. Talcott the club proceeded to 2nd reading, and the bill was again decided in the Affirmative. On motion of same gent. the Com. of Wh. was proceeded with, Mr. Webster taking the chair. Com. of Wh. reported to the house that they had decided the bill in the affirmative. Mr. Talcott moved a recess of ten (10) minutes. C-d. House then called to order after ten (10) minutes, when, at the request of the Pres., the next meeting was assigned for discussing the question: "Do the interests of England demand the disestablishment (and disendowment) of the Eng. Church.["] Adjourned to meet next Sat. eve.

T. W. Wilson, Pres.
Hiram Woods, Jr. Sec. of S.

From Janet Woodrow Wilson

My darling Tommy,   Wilmington N. C. [c. Oct. 8, 1877]
   I have only time for a hasty note, in time to send to the P.O. I am sorry you have been annoyed about Dr. Hampton's bill.[1] I gave the bill to your father before we left Rome—but he had not enough money to pay it. So he begged your Uncle James to explain to Dr. H.—saying he would send the money as soon as possible. I fear James neglected the matter. But your father will attend to it. The church has not paid anything for several months—and that is embarrassing us—but he will write to Dr H. at once—so you need not worry about it at all. I love you my darling—so does papa & Josie. I will write in a day or two. God bless you. Are you *quite* well?

Your own Mother

ALS (WP, DLC).
   [1] A dentist in Rome, Ga.

From the Minutes of the Liberal Debating Club

Oct. 13, 1877.

House met at 8.30, there being a full attendance. There were no propositions for Membership, so, after the minutes had been read, Mr. Wilson, under the head of Mis. bus., made the following motion as an amendment to the Constitution: Res: "That after the words, 'questions of the present century,' in Art. V, Sec. I of the Constitution, there be inserted the words, 'or such Literary matters as the Club may see fit to discuss from time to time'." Mr. Woods moved as an amendment that for the words "from time to time" there be substituted the words, "every other Sat. night." The Amendment was lost, and the question was carried on its first reading. Mr. McCarter then moved the following as a *By-Law*: *Res.* "That the time of assembling the Club be 7.30 provided a quorum be present. Motion C-d. Mr. Woods then read from Cushing's Manual, after which Mr. Wilson's bill regarding the treaty of Paris passed through its 3rd reading, and was finally decided in the Aff. By unanimous consent Mr. Talcott was excused from reading the essay. Mr. Wilson's bill regarding the Eng. Church was then discussed on its 1st reading, and was carried. On motion of Sec. of S. the 2nd reading was proceeded with, when the bill was again carried. Mr. McCarter moved the Com. of Whole. C-d. Mr. Talcott took the chair, and the Com. of Wh. reported to the House that they had struck out the words "and disendowment," and had carried the bill as amended. Mis. Bus. being in order, the 2nd reading of bill amending Art. V, Sec. I of the Cons. came up, and was carried. Mr. Talcott moved Com. of Wh.—Cd. Mr. Webster took the chair, and reported the bill to the House, as decided in the Aff. On motion of Mr. McCarter Cushing's Manual was temporarily suspended, and the Club proceeded to the 3rd reading of the bill, and finally carried it; thus making it part of the Constitution. Mr. Talcott moved a recess of (5) minutes. C-d. The House, after five (5) minutes, was called to order, when Mr. Talcott moved another recess of five (5) minutes. Amended to read ten (10) minutes. Amendment lost, and the original question carried. After the lapse of five (5) minutes the House was called to order. At the request of Mr. McCarter the Club decided to discuss at its next meeting "The Province of History." Adjourned to meet Oct. 20.

T. W. Wilson, P.

Hiram Woods, Jr. Sec. of S.

From Wilson's Shorthand Diary

[October] 14th Sabbath. My efforts at journal-keeping are ludicrously spasmodic and it scarcely seems worth while to again renew the attempt which has so often proved a failure. But as this term promises to be one of unusual interest to me it may witness one more such effort. At some future time I may attempt a sketch of the past summer as it has been one of great interest and enjoyment to me. The occasions of the day are not worth recording and might, if recorded, recall unpleasant memories to my mind as I have not spent this Sabbath as a Christian should. I looked over some copy for the Princetonian which was anything but an occupation for Sabbath afternoon. God help me to be a better man in the future. I am constantly failing. This term has so far been one of hard work and my literary labors have already been almost as constant as they promise to be during the next few weeks. I wrote my usual weekly letter to mother this evening. Thank God for health and strength.

[October] 15th Monday. This is one of our busiest days as juniors [?] as we have four exercises during the day. Spent most of the day upon my regular studies. From 12 to 1 o'clock I spent in Bill Wilder's room correcting copy for the Princetonian and decided with Wilder about the manner in which the editors should express themselves in the editorial department with reference to the result of troubles between '78 and '79 in the game for college championship in baseball. The '78 men on the board of editors though they have the majority and might put in anything they please very kindly agreed that nothing should go in the editorial department of which Wilder and I did not approve as members of '79. I don't think that the account we agreed upon will agree with the views of many in the class but it is in strict agreement with facts. Spent most of the evening in writing: first a few points for debate next Friday evening[1] and second an introduction for my speech on Bismarck.[2] My progress with the introduction was comparatively satisfactory but I did not succeed in thinking of many points for my debate. The fact is I was thinking more of my speech than of my debate all the time. Thank God for health and strength.

1 See Whig Minutes for Oct. 19, 1877.
2 WW delivered this speech in the preliminary Junior Oratorical contest in Whig Hall on Dec. 6, 1877. It is printed at that date.

Marginal Notes

John Richard Green, *A Short History of the English People* (New York, 1877).

Transcripts of WW Shorthand Comments [c. Oct. 17, 1877]

Pp. 83-84:

The real work [of education], however, to be done was done not by these scholars, but by the King himself. Alfred resolved to throw open to his people in their own tongue the knowledge which had till then been limited to the clergy. He took his books as he found them—they were the popular manuals of his age—the Consolations of Boethius, the Pastorals of Pope Gregory, the compilation of Orosius, then the one accessible hand-book of universal history, and the history of his own people by Baeda. He translated these works into English, but he was far more than a translator, he was an editor for the people. . . . Before him, England possessed in her own tongue one great poem, that of Caedmon, and a train of ballads and battle-songs. Prose she had none. The mighty roll of the books that fill her libraries begins with the translations of Alfred, and above all with the Chronicle of his reign. It seems likely that the King's rendering of Baeda's history gave the first impulse toward the compilation of what is known as the English or Anglo-Saxon Chronicle, which was certainly thrown into its present form during his reign. The meagre lists of the kings of Wessex and of the bishops of Winchester, which had been preserved from older times, were roughly expanded into a national history by insertions from Baeda, but it is when it reaches the reign of Alfred that the Chronicle suddenly widens into the vigorous narrative, full of life and originality, that marks the gift of a new power to the English tongue. Varying as it does from age to age in historic value, it remains the first vernacular history of any Teutonic people, the earliest and the most venerable monument of Teutonic prose. The writer of English history may be pardoned if he lingers too fondly over the figure of the king in whose court, at whose impulse, it may be in whose very words, English history begins.

If there were no other passage in this book to establish Mr. Green's reputation as a master-writer this description and estimate of Alfred would be sufficient: nothing can surpass its condensed vigor and beauty.

P. 522:

Pym alone remained, resolute, patient as of old; and as the sense of his greatness grew silently during the eleven years of deepening tyranny, the hope and faith of better things clung almost passionately to the man who never doubted of the final triumph of freedom and the law. At their close, Clarendon tells us, in words all the more notable for their bitter tone of hate, "he was the most popular man, and the most able to do hurt, that have lived at any time." He had shown he knew how to wait, and when waiting was over he showed he knew how to act.

Some marked resemblance between Pym and Bismarck as statesmen.

P. 523:

He [Pym] saw that as an element of constitutional life Parliament was of higher value than the Crown; he saw, too, that in Parliament itself the one essential part was the House of Commons. On these two facts he based his whole policy in the contest which followed. When Charles refused to act with the Parliament, Pym treated the refusal as a temporary abdication on the part of the sovereign, which vested the executive power in the two Houses until new arrangements were made. When the Lords obstructed public business, he warned them that obstruction would only force the Commons "to save the kingdom alone." Revolutionary as these principles seemed at the time, they have both been recognized as bases of our constitution since the days of Pym.

Both Pym and Bismarck first to shape and defend the Constitution of their country.

P. 697:

Now that the House of Commons, however, was become the ruling power in the State, a change was absolutely required to secure steadiness and fixity of political action; and in 1716 the duration of Parliament was extended to seven years by the Septennial Bill.

A similar change is sadly needed in this country.

P. 708:

Whitefield's preaching was such as England had never heard before—theatrical, extravagant, often commonplace —but hushing all criticism by its intense reality, its earnestness of belief, its deep, tremulous sympathy with the sin and sorrow of mankind. . . . On the rough and ignorant masses to whom they spoke the effect of Whitefield and his fellow

This movement bears some slight resemblance to that of Moody and Sankey as those leaders bore more weight on account of superior mental abilities. Moody and

Methodists was terrible both for good and ill. Their preaching stirred a passionate hatred in their opponents. Their lives were often in danger; they were mobbed, they were ducked, they were stoned, they were smothered with filth. But the enthusiasm they aroused was equally passionate. Women fell down in convulsions; strong men were smitten suddenly to the earth; the preacher was interrupted by bursts of hysteric laughter or of hysteric sobbing. All the phenomena of strong spiritual excitement—so familiar now, but at that time strange and unknown—followed on their sermons; and the terrible sense of a conviction of sin, a new dread of hell, a new hope of heaven, took forms at once grotesque and sublime. Charles Wesley, a Christ-Church student, came to add sweetness to this sudden and startling light. He was the "sweet singer" of the movement. His hymns expressed the fiery conviction of its converts in lines so chaste and beautiful that its more extravagant features disappeared. The wild throes of hysteric enthusiasm passed into a passion for hymn-singing, and a new musical impulse was aroused in the people which gradually changed the face of public devotion throughout England.

Sankey felt the want of a *John Wesley*. Only such as he can give prominence to such movements.

From the Minutes of the American Whig Society

Whig Hall. October 19th 1877.

. . . Debate, 9th Division.

"Resolved, That a liberal education is to be preferred to an exclusively practical one."

Affirmative		Negative
Performed, Vinton, Failed,	Waller, Performed,	H. Woods Failed,
Weed,	S. Woods,	Voorhis
Wilds,	Wylly.	Webster,
Wilson.		Wiggan,
		Williams
		Worl.

The debate was decided in the Affirmative. H. Woods was chosen for the Inter-Division Debate. . . .

From the Minutes of the Liberal Debating Club

Oct. 20, 1877.

House met at 7.40 there being a full attendance. Prop for membership being in order, Mr. McCarter proposed Mess[rs] Sheldon of N. J., and Elsing of Ill., and Mr. Talcott, Mr Harlow of N. Y. Each of the above Gents. were elected. The Minutes were then read. Miss. bus. then coming up, the Sec. of S. proposed the following amendment to the Constitution: *Res.* "That in Art. VII for the words 'of 50¢,' there be substituted the words 'of 20¢'." The Club carried this resolution on its first reading. On motion of Mr. McCarter the bill was taken through its 2nd reading, and was again carried. On motion of Mr. Talcott the Com. of Wh. was proceeded with, when the bill was again carried, Mr. McCarter taking the chair, and reporting to the house the decision of the Com. Mr. Wilson's bill regarding the Eng. Church was then carried on its 3rd reading. After an interesting discussion on the question proposed at last meeting regarding the "province of History," at the request of Mr. Talcott the Club decided to discuss at next meeting the following: *Res*; "That the 3rd Republic of France has been more beneficial to the French People than any other form of Government wd. have been." The meeting the[n] adjourned to meet next Sat. Eve.   T. W. Wilson, P.

Hiram Woods, Jr. Sec. of S.

From Wilson's Shorthand Diary

[October] 20th Saturday. Nothing worthy of much notice has transpired during the last four or five days. My speech on Bismarck has progressed very satisfactorily during these days however and I wrote the last portion of it during the afternoon and evening of this day, Saturday. Of course since I wrote an elaborate essay upon Bismarck's life and character[1] during the summer this speech is little more than a condensation and improvement upon that essay. I think that when I have written it over several times with special view to increase in force and clearness of expression and boldness of thought it will be very suitable for delivery upon the occasion for which I intend it. I think that it will admit of more effect in delivery than the speech I wrote this summer upon Thomas Carlyle. I do not think that the literary man offers as fine a subject for a speech as a statesman and especially such an eminent statesman as Bismarck[,] Thiers and others. Spent a very pleasant instructive evening in the L. D. C. I enjoyed the discussion which was upon the province of history more than I have ever enjoyed any of our discussions yet. Thank God for health and strength of body and mind.

¹ Printed at Nov. 1877.

[October] 21st Sabbath. Nothing worthy of particular note has transpired today. In consequence of oversleeping myself I did not rise until 10 o'clock. Immediately after getting my breakfast I went to church and heard a long but rather instructive sermon by some minister unknown to me.¹ Spent the evening writing letters as also afternoon. Some of the evening however was spent in Bridges' room with Bridges[,] Woods[,] Talcott and Frank Lord.² I have to record another Sabbath unprofitably spent. May God give me strength to live a more Christian life. Thanks be to Him for his mercies past and for present health and strength and temporal prosperity.

¹ He was the Rev. Archibald Alexander Hodge, D.D., then Associate Professor of Exegetical, Didactic and Polemic Theology at Princeton Theological Seminary.
² Frank H. Lord, '79.

From Joseph Ruggles Wilson

Home [Wilmington, N. C.], Tuesday, 23d Oct. 1877

My darling boy—

We receive semi-occasional letters from your unprolific writing utensel, which cheer us with such light as we covet more and more of. The frequency of my paternal epistles you-ward entitles me to a complaint now and then! But then it is quality, you know, not *quantity*, that tells; and you can take this observation for a compliment to yourself if you are unwilling to allow it to me.

It is to be hoped that, however fishy you may be in some respects, you will hereafter make free to reject the bones of the literal finny fellows whose facility for being swallowed in toto is proverbial. Seriously do you think that bone which was surgically extracted from yr throat left no evil effects in the way of hindering your elocution? This is the principal bad consequence that I have feared. Your maw (not yr ma) is to be yr. chief dependence as a public speaker—and you ought to guard all its approaches with a care equal to its importance. Sometimes, then, it is what goes *into* a man that helps to ruin him, as well as that which comes out of him.

I am happy to report that yr. dear Mother is stronger than she was when you left her in Rome. Not that it was *yr.* leaving her that was so beneficial—but her getting *me* back! ahem! Since her return here she has revived very perceptibly and hopefully. . . .

As to myself—less said the better. I may learn to preach after a half century more of experience. Tomorrow I expect to leave for Synod (at Charlotte)—to return Monday the 29th. . . .[1]

Your aff. f. J. R. W.

ALS (WP, DLC) with WWhw notation on env.: "Ans."
[1] The Synod of North Carolina met in Charlotte, Oct. 24-27, 1877.

From Janet Woodrow Wilson

My precious Son,   Wilmington N. C. Friday—Oct 26. [1877]

I received your last sweet letter yesterday. Yes, dear, your letters give us perfect satisfaction. We always look for them anxiously—and when we receive them we are not disappointed. Of course we dont expect "news"—in the general sense of that term. Anything that interests you, however, is interesting to us—so that when you feel like telling us what matters are particularly engaging your thoughts, we are very much gratified. The more we hear of each other this way, the less painful—more endurable—our separation —dont you think so, dear? Of course the essential points to be treated in your letters are, your health and happiness—and the assurance of continued love for us—who love you so dearly. Did you get your father's letter? written last Monday, I think? He left for Synod, at Charlotte, on Wednesday morning—and will not return before some day next week. He did not anticipate much pleasure from the meeting—indeed quite the contrary—for it seems the Mecklenburgh Pres[bytery] will make an effort to have the Synod send up to the Assembly an Overture—the object of which shall be, to have the present Clerks—Stated and Permanent—ousted. In this way: they propose that these officers shall be elected every two years—for the reason that the present plan gives these men too much power—which they are in danger of using for personal ends! It seems that Mr. Taylor Martin[1]—Rev—started the idea. He privately charges Dr. Brown[2] with having so misused his position. The whole thing is the result of some private spite & jealousy. Your father, as you know, is tired enough of his office—but he has no notion of being put out in that way, you may be sure. They assure him privately that they have every confidence in *him*. But your father will not be so easily satisfied—and besides, he says the charge against Dr. B. is utterly false. He is a miserably *poor clerk* —and gives your father endless worry—but that is the worst that can be said. He has not done what is charged. So it is not any wonder that your father rather dreaded what he would have to meet at Synod. I would like to hear the speech he will make–if they drive him to it. He is fully prepared to meet them. Of course I will tell you all there is to tell–when I hear the end.

Everything is going on very quietly here. This is a stupid place. I will get your father to answer the question in your last letter as soon as ever he comes home. Be sure and send us a copy of your speech if you can.

Where are the Pope's, do you know?

I have not been so well the last few days; but am feeling better again. Josie joins me in unbounded love to you[.] Good bye my darling.   Your own Mother.

You should be very careful not to sit without fire this damp weather.

ALS (WP, DLC) with WWhw notation on env.: "Ans."
   1 The Rev. S. Taylor Martin, president of the Charlotte Female College.
   2 The Rev. William Brown, D.D., editor of the Richmond *Central Presbyterian*, 1860-79, Permanent Clerk of the General Assembly of the Presbyterian Church, U.S., 1865-84.

From the Minutes of the Liberal Debating Club

Oct. 27, 1877.

House met at 8 P.M., there being a full attendance. Messrs Sheldon and Elsing were introduced into the Club. Miss. Bus. being next in order, the Club proceeded to the 3rd reading of the bill proposed by the Sec. of S., amending Art. VII of the Constitution. The amendment was carried on its third reading, and became embodied in the Constitution. Owing to the lateness of the hour the reading of Cushing's Manual was omitted. The debate being next in order, the Club proceeded to 1st reading of Mr. Talcott's bill regarding the French Republic. The question was carried. On motion of Mr. McCarter the Club proceeded to 2nd reading, and the question was again decided in the affirmative. Mr. McCarter moved the Com. of Wh. C-d. Mr. Talcott took the chair, and the Com. reported to the House that they had carried the bill. At the request of Mr. McCarter, the Club decided to discuss at their next meeting the subject–"Poetry." The Club then adjourned to meet next Saturday Evening.   T. W. Wilson, Pres.

Hiram Woods, Jr. Sec. of S.

Woodrow Wilson's Birthplace, Staunton, Virginia

The Presbyterian Church of Staunton, Virginia

Joseph Ruggles Wilson about 1870 and 1874

Annie and Marion Wilson

Janet Woodrow Wilson about 1874

The First Presbyterian Church

of Columbia, South Carolina

The Wilson House

in Columbia,

South Carolina

"Old" Chambers Building of Davidson College

Princeton College about 1879

Lyman Hotchkiss Atwater

James McCosh

Theodore Whitefield Hunt

Arnold Guyot

The Alligators in 1879

Wilson's class picture

Thomas W. Wilson
1872 Columbia,
S.C.

T. W. Wilson
Room 9, North

Thomas W. Wilson
1874 Wilmington
North Carolina

The evolution of Wilson's handwriting

Your loving brother
Thomas

Respectfully Submitted

J. A. Wilson, N.C.,
First Comptroller

Norse Cove, N.C.,
July 30th/79

Dear Bob,

Why haven't you written to me,
old fellow; you don't know how longingly I've been waiting for a letter from

John B. Minor

The University of Virginia about 1879

A Biographical Essay

[Nov. 1877]

Prince Bismarck

Few centuries seem to have been more fruitful in crisis, in revolutions and counter-revolutions, in the establishment, convulsion, and overthrow of empires and kingdoms than our own. From the period upon the teeming pages of whose history falls the glitter of the first and great Napoleon's sword to that which witnessed the sudden downfall of the third Napoleon, innovation and revolution have been the rule rather than the exception in Europe. With Thiers passed away the last of those illustrious men who figured amid the memorable events which crowded upon one another in rapid succession after the great revolution and its attending convulsions. With the appearance of Bismarck upon the political stage began the rule of a new line of statesmen. Stern Time had superseded Thiers. Upon his will had hung the destinies of France. He had seen his country at the zenith of her glory; he lived to see her in deepest degradation at the feet of Bismarck. He lingered only long enough to see his country once more recover some of her wonted energy and then reluctantly made way for a younger generation of statesmen.

The death of Thiers has naturally led us to think of those whom he has left behind him in the field of European politics. And upon the character and life of Bismarck, now the foremost figure of Europe, we would dwell for a little. We may, from the vantage-ground of disinterested observation, be able, in the light of the eventful sixty-two years of his life, to estimate his merits without the hatred of the Austrian, the fear-begotten bitterness of the Frenchman, or the prejudice of the Englishman, to warp our judgment.

Perhaps nothing would have appeared more improbable to the ordinary observer of thirty-five years ago than that the unpromising young aristocrat, the young man only now and then exchanging the pleasures of the hunting field and the drinking-bout for the moody perusal of miscellaneous literature and abstruse philosophy, the young Bismarck, would before his sixtieth year make himself the virtual master of Europe. In the youthful Bismarck, describing in frequent and characteristic letters to his sister, "the farce of shooting the fox," which he daily performed in company with his old and then somewhat simple-minded father, there appeared few indications of that power of intellect and that force of purpose which characterize his later manhood. Occasionally, indeed, he lets fall some expression of discontent at the narrowness of his circle of vision and the petty character of the daily events of his life; but there were, so far as we can learn, no croppings out of that genius now so greatly feared and so justly admired. He seemed, unlike [like] his ancestors, destined to pass his life in the humble position of a country squire, until in 1847, he was called upon to take his place as a representative in his provincial Diet.

The notable year 1848 was the first year of Bismarck's public life. Every one is familiar with the revolutions which then convulsed the eastern portion of Europe; every one remembers with what startling rapidity the revolutionary spirit spread into every corner of Europe. We can easily conceive that it was a time when every patriotic Prussian must have been filled with the gravest apprehensions with regard to his country's future. France seemed to weather the storm with unsapped strength and undiminished resources, while the apparent success of the revolution made every sovereign of Europe tremble on his throne. Russia was then little less than Dictatress of Europe. Austria was supreme in the councils of the Confederation and seemed likely to hold Prussia in perpetual subordination, and the safety of Prussia, which seemed to the more conservative threatened by the somewhat revolutionary tendencies of the Prussian Liberals, apparently depended upon the continuance of this subordination. Prussia was thus surrounded by powerful states of no very friendly character at the same time that she found herself obliged to fight a domestic enemy in the shape of radicalism. Entering public life at such a time and under such circumstances, Bismarck, with his aristocratic and monarchical sympathies, naturally saw only the dangers of what he regarded as a menacing spirit of democracy, and we find him standing up in the Prussian Assembly and, even after the humiliation of Olmutz, boldly advocating Prussian subserviency to the house of Hapsburg. He looked with deep apprehension at the alarming spread of revolutionary principles and was naturally convinced that a close alliance with Austria was the only means by which these principles could be successfully combated. Seeing the many dangers which threatened the interests of the Confederation, he felt that Austrian domination alone could fend off these dangers from Germany and saw nothing but frivolity and "revolutionary enterprise" in all schemes for the deliverance of Schleswig-Holstein. But eight years at Frankfort in the midst of all kinds of petty, partisan struggles and contemptible efforts to secure influence by improper means, revealed to Bismarck the "utter nullity" of the German Confederation and taught him to regard with hatred and distrust the Austria of whose power he had so lately been the eager defender. By affording him an insight into the affairs of Germany and by revealing to him the extent of Austria's power and the direction in which it was all exerted, his stay at Frankfort proved eminently useful to Bismarck. It imparted to his views of European relations and of the possibilities of Prussia that breadth and grasp which have ever since characterized them. Bismarck's early political career was such as to render him peculiarly fit for that authority with which he was destined to be invested, and it was well for Prussia that when, in 1862, a crisis of supreme importance came she could avail herself of the services of Bismarck's clear eye and trained hand. The Crimean war and the international complications which sprung from it had caused the opening of a widening breach between Russia and Austria. Napoleon was plotting against Austria for the purpose of promoting Italian unity and, in his eagerness for the friendship of Russia, was unconsciously playing into the hands of Gortschakoff. The Prussian nation was deeply agitated by the fierce contention of parties and the angry antagonism of king and parliament, at the same time that the French papers seemed eager to thrust a splendid destiny upon Prussia by loudly calling upon her to unify and thus save Germany. Bismarck seems to have quickly and skillfully availed himself of all the golden opportunities which, amid such confusion of interests offered themselves for the aggrandizement of Prussia. Beyond all opposition in parliament and all antagonism in the king's closet, he seems to have seen some prospect of an immediate realization of those hopes which he had so long cherished with reference to the increase of Prussian influence and the ultimate humiliation of Austria. He probably felt that in his own powers lay many bright possibilities; and, acting with his usual decision and energy he commenced with a firm and skilled hand to steadily lay the foundations of Prussia's future power and greatness. The late Prussian plenipotentiary to the Federal Diet was not long in making himself dictator of Europe; the keen diplomatist soon proved himself the master-statesman.

Events called into action the man from whose will so many events have sprung. In 1862, when every rumor indicated a close alliance between Russia, Prussia, and France, and every circumstance seemed to be calling upon Prussia for immediate and energetic action, William had need to call into his counsels a vigorous mind, and it did not long remain doubtful to whom the position of chief advisor belonged by right of statesmanlike genius. Bismarck's character and commanding talents rendered him a necessity to the king. In his new position, which proved to be the most responsible in Europe, he acted with a boldness and energy combined with foresight and prudence which have made him the most prominent figure in modern history. To sketch his career since 1862 would be to recapitulate the history of Europe for the last fifteen years and such a sketch cannot be attempted here. It will be our aim simply to delineate with all possible care his mental and moral character.

We can form no just conception of Bismarck's capacities as a statesman by comparing him with any of those great English statesmen to whom we have been wont to accord a large place in our notice and admiration, or with any of those honored men and able statesmen who brought our republic in safety and honor through the storms of her early existence. Neither those talents so necessary to the English statesman as a leader of Parliament nor those peculiar gifts always to be found in the guide of popular opinion and guard of popular institutions are necessary to the Prussian statesman. All the energies of the English or American statesman must be spent in gover[n]ing great popular assemblies, in manipulating parties, in directing and controlling popular opinion. The Prussian statesman, on the other hand, must exert all his powers in rendering himself supreme in the royal closet, his power does not depend upon popular assemblies whose favor he must win and whose support he must command, but rests entirely with his royal master; he is comparatively independent of party relations and ties. Besides great intellect, the English statesman must have eloquence and tact; in the Prussian statesman eloquence and tact are nothing unless accompanied by marked administrative and diplomatic talents and a controlling influence over the royal mind. The triumphs of the English statesman are gained upon the floor of parliament; those of the Prussian statesman are won in the cabinet of his King. The powers of the English statesman are apt to be dwarfed in being so constantly exercised for the acquirement of nothing more than skill in dialectic fence; intrigue is apt to bemean the powers and sully the character of the Prussian statesman. For all the officers of the Prussian ministry are directly responsible to the king alone, and the prime minister, exercising no direct supervision over them, must control his subordinates through the king, their common master. And, while many a triumph over external difficulties and opponents, many a masterstroke of policy, and many a victory in war have all combined to attest the pre-eminence of his genius, Bismarck's character is not altogether free from the stain which intrigue invariably brings. In his dealings with the diplomatic world or even with his royal master he has not always proved himself above deceit. But still he may justly be regarded as a grand type of his class of statesmen—men of independent conviction, full of self-trust, and themselves the spirit of their country's institutions. In Bismarck are united the moral force of Cromwell and the political shrewdness of Richelieu; the comprehensive intellect of Burke, without his learning, and the diplomatic ability of Talleyrand, without his coldness. In haughtiness, a rival of Chatham; in devotion to his country's interests, a peer of Hampden; in boldness of speech, and action, an equal of Brougham, Bismarck's qualities are in most unique combination.

Though intensely German in all his tastes and peculiarities, Bismarck is by no means distinguished for those acquirements so much valued by Germans. In proficiency in purely literary fields he can stand no comparison with his friend and ally, Gortschakoff. But, while ranking with few of his many eminent contemporaries in literary power, he stands among them all without a peer in those powers of cool judgment, quick determination, and masterly execution which make up the statesman's character. But he is a Prussian and his talents are such as are usually met with in the chief officer of state in a virtually unlimited monarchy. All his faculties seem moulded for administration and legislation, for framing statutes, negotiating treaties and organizing armies. And the singleness of his aim has concentrated his powers. The extension and firm establishment of Prussian empire has all along been the cause for which and under whose inspiration he has accomplished by a few master-strokes such enterprises as would have been regarded as chimerical by a more timid or less commanding genius. In 1866 one short week saw the humiliation of Austria and the thwarting of France. The pleasing results of that stupendous week's work were the transformation of Prussia's former strategic weakness into actual strength by making her territory one compact mass, and the consequent increase of Prussian influence in Europe. A campaign of almost unrivalled brilliancy and rapidity then brought proud France to the feet of Prussia, exposing the "misunderstood incapacity" of Napoleon and adding the smiling fields of Alsace and Lorraine to the already powerful kingdom; and the victor of Sedan ended his course of victory by placing an emperor's crown upon the brow of his King.

Ever since his contact with Austrian intrigue at Frankfort-on-the-Main caused the scales to fall from his eyes, all Bismarck's public actions have been indicative of keenness of insight, clearness of judgment, and promptness of decision. As a member of the Federal Diet, he quickly and accurately divined the motives and aims of Austria and promptly and providently arrayed himself in direct opposition to them. He saw that more than ordinary influence was to belong to the clearsighted man who then represented Russia in Frankfort, and, with his keen eye on the future, successfully cultivated the friendship of the great Gortschakoff. He seems to have been the first to perceive the true weakness of Napoleon's character and the real emptiness of all his schemes for Italian unity and for the general good of mankind. His penetrating glance discovered the really feeble condition of Austria and detected the gullibility of Napoleon. He had learned many an useful lesson in the severe school of diplomacy in which he had studied. No tricks of policy, no subtilties of diplomacy could mislead one who gained his early experience among political tricksters and who is himself the keenest of diplomatists. His keenness of insight, begetting vivid conceptions of every position in all its bearings, has mapped out before him every possible line of action; his clearness of judgment has, with almost unerring accuracy, pointed out the one which might be most advantageously adopted.

Bismarck's vivid conceptive powers are naturally combined with an impulsiveness, which, if not checked by judgment and restrained by circumstances, might betray him into rashness. But, being under the constant necessity of carefully thinking out every line of action and laboriously planning every mode of execution, in order that his measures may be acceptable to his royal master, every tendency to rashness has been counterbalanced and neutralized by the necessity for deliberation. And, though the great chancellor often chafes fiercely under the restraints thus imposed upon him, he, nevertheless, owes to this very restraint much of his success. William has always yielded in more important matters to the genius of his great subject, but frequently only after long and severe struggles, which have greatly worn upon the chancellor at the same time that they have purged his schemes of every rash element. The King possesses more force of moral character and stubbornness of will than clearness of intellectual insight and his favor, often so hard to win, is therefore essential even to the all-powerful Bismarck. Only an unconquerable energy and an indomitable will have prevented the premier from retiring from a position necessarily so harassing. Obstacles seem only to whet his activity and increase his power.

With unmeasured energy and surprising power of concentration are combined the firmness, the quickness of resolve, and the ability for prompt action so necessary to leaders. But Bismarck's firmness, while pointed with intrepidity, is disfigured by harshness. Nothing could be harsher than his means of removing from his path some antagonist or rival and he has often proved unscrupulous in the use of these means. But our condemnation of Bismarck's occasional bad faith should be surrounded by many qualifications and explanations. We can never justify the wilful disregard of justice or the wilful breaking of faith. But in a man who is conscious of great powers, whose mind is teeming and overflowing with great political plans and dreaming of grand national triumphs, and who, withal, is hampered on every side by almost every circumstance of his surroundings we can at least understand an occasional breach of honor, and, in the presence of so many grand and peerless qualities and so many noble purposes, can perhaps forgive a want of integrity which so seldom exhibits itself. And even when uprightness is wanting in his purposes or in his choice of means, its place is filled by uncommon wisdom in action.

Burke has somewhere spoken of what, in his usually happy manner, he has styled "retrospective wisdom and historic patriotism;" of these the wisdom and patriotism of Bismarck are the direct opposites. His is the wisdom that penetrates and provides for the future; his is the patriotism that impels him to exhibit his love for his country in constant endeavors to secure for her permanent power and prosperity.

The history of modern times furnishes few examples of such minds as that of this now famous German. We can find on record few instances in which a comparatively small and virtually dependent kingdom has been raised in eight years to the proud place of a first class power by the genius of a single man. Few indeed are the modern statesmen who have possessed even a small part of Bismarck's creative power backed and pointed by his insight and energy. The man who has of late modified and directed the whole course of European events; the man who was able to destroy the power of Austria, humble France, unify Germany, endow Prussia with immense and unwonted strength, and command the uniform support of Russia; the man who was bold enough to take all temporal power from the German Roman Catholic Church in the face of so many thousands of German Roman Catholics; the man who, by mere genius and force of character, has attained the proudest position in all Europe, will not soon be forgotten. Prussia will not soon find another Bismarck.

Atticus.

Printed in *The Nassau Literary Magazine*, XXXIII (Nov. 1877), 118-27. WW unsuccessfully submitted this essay for the *Magazine*'s prize. See JRW to WW, Nov. 5, 1877. WW's pocket notebook, begun c. July 1, 1877, contains WWsh outlines of this "elaborate essay," which WW's diary for Oct. 20, 1877, says he wrote that summer. The manuscript has not been found. The essay is printed at the date of publication on the assumption that this text was WW's latest version.

From the Minutes of the Liberal Debating Club

Nov. 3, 1877.

Owing to the absence of Messrs McCarter and Webster at the football match with Harvard, and the enthusiasm of Mr. Talcott and your Sec. which caused them to go to the Junction to meet the victorious team, there was no meeting of the evening of the above date.

Ruled not in Order

T. W. Wilson, Pres.
Hiram Woods, J. S. of S.

From Janet Woodrow Wilson

My precious Son—   Wilmington [N. C.]. Monday, Nov 5 [1877]

Your father received the copy of your Bismarck speech. He is *very* much pleased with it. He desires me to say that he will let you have it in a day or two. How I wish I could hear you speak it, dear! Please tell me *when* you expect to deliver your speech & under what circumstances. I sometimes try to imagine you as you appear when speaking in public. Do you know, I am filled with a sort of wonder, when I think of you—who was for so long my little pet & constant companion—taking your place in this conspicuous way, among your fellows. Col. & Mrs. Pope were in church yesterday—it seems they got home about a week ago. She told me that you had called to see her in Princeton—that you looked very bright & well &c. What a life she leads! I cant understand how she finds any satisfaction in it. Your father had a very pleasant time at Synod last week. Everybody was most cordial—and flatteringly attentive. He preached for Dr. M.[1] on Sabbath morning—and was Dr M's guest during his stay at Charlotte—which was very pleasant, except that, the house being full[,] he was obliged to sleep with his host! You know he cant bear that sort of thing. Mr & Mrs Robinson went to Synod with him but had to return after being there one day. Fred Robinson's[2] baby, which had been lying at the point of death apparently for many weeks, died after they left—and he telegraphed for them to return to attend the funeral! They did not like to refuse. While I think of it, Tommy dear, did you ever hear about Willie Leckie? I suppose you must have done so. I think it was one of the saddest things I have ever heard. Do you correspond with Douglas McKay still? Do you ever write to your sister Annie? If not *please* do. Have you written to your Sister Marion? . . .

Dear papa & Josie join me in warmest love to you

Your own Mother

ALS (WP, DLC) with WWhw notation on env.: "Ans."
1 The Rev. S. Taylor Martin.
2 Frederick G. Robinson, son of the C. H. Robinsons.

From Joseph Ruggles Wilson

Darling Son— [Wilmington, N. C.], Tuesday—Nov. 5 77

I enclose yr. Bismarck speech. In my judgment, it is excellent. I have taken the liberty to suggest several alterations which seem to me to make it stronger and less *essay*-like. A speech is something to be spoken—and so, its sentences ought to resemble *bullets*—i.e. be compact and rapid, & prepared to make clean holes.

I am hardly sorry that you failed in the "Lit." prize. It is well to learn that you have need of still greater and greater exertion. That you came so near to success is enough for *encouragement*.

Study *manner*, dearest Tommy, as much as matter: *naturalness* of manner as much as *strength* of matter. *Both* are essential.

We all love you & hope wonderful things of you. You have every reason to feel thankful for the powers God has given you. Mother & Josie send love. So does your affec father   J. R. W.

ALS (WP, DLC).

From the Minutes of the American Whig Society

Whig Hall. November 9th 1877.

. . . Report of the Committee on Hall Improvement.

Whig Hall, Nov. 9th 1877.

Your Committee on Hall Improvement would report as follows;—

In accordance with the instructions of the Hall, a meeting of the Senate, having been duly advertised, was held last Tuesday at 12 M. Your Committee offered a resolution as ordered by the House: this was declared out of order on the technical ground that the Senate could not suspend the action of the constitution in any instance. On motion the matter was referred to the house through its committee, suggesting that the measure be presented in the form of an amendment to the constitution. An informal vote being taken, the Senate was found to be unanimously in favor of the measure proposed for the improvement of the Hall. The Senate then adjourned until next Tuesday Nov. 13th at 12 M. Your Committee after careful consideration have decided to present the following new section to Article LXI. of the constitution, as being what would best accomplish the object in view.

Art. LXI. §7. This fund may be used for repairs to the Hall, which are proposed by the House and approved by the Senate.[1]

In order to go through the proper formalities, it will be necessary to read this same three times and pass it through the committee of the whole, this evening. As the necessity and importance of this is evident, it is hoped that this will be done. As a matter of interest, your committee would add that Prof. Lindsey has made a careful estimate of the cost of these repairs and has kindly expressed his willingness to supertend the work and see everything done in good shape.   Respectfully submitted,

Dulles, Lieb, Wilson, Bridges, Lawrence, Chairman . . .

Second Session.

. . . Speaking. 9th Division.
Performed, Webster,
   Wilson, Thomas Carlyle.
   H. Woods, Some Necessary Elements in a Reformer's
      Character. . . .

[1] This motion passed its third reading and was adopted at this meeting. A second motion, instructing the committee to proceed with the repairs, was also adopted.

From Janet Woodrow Wilson

My dearest Son,   Wilmington—N. C. [c. Nov. 10, 1877]

I received your Postal, enquiring about Willie Leckie, this morning. I am sorry you have heard nothing about the matter—for it is a sad story I have to tell you—and I am sure it will distress you not a little. I think you know that he was engaged in teaching somewhere in the country during the last year. Well, it seems that his first trouble was in consequence of a "love scrape." He fell in love with a girl in the house where he was boarding. His mother was bitterly opposed to his marrying her—as she was greatly his inferior. Then he was doing a great deal of night work—and his friends think that his mind was probably somewhat unhinged in consequence of over-work. Upon this account, it is likely that he was instable, and perhaps somewhat unreasonable, in his management of his school. At any rate, he was charged with having whipped with inexcusable severity one or more of his scholars. I think too that he dismissed one—but I am not sure. However, he went to the home of the parents of one boy about whom there had been difficulty. I suppose there is no certainty as to what passed —one story is that he went up to the house and enquired for the man of it—he was told that the man was not at home—and that then he turned and walked away from the house—and that before he had gone many steps, he was *shot dead*, from behind! The other version of the affair is that he, Willie, saw the man Dent—that they had words—that Willie had a cowhide with him—attacked Dent with it—and that Dent killed him in self defence. The latter was the version accepted upon the trial—and Dent was acquitted.

Now is this not the saddest thing you ever heard, dear Tommy? I was never more shocked at hearing anything—and you who knew & loved the boy so well, will certainly not be less so. The poor fellow expected to go to the Sem[inary] this year you know—had selected his room—put his name upon the door—all. His poor mother was so happy that all her highest hopes for her boy were about to be realized—and you know how she has worked & denied herself in every way. And this is the end of it all!—I must not forget to tell you that *everybody* speaks of Willie with loving pity. He seems to have been a favorite with all who knew him—greatly respected by his companions. I heard about it when we were in Columbia last—and Annie was so surprised that *I* had not heard it before, that I took for granted that you *had* heard. Write to her & get her to tell you all the particulars. She is very anxious to get a letter from you at any rate. It seems to me this unhappy affair should be a warning to every one—for who would have been considered less likely to meet a violent end, such as this, than Willie Leckie! We cannot distrust ourselves too much—or be too constantly on our guard.

I cant write more now, my darling. I am sorry to sadden you by this distressing story. How are you now? Do you need anything? By the way, did your cravats arrive safely? & how did they suit? Your father & Josie send unbounded love. God bless you my precious son—& deliver you from all evil.

Yours lovingly, Mother

ALS (WP, DLC).

From the Minutes of the Liberal Debating Club

Nov. 10, 1877.

House met at 8 P.M., Mr. McCarter being absent. Minutes were read and adopted. Mr. Webster then read from Cushing's Manual, after which the Club proceeded to the 3rd reading of Mr. Talcott's Bill regarding the French Republic. The Bill was decided in the affirmative. The Sec. of State, taking the negative view of the question, resigned his office. The Pres. said he would defer the appointment of a successor, until the next regular meeting. By universal consent the subject of "Poetry"—appointed for this evening for discussion—was waved, and the Club proceeded to the first reading of the Bill offerred by Mr. Elsing: Res. "That the Mohammedan Religion has been a promoting, rather than a retarding force in the progress of civilization." The Bill was carried on its first reading. On motion of Mr. Talcott, the Club proceeded to the 2nd reading, and again carried the Bill. On motion of the same gentleman the Club proceeded to Com. of Whole, Mr. Sheldon in the chair. The Com. of Wh. recommended to the House the adoption of the Bill. Mr. Wilson having been called from the room, on motion of Mr. Talcott, Mr. Sheldon kept the Chair, as Pres. *"Pro. Tem."* At the suggestion of Mr. Talcott the Club decided to discuss at its next meeting the subject—"Poetry"—after which they adjourned to meet Nov. 17.

E. W. Sheldon Pres. *Pro. Tem.*
Hiram Woods, Jr. S. of S.

From Joseph Ruggles Wilson

My darling boy— [Wilmington, N. C.] Tuesday 12th Nov. [1877]

Enclosed, please find $10.00. Small sums will have to do you until the Church replenishes my own small treasury. A new overcoat—is it *essintial* to comfort & health, dear son? If so you shall at once have it. If not—wait a little. Be perfectly candid—as I am. Our interests are *one*[.] I will sacrifice anything for you, as I am sure you will for me.

The Princetonian is capital, and *improve* from week to week. It is better than it stood last year. You have every reason to feel encouraged and the college to feel itself complimented.

Your dear Mother continues to be well—but is not yet strong. Strength will come with time.

She & Josie join me in unbounded love for our precious one, whom we both love & *admire*.   Your own Friend & Father

ALS (WP, DLC) with WWhw notation on env.: "Ans."

News Item in *The Princetonian*

[Nov. 15, 1877]

Owing to the increase of labor caused by his appointment to represent the College in Oratory, at their Collegiate contest in January, Mr. C. L. Williams has resigned his position as Managing Editor of *The Princetonian*. As the time required to do his work on the paper was greater than one man could well spare, the Board has deemed it advisable to appoint two men to take his place, till after the Contest. The members chosen were, Messrs. Dickens, '78, and Wilson, '79.

Printed in *The Princetonian*, ɪɪ (Nov. 15, 1877), 109.

From the Minutes of the American Whig Society

Whig Hall, November 16th 1877.

. . . Report of the Committee on Hall Improvement.

Whig Hall, Nov. 16th 1877.

Your Committee on Hall Improvement would report as follows:—The Senate at their meeting on Tuesday last passed the new amendment to the Constitution regarding the sinking fund; and as soon as copied up in the Statute Book by the Secy of Records, it will receive the proper signatures and become a law. The Senate also agreed to the resolution of the House appropriating the monies now in the "sinking fund" for improvements.

As soon as possible your Committee will proceed to work.

Respectfully submitted,

Com. ⟨ Dulles,
Lieb,
Wilson,
Bridges,
Lawrence, Ch'r.

Resolved, That Art. XX. Sec. 2 of By-Laws which now reads, "Each disputant shall speak not longer than 15 minutes nor less than 3," be amended to read as follows, "Each disputant shall speak on his first speech not more than 10 minutes nor less than 3. On his second speech he shall be allowed not more than 6 minutes."

Bridges,   Sheldon,
H. Woods,   Wilson.

Amendment moved that it read 12 and 8 minutes, Kerr. Lost. Original then lost. . . .

From Janet Woodrow Wilson

Wilmington [N. C.] Friday A.M. [Nov. 16, 1877]
My darling Tommy,

. . . As to the proposed Overture to the Assembly with reference
to the Assembly's Clerks—you will be glad to learn that the Synod
had sense enough not to receive it favorably. It was laid on the
table—upon the motion of the mover's own brother. Your father
did not say a word with reference to the matter. There were plenty
ready to squash it—the movement—if it had needed squashing—
and he was glad not to appear—as it might, & would no doubt, have
been thought that his interest was *personal.* . . .

Goodbye my darling son. May God bless you. I am sorry about
your cold. Do take care. Is there anything you need to make you
comfortable? With fondest love from us all.

Yours lovingly, Mother

ALS (WP, DLC) with WWhw notation on env.: "Ans."

From the Minutes of the Liberal Debating Club

Nov. 17th '77.
House met at 7-50 P.M. with all the members present. There being no Sec'y of State, the President appointed Mr. McCarter to
fill that position. A motion was made by Mr. McCarter to change
the order of business so that the reading of the minutes shall be
first, followed by proposition for new members etc. Carried. Mr.
Sheldon then read a selection from the Manual and Mr. Elsing's
Bill, "Resolved that the Mohammedan Religion has been a promoting rather than a retarding force in the progress of civilization["] passed its 3rd reading & was unanimously adopted.

This being a night for "Literary discussion" the sec'y of State
read the subject for discussion viz: "*Poetry*," and the house indulged in some well-timed remarks on that subject. Miscellaneous
business being again before the house Mr. Sheldon then proposed
the following bill: ["] *Resolved* that the American Republic owes its
past success to natural advantages found in the country & not to
any inherent practicability in Republican Principles." The Sec'y of
State placed next Saturday evening for the reading of the above
bill. The gentleman from N. J. Mr. Sheldon proposed the following
bill: *Resolved* that the President appoint at every meeting a member who shall *speak* before the club on the following Saturday evening—amended by Mr. Wilson to read that the speeches be original.
The mover of the original resolution having accepted the amend-

ment it became embodied in the amendment that the speeches be original or selected at the option of the speaker. Accepted by mover of resolution & embodied in resolution. The bill as amended then passed its first reading. Mr. McCarter then moved the second reading of the bill. Carried. The bill was then read for the 2nd time and *lost*. There being no further business, the Club adjourned to meet Nov. 24th.

T. W. Wilson   Pres.   Robt Harris McCarter   Secy of State

From the Minutes of the American Whig Society

Whig Hall. November 23rd 1877.

. . . Miscellaneous Business

Resolved, That we reconsider the resolution in regard to amending Art. XX. § 2. of the By-Laws.

(c-d.)	H. Woods,	Archer,[1]
	Wilson,	Bridges.

On motion, postponed one week.

Resolved, By-Laws &c., That J. O. contest be postponed one week.

	Bridges,	Shoemaker,[2]
	H. Woods,	Talcott,
	Gilman	Wilson.

Amended "from Tuesday until Thursday," and carried. . . .

[1] Robert Archer, '79.
[2] George E. Shoemaker, '79.

From Joseph Ruggles Wilson

My darling boy—   [Wilmington, N. C., c. Nov. 23, 1877]

Enclosed you will find the enormous sum of $5.00 which exhausts my generosity at this time!

I am almost prepared to feel sorry that you have allowed your time to be occupied and your temper to be tried by going into the *business* of printing. But, then, I have great confidence in your judgment, and assume that you acted for the best all things considered. Do you write for the P[rincetonia]n? *All* the articles are so well composed that I am disposed to think them all your own! . . .

I am myself well enough for all practical purposes[.] Certainly my heart is always strong as towards my dearest son to whom this scrawl is sent. All send love.

Your affc. father J. R. W.

ALS (WP, DLC) with WWhw notation "Ans" and WWsh notes on env.

From the Minutes of the Liberal Debating Club

Nov. 24th '77.

House met 7.53 P.M. In absence of the Prest. that office devolved upon the Sec'y. of State, Mr. McCarter, who appointed Mr. Sheldon to act as Sec'y of State *"Pro tem."* There being no miscellaneous business, the chair appointed Mr Webster to read a selection from the manual.

The Club then proceeded to the 1st reading of Mr. Sheldon's bill:—Resolved that the American Republic owes its past success to natural advantages found in the country & not to any inherent practicability in republican principles. The bill was lost on its first reading.

Miscellaneous business being in order Mr. Talcott moved that the literary subject for discussion on next Saturday evening be the province of Fiction. Mr. McCarter then moved the following bill—*"Resolved* that at every meeting the President appoint a member to speak before the Society on the following Saturday night, or at the next meeting of the Society, an original speech," amended by Mr. Woods that speeches be original or selected at option of speaker—Seconded, and lost. Amended by Mr. Sheldon that the speeches be not less than four (4) & more than eight (8) minutes in length—Seconded & embodied in original bill. *Accepted.* Amended by Mr. Sheldon that the President also appoint a member to write a written criticism on the speech to be read at the meeting following the recital of the speech. Amended that on night of speaking oral criticism be made on matter & manner—accepted. Bill as amended passed its first, & second readings, committee of the whole, & Cushing's Manual be for the time lain aside, it passed its third reading & was finally adopted.

The President appointed Mr. Sheldon to speak & Mr. Elsing to criticise.

The meeting then adjourned to meet Dec. 1st.

T. W. Wilson N. C.   Robt Harris McCarter N. J.
    Prest.   Sec'y of State

From Janet Woodrow Wilson

My darling Son,   Wilmington [N. C.]—Nov. 30th [1877]
  ... How are you getting on with your speech, my dear? How I wish I could hear you utter it, my darling! I wish I could know the exact hour when you are speaking! God bless you my precious child! ...

Papa & Josie send unbounded love to our sweet Tommy. My heart is *full* of love for you.   Your own Mother

ALS (WP, DLC).

From the Minutes of the Liberal Debating Club

Dec. 1st 1877.

House met at 8-9 ¾ P.M. The Sec'y. of state being absent, the Prest. appointed Mr. Sheldon to fill that office. Miscellaneous business being in order Mr. Sheldon moved that on all questions of Definition, Pronunciation and orthography Worcester's dictionary be the authority of the Club—Carried.

Mr. Elsing then read chap. V of Cushings Manual. Mr. Talcotts question was then discussed with great éclat. It was the "*Province of fiction.*"

Mr. Wilson proposed the following bill—Resolved that the resumption of specie payment in accordance with bill of 1875 is essential to the welfare of the United States. Sec'y of State appointed the next regular meeting for the discussion of the subject.

Mr. Woods then spoke being appointed in the place of Mr Sheldon who was excused. Mr. Woods subject was "*Rowe's most precious treasure.*"

On motion of Mr. Woods the club adjourned to meet the first saturday of next term.

T. W. Wilson N. C. Prest.   E. W. Sheldon, N. J. Sec'y *Pro tem*

From Marion Woodrow Bones

My dearest Nephew,   Rome, Ga. Dec. 6th '77.

Shakspeare, or some one else, says "A letter timely writ"—does something desirable. . . . But yet, though I did not write you a "timely" letter, I call upon you to believe that I enjoyed your letter extremely, as indeed, we all did. Your letter to Jessie made its appearance yesterday, to her great delight, and it gave birth to a great many resolutions on her part to write you ever so long a letter "right away," and to keep on writing you at the most wonderful rate, always thereafter. . . .

It seems to me it would have been so very nice if I could have felt as well as I do just now while you and your Mother were here—but then of course I know it was better as it was. I think you are a most uncommonly dear sweet boy to be as satisfied and pleased as you express yourself, with a summer which most young men would have considered as tiresome & dull as possible. It takes one with a very unusual supply of brains & heart to get on without more outside pleasure than you had last summer. But then you *gave* a great deal of happiness, and that must have been a satisfaction. . . .

Your loving Aunt, Marion W. B.

ALS (WP, DLC) with WWhw notation on env.: "Ans."

From the Minutes of the American Whig Society

Whig Hall December 6th 1877.

Junior Orator Contest.

House met, roll called. The Judges took their seats and the Clerk read Art. 35 of the By-Laws. These gentlemen contested,—

E. A. Stevens, N. J.	A Glimpse at Bismarck.
A. J. Kerr, Ill.	Enthusiasm.
E. W. Sheldon, N. J.	Euthanasia.
T. W. Wilson, N. C.	Bismarck.
R. W. Blackwell, N. Y.	The Lesson of the Great Strike
T. M. McNair,[1] N. Y.	Elizabeth's Policy and Success.
C. C. Polk,[2] N. J.	The Jews.
C. Talcott, N. Y.	Thiers.
H. B. Smith, N. Y.	Macaulay.
x R. H. McCarter, N. J.	Thackeray.
x J. D. Davis, Pa.	The Might of Character.
x S. A. Harlow, N. Y.	Time, the Vindicator of Truth.
R. Bridges, Pa.	Zenobia.
x W. T. Elsing, Ill.	The Struggle of Holland for Independence
L. Helm,[3] Ill.	Thoughts that Glow and Words that Burn.
M. G. Emery, Jr., D. C.	The Triumph of Defeat.
A. B. Stewart,[4] N. J.	Be Helpful to Thyself.
J. L. Reynolds,[5] N. J.	The Noble Aim.
S. Alexander, N. Y.	The War in the East.

x Appointed . . .

[1] Theodore M. McNair, '79.
[2] Charles C. Polk, '79.
[3] Lynn Helm, '79.
[4] Anson B. Stewart, '79.
[5] James L. Reynolds, '79.

A Speech

[Dec. 6, 1877]

Bismarck

Bismarck grown old, clothed in authority, invested with power, the centre and soul of European politics, is as familiar a figure to us of to-day as was Frederic the Great to the Englishman of 1765. The world is not unfamiliar with the grim yet frank and genial man, the cool, clearsighted, consummate statesman who has made complete and firm the power of that Prussia whose history had already been rendered brilliant by the diplomatic talents and conquering swords of the great *Hohenzollerns* before it was lit up by the glory of the greatest subject that has ever owned allegiance to that royal house. To Otto von Bismarck every German owes a debt of gratitude, every Frenchman a debt of hatred, the world a debt of admiration and impartial judgment. As Americans, we can, from the vantage ground of disinterested observation pronounce upon the merits and demerits of this eminent Prussian without the repugnance of the Austrian, the bitterness of the Frenchman, or the prejudice of the Englishman to warp our judgments.

It would be difficult to recognize in the dignified and somewhat stern chancellor of to-day the excentric, hard-drinking fox-hunting young squire of thirty-five years (35) ago. But a crisis in national affairs finds him upon the floor of a stormy Assembly, where, strange to say, he feels bound to advocate Prussian subserviency to the house of Hapsburg even while his country's heart is still sore with the terrible humiliation of Olmutz. Yet can we be surprised that every word which the stalwart young aristocrat that day dealt out from the tribune was a blow to the Liberal party of Prussia? Can it seem strange to us that the demon of revolution, even though it bore the name of democracy, should seem terrible to him? From Austrian domination alone a little gleam of hope then seemed to him to flash athwart the oppressive darkness. But contact with Austrian intrigue soon rudely awakened him to the real position, the real duty, the real possibilities of Prussia. At Frankfort-on-the-Main the grim, silent, and thoughtful Prussian, planning in the declining light of the past not only, but in the rising dawn of the future as well, probably first conceived his vast schemes for the aggrandizement of Prussia. Here, too, he learned the lessons which were to fit him for taking the helm of state amid fierce contests between King and parliament and while international complications hung like a cloud over Europe, bringing many an anxious frown to the brows of English and European statesmen and seeming to threaten a wide-spread storm.

Both Bismarck's virtues and his faults, both his greatness and his littleness, have been developed and modified by the circumstances of his position. The chief and most trusted advisor of a monarch whose princely prerogatives are virtually unlimited, he has gained for himself a position of authority and command; the first minister of a powerful court, the leading figure of an exclusive and potent aristocracy, he occupies a place of peculiar advantage; wielding a mastery whose very existence depends upon his influence over the royal mind, his position is one which exposes him to temptations which are well-nigh irresistible. And, whilst many a triumph over surrounding difficulties and opponents, many a master-stroke of foreign policy, and many a brilliant victory in war have combined to attest the preëminence of his genius, his character is not altogether free from the strain which intrigue invariably leaves.

Bismarck's wondrous powers are seen in their true greatness in the conception and execution of political plans. He is not a great debater, yet there is a sort of rugged strength and beauty in his speeches and an occasional lucidity and even brilliancy of statement. Habitual terseness and frankness engrave his words upon his hearers' memories, imprint his sentiments upon their hearts. His eloquence partakes of the stern magnificence of the storm, rather than of the soft brilliancy of the cascade or the quiet beauty of deep, still waters. He stands without a successful rival as a diplomatist, without a peer in powers of cool judgment, quick determination, and masterly execution. Mark, too, the amazing quickness of insight which revealed to him the really feeble condition of Austria and the "misunderstood incapacity" of Napoleon; the penetrative sharpness of judgment which, amid untold difficulties and perplexities, enabled him to choose the path which led to the rapid augmentation of Prussian power. Bismarck's naturally impulsive nature has often threatened to betray him into rashness. But his tendency to indiscretion has been counterbalanced and neutralized by the necessity for deliberation which the Emperor's force of character and stubbornness of will impose upon him. But above all Bismarck is singularly a man of oneness of aim and, accordingly, brings to the aid of his purpose his entire powers concentrated into one intensely heated focus which enables them to *burn* their way to success, when success is a possibility. To the quickness of resolve and ability for prompt action so necessary to leaders there is added in Bismarck a calm firmness which receives all opposition like a wall of granite. But this firmness, grand as it sometimes is, is occasionally disfigured by harshness and sometimes even by unscrupulousness. Many violent actions, too, have thrown a shadow upon Bismarck's otherwise fair name; but this shadow only serves in his case to bring out into greater prominence many a shining virtue. We can never justify the wilful disregard of justice or the intentional breaking of faith. But in a man who is conscious of great powers, whose mind is teeming and overflowing with great political plans and meditative of grand national triumphs, and who, withal, is hampered by almost every circumstance of his surroundings, we can at least understand an occasional contempt of strict duty and, in the presence of so many grand and peerless qualities, so many noble purposes, we can, perhaps, forgive a want of integrity which so seldom exhibits itself.

In many characteristic qualities the immortal interpreter of Englands constitution and the princely man who has given a definite form to the constitution of United Germany resemble each other. Like England's great and not-enough-considered *Pym*, Bismarck, with a growing sense of his own greatness, remained resolute and patient until the time for action came, the time for proving himself as peerless in action as patient in waiting.[1] Like Pym's eloquence, the eloquence of Bismarck convinces and guides by virtue of its massive and logical force. Like Pym, Bismarck is the only one of his contemporaries who can clearly foresee and definitely determine how to meet the difficulties which lie before him. Like Pym, Bismarck unites genial and fascinating manners to his sternness of resolve. The very words in which a master-hand has summed up the powers of Pym seem to have been intended for a description of Bismarck: "A striking combination of genial versatility with a massive force in his nature marked him out from the first moment of power as a born ruler of men. He proved himself at once the subtlest of diplomatists and the grandest of demagogues. He displayed . . . . the qualities of a great administrator, an immense faculty for labor, a genius for organization . . . . tact . . . . an immovable courage, an iron will."[2] In Bismarck are united the moral force of Cromwell and the political shrewdness of Richelieu; the comprehensive intellect of Burke, without his learning, and the diplomatic ability of Talleyrand, without his coldness. In haughtiness, a rival of Chatham; in devotion to his country's interests, a peer of Hampden; in boldness and versatility, an equal of Brougham, Bismarck possesses all the peculiar qualities of a statesman in unique and brilliant combination.

When the great chancellor shall have passed away; when the

prejudices and passions of his age shall have ceased to influence mankind; when impartial History shall have given him his just meed of praise and blame; when future generations shall have recognized his mighty powers and virtues, forgiven his faults, his misdeeds; when, standing back upon the great field of the past rather than forward upon the immediate theater of action, he shall have taken his place among the finished figures of history, then shall be seen deep-graven upon his country's history his course of power, the traces of his lightening-like strokes of genius. History will not be blind to his faults, but it will look with a proud and kindly smile upon the frank, grim Prussian, upon the ample intellect bounded by an iron will, and will place his name among the master statesmen, the men who have set the pages of history aglow with the record of noble endeavor and accomplished deed, men who have established principles and crowned causes with success. The tribute of posterity to the

"Man whose mighty will, with giant power combined,
The noble fabric reared his genius had designed,"

to the stalwart man whose word is law to king and peasant alike, upon whose will the destiny of nations hangs, will be: "This was the noblest German of them all . . . . the elements so mixed in him that Nature might stand up and say to all the world, *This was a man*."[3]

WWhw MS. (WP, DLC).
[1] See WW's marginal notes in J. R. Green's *Short History of the English People*, comparing Pym and Bismarck, printed at Oct. 17, 1877.
[2] WW's elisions.
[3] WW's elision.

From the Minutes of the American Whig Society

Whig Hall, December 7th 1877.
. . . Resolved, By-Laws &c., That the officers be elected tonight and that we have no Constitutional Meeting on next Monday evening.

c-d. Kerr. . . .

The election resulted as follows,—
For Speaker, J. D. Davis.

1st Compr. T. W. Wilson
2nd " R. Bridges.
Sub-Com. Messrs. Sheldon & Stevens.

Secy Treasy. Mr. Orbison.[1]
" Library " Kerr.
" Dip. " Gilman.

" For. Aff. " Woods.
" Records " Withington.
Sergeant   " Webster.
 Auditors   Messrs McLaren[2] and Henderson.
 Clerk   Mr. Galbreath.[3]
Commissioners of Sinkg Fund, Dr. Cameron, Messrs B. Greene
& Orbison. House adjourned to meet after Chapel, Friday evening,
Dec. 14th 1877. . . .

1 John H. Orbison, '79.
2 Donald C. McLaren, '79.
3 James M. Galbreath, '80.

From Joseph Ruggles Wilson

Home [Wilmington, N. C.], Monday, [Dec.] 10th [1877]
My darling Son
 Enclosed you will find my check for $20.00 a Christmas gift
from us all. As to yr coming home during the coming short vacation, that must depend upon Pope. How we *long* to see you I need
not try to tell; but the painful sense of impecuniosity (this together
with a knowledge of the dangers of travel in winter) makes it
necessary for both yourself and us to "grin and bear" our disappointment. I think you would find a visit to Brooklyn pleasant and
profitable. . . .   Your aff father J R W

ALS (WP, DLC) with WWhw notation on env.: "Ans."

From the Minutes of the American Whig Society

Whig Hall December 14th, 1877
. . . Report of Com. on Hall Improvement.

Whig Hall. Dec. 14th, 1878[7]
 Your Committee on Hall Improvement would report as follows:—The Exterior Painting was bargained for with J. L. Briner
for the sum of ....$ 50.
Bids have been received from two contractors for the Car-
penter's work including the Library & all the proposed alterations, the lowest bid being ....$425.
Bids being received for doing the heating and ventilating
for ....$300.
Bid for making repairs to the roofing and painting of same ....$ 35.
 For general straightening-up & repairing of interior &
painting ....$ 35.
                                            $845.

In addition to this there will be erected new steps of white
pine at ....$ 60.
And a new combination-lock about ....$ 20.

The painting of the exterior was not mentioned in Prof. Lindsey's original estimate: this was done by the direction of the Committee, as it was much needed.

The repairs to the roof are now being made, after which a thick
coat of metallic paint will be put on. The repairs to the Interior
will be commenced next Wednesday, in order not to interfere with
the use of the Library in term time. The Library will have to be
closed during vacation: the books will be taken down by the
Librarian & several members of the committee, & afterwards replaced. The committee, although this work could have been done
a week ago, have thought best that it be done during vacation, &
hope to have it finished by the beginning of next term: it may
however require several days more to finish it.

Proposals for stone & pine steps have been received and in as
much as the stone steps would cost twice as much as pine, the
committee have thought best to have them of pine. Your committee will present a final report next term.[1]

Respectfully Submitted

Henry C. Cameron,	Wm Dulles Jr.	T. W. Wilson
chairman	D. M. Lieb.	W. W. Lawrence....
L. S. S. Orris[2]	Robt. Bridges	
H. S. Osborne[3]		

[1] See Minutes of the American Whig Society, June 14, 1878.
[2] The Rev. S. Stanhope Orris, Ewing Professor of Greek Languages and Literature.
[3] Henry Fairfield Osborn, '77, a graduate student. The scribe misspelled his
name.

From Janet Woodrow Wilson

Wilmington N. C. Tuesday evening, [Dec. 18, 1877]
My precious Boy,

Mrs. Pope sent me this morning an enclosure which I suppose
means a free ticket for you home. Do just as you like about it, my
darling—though I can scarcely doubt that you will come. I am too
much excited at the unexpected prospect of seeing you so soon,
darling, to write. I will send to the P. O. at the same time that I
send this, an order to Mr. "W. H. Fitzgerald of German St. Baltimore, Md." for your ticket. I suppose it is a ticket similar to that of
last Xmas—but your father says you had better reserve funds *for*

fear it should not be[.] I enclose your father's cheque for fifty five dollars.

Good bye, my precious boy. Telegraph us when we may expect you. Do guard yourself from cold. May God bless you, and keep you from all danger my precious son. Love from father & brother
Your own Mother.

ALS (WP, DLC) with WWhw list of articles purchased and WWsh notation on env.

From Annie Wilson Howe

My precious Brother,   Columbia, Dec. 20th/77
. . . You asked me to tell you about Willie Leckie. We have heard so many versions of the story that it is hard to know which to believe. The one which seems to come more directly, is this. One of the boys in his school brought with him one day a bottle of *whisky*; which when Willie found he threw out of the window, and then he gave the boy a severe whipping. The father of the boy was enraged and spread it abroad that his son had been so severely beaten that he was seriously injured by it. Willie heard this and went to see the father, carrying with him a *cow-hide*. He called him out and told him that he had come to whip him—and I believe struck him once. The father then drew his pistol and shot Willie, *dead*. The cause of it all, they say, was that Willie was in love with some girl in the house where he was boarding and his mother was bitterly opposed to his marrying her. He had just been home on a visit to his mother, and was worried and out of sorts altogether. . . .
Your devoted, sister Annie.

ALS (WP, DLC) with WWhw notation on env.: "Ans."

From Joseph Ruggles Wilson

Wilmington, [N. C.] Saturday, [Dec.] 22nd [1877]
My darling Son—
We all sympathize with you in the matter of your contest disappointment.[1] It must have been a sore grief—and the sorer because unexpected. But, let it go. It is not killing: only *stunning*. You will recover and be all the stronger for the blow. Indeed, to tell you the honest truth, I am not inconsolable by reason of your failure: I rather like it. It will help to reveal your true worth, both as to quality and quantity; will show the stuff you are made of. If you shall continue to be disheartened—much more if you should become despairful—in view of what has happened—well, you can't

be good for much. But, if, after the first days of depression shall have passed, you arise with new resolution and with at once an humbler and a mightier purpose to achieve success—trusting hereafter in God *and* yourself not so much in yourself alone—well, this will be prophetic of a noble and honorable manhood. I failed twice in pretty much the same way: but my competitors have never been heard of since—and I count myself as having only ordinary capacity.

My darling, make *more* of your class studies. Dismiss *ambition*—and replace it with hard industry, which shall have little or no regard to *present* triumphs, but which will be all the time laying foundations for future work and wage. *I* know you. You are capable of much hard mental work, and of much endurance under disappointment. You are manly. You are true. You are aspiring. You are most lovable every way and deserving of confidence. But as yet you despise somewhat the beaten track which all scholars and orators (almost) have had to travel—the track of patient study in mathematics, in languages, in science, in philosophy. Dearest boy, can you hope to jump into eminency all at once? You say, though, that others who seem to be less worthy are succeeding where you fail. Pshaw, this is always the case, in all life. Brass is mightier even than gold—and favors are showered upon fools often until they are saturated, whilst the wise are forgotten. Buckle on the harness again. You are skirmishing, now, remember: the battle is to come: and let the recollection of partial defeat in the earlier fights only serve to keep you more and more vigilant in view of the prolonged tug of war. Your dear mother and I are not cast down by reason of your failure: our sorrow is that you should have sorrow. I cannot tell you how dearly we love you, and now more than ever if possible. Keep a stiff upper lip.

Yes—destroy that check. I enclose $20.00 in draft on N. York.

Your affectionate father J R W.

ALS (WP, DLC) with WWhw notation on env.: "12/24/77."
1 WW's recent failure to win appointment as a Whig representative in the Junior Oratorical Contest. See Dec. 6, 1877.

From Janet Woodrow Wilson

My beloved Son,   Wilmington N.C. Dec. 29th 1877.

It is not possible for me to write a letter today—but I cannot let the day pass without sending you a few lines. Just to think, dearest child, that you are *twenty one* years old! You know you were born about midnight of the 28th but we do not know whether it was a little after midnight or before. Well, my darling—you have never been anything but a comfort & blessing to me all your life. Are you glad to know that? . . .

We received your report this morning. Your father is very much pleased with it. Isn't it a good deal better than any previous report? Still, it seems to me, your *"Sessional* Grade" is not in proportion with your *"Department* Grades"—as the average of the latter is much above what they give you in the former—and that is the only fair way to give it, surely. . . .[1]

Your father & Josie send warmest love. I love you with all my heart.   Your Mother

ALS (WP, DLC) with WWhw notation on env.: "Ans." Enc.: College of New Jersey, Official Report, Dec. 28, 1877, of standing of WW for session ending Dec. 19, 1877; signed by H. N. Van Dyke, Registrar.
[1] WW's sessional grade was 92.8. Whereas seven out of eight courses were graded between 94 and 99.8, only physics, 84, fell below the term average. The discrepancy which troubled JWW arose from the variable weighting of the several courses according to class hours in each.

Five Editorials in *The Princetonian*

[Jan. 10, 1878]

The Winter term, which is generally the most stupid of the academic year, as far as all entertainment outside of that to be found in the studies of the course are concerned, seems apt, this year, to be unusually dull, unless we have some course of interesting lectures, or some other sources of enjoyment and instruction afforded us. One of the most practicable methods of spending the long cold evenings of the term—a method which is, withal, not ill-suited to our academical surroundings—is, to take up a course of reading with some friends. In short, we advocate the formation of reading clubs among us. We do not mean that clubs such as the late abortive Shaksperian Club, would be of any substantial advantage to any. But the reading and common study of some of the masters of literature, by a small and select company of friends, is both highly entertaining and eminently instructive. We learn more of any author in reading his works with intelligent companions and by comparing our opinions of him, his style, and his sentiments, with those in whose judgment constant companionship has taught us to trust. In this way, we not only become more really acquainted with an author and his hidden shades of thought, but also gain some clearer insight into our own minds and into the hearts of our companions. Reading clubs, if properly formed, would also afford us the best means of keeping abreast of our course in English literature. Why not try them?

✧

Unless the Lecture Association be revived during the cold months which are already upon us, this term will be one of the dullest within our remembrance. There is absolutely nothing in prospect for this, the Winter term. The Lecture Association of last year came out of the season's work with an alarming deficit in their treasury, and an unfulfilled programme; but we must say that they have no one to blame for this but themselves. They were entirely too ambitious. Not content to follow the precedent course of the Associations of the two preceding years, they launched forth upon a series of the most expensive concerts, engaging the services of some of the best New York singers and musicians. They thought, perhaps not unnaturally, that the programme which they promised would attract a larger than usual amount of patronage from the students. But this expectation proved to be unfounded. They were unfortunate, but we can see nothing in their experience which ought to discourage the securing of such a course of lectures as we had year before last. We are confident that such lectures as we had in the Winter of 1875, '76 would command large audiences. We heartily hope that another Association will be formed, and can confidently predict that with proper management failure would be highly improbable, if not impossible. The Scientific Lecture Association of last year, gave us an opportunity to hear some of the first scientific men of the country, and were free from all financial embarrassments at the close of the season. Surely we can count upon enough enterprise among us to secure able lecturers for us during the rest of the academic year. And we would offer a few practical suggestions concerning the style of lecture which will be most likely to prove acceptable. We want men who can present to us in proper form and in an intelligent manner, some of the many live questions of the day, both of science and politics. We could enjoy a speech on the Silver Question or upon Free Trade from such a man as Evarts—and we do not think it at all impossible to get such men—than a flowery and insipid effusion from Adirondac Murray,[1] or a piece whose wit is all dried up in the process of elaboration, from Bailey. Prominent men are seldom unwilling to address such a community as this, when they have the promise of a large audience, and can come without expense to themselves. Can we not count upon some such lectures?

[1] Identified at Feb. 13, 1879.

When we look upon the difficulties which he has had to meet and overcome, we find much reason to congratulate the proprietor of the Nassau Hotel on the success which has, up to this time, attended his efforts to keep a comfortable house, and a table at which students could find cheap and excellent board. Since the time when the Commons passed quietly out of existence, and the Commons Hall was cut up into ill-proportioned bits, we have needed, more than ever, some establishment where the large number of students who cannot find satisfactory board at the private boarding houses in the town, could be accommodated with comfortable meals at a moderate price. Such an establishment Mr. Atwood was about to open for the accommodation of one hundred students, when our Faculty issued one of their mysterious notices, forbidding all students to either board or take lodgings at his house. Now we are loth to believe that the Faculty took such action on this matter without some sufficient reason, or without any reason at all. There must have been some causes to lead to this extreme measure on the part of our learned guardians. We have heard that they took alarm at the fact that there is a bar connected with the Nassau, and that they were haunted by the fear that it had degenerated into a grog-shop. We hesitate to criticise their action before we are certain of the motives by which it was prompted. But we have ourselves taken an occasional meal at this hotel, and can corroborate the favorable testimony of those who take their meals there regularly. We have never seen anything but gentlemanly conduct at its tables. We have heard of only one or two cases in which any drinking was indulged in at its bar; and never was this drinking carried to an excess. We do not really believe that there is any less drinking at the private eating clubs than at the tables of the Nassau Hotel; and we know that there is little at either. The Nassau is a thoroughly respectable hotel, and well deserves the patronage of the College. We are sorry that the Faculty have adopted a course which seems to be founded on so slight a basis of reason. Why have they done so?

❖

While we are on the subject of hotel patronage, we wish to speak a few words about the University Hotel. We consider it a valuable addition to our comforts here in this little academic town, and we could, therefore, wish that it was conducted in a manner to make students, who are its chief patronizers, thoroughly at ease in their intercourse with its managers. But this, we are sorry to say, is far from being the case. On the contrary, the recent experience of some of our number has shown that, in our dealings with its officers, we cannot be sure of being treated with even that degree of politeness which is every gentleman's due. We need not be more specific. We know that the attention of the hotel authorities has already been called to the case in which an upper-classman was grossly, and without provocation, insulted by an officer of the hotel; and we are confident that their gentlemanly instincts, as well as their most evident interests, will prompt them to see that there shall be no recurrence of such shameful misconduct on the part of their employees. We would ask them to secure the services of officials who are gentlemen.

Of all the types of College character, the most despicable is the habitual loafer. Not that this character is peculiar to the College world—every order of society, every Christian, every heathen, community affords more than one example of systematic idlers. But we believe that nowhere, more than at College, is the presence of such dead-weights upon life and activity more to be deplored. Few College men realize what College and College life are. Our educational institutions are nothing more nor less than great centres of activity—centres from which flow the learning and the mental training which is to cultivate the naturally arid fields of society, sowing in them the seeds of mental and moral nobility. Without the higher, broader, richer education which they afford, liberal institutions, political freedom, universal suffrage would be, one and all, the worst mockery of freedom, the sorest curse of humanity. Unless that part of man which alone makes him noble, and which distinguishes him from the beast of the field—his mind, his soul— be developed, and thus raised nearer to the likeness of divinity, he is, of all animals, the most dangerous. Now, when we think what a land would be—what many lands are—without education, we gain some little insight into the position into which each great educational centre sustains in relation to the political system of which it is an essential part. We then see how much of national stamina, of national integrity, and even life, depend upon national education. Now, in view of these undoubted principles, how high a sense of responsibility we, as students, should feel; and how mean is the College loafer. Every nation is full of loafers, and its universities have been established for no other purpose than that of counteracting and neutralizing the influence of this vicious class. The prime object of every College is to furnish young men with a solid foundation, upon which to base a broader career—to send forth, in all directions, men who can raise the people to the level of right and truth. With the loafer, this basis is a huddled mass of facts: the career built upon it, an obscure failure. He acts in direct opposition to his class-mates, by endeavoring to impart to those around him his own incoherent ideas. The loafer is not of as much use in a College community as is the drone in a bee-hive. He is not entitled to as much respect as would be the due of a sightless mole in the company of bright-eyed eagles, for the mole, though sightless and groveling, is always active. In the naturally gifted young man, who spends his four years of College life in worse than unprofitable idleness, you see, perhaps, the man who will one day command the attention of large audiences by his elegant and profoundly obscure utterance of garnished commonplaces, or only half-told truths—a man who will give his auditors such ideas of great truths and grand principles as will induce the comfortable but death-bearing habit[,] mental loafing. He will hold up to ridicule the earnest self-disciplining men who are eagerly, intelligently, and boldly seeking for the truth in all its fullness and beauty, and will laud those who, like himself, are content to loaf through life and its innumerable responsibilities, upon half-digested error.

As College may be considered the door to every life-work, so we may say, with some approach to the truth, that from the threshold of this door we may gain an insight into the whole after-career. Genuine hard work is as necessary to the mental life as is food to the physical system, and the man who takes his work in ill-assorted heaps, is the mental dyspeptic; the loafer, to whose mind work is unknown, is the mental weakling. The camp-following hangers-on of the great army of truth-searchers, are those who have, all their lives, been loafers. The performance of duty is the standard by which every man's worth is judged, and the idea of duty necessarily includes that of work: duty lies in the performance of the portion of work allotted to each. The loafer is the constant shirker of work, and, therefore, the constant neglecter of duty. The man who idles away precious time, is not one whit less blameworthy than the picket who deserts his watch-post before the enemy's lines. Every College student who makes a habit of loafing, is, in reality, simply refusing to perform active picket duty for Truth, and thus wilfully leaving her ranks and strongholds the more exposed to the assaults of Error's countless supporters. Such negative existence is actual confederacy with wrong. We do not wish to preach: it is not our province. But we do desire to see right views upon matters affecting our every-day life, prevail.

Printed in *The Princetonian*, II (Jan. 10, 1878), 145-49.

From Joseph Ruggles Wilson

My dearest boy—   Home [Wilmington, N. C.], Jan 10 78

Yours of the 8th was rec'd to-day. You neglected to enclose college bill. I send you the $5.00 you ask for.

It is one thing to be a "forcible" writer and another to be an *entertaining* writer. In order to the latter imaginative illustration is important. In order to the former, there must, indeed, be illustration, but only such as the subject naturally picks up, so to speak, in its progress. This is the only sort that Webster had, or Calhoun. The *soul* of oratory is thought, the *body* of oratory is the suitable expression of this thought:—and usually the *simplest* words give this expression the best. To a lawyer—to a *judicial* mind—*logic is everything*—and true oratory, whether of the bar or the pulpit or the hustings, consists in the statement of connected thought (i.e. logical statement) uttered with the energy and courage of *conviction*. If the speaker be in earnest, he will set fire to his logic as he proceeds; and out of this fire will spring the very illustrations he most needs. In *writing* it is somewhat different. Then the blood is cold, comparatively. Yet, even in the act of writing, if the composer be absorbed in what he is penning he need not fear that his style will be bald. As an instance I refer you to yourself. You are very far from being a dead and doughy writer. When you have anything to say to us at home—in your letters—you uniformly say it with vividness, and with a coloring that betrays no lack of the imaginative brush. Your difficulty may be—probably is—that you don't *let yourself go* when you begin to write. Every beginner—yea, every proficient—in the art of forceful composition, must learn to go through his subject in great leaps or jumps, putting down what comes first, having little or no regard to coherency; except that he must be careful to see that the subject is *expanding*: and he can go over the whole afterwards, putting all into shape, retaining those illustrations which his rapid pen may have hinted as it touched and went. It is probable, dearest son, that in your writings, intended for public criticism, you have *people* too much in view. Dismiss the imaginary audience, and concentrate yourself wholly upon yr. *subject*: being sure that if you master that you shall master your audience. And, besides, don't be afraid of commonplaces. It is not these that render a piece flat. It is the way in which they are *put*. Originality does not so much invent as *put*. The art of *putting things* is the art of taking and striking and persuasive composition. Others may have said the same things, and said them better—but you must say them, *for yourself*—and therefore you concatenate them differently, so differently as to make them seem new: i[.] e[.] you give them the impress of *yourself* and *your*self is not any *other* self. But put them from yr point of view. The pattern is thus placed with a stitch it never had before. In short, dear one, don't get discouraged. You have many reasons to feel the very contrary. Study words, so as to give *variety* to your sentences—and you will get on admirably with due industry and study. By studying *words* I mean *synonyms* as they are called.

But I must close. We are all well, and our love for our darling Thomas is just unbounded.

Write me freely & fully as to *all* your perplexities, I entreat you.

Your own & affc Fr. J. R. W.

Mother sent you two letters this week. Josie grumbles over your neglect of his late epistle

ALS (WP, DLC) with WWhw and WWsh notation on env.: "Received [WWsh] 1/12/78."

From the Minutes of the Liberal Debating Club

Jan 12th 1878.

Meeting called to order at 7-50 P.M. Messrs Elsing, Woods, & Webster being absent—the minutes of the last regular meeting, and after some discussion, those of a special meeting were read. This being the night for the election of President, after five ballots Mr. Woods was declared elected. The gentleman being absent, Mr. Sheldon was called upon to fill the chair by the retiring president Mr. Wilson. Mr. Talcott then read Section IV, chap XII of the manual. Debate being next in order the question *Resolved* that the resumption of specie payment in accordance with the Bill of 1875 is essential to the welfare of the United States, was read & seconded, the Sec'y of state taking the affirmative. Mr. Woods now entering took the chair to which he had been newly elected, & the discussion of the question was then continued. The bill after some debate passed its first reading, Messrs. Sheldon & Elsing alone voting in the negative. The bill then passed successively thro' the second reading and the committee of the whole & was reported favorably to the house. report adopted—The debate being over Mr. Talcott offered the following subject for discussion next Saturday evening: "Macaulay & Carlyle as essayists" which was adopted. After which Mr. Elsing read an able criticism on the speech which Mr. Woods delivered at the last regular meeting. Miscellaneous business was next in order & the President appointed Mr. Wilson as orator & Mr. McCarter as critic for next

Saturday evening. The minutes of previous meeting came up for adoption & those of the special meeting were ruled out of order. Mr. Sheldon moved that the J. O.'s let up—lost. Meeting adjourned at 9-00.

H. Woods, Jr.   Robt Harris McCarter
       Pres.   Sec'y of State

Joseph Ruggles Wilson's Advice to His Son

[Jan. 14, 1878]
Guide in Writing

It is one thing to be a "forcible" writer and another to be an entertaining writer. In order to the latter imaginative illustration is important. In order to the former, there must, indeed, be illustration, but only such as the subject naturally picks up, so to speak, in its progress. This is the only sort that Webster had, or Calhoun. The *soul* of oratory is thought; the *body* of oratory is the suitable expression of this thought:—and usually the simplest words give this expression the best. To a lawyer—to a *judicial* mind—*logic is everything*—and true oratory, whether of the bar or the pulpit or the hustings, consists in the statement of connected thought (i.e. logical statement) uttered with the energy and courage of *conviction*. If the speaker be in earnest, he will set fire to his logic as he proceeds; and out of this fire will spring the very illustrations he most needs. In *writing* it is somewhat different. Then the blood is cold, comparatively. Yet, even in the act of writing, if the composer be absorbed in what he is penning, he need not fear that his style will be bald. . . . Every beginner—yea, every proficient—in the art of forceful composition, must learn to go through his subject in great leaps or jumps, jotting down what comes first, having little or no regard to coherency; except that he must be careful to see that the subject is expanding: and he can go over the whole afterwards, putting all in shape, retaining those illustrations which his rapid pen may have hinted as it touched and went. In writings intended for public criticism, dismiss the imaginary audience, and concentrate yourself wholly upon your *subject*: being sure that if you master that you shall master your audience. And, besides, don't be afraid of commonplaces. It is not these that render a piece flat. It is the way in which they are *put*. Originality does not so much invent as *put*. The art of *putting things* is the art of taking and striking and persuasive composition. Others may have said the same things, and said them better—but you now say them, *for yourself*—and therefore you concatenate them differently, so differently as to make them seem new: i.e. you give them the impress of *yourself* and *your* self is not any *other* self. Just put them from your point of view. The pattern is thus placed with a stitch it never had before. Study words, so as to give *variety* to your sentences. . . . By studying *words* I mean synonyms as they are called.

1/14/78   Copied from one of father's excellent letters[1]

WWhw copy (WP, DLC) of extracts from JRW to WW, Jan. 10, 1878. Apparently JRW's advice on how to acquire a vigorous prose style made such an impression on his son that WW copied these extracts so that he might have his father's words before him in a more legible and convenient form. WW indicated by ellipses some but not all of the omissions from his father's advice. In some instances he even altered slightly JRW's phraseology, mainly to make the advice less personal. A shorthand copy of these extracts appears in WW's pocket notebook, described at July 1, 1877.
[1] "from one of father's excellent letters" transcribed from WWsh.

From the Minutes of the Liberal Debating Club

Jan. 19th 1878.

Meeting called to order at 7-55 P.M. Mr. Elsing the only member absent. Miscellaneous business being in order Mr. McCarter suggested that after the adjournment of our meetings the members remain to read in company any author who may be pleasing to them—the suggestion met with approval and it was decided to read Shakspeares King Henry IV on next Saturday evening after adjournment. Mr. Sheldon then read section VI, chap. XII of the manual.—The third reading of Mr. Wilson's bill: ["]Resolved that the resumption of specie payment in accordance with the bill of 1875 is essential to the welfare of the country" came up & the bill was finally adopted, Mr. Sheldon alone sustaining the minority. The Literary discussion on the subject "Macaulay & Carlyle as essayists" then received the careful attention of & discussion by the members of the Society. The opinion of the Society seemed to be that Carlyle was the greater thinker, but Macaulay the greater essayist. After the discussion, Mr. Wilson being the gentleman appointed by the President, spoke before the Society & criticism by the members on both the matter of the speech & the manner of delivery was then offered. Mr. Talcott then offered the following bill. *Resolved* that Free Trade would be beneficial to the Country's interest, & Sec'y of State appointed next Sat. evening for the discussion. The President then appointed Mr. Elsing to speak on next Saturday evening with Mr. Talcott as his critic. There being no miscellaneous business the house adjourned to meet next Saturday evening.

Hiram Woods Jr.   Pres.   Robt Harris McCarter, Sec'y of State

From Janet Woodrow Wilson

My dearest Son,   Wilmington [N. C.] Tuesday. [Jan. 22, 1878]

I received your somewhat despondent letter this morning. My darling—dont indulge in anxious thoughts as to your future. Just apply yourself resolutely to improve every advantage of the *present* to the utmost—and let your future take care of itself. This is the *only way* you *can* take care of the future. Dont be too ambitious, dear—for that kind of ambition brings *only* worry—unhappiness. I confess I have no fears as to your getting on all right when the time comes—but present worry on your part will only hinder you— every way—so try with all your might to dismiss such anxieties my precious boy. Your father will write you in a day or two. He is suffering today from severe cold. You see he preached every night for two weeks—and was in an exhausted condition, so that he was very liable to cold. He is rather better today, however, than he was yesterday. . . .   Your own Mother

ALS (WP, DLC).

Music Criticism in *The Princetonian*

[Jan. 24, 1878]

We enjoyed, on last Monday, the 21st, one of the finest concerts we have ever heard in Princeton. We will not comment upon the performance of the Boston Philharmonic Club on that occasion, as they are sufficiently noticed in our Reporter; but we wish to express our satisfaction in the matter of this concert. We mourn the fact that we do not have more frequent opportunities of delighting in musical treats of this character. We never remember having heard a clearer voice than that of Miss McQuesten, or more perfect artists than the members of this Club; certainly not in Princeton, at any rate. The audience, last Monday evening, exhibited, we are sorry to say, some signs of what seems to be a prevalent lack of discriminating taste, in bestowing more applause upon pieces of comparatively inferior merit, than on those which were most harmonious, and most perfectly executed. But this was less noticeable than usual. Certainly the harp solos were deserving of the overwhelming acclamation they received, as nothing could have been more exquisite than they. If the members of the Philharmonic understand the character of a Princeton audience, they must certainly feel gratified at the manner in which they were received, for we have seldom seen a more appreciative and enthusiastic set of listeners here.

Printed in *The Princetonian*, II (Jan. 24, 1878), 157.

Three Editorials in *The Princetonian*

[Jan. 24, 1878]

We think that the example of the Fifth Division of Chapel Stage, in securing the services of the Glee Club to furnish music at the Saturday orations, is one which is worthy of imitation. We have always enjoyed most thoroughly the music furnished on several similar occasions by the Orchestra, and have been surprised that the Glee Club, its sister organization, did not appear more frequently under like circumstances. We have had our suspicions that it was because the Club did not feel that it was familiar with enough suitable pieces to sing in public too frequently, and it is this suspicion that has led us to pen these few lines. And we wish to say that we would offer some suggestions, with the best motives. We would recommend to the leader of the Club that, on such occasions, he confine himself to College songs. Not because the Club fail in rendering other and more elaborate pieces, for they uniformly sing remarkably well, but because we are inclined to believe that many of our College songs are peculiarly appropriate under such circumstances, and would be received with universal applause. To the majority of us they never become stale or tiresome, and, as far as our experience goes, they are, in all cases, shown to better advantage by trained voices than by any others. Can't we have them?

✧

In connection with the Chapel Stage exercises, we would say a few words as to the speeches themselves, or rather concerning their delivery. A somewhat extraordinary, and yet to us pleasing thought concerning this matter, has been suggested to us. It is, that it seems to be the duty of every speaker upon Chapel Stage to deliver his oration in as poor and slip-shod a manner as possible. The reason is, that we receive not only inadequate, but absolutely hurtful instruction in elocution. When an oration is well delivered upon Chapel Stage, the action and grace of the speaker, and his control of his voice, does not represent the training he receives here, but his own natural ability or persevering self-culture. If, then, all would persistently do their worst, it might shame the authorities into securing for us some competent instructor in voice-training. We have urged this upon them in every imaginable way, and on every timely and untimely occasion, and have not even induced them to make a single move in the matter. Although the method of arousing them which we have suggested is one which is probably very unusual, and which will, in all likelihood, be rejected as silly, it might be effectual, because humiliating to those with whom the blame properly lies.

We do not, of course, seriously advocate it, but we would gladly accomplish the end to which it would operate.

✦

Another Inter-Collegiate contest in oratory has taken place in the Academy of Music, New York. Every year, our faith in the association and our approval of its work, grow materially weaker. We are now prepared to say that we are convinced that it has not accomplished the ends which it was intended to subserve. Now, we are confident that our lack of trust in this institution, following, as it does, close upon the heels of eager support of it on our part, will be attributed to the operation of repeated disappointments on our feelings. In other words, it will be said that Princeton, who was the first to advocate the formation of such an association, and who has hitherto been its most prominent defender, has now concluded that it is no longer worthy of her patronage, for no other reason than that she has been unable to put forward men who were able to stand the test of a competitive examination. This imputation is, perhaps, natural under the circumstances. But we are certain that no one who understands the nature of our course of study can fail to see that our failures in these contests have been neither unnatural nor dishonorable, or can hesitate, in view of these facts, to exonerate us in all charges of unworthy motive. Our course is an essentially liberal one, and we have among us no *specialists* in any branches, except those which are distinctively scientific. Other Colleges have usually, and very properly, been represented in Latin, Greek, and mathematics, and, until the withdrawal of Hamilton, in oratory, by persons who had made a special study of these several branches. Princeton could send no such representatives, since, in these departments, she had no special courses. With mental science, it has been different. To this branch, we do pay special attention, and in it we have been uniformly successful. We have always acquitted ourselves most honorably in oratory, as has been acknowledged by the press. We can, therefore, treat with unconcern all insinuations against us. We feel that we are free from prejudice, when we say that, in our opinion, the I. C. L. A. has failed to bring about the increased enthusiasm in educational matters and the advancement and mutual improvement which we had hoped to see issue from its labors. We would gladly endorse Princeton's withdrawal from it, as we are sure that there is an almost universal feeling among us in favor of such a course.

Printed in *The Princetonian*, II (Jan. 24, 1878), 157-59.

To the American Whig Society

Whig Hall, Jan. 25th/78

Your First Comptroller would report that Council met last Tuesday evening, Jan. 22nd, and excused fines as follows:—

Polk	.80¢
Archer	$1.00
Gilman	.35¢
Webster	.20¢
Total	$2.35

Respectfully Submitted   T. W. Wilson, N. C.   *First Comptroller*

WWhwS report, "Reports of the Comptroller, American Whig Society, Mar. 16, 1877-Nov. 2, 1883" (NjP); copied in American Whig Society Minutes, Jan. 25, 1878.

From Joseph Ruggles Wilson

Home [Wilmington, N. C.]—Friday [Jan. 25, 1878]

My dearest Son

I enclose yr. college bill which calls for $172.00. I send a draft for $182.00. The Church is so far behind in the payments on a/c of salary that I dare not send more.

Your last letter to yr mother I read with great interest. It is not now my purpose to preach to you upon the subject of "ambition." Within bounds the desire to attain distinction is commendable. But, to *deserve* distinction is a far worthier aim than distinction itself[.] To deserve it, you have only patiently to plod on, doing with your might what your hands find to do, making the most of opportunity, and, letting the vast clouded future *wait*. I do not wish that you shall cease to *aspire*; but let your chief aspiration be —to discharge present duty with all fidelity—for, rest assured, in the duties that *lie just about you*, is contained all the to-come, i.e. all *that lays ahead*. You *have* talents—you have *character*—you have a manly bearing. You have self-reliance. You have almost every advantage coupled I trust with genuine love for God. Do not allow yourself, then, to feed on dreams—daydreams though they be. The roast beef of hard industry gives blood for climbing the hills of life. It is genius that usually gets to the highest tops—but, what is the secret heart of genius? the ability to work with pains-taking self-denial. Through this work success comes—and comes as a *matter of law*—therefore, *must* come. At present the world—certainly our western world—seems to be governed by asses. Look at this petty Congress! If, however, you should search out the cause at the root of this dire effect, it would be seen in this: the men in temporary power have never learned *to think*. The great mass of them have been merely *ambitious*. You know what this word comes from: "ambio"—to go around as candidates do requesting votes! It was this custom among the Romans that gave the word to the Lat-in language & thus to our own. But he who has learned to think (by laborious plodding and much painful self-discipline) cannot be ambitious in that way: desiring place just because it is *place*: he will, on the contrary, be sought after and raised despite himself almost: and, like Gladstone, command just as widely *out* of office as he does *in*[.] In short, dearest boy, do not allow yourself to dwell upon *yourself*—concentrate your thoughts upon *thoughts* and *things* and *events*[.] Self-consciousness is a torment: was mine at your age: has, often since then, been such. Go out from your own personality. Do not regard ego as the Centre of this uni-verse. Reflect: I am not charging egotism upon you. Far from it. I am only warning you against an evil, common to youth. They are apt to *taste themselves* too much! You will understand what I mean.

Write me freely, my darling, as to all your feelings—and trust us both, in the future as in the past, with all your secret desires—being *sure* that we are your truest friends.

All send love unbounded   Your affc far   J R W.

ALS (WP, DLC) with WWhw and WWsh notation on env.: "Received [WWsh] 1/28/78."

From the Minutes of the Liberal Debating Club

Jan. 26th 1878—

House met at 8.00 oclock P.M. Messrs Wilson & Talcot being absent. The minutes of the previous meeting were read corrected and adopted. As there was no miscellaneous business, Mr. Web-ster read chap. XIII, Sections 232-238, exclusive from Cushings Manual. During the reading of which Mr. Talcot entered the room being tardy as usual. The Debate then came up on the bill—*Re-solved* "that free trade would be beneficial to the country's in-terest," Mr. Talcot moving the bill & the Sec'y of State taking the affirmative. It passed the first, second readings, & the committee of the whole, unanimously & was reported to the House favorably —report adopted. Mr. Elsing being the regularly appointed speaker of the evening, then read a speech on the subject "Our Country & the Poor" and criticism was offered by the members. The President then appointed Mr. Sheldon to speak at the next meeting with Mr. Wilson as critic. Miscellaneous business being in order, Mr. Talcott moved that *Resolved* we no longer adhere to the precedent of discussing a "literary subject" every alternate week. Motion carried. Mr. Sheldon then moved—*Resolved* "that the cabinet officers should have a seats & a votes in the House." The sec'y of State appointed the next regular meeting for the discussion of the bill. As there was no further business the House adjourned at 9.00 P.M. Hiram Woods Jr.   Prest.   Robt Harris McCarter, Sec'y of State

A Political Essay

[c. Jan. 30, 1878]

Some Thoughts on the Present State of Public Affairs.

While it is always unreasonable and unprofitable to regard the past as in all cases better than the present, it is the part of wisdom and prudence frequently to draw from the stores of experience which preceding generations have gathered in the stormy passage of centuries. In most cases we can derive both pleasure and instruction in looking back over the deeds of our sires. Indeed we cannot too often pause to assure ourselves that we have not unadvisedly ventured upon a path which our fathers have already found, to their sorrow, to be one of danger or disgrace. He is no statesman who has not thoroughly learned the lessons which the past teaches. But it requires more than ordinary insight and judgment to perceive when the experience embodied in any particular period of historical development throws any light upon a present emergency, since the principles by which we seek to be guided appear only in the results of long series of events and we can, therefore, justly apply them to any one event only after we have shown it to be one of a similar series.

Our government, as it has had no parallel in history seems to be without precedents for its guidance, except such as the insufficient experience of one short century has established. It is said that there is no need for American statesmen to look for precedents since the government which they are called upon to administer has for its foundation broad and clearly enunciated principles drawn with consummate wisdom from the crowded experiences of the English race, by men who added no small amount of grandeur to the crisis which called them into action. And it is undoubtedly true that these principles have been in successful operation for one hundred prosperous years. But the whole history of England is full of important and pertinent examples the principles of which cannot be found embodied in our Constitution. Since it is claimed for ours that it is the best and purest of representative governments, surely the history of representative government should be the well-thumbed text-book of every American statesman. Such is the history of England; and, as it traces the historical development of the representative system, it is pregnant with lessons for our public men. Whether our institutions, when subjected to this historical test, exhibit principles of vitality or symptoms of decay is now an interesting and all-important question whose truthful answer is fraught with weighty consequences. There are certainly grave facts and graver tendencies whose undoubted existence should make us scan with a searching, though loving, eye the noble system which has stood so long and so well. If elements of decay exist, we have reason to believe that they are not uneradicable. But no true American who calmly and dispassionately surveys the position of the government at this moment can restrain the feeling of deep concern which creeps over him. There have, in truth, of late years been few signs in our political horizon calculated to impart cheer to the hearts of the thousands of thoughtful earnest men to whom the principles of this American republic are dear. It is manifest to every intelligently observant man that the practical issue of the operation of our system has been the entire and almost fatal separation of power and responsibility. For instance, it is in the power of a Congressional majority through the Chairman of the Committee of Ways and Means to force a budget upon the Administration, and for this budget no one is responsible except that indeterminate mass of men, called a party, which happens to have control of the majority, and which, from natural causes, the people cannot well punish. Irresponsibility is known to be the nurse of despotism. And what despotism can be more intollerable to a commercial people than that which a practically irresponsible convention can exercise in using for sectional or party purposes their control of the national finances, of the national credit? Administrations have with us come to be mere machines for carrying out policies in the framing of which they have scarcely any voice, and for which they are not in any way responsible!

In this country it has become a political axiom that the dominion of party spirit means over-throw; and who can characterize in sufficiently denunciatory terms the party, or rather factional, spirit now for so long displayed in the nation's highest tribunal? We hope, perhaps with reason, that this threatening spirit of faction will not, before it is checked by the intelligent co-operation of patriots, so disable our political system as to destroy all possibility of its regeneration; but, while we cherish this hope, we have constantly in our ears the ring of those prophetic words which Webster uttered in one of those passionate bursts which mark his manly tribute to the character of Washington: "Undoubtedly, gentlemen, it (party spirit) is the greatest danger of our system and of our time. Undoubtedly, if that system should be overthrown it will be the work of excessive party-spirit acting on the government, which is dangerous enough, or acting *in* the government, which is a thousand times more dangerous; for government then becomes nothing but an organized party, and in the strange vicissitudes of human affairs it may come at last, perhaps, to exhibit the singular paradox of a government itself being in opposition to its own powers, at war with the very elements of its own existence. Such cases are hopeless. As man may be protected against murder but cannot be guarded against suicide, so a government may be shielded from the assaults of external foes but nothing can save it when it chooses to lay violent hands on itself." While few thoughtful men can hesitate to agree that the state of affairs which has existed in this country for more than a decade has come almost fatally near to coincidence with that state of affairs so vividly suggested in this brilliant passage, we may be allowed the hope that this suicidal course has not so impaired our system that loving hands may not heal its wounds.

And these foreboding and painful facts are not, let it be understood, brought forward in a spirit of dispair, but with the conviction that it is time for us to face the stern facts of our position, however humiliating these facts may be; that we cannot too soon fortify ourselves by becoming thoroughly acquainted with the character of the foes, be these foes persons or principles, which we shall sooner or later be compelled to face. It is well to sum up in plain words the lessons which the public mind has been for some time learning in the presence of unpalatable facts. Let us look at these defects in our institutions, if defects they be, in the hope that, by understanding them, we may, in time, discover the proper means of eradicating them.

The history of affairs both in this country and in England seems to prove in an unanswerable manner, that the permanent health of a representative government depends in great measure upon the existence of a large body of upright and intelligent men who make politics a career. Large numbers of the ablest, sturdiest young men in America carefully prepare themselves for the profession of the Law, recognizing the fact that success at the bar depends almost as much upon thorough preparation as upon natural ability. None but men of the highest ability and most thorough training are thought fit to administer the laws of the land; and yet, strange to say, we pardoxically act upon the principle that it requires less of ability and less of training to frame our laws than to execute them. At the bar only the most learned, the judges, administer the law. But in the popular assemblies which frame the laws of our land the most able and learned can rule only after long and complete training has made them parliamentary masters. Otherwise intrigue and cunning rule. Legislation can be properly conducted only by those who are so far veterans in parliamentary government as to have learned its true sphere and offices and to have become thoroughly convinced of the responsibility of the Legislature, as a whole, to the people, to the country. Hear the words addressed only two months ago to the English people by one who is at present the first of English public men: "That union of suppleness and strength, which is absolutely requisite for the higher labors of the administrator and the statesman, is a gift the development of which, unless it be exercised betimes, nature soon places beyond reach. There is, indeed, scope and function in Parliament for the middle-aged man . . .[1]; but nothing can compensate for a falling off in the stock of young men whom we need for the coming time; and we need the choicest of the country. The only education for the highest work in the House of Commons is, as a rule, that given in the House of Commons." Thus says Gladstone. And in deed no thinking man can fail to see that fitness for those duties, which are, politically considered, of the very highest nature, must result from long training alone, and can be successfully and honorably accomplished only by men of character and capacity. In England politics is a career for which men, who in character, capacity, or position rank among the first in the empire, begin to train in early life. In the House of Commons both the majority and the Opposition are ruled by men who confidently expect to spend all the active years of their lives in the legislature; their honor and reputation is staked upon this their life work; and they are thus led to look upon power as merely a means of carrying out in a definite line of policy the principles for the establishment and main-

[1] WW's elision.

tenance of which they have entered a noble profession—the public service of their well-loved country. Ever since the death of the younger Pitt every Prime-Minister of England if we except Wellington has been a parliamentary veteran surrounded by a Cabinet composed of men only less skilled than himself in parliamentary government. Our national Congress, on the other hand, is a changing body of men the most able of whom do not make the service of their country their business but for short periods sacrifice their private interests to the unfamiliar duty of legislation. Yet the unskilled leaders of this ill-sorted body of undisciplined men have almost as much to do with forming our national policy as have her Cabinet in forming that of England. Our representatives temporarily neglect their private affairs to serve the country in a capacity of the duties or responsibilities of which they know little or nothing. They find that, in the absence of training for their new and peculiar commission, their natural ability cannot gain permanent influence for them unless it be seconded by intrigue. They have entered public life too late to become efficient public servants. Men of week characters, feeling that their life work is not in Congress and that, if they are to make any reputations in this field of new and temporary labor, they must make them in a year or two, seek to win cheap notoriety by random, and often corrupt, legislative measures. They see, too, that with our peculiar institutions power has no necessary connection with positive action or real responsibility, and are eager to sieze upon the administration of the government at the earliest opportunity only that they may win the *spoils*. The fruits of this state of affairs have been many. Every two years a few thoughtful and able men, finding themselves powerless to advance the permanent interests of the country in Congress, retire into private life and make way in most cases for middle-aged men of mediocre ability who accept the offices of representatives because of the honor connected with them and commence a parliamentary career when they are too old to learn to make themselves really felt in Congress until they consent to dispense with all encumbering scruples.

This state of affairs is the direct outgrowth of our institutions and serves to illustrate the truth that progress and its attendant prosperity are the severest tests of national character and national institutions. But we are an essentially English people inheriting all the traditions and characteristics of our noble mother race; and, unless we are to disbelieve the capabilities of that Anglo-Saxon character which has stood the test of so many centuries of progress, unless we are to believe that the foreign elements which have been introduced into our national life have sapped the natural strength of our English stock, we must adopt the opinion that there are large capacities and possibilities for improvement and regeneration in American public life. That this purification or revivification may be more or less completely realized[,] history would seem to prompt us to believe. Perhaps one of the most direct means of bringing about this hoped-for elevation of our national energies would be the correction of that deficiency in our system which, as lying at the root of most of the evils already alluded to, is one of the most serious and weakening in its effects: the absence from Congress of any considerable body of the country's most promising young men. And, in dealing with this feature of our Legislature we are brought into direct contract [contact] with the principle of universal suffrage. The qualifications which are most apt to win for a candidate the favor and suffrages of a popular constituency are station, talents, character, former service, commercial eminence, and money. Now it is at once evident that upon none of these qualifications can most young men rely for successful candidacy except upon character and talents. Before they have been able to acquire the other and more popular qualifications they are past that period in life in which parliamentary training should be commenced.

This is one side of universal suffrage; look at the other. While it is indisputably true that the people can comprehend great truths, is it not as true that they are not primarily acquainted with these truths and that they must be educated into an acceptance of them? Now the judgment of the masses is in most cases clear and discriminating to a wonderful degree and they can be educated into permanent acquiescence in grand principles by none but those whom integrity and a long experience in the matters of which they speak recommend to a hearing. Those who have served the public long, faithfully, and ably, will always command a ready hearing and a numerous following in the nation. Why is it that Gladstone and Bright have so often been able to control and direct the current of public feeling and conviction in England? They give weight to any principle, power to any cause, from the mere fact that they represent an ability and integrity which the nation have seen tested by long public service. They represent a great party because that party is united on the basis of the great principles for which they have made a life-long fight. These men, like so many others of England's distinguished leaders, early sought to ingraft upon the national policy the principles which they had early espoused. To see their cause triumph they have undergone severe and unintermitted training in that field of labor in which alone real, permanent success is possible—in Parliament. No policy could become national unless it triumphed in Parliament and English leaders know, what Americans do not seem yet to have learned, that to win a victory in a popular assembly requires full as much genius and skill as to win a victory in war; that, like the victor on the battle field, the victor in a popular assembly must consent to train untiringly before he can hope to command with effect and success. There are, of course, exceptions to this rule. But it is as idle for us to wait for an American counterpart of a Pitt as it would be unreasonable in time of war to look for another Washington. It is as necessary for an American statesman to command the support of Congress as it is for an English statesman to command that of Parliament. American statesmen of the future must rule through the instrumentality of Congress and they cannot too soon learn that a popular assembly is an instrument so easily abused because of its delicate nature that its proper use is possible only to those whom years of the most laborious training have fitted for its use. The people will gladly and safely follow those whose practical wisdom has been established by that surest of all evidence: the beneficient operation of their avowed principles. Webster, Calhoun, and Clay, whose hearts seem to have been lighted up with some of the heroism of the Revolution, devoted their lives to implanting the principles which they represented and died the idols of the people. Unless we can send to the Halls of Congress the very first young men of the country that they may make the study and upholding of national interests the duty of the best years of their lives, we cannot reasonably hope to see our counsels led by worthy successors of these great statesmen. Unless the public service becomes an honored profession we cannot hope that universal suffrage will prove the blessing it is capable of becoming. The people will rather trust to their own blindness than follow blind demagogues.

How the salutary changes in the composition of Congress, here indicated only as an echo of the now audible public voice, are to be brought about is a problem which demands earnest study. A change in the habits of thought among the young men of our colleges upon questions of public importance might go far towards solving it. If the thirty thousand young men who are pursuing studies at the different colleges of this country would endeavor to throw off the party spirit which has been rooted in their natures by education and would undertake to study each political question for themselves, forming their opinions intelligently and independently, and would, moreover, strive to uphold and advance in every way within their power the principles which they have accepted only after mature consideration, there would be little to fear concerning America's future. That this course of action is nothing less than the plain duty and great privilege of the youth of a free country is perfectly evident. If men in their youth allow blinding party prejudice to rule them there is the less hope that they will throw off its shackles in later life. If, on the other hand, they conscientiously and thoroughly study the interests of the country, they will flood the land with vitality; will go forth prepared to lift the people to the comprehension of the great principles of political economy: raising the masses to the level of each great principle rather than lowering the principle to the level of the masses and thus degrading both. Then can we hope with some color of reason that parties will form themselves under the leadership of able men who have avowed principles and opinions which have stood the test of practice; that personal independence of conviction will be made the basis of allegiance to party; and that we will see true leaders in the persons of men who by force of genius will elevate the people to the heights of principle and justice in spite of themselves. Under such circumstances there would be no room for the fear that the condition of our country would form a painful or humiliating contrast to its high position in those days of prestige and glory which elapsed between the Revolution and the struggle which preceded our terrible civil war. What can America expect from her young men, disgrace or manly support?

Junius

WWhW MS. (WP, DLC). Wilson's quotation from the "words addressed only two months ago to the English people" was from W. E. Gladstone, "The County Franchise and Mr. Lowe Thereon," London *Nineteenth Century*, II (Nov. 1877), 555, and is the most obvious clue to the date of composition. Actually, "Some Thoughts on the Present State of Public Affairs" seems to have been a very considerable revision of Wilson's earlier speech, "Independent Conviction." He completed the latter on July 20, 1877, for future delivery in the American Whig Society but was so dissatisfied with his effort that he discarded it and, instead, prepared and delivered a speech on Bismarck. Wilson must have gone back to "Independent Conviction" in January 1878 and rewritten it completely, changing its focus but retaining some of its ideas and subject matter in the new version. His use of the pen name "Junius" suggests that he also submitted "Some Thoughts" to the *Nassau Literary Magazine*, for he had just used the pen name "Atticus" in signing the article, "Prince Bismarck," which appeared in that magazine in November 1877.

To the American Whig Society

Whig Hall, Feb. 1st 1878

Your First Comptroller would report that Council met last Tuesday evening, Jan. 29th, and excused fines as follows:—

Galbreath	60¢
Hamilton[1]	50¢
Duncan[2]	$4.50
Dunning[3]	80¢
Isham	$1.30
Davis	$1.25
Wilson	20¢
	$9.15

Respectfully Submitted   T. W. Wilson, N. C.,   First Comptroller

WWhwS report, "Reports of the Comptroller, American Whig Society, Mar. 16, 1877-Nov. 2, 1883" (NjP); copied in American Whig Society, Minutes, Feb. 1, 1878.

[1] George P. Hamilton, Jr., '80.
[2] Alexander B. Duncan, '80.
[3] Probably George A. Dunning, '80.
[4] William B. Isham, Jr., '79.

From the Minutes of the American Whig Society

Whig Hall. February 1st, 1878.

. . . Special Meeting

House met immediately after adjournment, at call of Speaker. On motion, calling of the roll was dispensed with; the following then called for:—

Resolved, By Laws &c. That there be no Constitutional Meeting on Monday evening, & that we now proceed to the election of Officers.

        (c-d)   Kerr.

Officers were then elected as follows:—

For Speaker.	T. W. Wilson
" 1st Comptr	R. Bridges
" 2nd "	Talcott.
Sub. Com.	Messrs. Elsing & Harlow.
Sargeant	Kerr
Secy For. Affairs	Shoemaker
Auditors	Messrs. Smith & Davis
Clerk,	Scribner[1]
Librarian's Assistants	Messrs. Wilds, Scribner & Kimball.[2]
Treasurer's " "	Voorhis & Reed[3]
Recorder's Assistant, McGarvey[4]	

House then adjourned to meet on Friday evening Feb. 8th immediately after Chapel. . . .

[1] Charles W. Scribner, '80.
[2] Arthur L. Kimball, '81.
[3] Probably Alexander T. Reid, '81.
[4] William C. McGarvey, '80.

From the Minutes of the Liberal Debating Club

February 2nd 1878.

House met at 8.00 P.M. Minutes of last meeting read & adopted. Miscellaneous business being in order Mr. Elsing stated that he had neglected to give his speech to Mr. Talcot for criticism but would do so immediately. Mr. Talcot then read Sections 240-245 of the Manual after which the bill: Resolved ["]that free trade would be beneficial to our country's interest" came up for its third reading & was finally adopted. By the appointment of the Sec'y of State Mr. Sheldon's bill Resolved "that the cabinet officers should have votes 2 & seats 1 in the House of Representatives," came before the Society and passed its first & second readings, the committee of the Whole, & was reported favorably to the House. Mr. McCarter then read a criticism on Mr. Wilson's speech delivered two meeting past, after which miscellaneous business again came up. Mr. Elsing offered the following bill "Resolved that the interference of England in the Eastern struggle would be beneficial to the cause of civil liberty" & the Sec'y of State appointed the next regular meeting for the discussion of the bill. Mr. Elsing also moved that when the treasury be sufficiently full the Society purchase 7 *Cushing's Manuals* to be presented to the members of the Society—motion carried. Then Mr. Sheldon stated that from want of time he had been prevented from preparing a speech for the Society & the President allowed him another week in which to write the speech. There being no further business the Society adjourned at 9-45 P.M   Robt Harris McCarter   Sec'y of State Hiram Woods Jr.   President

Two Editorials in *The Princetonian*

[Feb. 7, 1878]

The preaching to which we had the pleasure of listening on the last day of January, the day of prayer for Colleges, was characterized by peculiar power. Dr. Cuyler's[1] remarks in the afternoon Chapel exercises were very earnest and unusually impressive.

Those who did not take advantage of the opportunity of hearing Dr. Duryea[2] in the evening, missed some thorough enjoyment as well as much valuable instruction. Dr. Duryea is an orator such as Princeton seldom hears, and as a Christian minister, his power is consummate. The charm of the vivid and noble thought which he poured forth in such rich abundance, was rendered over-mastering by his manly bearing, by his forceful and brilliant delivery. If we had more of this eminent gentleman's stern simplicity of oratory and power of deep and sharply-enunciated convictions, more of us could hope for some measure of the success which was his theme.

[1] The Rev. Theodore L. Cuyler, D.D., Pastor, Lafayette Avenue Presbyterian Church, Brooklyn, N. Y.
[2] The Rev. Joseph T. Duryea, D.D., Pastor, Classon Avenue Presbyterian Church, Brooklyn, N. Y.

✧

Dr. Atwater's kindness and wisdom in giving us the chance of hearing his well-founded, because carefully-formed, opinions upon the Bland Silver Bill, cannot be over-estimated. His just reputation as a financier[1] of unusual ability, certainly recommended him to a hearing upon this now all-important question. It is needless to say that his lecture was an able one. He recapitulated the many unanswerable arguments for a gold standard which have been so ably urged upon Western inflationists by our most capable public journals, and to which the silver men so persistently turn a deaf ear.

This is the first discourse of the kind that we can remember to have been delivered here, and we most sincerely hope that it is only the first of many similar ones. One of the greatest evils which this country has to labor under is the utter and disgraceful ignorance of her young men on great public questions. We have long thought it the duty of College Professors to do all in their power to enlighten the youth under their care, as to all the principles of those branches upon a thorough knowledge of which, on the part of public men, the welfare or, perhaps, the very existence of the government depends. If instructors allow young men to go from under their care without having made at least an honest effort to clear up their hazy ideas upon pressing public questions, the responsibility of bad government rests, in great measure, upon their shoulders. Dr. Atwater seems to have recognized these facts and has acted accordingly. From him instruction upon such subjects as those of finance comes with all the greater authority and force, because of his known intimacy with such topics, and the fact that we can rely upon his speaking without any party bias or any sectional prejudice or personal interest. Most of his arguments were based upon scientific principles, though there was an ever-present vein of practical observation in them. He treated his subject in a philosophical manner as well as with a philosophical spirit. We most heartily thank him, and must say that there is now no excuse for any one among us entertaining such puerile theories upon finance as are now so shamefully prevalent among the nation's representatives. (Save the mark.)

Printed in *The Princetonian*, II (Feb. 7, 1878), 170.
    1 The Professor's chair roomily embraced logic, metaphysics, ethics, political science, and economics. Though his chief interest was divinity, he contributed articles on finance to the *Princeton Review*, and was a diligent money-raiser for the College as well as watch-dog over the expenses of the Theological Seminary as its committee-man for grounds and buildings.

To the American Whig Society

Whig Hall, February 8th/78

Your First Comptroller would report that the Council met last Tuesday evening, Feb. 5th, and excused fines, as follows:—

McCarter	$1.30
Worl	.90
J. Farr	4.65
Polk	2.00
Miller[1]	1.90
Van Hoesen	1.50
Vanuxem	3.15
Reid	.60
Total	$16.00

In accordance with the provision of the By-Laws contained in Article XXIX Sec. 2nd the name of Mr. J. Garmany[2] is hereby reported for suspension.

Your First Comptroller is glad to be able to say that this is the only gentleman whose name he has been compelled thus to bring before the House, during his term of office.

In leaving the office of First Comptroller the present incumbent feels confident that he is resigning it to one who is in every respect competent to fulfill its duties

Respectfully Submitted   T. W. Wilson, N. C. F. C.

WWhwS report, "Reports of the Comptroller, American Whig Society, Mar. 16, 1877-Nov. 2, 1883" (NjP).
    1 William Miller, Jr., '80.
    2 Jasper J. Garmany, '79.

From the Minutes of the Liberal Debating Club

Feb. 9th 1878.

Meeting called to order at 8-3 1/3 P.M, Mr. Webster being absent—Miscellaneous business being in order, Mr. McCarter moved to strike out Art. XXIII Section III of the Constitution, seconded & passed respectively the first & second readings & the committee of the whole & was reported favorably to the house. Mr. McCarter moved that we no longer adhere to the precedent of confining our list of membership to members of Whig Hall—carried. Mr. Wilson then read sections 246-259 of the manual. The President, after the reading of which, called upon Mr. Sheldon to speak & the gentleman then addressed the Club on the subject Molière's *"Misanthrope"* on which criticism was offered by the members. The President then appointed Mr. McCarter to speak at the next meeting with Mr. Sheldon as critic. The third reading of the bill ["] Resolved that the cabinet officers should have seats & votes in the House of Representatives" then came up & the bill was finally adopted. The Sec'y of State then read Mr. Elsings bill "Resolved that the interference of England in the Eastern struggle would be beneficial to the cause of civil liberty," the Sec'y of State siding with the negative. The first reading was carried but the bill failed to pass the second reading, Mr. Elsing alone supporting it. Mr. Woods then offered the following bill—Resolved "that the right of suffrage should be limited by a property qualification" & the Sec'y appointed the next regular meeting for the discussion. The Club then adjourned at 10-05 P.M.

Hiram Woods Jr.   President   Robt Harris McCarter   Sec'y

Feb. 16th, 1878

House met at 8.07 P.M. Minutes of previous meeting read, corrected and adopted. The bill to do away with Art. XXIII, Section III of Constitution passed its third reading & was thus finally adopted. Mr. McCarter then spoke before the Society on "Culture & Riches —which?" and criticism was offered by the members. Mr. Wilson moved we return to election of members, c'd. He then proposed the name of Mr. Harold Godwin for membership & the gentleman was elected & the president appointed Mr. Wilson a committee to inform the gentleman of his election. The first reading of the bill ["]Resolved that the right of suffrage should be limited by a Educational Qualification" came up & the bill passed the first & second readings & was reported favorably to the House by the committee of the whole. Miscellaneous business being in order, Mr. Sheldon offered the Topic *"Bacon"* for discussion at the next meeting, after which Mr. Talcott read a a [*sic*] criticism on Mr. Elsings, and Mr. Wilson a criticism on Mr. Sheldon's speech. The club then adjourned at 10. P.M.

Hiram Woods Jr.   Prest.   Robt Harris McCarter, Sec'y of State

News Item in *The Princetonian*

[Feb. 21, 1878]

'79's *Editorial Elections.*—The Juniors elected their *Lit.* and *Princetonian* boards much earlier than usual this year, the election occurring on Friday, February 15th.[1] Nothing unusual marked the day, but the election of both boards on six ballots. Some days afterwards the editors elect divided, with the following result: *Lit.* —R. Bridges, E. P. Davis,[2] F. Durell,[3] H. Godwin, C. Martin,[4] M. Pitney,[5] E. W. Sheldon, W. R. Wilder. *Princetonian*—M. G. Emery, Jr., W. F. Magie,[6] R. H. McCarter, C. Talcott; T. W. Wilson, Managing Editor.

Printed in *The Princetonian*, ii (Feb. 21, 1878), 190.

[1] A letter from Robert Bridges to his father, finished at 11:25 that night reports the excitement felt by "our crowd" over the elections. "Last night," he wrote, "Wilson, Talcott, Woods & myself talked the thing over until 12 o-clock. . . . Of course we hoped we would all be elected but hardly expected it." WW won 96 votes, Wilder 93, Godwin 88, and Bridges 86. Robert Bridges to his father, Feb. 15, 1878. Papers of Robert Bridges (PCarlD), quoted by permission of the librarian of Dickinson College.

[2] Edward P. Davis, born Sept. 16, 1856. A.B., College of New Jersey, 1879; M.D., Rush Medical College, 1882. Professor of Obstetrics, Jefferson Medical College, 1898-1924; editor, *American Journal of the Medical Sciences*, 1890-98; author of several textbooks on obstetrics. Died Oct. 2, 1937.

[3] Fletcher Durrell, '79.

[4] Chalmers Martin, '79.

[5] Mahlon Pitney, born Feb. 5, 1858. A.B., College of New Jersey, 1879. Studied law, admitted to New Jersey bar, 1882. Republican member of United States House of Representatives, 1895-99; member of New Jersey Senate, 1899-1901. Associate Justice, New Jersey Supreme Court, 1901-08; Chancellor of New Jersey, 1908-1912. Associate Justice, United States Supreme Court, 1912-1922. Died Dec. 9, 1924.

[6] William F. Magie, born Dec. 14, 1858. A.B., College of New Jersey, 1879; Ph.D., University of Berlin, 1884. Professor of Physics, Princeton University, 1885-1929, Dean of the Faculty, 1912-25. Died June 6, 1943.

From the Minutes of the Liberal Debating Club

Feb. 23rd 1878.

House met at 8-10 P.M. Mr. Webster the gentleman appointed to speak was allowed one more week for preparation. The bill relative to the restriction of suffrage came up for its 3rd reading & as there was a tie vote the opinion of secy. state was sustained—

aff. Motion to postpone the regular question cd. Adjourned at 9-20.
H. Woods Jr.   Pres.   Chs. Talcott, P[ro] t[em]

From Janet Woodrow Wilson

My darling Son,   Wilmington, N. C. Feb 23rd 1878.
. . . We have been very much shocked at the accounts we see in
the newspapers, of the difficulty between some of the Sophomores
& Freshmen at Princeton.[1] What is the truth with regard to the
matter? I never know how much to believe of what I read in the
papers. However I was not very much surprised to hear of serious
trouble resulting from that frightful sort of fun. I am so relieved
to know that you belong to neither of those classes—for it does not
seem to depend altogether upon a student's own will as to whether
he will be mixed up in these things or not. Dont forget to give us
the true version of the affair in your next. . . .

Tommy, dear, how would you like to settle in *Nebraska,* when
you get through with your studies? I have been thinking lately
that it would be wise for us to have such a plan as this before us.
You know we have some very beautiful land near Fremont—and it
seems to me that it would be a wise thing for us to go there in three
or four years, and settle a home—and it is more than likely that a
good opening for you might be found "there-abouts." Think about
it—if you have time. . . .

God bless you, Your loving Mother.

ALS (WP, DLC) with WWhw notation on env.: "Ans" and WWsh notes, apparently for reply to his mother. Transcript of these reads: "As to the Neb. affair and
some thoughts of mine with career suggestions *National Committee* etc as to
many different residences etc."
  [1] This was a riot set off by a fight between freshmen and sophomores on Feb.
18, 1878. It prompted the faculty to expel seven sophomores guilty of hazing and
to suspend twenty-five additional sophomores for rioting. See *The Princetonian,*
II (March 7, 1878), 201-203, and the editorial printed at that date.

From the Minutes of the Liberal Debating Club

Feb. 30th [March 2?] 1878—
House met at 8. p.m. Messrs. Talcott & Elsing being absent.
The new member Mr. Godwin was introduced to the Club, & the
minutes of the two previous meetings were adopted. There being
no miscellaneous business & no manual at hand, the subject for
discussion came up viz *"Bacon."* After the close of wh. Mr. Webster addressed the club on the subject *"The Pilgrim Fathers"* and
criticism was offered by the members. The President appointed
Mr. Talcott to speak at the next meeting. Mr. Wilson then offered

the following bill "Resolved that the Missouri Compromise was impolitic" & the Sec'y. of State appointed the next regular meeting for the discussion of the bill. The meeting adjourned at 9-30 P.M
Hiram Woods Jr.   Prest.   Robt Harris McCarter   Secy of State

Editorial in *The Princetonian*

[March 7, 1878]

The reasons that, in our last issue, we said so little about the late disturbance between the Sophomores and Freshmen were these: The fracas began just after we had gone to press. It, therefore, was almost impossible to give any very extended account. In the second place, we desired to wait until perfect order was again restored among the refractory portion of our students. In our "Reporter's" column may be found a *true* account of the whole affair, beginning with the hazing of the Freshman Lang, and ending with the latest decisions of the Faculty. We have given considerable space to this matter in this issue, mainly because up to the present time of writing, March 4th, no *impartial* and *correct* statement, so far as we know, of "hazing in Princeton," has been given. It is at best unpleasant for any alumnus and under-graduate of old Nassau to know that such proceedings as those of the last two or three weeks should occur within the walls of our *Alma Mater,* but it enlarges to a harrowing indignation and distends to a festering grief to know that we have been so ungraciously, so diabolically misrepresented by certain newspapers.

Printed in *The Princetonian,* II (March 7, 1878), 193.

From Janet Woodrow Wilson

My precious Son,   Wilmington N. C. Thursday, [March 7, 1878]

I am so glad to think of your dear father having been with you. Were you not glad to see him? I have been so happy to think of the pleasure that a sight of him has given you—and the keen happiness that a sight of his precious son has given him. He does love you *so* dearly, my sweet child. It should always be a comfort to you to know, that you are such a comfort to us, who love you so dearly. You have never given us a heart-ache except, indeend, such as has been caused by our longing for your presence—& our anxiety for your happiness. . . .

I am so sorry about Paul's[1] trouble. I do hope your father will be able to accomplish something in his behalf. Why, it will ruin the boy for life, if he is so disgraced! He had not much chance to begin with! In my opinion, they, the Faculty had no right to *go back* in that way. I cannot forget how they would have disgraced *you* upon the slightest pretext—when you innocently made the mistake of supposing you were only risking an *absent* mark. *Character* seems to go for nothing with that Faculty. But I must close now. I have to write a note to Marion & Annie in time for the mail—and a note to Mr. Worth—asking him to conduct the service tonight. Josie joins me in warmest love to you[.] God bless you my darling—

Your own Mother.

ALS (WP, DLC) with WWhw notation on env.: "Ans."
1 Paul Pope, who was involved in the student riot.

From the Minutes of the American Whig Society

Whig Hall March 15th, 1878.

    . . . Second Session
    . . . Resolved, By-Laws &c. that we elect officers for the next six weeks, tonight; and that we have no Constitutional meeting next Monday night.
c-d.   Woods.
The House then proceeded to elect the following officers:—

For Speaker.	Robt. Bridges.
" First Compt.	Chas. Talcott.
" Second "	McCarter.
" Sub-Committee,	Mitchell and Emery.
" Auditors,	Handy and J. Kerr.
" Secy. of For. Affairs,	McNair.
" Clerk,	Parkhill.[1]
" Recorder's Assistants,	McGarvey and Thom.[2]
" Treasurer's "	Voorhis and Reid. . . .

1 James W. Parkhill, '80.
2 Henry C. Thom, '81.

From the Minutes of the Liberal Debating Club

March, 16th 1878

House met at 7.55, the president, Mr. Woods, and the Secretary of State, Mr. McCarter being absent. On motion of Mr. Wilson, Mr. Sheldon took the chair. The president pro. tem. then appointed Mr. Wilson to act as Secretary of State. There was no miscellaneous business. Mr. Godwin read Chap. XIV of the Manual. Mr. Wilson moved "that the regular order of business be postponed for one week." Mr. Godwin offered the amendment "that the regular speech of the evening be not dispensed with." This was accepted and incorporated in the motion. The motion was then carried as amended. Mr. Wilson then moved "that this house resolve itself into a Committee of the Whole for the purpose of discussing the political prospects of the United States, especially with reference to the reformation of parties." This motion was carried and Mr. Talcott, of New York took the chair. Mr. Sheldon opened the debate. An extended discussion took place. During the progress of this debate the president, Mr. Woods arrived. The Committee then rose and the president took the chair. Mr. Godwin then read an oration entitled "The Scandinavians in History." One or two remarks by way of criticism were offered and Mr. Wilson was appointed to write a criticism upon the subject-matter of the oration. Mr. McCarter not being present it was determined to postpone the reading of Mr. Sheldon's criticism upon the subject-matter of his speech for one week. Mr. Elsing then read a written criticism upon Mr. Webster's speech upon "The Pilgrim Fathers." There being no miscellaneous business, the house was then adjourned at 9.40.

Hiram Woods, Jr.   Pres.   T. W. Wilson, Acting S. of State.

Editorial in *The Princetonian*

[March 21, 1878]

Is it Sufficient?

We know that we tread on dangerous ground when we criticise any action of the Faculty. They undoubtedly did what they thought best in the late hazing troubles. What—if at all, any—action will be taken in regard to a certain select "logic spree"[1] is yet unknown. If any, we trust it will be radically different from the former. The court has committed some innocent men; it remains for them to find the guilty. We fear that the desire to have numbers rather than kind, quantity rather than quality, is injuring the College. Fifty were lately suspended, some few will probably be expelled, but nearly all, it is likely, will be allowed to return. One-half or less of them we may see back again among us. The remainder will go to other Colleges. So, by their very action, one of the ends of the present management seems to be defeated. We are positive that the result of the Faculty's action would have had a healthier effect if some ten or fifteen had been sharply and summarily *expelled*, and the remainder allowed to remain under the threat of similar treatment. Punish all and no one is punished. We regard it as betraying the trusts of parents in distant states, and manifesting an almost criminal disregard for the morals of the suspended boys, to send them off to the large cities for a "couple of weeks, till quiet is restored." Numbers of them, especially those who live in remote states, have been engaged in a succession of "larks" in Philadelphia and New York for the past four weeks. Their riotous conduct would pain any member of the Faculty, and convince him that not much time was wasted in repentance and contrition. The punishment, directly upon the parents' pockets, and indirectly upon the boys' moral natures, is unquestionable in fact, but questionable in its character.

"Suspension for a few weeks" means, to the youth "punished," a more or less pleasant vacation; to the thoughtful men in College, a most sorry travesty upon College discipline.

We have no complaints to make that "rows" and "sprees," which, two years ago, were entirely unnoticed, are now howled from Dan to Beersheba by an enterprising press. We feel confident that now is the opportunity to make our old College more powerful and influential than it has ever been. We can well afford to lose twenty-five or fifty students, as we may yet, but let it be done in a manner worthy of the College. Too much maudlin sentiment is felt for the feelings of parents, and not enough proper sympathy expressed for the wounded honor of the College. Men who violate the laws of the College and humanity, men who willfully disregard the wishes of their class and the best interests of their College, have no claim upon the sympathy of any one. Nor should the parents of such scape-graces be allowed to cherish the notion that their feelings deserve more consideration than the weal of the College.

As long as desire for numbers prevails over a rigid discrimination in selection, so long the present policy of half-boarding-school, half-university discipline must last. We know of no better opportunity than the present to eradicate the rapidly spreading notion that Princeton College contains some ignorant rowdies and puerile idiots, subject to a discipline that smacks of a mockery and a farce.

B.

Printed in *The Princetonian,* II (March 21, 1878), 209-10.

1 The word, "spree," was generic for teacher-baiting and classroom disorder. Serenading a professor with horns was a "horn spree," disorder in logic class a "logic spree," and of course there was the "cane spree."

From the Minutes of the Liberal Debating Club

March 23rd 1878.

Meeting called to order at 8-30, Messrs Sheldon, Elsing, McCarter and Webster being absent. In the absence of the Secretary of State, Mr. Talcott was appointed to fill that position Pro. tem. Mr.

Wilson read chap. III Article 1st of the Manual. Mr. Talcott was excused from speaking. Mr. Wilson moved that the discussion of the regular question be laid on the table—carried. It was then moved by Mr. Wilson that a committee of two be appointed to consider the advisability of holding Public debates—carried. The committee was appointed Mssrs McCarter & Wilson. Mr. Wilson then proposed the following bill *Resl'd* ["]that it would be a national benefit to have a national university provided the charter of such a university would not be under the immediate supervision of of [*sic*] the legislature" & the sec'y of state placed the next regular meeting for the reading of the bill. The House then adjourned.

Hiram Woods Jr.   Prest.   Chas' Talcott   Sec'y. Pro. tem

From Janet Woodrow Wilson

My darling Son,   Wilmington N. C. March 23–[1878]

I hoped to write you a long letter at my leisure before this—but it seems to me that I am fated to live in a hurry—not having my time at my own command—and not accomplishing very much of anything in any direction.

Your father was greatly delighted by his little visit to you. He was so gratified at being able to see how you looked in your own room. He was so struck by the *neatness* of your room. And, above all, he was so glad to find you so well, and so happy.

By the way, Tommy dear, you *must* have a lounge & arm-chair for next year—as well as curtains of some description. Take the measure of your windows at once—and put down in your Mem. Book. Then I will prepare some pretty things for your mantlepiece —in addition to the jars I have already decorated, and I will be better satisfied with your surroundings. I have gotten a N. Y. furniture Catalogue—from which we can furnish any want in that line. . . .

God bless you, my precious son.   Your loving Mother.

ALS (WP, DLC) with WWsh and WWhw notations: "Received [WWsh] 3/25/78" and "Ans 3/31/78."

From the Minutes of the Liberal Debating Club

                                                  Mar. 30th '78

Meeting called to order at 7.55 Messrs McCarter[,] Sheldon & Wilson being absent. Mr. Webster was appointed to fill the vacant chair of the sec'y of state. Mr. Talcott asked to be excused from speaking his speech granted. Mr. Elsing then read a selection from the Manual after which Mr. Talcott read his speech. During the reading of which Mr. Wilson entered the meeting. The Debate being then called for the following question was read by the sec'y of state ["] Resl'd That it would be a national benefit to have a national (benefit) university provided the charter would not be under the immediate supervision of the legislature" the bill then passed its first reading and Mr. Wilson moved to lay on the table, c'd. Mr. Wilson then read a criticism on Mr. Godwin's speech subject the "Scandanavian[s] in History" after which the same gentleman read the report of the committee on the advisability having public debates. Motion to adopt was not Seconded, & the report was then laid on the table for further consideration. Moved to adjourn till the next Session of next term.

Hiram Woods Jr   Prest.   J. E. Webster   sec'y Protem

Editorial in *The Princetonian*

[April 4, 1878]

   Whether it shall be a custom among us, for each retiring Board of *Lit.* and *Princetonian* Editors to elect their successors, is a matter that seems to be agitated quite generally. The new Boards, we are informed, are unanimous in the opinion that, hereafter, this should be the mode of election. We hope that some of those who are interested, will give us their views, and will join us in a discussion of this matter. So far as we are concerned, we think the present way of securing editors of our College periodicals, is not so good as the new one proposed. We are in favor of a change. These are our reasons:

   First—More men would be stimulated to write for the College papers, and those who do write, would do so with more interest and care. It would be a matter of ambition for a man to become one of the editors through the right channel of fitness. More enthusiasm would be excited in that kind of writing which enables a man to write an essay or a speech a hundred miles from any library. An every-day and easy style of composition, which comes from large practice, would be more general. It would tend to bring out men who aspire to become journalists.

   Second—Men best fitted for the several departments of the paper, would be more likely to be secured. For example: To be a good "reporter," requires a special kind of talent. If, then, a contributor to the paper shows a special aptitude in this direction, he, by all means, should, for the highest success of the paper, be on the Board. Almost every man thinks he can report a ball game. Many think they can work up a good report of a musical concert, but the fact is, that not more than three or four in the whole College can do this with anything like adequateness or justice. The exchange department requires men of correct literary taste and comprehensive judgment. They should have facility and variety of expression. They should be able to say sharp things, in a sharp way. They should represent the best critical ability of the Board.

Third—Those who have not the least fitness for the editorial work of a College paper, would be kept off the Boards. In almost every election, it happens that one or more weaklings are put on the Boards, sheerly because they are popular in the class. They are without experience, and they do pretty well if, at the end of their term of office, they learn to do what they should have learned before they were elected. This, mind you, can be done only at the expense of the papers' reputation, and entails upon those who are well qualified, an extra amount of work and anxiety. Under the present system, there must almost always be some mere figure-heads. They are just like so many wooden wheels under a rail-road car. Their enthusiasm dies out with about the third number of the volume. During the rest of the year, they sort of hang on, and let others do the work they virtually promised their class they would do. If, in the course of human events, the Board should, collectively, be sentenced to thirty lashes, they might be of some comfort to the Board then, perhaps, if they should take their proportion.

The work of conducting a College paper is hard, and he who does it has to make a large sacrifice of time and energy. What does he get in return? He gets a salary of what is called honor, and, as a perquisite, a few words from some incensed reader, which remind him of his latter end. But all this he can endure, if every one of his colleagues is a man who comes up to the full measure of duty to the paper.

Fourth—This plan works well elsewhere. Why not here?

None will deny, we presume, that the *Harvard Advocate* and the *Yale Courant* have, for a long time, been uniformly the best conducted College papers in the country. Editors of each are elected in this way. Cornell, with its accustomed enterprise, is agitating this subject. All these things show that there must be excellence in the system. We hope that in our next contribution column, we shall be able to hear the other side, or something more on the side we have taken up. It will do no hurt to stir up the matter.

Printed in *The Princetonian*, II (April 4, 1878), 218-19.

From Joseph Ruggles Wilson

My darling Son—   Wilmington [N. C.], Ap[ril] 9 1878

Enclosed find a draft for $50.00, with which I desire you to go to Wannamakers and fit yourself with such garments as you may need. The perfect confidence we have in you renders unnecessary any specific directions. . . .

Your affc &c   J. R. W.

ALS (WP, DLC) with WWhw notation on env.: "Ans."

Classroom Notebook

[c. April 17-Dec. 18, 1878]

Inscribed on front page (WWhw): "Metaphysics."

Contents:

(a) WWsh notes with WWhw headings taken in Professor Lyman H. Atwater's metaphysics course, third term, April 17-June 20, 1878.

(b) Additional WWsh notes on Professor Atwater's course, civil government, first term, Sept. 11-Dec. 18, 1878, for main body of which, see the second of the three notebooks described at Sept. 11, 1878.

(c) First notes on Professor Atwater's course in ethics, the same first term, for continuation of which see the third of the three notebooks described at Sept. 11, 1878.

(WP, DLC). This is a notebook made by folding pages 12" x 9 3/8", making pages 6" x 9 3/8".

Five Editorials in *The Princetonian*

[May 2, 1878]

Upon donning the editorial harness and taking upon themselves the responsibilities and duties of their predecessors, '79's *Princetonian* board do not feel called upon to preface their work by many words of self-introduction. A salutatory editorial from a new board must be either a budget of promises or a moralizing essay. Promises of the performance of plain duty are superfluous; sermons sound ill from such a pulpit. *The Princetonian* was meant to be an impartial record of College incident and a medium for a bold, frank, and manly expression of College opinion. Such it is '79's duty and aim to keep it. They would, therefore, advocate such a change in the manner of electing future boards as has already been spoken of at length in these pages. This change they regard as the only thing needed to make the paper in every respect what it should be.

There is one prominent fact about our College life that seems to furnish a plausible excuse for Mr. Jackson's proposition that a prize should be offered for the best essay on College Discipline. Almost every year the post office boxes bristle with envelopes coming from the Treasurer's office and containing a new set of rules and regulations for our guidance in our intercourse with the College authorities. However crude might be the suggestions which the proposed essay would venture, they could scarcely fail to throw some light upon the apparently bewildered minds of certain College officials. Certainly no wise man would recommend that College students be hedged in on all sides by a multitude of rules, that a College be converted into a kinder-garten. And yet we seem to be rapidly approaching such a state of things. The latest departure in the line of law-making is an elaborate set of provisions with reference to engaging and holding rooms in the College dormitories. One of the most remarkable and most unnecessary of these provisions is that "whenever a student desires to occupy a room in one of the College buildings he and his parent or guardian shall be required to sign a room agreement, engaging to pay the rent and charges of said room for the ensuing academic year, or for the remainder of the current year, as the case may be." Now if the Treasurer had had in the past any difficulty in collecting from the students within a reasonable time all room rent and charges, there might be some color of an excuse for such a rule as this. We have good reason to believe that no such trouble has ever been experienced. The rule is, then, merely an uncalled-for blow at the honesty of the students. We are virtually told, "you have never given us any reasonable ground for supposing that you will ever refuse to pay all legitimate and equitable charges, &c.; we have always found you honest; but we think it best to bind both you and your parent or guardian to the fulfillment of just obligations, to require from you a written promise of honesty."

To this singular regulation something quite as unnecessary, though not quite so insulting, is added. It is, and always has been, perfectly well understood that when one engages a room he agrees to keep it at least until the end of the academic year. It is also well known that if, in the meantime, he vacates the room he is responsible for its rent, unless some one else is found to occupy it. Notwithstanding the fact that this is a common and universally understood rule, applying out of College, as well as within it, we are compelled to sign, in conjunction with our parents or guardians, an agreement to obey in this matter also the law of honesty and fair-dealing. This may seem a small matter. These rules are

contemptible and cannot do more than subject us to petty harass-
ings and annoyances. But they are indicative of a tendency in the
actions of the College authorities which we have for some time
been watching with growing uneasiness. We allude to the tendency
toward overlegislation, toward a multiplication of rules which are
not needed and can serve no other purpose than that of irritating
us. We deprecate all such action and ask the trustees to deal with
us as with men and not to yield to what appear to be the suggestions of some unlettered savage. This is not discipline, but empty
folly. In matters of real discipline we bow to the wisdom of our
elders; but when our honor is impugned we feel bound to enter our
protest.

It is pleasant to turn from these vexatious rules and regulations
to Dr. McCosh's clear, candid, and sensible remarks upon College discipline in the last number of the *North American Review*,
though we do not find in his article exactly such a treatment of the
subject as we expected. We had looked for a paper devoted to practical suggestions as to the government of large numbers of young
men. We had hoped to see much light thrown upon the vexed
questions of College discipline. Instead of this, our honored President has reviewed the methods of discipline in force in the most
prominent educational institutions both at home and abroad. Between these different methods he has drawn a discriminating comparison. He points out with clearness and by means of happy illustration the principles which lie at the foundation of the various
systems. He sketches in outline the policy which is recommended
by wisdom and morality. His conclusions are, upon the whole, favorable to American Colleges, and he can see little in the discipli-
nary regulations of foreign institutions which is worthy to be transplanted to American soil. We are gratified to see that he does not
even allude to the visionary schemes which have recently been
floating before the troubled minds of some puerile graduates. His
practical wisdom is sufficient to show him that no such means as
they proposed could be adequate to meet the many and peculiar
difficulties which beset the College disciplinarian. He repudiates
all quack remedies for existing evils and recognizes the fact that
we need, not more rules, but an intelligent, kind, and firm enforcing of the common rules of order and morality. We can heartily
endorse all his sentiments and must only regret that he did not
carry his remarks and suggestions to a greater length.

We are glad to see the general good-will which exists this season towards the University Nine. The spirit of fault-finding, prevalent in previous years, was not only unjust in itself, but also robbed the nine of that moral support, without which success is impossible. We do not refer to just and unprejudiced criticism, which should be nourished rather than condemned. What we censure is that unpatriotic element in our College, which prophesies defeat as often as any College organization takes the field. Those were not few, last autumn, who prophesied defeat in foot-ball. There were some even who assigned the team's victory over Harvard to chance, and were only silenced by the subsequent struggle with Yale. We hope that this spirit will not be revived but that the support which has thus far been extended to the nine, will continue throughout the entire season.

And while great interest is taken in our own nine and hopes for its success entertained, the College should not fail to extend a gentlemanly courtesy to each College nine that visits Princeton. Against one College, in particular, feelings of enmity exist, which time cannot allay, because each year brings fresh cause for bitterness. We may attempt to excuse each act of rudeness by calling it "revenge," or by saying that we are only "getting even" with these men for past injuries. The act, nevertheless, remains a rude one; and as such cannot fail to detract from our reputation as gentlemen. We should also recollect that such petty acts, committed for revenge, degrade us to the level of those against whom they are directed, and take from us the privilege of criticizing their actions in the future. We should endeavor to treat the visiting nines with equal fairness; and if we can add nothing to our fame as ball players, let us see to it, that we take nothing from our reputation as gentlemen.

The contribution on the election of editors, which may be found in another column, and which supports the present mode of electing editors for our College press, contains, as far as we can see, all the arguments in favor of that side of the question which can be made in any way specious. The plating of sound argument, however, is so thin that it takes a vast amount of burnishing to give it the appearance of solid metal. Our contributor has, perhaps, done as well with his materials as was possible; but his materials were poor. He makes a great parade of the argument of Hall prejudice and of favoritism, and would have us believe that no one in College can act without being influenced by them. Granted, to a certain extent; denied, to the extent to which he would press it. If we thought that there were no men in Princeton able to vote in a class election without being influenced, so far as their votes were concerned, by Hall prejudice, we would feel inclined to pack our trunks and leave in search of more sensible company. In actual practice, the question of Hall enters very little into such matters, and never to such an extent as to influence votes. There are few, we believe, in each class, who cannot sink the petty question of Hall out of sight when the interests of the whole College are at stake. The argument of Hall prejudice reacts upon itself. A small body of men, representing more or less completely, the talent of their class, and wedded to the paper by one year's service upon its editorial staff would be much less apt to act from prejudice, and more apt to act for the real interests of the paper, than that heterogeneous body called a class. They would act more intelligently and more systematically.

The objection of favoritism, as indeed the one just noticed, can be answered briefly thus: the retiring boards, under the new plan, are to elect their successors *on the basis of contributions*. It is hard to conceive of a set of men so shameless as to deliberately give to one candidate a position which had been rightfully won by another, especially when their injustice could not possibly be concealed.

The last point made by our contributor we need not dwell upon. We would be loath to deny, in republican America, that a democracy is a good thing; and yet an argument founded upon the democratic principle seems to us to be based on a pleasing sentiment rather than on reason. When the serious remark is made, that the papers will get out of student control and will cease to represent the College, we can only reply that, as the power of election was given to the retiring boards, so it can be taken away from them. The students can practically regulate the tone of the papers by refusing to subscribe for them unless the editors continue to be in sympathy with College sentiment. In short, the change appears to promise greater efficiency, greater excellence. Will it not be well for us to try that which can do no harm and promises much good?

Printed in *The Princetonian*, III (May 2, 1878), 1-4.

Review of Green's *A History of the English People*

[May 2, 1878]

Within the last three years another and now exalted name has been added to the noble list of English historians. The candor of

Carlyle, the concise expression of Gibbon, and the brilliancy of Macaulay seem to be combined in Green. "A Short History of the English People" was received by the English-speaking world with the enthusiasm it richly deserved. To the Englishman it was a welcome summary of the great deeds of his great fathers. To the American it was a vivid outline sketch of the progress of a people whose blood was coursing through his own veins, and whose traditions he was proud to claim as his own.

And now the first two volumes of a larger and fuller work have come from the same master hand, and are in the hands of the public. Three more volumes are promised, and all are expressing the hope that the great author may live to complete his great work.

The overmastering charm which this work exercises over all its readers is explained by the fact that it is suited to every taste. The cold, matter-of-fact man of books finds in its pages a knowledge of great authors which commands his respect; the scholar discovers in it the ripest scholarship; the rhetorician yields his homage to its marvelous purity of style; the orator is moved by its manly and stirring eloquence; the politician may go to it for a distinct outline of English constitutional history, for a clear insight into national policy; the statesman may learn of it the philosophy of history; to its subtle fancy the poet must give his admiration; to the common man it is a clear and simple record whose every line is intelligible to him, and through whose sentiments he can recognize the beatings of a heart which is in sympathy with his humble wants and ambitions, which understands his joys and sorrows.

Mr. Green's powerful delineation of character adds a peculiar vividness to the history. In this power, in which Macaulay surpassed, he surpasses Macaulay. To one who has read the opening passages of his history, the life of the Angles, Jutes, and Saxons amid the German forests in which the English race was cradled, is no longer shrouded by myths. After a perusal of the moving record, we feel that we have mingled in everyday intercourse with those sturdy pioneers of English civilization; that we have lived in the court of every English monarch from William the Conquerer to Victoria; that we have participated in the conquest of every province of the vast British Empire; that we actually hear the "morning drum beat," which, "following the sun and keeping company with the hours, circles the earth with one continuous and unbroken strain of the martial airs of England." English history is now an actuality in our minds, a reminiscence, an *experience*.

It is a grateful thought that this History of the English People is a history of the American people as well; it is a high and solemn thought that we, as a lusty branch of a noble race, are by our national history adding lustre or stain to so bright an escutcheon.

We profess to be building upon the grand principles of liberty in whose development nine centuries have been consumed. With what diligence, then, should we guard so precious a legacy of privileges! How careful should we be that in this experiment of ours, in which sacred principles are stretched to their utmost, the place of the Goddess of Liberty be not usurped by the Harlot.

License.

Printed in *The Princetonian*, III (May 2, 1878), 7-8.

From the Minutes of the Liberal Debating Club

May 6. [1878]

House met at 7-55, minutes of last meeting read & approved. Talcott, Sheldon, Godwin & Elsing were absent[.] Mr. Webster read a selection fr the Manual during which Mr Talcott entered the Room. McCarter moved that Mr. Woods be reëlected by acclamation—lost. Voting for President then followed. In the 1st ballot there was no election. On the second Mr Sheldon was elected. The Debate then followed upon the "National University" bill which was at the previous meeting tabled by a motion of Mr Wilson— Re.tabled. Debate upon the bill Res. that the "Missouri compromise was impolitic" passed 1st & 2nd readings & committee of whole, in wh. Mr Webster took the chair. Committee reported favorably to the House, Mr. Webster was excused fr. reading a criticism on Mr Talcotts speech. House adjourned at 9-20.

Hiram Woods Jr.   Prest.   Robt Harris McCarter   Sec'y of State

From Joseph Ruggles Wilson

My darling Son—   Home, [Wilmington, N. C.] May 9 78.

I enclose the order for which you ask, and for which I can see no necessity. The editorial in the last Princetonian touching the want of confidence the col. authorities repose in the students is capital, and ought to make the Trustees open their eyes somewhat. I do not see any reason why that College should continue to prosper. They who manage its affairs certainly seem more anxious to deter than attract patronage.—I cannot help thinking that the P. under its new editorial staff is an improvement when compared with what it was. It is more dignified whilst not less racy. Your mother and I read it through—our perusal being limited alone by the advertisements between the two bodies of which the main contents are sandwiched. I wonder that the great New York papers do not copy from it and give it prominent notice. May-be they do, though, without my seeing the references. . . .

Your affectionate F.   J R W

P.S. I trust you rec'd the $110.00 all right.

ALS (WP, DLC) with WWhw notation on env.: "Ans."

From Janet Woodrow Wilson

My precious Son,   Wilmington–[N. C.] May 11th [1878]

. . . Your father wrote you early in the week—sending you the order you desired. How disgraceful to the Col authorities to have made such a rule! Their object seems to be to distroy all self-respect on the part of the students—and such will be the effect upon weak minds. Your father expects to leave for the Ass[embly] at Knoxville on Monday night.[1] He is quite well just now—and I hope he will enjoy the Assembly more than he usually does, in consequence. Did you get his enclosure for paying your bill? He sent it last week. . . .   Yours lovingly   Mother

P.S. by JRW omitted. ALS (WP, DLC) with WWhw notation on env.: "Ans."
[1] General Assembly met in Knoxville, May 16-25, 1878.

Editorial in *The Princetonian*

[May 16, 1878]

The Inter-Collegiate Literary Association is fast nearing the death agony. One of the most energetic and influential of its members, Lafayette College, has recently followed the example set by Hamilton, and withdrawn, and it seems likely that others will follow. The temperate and sensible reasons given by Lafayette, for her action, will apply equally well to every other College which is now a member of the association. The question of our withdrawal has been discussed here, time and again, until further words are useless. We are glad to hear that there is a prospect of our being called upon, at no very distant date, to act in the matter. We understand that a meeting of those interested will soon be called, when the question as to whether or not we shall sever our connection with the association, will come under consideration. In the present state of the under-graduate mind, it requires no prophet to predict the answer that will be given to this question.

Printed in *The Princetonian*, III (May 16, 1878), 13-14.

From the Minutes of the Liberal Debating Club

May 18. [1878]

Meeting called to order at 8 oclock. Mr. Sheldon the President being absent Mr. Webster took the chair. No Miss. business. Mr. Woods was excused fr. speaking. Mr. Talcott read section IV. chap XV of manual, Third reading of Missouri Compromise bill came up & Mr. Woods moved that the question be post poned until the leader of the opposition Mr McCarter should return. Cd. The bill in regard to National University then came up for its 1st reading and after its first discussion passed 1 reading—Second reading moved & carried. Committee of whole moved and carried. Committee rose & reported favorably to the House. Mr. Webster was excused from reading a criticism on Mr. Talcotts speech. No miscellaneous business. Mr. Elsing moved the following question *Resl'd* ["]that Morality does not keep pace with civilization." House adjourned at 9-30

Webster   Ch'mn   T. W. Wilson N. C.   Sec'y Pro tem.

From the Minutes of the American Whig Society

Whig Hall May 24th 1878

. . . Resolved. That Article XVIII of the by-laws be amended as follows:

In Sec. 1—Strike out the last clause reading: "When there are no more than three competitors, only one medal shall be awarded" and insert: "If there are less than eight competitors, no prize shall be awarded."

Section 3 by adding: "Nor one alredy used as a College exercise"   Davis   Wilson   Bridges

A motion to adjourn was lost

 "   "   "   table   "   "

The Resolution was lost.

Res'd That for the remainder of this term, while forty-five members constitute a quorum for Literary exercises, that the same number constitute a quorum for Initiation and for transacting any business relating to Literary exercises and also that it have the right to adjourn itself on motion

c-d   Wilson   Woods—. . .

. . . Second Session

. . . The Ninth Division Messrs Voorhis and Wylly inclusive then debated the following:

Resolved that a Protective Tariff is now no longer necessary for the protection of our home industries

Performed on the affirmative Mr. Wilson . . .
Performed on the Negative Messrs Warren,[1] Webster[,] Wills[2]
. . .

The Sub. Com. decided the question in the aff. and together with the 1st Compt gave the appointment to Mr. Wilson. The House then decided the question in the Neg. . . .

[1] Albert D. Warren, '79.   [2] David Wills, '80.

Three Editorials in *The Princetonian*

[May 30, 1878]

It is with extreme regret that we notice Mr. W. E. Dodge's resignation of the captaincy of the Foot-ball team. We regret it, not because of any lack of confidence in Mr. Ballard,[1] his successor, but because of the splendid work Mr. Dodge has done for the College in the past. When a man's skill is tried and his fitness for a position of command and of high responsibility is fully established, his services have become invaluable and his loss is a real and severe misfortune. Such a man Mr. Dodge had proved himself to be under circumstances the most trying. Both his character and his powerful playing rendered him one of the best captains we ever saw upon the field. But he has found it his duty to resign; and, under the peculiar circumstances, we have no right to question the wisdom of his course. But we most heartily thank him, on behalf of the College, for his past brilliant and fruitful services. We wish for his successor the same measure of support and success.

[1] Bland Ballard, Jr., '80.

✧

Our success at Mott Haven,[1] as the records show, was highly creditable, both to the gentlemen who participated in the games and to the College. Princeton has always been famed for fine athletes. Whatever our success in base-ball, or at the oar, our excellence in other athletic contests is conceded on all hands. Nor has our reputation been marred in this year's games. It is to be hoped that our renewed success will revive the flagging interest of the College in athletics. The training and practice necessary as a preparation for a contest of strength or skill is so dependent upon individual effort that the majority are apt to overlook the fact that success, when achieved, is a matter of congratulation to the whole College, as well as to those who have won the honor. We ought to regard our athletes as we do our ball nine: as representatives of the whole College, and, as such, claimants upon our hearty good-wishes and applause. We hope, too, that the Caledonian Games at Commencement will be contested by a number of new men. Too commonly men, who have been successful in some contest back in Freshman year, acquire, by that success, such a reputation as to deter others from afterwards contesting the palm with them. Thus, almost every contest presents the sorry spectacle of some half a dozen men carrying off prize after prize, in what are practically walkovers. Such a state of things might easily be remedied, if only some of the "dark horses," sound in wind and limb, but yet undeveloped by practice, would exert themselves with that end in view. There are many men in College who might, with the aid of sufficient practice, force the present champions to put forth their utmost powers to retain their positions. The more the men can be induced to train faithfully, the surer our chances of success in the Mott Haven games next year. The records show that we could have won first place this year with ease, if more of our men had gone down. We have two men in College who could have taken first and second places in the hurdle race with little trouble, had they entered. Let not our record be spoiled by such negligence again.

1 At the Inter-Collegiate Athletic Association field-meeting at Mott Haven, New York, on May 18, 1878. Princeton won seven first and two second prizes.

Those who attended the Mott Haven games report that they were excellently managed, but that the time consumed by them was so long as to render them wearisome. We have heard it suggested that, for the future, some way should be devised by which the time might be shortened, and the tediousness thus obviated. It has been proposed that it might be well to have two events take place at the same time: the mile-walk and throwing the hammer, for instance. But the impracticability of this plan is evident when it is remembered that the games must be so arranged that anyone may compete in any or all of the contests, if he so wishes; and also that, under such circumstances, it would be necessary to have two sets of judges and referees. The only feasible way out of the difficulty seems to be that of having the games extend over two days, as did the preliminary contests at Dartmouth. In our Fall and Spring meetings, at least, this might be tried; and we do not see any insuperable difficulty in the way of doing it even at Commencement. If the managers of the coming games would so arrange them as to relieve the tedium always incident upon them hitherto, they would be repaid for any extra trouble they might incur by seeing a far larger number of spectators in attendance.

Printed in *The Princetonian*, III (May 30, 1878), 25-26.

From the Minutes of the Liberal Debating Club

June 1 [1878]

Meeting called to order at 7-55 Mr Sheldon in the chair, Mr Elsing was not present. Minutes of last meeting were read & approved. Miscellaneous business coming up Mr. Woods moved that the Report of the Committee on inquiring into the advisability of holding Public Debates, be adopted. Mr Wilson read the Report and Mr Woods moved that the Section in regard to the "procuring a suitable room" be stricken out. Amendment accepted & incorporated. Mr. McCarter moved amendment that "the 2nd meeting of each month shall be public Each member being priveleged to invite any friends to the meeting—sec'd—Mr Woods moved amendment "that any member be permitted to bring any friends to the meetings" accept. & incorporated—Report as amended then passed.

1st reading of amendment to Art XIII was moved & c'd & bill passed. Mr Woods read Section 5, Chap XV of Manual, after which the 3rd reading of the bill in regard to the Missouri Compromise came up before the Club & was lost, the sec'y thereby losing his position.

Bill in regard to National University came up for 3rd reading & was c'd, moved to lay the bill in regard to ["]progress of morality & civilization" be laid on the table carried.

Mr Webster read a criticism on a speech of Mr. Talcotts delivered some time since after wh. Mr Woods moved that the Club meet on the Second saturday of next term—c'd.

Mr. Wilson moved 1st reading of the amendment to Art II, Sect I, of Constitution c'd—& amend. passed.

Club then adjourned

E. W. Sheldon   Prest.   Robt. Harris McCarter   sec'y of state

From the Minutes of the American Whig Society

Whig Hall   June 7, 1878

... Your Com. appointed to consider the advisability and means of securing an endowment fund for the Hall would recommend as follows:

I That the Hall adopt the following resolution:
  Res'd that this House think it eminently advisable that the Senate take the proper steps for securing for *American Whig Society* an endowment fund of $10,000

II That the following resolution be brought before the Senate
  Res'd *First*, that there be appointed by the Senate a joint-com-

mittee consisting of 3 members of the Senate and 2 members from the House of Undergraduates, whose duty it shall be to make every effort to obtain from the Alumni and the friends of the American Whig Society the sum of $10,000 to be used as an Endowment Fund for the Society.

Second, that this money, when obtained, shall be invested in United States 4 per. cent. registered bonds.

Third that the joint committee of five be instructed to draw up additional articles to the Constitution, providing for the receipt and expenditure of the interest of the Endowment Fund as it may accrue from time to time

Respectfully submitted   Mitchell
Weed   } Committee
Wilson

. . . Res'd That Drs. Woods and Mitchell be instructed to purchase a good fresh skull and bones for the Society this summer, the same not to exceed in cost $5.00[1]

c-d   Wilson McCarter Helm Bridges Elsing
Res'd That the Committee's report on Endowment Fund be adopted
c-d   Mitchell Weed Wilson . . .

[1] The Minutes of the American Whig Society, Sept. 20, 1878, contain the following entry: "Resolved By-laws etc. That the Treas'r. be instructed to cancel the sessional fees of Messrs Mitchell and Woods in consideration of the $5.00 spent by them in purchasing a skull and bones for the Society.   c-d   Wilson"

From Joseph Ruggles Wilson

My dearest son   Wilmington, [N. C.] Monday, [June] 17th [1878]

Enclosed please find $20.00 which I dare say will amply meet all your expenses. I hope that you have sent for yr ticket to Baltimore. We will confidently expect you by Saturday night. If I should not be at the depot, it will be because you have requested me not to be. I need not try to tell you how welcome you will be.

I am to leave home on Monday 24th for Tuscaloosa, Ala., where I am expected to deliver the baccalaureate on the 30th[.][1] I go via Davidson where the Board meets on Tuesday 25th. My leaving home will not be so painful when *you* are here, on whom yr dear mother can lean with such confidence[.] All send love.

Your affc father   J. R. Wilson

ALS (WP, DLC).
[1] At the University of Alabama. For a brief report of JRW's sermon, see the Tuscaloosa (Ala.) *Gazette*, cited in the Wilmington *Morning Star*, July 25, 1878.

From the Minutes of the Senate of the

American Whig Society

Whig Hall. June 19th, 1878.

. . . The report of the Com. of the House, Messrs. Mitchell, Wilson, & Weed, was then recd.[1] It was moved by Mr. W. B. Greene, Jr. that this report be referred to a committee of three members of the Senate and two members of the House of Undergraduates who shall have power to submit such action as they may recommend to the House of Undergraduates for consideration.

It was moved as an amendment that the committee from the Senate be made five. Seconded and carried.

It was moved by Mr. Lowrie[2] that the committee from the House of Undergraduates be likewise made five. Carried.

The Committee on the Renovation of the Hall appointed @ a special meeting Nov. 13th 1877, and of which Prof. Cameron was chairman, then presented their report, which was accepted and the committee discharged with thanks. . . .

The history of the Society[3] was then read, accepted, and placed on file. . . .

Hw entry, bound ledger book (NjP).
[1] See Whig Minutes, June 7, 1878.
[2] Reuben Lowrie, '81.
[3] Not found, but see the extract printed in Jacob N. Beam, *The American Whig Society of Princeton University* (Princeton, N. J., 1933), p. 188.

Editorial in *The Princetonian*

[June 27, 1878]

The class of '81 showed poor taste in their manner of celebrating the arrival of Sophomore year. The Sophomore and Junior classes were still busy with examinations, and were disturbed in no small degree by the noise and uproar which was created. A year ago the class of '80 had a celebration of the same character, and the Faculty promptly suspended them. We sincerely regret that a like punishment was not inflicted on the class of '81. If we should strive to possess anything here in College, it is a kindly respect for the convenience of others, endeavoring to discover the consequences to which any act of school-boy frivolity may lead. The class of '81 did not take this into consideration, but were content to injure their good reputation by their carelessness and want of consideration. It may be remarked, in extenuation of this action of theirs, that an example was set by the Seniors on the Tuesday evening preceding. Indeed, it may be said that the Seniors are worthy of far greater blame, because of the greater difficulty of the examinations then at hand, and because of the total sacrifice of that dignity which we are accustomed to credit Seniors with possessing. But it is dangerous to follow the example of those who have passed their last examinations, and, for our own part, we are extremely sorry that propriety does not admit the suspension of such offenders. The class of '81 can certainly consider that excuse of little value which would only shield their errors behind the greater faults of others. In whatever light it is viewed, this disturbance cannot be explained away, but must stand as hasty, inconsiderate, and worthy of condemnation. An act of this kind sets a bad example to succeeding classes, and our criticism of it cannot be too strong, while there is danger of it becoming a firm and established custom.

It is far from our intention to find fault with any display of class feeling. But we believe that every such display of feeling should be tempered with a sense of propriety—that it should never be permitted to seriously interfere with the work and convenience of others. It is to be hoped that the class of '81 will conduct themselves as Sophomores with increased dignity, and that they will never yield to the promptings of a foolish vanity, which cannot but cover their good name with ridicule and reproach.

Printed in *The Princetonian,* III (June 27, 1878), 50.

To James Edwin Webster

Dear Ed., alias Daniel: Columbia, So. Ca. 7/23/78
I suppose that my long delay in writing to you has filled you with secret joy because you promised to write to me only on condition of receiving first an epistle from me. But I have not by any means forgotten my promise and I do not intend to leave you any excuse for not writing to me but that of disinclination[.] You need not think that you are the only one whom I have neglected in the matter of letter-writing. I have been neglectful of all alike. Talcott was the first to be favored (?) by me and it is but two or three days since I wrote my first letter to him. I promised to write to "Pomp,"[1] Woods, and Bridges but have yet written to none of them. They all seem to expect me to open the correspondence for some reason or other, I hardly know why. I suppose, however, that they think my writing powers—my gift of gab—unlimited. Although the vacation is well-nigh half over, I give you fair warning that I shall expect no less than two letters from you before College opens

And now I proceed to ask the all-important question, *How's Buffalo?* I hope that your correspondence with the fair inhabitant

of that fair city flows happily on. Have you yet succeeded in re-
placing the lost watch ornament?

As you will see by the heading of this letter, I am in Columbia
on a visit to my younger sister. I have been here for a week and
will leave for home in a few days. The weather has been oppres-
sively warm here but, by keeping quiet and idle I am managing
to keep comparatively comfortable. I believe that you know that
I lived here for some four or five years just before I went to Princeton. I feel at home upon coming here where I have quite a large
number of acquaintances, some of whom it is very pleasant to
meet again. Columbia is the scene of some of my old love adventures of which I have from time to time given you some partial
accounts. You may naturally imagine that this place, therefore,
recalls some strange memories to my mind. I have made a considerable fool of myself here in times not very long past. The Columbia people have a good deal of the old South Carolina hospitality and hearty warmth of manner and make very kind and
pleasant friends. The fair ones especially are most of them free
from affectation and pretense. I have just returned from calling
on a whole family of girls who are all old acquaintances. They all
knew me as a boy and embrionic young man and know me as
"Tom." I always enjoy getting among people who know me well
enough to throw aside the formal prefix, *Mr.*, and call me *Tommie*,
simply.

Much of my leisure time I employ in the undignified occupation
of romping with the younger of my two bright nephews here. He
delights in having me chase him on *all fours*, and I constantly indulge him to the material detriment of my breeches. The little
chap has an immense amount of determination housed in his
diminutive frame and can rule me with ease. He will be master
of those with whom he comes in contact as long as he lives, probably. He has already interrupted me more than once in the writing of this letter and I am finishing it while his morning sleep
gives me temporary freedom. I believe I am quite a willing slave,
however.

One would not think that this was the same city that it was
during the campaign of '76. Hampton has now long been in quiet
possession and has administered the government of the state with
more ability and success than might have been expected in view
of the fact that he is in most respects a very ordinary man. He is
certainly no statesman—little more than a rough an[d] honest
soldier with a soldiers aptness at orderly administration and the
control of the rank and file of his followers. As usual politics is the

all-engrossing topic of conversation. Southerners seem born with an interest in public affairs though it is too often of late a very ignorant interest.

I have not received Woods' scrawl yet nor a letter from Bridges with its quaint caption: "Friend Wilson." I hope soon to hear from you however—the sooner the better

Your very sincere friend   T. W. Wilson

ALS (photostat in RSB Coll., DLC).
    1 Probably R. H. McCarter.

To Robert Bridges

Dear Bobie: Wilmington, N. C. 7/27/78

I have just returned from Columbia, S. C., where I have been on a visit to my younger sister, and find a letter from you awaiting me.[1] I need not tell you that I was thoroughly pleased at seeing it. I can hardly tell why it is that I have delayed writing so long. You are by no means the only one whom I have neglected. After reaching home I determined to spend the first week or two in perfect idleness that I might have complete rest after the heat and hurry and fatigue of Commencement week. But the one week passed into two, the two lengthened into three, and I was off for Columbia, and not a single letter was written. I promised to write to "Pomp.," Talcott, Woods, and Daniel, as well as to yourself, and I felt that it was a task too stupendous for hot weather to open so wide a correspondence. But I have now thrown off my laziness with an effort and Wilson "is himself again," with his correspondence hopefully opened and his P. O. box longingly awaiting his friends' epistles. But all except you seem to have expected me to open the correspondence, Daniel confessedly because of laziness, Talcott for much the same reason, no doubt, and "Pomp." for some cause yet to be revealed. As for the Cow,[2] I intend to keep cold silence until he writes to me. I have not heard a word from the rascal

I most heartily pity you on account of the heat wave. The two sections of the country seem to have changed their relative positions as regards heat. The South seems to have been the cooler portion this summer. The thermometer here has seldom ranged higher than 91 and its average has been about 85. A Harvard fellow here says that it seemed to him to grow cooler as he came South.

My report was eminently unsatisfactory, bringing me down to 37th in consequence of my non-attention to Physics and the injustice of old Guyot,[3] Pscych, 98.8, Dad 97.,[4] Greek 94.5[,] Butler[5] 95, Geol. 71, Lat. 96.5, Eng. 90, History, 95, Physics 78. I never got down in the *seventies* before! As for the *bet*, go to see the "ten-mile girl" before being rash enough to brag. Now *I* have some reason to boast. I have been to Columbia, the home of pretty girls and the scene of many of my old love scrapes, and my heart has not so much as beat any faster than usual. I think that we will take creams, for Wilmington girls are not apt to charm me very speedily. The names of Rose Thurston and Robert Henderson will dwell side by side in my memory! Bob is easily teased, and he will no doubt hear enough of Rose. Your imagination is stronger than mine so you may make up the yarn.

You are very courageous to write reports in such weather as you have been experiencing. The only writing I have done has been a rough, outline sketch of an essay on Chatham.[6] I doubt if it will ever be developed into a full-fledged essay. But the subject is one of engrossing interest to me and I can perhaps write as well on it as on any.

I have been devouring Green's larger History of the English People with great avidity. I have seldom been so completely charmed by any work. It has the same fascination for me that I believe Hawthorne has for you. His style is richer than Macaulay's, though sometimes not quite so uniformly brilliant. But I have often expressed to you my admiration for Green and his work and need not again repeat his praises.

The Commencement number of the *Princetonian* came and proved a little more readable than I had expected, though there were some ridiculous typographical errors in it, such as "*Lawyers* in the circle" instead of "*Sawyers* in the circle."[7] Some *may* be at a loss to see the point of the joke, for *joke* it was intended to be.

The address you put on your letter to me was sufficient, though it might be safer to put, *care* Rev. J. R. Wilson, D.D., box 586. Then there *could* be no mistake.

My life since leaving College has been quite quiet. I had rather sit at our Western windows and enjoy the sea breeze than stir upon any of the numerous excursions which are constantly going out to various neighboring points. Bob, how is your Grandmother, whose sickness called you off so suddenly? Please write very soon to　　　　　　　Your very sincere friend　Thos. W. Wilson

ALS (Meyer Coll., DLC).
  [1] R. Bridges to WW, July 20, 1878, ALS (WP, DLC).
  [2] Hiram Woods, Jr.
  [3] Arnold Guyot, Blair Professor of Geology and Physical Geography.
  [4] Atwater's course on logic and metaphysics,

⁵ Shields' course on science and religion, the text for which was Butler's *Analogy.*

⁶ Printed at Oct. 1, 1878.

⁷ WW's reference is to a brief item in the "Here and There" column, *The Princetonian,* III (June 27, 1878), 62.

Marginal Notes

John Richard Green, *History of the English People* (4 vols., New York: 1878-80).

Transcripts of WW Shorthand Comments

Vol. I, 93:

In the "great meeting" of the Witenagemote or Assembly of the Wise lay the rule of the realm. It represented the whole English people, as the wise-moots of each kingdom represented the separate peoples of each; and its powers were as supreme in the wider field as theirs in the narrower. It could elect or depose the King. To it belonged the higher justice, the imposition of taxes, the making of laws, the conclusion of treaties, the control of wars, the disposal of public lands, the appointment of great officers of state.

[c. July 27, 1878]

The folly of America in taking away from the national assembly the reverent custom of appointing the great officers of state! Parliament still possesses this power.

Vol. I, 95:

The death of Eadwig a few months later restored the unity of the realm; but his successor Eadgar was only a boy of fourteen and throughout his reign the actual direction of affairs lay in the hands of Dunstan, whose elevation to the see of Canterbury set him at the head of the Church as of the State. The noblest tribute to his rule lies in the silence of our chroniclers. His work indeed was a work of settlement, and such a work was best done by the simple enforcement of peace. During the years of rest in which the stern hand of the Primate enforced justice and order Northman and Englishman drew together into a single people. Their union was the result of no direct policy of fusion; on the contrary Dunstan's policy preserved to the conquered Danelagh its local rights and local usages. But he recognized the men of the Danelagh as Englishmen. . . .

This is always the proper policy in similar cases and had the North acted upon that principle in her dealing with the South after the war there would have been less subsequent trouble between the two sections.

Vol. I, 208:

As in other townships land was a necessary accompaniment of freedom. The landless man who dwelled in a borough had no share in its corporate life; for purposes of government or property the town consisted simply of the landed proprietors within its bounds. The common lands which are still attached to many of our boroughs take us back to a time when each township lay within a ring or mark of open ground which served at once as boundary and pasture land. Each of the four wards of York had its common pasture; Oxford has still its own "Portmeadow."

A proper and necessary order of things. No other basis of the franchise can be a *natural* one, none other can be a wise one. All advance in principles of the franchise must be in the same direction a development of the same principle, and not in the opposite or different direction, the development of a foreign principle.

Vol. I, 246:

The Great Charter met this abuse by a provision on which our constitutional system rests. "No scutage or aid [other than the three customary feudal aids][1] shall be imposed in our realm save by the common council of the realm," and to this Great Council it was provided that prelates and the greater barons should be summoned by special writ and all tenants in chief through the sheriffs and bailiffs at least forty days before. The provision defined what had probably been the common usage of the realm; but the definition turned it into a national right, a right so momentous that on it rests our whole Parliamentary life. Even the baronage seem to have been startled when they realized the extent of their claim; and the provision was dropped from the later issue of the Charter at the outset of the next reign. But the clause brought home to the nation at large their possession of a right which became dearer as years went by. More and more clearly the nation discovered that in these simple words lay the secret of political power. It was the right of self-taxation that England fought for under Earl Simon as she fought for it under Hampden. It was the establishment of this right which established English freedom.

A right thence which was taken out to English America a struggle for which gave birth to the United States. But in establishing this claim to the ancient right of their race Americans seemed to have forgot some of the wisest and most fundamental of those principles of government which had been washed in the blood of their ancestors. Is the principle of universal suffrage for instance consistent with those principles of government which bear the sanction of the wisest Englishmen of 8 centuries and which have secured personal freedom and political liberty to a great nation for more than 8 hundred years? Is it necessary or even compatible with the healthy operation of a free government?

[1] Brackets in original text.

Vol. I, 248:

While Innocent was dreaming of a vast Christian Empire with the Pope at its head to enforce justice and religion on his under-kings, John believed that the Papal protection would enable him to rule as tyrannically as he would. The thunders of the Papacy were to be ever at hand for his protection, as the armies of England are at hand to protect the vileness and oppression of a Turkish Sultan or a Nizam of Hyderabad. His envoys were already at Rome, pleading for a condemnation of the Charter. The after action of the Papacy shows that Innocent was moved by no hostility to English freedom. But he was indignant that a matter which might have been brought before his court of appeal as overlord should have been dealt with by armed revolt, and in this crisis both his imperious pride and the legal tendency of his mind swayed him to the side of the King who submitted to his justice. He annulled the Great Charter by a bull in August, and at the close of the year excommunicated the barons.

How unworthy a successor of such men as Earl Stephen Langton is such a minister as a fickle though plausible Disraeli! He used the power of a great and free nation to strengthen the rule of vile oppressors.

Vol. I, 255:

The zeal of the Spaniard Dominic was roused at the sight of the lordly prelates who sought by fire and sword to win the Albigensian heretics to the faith. "Zeal," he cried, "must be met by zeal, lowliness by lowliness, false sanctity by real sanctity, preaching lies by preaching truth."

A great truth applicable as much perhaps in the political as in the religious sphere. The power and influence of demagogues and petty politicians who pander to the blind masses is shortlived because they do not recognize this truth.

Vol. I, 266:

But the importance of the Friar's work lay in this, that the work of the scholar was supplemented by that of the popular preacher. The theory of government wrought out in cell and lecture-room was carried over the length and breadth of the land by the mendicant brother, begging his way from town to town, chatting with farmer or housewife at the cottage door, and setting up

The English people were then educated in their political rights and in principles of state-craft much as were the Athenian people—by direct instruction from popular orators. Might not Demosthenes have mingled religious truth with political his portable pulpit in village green or market-place. His open-air sermons, ranging from impassioned devotion to coarse story and homely mother wit, became the journals as well as the homilies of the day; political and social questions found place in them side by side with spiritual matters; and the rudest countryman learned his tale of a king's oppression or a patriot's hopes as he listened to the rambling passionate, humorous discourse of the begging friar.

teaching had he known Christianity?

Vol. I, 292:

A royal proclamation in the English tongue, the first in that tongue since the Conquest which has reached us, ordered the observance of these Provisions. The King was in fact helpless, and resistance came only from the foreign favourites, who refused to surrender the castles and honours which had been granted to them. But the Twenty-four were resolute in their action; and an armed demonstration of the barons drove the foreigners in flight over sea. The whole royal power was now in fact in the hands of the committees appointed by the Great Council.

These committees were the committees of Congress in very crude form. It is strange that the form of government established by our Constitution has resulted in the adoption of [an] impractical and a calamitous scheme of regulating affairs of state through committees rather than directly through responsible ministers. We have thus to a considerable extent kept the rudder and lost perfect sight of the English Constitution.

Vol. I, 440:

. . . it was in the preaching of John Ball that England first listened to a declaration of the natural equality and rights of man. "Good people," cried the preacher, "things will never be well in England so long as goods be not in common, and so long as there be villeins and gentlemen. By what right are they whom we call lords greater folk than we? On what grounds have they deserved it? Why do thay hold us in serfage? If we all came of the same father and mother, of Adam and Eve, how can they say or prove that they are better than we, if it be not that they make us gain for them by our toil what they spend in their pride? They are clothed in velvet and

Almost the very words of the men who are now advocating such doctrines in America!

warm in their furs and their er-
mines, while we are covered with
rags. They have wine and spices
and fair bread; and we oat-cake
and straw, and water to drink.
They have leisure and fine houses;
we have pain and labour, the rain
and the wind in the fields. And yet
it is of us and of our toil that these
men hold their state." It was the
tyranny of property that then as
ever roused the defiance of socialism.

Vol. II, 6:

But with the close of the struggle for the succession this liberty
suddenly disappeared. If the Wars
of the Roses failed in utterly destroying English freedom, they succeeded in arresting its progress for
more than a hundred years. With
them we enter on an epoch of constitutional retrogression in which
the slow work of the age that went
before it was rapidly undone. From
the accession of Edward the Fourth
Parliamentary life was almost suspended, or was turned into a mere
form by the over-powering influence of the Crown. The legislative
powers of the two Houses were
usurped by the royal Council. Arbitrary taxation reappeared in be-
nevolences and forced loans. Personal liberty was almost extinguished by a formidable spy-sys-
tem and by the constant practice
of arbitrary imprisonment. Justice
was degraded by the prodigal use
of bills of attainder, by a wide extension of the judicial power of the
royal Council, by the servility of
judges, by the coercion of juries.
So vast and sweeping was the
change that to careless observers
of a later day the constitutional
monarchy of the Edwards and the
Henries seemed suddenly to have
transformed itself under the Tu-
dors into a despotism as complete
as the despotism of the Turk. Such
a view is no doubt exaggerated and
unjust. Bend and strain the law as
he might, there never was a time
when the most wilful of English
rulers failed to own the restraints
of law. . . .

The Wars of the Roses and
Civil War in America issued in
results not altogether dissimilar:
with the triumph of the House
of York unrestrained and irresponsible power passed into the
hands of the royal Council; with
the death of the Confederate
cause in America unrestrained
and irresponsible power began
to be exercised by Congress; thus
creating a nursery for corruption and threatening death to
free institutions.

Vol. II, 93:

Flushed with this new glory, the young King was resolute to continue the war when in the opening of 1514 he found himself left alone by the dissolution of the League. Ferdinand had gained his ends, and had no mind to fight longer simply to realize the dreams of his son-in-law. Henry had indeed gained much. The might of France was broken. The Papacy was restored to freedom. England had again figured as a great power in Europe. But the millions left by his father were exhausted, his subjects had been drained by repeated subsidies, and, furious as he was at the treachery of his Spanish ally, Henry was driven to conclude a peace.

To the hopes of the New Learning this sudden outbreak of the spirit of war, this change of the monarch from whom they had looked for a "new order" into a vulgar conqueror, proved a bitter disappointment. Colet thundered from the pulpit of St. Pauls that "an unjust peace is better than the justest war," and protested that "when men out of hatred and ambition fight with and destroy one another, they fight under the banner, not of Christ, but of the Devil." Erasmus quitted Cambridge with a bitter satire against the "madness" around him. "It is the people," he said, in words which must have startled his age,—"it is the people who build cities, while the madness of princes destroys them."

Vol. II, 104:

More than a century before William of Orange [Sir Thomas] More discerned and proclaimed the great principle of religious toleration. In "Nowhere" it was lawful to every man to be of what religion he would. Even the disbelievers in a Divine Being or in the immortality of man, who by a single exception to its perfect religious indifference were excluded from public office, were excluded, not on the ground of their religious belief, but because their opinions were deemed to be degrading to mankind and therefore to incapacitate those who held them from governing in a noble temper. But they were subject to no punishment, because the people of Utopia were "persuaded that it is not in a man's power to believe what he list." The religion which a man held he might propagate by argument, though not by violence or insult to the religion of others.

Much the same doctrine as that held by some modern advocates of "peace at any price."

The proper ground to be taken against such as [Robert] Ingersoll.

Vol. II, 105:

[Green's summary comments on Sir Thomas More's *Utopia*]

Those who delight to notice coincidence will not fail to remark that More describes this kingdom Nowhere as situated in this Western world of ours where its institutions have since been established almost in their fullness; but these same persons could have in all likelihood overlooked the fact that most of the principles set forth in the "Utopia" found their triumphant establishment in England itself before the United States came into existence and were merely *transplanted* to this continent.

Vol. II, 357:

Elizabeth adopted the system of her two predecessors both in the creation of boroughs and the recommendation of candidates; but her keen political instinct soon perceived the inutility of both expedients. She saw that the "management" of the Houses, so easy under Cromwell, was becoming harder every day. The very number of the members she called up into the Commons from nomination boroughs, sixty-two in all, showed the increasing difficulty which the government found in securing a working majority. The rise of a new nobility enriched by the spoils of the Church and trained to political life by the stress of events around them was giving fresh vigour to the House of Lords. The increased wealth of the country gentry as well as the growing desire to obtain a seat among the Commons brought about the cessation at this time of the old payment of members by their constituencies. A change too in the borough representation, which had long been in progress but was now for the first time legally recognized, tended greatly to increase the vigour and independence of the Lower House.

A momentous fact. England was thus safe from the professional politicians[,] men who make a living in public service.

From Robert Harris McCarter

My Dear Tommy—Sea Bright, Monmouth Co. N.J., 5th Aug. 1878.

. . . Remembering your praises I began the other day Curtis' life of Dan'l. Webster & I am perfectly charmed. It is a strong book of a stronger man. I like to read biography. It is the true way to

read history. It takes the place of novels. Why is it not more interesting to read the struggles and trials of a great man than of a
fictitious character who is never real. . . . Your opinion of Hampton I think, from what little I know of him, [is] true. After all it
strikes me that most all of the so called statesmen of the day are
nothing more than managers—they have it may be a skill for execution & for commanding & being obeyed, more as a servant
obeys his master than a citizen his ruler, but as for any true in-
born principle of right, of *statesmanship statesmanship,* [sic] why
Bah! . . .

Why is so little true interest taken in politics by the youth of our
land? Questions involving political interests have no audiences
and no supporters in Whig Hall. Let us wake up! Why cant we send
from Princeton some men who are honest & yet who are unselfish
enough to forget personal aggrandizement in public good and patriotism. I have yet great hopes of you Tommy. . . .

Yours very sincerely   Robt Harris McCarter

ALS (WP, DLC) with WWhw notation on env.: "Ans."

To Robert Bridges

Dear Bob: Wilmington, N. C. 8/10/78
I rec'd yours of the 6th in due time and was thoroughly pleased
with it, *save in one point.* The Cow in his letter[1] to me dropped
some hint about your connection with a *walk* and a kiss, and you
say nothing about such an exciting topic! Now, what does this
mean? Surely the "ten-mile girl" has no knowledge of this; or,
startling thought, she may be one of the parties interested! If I
did not misunderstand Hiram, *you* were certainly one of the
portion to the transaction. Do put me out of suspense.

Your description of the scenes to be met with at a large camp
meeting were very interesting to me. I have never seen one. They
are unknown in the South, at least on so large a scale. I should
not suppose from the descriptions of them that I have heard that
they would lead to any *real* spiritual growth—not among the young
at any rate. I think that there is every reason to believe that Whitefield, Methodism's great founder, would if he were now living
frown upon all such religious (?) demonstrations. In his time and
that of his greater coworker, Wesley, there was no other way of
gaining access to the people open to them. Good *may* be done, but
this good *must* be outweighed by the evil. Your description of the
different camp-meeting characters was both vivid and most evi-

dently faithful. I only wish that you had let it assume more the dimensions of "a regular book" than you did. I should imagine that such a meeting was *flirting made easy*. And certainly one can hardly find courage enough to blame the young men and women for yielding to a temptation which everything conspires to make almost irresistable. I know well enough that I could pretty safely predict my own course under such circumstances.

While you have camp-meetings, excursions, cousins' visits &c &c to tell of, my quiet, uneventful life furnishes few interesting topics for a letter. Not that there are no excursions, no girls, no Summer amusements here. There are plenty of them: Excursions on the river by moon-light &c, yacht regattas on the Sound, amateur concerts &c, and plenty of pretty girls. But I have been keeping away from all such simply because of disinclination to stir about much during the hot weather. I prefer reading quietly at home. One of the chief reasons why I don't go out into society more, however, is one which I have already mentioned to you. Coming here just a few months before leaving for Princeton, I have never become well acquainted with the people and am thus almost a stranger in my own home. During the Summer all whose acquaintance I care to cultivate are away from home, summering in the country or at some watering place. So I am well content to keep quiet and aloof from "society."

I let my inclination dictate each days occupation, sometimes reading, sometimes writing, sometimes reading some great orators productions aloud in the large church of which father is pastor and which adjoins our premises. I have in this way read several of Everett's best orations and Brougham's great speech on Parliamentary Reform delivered in the House of Lords when he held the office of Chancellor. It *is* a *very* great speech, one of the greatest I ever read.

The essay on Chatham which I purposed writing when I last wrote to you is now written and satisfies me ill. It is, I am afraid, rather a lame affair—some passages of it limp perceptibly and even painfully.

Has the Cow described to you his ride on horse-back, in a drizzle, with "a dear creature." It must have been a rich adventure. But that reminds me of your walk &c and, impatiently waiting to hear from you, I am, as ever,   Your sincere friend   Thos W. Wilson

ALS (Meyer Coll., DLC).
  [1] R. Bridges to WW, Aug. 6, 1878, and H. Woods, Jr., to WW, July 30, 1878, both ALS (WP, DLC).

Draft of an Unfinished Biographical Essay

[c. Aug. 10, 1878]

Daniel Webster and William Pitt.

Exercising their powers under entirely different conditions and at differing periods, Daniel Webster and William Pitt cannot be compared with each other. Did we look for some character in English history to whom we might with reason liken Webster, America's greatest statesman, his rank or prominence as a public man and many of his mental characteristics might recommend to us Chatham, England's most successful statesman and most consummate orator. Or we might select Burke, because on many important occasions he, like Webster, fought almost alone, after numerous failures, with little hope of ever seeing his own principles cut out in national policy, and yet, at the same time, claiming the esteem of his countrymen, the unbounded love and admiration of a large circle of devoted friends. There are, indeed, many English statesmen to whom Webster bears a much closer resemblance than he bears to William Pitt, though there is not one to whom he bears more than a very partial, incomplete, and unessential resemblance. But the names of Webster and Pitt might with propriety be placed side by side for purposes of contrast; because we find in them statesmen most characteristic of their respective countries; in order that through them we may gain, for purposes of comparison, a glance at the respective governments under which they lived, worked and won renown.

The period of the Revolution is the architectural and formative period of American history. It is a period whose annals bear high names of American history: Washington, Franklin, Hamilton, Jefferson, Adams a noble company of statesmen, born commanders. Following close upon the heels of this eventful and memorable era came the period of national development and progress; when our national life began to assume a unity and our national institutions added to themselves a definite and permanent form; when there sprang up a rank and file of public men[,] and great leaders were few. Then this American experiment matured into a determined reality and its governmental machinery was subject to wear and tear of daily work. In this period Daniel Webster lived, and of this period he is certainly, beyond a doubt, the most prominent figure. We live amid the moving scenes of a third period— a period of doubt and transition, [* * * *] and can thus look with some degree of impartiality upon those earlier times and judge of their leading spirits with some thought to this close view which is usually ascribed to Webster.

Viewed from this standpoint Daniel Webster seems to have come into history as an eminent example of that type of statesmanship which the institutions that have grown up under the shadow of the American Constitution are capable of fostering when at their best. He was a man of broader, though perhaps not deeper, genius than that of Calhoun or of Clay. The majestic flow of his eloquence vitally conveyed his life thoughts. He breathed the spirit of that Constitution whose every section and clause he revered and for whose integrity he fought; and yet the form of government to which that very Constitution had given rise was such as to prevent his powers from attaining that fullness of usefulness for which they were suited, such as to raise him high in honor and reputation without conferring upon him one iota of that power which would in any other country, belong of right to one of like endowments. He seemed in every way fit for political command yet he was not in any true sense a leader. His gift of brilliant and lucid statement rendered him a forcible expounder of principles but never drew a powerful party to his support. His very independence made it impossible to strictly identify him with any particular party.

Transcript of WWsh draft of speech (WP, DLC). This seems to be WW's first (and false) start on his essay, "William Earl Chatham," as the distinctive rulings by WW of the pages upon which he wrote this draft, and also that of the "Chatham," are not duplicated in any other WW document known to the editors.

Two Letters from Joseph Ruggles Wilson

My dearest son— Saratoga Springs [N. Y.] Friday 16th Aug 187[8].

Your welcome note came to hand on yesterday-evening:—and had a great deal of the home flavor about it.

I am sorry that you and Josie are in the hands of the dentist; but hope that you are not suffering—much. . . .

Your account of the services on Saturday afternoon would not flatter Mr. Payne's vanity, were he to see the same—yet it might do him a world of good. . . .

Kisses many to darling Mamma & to dearest Josie.

Yours as ever, "Father."

ALS (WP, DLC) with WWhw notation on env.: "Ans."

My dearest Son—   Bennington Centre, Vt., Aug 24 1878

Yrs. of Tuesday was received on yesterday Friday. . . . I am glad to hear that yr piece on Chatham is to undergo still another revision. It is very good, without alteration—but can be greatly improved by the process you propose, and the probable effect of which you express so happily: "more compactness because less breadth; more depth, because less surface[.]" One can write a far more interesting short essay on the thumb (say) than upon the entire body. . . .   Yours Most affy—Father

ALS (WP, DLC).

Notes on President McCosh's Syllabus for the History of Philosophy

[Sept. 11, 1878-June 18, 1879]

Hobbes A vigorous thinker but a very narrow thinker.

(a) The [*] sensationalist: 2 errors (a) All our ideas are got from sensation. The ideas we do not get from sensation are creations of fantasy and have no existence. (b) All our motive principles have regard to pleasure and pain.

(β) In following out this theory, the shutting out all ideas of thought would sustain the sensation but could not be derived from it.

It is not true that Locke was a sensationalist. Locke had two intellects and not one only, as Hobbes.

Hobbes, a utilitarian as well as a Sensationalist.

WWsh and WWhw notes on blank page opposite p. 112, James McCosh, *History of Philosophy From Notes Taken in the Lecture Room* (Princeton, 1878). (WW Library, DLC). This is one of many similar notes on blank pages or in the margins of this volume.

Three Classroom Notebooks

[Sept. 11, 1878-June 18, 1879]

Inscribed on cover page (WWhw): *"Greek Notes Prof Orris"*
Contents:

(a) WWsh notes with WWhw headings taken in Professor S. Stanhope Orris's senior Greek course, Sept. 11, 1878-June 18, 1879, along with WW's comparative word tables (in Greek, Latin, English, and German), extracts from Greek authors copied in Greek, and notes on Greek grammar and derivation written in Greek and shorthand.

(b) WWsh notes with WWhw headings taken in English literature course given by Professor James O. Murray, second and third terms, Jan. 2-June 18, 1879. Professor Murray lectured on Pope,

Swift, Hume, Gibbon, Dr. Johnson, Gray, Thomson, Collins, Byron, Wordsworth. A transcript of WW's sh notes on the Wordsworth lecture is printed at May 14, 1879.

(c) Four pages of loose notes, two recto and two verso, similar to contents previously described. On one of these pages is a quotation from Plato's *Republic* copied by WW in Greek and reproduced below.

[Sept. 11, 1878-April 9, 1879]

Inscribed on front page (WWhw): "History. *American Civilization.*"
Contents:

(a) WWhw and WWsh notes of a few lectures taken in Professor Charles W. Shields' history course during first and second terms of the academic year 1878-79 (Sept. 11, 1878-April 9, 1879). The Princeton catalogue for 1878-79 lists this course as being one both in English and American civilization and "European, American, and Universal History."

(b) WWsh lecture notes, with WWhw headings, taken in Professor Atwater's course, civil government, Sept. 14, 1878-Dec. 2, 1878. Transcripts of lectures 7 and 8 printed at Nov. 1 and 11, 1878, respectively.

[Sept. 11, 1878-June 18, 1879]

Inscribed on front page (WWhw): *"Science and Religion"*
Contents:

(a) WWsh and WWhw notes on Professor Shields' course, science and religion, taken during academic year Sept. 11, 1878-June 18, 1879.

(b) WWsh notes, with WWhw headings, taken in Professor Atwater's course in ethics, first term, Sept. 11-Dec. 18, 1878.

(WP, DLC). The last two notebooks made by folding pages 12" x 9 3/8", making pages 6" x 9 3/8".

From a Wilson Notebook

[c. Sept. 11, 1878]

WWhw entry in first classroom notebook just described. The following translation of this passage from Plato's *Republic* is by Robert F. Goheen:

"One must posit[, then,] that even if the just man experiences poverty, disease, or any other seeming evil, he will have these misfortunes finally work out
to his benefit, either during his lifetime or after death. For he surely will not
be overlooked by the gods, who has set himself earnestly to being just and,
through the pursuit of excellence, to becoming as much like a god as a man can."

The connective οὕτως ἄρα in the original text is omitted in Wilson's copy
[R. F. G.].

From the Minutes of the Liberal Debating Club

Sept. 21 [1878]

Meeting called to order at 8.15 P.M. Pres. Sheldon in the chair.
Messrs. Elsing, Godwin, and McCarter absent. Minutes of last
meeting read and approved. There being no miscellaneous business, Mr. Wilson read the concluding remarks in Cushing's Manual. Mr. Woods was excused from speaking, but read a speech
entitled 'Remarks Upon Ourselves.'

Mr. Wilson moved that the bill in regard to 'morality and civilization' be taken from the table.—Lost—

On motion of Mr. Wilson the meeting went into Com. of Whole
on a discussion of Pres. Hayes' administration after which the
following question was appointed for this night one week,—

Res: That the Anglo-Turkish convention was dishonorable to
the present English ministry—Wilson

Club then adjourned

E. W. Sheldon N. J. Pres.   Charles Talcott N. Y. Sec. of State.

From Wilson's Shorthand Diary

September 1878

26th Thursday. Spent the morning[,] after Murray's senior lecture upon Shakespere's Merchant of Venice, in the Library looking
among the books, and reading a life of Richard Cobden written
by one McGilchrist. It seems to be a book written with little taste[,]
spirit or method, but anything that gives the facts of such a man's
life and describes the tendencies of his days is extremely interesting. I look for inspiration to such a life as that of Cobden. This
afternoon, after sending off some copies of the *Princetonian* to
Wardlaw, I read some astronomy and appropriated this book for
more constant use. On account of a thunderstorm *and disinclination* I cut the recitation upon astronomy. After chapel I went to a
baseball meeting called in the interest of one Cuyler[1] of my class
who hopes to be elected president of the association. The meeting
was sprung upon us suddenly. The notice that the association

would meet after chapel was put upon the tree about noon. The usual time for this meeting and election has heretofore been the middle of October and everyone was taken by surprise by this sudden call. As soon as the meeting opened Talcott, at my suggestion, moved that the election be postponed until the 21st of October. He supported his motion in a particularly excellent speech. One of Cuyler's supporters endeavored to answer him but made a very weak case. He [Talcott] was supported by numerous good speakers and after feeble opposition his motion was carried by tremendous majority. Walked home from the meeting quite elated with our victory for a victory it was. One of the speeches made in favor of postponement of Cuyler's electioneering was by Dennis and he [Cuyler] has evidently lost almost all chance of election by this false and avidly "snide" move. This evening I spent some time in Woods' room. He is suffering from a very severe cold which if neglected might develop into pleurisy or pneumonia. He hopes to be improved rapidly however. After staying with him until some time after 8 o'clock, I came to my room and finished Morley's criticism upon Thomas Carlyle. A very discriminating criticism, making me vividly conscious of how sadly I have failed to understand and appreciate Carlyle heretofore. How could I learn to know Carlyle by reading only one of his works: the French Revolution? To know an author of genius one must read his every word. I have yet to learn Thomas Carlyle. See page 7, bottom. Thank God for health and strength.

¹ Cornelius C. Cuyler, '79.

Four Editorials in *The Princetonian*

[Sept. 26, 1878]

Some murmurs because of the subscription now being raised for the Foot Ball team have reached our ears. In view of the fact that the Treasurer of our Foot Ball Association last year reported a balance of $61, some seem to think that it is unreasonable to ask subscriptions for an organization which has escaped debt, with a margin of a few dollars. But scarcely a day passes that does not bring some new expense upon the Association. We are soon to play several of the neighboring Colleges and must be prepared to meet a portion of their expenses; the old suits are unservicable and the men must have new ones; this year we will have to play most of the games of the championship series either in New York or on the grounds of our opponents, and the aggregate of our travelling expenses will be very large. Only a portion of these expenses are paid by the Colleges whose teams we meet; some of them pay us nothing at all when we go to play them. Of course, then, we cannot start with an empty treasury. It is absolutely necessary that the Association have a couple of hundred dollars at once, and they confidently call on the students for small cash subscriptions.

✧

We come back, after the summer's vacation, to find that the zeal of Civil Service Reform has spread to our College officers, and sundry reforms have been instituted which move us to wonder, though hardly to admiration. We are inclined to look upon these late reforms in our civil service, which are quite as spasmodically effected as those of Mr. Hayes, as in every way as ridiculous as his. The men servants who last year did good service in the entries of the various dormitories, and proved such real comforts to the students, have been dismissed, and we are left to have all our work done by a few superannuated Irish women, who are required to do an immense amount of work in so short a time that they necessarily do it in a careless, partial manner, which is worse than absolute neglect. This change is said to be a step toward economy; we should prefer to denominate it an indication of parsimony. Perhaps if the room rent were lowered in proportion to the inferiority of the service we receive, we might hesitate to complain in such a case as this. But when our comfort is materially lessened and we are, at the same time, compelled to pay the same amount for accommodations, we are entitled to a word of protest. Our coal is to be brought to us in the winter, ashes removed, &c., but that is to be the extent of the service rendered us. We have been obliged to sign an agreement to pay the rent of the rooms we now occupy for the coming College year and are, therefore, forced to keep them, however much we are stinted as to the service for which we pay, however much is taken away from the comfort of our quarters. A false view of economy has led to the dismission of capable and trustworthy servants, and to a lessening of our comfort and convenience, without any corresponding lessening of expense.

✧

The disastrous close of the last base-ball season seems to have completely blighted the hopes which its opening had aroused. We do not believe with some that the failure of our nine was entirely due to any special mismanagement; that last year's managers were guilty of any unusual neglect. They were simply working out a system which had wrought mischief under their predecessors for several years; their failure was natural and, from the first, inevitable. In undertaking, therefore, to point out the errors of our base-ball administration in the past we are not attacking, not even specially blaming, those who have been connected with it. Our quarrel is with principles, not with the men who represented them. We are seeking, by explaining its inefficiency, to overthrow and supplant a system which has been working evil at least ever since the present Senior Class entered College, perhaps longer.

Hitherto it has been the custom of the base-ball autho[r]ities to announce each year, as winter drew nigh, that all candidates for positions on the University Nine should hand in their names, that the necessary training in the gymnasium might begin at once. Under this plan, candidates have almost always been volunteers, for little or no real, steady, systematic effort has been made to collect and develope the best material in the several classes. Men whom the experience of more than one season had proved to be utterly incapable of becoming good players were allowed to train, swelling the numbers with mere supernumeraries. Frivolous excuses, their laziness, or the mere difficulty of keeping them to their duty were considered sufficient grounds for allowing players of fine promise to give up their training. Those who gave some evidence of a willingness to learn and to undergo the proper discipline trained to no purpose for the simple reason that there was no one with energy enough to constantly supervise and direct their work. No one had sternness, determination, moral courage sufficient to reject at once those who refused to work faithfully. The results of such a system were natural and always ripened in due course. As the spring came on the nine was generally chosen from a limited number of perhaps inferior players, some of whom had not even applied for positions until the winter training was over and who had, consequently, none of the much-needed preparatory discipline. Then followed a season of listless practice and a series of disastrous games.

Now it is perfectly evident to all that an entirely new mode of action is an imperative necessity; and there can be no reason to hesitate as to the plan which might best be adopted. The voluntary system should be altogether done away with. The captain and president should seek out all the best players and all those who give any promise of good playing, and from these pick out the eighteen best for the preparatory work of the winter. It is just as real folly to allow any one and every one to train for a base-ball nine as it would be to let the weakest as well as the most powerful, the smallest as well as the largest, train for a boat crew. There is no good reason for believing that intelligent managers could not select the best material with comparative safety against mistake. From all but the Freshman class they could pick out the best men with but little trouble; and even in respect of the Freshmen there need be no reason for mistake in the matter of selection. Natural talent has much more to do with good base-ball playing than with excellence in any other equally scientific game, and managers could soon decide upon the capabilities of any new man to whom they might have their attention called during the autumn series of games between the classes. Selection would be a comparatively easy task, if undertaken with painstaking vigilance and energy. Nor would there be as much difficulty in getting the men selected to train as might be anticipated. They would be relieved of the responsibility of putting themselves forward and the very fact that they had been selected would inspire them with the hope which is necessary to all such work. Thus also the apparently formidable difficulty of securing hard and constant work during the winter and real, energetic practice in the spring would seem to be obviated. The personal influence of the managers would in this matter count for much. If the training did not go steadily on, it would be because the captain and president did not daily guide and encourage the men in their work, punishing with immediate dismission any continued shirking of duty on the part of any.

In past years the discipline of the nine finally selected has been lax because the winter's training had failed to develop enough men to take the places of those who proved themselves weak players. The voluntary system does not induce a sufficient number of men to sacrifice their immediate personal comfort so far as to train untiringly. Their training is a half-chosen work and many of them have no reason to believe that the managers think favorably of their chances of getting on the nine. They are discouraged from the first and soon give up, and the number of trainers decreases. In the spring practice games gross and inexcusable errors must, therefore, be overlooked. There is no one to take the negligent or weak player's place and he must continue to weaken the nine. The rule should be—and it should be a rule which is never under any circumstances departed from—that in practice, as well as in match games, every avoidable error is taken note of, and continued carelessness followed by dismission. But, of course, no such rule can be put into force unless several good substitutes are kept constantly in training, and for all effective work this must be done.

Now it is plain that every observation we have made in this attempt to throw some light upon a subject of some perplexity points to the patent fact that *everything* depends upon the character of the captain and president. With a good captain and an efficient president success is no longer a matter of doubt. A good captain gave us a brilliant success in foot-ball. In 1873 a good captain gave us success in base-ball. The old nine chooses the captain and the only duty of the College at large lies in the selection of the best president within their choice. It is not sufficient that he be well acquainted with the game. The majority of men in College are sufficiently familiar with the rules of the game to fill the office. The president must, above all things else, be a man of unbiased judgment, energy, determination, intelligence, moral courage, *conscience*. These are indeed high requirements and we can at best seek the man who possesses them in as high a degree as any. None other can command success.

❖

Foot-Ball.

In a late number of *Littell's Living Age*, there appeared, copied from an English magazine, an article which condemned Rugby foot-ball as most brutal and dangerous. The picture thus drawn is really horrible, and one likely to prejudice the ignorant against the game. But according to our American standard of experience, the account is most untrue. Some among us, who often look on but never play, believe that the danger is very great, and many outsiders, who witnessed the games last autumn, think, as did our English friend, that the law should forbid such rough and dangerous sport.

We speak to men who reason, in this way, for we will need all possible support this year, and in order to secure such support, all croakers in our midst must be silenced.

Rugby has a great advantage over the association game in the substitution of "tackling" for "bucking," and any one who has experienced both ways of reaching the ground, must prefer an embrace and easy tumble to the violent jar and fall following a hard blow from an enemy's shoulder.

But is Rugby, as it is at present played, too dangerous to be countenanced? Players disposed to harm one another can easily do so in any active game, and perhaps in foot-ball more than in any other, because of its greater activity, but a gentlemanly spirit has always prevailed in the foot-ball contests here in Princeton, and such a spirit is sufficient protection against intentional injury. If it is the English player's object to lay up as many of his antagonists as possible, it certainly is not our practice here. There is no reason why a man should be other than a gentleman while he plays.

Of course there is roughness connected with this, as with all active games, but a man of moderate strength and common sense can so take care of himself as to come off with few, if any, severe knocks. Granted that English insurance companies pay much for foot-ball accidents, need we cry out against the game until we have some such tangible proof of its horrors? It is not strange that gentlemen who witnessed our games last fall were shocked at their seeming roughness and danger, but any of us who played can testify that the real danger is far less than the apparent. To prove this we need only say that in our four principal foot-ball-playing Colleges the men severely injured last fall were very few. Indeed, there are only two principal causes of harm to players: the one proceeding from intention, the other from ignorance of the rules.

Inexperienced players naturally engage most roughly in the game. Skill makes a player more careful, both of himself and of others, since it is recognized as dishonorable to injure an opponent in order to stop his playing. Our last game with Harvard was unusually rough and spirited. Why, then, were no players hurt save one who strained an ankle? Simply because a gentlemanly spirit prevailed throughout the entire game. If this principle is recognized, and if players possess a moderate amount of skill, injuries in foot-ball are not of frequent occurrence.

After all, is there not danger in everything we do for exercise? Does not the gymnasium have its perilous feats? Is not danger present in the base-ball and cricket fields? If anybody is inclined to give up foot-ball, or to use his influence against it, because its players are likely to receive an occasional strain, let him consider the great amount of exercise to be gained by playing one hour daily, an exercise which is most beneficial because it is in the open air, and affords so much relaxation and enjoyment. There is capital mental practice, too, connected with the game, for to play well requires quick thought and cool judgment.

Princeton has had fair success in the past, and we must work hard during the present autumn, in order that we may keep what honor and excellence we now possess. To accomplish this end it is necessary for every one who can play to engage in the game—at any rate, let no one hold back his support because of supposed danger. Whoever has fairly tried the game must acknowledge that the exercise, if not the sport, justifies the incurrence of all danger connected therewith.

Printed in *The Princetonian*, III (Sept. 26, 1878), 64-66, 70-71.

From Wilson's Shorthand Diary

[September] 29th Sabbath. An uneventful day of quiet. Rose about 7½ o'clock and had breakfast at 9. Heard a sermon in the chapel from Dr. Duffield. Spent the afternoon writing letters to mother, cousin Hattie,[1] and sisters. In church at night had hard fight to keep awake. Last Friday I spent the morning laying out the football ground. Saturday afternoon I spent reading Cobden's Life, and superintending the playing of football on the University ground. I have done little or no reading since last Thursday. I intend this as a diary of thoughts and record of reading, rather than anything else. Thank God for health and strength.

[1] Harriet Augusta Woodrow.

A Biographical Essay

[Oct. 1878]

William Earl Chatham

Beneath Westminster Abbey's arched roof, with commanding mien, haughty features, and gesture of authority, stands the statue of Chatham. Visitors to the venerable old church may see in the hard lines of the cold marble the lifeless yet life-like reproduction of the striking form of the great statesman; but to all who have learned, in the pages of history, to comprehend the character and work of Chatham, this piece of stone must seem to fall very far short of bringing before their imaginations the real person of the great Commoner. A skillful sculptor might trace the lines of cunning policy and of secret scheming, the habitual air of authority upon the face of a Metternich, and we would recognize the man himself in his effigy; he might chisel the marks of cruel purpose, of uncurbed and defiant ambition, of pitiless despotism upon the spare visage of a Richelieu and we could wish for no better reminder of the man; he might preserve the deep-cut wrinkles that spoke of thought, the firmly-set mouth that indicated an inflexible determination, upon the open countenance of a Hampden; but the marble must have the warmth of life infused into it by the hand of God before it could resemble the dwelling of Chatham's high-wrought, passionate, many-sided nature.

It is indeed the diversity of his genius which first strikes us as we look back to the elder Pitt. In him consummate powers kept company with small weaknesses, strong wisdom stood side by side with weak folly, truthfulness and earnestness were contrasted with affectation and pedantry. To the careless student of history Pitt's character, made up as it was of qualities the very opposites of each other, might at first seem to have been inconsistent with itself. But it was a character of great power, because in reality of singular unity. His many talents, his capacity for good, his capacity for evil, his wisdom, his folly, his strength, his weakness, apparently at war among themselves, were reconciled and brought into harmony by the concentrating power of strong convictions. Prior to a thoughtful investigation of the history of his times, however, there would seem to be some cause for surprise that such a man as Pitt should have risen to the head of the state when he did; for few men's tempers ever clashed more roughly with their surroundings, ever sympathized less with the tastes and tendencies of the day, than did the temper of the great Commoner. Indeed he harmonized with his age in nothing but in affectation, and even his affectation had an earnestness and a frankness about it which did not belong to the all-pervading affectation of the society around him. He was in everything enthusiastically earnest, and his age laughed at earnestness; he was vehement, and his age affected coldness and indifference; he was sternly virtuous, scorning corruption, and his age was skeptical of virtue, nursing corruption; he had eager, burning beliefs and was actuated by a warm love for principle, and his age delighted in doubtings and questionings, was guided by no principle save that of expediency; he was used constantly and confidently to appeal to the higher, brighter, purer instincts of human nature, and his age doubted the existence of any such instincts, nay, even argued from its own experience that all human nature was low and pulseless. He stood, in fact, almost alone—above the masses who, from sheer admiration, supported him, and in their enthusiasm idolized him; separated by all his tastes and sympathies from those classes of society with which he was naturally thrown by virtue of his high public station.

That a man thus isolated from his fellows should wield undisputed power over them seems at first beyond explanation. But as we study his character more closely the mystery which hangs around his ability to exercise unquestioned authority over those who were entirely out of sympathy with him clears rapidly away. The elements of his power are not far to seek. They lay almost altogether within himself. Outwardly he was every inch a leader. Every attitude, every gesture, each play of feature, each tone of voice bore witness of a will that must be master. And men were speedily convinced of the depth and strength of the nature thus outwardly shadowed forth. They bowed to a will which itself bent to no obstacle; they feared, even while they sneered at, the personal purity which gave such a keen edge to his attacks upon corrupt opponents. Their hearts instinctively warmed toward a man whose patriotism was so real. Selfish policies fell beneath the onsets of a man whose great intellect gave such resistless force to the convictions he so boldly avowed.

Pitt's nature was so passionate as to be almost tragic, rendering his career an essentially dramatic one. Passion indeed was the ground-work of his character; and because, led on by ardor, he trod steadily onward toward the ends he had marked out for himself, the name of Chatham has become to Englishmen a synonym of the highest statesmanship. And certainly, if we conceive of statesmanship as being that resolute and vigorous advance towards the realization of high, definite, and consistent aims which issues from the unreserved devotion of a strong intellect to the service of the state and to the solution of all the multiform problems of public policy, Pitt's statesmanship was of the highest order. His devotion to his country's service was as intense as it was entire; and the intellect whose every power he brought to bear upon the direction of her affairs compassed its duty with a vigor commensurate with its colossal proportions. To enquire why Pitt so completely identified himself with the fortunes of England would be an invidious task. The motives which prompt to great deeds are often as hidden as the deeds themselves are conspicuous. Pitt's self-love was boundless, and small men can, therefore, see nothing in his high aims but an inordinate desire to gratify ambition, to exalt self. But to those who believe that there is some nobility in human nature, and especially to those who can see how small a part of his real character Pitt's egotism constituted, his ardent, absorbing patriotism is sufficient cause for the belief that there was much of true disinterestedness in his great career.

Each quality of Pitt's mind bespoke the ardor of his nature. Even his affectation and his pedantry, like his love and determination and pride, had caught the hue of passion. It was impossible for such a man to espouse any cause with coldness. With him every act must be an act of warm enthusiasm. His mind was strong and clear, his will was unswerving, his convictions were uncompromising, his imagination was powerful enough to invest all plans of national policy with a poetic charm, his confidence in himself was implicit, his love for his country was real and intense. Of course, then, he entered into the realities of public life with all the vigor of a large and earnest soul, with all the keen interest imparted by a vivid imagination, and it is not strange that his policy was well-defined and determined, straightforward and brilliant. The startling, far-reaching results of his administration, moulding the future history of the world, were such as appealed to the admiration and won the approbation of a people the very marrow of whose nature is a spirit of adventure, enterprise, conquest. What could be more impressive than a policy which, in winning India for the English Crown, built a great empire in the far East; in driving the French from America, made our great republic a possibility in the far West; and, in lending constant and effective aid to Prussia's great Frederick, prepared the destiny of her greater Bismarck? Such having been the work of the elder Pitt, Englishmen may justly regard him as high among the greatest statesmen of a great race. And yet his errors were many and grave. They were, however, such as are incident upon a policy whose authors seek, with whole-souled ardor, with keen enthusiasm, to carry out great principles in all their integrity. Such a policy is always admirable in the abstract, but, in practice, is seldom safe. In a free government, founded upon public opinion, the governmental machinery is so nicely balanced, opposite parties, opposing forces of thought, generally exercise powers so nearly equal, that great principles must be worked out cautiously, step by step, seldom attaining triumphant ascendency by a course of uninterrupted success—by only a few bold and rapid strokes. Public opinion must not be outstripped, but kept pace with. Time, indeed, has traced out to their end all the greater lines of policy which, in their beginnings, bore indications of the strokes of Pitt's decided hand. But he had lain in his grave many years before some of the most prominent measures which he had advocated were carried out in their fulness; and during his lifetime, while he was still a power in the state, even his towering influence fell powerless when he sought to force his country to follow the paths of foreign policy which he had cleared for her, and which he had shown to be the only roads to honor and safety. The enormous strain which war had brought upon the Treasury was thought to be cause for serious alarm, and the reaction thus brought about, seconded by the sinister influence of an unscrupulous king, thrust a ruinous peace upon the country. Pitt left the Cabinet to be re-stricken by the disease which finally sapped the strength of his imperial intellect. His life drew rapidly toward its close; but he had done enough to set a seal to his fame— enough to mark *that* as the highest type of statesmanship which, with conscientious purity, by an undeviating course, with cool judgment and prompt determination, with a bright hope and a passionate patriotism, overpowering opposition, subordinating party to national interests, constantly and confidently seeks to build a great policy upon broad, deep, homogeneous principles. Such, with all its small follies and minor inconsistencies, despite disfiguring arrogance and overbearing pride, was the statesmanship of William Pitt.

If, because his statesmanship was whole-souled and dazzlingly successful, we do not wonder that William Pitt has been considered worthy of a place among the very first of English statesmen, still less can we be surprised that he has been called the first of Parliamentary orators. If the passionate intensity which entered so largely into the texture of his character lent so much of force, so much brilliant boldness, to his plans of administration, what masterly power must it have imparted to his oratory! Passion is the pith of eloquence. But it alone cannot make the consummate orator; for while it gives strength, it may be rugged and cumbersome. Imagination must be present to give it wings and a graceful flight. And one of the most striking features of Pitt's mind was "a poetic imaginativeness" which set his words fairly aglow with beauty. While vivid passion blazed out in his orations, the reality of the convictions he so fearlessly uttered hid the exaggeration of his diction, transfiguring all that was bombastic and ungraceful, and clothing with real grace his theatrical airs. Unfortunately our only trustworthy information concerning his oratorical powers comes from meagre tradition. Those who had seen his noble figure in striking action, his eagle eye alight with the thoughts that stirred within him, have left us only some scanty outlines of his more brilliant thoughts and most memorable flights of rhetoric. The main bodies of all his great speeches, those thoughts which constituted the warp and woof of his masterly statements of political truths and his moving appeals in behalf of a broad, patriotic, and consistent state policy, are irretrievably lost to us. But, aside from the unanimous testimony of his contemporaries, the fragmentary utterances which we know to have fallen from his own lips bear ample witness to his unrivalled powers, being laden, even for us, with much of their old potency. Even upon the printed page, the echo of his impassioned accents seems yet to linger about his words. Although in his youthful studies of Demosthenes he had failed to catch the great Athenian's purity of style, he recognized, as the movings of a kindred spirit, his burning vehemence. Athens had at times responded as one man to the rapid, vehement, cogent sentences of Demosthenes; the British Parliament, the English nation, harkened with glad eagerness to the organ tones of Pitt's eloquence, and dared not disobey.

William Pitt was the second of that long line of great commoners of which gifted, wise, unscrupulous Robert Walpole was the first, and which has moulded English policy down to the day of shrewd, fickle, brilliant, plausible Benjamin Disraeli. In one respect Pitt resembled the now exalted Jew: he had an unhesitating, almost boundless confidence in himself, in the wisdom of his own aims. But Beaconsfield loves and has confidence in himself alone; Pitt loved and trusted the English people as well—for he was himself an Englishman!

With Pitt's acceptance of an earldom not only his official power but also much of his innate greatness passed away. Disease had unmanned him, and he refused to aid his country at a time of sorest need, thus, in a moment of folly, well nigh undoing the great work of a memorable lifetime. William Pitt was a noble statesman; the Earl of Chatham was a noble ruin. But in his death we catch a faint glimmer of his old manhood. Under the deepening shadow of a gathering storm we obtain a last glimpse of Chatham, as he stands, himself a wreck, holding up before a blind Ministry a picture of the dark ruin which was awaiting them. With some of his old haughtiness the austere old man rises to answer one who had dared to reply to him, and falls, never to rise again.

Printed in *The Nassau Literary Magazine,* xxxiv (Oct. 1878), 99-105. This essay was designated the Magazine's prize essay. There is an undated WWsh draft in WP, DLC, the transcript of which shows it to have been WW's first extended draft.

From Hiram Woods, Jr.

Dear Tommy,   Baltimore, Oct. 1, 1878.

I arrived home all right side up last evening. The telegram you sent had reached Pa about 2:30, and I found that he had kept the matter entirely to himself. Today I am feeling much better. I have spent the day quietly at home. . . .

Please report to the Alligators[1] the continued convalescence of the disaffected member, and to all enquiring for me report improvement. Specially remember me to all those most closely connected with my sickness.   Yours Affectionately, Hiram Woods, Jr.

ALS (WP, DLC).
[1] An eating club, formed in 1876, which WW joined the next year. Other members between 1877 and 1879, all of the Class of 1879, were Dennis, W. Earl Dodge, Farr, Godwin, McCarter, Pitney, Stewart, Talcott, and Woods. Also four not previously identified: Philippus W. Miller, Elwood O. Roessle, Edward H. Trotter, and Jacob R. Wright.

From the Minutes of the American Whig Society

Whig Hall October 4, 1878

. . . Whereas, at a meeting of the Senate held June 19th 1878 a resolution (in responce to an overture from the House, dated June 7, 1878) was passed, providing for the appointment of a Committee of the Senate to cooperate with a similar Committee of the House in endeavoring to raise an endowment fund, and to draft such amendments to the Constitution as may be necessary, therefore

Resolved, That a committee of six be appointed: and that they be empowered to take whatever action, they may deem necessary in the premises. Weed . . .[1]   c-d

---

[1] WW was not appointed to this committee. For the committee's report, see American Whig Society Minutes, Nov. 15, 1878.

Eight Editorials in *The Princetonian*

[Oct. 10, 1878]

We call the attention of '79, as we did that of '78, to the matter of Class Day Elections. It has become the custom here to crowd all the work which devolves upon the Seniors aside of their regular College studies into second and third terms, instead of getting as much class business as possible off their hands during the comparative leisure of first term. We urge upon '79, therefore, the advantage of holding Class Day Elections this term. Delay can secure no advantage. Intelligent selections can be made now as well as later; and much electioneering can be prevented by early elections. We believe that the exercises of Class Day will be much more entertaining and creditable to the class, if its representatives be chosen now, than if the choice of them were postponed until next term.

❖

Although the question as to the proper mode of electing the editors of our College periodicals, which was so much mooted during the last term, has apparently ceased to interest as it did then, it is none the less of vital importance, and demands an immediate and authoritative answer from the College. The present editors of the *Lit.* and *Princetonian* have therefore determined to bring the matter before the College at the meeting which is to take place on the 21st of Oct., for the purpose of electing a president of the Base Ball Association. After the election there will be a favorable opportunity of ascertaining the sense of the College in this matter. A carefully sketched plan will then be submitted by the *Lit.* and *Princetonian* boards, to be discussed and voted upon. We thus give previous notice in order that all may have the matter before their minds, and prepare themselves to vote dispassionately and intelligently.

The Inter-Collegiate Literary Association is almost at its last gasp. It has determined to give certificates, instead of prizes, to successful competitors in the coming contests. Lack of cash has been met and overcome by the method which is seemingly now in favor with the American people: the issue of *fiat* money, in the shape of certificates, in lieu of prizes. The crisis has been passed, and passed unfavorably. The Association, always sickly enough, has now gone into a decline from which it can never recover. The one plausible plea for its continued existence can now no longer be urged. For it has always been the watch-word of the Association's defenders that its prizes would serve as aids to the prosecution of further studies on the part of those who gained them; and now these prizes are no longer offered. Surely then these contests no longer accomplish any real good or serve to advance scholarship.

Our representative in the meeting at which this suicidal step was taken, strenuously opposed himself to any such action, suggesting the postponement of the contests until April, in order that time might be given for the collection of the requisite funds; but an overwhelming majority insisted upon sealing the doom of the organization.

Now we cannot bring ourselves to mourn on account of the approaching dissolution of this decrepit institution. It is a notorious fact that the students of this College have long looked upon it with the utmost indifference, if not with hostility; and the only wonder is that we have remained within it so long. At the December meeting of the Princeton branch of the Association the motion will be made that we withdraw after the approaching contests; and there can be little doubt about the fate of this motion. The only doubt is as to whether or not there will be any Association to withdraw from.

The severe defeat which '81 experienced last Saturday at the hands of the Sophomore nine of Lafayette furnishes food for thought, and affords us a text from which to preach the Base Ball doctrines which we have recently been upholding. The Lafayette nine was an unusually strong one; but, with the possible exception of the pitcher, its men were, individually, no better players than our own Sophomores. Their strength lay in *discipline,* in the way they supported each other, in organization. It is said that it was no disgrace to the Sophomores that they were beaten by so excellent a team. True—yet very false. It might be said, with equal color of plausibility, that it was no disgrace to our University nine to be defeated by such a nine as Harvard's of last year. Defeat does not necessarily imply disgrace, by any means. But disgrace *is* brought home to us when the causes of our defeat appear. The principal cause was not a lack of fine material, but the want of firm discipline. And in this the Sophomores were brought into discredit on last Saturday. Their class contains as good players as any on the Lafayette nine, but their nine did not give evidence of discipline and training, as did that of their opponents. The present Junior nine has worked and trained together more than any of the other class nines, and for that reason, more than any other, now stands nearest to the class championship. In short a *"scrub"* nine, even if made up of the best players, is always weaker than a nine composed of inferior players who have long and faithfully played together. We have never seen a Princeton nine in which the men knew how to support each other properly. Until we do see such a nine victory will be a stranger to us. Natural talent alone will never win us a game. This is the special lesson taught by last Saturday's game.

✧

Princeton has long felt the need of an elective course in Anglo-Saxon, it is owing to the spirit and energy of Professor Hunt that this need will be felt no longer. Prof. Hunt has volunteered to instruct a class in this branch. The course will consist of one hour a week for two years. It is begun in Senior year and continued during the post graduate course. Any Senior entering the class is expected to pursue this branch as a post graduate, if he returns to Princeton as a student after his graduation. Those who do not return are under no obligation to continue the study.

During the first term of Senior year instruction will be given in elementary grammar; during the second and third terms, "a reader, an Anglo-Saxon version of the Gospels, and other light literature" will form the basis of study. At the end of Senior year the student will have become thoroughly instructed in the fundamental principles of grammar, and enabled to read the language with readiness.

A wider field is entered during the second year; comparative grammar is investigated and the etymological relation of the language to English is considered. The Epics, Caedmon and Beowulf, together with other works extant in the original are read and criticized. When the entire course has been completed, it is Prof. Hunt's opinion that each student will have such a thorough knowledge of the subject as will render him capable of teaching it.

When the plan, which has been briefly outlined, was laid before Professor Marsh,[1] the eminent Philologist, and his opinion asked regarding it, he said that the course was the best possible which could be pursued. Thus it is evident that we will have as good opportunities for entering upon the study of Anglo-Saxon as can anywhere be found. And we believe that the introduction of this elective will be a source of great profit to the student of philology and literature, that it will be attended with great success, and be the means of effecting a broader culture.

[1] George Perkins Marsh, man of affairs and author of two books on philology that were widely studied by Wilson's college generation.

✦

During the latter part of this term and the first part of next, Seniors have the opportunity of enjoying what is, to some minds, the best joke of their College course. Chapel Stage in the abstract is certainly humorous, but in the concrete we are able to discover the serious side of this old and venerable institution. Viewed as the first and only compulsory appearance of the Princeton student, it embodies the leading elements of humor. But when we call to mind the hurried palpitation of individual hearts, the violent trembling of individual knees, and the general confusion of individual minds, Chapel Stage seems to have a pathetic phase.

It is the poor and friendless, however, who suffer most from Chapel Stage. The rich man can buy, the popular man can borrow, an oration. To the poor and unpopular it means eight hundred and forty words which must be either cribbed, or written at the expense of many forcible expressions which do not find a place in the orator's manuscript. It is true that there is some comfort in cribbing; there are innumerable Encyclopaedias, Reviews, and other books of reference which are great sources of comfort and legitimate sources of thought. Originality is not expected; for, you know, when ideas once appear in print, they become public property. Yet the necessary change of style from the essayical to the oratorical requires no little ingenuity and involves no little labor. Some men are ambitious enough to attempt a new arrangement of ideas; but such rash ambition is rare.

Chapel Stage is a truly wonderful institution; for it performs in one exercise what some other Colleges waste four years in accomplishing. No one will have the temerity to say, however, that the good obtained from Princeton's course in oratory is, either in amount or degree, less than that obtained from the course of any other College in the land. To assert such a thing would be ingratitute indeed. Why is it that so many Princeton graduates become eminent in the pulpit or at the bar? Why is it that a Princeton student has never been known to lose his self-command in the presence of a female seminary? Why is it—but we pause. You have anticipated the answer, it is—Chapel Stage.

We would say, in conclusion, that the public derive no little benefit from Chapel Stage; for poor speakers are so badly frightened in the first oratorical effort, that they never make a second attempt to address the public. Can any one, then, contemplating the great good done by this institution, fail to wish for the future prosperity of Chapel Stage?

Dry.

No doubt every under-graduate is pleased with most of the improvements which have been made in and around the campus, during the last few years. There is one subject, however, which seems to have been entirely overlooked. While Lake McCosh has lent its placid waters to beautify the grounds and cleanse the students of the College of New Jersey, there has been a lamentable neglect of that time-renowned institution known as the Pump. In former days the campus boasted of three pumps. These were neither remarkable for their beauty nor for the excellence of the beverage which they furnished, but the water obtained from two of them was at least drinkable. Now, but one solitary pump remains. This we could endure, had not the quality of the water deteriorated in a geometrical ratio with the decrease in the number of pumps. Every year impurities have *crept* in, until it would be almost a straining of conscience to say that fifty per cent of the liquid which flows from the nozzle of the pump at the eastern end of north,[1] is water. The need of a good College pump is manifest. Students will get thirsty, and if good water cannot be obtained readily on the campus, there are places not very far off where something—possibly stronger than water—to allay thirst can be procured. "Committee on Morals and Discipline," please note this. The present pump, with all its failings, is in constant use at all hours of the day and night. What better argument could be adduced in favor of procuring a new one more capable of satisfying the wants of the College community? Besides this, the water now furnished cannot fail to injure, sooner or later, those who drink it. But to remove even a poor pump, and not replace it with a better, would be only making bad matters worse. We speak, therefore, for a new pump. The question of expense ought not to hinder such a request being complied with; and there certainly are springs in or near the campus, where good water can be obtained, if the proper means were employed. If the Board of Trustees do not like to disfigure the campus with a common pump, let them give us a handsome affair—an ornament not unworthy of its surroundings. What a place of resort such a pump would become! How many weighty questions would there be discussed! Pumps have played no unimportant part in the history of our country, and who knows what influence a good College pump would have, physically, socially, morally, on a College community? By all means, gentlemen of the Trustees, let us have a new pump, where we can obtain pure water. The thanks of the present generation shall be yours, and it may be that, in the time to come, venerable Alumni will come back to their *Alma Mater*, and as they quaff a cup of the clear, cool water, they will think of the good days "when this old pump was young."

1 Nassau Hall, called North College or Old North.

The I. C. L. A.

At a meeting of the Inter-Collegiate Literary Association, held on September 27th, in New York, it was decided that no money prizes should be given to contestants, this year, but written certificates. Provided, however, the debt of the association be paid—a debt of $1500—any surplus that might then be in the treasury would be equally divided among those taking honors. The treasury is now empty; the prospects of its ever being filled again are very few and insignificant. Mrs. Astor promises an endowment of $500 a year, if only the debt is paid off; in event of which, the association may hope again to give a moneyed interest to her prizes. Again, it was decided that not even a certificate should be given in essay or mental science this year, as the prizes in those departments for last year are not yet paid. Such were the most important conclusions arrived at directly in the Council of Regents.

There came up, however, a question for discussion which involves more than any of the above questions, in that the future prospects of the association may be more or less positively gleaned from it. After discussing finances for awhile, a motion was made at the instigation of the Secretary, to postpone the time of examination some three months. By that time the debt might be paid, and a moneyed value attached to the prizes. This question evolved [evoked] a few signs of life from the Regents, who, on the ground that such a postponement would bring complete ruin upon the association, voted it down. The question was therefore satisfactorily settled to the minds of all present, that the association would live, and certificates should be given.

But, in face of the fact that the Regents believe they have pursued the best course, the arguments for a postponement are not to be set aside. Perhaps a postponement would be its death; would reveal to the world the poverty-stricken condition of the association; would discourage men from working, both through fear that a postponement meant the ruin of the organization, or, that men had other things which they counted upon doing during the time intervening between now and next March. But such arguments react upon themselves, and mean nothing. An organization which cannot postpone its exercises for three months without dying, cannot certainly expect to live and pursue the policy adopted by the Council of Regents on the 27th of last September. What, pray, can the certificate of such a corporation be worth? It certainly cannot be doubted that the greater part of the interest excited among students by the association was the influence of their liberal prizes. It was this value which was first considered and made it worth while to work. To this was added last year the *certificate*. As a flourishing institution, its seal and stamp lent additional value to the prize. But take away the moneyed value, give a certificate from a foundering institution, and the interest first among students is lost, and then the reputation also of the institution. To have had a valuable prize beside the certificate—to have honorably discharged its past debts, would not have been the death of the I. C. L. A. The interest indeed which would have been lost by those who had other things to do, if not speedily restored in view of a handsome prize, would have been quickly substituted by the entrance into competition of many others who are now driven away by the puny advantages they offer. Does it take more than the sagacity of a Pythian oracle to predict the association's death, as it is? To be sure, in oratory, more or less inducement will always remain so long as there is speaking before a large house; but to have destroyed, above all, the contest for essays, and not even give a certificate here, which costs nothing, eliminates just so much interest from being manifested in the maintenance of the association. Taken altogether, the prospects are not of the fairest, and cannot be, by making a departure so manifestly to its own hurt.

The question also of our withdrawal, so often mooted, might be mentioned. We are asked to support the institution, and have supported it, ever since it has left our hands. Repeatedly we have expressed our disapproval of its procedure. We are not in full sympathy with it—our prizeman has not been paid—it continues on a course which cannot but be opposed to our wishes and the wishes of those from among us who were so zealous in its formation. Is it not, therefore, advisable at this juncture quietly to withdraw, and let the association pursue its own line of action, while we pursue ours?

Printed in *The Princetonian*, III (Oct. 10, 1878), 75-81.

From Joseph Ruggles Wilson

My darling T.   Wilm[ingto]n [N. C.] Oct 10 78

Yesterday I returned from Charleston where I left yr dear Mother and Josie with Bella as her nurse. The Dr. has pronounced her case as having no alarming complications.[1] She will remain for a few weeks and no doubt return O. K.

Upon getting home I found a dunning letter from Mr. Harris Treasr of yr. concern enclosing bill, and insisting upon immediate payment. I immediately sent the check demanded,—without comment.

Yr. last to Mother I will send down to her to-day. Her address is "care of G. L. Pratt, No. 6, Beaufair street, Charleston, S. C."

I am as usual.   With great love, your Father.

P. S. I wrote you a note before leaving N. Y. informing you of the train I wd. take, homeward bound.

ALS (WP, DLC) with WWhw notation on env.: "Ans."
[1] The nature of JWW's illness is not clear from the evidence. Bella was a family servant.

From the Minutes of the Liberal Debating Club

Oct. 19 [1878]

Meeting called to order at 8.00 P.M. Pres. Sheldon in the Chair; absent messrs. Elsing, Godwin, McCarter. There being no miscellaneous business Mr. Woods read sections 59 and 60 of Chapter 5th of Cushing's manual. Mr. Wilson was excused from speaking and handing in speech for criticism.

The following question past passed [*sic*] its 1st and 2nd:

Res. That the Anglo-Turkish Convention was dishonourable to the present English ministry—Wilson

The meeting then went into com. of whole, on the above, and reported favorably.

Miscellaneous business:

Res. That section *first* of Article *second* of the Constitution be amended, by striking out the word 'eight' and inserting the word 'ten'—Woods.

The resolution of [blank] passed its first and second readings. On motion of Mr. Wilson the society went into com. of whole. Carried—The com. reported favorably.

The following subject was proposed for discussion this night, one week—Richard Brinsely Sheridan

The meeting adjourned at 10 P.M.

E. W. Sheldon N. J.   Pres.   Charles Talcott N. Y.   Sec. of State

Two Letters from Joseph Ruggles Wilson

My dearest Son—   [Wilmington, N. C.] Saturday, Oct. 19 78
Your Mother writes me a note every day. This morning I received one which informs me that her trial is almost over, and *successfully* over. She hopes to be out of bed to-day or to-morrow:—and probably will get home about the 29th of this month, the day after my return from Synod at Goldsboro. The blessed prospect now is that the dearest lady living will quite regain her health and begin to have that enjoyment in life which her virtues deserve.

I am "rocking along" as usual—trying to improve my preaching. I have been more successful than usual in speaking without manuscript—which I attempt each night at 2n Church—and will continue at my second service during the winter. There is a positive luxury in speaking—free—when the machine is working easily & oilily.

How are you progressing in yr. studies, dear one? I trust that this yr. last year will be your best year. Give close attention to each part of the curriculum. Not many who have neglected their classroom recitations have been known to become eminently successful in after life. But I trust you every way.

May the Lord abundantly bless and keep you, my precious son. Love *Him* more and more.   Your affectionate Father

My darling son—   Wilmington, [N. C.] Oct 22, '78
I have received the no. of the "Lit" you were kind enough to forward me. Your prize essay is just admirable. I read it with equal care and pleasure. I offer you my sincere gratulations and also my

hearty thanks. It will be altogether your own fault should you fail to become a great writer. Your imagination, only, needs especial cultivation. I mean by this that you ought to practise upon *illustrative* argument. The present piece is not deficient in this respect, or very little so. But, look into Macaulay, and you will know what I mean—although he is too exuberant in this direction.

I enclose $5.00 as part pay for the pleasure you have given me and the paternal pride you have awakened. . . .

Believe me, dearest of sons,
Your affectionate Father

ALS (WP, DLC).

Two Editorials in *The Princetonian*

[Oct. 24, 1878]

A rumor has reached our ears to the effect that '82 expects to organize a class foot ball team for the purpose of playing the Freshmens' teams of other colleges; but we refuse to believe the report. We have on several occasions watched the Freshmen's foot ball practice and cannot see any possibility of their forming any team of more than ordinary strength; and we are sure that they would not risk Princeton's foot ball reputation by going into the field against other college teams with a comparatively weak team. We sincerely hope, at least, that their inexperience will not lead them into any enterprise so rash.

✧

We have heard some complaints about the large admission fee charged at last Saturday's foot ball game with the University of Pennsylvania's team. This complaint is unreasonable, because it arises from an entire misapprehension. These admission fees are looked upon by most as merely a means of defraying the expenses of the visiting team, whereas they are, in reality, subscriptions to the Treasury of our Foot Ball Association. This Association is unable to raise money in any other way and must, therefore, resort to the plan of charging a moderately high admission fee to each of the games played here upon our own grounds. The expenses incident upon the team's visits to other grounds will be very heavy indeed and will by no means be met by what they receive from the teams whose grounds they are to visit. What more equitable plan of raising money could be devised than that of placing the fees of admission to the games played here at a figure high enough to enable the Association not only to pay all present expenses, but also to meet their engagements with Harvard and Yale? When looked at in this light, a fee of fifty cents cannot seem exorbitant to any fair-minded person.

Printed in *The Princetonian*, III (Oct. 24, 1878), 87, 88.

Two News Items in *The Princetonian*

[Oct. 24, 1878]

Since our last issue, Mr. Chas. B. Wigton '79 has been elected captain of the University nine, and Mr. Thos. W. Wilson '79 president of the Base Ball Association. We wish them abundant success and promise them our hearty support in any course which may lead to success.

COLLEGE MEETING.—A College meeting was called last Monday, after chapel, for the purpose of electing a President of the Base-ball Association, and to consider the method of electing editors of the *Lit.* and PRINCETONIAN. Mr. T. W. Wilson, '79, was elected to the Presidency of the Base-ball Association.

The question in regard to the election of editors then came before the meeting, and Mr. Bridges, '79, moved that the following method of electing editors of the *Nassau Lit.* be adopted:

About the 20th of March in each year the *Lit.* Board (all literary editors being present) shall nominate, from their contributors of the Junior Class, ten men, eight of whom shall be mentioned in one group and two in another. This list shall be handed to the President of the class, who shall immediately call a meeting to vote on the nominees. The editors are to be eight in number. It shall take a majority vote to ratify the eight of the first group, or to set aside any one or two of them and elect from the second group in their stead; but a two-thirds vote shall be necessary to elect any one not nominated by the Board, and to set aside any or all of the nominees. The Treasurer shall be chosen by the class whenever they deem fit. The Board shall keep a record of all contributions from lower classmen, and this is to be handed to the succeeding Board and taken into account by them in the choice of editors for the following year.

After a few remarks by Mr. Bridges, the plan was unanimously adopted.

Mr. Wilson, '79, then moved the following plan of electing editors of THE PRINCETONIAN:

At a full meeting of the literary editors of THE PRINCETONIAN Board, to be held about the 20th of March in each year, they shall elect from their contributors four editors from the Junior Class (three Academics and one Scientific), one from the Sophomore Class and one from the Freshman Class. The two Juniors and one Sophomore on the retiring Board shall continue to hold office during the following year or years, unless requested to resign by a majority of the editors; when, if they (the editors so resigning) desire it, the matter of their continuance in office shall be left to their class. The Treasurer is to be elected by the Junior Class. If, however, the College seems dissatisfied with the choice, any twenty men may call a mass-meeting, by which it shall be decided by a majority vote whether the elections of the Board shall stand or not. If the vote is in the negative, the election of the editors shall be referred to their respective classes. If THE PRINCETONIAN and *Lit.* shall choose the same man or men, his choice in the matter shall be considered final. The nominees of both Boards shall be notified before their nominations are made public, in order that any resignation or conflicting choice, like the above, may be regulated.

Mr. Cutts, '80,[1] moved, as an amendment to this plan, that the retiring Board nominate four (4) men and two (2) substitutes from the Junior Class and one (1) man and one (1) substitute from each of the two lower classes. This amendment was adopted, and the original plan, thus amended, carried by a large majority.

It is a well-known fact that during years past some of the College organizations have, at times, been extravagantly managed, and that the mass of the students have been obliged to make up any deficiency in their bank accounts. For this reason Mr. Lee, '80,[2] moved the following resolution:

Resolved, It is the will of this meeting that all the business of the various associations of this College be hereafter conducted on a cash basis, and that we, as a College, will never be responsible for the future debts of any of these associations.

This resolution passed without a dissenting voice. The meeting, in which the best of order had prevailed, was then adjourned.

Printed in *The Princetonian,* III (Oct. 24, 1878), 89, 94-95.

[1] Harry M. Cutts.

[2] Blair Lee, born Aug. 9, 1857. A.B., Princeton, 1880; LL.B., Columbian (now George Washington) University, 1882. Practiced law in District of Columbia and Montgomery County. Md. Elected to Maryland Senate 1905 and 1909. Served as Democrat in United States Senate 1914-17. Died Dec. 25, 1944.

From the Minutes of the American Whig Society

Whig Hall   Oct. 25, 1878

. . . Resolved, By-laws, etc. that we now proceed to the election of Officers

c-d   Bridges

The following officers were then elected.

Speaker	McLaren
1st Compt.	Sheldon
2nd "	Woods
Sub. Com.	Wilson and McNair
Sec'y. For. Aff.	Mitchell
Auditors	Bridges and McCarter
Sargeant	Helm
Clerk	Harlan[1] . . .

Second Session

. . . Resolved, By-laws etc. that I be allowed to resign the office of Sub-Committee-man

Wilson

Amended, by adding the clause, "and that we now elected a successor.["]

c-d

Mr. W. E. Dodge was then elected to fill the vacancy . . .

[1] Richard D. Harlan, '81.

From the Minutes of the Liberal Debating Club

Oct. 26 [1878]

Meeting called to order at 8.05, Pres. Sheldon in the chair.

Miscellaneous Business

The amendment to Sect. 1 Art. 2nd of the constitution—

Mr. Mitchell['s] name was proposed. The gentleman was elected.

Mr. McCarter read Chap. 8 of Cushing's Manual.

Mr. Elsing delivered a speech upon Louis Kossuth—Mr. Wilson was appointed to write a criticism upon the subject matter.

The bill in regard to Anglo-Turkish Convention then passed its 3rd reading.

The life, character, and work of Richard Brinsely Sheridan were then discussed.

Percy Byshe Shelley was proposed for discussion this night, one week. Misc. business: Res. That Cushing's Manual be purchased for each member of society—Elsing   c-d-

The meeting then adjourned.

From Janet Woodrow Wilson

My darling Son, Charleston. S. C. Saturday. Oct. 26th 78.

I have delayed writing you from day to day hoping that I would be better—so that I could write more satisfactorily. But I have suffered more in the last forty eight hours, than I did altogether before that time. The pain I have had to endure during the last two days and nights, has seemed almost intolerable. But the doctor relieved me this morning, and assures me that the worst is over. If everything continues to go on well, I may hope to be at home before many days. I will have to get back a little strength after I get out of bed you know. . . .

Write to me here again, please dear. I cannot hope to get off from here before Monday week—and your letters do me so much good. Your father wrote me about your getting the prize. I am *so* *rejoiced*. Please tell me *all* about it. Why did you not speak of it in your letter of last week[?] I cannot tell you how glad I was about it.

I am tired dear & must stop for the present. Of course I will write again before we leave for home.

Josie joins in unbounded love to you. Bella was *much* pleased at your remembering her. God bless you, my darling—

Yours lovingly   Mother

ALS (WP, DLC) with WWhw notation on env.: "Ans 10/28/78."

Wilson's Notes and Topical Headings on Professor Atwater's Lectures on Civil Government

Lecture *Seven* 11/1/78

The next great question of the Vatican Infallibility the infallibility of the Pope. The Protestant doctrine on the other hand of private judgment applicable alike to rulers and people. This is not merely a theological question but affects political questions largely. According to the doctrine of private judgment while all of us must get what little we can from his clergy yet after all we must judge for ourselves what God requires in his Word and indeed whether it is his Word at all and we are personally responsible. Each one is responsible for his own answer to the question "What say I that I am."

Papal infallibility vs private judgment

Everyone is required to search the Scriptures. This doctrine applies to every sphere of life. This doctrine puts the ruler like all other people in the same attitude with reference to the church. Of course the minister is not infallible any more than the Pope. But the minister gives instruction. If the instruction be wrong we are not apt to obey it. This leaves room for religious and political liberty while it subjects us all to the Word of God and morality. The contrary doctrine of papal infallibility in itself and in its relations to political institutions, etc., discussed by Mr. Gladstone we cannot here discuss. It is becoming a power not only in European but also in American politics. Ex cathedra speeches of the Pope. Infallibility of the Pope is his prerogative. Once he speaks all parties[,] governments[,] as well as subjects are bound thereby. This gives the Pope power to govern all rulers to the extent of his own will. This is the logical outcome of the doctrine. This doctrine however has some half truth in it. There is a real infallible knowledge not belonging to any organization or head of an organization but belongs to each Christian individual. For instance in answering the question "Who think you that I am?" the knowledge of those who answer this is infallible. It is safe to say that the doctrine of the incarnation, resurrection, etc., in themselves in their substance are infallibly known by the whole Church of God, that is by all true Christians. All these fundamental doctrines are known infallibly. We do not hereby necessarily mean that each can give an adequate definition of his knowledge. Of this true doctrine the doctrine of papal infallibility is the shadow. The claim of the Pope is the last extreme to human presumption. It is only because of this shadow of truthfulness that this doctrine can take any lasting hold upon the world. *Some shadow of truth in the former*

The infallibility of the human mind holds only in respect of fundamental customs which constitute the foundations of all acquired knowledge. These customs are the fundamental portions of knowledge and are of course infallible. Other men are just as infallible as the Pope at Rome. *Infallibility of the Human Mind*

Is this a Christian nation; is Christianity the law of the land? If the question, is this a Christian nation, means do the majority of the people lead a moral and Christian life[.] But if the question be is it the religion which is the religion of the great mass of the people, is it that which has molded our national life[,] institutions[,] laws, that which is recognized by the nation on Sabbaths, upon Thanksgiving; the answer is emphatically this is a Christian and less emphatically a Protestant nation. We are a Christian in contrast to being a heathen or pagan or atheistic nation. Christianity is the law of the land in the sense that (1) the common law of Great Britain which provides our judicial proceedings found its underlying principles in Christianity. (2) Our laws aim to *This a Christian Land?* *This nation governed by the laws of Christianity* carry out the commands of the Bible.[1] (4) It is universally acknowledged that no legislation should be adopted which is contrary to Christianity. (5) It is constantly recognized as a sufficient argument for one thing that it is demanded by or in accord with Christianity.

State Education and Religion

How far should the state be an educator, how far should it impart moral and religious instruction? Should it require or permit the use of the Bible or any kind of worship in its public schools. This became a serious question when the Roman Catholics poured into this country. The fact that the Church had no control over the schools[,] that the schools were entirely secular[,] did not suit them.

Various modes of solving this problem have been proposed. One of these is that the reading of the Bible[,] any form of prayer or singing in the schools makes the state a teacher of this particular sort of religion. This is claimed to be in violation of the national

Bible in the Public Schools

Constitution which forbids passing any law in respect of the establishment of religion or prohibiting the free exercise thereof. It is contrary to the letter of our national Constitution that any favor should be shown to any particular religious denomination. But this was not considered to mean before the vast Catholic immigration era that the Bible which is the foundation of all Christian sects might not be read in the public schools or that the child might not be taught simple Christian and moral duties. Nor has it been considered to mean that there should not be chaplains etc. and that courts might not be opened with prayer. This has not been supposed to bring about any union between any church and state. Wherever a silent majority of the people wish these exercises in public schools they have been permitted without thought of unconstitutionality. That the permission of these exercises in the public schools is sanctioned by the Constitution if the people in general so interpret the Constitution. This is the interpretation of the history of the country. The schools are to prepare the children to be good citizens and in order to this it is necessary that those fundamental truths of Christianity be taught them. Thus deepen the moral impressions of the children and promote good citizenship. The constitution of the state of Massachusetts indicates that the fundamental principles of piety and Christianity must be taught in the public schools of the state.

Transcript of WWsh notes in the second of the three notebooks described at Sept. 11, 1878.
[1] WW missed point (3). It is to be found in Atwater's "Civil Government and Religion," *Princeton Review*, 3rd Ser., v (April 1876), 224-45.

From the Minutes of the Liberal Debating Club

Nov. 6 [1878]

House called to order at 8.15. In absence of Pres. Sheldon, Sec. Talcott took the chair. Mr. Woods was appointed Sec. of State pro. tem. The minutes of preceding meeting, read, corrected, and adopted. Mr. Mitchell[,] the new member, was introduced and read Sec. 1 ch. 9 of Cushing's Manual. Club then proceeded to discuss the life, character, and writings of Percy Bysshe Shelley. Mr. Wilson had no criticism to read on account of Mr. Elsing's failure to hand in his speech, which omission was caused by Mr. Elsing's having friends in town. Mr. Elsing proposed John Milton for discussion. Sec. of State appoint next regular meeting but one for the question. Res. That the course of Bismark in dealing with Socialism in Germany was neither wise nor politic—Wilson.

Sec. of State appointed next regular meeting. Adjourned at 9.45.

Chas. Talcott   Pres. pro. tem.

Hiram Woods   Sec. of State pro. tem.

Five Editorials in *The Princetonian*

[Nov. 7, 1878]

The new method of electing editors now goes into force, and we would urge those who intend trying for editorships to contribute *constantly*, not simply once or twice. The present board of editors intend to make a conscientious endeavor to select their successors only on the ground of work done, and not at all on the ground of reputed ability. Let it be remembered that, in a certain sense, every department of the paper is open to contributors. Pointed comments on live College topics; poetry; short, spicy stories, and well-told anecdotes; notices of events interesting to College men; items of College news and current College jokes; information as to the whereabouts and employments of alumni; and brief, pungent criticisms of magazine articles and books whose subject-matter is of immediate interest to us here, will always, when properly written, find a place in our columns and entitle their writers to a consideration in the final choice of editors. As for the mere manual part of this contributing, all contributions must be written on one side of the paper only. If any of the communications which are handed in fail of gaining admission, that in itself should not be matter of discouragement. Only constant practice can fit *any one* for the peculiar kind of work required from the editor of a College paper. We would remind '82 that one editor is to be chosen from their class and that all candidates should begin contributing at once.

❖

Chapel Stage may or may not be an evil. But as long as it is a necessity, as long as the evil, if such it be, must be endured, surely it should be made as bearable as possible. We do not now address ourselves to the speakers, whose business it is to be as entertaining as they can, but to the audiences—or rather, to those who should compose the audiences. To use the words of plainness and truth, the way in which Chapel Stage speaking is attended is disgraceful. The small number of those who hear the first speaker of each division is sadly diminished by the time the last speaker rises. We need hardly say that it is to the last degree annoying to speak to so pitiably small an audience; it does seem necessary to remind some that it is positively impolite to rush out of Chapel just as a speaker is being introduced. Surely the orators speak under enough disadvantages, without being subjected to the mortification of speaking to empty benches. Inspiration may be too strong a word to use in relation to a College speech; but certainly there is an inspiration to be caught from a large audience which no amount of artificial ardor can counterfeit. There can be no doubt but that an appreciative hearing is an immense help to any speaker. This the College has it in its power to give. Instead of the scattered few who now attend, the seats might easily be filled. It is certainly not too much to ask that everyone who can do so without any great inconvenience to himself will give the Chapel Stage speakers the encouragement of his presence. The Seniors especially should turn out to a man. The exercise is most particularly theirs as a class, and to them the speakers, their classmates, must look for their principal support.

❖

The foot-ball season is now well advanced and we have many reasons to feel considerable confidence in our team. In many respects the fates seem to have been against us. In the beginning of the season we were deprived of the services of two of our best players, and now in the midst of the season another of our most tried and valuable men, Mr. Lee, '80, is compelled to give up playing. But fortunately the practice of this year has developed enough men to fill the vacant places on the team, if not to entirely make up for the losses we have sustained. As far as individual excellence is concerned, this year's practice has been as full of promise as that of last year. But, as a team, our men sometimes manifest a sad lack of steadiness. There is a variableness in their playing which furnishes some cause for uneasiness. In the first game of the season, that with the team from the University of Pennsylvania, the team showed the want of experience. In the game with the picked team from Stevens Institute and the St. George Cricket Club, on the other hand, they played together remarkably well—working as a team, mutually supporting each other. In the game with the Rutgers team, however, they again played recklessly, passing poorly, each man working separately and spasmodically. Of course their carefulness or carelessness depends largely upon their estimate of the strength of the opposing team; but carelessness is only too apt to become a habit. Capt. Ballard is to be congratulated, however, on the manner in which he has managed and worked his men. He has only to continue to sternly insist upon careful and united playing to insure to us the championship. The only thing worthy of serious reprehension in the playing of the team is the stubborn manner in which some of the men shut their ears to the commands of the captain. Until they learn to obey they will never learn to play with effect.

✧

The games with Harvard and Yale are now definitely and finally arranged for the 16th and the 28th respectively. The game with Harvard will have taken place, the weather permitting, before our next issue. Of course there was much correspondence before Yale settled down to a definite arrangement. After agreeing to play us in Hoboken on Thanksgiving Day, they endeavored to change both the place and the time of the game. They have now, however, resigned themselves to abiding by their word. Of course there can be no objection to their trying to suit their own convenience as perfectly as possible. But why not think of these things at first and cease having constant misunderstandings about such simple matters as the time and place of a game.

✧

Past experience would almost lead us to believe that it is impossible for any athletic organization to exist here free from a burden of debt. Unless resort is taken to subscriptions, deficits must almost invariably appear on their books at the close of each season. Of course the *amount* of these deficits depends in large measure upon the business-gifts of the several managers; but, however good the management, some deficit is hardly avoidable. This year, as last, a large debt appears on the accounts of the Base Ball Association. This debt now amounts to about two hundred and thirty-six dollars. We can scarcely wonder at its size. We may rather be surprised that it is no larger, when we look back upon the history of the past season. The Association then met with almost no support from the students. At many of the games with professional nines there were scarcely so many as twenty spectators; and, as each of these nines was paid about sixty dollars, some of them more, and on each such occasion the Association had to pay for the use of the grounds, its losses were many and frequent. In fact about forty dollars were sunk in each game with professionals. All the debts of the Association, except some to local organizations, were, however, completely discharged. Of the existing debt, one hundred and ninety-five dollars are owed to the Athletic Association for the use of the University grounds, and the remainder, forty-one dollars, to the College Treasury in repayment of a loan. This is a very serious and exceedingly discouraging state of affairs. It seems almost hopeless to appeal to the College for subscriptions now, while the debt of the Boating Association remains unpaid. But such an appeal must be made ere long; for, in view of the resolutions passed at a recent mass meeting of the College, the present management will feel compelled to refuse to put any nine in the field unless the present debt be paid before Spring comes. To enter upon a new season with a large debt unpaid would be to invite failure. The present managers feel justified, therefore, in calling upon the students to aid them in this matter by as liberal cash subscriptions as possible.

Printed in *The Princetonian*, III (Nov. 7, 1878), 99-101.

Wilson's Notes and Topical Headings on Professor Atwater's Lectures on Civil Government

Lecture Eight   11/11/78

Religion in the Public Schools

Same subject completed: If we have come to ignore God in our public schools because that will come athwart visions of some difficulties or because we cannot afford any sort of religious or Christian recognition without debate of our form of religion and religious rites which constitute popery, we cannot stop there. There are those who disbelieve in any moral obligation, whose creed is that of mere secularism, whose visions are violated by any inculcations of morality. Following this out we must exclude all recognition of moral obligation. There can be no standard of right and wrong in our schools, no demanding avoidance seen, or keeping of faith, etc. If we are compelled to exclude the Bible in order to avoid taking knowledge of those whose beliefs are anti-Christian we must go further, even to the furtherest end. The exception that has been taken to Dr. Walton's book by a New York paper because he has said that no crime which does not *deserve* punishment should be punished. The exception taken on the ground that this would be established religious tendency. If desert does not come into the consideration of punishment we must leave discretion with rulers, allowing them to determine whether or not this crime is antagonistic to the interests of the state. This would be dangerous in the highest degree. This is a kindred subject to that of religion in the public schools.

Some say that the state cannot have any moral principles at all without treading on the religious convictions of someone and therefore it is necessary to reduce to a minimum the religious element in public education. Is there no flaw in this line of argument, or some oversight? Some say follow your logic no matter in what vortex it casts you. But seek and follow any premises. Unsectarian in the state and remember your minds are of two drifts in public affairs. Man is in a state of unrest thinks God. The state does not hesitate to punish blasphemy and other offenses against God. A simple argument that they stand as offenses against order and not as against God. But we must find in these prohibitions of the state a moral element beyond mere expediency. There is an element of fear of God. See page 532, second column, Dr. Walton's Political Science.

The Roman Catholics would have the Bible supplanted by teachers of their own denomination. They would also receive monies from the state as endowments of their own schools. The state will never support denomination schools by taxation. It will maintain [them] as common schools on a footing which will not exclude any reasonable persons. *Roman Catholic aggressions*

If every denomination had schools supported by the state, these schools would be too small to command good teachers. There should be such school hours and recesses that all parents might have the opportunity of giving their children such religious instruction as they desire that they should have. Some Christians say that the Bible should be excluded from the public schools in order that we might gain the cooperation of the skeptics. Non-religious education can only be simply hardminded. We could under such education gain only formal knowledge, such as would enable us to learn facts and principles. How can we learn history and ignore the sources and forms of Christianity[?] If religious [education] is excluded the schools must be confined to the most elementary instruction. Hence a proper state university becomes an impossibility because unable to teach history and science. 408 page second volume of Woolsey with reference to teaching science as related to the exclusion of the Bible from the schools. There are movements towards a mode of settling this question. A year ago or more the board of education in the city of New Haven ordered all religious exercise banished from the school. This immediately created dissatisfaction and later action reversed this decision. The *Catholics* united with that portion of the residue of the people who desired not to have religion banished from the schools in voting down the action of the board of education and did this under explicit directions from their priests. Then the practical question arose how to carry out the will of the people thus expressed. In order to settle this question a committee was appointed on the part of the Protestants and they had conferences with the Roman Catholic priests and the result was the adoption of a short exercise containing not [sic] nothing distasteful to any and yet embody[ing] the elementary truths of Christianity. In addition to this the Romanists would have thrown in something more but did not. In cases in which the Roman Catholics constitute 30 per cent of the scholars they might go into an adjacent room by themselves and there have exceptional devotions. Thus a liturgy was made to take the place of other religious exercises in the schools. Whether this amounts to a perfect solution of the matter or not it suggests what *may* amount to a satisfactory solution: i.e. a converse of those who represent the different religious elements[—]a brief exercise such as is offensive to no one but theorists may be adopted to be heard in the schools with the exception given above.

Transcript of WWsh notes in the second of the three notebooks described at Sept. 11, 1878.

From the Minutes of the American Whig Society

Whig Hall Nov. 12, 1878

... This being the night appointed for the Competitive debate[,] upon the arrival of the Judges, Messrs Ormond,[1] Kerr and Slemmons, the following question:

["]Res'd that abolition of the Prepective [sic] Tariff would be injurious to the interests of the United States" was debated by following gentlemen

Aff.	Neg.
Mr. Blydenburgh[2]	Mr. T. Wilson
" Galbreath	" R. McCarter
" Davis	

After the debate, the judges retired. On motion of Mr. Elsing, the House voted on the question of the evening and decided it in the Affirmative.

On motion the roll was called.

The judges then returned and through Mr. Ormond awarded the medal to Mr. Davis, the 1st place on the Fancy Debate to Mr. R. McCarter; and the 2nd place to Mr. Galbreath and decided the question in the Aff. . . .

[1] Alexander T. Ormond, '77, a graduate student who was Chancellor Green Fellow in Moral Science.
[2] Benjamin B. Blydenburgh, Jr., '81.

From Janet Woodrow Wilson

My precious Son,   Wilmington N C Wednesday Nov 20th [1878]

. . . Dear Tommy, if I were you, I would resign the Presidency of that Club[1]—for the reasons you assign. It is very pleasant to think that your fellow-students have such confidence in you—their action in this matter is very flattering indeed. But it would be wrong to put aside your more important interests—for the sake of a temporary interest of that sort—and you would lose nothing in any way by declining to continue in your present position. You will make a great mistake if you allow anything of the kind to come in the way of your doing your utmost in the direction of your *future* interest. I want to speak of another thing in this hurried note. Christmas is very near—what are your plans with reference to it? I need not tell you how I want you to come home. But your father always objects to the risk of your journey at such a season for such a short time. I just want to repeat, darling, what I said to you last summer—viz. that if you have any desirable invitation for the holidays—to some place where you would have such recreation as would be really pleasant to you—I beg you will accept it. I want you to have a taste of this kind in this your last year in the North. Of course you shall have your new overcoat. I will endeavor to send the money before many days—there will be no difficulty about it. . . .

God bless you my own dear son. Papa & Josie join me in fondest love.   Your Mother

ALS (WP, DLC) with WWhw notation on env.: "Ans."
[1] The Base Ball Association.

Editorial in *The Princetonian*

[Nov. 21, 1878]

Some time ago the Harvard *Advocate* expressed the opinion that the game between Yale and Harvard on November 23d would be the great event of the foot-ball season. No doubt it will be a very interesting game indeed; but does the *Advocate* still adhere to its opinion concerning its relative importance in view of the events of November 16th?

We cannot say that we were surprised at the result of last Saturday's game. Our team has had constant and thorough practice and fairly won its success at Boston. Our superiority lay not so much in the individual excellence of the men as in the collective strength of the team and its thorough acquaintance with the nicer points of the game. We played a much more scientific game than our opponents did. We were over-matched in weight, they in skill.

We hope that as many as possible will go down to the grounds every day to see the practice games until we play Yale. Even in practicing the team are stimulated by a large number of spectators. Had our nine been thus encouraged in their practice last year we might have had a victorious nine, as we now have a victorious team.

Printed in *The Princetonian*, III (Nov. 21, 1878), III.

From the Minutes of the Liberal Debating Club

Nov. 23 [1878]

House called to order 8.25 P.M. Messrs. Godwin, McCarter, Mitchell, Sheldon, Webster were absent. Minutes read, corrected, and adopted. There being no miscellaneous business Mr. Wilson read Sec. 2. Ch. 9 of Cushing's Manual. Mr. Wilson moved the postponement of the question for debate until next meeting and that a member be appointed to inform the absent members of time and place of next meeting.   C-d.

Mr. Wilson moved an adjournment to next Tuesday evening at 7.15 ocl'k and that Mr. Wood be the member appointed to inform the absentees.   C-d.

Meeting then adjourned. Chas. Talcott, N. Y. Pres. pro. tem—
Hiram Woods, Md.   Sec. of State pro. tem—

Nov. 26 [1878]

Meeting called to order at 7.45 p.m. Messrs. Godwin, McCarter, Sheldon, absent. Mr. Talcott took the chair & appointed Mr. Woods Sec. of State pro. tem. Minutes read, corrected, & adopted. Mr.

Webster read secs. 3 & 4 of ch. 9 Cushing's Manual, after which
the club proceeded to debate question postponed from last meeting. Carried on 1st reading.

Society proceeded with 2d reading C-d. Society then went into
com. of whole with Mr. Elsing in the chair. Com. reported favorably. Society then adj[ourned] until first Sat. evening of next term
at 7.30.

Chas. Talcott, President pro. tem.
Hiram Woods Sec. of State

From Janet Woodrow Wilson

My darling Son—   Wilmington N. C. Tuesday Dec. 3rd [1878]
I have been longer in writing than I wished to be. I had determined that I would not write again without sending you money
for your overcoat—and it is hard to get hold of it in the proper
shape. Your father has procured a *thirty dollar P. O. order*, which
I enclose. I enquired of Mr. Munson the other day what would be
the cost of a really good over-coat—and he said that no one would
desire a better one than could be bought for *twenty dollars* at present. If he is right, you will have something over—which will not be
inconvenient, I am sure. Where will you send for your coat? to
New York? I do hope you will be able to get a satisfactory one. I
would not get a very heavy one if I were you

I will be anxious to hear certainly as to your going to Baltimore.
I do hope you will make the visit you speak of—for I think you
would enjoy it. Let us know as soon as the matter is decided,
please. I wish you could *settle* in Baltimore, I sometimes think.
. . .

God bless you my dearest son. Papa & Josie join me in fondest
love to you.   Lovingly your Mother

ALS (WP, DLC) with WWhw notation on env.: "Ans."

Three Editorials in *The Princetonian*

[Dec. 5, 1878]

The editorial comments which appeared in our last number relative to the subscriptions for the boating club called forth from a
member of the Senior class a subscription, which he placed in our
hands with the request that we would hand it to the proper authorities. We are very happy to receive all such donations and will
take pleasure in seeing that all such reach the proper persons. But
in the note which accompanied this subscription the subscriber

took occasion to question our statement as to the reluctance, or at least tardiness, of the Seniors in responding to the boating association's appeal for contributions. He said that he knew of several, besides himself, who had not subscribed simply because they were waiting to be called upon by authorized collectors. We do not question this gentleman's statement, but his information as to the matter is evidently too limited to warrant his concluding, as he does, that our recent criticism of the Senior class must have been unjust. We were informed by one of the gentlemen who is acting as collector for the association that he himself had solicited subscriptions from no fewer than ninety members of the Senior class and that the result of this labor was eighty-nine unwilling promises and one payment of *fifty cents*. This speaks for itself.

✧

In consequence of the slow progress of the subscriptions for the payment of the boating debt, it seems as if some other method of raising money was needed. Subscriptions for the burial of a defunct association are notoriously difficult to get. We do not care to pay out our money for no value received.

The plan has been suggested, and there can be no harm in trying it, of giving an entertainment for the benefit of the association. There are men in College of decided histrionic talents who, we do not hesitate to say, would compare favorably with professional elocutionists. These could easily supply a very pleasant evening's amusements. We dare not suggest theatricals, but reading and recitation of selections, humorous and otherwise. We do not doubt that such an entertainment could be made very attractive, so as to charm the dollars from the most tightly-buttoned pocket. The difficulty would be to induce men to lend their services as readers, but those who are able might undertake the work for the sake of the object.

✧

Certainly the issue of the foot-ball season affords us every reason for self gratulation. On Thanksgiving Day our splendid team won the last of the long series of victories with which the past few weeks have been crowded. They gained the championship to which a long season of hard and unremitted practice had fully entitled them. Though our victory over them was a very decided one, the Yale team certainly proved themselves gallant antagonists. They played strongly and, at times, skilfully. Their comparative weakness lay in lack of skill, not in want of strength. While our men were quite their matches in point of strength, they were more than their matches in point of skill, passing the ball more surely and supporting each other more carefully. We only express the general opinion of the College when we say that Mr. Ballard has proved himself an admirable captain; and we only reflect the universal sentiment of the College when we offer him our hearty congratulations and thanks. In this game with Yale we played off the tie of last year. What was then left unsettled is now decided in our favor, and we now may claim, as we do, the championship of last year, as well as of this.

The overwhelming victory of our Sophomores over the Columbia Sophomores on last Saturday, Nov. 30th, was a fitting and significant close to Princeton's foot-ball season.

Printed in *The Princetonian*, III (Dec. 5, 1878), 123-24.

News Item in *The Princetonian*

[Dec. 5, 1878]

Class Day Elections

On Nov. 21st the Seniors held their elections for Class Day Orators and Committees. . . . Mr. A. W. Halsey[1] received the vote of the class for President, and Mr. W. E. Dodge for Master of Ceremonies. For Class Orator there were three candidates, Messrs. Chambers, Wilson and Elsing. After several ballots Mr. Elsing was elected. . . .[2]

Printed in *The Princetonian*, III (Dec. 5, 1878), 128.
[1] Abram Woodruff Halsey, '79.
[2] WW's only class office was membership on the "Photograph committee," to which he had been elected in May 1878. See *The Princetonian*, III (May 30, 1878), 35.

From Janet Woodrow Wilson and Joseph Ruggles Wilson

My darling Son—   [Wilmington, N. C.] Monday—Dec. 9th '78.

I am so glad you had the relief [So far Momma]¹ of, I suppose she was about to write, a trip to N. York and a participation in that Hoboken kicking. [Your Mother is tired, that's all]² You did well to go, although the rowdyism was—a little steep. We all rejoiced at Princeton's success, as if we had a personal interest in the same. I imagine *your* going yelling down and up 5th Ave! But wonders will never cease.³

We are all in our usual health. Indeed your mother seems to be improving from day to day. That trip to Charleston was truly a success so far as yet appears[.] My indebtedness to Dr. Robertson is very great and shall never be forgotten

You have received ere this your Mother's last letter—which crossed yours. It contained P. O. order for $30. We hope that you will visit Baltimore. If so, don't fail to see Dr. Leighton Wilson.[4] I *think* he boards at the Albion hotel, wherever that is. But any Presbyterian can put you upon the right track for finding him.— We have received no Princetonian since middle of November:— hope it is not suspended, either by neck or heels.

Your[5] father took this out of my hands a little while ago—saying he would finish my letter for me. I suppose he thought I looked so sleepy that he was led to fear that I might inflict upon you something very stupid indeed. I went out to make a few visits this morning—the first I have made, you know, in many months—and I have come home very, very tired.

I am wonderfully well—only not very strong. I am determined to continue to be very careful indeed.

I enjoyed so much your description of your little frolic. I am sure you must have felt benefitted by it. I am glad you are going to Baltimore—for I fancy the society there will be more congenial than that of New York.

Your Uncle James Bones was with us a few days a week or so ago—on his way to Staunton. He seems much as usual—and in spite of his distress at the failure,[6] is on the whole, greatly relieved at escaping from a burden which he was scarcely fit to carry. I would not wonder if you have had more news through your letters from Staunton, than I was able to get personally from James himself. I wont write more now—but will wait till I am wider awake than I am at present.

Your father & little Josie are quite well—and join me in fondest love to our precious Tommy.   Lovingly your Mother.

ALS (WP, DLC).
¹ JRW begins here. His brackets.
² JRW's brackets.
³ A reference to the celebration following the Princeton-Yale football game, which Princeton won by a touchdown and a goal, played on St. George's Cricket Grounds in Hoboken, N. J., on Thanksgiving Day, Nov. 28, 1878. See the *New York Times*, Nov. 29, 1878; *The Princetonian*, III (Dec. 5, 1878), 129-30; and Godwin's *History of the Class of '79*, pp. 57-58, for accounts of the game and its aftermath at Delmonico's and several theaters.
⁴ The Rev. John Leighton Wilson, D.D., of Baltimore, one of the founders of the American Presbyterian missionary work in Africa; secretary of the Committee on Foreign Missions of the Presbyterian Church, U.S.A., 1853-60; secretary of the Committee on Foreign Missions of the Presbyterian Church, U.S., 1861-86, and of that denomination's Committee on Home Missions, 1863-82.
⁵ JWW resumes letter here and continues to end.
⁶ James Bones had just gone into bankruptcy.

From Joseph Ruggles Wilson

My dearest boy— Wilmington [N. C.] Dec 10 78

Please find enclosed P. O. order for $20.00 which will surely meet all your present wants. I am sorry I have to send you money in such dribblets—but—but &c &c.

You were right in going to N. York for overcoat. It cost a little too much, I think. The one I am now wearing was $16.00, and no one c'd desire a better. But you are not good at bargaining.

You of course will write us befor going to B[altimore].

We wrote you a joint note yesterday.

All well and all love you with unbounded affection.

ALS (WP, DLC). Your own—Father

From Janet Woodrow Wilson

My precious Son, Wilmington N. C. Dec. 24th 78

I am so glad you are in Baltimore—for you cannot fail to have a nice time. It was very kind in you, dear, to think of sending us a telegram. It relieved us of all uncertainty as to your movements. I will not deny that it is a great trial to me to give up the hope of seeing my darling son during these holidays—but I am really glad to have you where you are. It will be a new experience to you— and one that I feel sure you will enjoy, & that will be beneficial to you besides. Dont expose yourself, please, to the chance of taking cold—for that would spoil all, you know. Enjoy yourself just the most you can—but *take care of your health* I entreat you. . . .

Papa & Josie join me in fondest love to you, and in wishing you a happy, happy Christmas. Yours lovingly Mother

ALS (WP, DLC).

From Marion Wilson Kennedy

Dear Tommy:— [Augusta, Ark., Dec. 28, 1878]

The enclosed letter is rather ancient, but I really have neither time nor *sense* to write another, so will just send it as it is. I have a dreadful cold, which may account to some extent for my want of my *usual sense*.

Today is your birthday and you are actually twenty-two years old, my big brother. May you have as many happy returns of the day as are desirable, and may each return find you ever so much better, wiser and happier than the preceding one! . . .

Your aff. sister, Marion.

ALS (WP, DLC) with WWhw notation on env.: "Ans 1/12/79." Enc.: Marion
W. Kennedy to WW, ALS (WP, DLC), Dec. 12, 1878.

From a Wilson Notebook

My Reading:—(Principal works.)   [c. 1879]

1876

Addison's Works, Vol. III.	
Woodfall's Junius, Vol. I.	
Lectures on Shakspere, Vol. II	Hudson
Milton's Poetical Works Vol I	Masson
Shakspere's Works Vol VIII	White
Macaulay's Essays, Vol II	
Jeffrey—Modern British Essayists.	
Boswell's Johnson Vol. I.	
Life of Goldsmith Vol. I	Foster
Addison's Works Vol II	
Dante's Inferno.	
Shakspere's Works, Vol XI	White

1877

Works of Dan'l Webster Vol I	
Life of " " "	Curtis.
Wilkes, Sheridan, and Fox,	Rae.
Shakspere's Works Vol VI	White
Words, Their Use and Abuse	Mathews
Hours with Men and Books,	"
Ticknor's Life and Letters Vol I	
Success and its Conditions	Whipple
French Revolution Vol I	Carlyle
" " " II	"
Junius	
Manual of the Constitution	Farrar
Edmund Burke, An Historical Study	Morley.
Life of John Locke Vol. I	H. R. Fox Bourne
Short Studies on Great Subjects	Froude

1878

Variorum Shakspere—Hamlet	Furness.
Practical Political Economy	Price
Richard Cobden	McGilchrist
Cobden and Political Opinion	Rogers
History of the Constitution of the U. S. Vol I	Curtis
" " " " " " " " II	"
Comparative Politics	Freeman

Critical Miscellanies (First Series)	Morley
Huskisson's Speeches Vols. I and II	
Recollections and Suggestions	Earl Russell
Greville's Memoirs, Geo IV and Wm. IV, Vol I	
Brougham's Works, Vol III.	
History of the English People Vols I and II	Green
Webster's Works Vol. III.	
Reminiscences of Dan'l Webster	Harvey.
The Federal Government	Gillet.
Life and Speeches of Henry Clay	
Life of Dan'l Webster Vol. I	Curtis
The Great Conversers	Mathews
The English Constitution	Bagehot.
Life of Alex Hamilton Vol I	Morse.

1879

Critical Miscellanies (Second Series)	Morley
Sartor Resartus	Carlyle
Oratory and Orators	Mathews
Beauties of Ruskin	
Growth of the English Constitution	Freeman
Brief Biographies of English Statesmen	Higginson
History of the Constitution of the U. S. Vol II	Curtis
Samuel Johnson	Stephen, Leslie
Speeches of John Bright Vol II	
Lieber's Political Ethics Vol I	
" Civil Liberty and Self-Government.	
History of English Literature Vol II	Taine

WWhw list, in notebook described at Sept. 7, 1875. WW probably made this list near the end of his senior year, and almost certainly before the summer of 1879.

From Joseph Ruggles Wilson

My dearest Son—   [Wilmington, N. C., c. Jan. 10, 1879.]
    We were made glad by the reception of yrs from Princeton this morning. We share your surprise and yr indignation in view of the extraordinary "report."[1] Be assured, though, that we accept of *yr.* report rather than that of the faculty. We are perfectly certain that strict truth would place you above the grade allowed by yr. teachers —and considerably above. One reason for their grading you as far

down as they dared is that you have never taken pains to "cringe the pliant knee." At least I fear that such is the case. Be not disheartened dear boy. Your course has been upward—and will continue to be. Certainly your parents are satisfied, and feel that they have good reason to be. And in addition to this, you have what is almost better, the satisfaction of yourself. If you feel that you have neglected no duty which might have been discharged—have slighted no study which might have been diligently pursued—and have comported yourself as a gentleman and a Christian should— why, who cares for the rest?

I enclose the request to the faculty which you desire me to send.

Your dear Mother & Dode[2] are quite well. The former is always busy—the latter always lazy. They send plenty of love.

Your affectionate & trustful Father

P. S. Please fill up blank in my note to faculty.

ALS (WP, DLC) with WWhw and WWsh notations and "doodles" on env.

  [1] The Registrar's record book, "Grades of the Seniors December, 1878," (NjP) shows three subjects, including history, in which WW received 98, with 94 in ethics, 93 in political science, and 92.5 in English. His worst grades were 82 in chemistry and 73 in astronomy, "as far down as they dared," since grades below 70 were disregarded in class rankings. WW's average for the first term was 88.6, and his class ranking was 44th. At his graduation, his average was 90.3, and his ranking was 38th in a class of about 167.

  [2] Joseph R. Wilson, Jr.

Two Editorials in *The Princetonian*

[Jan. 16, 1879]

We take advantage of this opportunity, the occasion of Mr. Elsing's gratifying success in the Inter-Collegiate Oratorical Contest, to again urge our withdrawal from the Association. We said before this contest, it will be remembered, that, whatever its issue, it should be Princeton's last. We are informed that a meeting of the College will be called at an early date to consider the advisability of tendering a formal withdrawal from membership. According to the Constitution of the Association, no College which is a member of it can withdraw, except by an unanimous vote of its students. Consequently any one who dissents may himself remain a member of the Association, and, upon payment of the necessary entrance fee, enter into competition for any honor or prize offered by it. It is, however, hard for us to conceive of any one's having assurance enough to enter a contest despite the discouragement and disfavor of a large majority of his fellow students. It is by no means certain that the Association will out-live another year. Certainly some of its recent acts seem indicative of the imbecility which is often the immediate precursor of dissolution. One instance will suffice to illustrate this. Last year, as in the previous years, our representative was awarded the Mental Science prize. Failing of funds wherewith to pay the amount of the prize, the Association cooly requested us to raise the money to pay our representative what it had promised him. This we very justly and very naturally refused to do; and it was thereupon announced that, *because* of this refusal on our part, there would this year be no prize offered in the branch of Mental Science. We move a withdrawal.

✧

When the Autumn class races were given up, we thought that we had seen the last of boating in Princeton. But we are now told that there is a movement on foot, which looks to the selection and training of a university crew to take part in races at Newark with other crews as opportunity may offer. This is, to say the least, ill-advised. If we had convenient access to a moderately good course for training purposes, or even if, with only a canal to row on, there were any immediate possibility of our ever meeting any representative College crew upon any eligible neutral watercourse, we would never for a moment think of opposing the organization and careful training of the best crew we could muster. But, there being no such possibility, why is a crew to be maintained, and why are the considerable expenses attendant upon its maintenance to be incurred? We are just now paying off a heavy debt left us by our last university crew; are we to burden ourselves with further debt? True, it is not now a question of such a large outlay as was necessary to send a crew to Saratoga; the expenses of such a crew as is proposed would be comparatively light and easy to meet. But why go to any expenditure at all? An altogether wiser course would be to devote all our resources to foot-ball and base-ball, in which alone we are able to meet our great antagonists, Harvard and Yale, on equal ground. There is no possibility whatever of our being able to meet any worthy rival on the water with much hope of success. Is it not, then, the part of wisdom to devote all our energies to gaining and retaining the championship in those sports in which we can meet, have met, all competitors, without any odds given or taken?

Printed in *The Princetonian*, III (Jan. 16, 1879), 136.

Review in *The Princetonian*

[Jan. 16, 1879]

The December Lit.

This last number of the *Lit.* is, taken all in all, both interesting and well-written. We cannot, however, bestow upon it as
unqualified praise as its predecessors of this volume have deserved
and received. It lacks that character of sustained ability which has
hitherto signalized the work of the present board. In writing of
what he is pleased to call "The Modern Epic" Mr. Van Dyke[1] proves
himself master of a vigorous style which is far from lacking beauty
and finish. Few, we believe, would feel themselves prepared to
agree with him, however, in looking upon Tennyson's Idyls as a
complete Epic. Mr. Van Dyke may demur to the generally accepted
definition of an Epic and speak slightingly of "the mathematical
rules of art," but it is useless for him to attempt to establish the
claim of a series of short poems, whose connection is so slight as
to be detected "more by their secondary meanings, by the histories
and changes implied in some hasty sentence or light word, than
by their leading ideas," to be classed among those great poems
whose essential characteristic is a connected story, not merely a
pervading *theme*. His arguments are, in their first impressions
upon the reader, plausible and even ingenious, but they are far
from being final or convincing. We need not strive to place the
Idyls among the great Epics; they may almost be said to form a
class of themselves. Their beauty and enduring value will not be
enhanced by placing them where they do not belong. The general
impression left by this essay is good, very good, and the estimate
of the great laureate's work seems, on the whole, a very just one.
There is something unsatisfactory, however, about a criticism of
this kind. Being little more than an analysis of the Idyls, we get
very few of the writer's own ideas, and if we have read these Idyls,
as who has not, leave the matter about as it was before we read
Mr. Van Dyke's critique.

The *Reminiscences of an Indian Orator* are well told and possess
no small interest to the general reader. They are certainly not of
the usual style of story, and their attraction may lie partly in their
novel theme. In *A Claim to Recognition* our attention is called with
considerable force to that race to whom our English stock owes its
manlier, more progressive and aggressive qualities, the rude, noble
Norseman. Indeed he has many and strong claims to our recognition. The style of this piece lacks directness, straightforwardness. Then, too, an introduction of almost a page in length seems

rather too elaborate in a piece which covers only four pages in all.

The Snow-Angels is a poetical bit of rare beauty. The idea suggested by its title is not unfamiliar in poetry. The imaginations of not a few have pleased themselves with the fancy that the snow has its accompanying elves or spirits. But the author of this poem has given an original stamp to this not unfamiliar idea. He sees angel faces in the weird, spirit-like forms which the drifted snow assumes when the soft, cold light of the moon falls upon it. In the arms of these spirit-forms a maiden, saved from suicide, falls into the sleep of death. The melody of the verse is remarkable, its sweetness and subdued beauty chiming in perfect harmony with the sad but healthy thought. To tempt our readers to read this poem, we give a specimen stanza, the first:

> "White lies the snow
>   On the face of the fields,
> And the North Wind's bow
>   Its arrows yields
> In a swift and biting shower;
>   For the Archer old
>   Has tipped each dart
>   With a feather, cold
>   And loathe to part
> From its snowy northern bower."

Of the *Death of Little Tad* we are in doubt what to say. Looked at from one point of view, it is excessively tame; looked at from another, it is more than ordinarily good. When extricated from the overgrowth of verbiage which surrounds it, the incident described is simple and quite commonplace. The redeeming features of the sketch are one or two admirable descriptions of natural scenery which relieve its monotony.

The "Statistics" published in the *Olla-Pod.* are, in a certain sense, interesting, but they are almost meaningless. The number of touch-downs secured by a player is no index of the work he has done. Often some of the most effective playing is done by the Backs, yet a Back seldom, if ever, gains a touch-down. Some of the very best players, again, never score a touch-down. Such statistics have no such value or meaning as a nine's batting or error record.

Printed in *The Princetonian*, III (Jan. 16, 1879), 137-38.
1 William D. Van Dyke, '78.

From the Minutes of the Liberal Debating Club

Jan. 18–[1879]

Meeting called to order at 7.55 P.M. Messrs. Godwin, Mitchell, & Webster being absent. President being absent Mr. Talcott took the chair and appointed Mr. McCarter Sec'y of State pro. tem. Minutes for previous meeting were read and adopted. Misc. Bus. being in order Mr. Elsing moved that we suspend const[itution] and elect Mr. Emery to the Society. Mr. Talcott moved as an amendment that the gentleman absent from meeting be visited by Sec'y of State during the week and informed that a ballot on Mr. Emery's name will be taken at the next meeting and requesting them to be present or send proxy votes—Embodied. Mr. Elsing read sec. 5 art. 94-102—of Cushing's Manual. After which Mr. Woods delivered a speech on State Sovereignty, upon the delivery of which criticisms were given by the members. It being the night for the discussion of a literary subject, John Milton was discussed, after which Mr. Wilson offered an explanation for not being prepared with a criticism on Mr. Elsing's speech.

Mr. Wilson then moved the following:

Res. That the action of the British Ministry in undertaking the Afghanistan War was an unjustifiable aggression upon the Ameer.

The Sec'y of State appointed the next meeting for discussion of this bill. House then adjourned at 9.57 P.M.

R. H. McCarter.   Chas. Talcott

Sec'y of State, pro. tem.   Pres. pro. tem

From Janet Woodrow Wilson

My darling Son,   Wilmington N. C. Jan. 20th 79.

. . . I feared that you would be distressed at your report.[1] It came to us while you were in Baltimore—and I understood it to be miserably unjust. I knew that you had reason to expect a better report than usual. The only feeling I had was that of indignation at what I knew to be injustice—and sorrow for what I knew would be your feelings with regard to it. . . .

Lovingly   Mother.

ALS (WP, DLC).
[1] See n. 1 at Jan. 10, 1879.

From the Minutes of the Liberal Debating Club

Jan. 25. [1879]

Meeting called to order at 8.15. The minutes of preceding meeting read & adopted. Mr. Emery's name was then proposed for membership & the gentleman was elected. Misc. Business being in order, Mr. Elsing moved that Mr. Woods be reprimanded. Lost. Election being in order Mr. Godwin was elected President. There being no misc. business, Mr. Woods read sec, 1 & 2 of ch. II Cushing's Manual.

Mr. Talcott moved that Mr. Sheldon be excused from speaking— C-d—The question for debate then came up; Res: That the action of the British Ministry in undertaking the Afghanistan War was an unjustifiable aggression upon the Ameer. Wilson.

The society proceeded to first reading and the question carried. In Second reading question carried. Society on motion went into com. of whole with Mr. Elsing in chair. Question carried and report adopted. Mr. Talcott was appointed to criticise Mr. Sheldon's speech. John Dryden was appointed for discussion next week. At 9.20 Society adjourned.

Charles Talcott N. Y.   Harold Godwin N. Y.
  Sec'y of State.   Pres

Two Editorials in *The Princetonian*

[Jan. 30, 1879]

The Secretary of the St. George Cricket Club recently addressed a letter to Capt. Ballard, as the most prominent representative of Princeton athletic interests, in which he advocates the organization of a team here. The letter will be found in another column. The St. George Club make very generous offers of assistance to all those who care to see the game established here. Certainly if any wish to make an effort in this direction, they could not do better than to take advantage of these offers. And why should not some one wish to do so? The effort is worth making. Cricket is an interesting, healthful, inexpensive game, in every way suited for those who do not wish to enter into rougher sports like foot-ball, and for whom base-ball has lost its attractions, because of the immense amount of training requisite for the acquirement of any real proficiency in it, and because of its having fallen into the hands of those who have made it a profession and reduced its methods to a science. We do not believe that cricket will ever gain the favor here which it has so long enjoyed over the water; it cannot become a great national game. It is too distinctly an exotic; and, moreover, it has too little excitement about it to become universally popular among Americans. But it is, beyond doubt, a pleasant and eminently gentlemanly game, and we would gladly see it introduced into Princeton. We would urge an early acceptance of the assistance offered by the St. George Cricket Club. We are certain that there are not a few in College who are interested in the game, and these will no doubt appreciate the letter printed elsewhere in our columns.

✧

" 'English Lit. One Hour' "

As descendants of one of the noblest races and consequently lovers of the language of such ancestors, one can but feel that in the prescribed course in this College enough time is not given to the study of English literature. While I would say nothing in regard to the manner in which it is taught, it seems to me that the time devoted to it should be considered more seriously. To this one branch, which merits the most careful study, one hour a week is given, and part of that time, during Junior year, is devoted to reading Chaucer and finding, in the Canterbury Tales, a remnant of our original language. Among an English-speaking people the great lack of a proper understanding of our language and the works of the men who have done so much to elevate it by their genius and labor, is felt. It is preposterous to assume that any knowledge, worthy of the subject, can be obtained here in the time allotted. True, those who are thoroughly aroused to the importance of the study may extend their knowledge by means of the library, but such reading is not so systematized that we would be profited as much as if an extra lecture were given each week, or some exercise that would tend to the more careful investigation of this branch. Some have not that great power of converting the toil of others to their own use, and some assistance in this way would not be "seed thrown on stony places." There is a complaint of the dry, metaphysical way of dealing with subjects in this College, and it is attributable to this one thing. Perhaps it is assumed that English Lit. being such an important branch, and mankind seeing the necessity of such a knowledge, because it is loved for its own sake, and is its own reward, therefore the study will be taken up without more time being given to it in the lecture room. Why then attend College? Surely, we as a people, see the necessity of an education and a thorough discipline of the mind. The same will hold in any branch. What we need is the assistance of men who are acquainted with the beauties and values of the language to give us a taste of the good things; as it is now, we know nothing of the dainties. If men ask why we as a College do not have more graduates who figure conspicuously in the literary world, it would be proper to say *only one hour per week is devoted to the study of English Literature*. Every lover of the English language feels this great need, and if an united effort were made to have this rectified we would succeed. At any rate, let us hope that it will receive the attention of "the powers."

Printed in *The Princetonian*, III (Jan. 30, 1879), 147, 150.

From the Minutes of the Liberal Debating Club

Feb. 1 1879.

Meeting called to order at 7.50 P.M. Messrs. Godwin, Sheldon absent. Mr. Emery, the newly elected member was introduced. Misc. Business: Mr. Wilson moved that sec. 1 art. 5. of Constitution be amended by striking out words "or such literary matters as the club may see fit to discuss from time—" Lost.

Mr. Wilson then read Sec. 18 Chap. 9 of Cushing's Manual. Mr. Sheldon being absent speech was dispensed with & the literary subject "Dryden" was discussed.

There being no misc. business the following quest was appointed for discussion one week from tonight—[1] Meeting then adjourned—M. G. Emery   Chas. Talcott N. Y.

Sec. of State pro. tem.   Pres. pro. tem.

[1] "Res: That it would be for the best interests of France for M. Gambetta to accept office at the present time. Wilson." See at Feb. 8, 1879.

From Janet Woodrow Wilson

My darling Tommy,   Wilmington. N. C. Febry 4th. [1879]

. . . I do hope you are being careful dear—& that you will be able to escape taking cold.

You may imagine how glad we were to get your likeness. I think it is very good indeed—and a wonderfully clear & finely executed picture. Your father & Josie are not satisfied. Josie says it is not "half so handsome as brother is!" Of course it does not give your face as I would like to have it—but I have learned not to expect that from a picture. I had a letter from your Auntie[1] this morning. They were delighted with the picture you sent Jessie. It seems that Hattie and Jessie addressed their last letters to "Princeton" simply—

and are afraid that you did not receive them? What sort of letters do they write?

We received the last number of the Princetonian day before yesterday. I enjoy it so much—because there is so much of you in it. Could you not put a cross or some little mark to your pieces—so as to make perfectly certain?

I am very sorry to hear about your eyes my darling. As you have not said anything about them this winter, I was hoping that they had ceased giving you trouble. I cannot tell you how I shrink from the idea of your putting yourself in the hands of a doctor. Your father was very much disturbed about it. It seems he has not known anything about it. You see, you and I talk over such matters here in the summer—and are apt to forget that he does not know all that we talk over. I wish you would write *to him* particularly about this matter—giving all possible particulars. How would you manage in going over to N. Y.? I suppose the way to do, would be, to make an appointment beforehand—then go & return the same day—would that be possible? The truth is, dear Tommy, that this miserable people is giving your father much trouble as to money matters. They are *far* behind in their payments—farther than ever. So that we must manage everything in the least expensive way possible. Your father is preaching *just wonderful* sermons this winter—but he is not well—sometimes I feel very uneasy about him. He looks wretchedly at present. The people seem to be as enthusiastic as ever in their affection for & pride in him—but they are an utterly selfish people. Your father seems to have an utter distaste for the whole affair—and would leave them if he could. They dont know what they are risking by their want of honesty. And yet, strange to say, there seems to be an unusual amount of seriousness among the people[.] We have some faint hope that there is in prospect a season of revival—and that would make up for everything that is wanting. I would rather not tell you anything, dear, that is not altogether pleasant—but I think you would rather know all about it.

What about your Essay?[2] I have been looking anxiously for it. Is it not finished? God bless you my dear, dear child. Take care of your health. Josie is sick with cold today—I am *much* better. Papa & Josie join me in fondest love to you my precious Son.

Lovingly   Mother

ALS (WP, DLC).
    [1] Marion Woodrow Bones.
    [2] A reference—the first in these documents—to WW's essay, "Cabinet Government in the United States," printed at Aug. 1, 1879.

Two Editorials in *The Princetonian*

[Feb. 6, 1879]

Among the many changes that have been proposed with a view to increasing the interest taken in Commencement Exercises, none seems to us more feasible than the reduction of the number of speakers on the Commencement Day. We are aware that the custom of assigning to a certain proportion of every graduating class speeches in public, which must be delivered on pain of forfeiture of the coveted diploma, is one of great antiquity. We are aware that in the College days of Madison and Breckenridge the "Commencement Speech" was already a time-honored institution. But in those days there were classes of twelve; and now we have them of ten times that number. The proportion of about one-third of the class, which comes within the limits which entitle one to an oration, a very proper limit for them, becomes almost unbearable for us. A very ordinary speaker can make a single speech more or less interesting. But the genius of a Burke or a Webster would be balked when there is not one nor two, but thirty speeches.

The Commencement Exercises, as at present conducted, are about as "state [stale], flat, and unprofitable" as the most ardent admirers of mediocrity could wish. They drag along from ten o'clock until after two with a drowsy stream of so-called oratory, interrupted only by momentary intervals, in which one victim retires and another takes his place. The audience is composed of the appreciative relatives of these victims aforesaid. These relatives, when anyone but their own peculiar pet is speaking, drift off into promiscuous whispering; the performance is diversified by the slamming of doors and the squeaking boots of some late arrival, or the rattle of some newfledged and inexperienced Sophomore's cane; the sun beats down upon the roof of the church until the interior is as hot as an oven; and the peculiar rustle of fans, which the heat necessitates, prevents even the speaker's words— if haply they are worth hearing—being distinctly audible. The complaint has often been made that Commencement Day is losing all its old attractions, now that Class Day has become a permanent institution. We see the reason in the facts we have noticed. How can there be any interest taken in exercises such as these? And that the picture is not over-drawn a half hour spent in the church at commencement will convince anyone. The speeches are so numerous and the exercises so lengthened out that even enthusiasts in oratory cannot endure them all. The fault clearly is that there are altogether too many speakers.

The remedy for this evil—for an evil it certainly is—cannot be so easily pointed out. The number of orators must be cut down, but whether orations shall only be given to the "honormen" as heretofore, or whether they shall be bestowed for especial merit in oratory and in literature, is not so easily determined. We are inclined to believe that a compromise between these two methods might be made, by which the first five honormen should be given speeches, and five other men in the class, distinguished for their writing or elocution, should also be favored. Of course the valedictory should be bestowed as at present.

The only real objection to some such plan would come from those who would neither be included in the list by their stand nor their oratorical ability, but who would, on the present system, get a chance to exhibit themselves to the world. We believe that there are few of this sort; few, we hope, care so much to be talked about as to be willing to pillory themselves to accomplish that end. When men can gain neither honor nor profit by taking a part in the exercises on the commencement stage, it will be strange indeed if they are not willing to give up the privilege in the matter which they now possess.

We believe that a change in the Commencement Exercises is necessary, if they are ever to regain their ancient pre-eminence in College life; and we see no more feasible plan than the above for accomplishing this change. It is not radical by any means, but only proposes a modification of existing and well established customs; and a modification, too, which the size of classes renders almost absolutely imperative.

❖

Social Debating Clubs.

Frequent complaint is heard that as a College we aim at filling instead of strengthening and polishing; that too little attention is paid to social culture; that our graduates are practical and energetic enough, but have no generous love of literature; that not enough time is devoted to the arts, to writing, to oratory, in short to the attainment of all those accomplishments which constitute so much of the benefit that a College course is expected to impart.

Some charge it to the small time allotted to the English course, others to our lack of regular instruction in oratory, while a few suggest that the absence of the Greek-letter Societies takes from us a valuable source of social improvement. That our curriculum is faulty in this particular is undoubtedly true, but the remedy is largely in our own hands. In the first place, the Halls, if properly sustained and employed, are capable of doing noble work in this direction. They offer strong inducements to effort and afford considerable opportunity for practice, but they labor under the disadvantage of being too large and too promiscuous in their membership, to alone remedy the evil. But there is a new element appearing in our College life which may do most efficient service in this respect. It is the small literary and social clubs that are springing up, several of which have long existed in the present Senior Class, and have proved valuable allies of the Halls. True, they involve some work, but that is a postulate in all improvement. Their benefits are numerous. They give a practical acquaintance with literature and history, which is the condition of any profitable enthusiasm in those departments. To be sure, the study may be desultory and lack the direction of an instructor, but this objection becomes very slight when we remember that each one receives the benefit, not alone of his own work, but of that of his companions. Then, too, the style of oratory developed in such societies is just that which will help us the most out of College. The tendency of all College speaking is to become mere declaiming. Notice the Chapel Stages. How many speakers give the impression that they care for what they say, except that it may sound well?

Few men can develop much earnestness when their sole object is to make a good appearance. But in these societies there is little inducement to make a display, for each one knows that his calibre is already measured. The object of the discussion is to arrive at the truth, or to influence the opinions of his comrades. Does any one object that such discussions must be uninteresting; let him make the experiment, and he will find that there are generally enough conflicting opinions in any dozen of well-read fellows to make a lively evening, if it can only be started. But, perhaps, their greatest advantage lies in the fact that they form social organizations of the highest type. A recent *Lit.* essay ably maintained the value of conversation as an educator. Where could we have this better exemplified than in the intelligent and animated conversations which such societies encourage? Select, but not exclusive, they promote the most desirable kind of College friendship. They have most of the advantages without the dangerous temptations, and the compulsory element of the fraternities. Affording valuable opportunities for social and literary culture, they certainly seem a very excellent addition to our College world.

Printed in *The Princetonian*, III (Feb. 6, 1879), 161-62, 164-65.

From the Minutes of the Liberal Debating Club

Feb'y 8. 1879—

Minutes read and adopted. The sec'y of State reported in regard to the purchase of books, report accepted. There being no Misc. business Mr. Mitchell read chapter 3. Cushing's Manual. Mr. Sheldon was excused from speaking. The following question was then discussed:

Res: That is would be for the best interests of France for M. Gambetta to accept office at the present time. Wilson.

The question passed its first and second readings. The society went into Com. of Whole with Mr. McCarter in the chair; after a short discussion the committee rose and the mover of the question with the consent of the society withdrew the question.

The sec. of State appointed dates for the following questions:

For Feb. 15—Res: That the Eng. Church should be disestablished—Emery

For Feb. 22:—Res.—That Pope was a greater poet than Dryden—Elsing.

For M'ch 1;—Res: That the administration of Lord Beaconsfield's Cabinet has been highly prejudicial to the British Empire, and that a liberal triumph would accrue to its best interests. Wilson

For M'ch. 8; Res: That Home Rule would be prejudicial to the interests of Ireland. Wilson—

For M'ch. 22, Res: That prohibition by Congress of Chinese immigration would be unjustifiable—McCarter.

There being no further business before the society, adjournment took place at 9.50 P.M.

Charles Talcott N.Y.　Sec of State　Harold Godwin N.Y.　Pres—

From Annie Wilson Howe

My precious Brother,　　　　　　　Columbia Feb. 9th 1879.

I have only time to write a line or two, but I want to thank you for the picture. It is *splendid*. I never saw a better likeness and it is so beautifully finished. I wish the artist who took it would step down this way and take some photographs of my little family. Some of the students looking at your picture the other night said that you looked younger than you did when at Davidson. . . .

Your devoted Sister, Annie

ALS (WP, DLC) with WWhw notation on env.: "Ans 3/2/79."

Editorial in *The Princetonian*

[Feb. 13, 1879]

We have every reason to congratulate ourselves on the prospect of hearing Mrs. Scott-Siddons[1] and as many reasons to be provoked that no better lecture-room could be procured for her. The Methodist Church is small and dingy; in fact is not the best room that even Princeton can furnish. From that best room Mrs. S. has been excluded by pure caprice. Of course the officers of the Second Presbyterian Church have an unimpeachable right to make what use they will of their building; and, as that organization has at length freed itself from a debt full of convenience to the amusement attending community, we must expect to find it more scrupulous and discriminating than heretofore about the means of acquiring lucre. But it requires a nicer conscience than the children of this world possess to discern the religious principle which, while it throws open the doors of that sacred edifice to "Adirondack" Murray's[2] jokes, Helen Porter's mimicking and a quack phograph [*sic*] manipulator, slams them in the face of Henry Ward Beecher and Mrs. Scott-Siddons.

Printed in *The Princetonian*, III (Feb. 13, 1879), 173.

[1] Mary Frances Siddons, a famous beauty and former actress, who was to give dramatic readings at the Methodist Church on Feb. 19. See WW's review at Feb. 27, 1879.

[2] William Henry Harrison Murray, a Congregationalist minister and author of several volumes of sermons, who was an early enthusiast for going back to nature. He popularized the Adirondack region in lectures and many books, including *Adventures in the Wilderness or Camp-life in the Adirondacks* (Boston, 1869), and *Adirondack Tales* (Boston, 1877).

From Janet Woodrow Wilson

My darling Son,   Wilmington N. C. Feby 14th '79.

... At what time do you think it would be best for you to go to N. Y? and what would be the amount of your expenses—in addition to the $15 you mentioned? Dont forget to let me know—so that the arrangement may be made as early as you desire. I am so relieved to know that there is to be no operation upon the eye—for I believe it is always a dangerous experiment.

Thank you for marking your pieces in the last Princetonian.[1] We read them with so much pleasure. Your father takes great delight in the P. Says he would regard it as invaluable, if he were one of the Professors. Its influence is always on the right side, not only—but it informs the Professors of all they need to know with reference to the students—which he thinks must be of the greatest advantage if they use it rightly. Goodbye now my darling. I will try &

write early next week. No news of course. Your father & Josie unite with me in unbounded love.

Lovingly   Mother

I see you are having entertainments—and I fear you have no "spondulics." I enclose $1. that will do for one I suppose.

ALS (WP, DLC).
    ¹ Copies marked by WW are missing.

From the Minutes of the Liberal Debating Club

Feb. 15 1879

Meeting called to order at 8 P.M—with Pres. Godwin in the chair. The minutes were read and adopted. Misc. business being in order, Mr. McCarter moved that a committee be appointed to arrange a debate between the members of the L. D. C. and the members of the Cyclops.¹ After being briefly commented upon the motion was laid on the table.

Mr. Webster then read sec. 1 chap. 12 of Cushing's Manual, after which the following question was discussed:

Res: That the Eng. Church should be disestablished. The question passed its first and second readings. The com. of the whole reported favorably and the report was adopted.

Misc. business: Mr Wilson moved that art. 13 of Constitution be stricken out. The resolution passed first & second readings & com. of whole. There being no further business, the Society adjourned at 9.45 P.M.   Harold Godwin N. Y.   Pres—
Charles Talcott N. Y.   Sec. of State

    ¹ This group is mentioned in Godwin's *History of the Class of '79*, p. 16.

Two Letters from Joseph Ruggles Wilson

My darling Son—   Wilmington, [N. C.] Feb 19   1879.
    I enclose draft on N. York for $25.00 for Eye purposes, &c.
    I have sent to "Wm Harris, Treas." the am't of quarter's bill.
    The Church treasury here is so far in arrears that I am becoming embarrassed pecuniarily. If matters continue as they are, your going to Law School will be very doubtful.
    I am thankful that your health is so good and your spirits so cheerful. As to the publication of yr Essay I can better judge when I see it. If it be really good—as I am sure it is—I don't see why I may not get it inserted in some review. I certainly will try for it.

How dearly we all love you cannot be put into words—and we are proud of you besides.

Your ever loving & ever hurried Father.

I will write more at length when yr. piece comes.

ALS (WP, DLC).

My dearest Son—   Wilmington, [N. C.] Feb 25 1879

I return you the Mss containing your discussion of Cabinet gov't. I have read it and re-read it, and have ventured to make a few verbal corrections. My hope is that it will find speedy publication in one of the Quarterlies. It deserves at least that much distinction. Suppose then that you send it to the North American Review, after taking a copy for trial elsewhere should it be refused there. Your arguments are quite to the point, and ought to be given to the thoughtful public for the purpose of eliciting a wide discussion into which you might enter with a second piece. I need not say that I entirely approve of the positions you have taken and so well maintained. But I will say that your manner of presentation is worthy of my sincerest commendation. I do not think you could improve the composition. It is neat, terse, manly, and sufficiently flowing, leaving fewer marks of inexperience than many writings of older heads which yet have found a place in our review literature. It might, with advantage, be made to *glow* a little more. It is, to a certain extent, cold; but then, in such a discussion rhetoric can afford to dispense with warmth if it have enough of *light*: and this your piece unquestionably has. Imagination has not here much room. What is most needed is clearness, and clearness does not necessarily require the ornamentation of color. That you are yourself dissatisfied with your own performance I am glad to know. For dissatisfaction with present achievement implies future progress. And *I* do not pronounce what you have written, perfect. It might be considerably improved—and you *will* improve upon it. Let, however, *this* essay remain just as it is. The probability is that, were you to rewrite it many times more, you would succeed only in *stiffening* it. Send it out unmended, to take its fate. You are perhaps correct in thinking that long-hand writing is more favorable than short hand, to composition which ought, like a tree, to grow rather than, like a house, to be built. You should use your short-hand as a rapid limner rather than as a filler-in of details. Or—let me make this suggestion. When you *first* are studying a given subject, place it upon paper in short-hand:—then make *no direct use* of that, but, quitting it altogether, commence afresh in long-hand as if you had not previously written at all. The one operation would give you the advantage of rapid and connected *study*—the other that of slow and connected *expression*. To say a thing is not *merely* to say it, but to say it suggestively—i.e., so as to leave the impression that there is much more which *might* be said, at which you *hint*. This conveys idea of mastery and power. Thus, expression of thought is itself thought, and so, the more *free* this expression is—the more it *swings* in its subject the more telling and taking it is—for, the more it seems to embrace. Well, one can thus swing only when heated with his matter—*after having studied it in cold blood*—i.e. getting the definitions all right, the facts all marshalled, the arguments all nakedly stated. This done (say in short-hand) then, without risk of inexactness, the writer can give scope to his pen, a scope that has no limits except of taste.

But you will find that *practise* is, in this as in all else, another name for perfection. *You* have only to persevere. As it is, I feel proud of you, and send you thanks for the pleasure this essay has given both your dear mother & myself.

I am not able to write more now. God bless you, my boy. Do not forget to ask His blessing upon your efforts, every day for yourself.

All send unbounded love.   Your affectionate Father.

ALS (WP, DLC). Att.: JRW to WW, "Saturday 13th," printed at Dec. 13, 1879.

Drama Criticism in *The Princetonian*

[Feb. 27, 1879]

That Mrs. Scott-Siddons' reading was highly appreciated was very clearly manifested by the vociferous and somewhat undiscriminating applause of her audience. And as a whole it was very enjoyable indeed. Her chief fault is an exaggeration, which seems to be affectation. Perhaps this exaggerated style of acting is excusable in one who acts, as she did, without the aid of those almost essential auxiliaries, costume and scenery. Without these an extra effort seems necessary to rouse the imagination of the audience, and it requires a higher genius than Mrs. Scott-Siddons possesses to make this extra effort without over-doing the matter and sometimes degenerating into affectation, into mere staginess. Her worst manner was illustrated in her reading of the selection from the play of "As You Like It," her best in "The Legend of Bregenz" and her special part, the sleep walking scene from Macbeth. In the two latter she was thoroughly at home, and, consequently, thoroughly natural. She certainly did not want for encouragement from her audience, receiving from them as hearty cheers as those which, on her last visit to Princeton, three years ago, drew from her the exclamation: "I would go a thousand miles to read to such an audience." And most of the applause was well-deserved.

Printed in *The Princetonian*, III (Feb. 27, 1879), 183.

Three Editorials in *The Princetonian*

[Feb. 27, 1879]

We found in the *Voices* of the last *Lit*. an article on College debating which impressed us as being in every way admirable. It pointed to the undoubted fact that we have witnessed here a divorcement of oratory from debate; that this has been brought about by false, undiscriminating criticism which exalts correctness to a supremacy—an undisputed throne—which does not of right belong to it; and that, as a result, we are coming to witness the death, the utter extirpation, of all true excellence in debate. That these errors are fostered by the rules under which the Lynde Debate is conducted is, we think, beyond question. For the debaters are generally given a broad, many-sided question to discuss and are required to pack their main arguments into the compass of twelve minutes. They *must*, it seems, from the necessity of the case, throw away all ornament and content themselves with a bald, bare statement of facts and a spare outline of the logical phases of the matter in hand. The debater must do this, or else confine himself to the elaboration of a small part of the subject and expose himself to the charge, from the unthinking, of shallowness or narrowness. Now, debate is the chief field of oratory, outside of the pulpit. A lawyer's life must be spent in the atmosphere of eager debate; a statesman must constantly breathe the air of public discussion and win his way to honor and power as a master of dialectic fence—his life is a life of discussion. The hustings is a place of debate. The lecture platform is the exception. And certainly any one who hopes to make all his extemporaneous expression "quadrable by the classical formulae" hopes against possibility. We look anxiously for reform in this matter—or rather for a clearing up of College opinion. Until we eschew declamation and court oratory we must expect to be ciphers in the world's struggles for the settlement of principles and the advancement of causes. Oratory is persuasion, not the declaiming of essays. The passion and force of oratory is spontaneous, not carefully elaborated. Logical statement pure and simple is not oratory; nor is a polished style always eloquence.

✧

In deciding to take the excellence of the speeches handed in, as well as the standing of their authors, into consideration in making appointments for Commencement Stage, the Faculty have undoubtedly taken a step in the right direction, but only one step. We perceive it with gratification not because we look upon it as the adoption of an entirely rational system, but because it is a move which indicates a partial recognition of the necessity for some new system and gives promise of better things to come. We have recently outlined in these columns what seemed to us a much juster and much more reasonable basis of appointment to Commencement honors. It is common matter of everyday talk among the students themselves, that, under the forms and methods of education which obtain among American educational institutions, there is almost always found to be a set of men in each class which pursues the "classical" curriculum who stand below the honor list and are yet among the brightest men of their class. They devote much of their time to outside reading; to study whose field lies without the course; to the work of literary societies; or the acquirement of skill in writing, speaking and debate. In order to pursue such a course they partially neglect some of the regular studies which are required of them, and thus, while winning and holding a creditable stand in their classes, fail to carry off any College honors for scholarship. These men are not infrequently hard and conscientious workers. They are often men who are sure to do their life work well and to bring honor upon their College. They are preparing themselves, amidst the varied requirements of a general classical course, for the special work which awaits them after graduation. And this work of theirs certainly deserves some recognition from the Faculty. We hope in future to see the number of Commencement speakers limited to fifteen, of which number ten may be appointed for scholarship and five for literary or oratorical excellence. Under such a system the Professor of Eng. Lit. would see the character of the essays handed in to him rapidly improve. The regular essays of the class in Eng. Lit. are now often regarded by many as interferences with their private work; they would then be part of it. To adopt such a system would not be to encourage neglect of regular college work, but to encourage men to supplement the course by such literary work as will prepare them to make Princeton famed in those fields in which it is commonly said she has no fame.

❖

Exchanges

One of the Regents from Williams of the Inter-Collegiate Literary Association sends a short communication to the *Athenaeum* in regard to the prospects of the association. He reports interest more lively as proved by the fact that one more College has joined. But there is no knowing how soon it will want to get out again. Almost every College in the association would like to leave it now; Cornell is restless, Madison is grumbling, even Williams we suspect is not as firmly established in its allegiance as this Regent would wish. He tries to awaken enthusiasm by stating that at the next meeting of the Board of Regents there will be discussed a motion to offer a money prize in oratory; and by applauding what he justly calls the common sense policy of filling the offices with influential men, instead of students and recent graduates. We do not wish to darken his bright dream, but yet we fear that all money prizes will end as the one did last year; and that even influential men will not be able to interest people in this moribund association to the extent of influencing their pockets. We await with some interest the decision which Williams must come to sooner or later in regard to her further connection with the association.

Printed in *The Princetonian*, III (Feb. 27, 1879), 183-84, 192.

From the Minutes of the Liberal Debating Club

March 1st 1879.

Meeting called to order at 7.45 P.M. with Mr. Godwin in chair. Absent, Messrs. Elsing, Mitchell, & Sheldon. The minutes were read and adopted. Misc. [business] being then in order it was moved to take from the table the question in regard to a debate with the Cyclops. The question was taken from the table, & coming before the society, was lost. Mr. Woods read Sec. 2 Ch. XII of Cushing's Manual. Mr. McCarter was appointed to deliver a speech at next meeting. Debate being in order, the question regarding the disestablishment passed its 3d reading. The Society then considered the following question—

Res: That the administration of Lord Beaconsfield's Cabinet has been highly prejudicial to the British Empire and that a liberal triumph would accrue to its best interests.

The question passed its 1st and 2d readings. The society went into Com. of Whole with Mr. Elsing in the chair; the com. reported favorably and the report was accepted.

There being no further business before the Society, adjournment took place at 10 P.M.   Harold Godwin N. Y.   Pres.
Charles Talcott N. Y.   Sec. of State.

Mar. 8th 1879

Meeting called to order by the Sec'y of State, the Pres being absent. Mr. McCarter was appointed Sec. of State pro. tem. There being no misc. business Mr. Emery read from Sec. III of Cushing's Manual. The debate being next in order the question in regard to Beaconsfield's policy coming up for its 3rd reading, was carried. The regular bill of the evening next came up: Res: That Home Rule would be prejudicial to Ireland's interests. This bill passed its first and second readings and Committee of Whole, Mr Elsing in the Chair.

The orator of the Evening Mr. McCarter spoke on the subject The Government of the Future. There being no Misc. business the meeting adjourned at 9.30

R. Harris McCarter   Chas. Talcott Pres. pro. tem.
Sec. of State pro. tem.

From Janet Woodrow Wilson

My precious Son,   Wilmington N. C. Tuesday [March 11, 1879]

... I hope you are keeping quite well my darling. You should be very careful during this warm weather. I am really glad you are so nearly through with the Princetonian. It gives me *great* pleasure to read it—but I can't help thinking of the labour it must be to you. The last number was perfect. I think you have reason to be proud of your success. What of your Essay? Your father was so delighted with it. He thinks that it would suit the "Princeton Review," if the "North American" is stupid enough to reject it. You wont be too easily discouraged, I trust—for you have some idea of how such matters are worked. You cannot fail to succeed in gaining the ear of the public if you persevere....

God bless you, my darling. I will write again before leaving for Columbia.   Yours lovingly   Mother

ALS (WP, DLC) with WWhw notation on env.: "Editors Int. Review 31 Beacon St. Boston."

Editorial in *The Princetonian*

[March 13, 1879]

The disorder of which the Seniors are guilty in Professor Guyot's room is disgraceful. Professor Guyot now stands at the head of the Physical Geographers of the world, and a large majority of his class are naturally anxious to take full notes on his admirable lectures; many of them are, however, prevented from doing so by the continual buzz of conversation which is kept up in the back part of the room, and amidst which it is impossible to hear half of the lecture. Even if Professor Guyot were an uninteresting lecturer and the number of those wishing to take notes small, the remainder of the class would have no right to prevent those who did wish to do so. We would even prefer to see those who can not keep quiet, cultivate the not very creditable habit of sneaking from the room, as some now do. This, of course, is arguing the matter on the narrow ground of individual comfort and privilege, and of mutual consideration and general gentlemanliness. It is leaving altogether out of view the disrespect to the lecturer, which is thus manifested, and the neglect of duty on the part of the disturbers of quiet and order. But these latter phases of the matter have so often been dwelt upon at length, without producing any effect upon class-room habits, that we now seek to call attention to the more practical feature of it, the feature of personal right. We each have a right in this matter, which others, as gentlemen, are bound to respect. As we have before said, Professor Guyot's room is none of the best for hearing, even under the most favorable circumstances, and the most perfect order and quiet, is therefore, all the more imperatively necessary. We would fain believe that those who talk thus loudly and constantly, do so from thoughtlessness; we hesitate to attribute their conduct to malicious motives. And, believing thus, we hope that it is only necessary to call their attention to the fact that they are inconveniencing, even wronging their class-mates, by so disregarding propriety and the comfort of others.

Printed in *The Princetonian*, III (March 13, 1879), 197.

Music Criticism in *The Princetonian*

[March 13, 1879]

CONCERT.—A concert was given in the Second Presbyterian Church on Thursday evening, March 6th, by the Glee and Instrumental Clubs, assisted by Miss Maud Morgan, of New York, and Mr. Edward Giles, of Philadelphia. The audience was very large for a winter entertainment. Miss Morgan, although a harpist of but four years experience, made a most favorable impression. She rendered the more difficult pieces with expression and ease of execution, but it was the old and familiar tunes that drew forth the longest and loudest applause. Mr. Edward Giles has a powerful and well-trained voice. He gave the Two Grenadiers and the

Bass Solo in good style, but on one or two occasions was unfortunate in selecting pieces unsuited to his age.

The Instrumental Club never appeared to better advantage than in its rendering of the selections from Weber and Mozart. There was, as a rule, perfect harmony, the Club showing that it had worked patiently with able training. Its rendering of the selection from Strauss was less fortunate, the first violin not showing a sufficient acquaintance with the music.

The Glee Club was never more warmly received. The Waltz and College Songs were well rendered and received double *encores*. But it was the chorus from the Pinafore which particularly delighted the house; the solos of the Admiral, the Captain, and little Buttercup were all well rendered, and if more selections had been prepared the audience would have kept the Club singing until a very late hour. The only thing to be regretted is that fewer College Songs were prepared: one was repeated as an *encore*. No one, however, went away dissatisfied with the Princeton Musical organizations.

Printed in *The Princetonian*, III (March 13, 1879), 202-203.

From Joseph Ruggles Wilson

My very dear Thomas—   [Wilmington, N. C.] Mar 20   79

You would do right, I think to contest for a place among the senior debaters. Only make up your mind to fail, and there need be no feeling of regret. The fact is, no one ever becomes much unless he knows how to *conquer* failure—which is best done by treating it as a spur to the success which laughs at failure by and by. I am greatly pleased to know that extemporaneous speaking is your forte. By all means cultivate the gift or rather the assemblage of gifts. It is rare, and as valuable as rare. It is the *diamond* among those accomplishments which ensure the future of a public man. Try for the "Lynde Debate." And you can try *best* by not having any anxiety as to whether you shall be chosen or not: for anxiety is partial paralysis. I am glad that you are by this time rid of the base ball presidency. Yet it is well to have "tried it on"—for something was learned and something enjoyed. . . .

Goodbye, beloved son,   Your affc Father

ALS (WP, DLC) with WWhw notations on env.: "Ans."; "*Carmina May 1st*"; and "Alfred S. Niles." Also WWsh notes: "Do the advantages of universal suffrage excuse [?] its failures in the United States." *Carmina Princetonia* was the title of a series of Princeton song books first published in 1869. The edition of 1879 was published in Newark, N.J.

From the Minutes of the Liberal Debating Club

Mch. 22d 1879

Meeting called to order, pres. in the chair. Minutes read and adopted. There being no misc. business Mr. Elsing read sect. 1st Chap. XV Cushing's Manual. The debate being in order the question, Res. That Home rule would be prejudicial to Ireland's interests, passed its 3d reading. The regular bill of the evening was then considered: Res. That prohibition by Congress of Chinese immigration would be unjustifiable. The bill passed its 1st & second readings & com. of whole with Mr. Elsing in the Chair. Miss. business being in order, Mr. Wilson was elected to deliver the Valedictory address at the last meeting of the society. The society adjourned at 10.5 P.M.

Charles Talcott, N. Y.   Sec'y of State.

Harold Godwin, N. Y.   Pres.

Five Editorials in *The Princetonian*

[March 27, 1879]

Modesty is not a fashionable virtue at the Gymnasium. Some of the gymnasts, especially some Freshmen who are, as yet, called gymnasts only by courtesy, seem to delight in showing as much bare flesh as possible. Not only is it the style, among some, to have no sleeves to their shirts—there could be no objection to bare arms, simply—but the arm-holes take the form of a long opening, which discloses no small portion of the wearer's side. This is a very delicate subject for editorial comment, but we mean to speak plainly, even here. We do not care to take lady visitors into the galleries of the Gymnasium, when they are likely to see men dressed in a style which is disgusting even to our more hardened eyes and sensibilities; and we know that many have refrained from visiting the Gym. for this very reason. Gentlemen will be careful; others should be forced to be so. Their natural beauties, when unadorned, are not so pleasing (are even disgusting) to us, however much they themselves may admire them.

✧

Have the Faculty, or whoever is the authority in the matter, fully and finally determined not to change the time which had been fixed upon for Lynde Debate? If so, they are acting most unwisely, and are threatening the Debate with absolute overthrow. It has been announced to take place on the evening of Class-Day.

For that same evening, is appointed the Sophomore Reception. Now, we need hardly say that, to most of the people who visit us at Commencement, a debate is not, of itself, a very attractive exercise. Not a few of the young people who attend, certainly go simply because it is one of the regular exercises, and, being here for no other purpose than "taking in" all the events of Commencement week, they do not wish to miss it. Then, too, there is a whole evening to be whiled away, and it may be best gotten through with by availing oneself of the only amusement provided. But, let there be another and more attractive entertainment offered, and there is little reason to suppose that the decision would be in favor of the Debate. And, certainly, after the fatigues of Class-Day exercises, very few of our fair visitors will care to wait in a crowded and hot church, for the hour of the Reception to arrive, especially with a painful and ever-present consciousness that their evening dresses were becoming crushed out of all shape. But the fatigues of Class-Day would affect the audience less than the debaters. The debaters are all Seniors, and must, of course, have been prominent in the exercises of the day, unless, indeed, they were kept away from the exercises of their classmates altogether because of the anxiety and necessity for study, if not for some rest, which would rest upon them in view of the duties of the night. In either case, they would be placed at an unfair disadvantage. If they did their duty, they would be deprived of the pleasure of witnessing and taking part in the exercises of a day which, to them, as Seniors, would be *the* day of the Commencement season. If they regarded the pleasures of the day before the duties of the night, the latter might be performed in so negligent a manner as to give the audience good reason for thinking the Debate a bore, if not a farce. We are here only adding further emphasis to facts which were well brought out by a contributor, in a recent number.[1] The matter is a really serious one, and should be looked to immediately. Why could not Lynde Debate come on Saturday evening? We know of no event which has been appointed for that time, as yet, for the Glee and Instrumental Clubs do not intend giving their concert then, as heretofore.

[1] The communication, "Lynde Debate on Class-Day Night," *The Princetonian,* III (Feb. 13, 1879), 176-77.

✧

In our criticism of the playing of the Instrumental Club, at the last concert, we failed to make mention of a very commendable feature in their performance. We refer to the excellence of their selections. Their programme was never before so good. To be sure, the Club did not win their wonted fill of glory and applause, on that occasion. But the correct explanation of the comparative coldness with which they were received, was given in our last issue. The execution of the music, and not the music itself, failed to satisfy the audience. In fact, good music has always been enthusiastically appreciated by the fellows. We need only refer, in illustration, to the popularity of the "Surprise Symphony," "Fest March from Tanhaüser," and the oft-repeated "Overture to Massainello." The Club has no reason, therefore, to be discouraged from elevating, as far as possible, the musical character of its *repertoire*. This fact, and the steady advance that has been made during the past two years, from polkas, gallops, quadrilles, and the lightest waltzes, to thoroughly classical music, encourage us to suggest to the Club that they can in no way make their concerts so agreeable to us as by introducing into their programmes a greater proportion of operatic airs, and of that style of music so perfectly exemplified in Mendelssohn's songs without words. No music is more enjoyable or better enjoyed, at Princeton—none so excellently adapted to the number and combination of instruments in our little Orchestra. There has been, heretofore, we think, rather too strict an adherence to the heavier forms of classical music, to overtures, marches, etc.; and, in truth, the rendition of these has been creditable and, for the most part, very acceptable. But, although the performers have, in every case, made as much noise as they very well could, a certain want of fullness must have been sadly apparent to those who have listened to these same selections as rendered by an approximately full Orchestra. Furthermore, in lieu of the proper instruments, the piano is forced to do a vast share of the work, greatly to the discomfiture of second violin, bass, and flute, which are often hardly audible. Occasionally, and for variety's sake, overtures are to be recommended; but we think that the less ambitious style of music above suggested, with its comparative ease of execution, its popularity and capacity for nicety of expression, could much more suitably form the body of the *repertoire* of the Instrumental Club.

❖

A matter of importance presents itself to us and, although it does not press itself as of immediate importance, yet such things ought to be brought before the College in time to give ample opportunity for careful consideration. It is in regard to the election of University base-ball captains. By the system which has been followed for the last few years, the captain is elected by the remaining members of the past year's University Nine at the beginning of the year following their season, and the captain must be chosen from this remnant. Now, it may to some seem reasonable to suppose that the best man could be found in this number and that they are better fitted to choose the right man; but strong objections may be urged against such a system. By the loss of the Senior Class, it is possible, although hardly probable, that none of the old nine remain; in such a case there can be no captain elected by the present rule. It is possible that only two of the former nine be left; in this case there can be no election, unless one man votes for himself. But, to state a general case, what usually happens, say four or five men remain. These four or five must elect a captain from their own number, however excellent a man, pre-eminently fitted for the place, may be in College at the time, outside of this number. The captain must be elected from this remnant. Another objection is that the College has nothing whatever to say on a question of great interest to the College. The whole power rests with a few men, from ten or eleven to an indefinitely small number. The original plan was for the retiring nine to elect before disbanding, but this has degenerated into the present plan. The former is preferable, but neither is right. The ultimate decision ought to rest with the College and we would suggest a middle course combining both. Give the vote of the old nine some preference, let them nominate a man either from their number or from outside before they disband, and, while giving first consideration and some preference to this nomination, let the College still retain the power of final election. The present plan is obviously unjust and impracticable, and something of the kind ought to be done this year. The College is mainly interested and with the College ought to rest the real power. We call the attention of base-ball men and others to this matter in the hope that some action will be taken before the present season is over. It is, of course, farthest from our intention to be personal; no reflection is cast on past captains nor on our present excellent one. We are writing against a system and not against any particular man.

The struggling Boating Association seem to be making preparations for putting a crew upon the water. The debt is said to be now nearly liquidated, and the officers of the association are considering the best means of raising an amount of money sufficient to put the boat-house and some of the better boats in repair and to allow them enough surplus to commence the season's work without the terror of bankruptcy before them in the immediate future. Now, we sincerely hope that the debt may speedily be paid, and, were the association able to point to any prospect of promise; were they able to hold out any reasonable expectation that they will be able to meet the expenses incident upon an active rowing season; could they make it appear to the satisfaction of the College that our crew would have any good opportunity of meeting crews which really represented any of the larger Colleges, any really worthy antagonists, we would not for one moment allow ourselves to put any obstacles in their way. We would not feel justified in giving them anything but a most hearty and constant support. We would, as in the past, do all in our power to further all the athletic enterprises which gave any reasonable ground for hope of success or advantage to the College, now or in the future. But it would be both unwise and unpatriotic to conceal from ourselves the real facts as to this matter of boating in Princeton. Experience has taught us one or two things, to forget which would be to invite and to deserve failures as disastrous as those of the past. And one of the most prominent of these teachings is, that no association can flourish here unless it be self-supporting. Foot-ball and base-ball associations have their treasuries supported by gate money. They are not compelled to depend upon mere donations from the students and liberal friends of the College for means of subsistence. They have numerous games with outside teams and nines, and the money paid by those who wish to witness these games—and those who do wish to see them are by no means few, under ordinary circumstances—is sufficient, with provident and economical management, to defray all necessary expenses. With boating it is manifestly far otherwise. There is no gate money at a boat race; and yet the expense which must be undergone in the training and preparation which culminates in one day's racing, in one short race, is often, nay generally, equal to, if not greater than, that of the busiest foot-ball or base-ball season. To student subscribers it seems so much money sunk, or, at most, given in order that some of their number may have the pleasure of a season's rowing; for in our case there is no success to look back upon, and no prospect of success, over very formidable antagonists at least, in the future. These are the stern realities of the matter; and, in view of the recent action concerning incurring debts, it would be well for our boating men to face them at once.

Printed in *The Princetonian*, III (March 27, 1879), 207-209.

From the Minutes of the Liberal Debating Club

Mar. 29th 1879—

President being absent meeting was called to order by Sec'y of State. Mr. Sheldon appointed Sec. of State pro. tem. The minutes of last meeting were read and received. Misc. business being in order, the closing exercises of the society were considered in a com. of the whole, Mr. Wilson in the Chair. On motion of Mr. Woods as amended by Mr. Emery the com. resolved to report in favor of appointing a com. to make the necessary arrangements and to report at a special meeting Tuesday April 1st after Evening Chapel.

Mr. Emery then read sec. 2d chap XV of Cushing's Manual. Mr. Webster being unable to perform in speaking, Debate was in order. The question relative to Chinese immigration then passed its 3d reading.

The subject for the evening, Samuel Johnson was next discussed. There being no misc. business the meeting adjourned at 9.15 p.m.

Chas. Talcott, N. Y. Pres. pro. tem.
Edward W. Sheldon   Sec. of State pro. tem.

From Janet Woodrow Wilson

My precious Son,   Wilmington—[N. C.] Tuesday. [April 1, 1879]

We received your last sweet letter today. We think just as *you do* as to the matter of clothing. I suppose a great deal the best plan will be for you to go to Wannamakers and get what you need for the coming season. You will find a stock there from which you can choose just what will suit you. The stock here is miserable—and besides it is all picked over by the time you get home. I suppose you will want your nice suit for Commencement at any rate. In you[r] next you must let us know as nearly as you can how *much money* you will need—and *when* you would like to get the clothing. I really dont' think it is wise for you to get any clothing here whatever. I wish you could get your coats made by Roger & Peet of N. York—but they confine themselves to clerical clothing, I think. Can you believe it? Your father got a fine broadcloth coat from there a week or two ago—made to order—a perfect fit—a perfect coat in every respect, for fifteen dollars! Did you ever hear of such a thing? Your father was so pleased with it that he ordered a duplicate at once. It seems clothing is very low at present. I must tell you of another bargain which your father got when he was in N. Y. I had insisted upon his getting a new over-coat before he went to Princeton. I wanted him to stop at Wannamakers on his way there—for I wished him to look his best when he went to see you—but it seems he was disobedient in the matter. But when he went to N. Y. he got a "diagonal" Spring over-coat—long, and stylishly made for *twelve* dollars! Incredible isn't it. Something new for him to get bargains you know.

When you get your clothing I would advise you to look patiently till you find just what you want. It is a great mistake to take the first thing offered—for a suit of clothing lasts you a long time—you take such nice care of your clothes too—and it is very unpleasant to have to keep on wearing anything that does not suit you. You are very far from being hard on your clothes, my darling—just as far as possible. No one could take more care than you do—so that you deserve to have something worth taking care of. It is, as you say, every way the best economy to get clothing of the best discription. You must not fail to write particularly as to this matter at once—for you know this is *April. . . .*

Goodbye my precious son. Your father is pretty well. Josie quite so—and we all love you so dearly.

Lovingly   Mother.

ALS (WP, DLC).

To Francis Champion Garmany

Dear Frank,   Princeton, April 2nd/79

Although our friendship has not been as close as our common sympathies would have warranted, I have always looked upon you, as I hope you have looked upon me, as one on whose friendship sure reliance may safely be put. I, perhaps, am colder and more reserved than most of those who are fortunate enough to have been born in our beloved South; but my affection is none the less real because less demonstrative. It shall always be my aim to claim and win and retain and, if possible, deserve the love and intimate communion of all who yet cultivate the courage, chivalry, and high purpose which have hitherto been the birthrights and most cherished virtues of Southern gentlemen; and among the number of these may I ever remember Frank Garmany.

Yours sincerely   Thomas W. Wilson
Wilmington, N. C.

ALS in Francis C. Garmany senior class book (NjP).

From the Minutes of the Liberal Debating Club

Tuesday, April 2d 1879–Special Meeting.
The meeting was called to order at 5.20 p.m. by Sec'y of State,
Mr. Wilson was appointed Sec. of State pro. tem. The committee
appointed to make arrangements for closing exercises of the Society having no report to offer[,] the society went into committee
of whole on this business with Mr. Mitchell in the Chair. Mr Woods
moved that the society have a spread in the room of one of the
members on Saturday evening, April 5th. Mr. Talcott moved as an
amendment that the cost do not exceed 75¢ per. head and that a
committee of arrangements (3) be appointed to complete the arrangements. The amendment was accepted & the motion as
amended was carried; the proceedings of com. of whole being reported to the society were accepted with the amendment that the
pres. pro. tem be chairman of com. of arrangements. The meeting
adjourned at 5.40 P.M.

Thomas W. Wilson   Charles Talcott
    Sec. of State pro. tem.   Pres. Pres. [*sic*] pro. tem.

Two Editorials in *The Princetonian*

[April 10, 1879]
The Base Ball season has come and the Nine have commenced
earnest work. A provisional nine is all that has yet been chosen,
but its composition will probably not be materially changed. Of
course it is as yet too early to forecast the fortunes of the season--
it will not be safe to do so until several games with professional
nines shall have steadied the nerves of the new men. But the prospect seems far from gloomy; and the conscientious character of
the officers of the Association, and the steady habits of the players
give promise of careful practice and rapid improvement and progress. We may be fully justified in placing implicit confidence in
the managers of the Nine's affairs, and may thus throw off the
nervous distrust which paralyzed interest last year. Our first College game will come very early this year, on the Third of May, and
numerous practice games are, of course, imperatively necessary as
a preparation for that game. We must urge the students, therefore, to attend all the games, and thus enable the nine to prosecute
its training vigorously; for, unless supported liberally and constantly, it will give over all work. Much persuasion to this end will
not, we are sure, be necessary if the Association are perfectly
frank with us as to the state of their treasury; and they can hardly

find better means of keeping us informed on this matter than those suggested by a contributor in our last number. The College is not deaf to calls for aid when shown just where it is needed and just how they may most effectually render it. If the Nine gives us good playing, we will assure them of our hearty good will and generous support. We will not support carelessness, but we will encourage hard work; and there is, we believe, every reason to expect careful work this season. Work in Base Ball, such as we saw in Foot Ball, will ensure the Nine success such as that of the Team.

But it is not for the example of hard work only that we owe the Foot Ball Team thanks. As will be seen from the report of the Treasurer of the Association, published in our last issue, a handsome surplus remained after all the expenses of a very busy season had been met. The Base Ball Association, on the other hand, found itself at the opening of the present year under the burden of a large debt consequent upon its inability to pay the expenses of its last campaign. At a recent meeting of the Foot Ball directors, therefore, it was resolved to contribute one hundred dollars toward the liquidation of the Base Ball debt. The latter Association is thus almost entirely freed from embarrassment. This is certainly a most handsome action on the part of the officers of the Foot Ball Association and argues the existence of a very praiseworthy spirit of good-will, of a very laudable desire to contribute all in their power to the success of a less fortunate organization. We could wish to see this purpose of mutual helpfulness grow and become permanent among our various organizations. If properly regulated it need not deprive any of them of that self-reliance which each must cultivate. It need not militate against independence; it may, on the contrary, be made to advance it.

❖

Lynde Debate must, it seems, be sacrificed to the necessity of shortening the Commencement season by one day. We believe that the Faculty have done all they could to arrange the exercises as conveniently as was possible under the circumstances, but it is impossible to crowd so many exercises into three days without slighting some one of them. But still we believe that there is patent in this matter a very queer case of self-deception. In order to shorten the season, Thursday is left out, and Wednesday made Commencement-day; but at the same time several of the College organizations are urged to have their exhibition on the Saturday preceding Commencement-week proper, and thus to lengthen the season at the other end, as it were. It will be just as long and tedious if it begins on Saturday and closes on Wednesday as it would be if it began on Sabbath with the Baccalaureate sermon and closed on Thursday. Visitors must, then, come Saturday morning and spend five days here, or organizations such as the Athletic Club and the Glee and Instrumental Clubs must exhibit in an empty field, play and sing to an empty house. We cannot see how matters are much bettered by this new arrangement. But, to come back to the Lynde Debate. It must take place on the evening of Class-Day, and must on that account, we believe, be deprived of some of its value. For, in view of the fact that the debaters would in all probability be deprived of the enjoyments of the day, were the sides allotted to them on that morning as heretofore, it has been decided to announce the sides on the morning of the Saturday previous. Now, our fear is that in so doing the Faculty will in great part take away from the debate that extemporaneous character which has been its most essential and most admirable feature. This is unfortunate, and we would fain believe that it could be obviated, next year at least, if not this. Lynde Debate is one of the most important events of Commencement-week and should be honored accordingly.

Printed in *The Princetonian*, III (April 10, 1879), 220-21.

Two Letters from Joseph Ruggles Wilson

My dearest Son—   Wilmington, [N. C.] April 10, '79.
    . . . That note from Lodge[1] of the International is very gratifying[.] You acted wisely in leaving the Mss. at his disposal. The article will appear after Congress shall have adjourned and when the public mind will be at leisure to turn to such topics as you present. Delay will thus be an advantage[,] I was much interested in yr account of the debating club. It must be very pleasing to you to reflect that it was your speech which changed the current from gay to grave; and it ought to encourage you to feel that you possess *power* over the minds of others. So influential upon my life has been the belief that *I* had no special claims to superiority—that I am anxious to see you escape this practical blunder,—I would rather have you think too much than too little of yourself and your mental forces. . . .

                                        Your loving Father

ALS (WP, DLC) with WWhw notations on env.: "Rec'd April 12th/79"; "Ans April 13th/79." Also on env.: WWsh draft of three sentences of "Cabinet Government in the United States."
    [1] Henry Cabot Lodge, then "Junior Editor" of the *International Review*.

My darling Son—   [Wilmington, N. C.] April 17   79

Please find enclosed $10.00—all I can now spare.

I am surprised that the question for debate does not interest you.[1] I know of none of greater importance in view of the future of this country. Either a limitation of suffrage or anarchy in twenty-five years or sooner. I do not refer to the Negroes any more than to the ignorant Northern voters. The true principle unquestionably is: the owners of a country ought to be its rulers. That is, let there be property qualification—and all the more, because, *ordinarily*, property and intelligence go together. The Statesman who shall find an effectual and yet a peaceful remedy for universal suffrage will be the foremost leader in the U. States. . . .

Your affectionate   Father

ALS (WP, DLC).
[1] See the editorial note, "Wilson's Refusal to Enter the Lynde Competition."

From the Minutes of the American Whig Society

—Whig Hall—April 25th 1879.

. . . Literary Exercises being next in order, the Ninth Division spoke.
Performed:—Messrs. Wilson, Woods, Young.[1]
Failed:—Messrs. Weed, Westervelt,[2] Wilcox,[3] Wilds, Williams, Withington, Worl.

[1] Frederick B. Young, '82.
[2] George Westervelt, '82.
[3] Hallet D. Wilcox, '82.

From Janet Woodrow Wilson

My darling Son,   Wilmington—[N. C.] Saturday [April 26, 1879]

. . . I am glad that you were able to do your shopping satisfactorily. Cousin Emma was telling me of a house in Phila. which is considered very reliable—Hoyt & something. She says they have great pride as to the *style & fit* of their goods—are not willing to put off a poor fit on anybody—as she says Wannamaker's clerks will do. She thinks that if you are particular to insist on a perfect fit, you get nice & cheap things there—but they seem to have no pride in it for their own sake as the other firms have. However, the failure in your over-coat, would put you on your guard—and you would be more particular. Tell me particularly about your nice suit. I like to imagine how you look. Next time you are getting anything, you might look at the other place.

But I must close now, darling. I am so thankful that you keep well & happy. Dont let the "Hypocrite" distract [?] you. There must be such it seems. God bless you, my precious child. Your father is at Presbytery. Josie joins in warmest love

Lovingly, Your Mother

ALS (WP, DLC) with WWhw notation on env.: "Ans."

From Joseph Ruggles Wilson

My dearest Son—   [Wilmington, N. C.] Tuesday—29th Ap. 79

Enclosed you will find draft on New York for $125 [$155?] being $12 more than you have asked for. Please acknowledge receipt at once.

I see that [Senator George H.] Pendleton of Ohio is stealing yr. thunder as to Cabinet gov't. Have you seen his "bill" or read his speech? . . .[1]

In great haste and great love   Your affc   Father

ALS (WP, DLC) with WWhw notation on env.: "Ans."
[1] See the editorial note, "Cabinet Government in the United States," n. 6.

Two Editorials in *The Princetonian*

[May 1, 1879]

With this number SEVENTY-NINE's work on *The Princetonian* ends and the editorial pen falls to other and, we believe, not less able hands. To us the duties of editing have been both pleasant and profitable, for they have placed us in a position from which we could obtain a closer and more perfect view of College life and affairs both here and at other institutions, and have brought us into a more thorough acquaintance and a fuller appreciation of the needs and excellencies of our course than we could otherwise have gained. How far we have succeeded in keeping pace with College events and in interpreting or guiding College opinion we leave others to judge. Of ourselves we can say that we have worked with a will and with every endeavor to accomplish the best results, and that our efforts have been eminently successful as far as [our] own personal improvement and pleasure in the work have been concerned. During long Winter months when news was scarce and editorial topics scarcer we have not found our task by any means an easy one, but we have seldom found it an irksome one; and however ill it may have been performed, it has always been attended to with prompt and hearty energy. We have sought to keep the paper strictly within its own peculiar province, the province not of literary criticism or of sketchy anecdote, but of close sympathy with Princeton interests both in athletics and in scholarship, and of earnest endeavor to set the current of College sentiment in favor of just and temperate conduct in College affairs. Our hope is that our work will be found to have been apace with our purposes, and that still higher and wider success may attend the labors of our successors.

✧

Princeton will once again take up boating. At a mass meeting of the students held on Thursday last, April the 24th, it was decided to accept the challenge of the crew of the University of Pennsylvania. This challenge was accompanied by a most generous offer to meet all the expenses of our crew and to make all the conditions of the race as favorable for us as they could well be. We are glad that the proposition was accepted, for such a race as is intended will be a trial of our boating capacities under the most favorable circumstances and may be instrumental in settling finally the question whether boating can ever flourish here. If we fail in this attempt, boating may well be looked upon as dead henceforth for Princeton; if we succeed, our rowing association may once again be placed upon a firm, perhaps a permanent, footing. We have before expressed our doubts as to the possibility of boating ever becoming a permanent institution here and we have as yet seen no reason to cast these doubts aside; but we realize the fact that the desire to revive the interest in rowing will not cease to lead to spasmodic and ill-timed efforts at organizing crews until the hopelessness of such efforts is fully and finally demonstrated by the failure of our crew when every circumstance favors. We would not be understood as hoping that our crew will be defeated in the coming race at Philadelphia; far from it. And we are free to confess that we may be mistaken in our views as to Princeton's boating possibilities. But we wish this race to determine once for all our position as a boating or a non-boating college, and for this reason we receive the decision of the mass meeting with satisfaction. We hope that a crew will be organized which will be worthy to represent us.

Printed in *The Princetonian*, III (May 1, 1879), 231-32.

From Janet Woodrow Wilson

My darling Son,   Wilmington–N. C. May 13th [1879]
  ... Did I tell you–that your father said that you were *perfectly*

right in your decision as to the Debate—so do I think so—but I was sorry that you could not enter the lists—i.e. that they chose a question that made it impossible.

Lovingly your Mother

ALS (WP, DLC) with WWhw notation on env.: "Ans 5/18/79."

EDITORIAL NOTE

WILSON'S REFUSAL TO ENTER THE LYNDE COMPETITION

The documents are not fully revealing about Wilson's refusal to enter the Lynde competition. The American Whig Society held its contest to choose its representatives in the forthcoming Lynde Debate on April 22, 1879, the subject being "Resolved that it would be advantageous to the United States to abolish universal suffrage." Seniors wishing to participate drew for sides. As C. A. Talcott to Wilson, May 21, 1879, makes clear, Wilson drew and then refused to defend the side he had drawn, but the minutes of the Society mention neither Wilson's drawing nor his refusal to participate. M. G. Emery, Jr., R. H. McCarter, A. J. Kerr, and Robert Bridges defended the affirmative side; S. A. Harlow, D. C. McLaren, and G. L. Prentiss, the negative. Bridges, Harlow, and Emery were chosen to represent Whig, with Kerr as alternate. Jacob N. Beam, *The American Whig Society*, pp. 191-92, suggests that since there were only three negative debaters, Wilson must have withdrawn from that side because he was unwilling to defend universal suffrage. This seems to be correct, although the letter from Wilson's father, of April 17, 1879, suggests that Wilson had not been very excited by the question when it was announced about a week before the drawing for sides.

The Lynde Debate took place at commencement, on June 16, 1879, in the First Presbyterian Church, the subject being "Ought Chinese Immigration to be Prohibited?" Emery, Chalmers Martin (from Clio), and Harlow debated the affirmative; Bridges, and Peter J. Hamilton and Abram W. Halsey, both from Clio, defended the negative. Halsey won the first prize of $130; Bridges, the second prize of $120; Harlow, the third prize of $100.

The account of this episode in William Bayard Hale, *Woodrow Wilson, The Story of His Life*, pp. 69-70, on which Ray Stannard Baker, *Woodrow Wilson: Life and Letters*, I, 105-106, is largely based, is in error in saying that Wilson, in the qualifying debate in Whig, refused to defend the protective tariff.

His refusal to defend universal suffrage in April 1879 was consistent with his father's views and his own. We find him writing in his diary on June 19, 1876, that universal suffrage was at the foundation of "every evil in this country." His shorthand comment on the envelope of his father's letter of March 20, 1879, reveals that Wilson was still concerned about the "failures" of universal suffrage in the United States. In the first paragraph of "Cabinet Government in the

United States," written in January and February of 1879 (printed at August 1, 1879), he said that universal suffrage was "a constant element of weakness, and exposes us to many dangers which we might otherwise escape." And Wilson, about a year later at the University of Virginia, spoke in favor of restricting the suffrage.[1]

[1] See Jefferson Society Minutes, at February 6 and 28, 1880.

Notes on Professor Murray's Lecture

Wordsworth   5/14/79

Over Wordsworth's poetry a long controversy has raged, as over that of Pope. Some denying to him any poetical talents; others saw in everything he wrote the highest poetical worth. He has however conquered his place. Test of time finds

(*a*) Wordsworth molded some of the best poetry and best literature of the day. Matthew Arnold is his most appreciative living critic and closely follows him. Traces of Wordsworth are to be found in Tennyson, George Eliot, Lowell, Emerson, etc.

(*β*) The best criticism of the day gives highest praise to Wordsworth's poetry. See Professor Shairp, Bagehot, St. Simon.

Born April 7, 1770, in Cumberland. Read a great deal of the fiction of all countries. School exercise: "Summer Vacation" "This is feebly expressed" he himself says but offered an important epoch ["]in my poetical history.["] Interpretation of nature here at this early date.

1787 Entered St. John's College, Cambridge. Graduated in 1790 and went to France during the second stage of the French Revolution (a) intellectual doctrine (b) revolutionary emotions (best period) (c) revolutionary deeds. Wordsworth went to France during the second stage. He was in Paris some days after the deeds of September. 1792 returned to England. He returned with altered feeling, supporting the reactionary party. He found difficulty in finding a profession. He actually made some movements towards journalism. Calvert's bequest of 9 hundred pounds (plain living and high thinking).

Wordsworth's sister must be understood in order to understand Wordsworth himself. Dorothy. See her journal of a journey to Scotland. Through her Wordsworth was rescued from depressed state of despondency at the result of the French Revolution. She was a remarkable woman.

Home in Racedown in 1797. Solitary tendencies showed themselves in choice of home. Imitations of Juvenal unpublished[,] tragedy which was a dead failure. Then entered Racedown where he came into contact with Coleridge. 1798 Lyrical Ballads by both Wordsworth and Coleridge. Rime of the Ancient Mariner first in which Wordsworth assisted. Lines on *Tintern Abbey* were most characteristic tone of the poet. 3 epochs in Wordsworth's career (Shairp's)[1]

A. 1795-1808 period of Lyrical Ballads, springtime of the poet's genius (Alfoxden)

B. 1808-1820 midsummer of genius

C. 1820-1850 Scottish poems[,] ecclesiastical sonnets etc.

Natural qualities of his mind

(a) Mind rigid which amounts almost to austerity. If this tendency unchecked by his sister, it is hard to tell what his career would have been. This was softened by influence of his sister.

(β) Solitary influence. This natural trait, a love of solitude not from headaches of the world but love for necessary solitude in the fertilization of his mind. Indeed the poet owed so little to his fellow man. Studied poets very little indeed. Natural truths met unexpectedly thereby.

(γ) Absence of anything like structural power either as to plot or in the construction of the landscape. Only indicated resemblance[?]

(δ) Absence of humor result of austerity and rigidity.

Strong resemblance to Milton

(a) High reverence for the poet's art. Wordsworth was utterly unmoved by the storms of criticism. Had his appeal to future ages. No incidents in literary history like Wordsworth's standing almost alone in this way.

(b) In the joyousness of nature. Most devout Church of England man.

Prelude must be studied by all who wish to understand the poet. Theory[:] Exposition of the crises through which he passed. Men of science must work in the country according to Wordsworth. This mark of progress. *Taine* on Wordsworth absolutely ridiculous. Looked at the sun on clouds for 10 years.

Theory: To him nature was a living spirit and not a system of laws. A spiritual being in the tree. Love of nature is not all therefore. Life with unity of conscience but not selfishness. Nearness to the clouds a comfort to his life. No naturalist. Lines from Excursion disprove this. The universe a shell to the ear of faith. Natural signs and objects described by selection of one or two essential features bringing out the spirit of the sign. Newton, faith; Voltaire, sinner; Wordsworth, adoration. Hutton's analysis of this power in Wordsworth.[2]

(1) Nature exercises often a plastic influence in molding us into beauty.
(2) Eerie power to awaken passion (Ruth).
(3) Nature's tranquilizing influences on thought. The peculiar interest in human life in its moral and artistic aspect in Wordsworth too much overlooked by critics. Wordsworth as pronounced in this as Dickens, and Browning, etc. Wordsworth's reverence for the human soul always great. Thoughts on immortality. True poetry finds its outflow often in feelings of lowest. Wordsworth did not read enough to give poetry representing outflow of great deeds and men. He has opened up interests in beggars and gypsies. Cumberland beggar.

Wordsworth had singular power of concentrating feeling upon humanity[,] objects. Frugality this is called. He was not prodigal of feeling for instance. He is frugal in feeling. [*] is mentioned. "True description of emotions afterward remembered in tranquility"[3] is his definition of poetry.

Lyrical Ballads do not show him at his best. Not in narrative poems that really found his best efforts. Peter Bell etc. Sonnets are characteristic of Wordsworth because illustrating his frugality of passion or feeling; Dutton [Duddon] sonnets the best. There is want of inspiration in ecclesiastical sonnets. *Ode on Immortality* great in its influence upon Murray. Highest limit of poetry since the days of Milton. Highest limit of a tide of poetic inspiration since Milton. The peer of the greatest. Features of Immortality from recollections of childhood.

First four stanzas of this glory which has vanished from the earth.

5th The notion of preexistence is wrought out

6, 7, 8, Delineate childhood on the earth in which the vanished glory has come to the child

9, Glorious outburst of rapturous praise found at rare intervals in Wordsworth. Highest poetic rapture.

Excursion There are dead levels of prose in it yet also high levels of poetry[,] philosophy, description, sentiment, ingenuity, etc. [* * *] For impulse to the higher life, making the mind higher and better, none exceed Wordsworth.

Transcript of WWsh notes in notebook described at Sept. 11, 1878.

    1 J. C. Shairp, "Wordsworth," *Studies in Poetry and Philosophy* (2nd edn., New York, 1872), pp. 46-47.
    2 Richard H. Hutton. See his essay, "The Genius of Wordsworth," *Literary Essays* (Philadelphia, [1876]), pp. 222-23.
    3 This seems to be Professor Murray's paraphrase of Wordsworth's definition of poetry in the preface to the second edition of *Lyrical Ballads*: "I have said that poetry is the spontaneous overflow of powerful feelings: it takes its origin from emotion recollected in tranquility."

From Charles Andrew Talcott

My dear Tommy:—   Utica [N.Y.] May 21   1879
    . . . I have received the first two numbers of Vol. III of the Princetonian. Before your letter arrived they were my only source of Princeton news as Roessle neglected to send me the old board's last number. I think the paper promises well for the ensuing year but your hand will be sadly missed from the editorial colums. Would you please inform me when your article appears in the *International*. That periodical comes to Utica only for sub[sc]ribers.
    I was somewhat surprised to hear that Emery & Harlow got on Lynde debate. I hardly think they represent the debating talent of Whig Hall. I am very sorry you were unfortunate; in drawing: I think you were right in staying out: arguing against settled convictions, in my opinion, injures a man more than it benefits him. You can rest assured that if you had entered the debate under favorable circumstances an appointment would not have been denied you. . . .
                          Your sincere frie[n]d   Charles Talcott

ALS (WP, DLC) with WWhw notation on env.: "Ans 5/22/79."

From Janet Woodrow Wilson

My darling Son,   Wilmington N. C Friday—May 23. [1879]
    I am glad too,—very glad,—that your father was elected Moderator[1]—all the more as the manner in which he was elected was unusually flattering. He would have been Moderator long ago—has been proposed in private among the members at every meeting of the Ass[embly] for a number of years—but there were always some, who thought that as he was Stated Clerk, he could not with propriety be elected as Moderator. Well—now we ought to be satisfied, I think—for the Church has now conferred upon your father *every* honor in her gift. I am sure he will make the best Moderator possible—the best they have ever had. He appointed Dr. Park[2] of Knoxville to act as Stated Clerk. I receive a hurried note from him nearly every day—he is quite well—and in fine spirits

Three weeks from tomorrow we will be expecting our darling Tommy home! I dont wonder at your regret at parting from your congenial companions & friends. The probability is that you will never have much of the same sort of enjoyment after you leave College. Your father always speaks with loving and longing regret of the choice friends from whom he parted when he graduated. He has never found any to take their place. . . .

Good-bye my precious son. Josie joins me in "abundance of love." Lovingly yours Mother.

ALS (WP, DLC).
1 By General Assembly in Louisville on May 15, 1879.
2 The Rev. James Park, D.D., pastor, First Presbyterian Church of Knoxville.

Marginal Note

William J. Rolfe, ed., *Shakespeare's Tragedy of Hamlet, Prince of Denmark* (New York, 1879).

P. 87 (Act II, Scene II):

Hamlet. . . . for look, where my abridgments come.–

Transcript of WW Shorthand Comment

[c. June 1879]

Some assured commentator might find unsettled fancy in this word. Hamlet had set himself to play the mad man in real life. His life was to be a play. This player played but for a season; he was to play perpetually– they were his *abridgments*. Their plays were short, his might have been long.

From Charles Andrew Talcott

My dear Tommy:– Utica [N. Y.] June 1 1879

. . . The thoughts in your letter concerning our work after graduation deeply impressed me. I entered heartily into their spirit and my flagging energy was quickened. Such thoughts have often arisen in my mind but never so forcibly as after reading your letter. I have been especially prone to reflections of this nature since I have been thrown with the lawyers of this city. I can now plainly see how a disinterested man filled with the desire to benefit his country can accomplish much. Probably many of the lawyers with whom I am acquainted started in life with high motives, but they were soon lost because strength and firmness were wanting. These lawyers have all fallen into the same rut: they first strive for a living; then for a fortune. But plans by which others may be benefited never enter their minds. They at length become utterly selfish.

Society might be threatened with dissolution; the channels of government might be filled with corruption; they would hardly lift a hand to set affairs right unless their own petty interests were endangered. Their sentiment is that society and government can run themselves. Now such men are often called to seats in Congress; their characters are not changed by the election; they may be politic enough to appear zealous in the good cause but at heart they are as selfish and unpatriotic as ever. So I think that with the majority of Congress the honor and prosperity of the nation is a matter of secondary importance and the desire for political advancement and personal aggrandizement usurps the place which love of country alone should occupy. I am convinced that much can be done to correct this state of things: work can be done not only in the halls of Congress but among the masses of the people where the root of the evil lies. Both classes can be reached by the press; and, as you suggested, we should do all in our power during the first years of our professional lives to purify politics by using this instrument and gradually work ourselves into a broader field. I am certain that if every power I have ever dreamed of possessing were increased a hundred fold I could never become a Bright but I am equally certain that if your talents are well directed your influence in America will not be less than Cobden's was in England. . . .   Your sincere friend   Charles Talcott

ALS (WP, DLC) with WWhw notation on env.: "Ans 6/7/79."

From Janet Woodrow Wilson

My precious Son,   Wilmington–[N. C.] June 2nd [1879]
    One week from next Saturday! It sounds like a little while—and the time will pass rapidly with you—but it will seem a long while to us who are waiting at home. May God keep you well and strong —and bring you home in safety & happiness.
    I had a telegram on Saturday from your father—informing me of his safe arrival in Staunton—on Friday morning—and I have had letters since telling me that he is very pleasantly fixed at the Seminary[1]—that the four cousins[2] are affectionate, sweet, & pretty —& that he finds old friends unchanged in their affection. He was to deliver the Baccalaureate sermon yesterday—then an address to the graduates tomorrow evening—and then he expects to start for home tomorrow night—and to reach this on Wednesday night a little before 10 o'clock. I will be glad enough to see him, you may be sure. The length of his absence, has seemed interminable this time. . . .

Your father has been greatly praised & complimented at Louis-ville. I will enclose a slip from the Louisville Courier—that will give you an idea of the impression he made there. Please preserve the slip for me. . . .

We have not finally decided upon any particular place in the Mountains—but Annie is diligently enquiring—through the students from Western N. C. I would like to go to Virginia—but the cost of the journey is so much greater—& it is said that the resorts in this State are just as attractive. If you are at the University next year, as I hope, perhaps we can arrange to go to the Va. mountains next summer. . . .

Did I tell you, that your father's election to the Moderatorship was the most complimentary—the manner of it—that has ever taken place? He was greatly gratified at the treatment he received during the entire sessions, from the members of Ass[embly]—and you know that means a great deal. I must not scribble more now. God bless you my darling. I love you with all my heart—and do so long for a sight of your dear face. Think how long it is since I saw you last. Josie joins in unbounded love.

Yours as ever   Mother.

ALS (WP, DLC) Enc.: clipping from Louisville *Courier-Journal* on JRW's activities at General Assembly.

1 Augusta Female Seminary, now Mary Baldwin College, Staunton, Va.

2 Jessie W. Bones; Marion McGraw Bones, sister of Jessie; Jeanie Wilson Woodrow, daughter of Dr. James Woodrow; and Hattie Augusta Woodrow.

To Charles Andrew Talcott

Dear Charlie,   Wilmington, N. C. July 7th/79

Of course I meant to open our correspondence before this, but various things, some of them indefinable, have led to my delay, until delay has lengthened into tardiness. But for the last week or so I have been feeling far from well—and here at least is *some* excuse,—or rather *explanation; friends* need no *excuse*. Since leaving Princeton I have not been in the brightest of moods. The parting after Commencement went harder than I had feared even. It most emphatically and literally *struck in*. I expect you thought it a little queer that I did not some time during Commencement speak to you *definitely* upon the subject which had principally engrossed our thoughts in the correspondence which followed upon your early graduation. I had promised myself an opportunity of doing so when you should return—and yet I didn't. Well, the long and short of the explanation is, *embarassment*. When I am with any one in whom I am specially and sincerely interested, the hardest subject for me to broach is just that which is nearest my heart. An unfortunate disposition indeed! I hope to overcome it in time. I can at least speak plainly in writing. I have not yet hit upon any definite *plans* for the work we promise ourselves, except that we should, I think, lose no opportunity offered us by leisure moments to improve ourselves in *style* and *knowledge*, should leave nothing undone to keep ourselves fresh from the prejudices and free from foolish inaccuracies of those with whom we will constantly be thrown by the necessities of our law practice, in order that when the time comes for us to write and work for a cause we may be able to command a hearing, and m[a]y be strong for the struggle which, it is to be hoped, will raise us above the *pettinesses* of our profession. In my daily efforts at composition, and the preparation of my voice for public speaking, I try to keep these things in view. I am thus able to give such exercises more dignity and a thousand times more interest. Without some such definite aim I could not endure them. Write me what you think. I speak thus freely to *you* because you know me well enough to credit me with sincerity and acquit me of affectation—or mere *talk*, which amounts to the same thing in essence.

I rec'd a letter from El. Roessle yesterday.[1] He writes a very interesting—a very characteristic—letter. He seems well satisfied with the manner in which he passed the examinations of the Naval pay corps, and is hopeful of an appointment. He has gone with his family to Lake George as usual.

From the rest of the fellows there is as yet nothing but silence

I leave in about a week, in company with my mother and small brother, for the Blue Ridge. Address me (and please write soon) at Highlands, Macon Co., North Carolina (via Walhalla, S. C.) I'll tell you about the region we are to visit when I know more of it myself. It is as yet new ground for me. With much love,

Your sincere friend   Thos. W. Wilson

ALS (photostat in RSB Coll., DLC).
  [1] E. Roessle to WW, July 4, 1879, ALS (WP, DLC).

From Hiram Woods, Jr.

Dear Tommy,   Baltimore, Md. 7/25/79.

. . . I hope your study at the University [of Virginia] will be delightful. Now don't you pledge yourself to any Fraternity this Summer. Don't open your eyes too wide when you read this. I now wear a ΦKΨ pin! The Balto. Chapter took me in. We have some delightful fellows and I already have made some mighty good friends. Billy Whittelsy[1] and Jeff Davis, whom I saw yesterday in Washington, gave me a most hearty welcome. I want you to join at the University. I have no doubt you can get in. Don't give this unnecessary publicity in writing to the fellows. I tell you, but don't like the looks of telling everybody. I will look forward with great pleasure to the time when we can again "draw the old bonds close." We may change in the meantime, but I don't believe our friendship ever can change. . . .

Very Sincerely Your Friend, Hiram Woods, Jr.

ALS (WP, DLC) with WWhw notations on env.: "Recd 7/30/79"; "Ans 7/31/79."
  1 William H. Whittlesey, '76.

From Robert Harris McCarter

My Dear Tommy—   Sea Bright N. J. 29th July 1879
  I took up the August International on Saturday and ran my eye down the table of contents stopping at "Cabinet gov't in the U. S." as an article in the subject of which I felt an interest from an acquaintance with you and I began to read without noticing the authors name till I thought his style & sentiments were familiar when I saw that your name was appended. Of course I read with double interest after my discovery and write now to congratulate you upon your success. I agreed with my Uncle when he said it was hardly possible that a man so young as you should possess information so broad & at the same time technical enough to have written the article. . . .

Ever sincerely yours   Robert H. McCarter:

ALS (WP, DLC) with WWhw notation on env.: "Ans."

To Robert Bridges

Dear Bob,   Horse Cove, N. C., July 30th/79
  Why haven't you written to me, old fellow; you don't know how *longingly* I've been waiting for a letter from you. I think that I can candidly say that not a day has passed since the to us ever-memorable June season that I haven't thought of the canny Shippensburg Scot and our friendship which I hold so dear.
  I have been doing so many unaccustomed things of late that I scarcely remember whom I have written to and whom I have been neglecting. As for you, I suppose that the "ten-mile girl" or some other fair charmer has been making further conquest of you
  Here I am perched high on the Blue Ridge. I stayed at home about three weeks and then sought this cool retreat with a family party consisting of mother, my little brother, my younger sister,

and her three little ones.[1] The journey hither was simply terrible for such a party. Alone, I could have enjoyed it in a measure at least; but for delicate ladies and children it was trying in the extreme. We travelled about twelve hours in the cars and *fifteen* in a stage over rough, ill-kept mountain roads. We have certainly found a cool resort, however, and are very comfortably lodged here in "Horse Cove." This is apparently North Carolina's jumping-off place, being in her westernmost corner where she seems to be intruding herself upon her neighbors, Tenn. and Georgia, much as Virginia thrusts her "pan-handle" upon her neighbors to the North.

A Mr. Thompson (whose name, by the way, is *Jno R.*) has built here some very convenient frame houses, which comfortably accommodate some thirty odd boarders. His rooms are all full now; our fellow-boarders are for the most part families from New Orleans and Charleston who have left the low countries of the coasts in anticipation of the yellow fever, which is already doing such terrible work in Memphis. They are most of them quiet, pleasant, refined people, who make very nice boarding-house companions. We have horses to ride and picturesque mountain roads to explore. We have been kept indoors for the past four of five days by persistent wet weather. The clouds have crowded down close upon us, almost on our very roofs, here in the cove, hiding almost completely from us the neighboring mountain sides, and soaking us with their continued rains.

Except for its discomfort, the wet weather is not altogether disagreeable to me, however, for, by keeping me in my room, it forces on me many opportunities for work on my article on France,[2] at which I am still pegging with more or less satisfactory success. My article on Cabinet Government, by the way, is advertized to appear in the *August* International.

I have heard twice from Pete Godwin and once from El. Roessle,[3] from the rest *not a word*. Pete says that he has "written to Bob. Bridges again and presumes that he will before long be journalizing in N. Y." What exactly does he mean? any thing more than you have already told me. Do write me at once and fully concerning your prospects and purposes. You yourself cannot be more interested in them than I am.

Of my own prospects I have nothing new to tell. I have secured a room at the University of Virginia and am due there on the first of October. I still have some respite before I filter my enthusiasm for my profession through the dry dust of Law.

With much love,   Your devoted friend   Thos. W. Wilson

ALS (Meyer Coll., DLC).
1 Annie Howe and her children, J. Wilson, George, and Annie.
2 WW's first reference—in these pages—to his article, "Self-Government in France," printed at Sept. 4, 1879.
3 H. Godwin to WW, July 12 and 20, 1879, and E. Roessle to WW, July 4, 1879, all ALS (WP, DLC).

From Harold Godwin

My dear Tommy:—   Roslyn Long Island July 31st 1879
... First of all I must tell you what to me has been the great event of the season. To most young fellows who have left college I presume that nothing is more interesting than a quiet flirtation or some trivial pastime. Yet nothing could have brought me greater pleasure or surprise than to come accidentally upon an August Number of the International. I'm really so proud of you in every way—both as my own friend and as my classmate—that I show everyone the above referred to, and feed my own vanity on their compliments. You've taken a big step old cuss and I sincerely hope that the encouragement it will give you shall lead you to do so some more. I truly despair for myself and become every day more open to the all powerful conviction that all the fools in this world are not dead yet—at least not so long as I live—and the only real encouragement that one can get from this reflection is that it "takes a wise man to make a fool." But I have always thought this saying a little bit overdrawn, and probably invented just to suit such a case as mine. But really Tommy I think your article excellent, and if I am at all capable of making the remark, you seem to have said what you wished to say in a very able and clear way. The French subject I should judge very interesting but of course do not know exactly what you are looking for in that direction. The practice of Parliamentary laws will be there found and possibly you might draw from them some lesson intended to apply to the subject of which you have already written. But I judge that French Politics will ever be a poor illustration of aught but versatility. . . .

Heard from Lindsey[1] who thinks I should devote myself to Art criticism. He is very positive on this point. Many thanks for your kind word on the same subject. I must here end. My address will be ["](Care) Drexel Harjis and Co.—Paris." I want to hear from you often. Ever   Harold Godwin.

ALS (WP, DLC) with WWhw notation on env.: "Ans 8/18/79."
1 Professor Lindsey of Princeton.

"CABINET GOVERNMENT IN THE UNITED STATES"

"Cabinet Government in the United States" was both the culmination of Woodrow Wilson's concentrated study of Anglo-American
institutions and politics to 1879 and the point of departure for the
thought, research, and writings that found second and third climaxes
in "Government by Debate," written in 1882 and never published in
full, and Wilson's first and most famous book, *Congressional Government*, published in 1885.

The record to this point is so replete with evidences of Wilson's
admiration of British institutions that it would be gratuitous to repeat
it here. Wilson had been exposed to British newspapers and quarterlies ever since he could read. As a boy passionately interested in
military and naval affairs, he had found his models in the British,
not the American, army and navy. All his youthful reflections about
politics were based on the assumption that British institutions were
superior to American. As his constitution of the Liberal Debating
Club and his plan for reorganizing the national government, proposed to that group on April 5, 1877, both show, he was particularly
impressed by the British Cabinet system, which concentrates executive and legislative responsibility in a group of ministers whose tenure
depends upon commanding a majority in the House of Commons. It
was not surprising, to cite another example, that Wilson chose "Our
Kinship with England" as the subject for the senior thesis that he
read at the Princeton commencement in 1879.[1]

Admiration of the British political system and a deep interest in
his own country's political institutions and practices combined to
make Wilson particularly sensitive to events at home at least during
his last three years at Princeton, if not before. Rutherford B. Hayes
was President during most of this period. Hayes tried hard to clean
the Grantian stables and did in fact succeed in restoring popular confidence in the integrity of the presidential office. But Hayes was never
master of his own party, much less of Congress, and irresponsible
congressional supremacy was the overriding fact of American political life while Wilson was an undergraduate. But Wilson's reactions
were stimulated and then channeled into one highly concentrated
stream by the widespread discussion in the contemporary press and
forum of the causes of the decline of leadership in the government
and of the urgent necessity for some effective reform.

This discussion had been intensified by the publication in 1873 of
the American edition of Walter Bagehot's *The English Constitution*. It
compared the British Cabinet and American presidential-congres-
sional systems and found the former a model and the latter egre-
giously wanting. The book had not been off the presses very long before
Gamaliel Bradford had written a scathing indictment of congressional irresponsibility and was proposing to give Cabinet members
seats in Congress.[2] Not long afterward, another critic proposed to vest

[1] Delivered on June 18, 1879, in the First Presbyterian Church. *132nd Annual
Commencement of the College of New Jersey, Wednesday, June 18, 1879* (Princeton, N. J., 1879). WW's thesis not found.
[2] Gamaliel Bradford, "Shall the Cabinet Have Seats in Congress?" New York
Nation, XVI (April 3, 1873), 233-34.

all executive power in Congress by giving that body the right to elect the President.[3] These are only a few examples of the discussion which surely deeply affected Wilson while he was an undergraduate.[4]

Letters published earlier in this volume reveal that Wilson wrote "Cabinet Government in the United States" in January and February 1879, and also that Dr. Wilson edited one copy of the text. No manuscript copy of the article has survived, and the text printed below is that of the final, published version.

It would seem that Wilson was most influenced in his criticism of congressional government by Bagehot,[5] Bradford, and editorials in the New York *Nation*. Wilson could have derived his proposal to give Cabinet members seats in Congress from numerous sources.[6] What was unique about "Cabinet Government in the United States" and extended the frontiers of the contemporary debate was Wilson's radical remedy to make the Cabinet into a body of ministers directly responsible to Congress. This would be the main theme of his thought and writing about the American political system during the next three years.

[3] Charles O'Conor, "The President and Party Responsibility," *ibid.*, XXIV (May 17, 1877), 288.
[4] For a more extended discussion, see Arthur S. Link, *Wilson: The Road to the White House* (Princeton, N. J., 1947), pp. 17-19.
[5] Wilson read it in 1878. He read either the first American edition, published in Boston by Little, Brown, and Co., 1873, or *The English Constitution and Other Political Essays*, published in New York by D. Appleton & Co., 1877.
[6] But obviously not from Senator George H. Pendleton of Ohio, who in April 1879 introduced a bill to give Cabinet members a seat in either house with liberty of debate. Link, *loc. cit.*

A Political Essay

[Aug. 1879]

Cabinet Government in the United States.

Our patriotism seems of late to have been exchanging its wonted tone of confident hope for one of desponding solicitude. Anxiety about the future of our institutions seems to be daily becoming stronger in the minds of thoughtful Americans. A feeling of uneasiness is undoubtedly prevalent, sometimes taking the shape of a fear that grave, perhaps radical, defects in our mode of government are militating against our liberty and prosperity. A marked and alarming decline in statesmanship, a rule of levity and folly instead of wisdom and sober forethought in legislation, threaten to shake our trust not only in the men by whom our national policy is controlled, but also in the very principles upon which our Government rests. Both State and National legislatures are looked upon with nervous suspicion, and we hail an adjournment of Congress as a temporary immunity from danger. In casting about for the chief cause of the admitted evil, many persons have convinced themselves that it is to be found in the principle of universal suffrage. When Dr. Woolsey, in his admirable work on Political Science, speaks with despondency of the influence of this principle upon our political life, he simply gives clear expression to misgivings which he shares with a growing minority of his countrymen. We must, it is said, purge the constituencies of their ignorant elements, if we would have high-minded, able, worthy representatives. We see adventurers, who in times of revolution and confusion were suffered to climb to high and responsible places, still holding positions of trust; we perceive that our institutions, when once thrown out of gear, seem to possess no power of self-readjustment,—and we hasten to cast discredit upon that principle the establishment of which has been regarded as America's greatest claim to political honor,—the right of every man to a voice in the Government under which he lives. The existence of such sentiments is in itself an instructive fact. But while it is indisputably true that universal suffrage is a constant element of weakness, and exposes us to many dangers which we might otherwise escape, its operation does not suffice alone to explain existing evils. Those who make this the scapegoat of all our national grievances have made too superficial an analysis of the abuses about which they so loudly complain.

What is the real cause of this solicitude and doubt? It is, in our opinion, to be found in the absorption of all power by a legislature which is practically irresponsible for its acts. But even this would not necessarily be harmful, were it not for the addition of a despotic principle which it is my present purpose to consider.

At its highest development, *representative* government is that form which best enables a free people to govern themselves. The main object of a representative assembly, therefore, should be the discussion of public business. They should legislate as if in the presence of the whole country, because they come under the closest scrutiny and fullest criticism of all the representatives of the country speaking in open and free debate. Only in such an assembly, only in such an atmosphere of publicity, only by means of such a vast investigating machine, can the different sections of a great country learn each other's feelings and interests. It is not enough that the general course of legislation is known to all. Unless during its progress it is subjected to a thorough, even a tediously prolonged, process of public sifting, to the free comment of friend and foe alike, to the ordeal of battle among those upon whose vote its fate depends, an act of open legislation may have its real intent and scope completely concealed by its friends and undiscovered by its enemies, and it may be as fatally mischievous as the darkest measures of an oligarchy or a despot. Nothing can be more obvious than the fact that the very life of free, popular institutions is dependent upon their breathing the bracing air of thorough, exhaustive, and open discussions, or that select Congressional committees, whose proceedings must from their very nature be secret, are, as means of legislation, dangerous and unwholesome. Parliaments are forces for freedom; for "talk is persuasion, persuasion is force, the one force which can sway freemen to deeds such as those which have made England what she is," or our English stock what it is.

Congress is a deliberative body in which there is little real deliberation; a legislature which legislates with no real discussion of its business. Our Government is practically carried on by irresponsible committees. Too few Americans take the trouble to inform themselves as to the methods of Congressional management; and, as a consequence, not many have perceived that almost *absolute* power has fallen into the hands of men whose irresponsibility prevents the regulation of their conduct by the people from whom they derive their authority. The most important, most powerful man in the government of the United States in time of peace is the Speaker of the House of Representatives. Instead of being merely an executive officer, whose principal duties are those immediately connected with the administration of the rules of order, he is a potent party chief, the only chief of any real potency,—and must of necessity be so. He must be the strongest and shrewdest member of his party in the lower House; for almost all the real business of that House is transacted by committees whose members are his nominees. Unless the rules of the House be suspended by a special two-thirds vote, every bill introduced must be referred, without debate, to the proper Standing Committee, with whom rests the privilege of embodying it, or any part of it, in their reports, or of rejecting it altogether. The House very seldom takes any direct action upon any measures introduced by individual members; its votes and discussions are almost entirely confined to committee reports and committee dictation. The whole attitude of business depends upon forty-seven Standing Committees. Even the discussions upon their directive reports are merely nominal,—liberal forms, at most. Take, as an example of the workings of the system, the functions and privileges of the Committee of Ways and Means. To it is intrusted the financial policy of the country; its chairman is, in reality, our Chancellor of the Exchequer. With the aid of his colleagues he determines the course of legislation upon finance; in English political phrase, he draws up the *budget*. All the momentous questions connected with our finance are debated in the private sessions of this committee, and there only. For, when the budget is submitted to the House for its consideration, only a very limited time is allowed for its discussion; and, besides the member of the committee to whom its introduction is intrusted, no one is permitted to speak save those to whom he through courtesy yields the floor, and who must have made arrangements beforehand with the Speaker to be recognized. Where, then, is there room for thorough discussion,—for discussion of any kind? If carried, the provisions of the budget must be put into operation by the Secretary of the Treasury, who may be directly opposed to the principles which it embodies. If lost, no one save Congress itself is responsible for the consequent embarrassment into which the nation is brought,—and Congress as a body is not readily punishable.

It must at once be evident to every thinking man that a policy thus regulated cannot be other than vacillating, uncertain, devoid of plan or consistency. This is certainly a phase of representative government peculiar to ourselves. And yet its development was most natural and apparently necessary. It is hardly possible for a body of several hundred men, without official or authoritative leaders, to determine upon any line of action without interminable wrangling and delays injurious to the interests under their care. Left to their own resources, they would be as helpless as any other mass meeting. Without leaders having authority to guide their deliberations and give a definite direction to the movement of legislation; and, moreover, with none of that sense of responsibility which constantly rests upon those whose duty it is to work out to a successful issue the policies which they themselves originate, yet with full power to dictate policies which others must carry into execution,—a recognition of the need of some sort of leadership, and of a division of labor, led to the formation of these Standing Committees, to which are intrusted the shaping of the national policy in the several departments of administration, as well as the prerogatives of the initiative in legislation and leadership in debate. When theoretically viewed, this is an ingenious and apparently harmless device, but one which, in practice, subverts that most fundamental of all the principles of a free State,—the right of the people to a potential voice in their own government. Great measures of legislation are discussed and determined, not conspicuously in public session of the people's representatives, but in the unapproachable privacy of committee rooms.

But what less imperfect means of representative government can we find without stepping beyond the bounds of a true republicanism? Certainly none other than those which were rejected by the Constitutional Convention. When the Convention of 1787, upon the submission of the report of the Committee of Detail, came to consider the respective duties and privileges of the legislative and executive departments, and the relations which these two branches of the Government should sustain towards each other, many serious questions presented themselves for solution. One of the gravest of these was, whether or not the interests of the public service would be furthered by *allowing some of the higher officers of State to occupy seats in the legislature*. The propriety and practical advantage of such a course were obviously suggested by a similar arrangement under the British Constitution, to which our political fathers often and wisely looked for useful hints. But since the spheres of the several departments were in the end defined with all the clearness, strictness, and care possible to a written instrument, the opinion prevailed among the members of the Convention that it would be unadvisable to establish any such connection between the Executive and Congress. They thought, in their own fervor of patriotism and intensity of respect for written law, that paper barriers would prove sufficient to prevent the encroachments of any one department upon the prerogatives of any other; that these vaguely broad laws—or principles of law—would be capable of securing and maintaining the harmonious and mutually helpful co-operation of the several branches; that the exhibition of these general views of government would be adequate to the stupendous task of preventing the legislature from rising to the predominance of influence, which, nevertheless, constantly lay within its reach. But, in spite of constitutional barriers, the legislature has become the imperial power of the State, as it must of necessity become under every representative system; and experience of the consequences of a complete separation of the legislative and executive branches long since led that able and sagacious commentator upon the Constitution, Chief-Justice Story, to remark that, "if it would not have been safe to trust the heads of departments, as representatives, to the choice of the people, as their constituents, it would have been at least some gain to have allowed them seats, like territorial delegates, in the House of Representatives, where they might freely debate without a title to vote." In short, the framers of the Constitution, in endeavoring to act in accordance with the principle of Montesquieu's celebrated and unquestionably just political maxim,—that the legislative, executive, and judicial departments of a free State should be *separate*,—made their separation so complete as to amount to *isolation*. To the methods of representative government which have sprung from these provisions of the Constitution, by which the Convention thought so carefully to guard and limit the powers of the legislature, we must look for an explanation, in a large measure, of the evils over which we now find ourselves lamenting.

What, then, is Cabinet government? What is the change proposed? Simply to give to the heads of the Executive departments —the members of the Cabinet—seats in Congress, with the privilege of the initiative in legislation and some part of the unbounded privileges now commanded by the Standing Committees. But the advocates of such a change—and they are now not a few—deceive themselves when they maintain that it would not necessarily involve the principle of ministerial responsibility,—that is, the resignation of the Cabinet upon the defeat of any important part of their plans. For, if Cabinet officers sit in Congress as official representatives of the Executive, this principle of responsibility must of necessity come sooner or later to be recognized. Experience would soon demonstrate the practical impossibility of their holding their seats, and continuing to represent the Administration, after they had found themselves unable to gain the consent of a majority to their policy. Their functions would be peculiar. They would constitute a link between the legislative and executive branches of the general Government, and, as representatives of the Executive, must hold the right of the initiative in legislation. Otherwise their position would be an anomalous one, indeed. There would be little danger and evident propriety in extending to them the first right of introducing measures relative to the administration of the several departments; and they could possess such a right without denying the fullest privileges to other members. But, whether granted this initiative or not, the head of each department would undoubtedly find it necessary to take a decided and open stand for or against every measure bearing upon the affairs of his department, by whomsoever introduced. No high-spirited man would long remain in an office in the business of which he was not permitted to pursue a policy which tallied with his own principles and convictions. If defeated by both Houses, he would naturally resign; and not many years would pass before resignation upon defeat would have become an established precedent,—and resignation upon defeat is the essence of responsible government. In arguing, therefore, for the admission of Cabinet officers into the legislature, we are logically brought to favor *responsible Cabinet government* in the United States.

But, to give to the President the right to choose whomsoever he pleases as his constitutional advisers, after having constituted Cabinet officers *ex officio* members of Congress, would be to empower him to appoint a limited number of representatives, and would thus be plainly at variance with republican principles. The highest order of responsible government could, then, be established in the United States only by laying upon the President the necessity of selecting his Cabinet from among the number of representatives already chosen by the people, or by the legislatures of the States.

Such a change in our legislative system would not be so radical as it might at first appear: it would certainly be very far from revolutionary. Under our present system we suffer all the inconveniences, are hampered by all that is defective in the machinery, of responsible government, without securing any of the many benefits which would follow upon its complete establishment. Cabinet officers are now appointed only with the consent of the Senate. Such powers as a Cabinet with responsible leadership must possess are now divided among the forty-seven Standing Committees, whose prerogatives of irresponsible leadership savor of despotism, because exercised for the most part within the secret precincts of a committee room, and not under the eyes of the whole House, and thus of the whole country. These committees, too, as has been said, rule without any of that freedom of public debate which is essential to the liberties of the people. Their measures are too often mere partisan measures, and are hurried through the forms of voting by a party majority whose interest it is that all serious opposition, all debate that might develop obstructive antagonism, should be suppressed. Under the conditions of Cabinet government, however, full and free debates are sure to take place. For what are these conditions? According as their policy stands or falls, the ministers themselves stand or fall; to the party which supports them each discussion involves a trial of strength with their opponents; upon it depends the amount of their success as a party: while to the opposition the triumph of ministerial plans means still further exclusion from office; their overthrow, accession to power. To each member of the assembly every debate offers an opportunity for placing himself, by able argument, in a position to command a place in any future Cabinet that may be formed from the ranks of his own party; each speech goes to the building up (or the tearing down) of his political fortunes. There is, therefore, an absolute certainty that every phase of every subject will be drawn carefully and vigorously, will be dwelt upon with minuteness, will be viewed from every possible standpoint. The legislative, holding full power of final decision, would find itself in immediate contact with the executive and its policy. Nor would there be room for factious government or factious opposition. Plainly, ministers must found their policies, an opposition must found its attacks, upon well-considered principles; for in this open sifting of debate, when every feature of every measure, even to the motives which prompted it, is the subject of out-spoken discussion and keen scrutiny, no chicanery, no party craft, no questionable principles can long hide themselves. Party trickery, legislative jobbery, are deprived of the very air they breathe,—the air of secrecy, of concealment. The public is still surprised whenever they find that dishonest legislation has been allowed to pass unchallenged. Why surprised? As things are, measures are determined in the interests of corporations, and the suffering people know almost nothing of them until their evil tendencies crop out in actual execution. Under lobby pressure from interested parties, they have been cunningly concocted in the closet sessions of partisan committees, and, by the all-powerful aid of party machinery, have been hurried through the stages of legislation without debate; so that even Press correspondents are often as ignorant of the real nature of such special measures as the outside public. Any searching debate of such questions would at once have brought the public eye upon them, and how could they then have stood? Lifting the lid of concealment must have been the discovery to all concerned of their unsavory character. Light would have killed them.

We are thus again brought into the presence of the cardinal fact of this discussion,—that *debate* is the essential function of a popular representative body. In the severe, distinct, and sharp enunciation of underlying principles, the unsparing examination and telling criticism of opposite positions, the careful, painstaking unravelling of all the issues involved, which are incident to the free discussion of questions of public policy, we see the best, the only effective, means of educating public opinion. Can any one suppose for one moment that, in the late heated and confused discussions of the Bland silver bill, the Western papers would have had any color of justification in claiming that the Resumption Act of 1875 was passed secretly and without the knowledge of the people, if we had then had responsible government? Although this all-important matter was before the country for more than a year; was considered by two Congresses, recommended by more than one Congressional committee; was printed and circulated for the perusal of the people; was much spoken of, though little understood by the Press at the time,—the general mass of our population knew little or nothing about it, for it elicited almost no statesmanlike comment upon the floor of Congress, was exposed to none of the analysis of earnest debate. What, however, would have been its history under a well-ordered Cabinet government? It would have been introduced—if introduced at all—to the House by the Secretary of the Treasury as a part of the financial policy of the Administration, supported by the authority and sanction of the entire Cabinet. At once it would have been critically scanned by the leaders of the opposition; at each reading of the bill, and especially in Committee of the Whole, its weak points would have been mercilessly assailed, and its strong features urged in defence; attacks upon its principle by the opposition would have been met by an unequivocal avowal of "soft money" principles from the majority; and, defended by men anxious to win honors in support of the ministry, it would have been dissected by all those who were at issue with the financial doctrines of the majority, discussed and re-discussed until all its essential, all its accidental features, and all its remotest tendencies, had been dinned into the public ear, so that no man in the nation could have pretended ignorance of its meaning and object. The educational influence of such discussions is two-fold, and operates in two directions,—upon the members of the legislature themselves, and upon the people whom they represent. Thus do the merits of the two systems—Committee government and government by a responsible Cabinet—hinge upon this matter of a full and free discussion of all subjects of legislation; upon the principle stated by Mr. Bagehot, that "free government is self-government,—a government of the people by the people." It is perhaps safe to say, that the Government which secures the most thorough discussions of public interests,—whose administration most nearly conforms to the opinions of the governed,— is the freest and the best. And certainly, when judged by this principle, government by irresponsible Standing Committees can bear no comparison with government by means of a responsible ministry; for, as we have seen,—and as others besides Senator Hoar have shown,—its essential feature is a vicious suppression of debate.

Only a single glance is necessary to discover how utterly Committee government must fail to give effect to public opinion. In the first place, the exclusion of debate prevents the intelligent formation of opinion on the part of the nation at large; in the second place, public opinion, when once formed, finds it impossible to exercise any immediate control over the action of its representatives. There is no one in Congress to speak for the nation. Congress is a conglomeration of inharmonious elements; a collection of men representing each his neighborhood, each his local interest; an alarmingly large proportion of its legislation is "special;" all of it is at best only a limping compromise between the conflicting interests of the innumerable localities represented. There is no guiding or harmonizing power. Are the people in favor of a particular policy,—what means have they of forcing it upon the sovereign legislature at Washington? None but the most imperfect. If they return representatives who favor it (and this is the most they can do), these representatives being under no directing power will find a mutual agreement impracticable among so many, and will finally settle upon some policy which satisfies nobody, removes no difficulty, and makes little definite or valuable provision for the future. They must, indeed, be content with whatever measure the appropriate committee chances to introduce. Responsible ministries, on the other hand, form the policy of their parties; the strength of their party is at their command; the course of legislation turns upon the acceptance or rejection by the houses of definite and consistent plans upon which they determine. In forming its judgment of their policy, the nation knows whereof it is judging; and, with biennial Congresses, it may soon decide whether any given policy shall stand or fall. The question would then no longer be, What representatives shall we choose to represent our chances in this haphazard game of legislation? but, What plans of national administration shall we sanction? Would not party programmes mean something then? Could they be constructed only to deceive and bewilder?

But, above and beyond all this, a responsible Cabinet constitutes a link between the executive and legislative departments of the Government which experience declares in the clearest tones to be absolutely necessary in a well-regulated, well-proportioned body politic. None can so well judge of the perfections or imperfections of a law as those who have to administer it. Look, for example, at the important matter of taxation. The only legitimate object of taxation is the support of Government; and who can so well determine the requisite revenue as those who conduct the Government? Who can so well choose feasible means of taxation, available sources of revenue, as those who have to meet the practical difficulties of tax-collection? And what surer guarantee against exorbitant estimates and unwise taxation, than the necessity of full explanation and defence before the whole House? The same principles, of course, apply to all legislation upon matters connected with any of the Executive departments.

Thus, then, not only can Cabinet ministers meet the needs of their departments more adequately and understandingly, and conduct their administration better than can irresponsible committees, but they are also less liable to misuse their powers. Responsible ministers must secure from the House and Senate an intelligent, thorough, and practical treatment of their affairs; must vindicate their principles in open battle on the floor of Congress. The public is thus enabled to exercise a direct scrutiny over the workings of the Executive departments, to keep all their operations under a constant stream of daylight. Ministers could do nothing under the shadow of darkness; committees do all in the dark. It can easily be seen how constantly ministers would be plied with questions about the conduct of public affairs, and how necessary it would be for them to satisfy their questioners if they did not wish to fall under suspicion, distrust, and obloquy.

But, while the people would thus be able to defend themselves through their representatives against malfeasance or inefficiency in the management of their business, the heads of the departments would also have every opportunity to defend their administration of the people's affairs against unjust censure or crippling legislation. Corruption in office would court concealment in vain; vicious trifling with the administration of public business by irresponsible persons would meet with a steady and effective check. The ground would be clear for a manly and candid defence of ministerial methods; wild schemes of legislation would meet with a cold repulse from ministerial authority. The salutary effect of such a change would most conspicuously appear in the increased effectiveness of our now crumbling civil, military, and naval services; for we should no longer be cursed with tardy, insufficient, and misapplied appropriations. The ministers of War, of the Navy, of the Interior, would be able to submit their estimates in person, and to procure speedy and regular appropriations; and half the abuses at present connected with appropriative legislation would necessarily disappear with the present committee system. Appropriations now, though often inadequate, are much oftener wasteful and fraudulent. Under responsible government, every appropriation asked by an Executive chief, as well as the reasons by which he backed his request, would be subjected to the same merciless sifting processes of debate as would characterize the consideration of other questions. Always having their responsible agents thus before them, the people would at once know how much they were spending, and for what it was spent.

When we come to speak of the probable influence of responsible Cabinet government upon the development of statesmanship and the renewal of the now perishing growth of statesmanlike qualities, we come upon a vital interest of the whole question. Will it bring with it worthy successors of Hamilton and Webster? Will it replace a leadership of trickery and cunning device by one of ability and moral strength? If it will not, why advocate it? If it will, how gladly and eagerly and imperatively ought we to demand it! The most despotic of Governments under the control of wise statesmen is preferable to the freest ruled by demagogues. Now, there are few more common, and perhaps few more reasonable, beliefs than that at all times, among the millions of population who constitute the body of this great nation, there is here and there to be found a man with all the genius, all the deep and strong patriotism, all the moral vigor, and all the ripeness of knowledge and variety of acquisition which gave power and lasting fame to the greater statesmen of our past history. We bewail and even wonder at the fact that these men do not find their way into public life, to claim power and leadership in the service of their country. We naturally ascribe their absence to the repugnance which superior minds must feel for the intrigues, the glaring publicity, and the air of unscrupulousness and even dishonesty which are the characteristics, or at least the environments, of political life. In our disappointment and vexation that they do not, even at the most distressing sacrifice of their personal convenience and peace, devote themselves to the study and practice of state-craft, we turn for comfort to re-read history's lesson,— that many countries find their greatest statesmen in times of extraordinary crisis or rapid transition and progress; the intervals of slow growth and uninteresting everyday administration of the government being noted only for the elevation of mediocrity, or at most of shrewd cunning, to high administrative places. We take cold consolation from the hope that times of peril—which sometimes seem close enough at hand—will not find us without strong leaders worthy of the most implicit confidence. Thus we are enabled to arrive at the comfortable and fear-quieting conclusion that it is from no fault of ours, certainly from no defects in our forms of government, that we are ruled by scheming, incompetent, political tradesmen, whose aims and ambitions are merely personal, instead of by broadminded, masterful statesmen, whose sympathies and purposes are patriotic and national.

To supply the conditions of statesmanship is, we conclude, beyond our power; for the causes of its decline and the means necessary to its development are beyond our ken. Let us take a new departure. Let us, drawing light from every source within the range of our knowledge, make a little independent analysis of the conditions of statesmanship, with a view of ascertaining whether or not it is in reality true that we cannot contribute to its development, or even perchance give it a perennial growth among us. We learn from a critical survey of the past, that, so far as political affairs are concerned, great critical epochs are the man-making epochs of history, that revolutionary influences are man-making influences. And why? If this be the law, it must have some adequate reason underlying it; and we seem to find the reason a very plain and conspicuous one. Crises give birth and a new growth to statesmanship because they are peculiarly periods of action, in which talents find the widest and the freest scope. They are periods not only of action, but also of unusual opportunity for gaining leadership and a controlling and guiding influence. It is opportunity for transcendent influence, therefore, which calls into active public life a nation's greater minds,—minds which might otherwise remain absorbed in the smaller affairs of private life. And we thus come upon the principle,—a principle which will appear the more incontrovertible the more it is looked into and tested,—that governmental forms will call to the work of administration able minds and strong hearts constantly or infrequently, according as they do or do not afford them at all times an opportunity of gaining and retaining a commanding authority and an undisputed leadership in the nation's councils. Now it certainly needs no argument to prove that government by supreme committees, whose members are appointed at the caprice of an irresponsible party chief, by seniority, because of reputation gained in entirely different fields, or because of partisan shrewdness, is not favorable to a full and strong development of statesmanship. Certain it is that statesmanship has been steadily dying out in the United States since that stupendous crisis during which its government felt the first throbs of life. In the government of the United States there is no place found for the leadership of men of real ability. Why, then, complain that we have no leaders? The President can seldom make himself recognized as a leader; he is merely the executor of the sovereign legislative will; his Cabinet officers are little more than chief clerks, or superintendents, in the Executive departments, who advise the President as to matters in most of which he has no power of action independently of the concurrence of the Senate. The most ambitious representative can rise no higher than the chairmanship of the Committee of Ways and Means, or the Speakership of the House. The cardinal feature of Cabinet government, on the other hand, is responsible leadership,—the leadership and authority of a small body of men who have won the foremost places in their party by a display of administrative talents, by evidence of high ability upon the floor of Congress in the stormy play of debate. None but the ablest can become leaders and masters in this keen tournament in which arguments are the weapons, and the people the judges. Clearly defined, definitely directed policies arouse bold and concerted opposition; and leaders of oppositions become in time leaders of Cabinets. Such a recognized leadership it is that is necessary to the development of statesmanship under popular, republican institutions; for only such leadership can make politics seem worthy of cultivation to men of high mind and aim.

And if party success in Congress—the ruling body of the nation—depends upon power in debate, skill and prescience in policy, successful defence of or attacks upon ruling ministries, how ill can contending parties spare their men of ability from Congress! To keep men of the strongest mental and moral fibre in Congress would become a party necessity. Party triumph would then be a matter of might in debate, not of supremacy in subterfuge. The two great national parties—and upon the existence of two great parties, with clashings and mutual jealousies and watchings, depends the health of free political institutions—are dying for want of unifying and vitalizing principles. Without leaders, they are also without policies, without aims. With leaders there must be followers, there must be parties. And with leaders whose leadership was earned in an open war of principle against principle, by the triumph of one opinion over all opposing opinions, parties must from the necessities of the case have definite policies. Platforms, then, must mean something. Broken promises will then end in broken power. A Cabinet without a policy that is finding effect in progressive legislation is, in a country of frequent elections, inviting its own defeat. Or is there, on the other hand, a determined, aggressive opposition? Then the ministry have a right to ask them what they would do under similar circumstances, were the reins of government to fall to them. And if the opposition are then silent, they cannot reasonably expect the country to in-trust the government to them. Witness the situation of the Liberal party in England during the late serious crisis in Eastern affairs. Not daring to propose any policy,—having indeed, because of the disintegration of the party, no policy to propose,—their numerical weakness became a moral weakness, and the nation's ear was turned away from them. Eight words contain the sum of the present degradation of our political parties: *No leaders, no principles; no principles, no parties.* Congressional leadership is divided infinitesimally; and with divided leadership there can be no great party units. Drill in debate, by giving scope to talents, invites talents; raises up a race of men habituated to the methods of public business, skilled parliamentary chiefs. And, more than this, it creates a much-to-be-desired class who early make attendance upon public affairs the business of their lives, devoting to the service of their country all their better years. Surely the management of a nation's business will, in a well-ordered society, be as properly a matter of life-long training as the conduct of private affairs.

These are but meagre and insufficient outlines of some of the results which would follow upon the establishment of responsible Cabinet government in the United States. Its establishment has not wanted more or less outspoken advocacy from others; nor, of course, have there been lacking those who are ready to urge real or imaginary objections against it, and proclaim it an exotic unfit to thrive in American soil. It has certainly, in common with all other political systems, grave difficulties and real evils connected with it. Difficulties and evils are inseparable from every human scheme of government; and, in making their choice, a people can do no more than adopt that form which affords the largest measure of real liberty, whose machinery is least imperfect, and which is most susceptible to the control of their sovereign will.

Few, however, have discovered the real defects of such a responsible government as that which I now advocate. It is said, for instance, that it would render the President a mere figure-head, with none of that stability of official tenure, or that traditional dignity, which are necessary to such figure-heads. Would the President's power be curtailed, then, if his Cabinet ministers simply took the place of the Standing Committees? Would it not rather be enlarged? He would then be in fact, and not merely in name, the head of the Government. Without the consent of the Senate, he now exercises no sovereign functions that would be taken from him by a responsible Cabinet.

The apparently necessary existence of a partisan Executive presents itself to many as a fatal objection to the establishment of the forms of responsible Cabinet government in this country. The President must continue to represent a political party, and must continue to be anxious to surround himself with Cabinet officers who shall always substantially agree with him on all political questions. It must be admitted that the introduction of the principle of ministerial responsibility might, on this account, become at times productive of mischief, unless the tenure of the presidential office were made more permanent than it now is. Whether or not the presidential term should, under such a change of conditions, be lengthened would be one of several practical questions which would attend the adoption of a system of this sort. But it must be remembered that such a state of things as now exists, when we find the Executive to be of one party and the majority in Congress to be of the opposite party, is the exception, by no means the rule. Moreover we must constantly keep before our minds the fact that the choice now lies between this responsible Cabinet government and the rule of irresponsible committees which actually exists. It is not hard to believe that most presidents would find no greater inconvenience, experience no greater unpleasantness, in being at the head of a Cabinet composed of political opponents than in presiding, as they must now occasionally do, over a Cabinet of political friends who are compelled to act in all matters of importance according to the dictation of Standing Committees which are ruled by the opposite party. In the former case, the President may, by the exercise of whatever personal influence he possesses, affect the action of the Cabinet, and, through them, the action of the Houses; in the latter he is absolutely helpless. Even now it might prove practically impossible for a President to gain from a hostile majority in the Senate a confirmation of his appointment of a strongly partisan Cabinet drawn from his own party. The President must now, moreover, acting through his Cabinet, simply do the bidding of the committees in directing the business of the departments. With a responsible Cabinet—even though that Cabinet were of the opposite party—he might, if a man of ability, exercise great power over the conduct of public affairs; if not a man of ability, but a *mere* partisan, he would in any case be impotent. From these considerations it would appear that government by Cabinet ministers who represent the majority in Congress is no more incompatible with a partisan Executive than is government by committees representing such a majority. Indeed, a partisan President might well prefer legislation through a hostile body at whose deliberations he might himself be present, and whose course he might influence, to legislation through hostile committees over whom he could have no manner of control, direct or indirect. And such conditions would be exceptional.

But the encroachment of the legislative upon the executive is deemed the capital evil of our Government in its later phases; and it is asked, Would not the power of Congress be still more dangerously enlarged, and these encroachments made easier and surer, by thus making its relations with the Executive closer? By no means. The several parts of a perfect mechanism must actually interlace and be in strong union in order mutually to support and check each other. Here again permanent, dictating committees are the only alternative. On the one hand, we have committees directing policies for whose miscarriage they are not responsible; on the other, we have a ministry asking for legislation for whose results they are responsible. In both cases there is full power and authority on the part of the legislature to determine all the main lines of administration: there is no more real control of Executive acts in the one case than in the other; but there is an all-important difference in the character of the agents employed. When carrying out measures thrust upon them by committees, administrative officers can throw off all sense of responsibility; and the committees are safe from punishment, safe even from censure, whatever the issue. But in administering laws which have passed under the influence of their own open advocacy, ministers must shoulder the responsibilities and face the consequences. We should not, then, be giving Congress powers or opportunities of encroachment which it does not now possess, but should, on the contrary, be holding its powers in constant and effective check by putting over it responsible leaders. A complete separation of the executive and legislative is not in accord with the true spirit of those essentially English institutions of which our Government is a characteristic offshoot. The Executive is in constant need of legislative co-operation; the legislative must be aided by an Executive who is in a position intelligently and vigorously to execute its acts. There must needs be, therefore, as a binding link between them, some body which has no power to coerce the one and is interested in maintaining the independent effectiveness of the other. Such a link is the responsible Cabinet.

Again, it is objected that we should be cursed with that instability of government which results from a rapid succession of ministries, a frequent shifting of power from the hands of one party to the hands of another. This is not necessarily more likely to occur under the system of responsibility than now. We should be less exposed to such fluctuations of power than is the English government. The elective system which regulates the choice of United States Senators prevents more than one third of the seats becoming vacant at once, and this third only once every two years. The political complexion of the Senate can be changed only by a succession of elections.

But against such a responsible system the alarm-bell of *centralization* is again sounded, and all those who dread seeing too much authority, too complete control, placed within the reach of the central Government sternly set their faces against any such change. They deceive themselves. There could be no more despotic authority wielded under the forms of free government than our national Congress now exercises. It is a despotism which uses its power with all the caprice, all the scorn for settled policy, all the wild unrestraint which mark the methods of other tyrants as hateful to freedom.

Few of us are ready to suggest a remedy for the evils all deplore. We hope that our system is self-adjusting, and will not need our corrective interference. This is a vain hope! It is no small part of wisdom to know how long an evil ought to be tolerated, to see when the time has come for the people, from whom springs all authority, to speak its doom or prescribe its remedy. If that time be allowed to slip unrecognized, our dangers may overwhelm us, our political maladies may prove incurable.

Thomas W. Wilson.

Printed in the *International Review*, VI (Aug. 1879), 146-63.

From Robert Bridges

Dear Tommy,   Shippensburgh, Pa. Aug 2nd '79
   . . . I got the August International the other day with your article in it. Its even stronger than I expected. My father read it through and when he had finished he said, "Robert, that's a strong article— if Tommy lives we'll hear from him. There is not a boyish sentence in the whole piece." Father is not much on literature, for he is self-educated and self-made—but he has a great deal better judgment on matters of good sound sense and argument than many college graduates I know. I think he took about as much interest in the article as I did. He takes a big interest in all the boys I knew at college. I guess you are working hard on the French Political article. . . .   Your Friend   Bob Bridges

ALS (WP, DLC) with WWhw notation: "Ans."

To Robert Bridges

Dear Bob,   Horse Cove, N. Carolina, August, 8th/79

I was *delighted* to receive your letter, despite the outrageous supposition with which you opened it, that I had already forgotten my old friends. Your letter was duly forwarded from Wilmington, and rec'd yesterday, to be read several times and thoroughly enjoyed. I wrote to you, you dear old rascal, a week or more ago. If the letter has reached you, you already know my address; but, for fear it has not, I will give it again:

> Horse Cove,
> Macon County
> (via Walhalla S. C.)   North Carolina

Now write to that address immediately and apologize for your unwarranted abuse of me. If you don't, I'll be tempted to—to write to you again.

Your letter contained just enough about yourself; it reminded me of the old confidential conversations we used to have at College, and which I used to value so, as an aid and encouragement to myself and as a cement to our friendship;—for friends cannot be such in truth unless they *know* each other, every inch both of body and soul, unless their love is one of *knowledge*. When I hear from you I *want* to hear about yourself. You say that you can almost feel the crust of selfishness growing over you now that you are leaving the generous rivalries of College for the cold push of the world. Yes, so do I. But we can do this much, Bob, as far as each other are concerned at least, let's *remain* College boys *and classmates*. We can keep our hearts open to each other. Thank God, *our* interests need never clash! The thing I have most dreaded in looking forward to intercourse with my friends after my separation from them is, changes in them and in myself which might throw us out of sympathy with one another, and make our friendship a mere *recollection*. But we can guard against this—partially at least—in one way, and in one way only, it seems to me, that is, by making our letters heart-and-mind-openers—just such as yours was

As for your low spirits and discouragement, allow me to say that you are a *goose*. When hot weather is slackening all your nerves and debilitating all your faculties, do you expect to have the same capacity for work that you had during a sharp, Wintry term in College? I don't wonder that your imagination shrinks from the work of construction when the thermometer indicates a heat as great as that of the blood! "As for my single self," I have very few fears as to your future, my chiefest one being that you wont have confidence enough in yourself. The *story* I like *much*, so far as it goes; and the first hints are definite enough. Write me of its further progress. The characters will certainly be unusual—and the plot promises to surpass in interest anything you've planned yet. It will be somewhat more natural, and, therefore, stronger. I'm interested in the weaver's daughter already. You have my full sympathy, old fellow. As for the situation you are about to seek, I can't believe that it will be hard to find. And the harness may rub and irritate at first, but you'll soon meet the collar squarely. Now, Bob, do you think that moon-light riding with "auburn-hair" (whom I remember very well indeed from your description of her) is safe when you are seeking to fix your attention on a literary subject?

Be sure to work in the Satire on the Madison Ave. family—You mean the crowd who worship God in full dress, don't you?[1]

I appreciate and *value* your father's judgment of my *International* article very highly indeed. It is to just such sound, practical common-sense as his that I would prefer to address any such argument as that on Cabinet Govt., and to convince such would be my greatest triumph. Please thank him for me. You are a partial witness—your testimony is excluded, though I must confess to harboring a *little* satisfaction that my work is admired by my dear friend. I have seen few newspaper notices of the article—have seen few newspapers indeed—only one or two. The *Wilmington Star*[2] notices it editorially to the length of a column and a half, and the *New Orleans Picayune* quotes from it to about the extent of a half column. These are the only papers I have access to.

The French article progresses finely, much more so than it would had I been compelled to work in Summer's heat. Here in these splendid mountains I am above the worst of the heat and can work with comparative comfort. The first draft of the article is complete, as far as my present plan of treatment goes. Of course it must yet be subjected to a thorough recasting—possibly more than one. But the main structure of the thought is built. The style needs the pruning knife. My plan is a very simple one—I don't think I have outlined it for you before; have I? It is this in the main: First, I endeavor to point out—rather at once to point out and to demonstrate—that *the* French Revolution instead of ending in the establishment of the first Empire, is really *yet in progress*, the 'revolutions' of this century being only natural convulsions marking the turning points, or crises, of a social and political change which was as inevitable as it has been powerful. I then seek to trace the lines of political change—how republicanism has hitherto proved a weak force, and how all France's governments have been rooted in the completed centralization of power. Hence the French must have grown up in the habits of political servitude—of quasi-slavery; all the weight of the past drags them down. Without—totaly without—any habits of self-govt., then, France has entered upon its practice. Hence grave dangers, which are aggravated by the ignorance of the peasantry—which makes them poor learners—and the social habits of the *bourgeoisie*. On the other hand, the peasant is thrifty and thoroughly independent—both the peasant and the bourgeois are thrifty and prudent. Then, too, France has been built up in strength by successfully passing through several of the severest crises since the establishment of the present Republic. On the one hand are habits of revolutionary remedy for governmental evils, on the other, a few short years of experience in the methods of constitutional *liberty*. From these considerations, marshalling these facts with much more method, clearness, and order than is indicated by this scant and random analysis, I venture a few hints—scarcely predictions—as to the "Political Destiny of the French People," noticing in passing the omnipotential influence which Paris had exerted heretofore upon the fortunes of France (with explanation of what I regard as the source of that influence), and treating at some length the influence of the Church as exhibited in the opposition recently manifested to M. Ferry's schemes of educational reform[3]—an influence which takes its hold upon, and works its will through, the *women* of France, rather than through the men of the nation. In short, I endeavor to discover for myself, and for my *possible* readers, the political factors now most potent in France with a view of discovering the securities and the dangers of her present government, in order, if possible, to forecast her political future. I cannot give you a more perfect idea of the task I have been endeavoring to compass, or of my plans of work, without stretching this epistle beyond all reasonable bounds.

This French work has absorbed my attention almost entirely since College closed, so that I have done little reading besides what was necessary in the way of gathering materials. I have given you my mental history since we parted.

Do write soon and often to Your sincere and loving

Friend   Thos. W. Wilson

ALS (Meyer Coll., DLC).
  1 The references in these two paragraphs are to omitted portions of R. Bridges to WW, Aug. 2, 1879.
  2 July 30, 1879.
  3 See footnote 2 to document printed at Sept. 4, 1879.

From Robert Bridges

Dear Tommy,   Shippensburg, [Pa.] Aug., 25th '79
    . . . I like your plan for the French Article ever so much—especially the latter part. I think you can swing out strong in the contrast between the Bourgeois and peasant influence. It gives you a splendid chance to balance arguments and forces—in which I think you [are] at your best always. Do I make a wrong inference in regard to this? Don't you hold that the middle and lower classes counteract each other's faults and magnify virtues? (I mean with special reference to their fitness for self-government). . . .
                          Your Friend   Bob Bridges.

ALS (WP, DLC) with WWhw and WWsh notations on env.: "Received [WWsh] 8/28/79"; "Ans 9/4/79."

From William Brewster Lee[1]

My dear Tommie,   Paris, France, Aug. 26th 1879
    I received a letter from Bob Bridges the other day—upon reading it, I immediately went & purchased the "International Review" for August—not that I needed ocular proof of what he told me. I wished to own that particular number. Well, old man, accept my very heartiest Congratulations. I wish we could celebrate the event in due Style in the accustomed haunt at nine E. W.[2] Bob Bridges wrote me such a graphic description of what the proceedings would be under such circumstances, that I became blue thinking how impossible the meeting was. The followin just now are widely separated, but when we all meet again, I believe the friendships will be found to be as close as ever. Towards that meeting I am looking forward even now. . . .   Very Sincerely   W. B. Lee.

ALS (WP, DLC) with WWhw notation on env.: "Ans."
  1 Nicknamed "Chang" and "the Heathen." Born Waterford, N. Y., Feb. 27, 1856. A.B., College of New Jersey, 1879. After reading law, was admitted to the bar in 1882 and practiced law in Rochester. Died Sept. 8, 1931.
  2 Bridges' room at 9 East Witherspoon Hall.

An Historical Essay

[c. Sept. 4, 1879]

Self-Government in France

We ought to understand the French; but we do not. As Americans, and in a certain sense the most advanced representatives of what is called, in the cant of our times, the democratic idea, we should be, and are, keenly sensitive to all manifestations of republican principles abroad. Then, too, these later years of hard experience are rudely testing our faith in popular institutions. The somewhat blind ardor of youth is cooling into the more mature thoughtfulness of manhood, and we are beginning to cultivate that calmer temper which prepares us to recognize our shortcomings and deficiencies, and makes us less unwilling to cast aside the haughty self-sufficiency which has hitherto been in one sense our strength, and in many senses our weakness,—such a temper as disposes us to learn of others. When, therefore, we see France adopting forms of popular government with more deliberation and thoughtfulness and moderation than she has exercised since she first threw off the despotism of the Bourbons, we turn toward her with unusual interest, prepared to criticize indeed, but not unprepared to profit by her experiences. And we are drawn to her by still other motives. We can see in her present government the latest and fullest fruitage of the truths which have lain at the foundation of the great Revolution which was ushered in by the passionate deeds of '93, and which has hardly yet ceased to stir; and we feel our partialities warm as we look to that revolution, for we feel that in its beginnings, at least, it was closely connected with our own, by the bonds of sympathy if by none stronger. The French Revolution is not yet ended. The convulsions which have shaken France during this century, and which have seemed, to many, fresh 'revolutions,' have been only turning-points in the progress of the one great revolution[.] To those who witnessed its earliest storms it seemed to clear entirely away as the day of the first Empire dawned. But no such radical social revolution ever completed its work at one blow. When the very foundations of a great and aged society are broken away, years of laborious building are necessary to its restoration. A new and elaborate structure cannot be raised until the obstructions of the old ruin are cleared well away, and old materials shaped for their new uses. New France is not yet completely builded; old France is not yet thoroughly cleared away. We do not know France and her people as we should because we do not recognize all the bearings of this cardinal fact of her later history. Did we understand, we could still hear footfalls of her Revolution. So stupendous have been the events of her later years that our eyes have been drawn to them as to the progress of a drama. They have thus absorbed the most of our attention. But we have at most only distantly skirted the shores and become partially familiar with its most prominent headlands; for few have troubled themselves to look closer into the inner life of the nation: and to be ignorant of this interior life is to misunderstand France's past and to be hopelessly blind as to her future. Until we shall have acquainted ourselves, at least in a general way, with the tendencies and the latest outgrowths of the gradual Revolution which is remaking France, we are totaly unable to appreciate contemporary events in her history, to estimate the factors in her national life, or to forecast her political and social future.

Amid all the experiences through which she has passed since the days of Terror[,] France has been struggling, often languidly, sometimes unconsciously, towards institutions which our Anglo-Saxon race looks upon as peculiarly its own; she has, from time to time, endeavored to habituate herself to those methods of self-government which take their beginnings from our strong-hearted, rough-natured ancestors along the bleak coasts of German Sleswick; and we cannot but regard all movements in this direction with the keenest concern and the warmest sympathy. Our interest in France is, therefore, undoubtedly most real and most deep; but it is to be feared that it is also very ignorant. Even learned and perspicacious men among us do not trouble themselves to know the French as they really are; and we find them persistent in treating questions of French politics as they would points of English policy. Englishmen themselves, they think that all the world must hope and will and act as Englishmen, that the same instincts that have driven *our* race to its present advance pulsate in the blood of all other peoples. It is for this reason, principally, that so many persons who are seemingly well read in French history reason so wildly as to its meaning and its probable issue. It is for this reason that it is necessary ever and again to lay fresh emphasis upon the peculiar, distinctive character of the French *people* as it has issued, by the evolution of revolution, from the darkness and trials of political servitude into unaccustomed paths of self-government.

It was natural, nay inevitable, that France should be convulsed by the first shock of a revolution which was to change the whole face of her society. There has in fact been something almost bewildering in the rapidity of the transformation which society has undergone within her borders. Yet, notwithstanding the power of its onset, it was impossible that the Revolution should arrive at its completion during the life-time of a single generation. In England, freedom has been deliberately and gradually won; yet even in England the progress of political reform has been accompanied by many mutterings of civil war, and once or twice the storm has actually burst upon her. In France, the bonds of servitude were suddenly and violently burst; what wonder, then, that her passionate haste for the liberty of self-rule has brought a long series of painful convulsions upon her? And the Revolution must, of course, pass on into many further stages of progress; but must it pass into other paroxysms? The answer to this question is the solution of the political destiny of the French people. In endeavoring, therefore, to forecast the future of France we must carefully familiarize ourselves with the French, as far as it is possible to do so without coming into immediate intercourse with them. All our largest readings of their past must be employed to reveal to us their distinctive temper and habits of public life; for upon these must all our interpretations of their present, and all our reasonings as to their future, be builded. If Frenchmen have so far thrown off the habits of dependence as to be able to exercise the rights of self-government soberly and conservatively, France may be spared further convulsions in her body politic. If, on the other hand, they have taken upon themselves the great duties and solemn privileges of self-rule before their strength was equal to the burden, or the time was ripe for such a change in their condition, we may expect the storms of still further change to break rapidly upon her. What, then, is the political temper of the French people?

All perplexity as to the causes which have been chiefly operative in making the French nation what it is to-day, clears rapidly away in the light of our knowledge that her Revolution is still a vital force—the force which gives direction to her present drift—; and that all the 'revolutions' which have scarred her recent history have been only paroxysmal symptoms of the tremendous change which is passing over her. As the Revolution at its first outburst was a new revelation to philosophers and a dark puzzle to statesmen, so the progresses and retrogressions which have marked France's social and political history throughout this century are equally an enigma to those of our own day who are wont to look upon the fall of the first Empire or the setting-up of Louis the Eighteenth's throne, not as parts of the one great Revolution, but as themselves distinct and separate revolutions.

The bolder characteristics of French society as it existed under the old régime flash vividly out against the dark background of those first days of anarchy—the days during which the Revolution did its earliest and most terrible work. England, too, felt the movings of the spirit which she saw so triumphant among her neighbors across the channel. But contrast the orderly progress of reform in England with the rush of revolutions in France. On one side of the channel we find law supreme; on the other, force. In England, great reforms are wrought out by peaceful methods, by the moulding power of discussion, within the bounds of law; in France governments have ruled awhile by force, only to fall by force, amid carnage and fierce convulsions. Such contrasts are big with meaning. The Englishman's strength has been built up by centuries of self-government, he has grown old, and therefore self-controlled, in the exercise and defence of his liberties; while, on the other hand, all the weight of the past serves to drag the Frenchman down. He has been born and nurtured in quasi-servitude. As far back as his traditions go, he and his forefathers have bowed the knee to king and to nobles—to all wearers of power. He has inherited nothing but obligations; the Englishman has a heritage of privilege as well. These differences of political habit are so conspicuously evident that it is not a little surprising to find so accomplished and learned a historian as Alison so little acquainted with the spirit of his countrymen as soberly to predict, as the forces of reform were gathering stronger and stronger around its opponents, that those forces would drag the country through scenes which would rival in horror the Reign of Terror; certainly so were the franchise not effectually barred against the middle classes. His warning grew vehement as he appealed to English patriots to save their country from a ruin which was impending only in his own excited imagination. He uttered these fears while the reforms of '32 were gathering head and they seem absurd enough now to us who know how quietly those reforms were accomplished and how beneficent their influences have proved. Alison failed to see that, although the same spirit reigned in both France and England, Englishmen had long since learned to govern themselves, and to work out their own will by means at once peaceful and effective; while Frenchmen were still inexperienced in the exercise of liberty, and knew only how alternately to obey and to overthrow.

A special illustration of the political temper of the French, as it has been manifested hitherto, appears when we compare their revolutionary history with the history of the Revolution of 1688, which ushered in the present state of things in England. In order to appreciate the French *mood* we have but to note the order and soberness of the English revolution in the completeness of its contrast with any of the many convulsions which have given France a change of masters. And yet with William of Orange England received a new dynasty to her throne and strode into a new period of constitutional advance; while France did little more than assist despotism to a change of name and dress. So, turn whither we may in later French political history, we meet the same violent, ill-controlled humor. In public affairs the grain of the ordinary French mind seems to run at right angles to the law, and parallel with every dangerous extreme. It has become habituated to heroic remedies. Quick amputation of an offending limb has been preferred to the tedium of slow nursing

Other examples of the political qualities which have seemed, in the history of the last century, everywhere to hedge the Frenchman are not far to seek, and are as instructive and as impressive as they are numerous. They all point us in the same direction, teaching us the easy solution of the apparent enigma presented by the alternating rise and fall of free institutions in France.

In reviewing the progress of the Revolution, we at once recognize the fact that there are, speaking broadly, two principal elements in the national life of France, which are also most prominent to-day in the republican life she is trying to lead, viz., the *political* and the *religious*. Of these two we naturally direct our attention first to the political, as the more manifest, though not perhaps the more potent, in its influence. And here we at once come face to face with that most important of all political facts in France: the thorough-going and minutely-complete *centralization* which has always, through all her history, focused whatever powers of despotism her governments have possessed. History furnishes few, if any, parallels to the centralization of the old monarchy. One has only to read de Tocqueville's *Ancien Régime* to get a vivid idea of the omnipresence of its influence. That acute, able, and statesmanlike observer fully discovers to us that system in all its marvelous completeness and minuteness. Not content with mere sovereignty, the central government assumed the guardianship of all the interests of the people, of even their most private concerns. From the king to the smallest official of the most distant corporate town, there extended an unbroken line of officers, each, directly or indirectly, the nominee of the king, or of his Council, and each at the beck and call of the monarch or his representatives; each a thread in the net-work of power which centred in the throne. By virtue of the supreme authority of which he was the servant, each official was all-powerful within his own sphere. Every department, every town, was full of officers of the crown, who were carefully thorough in the exercise of their tyrannical agency. Men everywhere found their most private affairs, their closest family secrets, pryed into by the king's officers. Their property was drawn upon largely and without scruple, to fill the royal coffers. Their every right was dependent upon the will of their crowned master. This universal control and supervision on the part of the government was manifested in every conceivable form. Citizens could not associate, even for commercial or manufacturing purposes, without the express permission of the authorities; public discussion was allowed only on abstract questions of philosophy or religion; the press was jealously watched, sternly kept within bounds set by royal whim; local and municipal autonomy was now given; again taken away: to be restored only for a price. And, since the monarch thus undertook to assume all the duties of a universal guardianship of his people, to control them in every particular of public life not only, but in private matters as well, he, as personating the State, came to be *accepted* as the conservator of all interests. The government came to be regarded as the only agent competent for the accomplishment of anything. Private persons never dreamed of success without the paternal aid and advice of the government. Frenchmen began to think with something very like contempt of any one who refused to accept these their views as to the duties and capacities of the state. Turgot laughed to think that America should have imitated the English government by vesting authority in three coördinate branches: the Executive, the legislative, and the judicial, instead of concentrating all power in "the state." Indeed, so rooted and grounded in such habits of thought and action did the people become, that the common peasantry held the state to blame for everything that went wrong, for every extreme of weather even. But such convictions did not create that interest in the administration of public affairs which would have seemed natural under the circumstances. While each was ready to blame the government for every trifling ill, it never entered his head to make government or governmental principles matters of concern to himself. Government was no business of his.

The nobility, the higher classes, were shut out from participation in the work of government scarcely less than the *bourgeoisie* and the peasantry. And it is interesting, though somewhat foreign to my present purpose, to remark that to this fact, more than to any other perhaps, are we to attribute the onetime brilliancy and wit of French *salons* as contrasted with the stately stiffness and

stupidity of English parlors. The power and imposing magnificence of the court attracted all who were wealthy and all who were
needy, everyone who was learned and everyone who was ignorant,
the ambitious and the vicious, to Paris. But no part in government, no field of statesmanship, was open to most of the men of
learning and wit who found their way to the bustling capital.
Across the channel, public life was open to all, each could command a place in his country's confidence and a hearing on the
great questions which affected her welfare, if only he were thoughtful and able; most of the men who were prominent in London society were also eminent members of Parliament; some of them
were England's actual rulers. They did not, therefore, always add
life and interest to a polite evening reception or fashionable dining.
They had graver matters in mind than those which constitute the
staple of social chat, and were either stiffly unentertaining, or re-
tarded their own and others' digestions by discussing state policy
over the viands. They went to the entertainments to which the
rules of society dragged them, because politeness or policy demanded, not of their own deliberate choice. It was far otherwise
in the Parisian *salons*. In the fair capital of France men of letters,
artists, men of pleasure, the minister and the poet, the thoughtful
and the thoughtless, the sober and the gay, all alike made society
part of the serious business of their lives. Those who sought the
favors of the court frequented places of fashionable resort and
were always to be found at brilliant evening gatherings. Here were
the paths to popularity. To become master of Parisian society, by
whatever powers of fascination, was to gain entrance to court
circles and come near to the ear of the king, or of his favorites.
The rising artist advertized his talents by keeping himself as well
as his pictures constantly before his patrons. The literary man,
after a day of close application, after hours of work in the quiet of
his study, at evening took his place among the wits of the *salon*.
If by any display of wit or learning, if by any clever conversation,
he could win the smiles of that brilliant society, his latest work
was sure of success; his recent drama would be produced to full
boxes and an enthusiastic pit. In short, society was the only *public
life* France had. In its bright circles all men sought an audience
to play to; and it may easily be imagined how splendid a stage it
was.

Under the old monarchy the courts of justice were the only
nurseries of liberty. From her law courts France learned all of
liberty that she was then able to recognize, "the principle that all
decisions should be preceded by discussion, and subject to appeal;

the use of publicity, and the love of forms." Magistrates often purchased their offices, it is true; but they were irremovable, and could look for no promotion:—and they were therefore for the most part independent. They were almost the only checks to arbitrary methods. Everywhere else the government ruled or dictated without let or hindrance. And it was quick to overrule even the courts when their judgments crossed its wishes.

Such were the bonds of the old monarchy. It is not strange, then, that when the nation came to shake itself loose from this burden of wrongs with which it had been saddled for centuries, it found itself bound by political habits of which it could not so easily divest itself. So strongly had the idea that the *State*, the central government, was the only power for good—or for evil—taken hold upon the minds of Frenchmen, that even the most radical of the writers who sowed the seeds of the Revolution were not able to rid themselves of it. Even in the expression of their furthest desires, they asked, not for political liberty, but only for certain reforms which they looked to the *State* to bring about. The State had, in their view, all power to mould individuals, and to carve a new nation out of present materials. "The state moulds men into whatever shape it pleases," said Bodeau. In the words of de Tocqueville, these would-be reformers "attempted to combine an unlimited executive with a preponderating legislative body—a bureaucracy to administer, a democracy to govern. Collectively, the nation was sovereign—individually, citizens were confined in the closest dependence; yet from the former were expected the virtues and the experience of a free people, from the latter, the qualities of a submissive servant." Thus were even the imaginations of the most hopeful reformers enslaved by a pernicious idea of the functions of the state. To recognize in a government only the agent or instrument of the governed would have been to them as impossible as to efface all the past history of France. To them the state *was* the nation. This was the political habit which had completely encrusted the French mind. Yet a few Frenchmen undoubtedly got some glimpses of real liberty. It is a sudden spirit of freedom which speaks in the philosophical writings of the later days of the Eighteenth century and acts in its terrible close; but it is freedom gone mad and rioting in the garb of license.

Nor did the first gust of the Revolution uproot the despotism which had grown so strongly into the habits of the French people. It only tore away its old and decayed branches and left it to send out a new and stronger growth. The people themselves, when they had snatched power from the hands of Louis, knew not how to rule save by absolute methods, by bringing all France into complete subjection to Committees of Public Safety, to a Central Committee of the National Guard, or to a Directory. They were more cruel despots than ever poor Louis XVI dared to be or wished to be. Their wild, uncurbed tyranny drove France, rather than continue to live in anarchy, to accept, in the government of the first Napoleon, a despotism more extensive and more absolute than she had ever known before. And since then she has done little better—until the war with Prussia made her newest experiment a possibility. Destroying so many other features of the old *régime*, the Revolution retained and even strengthened its stupendous system of centralization: for it legalized it. It constituted it a part of the Napoleonic system, not by implication or sufferance, but by direct and specific grant. The imperial administration was authorized to show its hand and make its power felt everywhere. Official agents were exempted from the jurisdiction of the ordinary courts; and whilst the authority of these courts was defined and circumscribed with some strictness, and their rights guarded with some degree of jealousy, the right of the government to encroach upon, or even usurp, their domain was made matter of constitutional enactment, of fundamental law. The history of France, since the opening of the Revolution, has been little more than a record of the alternation of centralized democracy with centralized monarchy, or imperialism—in all cases of the sway of a virtual despotism. Louis the Eighteenth conducted the forms of liberal government so wilfully, so unwisely, so despotically, that his reign was bright and beneficent only by contrast with those that had gone before and that which was to follow after. And under the third Napoleon the chains of centralized despotism were drawn as closely and cruelly as under the first Empire. Forms, indeed, were changed. Louis Napoleon pretended to rule by popular sanction; he claimed that his people had voted him a throne; he several times went through the mockery of a *plebecite*; and he was always ready with hypocritical expressions of admiration for an universal suffrage. But all the quintessential features of despotism were carefully preserved, and were as prominent in this second Empire as in the earlier and greater. France's passion for liberty has hitherto proved "inexperienced, ill regulated, easily discouraged, easily frightened away, easily overcome, superficial, and evanescent."

It seems unquestionably true that this same spirit of centralization still lingers in France; that, with her, parliamentary government is even yet at best but a doubtful experiment; that the old spirit of ready acquiescence in whatever rule is thrust upon them, of quiet, quick, unmurmuring obedience to whatever authority is put over them, still weights the French people in their struggle towards freedom; and that self-government fits many French districts, fits even some most enlightened French cities, as ill as independence of parental authority fits a child. Open Jules Simon's interesting and historically invaluable work on the *Government of Thiers*, and we find the ex-president, the late lamented liberal statesman—the man whose liberal views were the fruit of his latest and ripest years—an urgent advocate of such measures as that which made the mayors of all towns of less than twenty thousand inhabitants subject to the supervision of the prefects of the departments and removable by the Executive; and limited their privileges, as those of the municipal councils by whom they are elected, to civil matters; the exact scope of these privileges to be defined by the central government! And in his advocacy of such measures Thiers may truly be said to have represented quite justly French habits of thought and action in matters of practical liberty. Although in his later days he seems to have become convinced that the depositaries of centralized power should be, directly or indirectly, the nominees of the people, he was always a consistent advocate of centralization. And in such opinions he is supported by the arguments of some of the ablest and most advanced thinkers among his fellow Republicans. He proposed that the mayors of the larger cities should be nominees of the government; and Simon himself hastens to his support with such an opinion as this: "An elected mayor at the head of a city of two millions of inhabitants could neither be subject to a king nor subordinate to a president." If this be true, France is not ripe for self-government; if it is not true, how can we hope to see France wisely and liberally ruled while her most enlightened statesmen are thus ignorant of the true principles and methods of practical political liberty, thus blinded by the instincts of despotism? To whichever conclusion we incline, we must realize the immediate jeopardy of the Republic.

Parliamentary government seems to work in France now as it has always worked in the past: clumsily and jarringly; with much violent friction; with variable strength; and often-recurring symptoms of instability. It is a conflict of passions, not a war of parties merely, nor a joust of policies simply. In the past it has ruled factiously in times of peace and order; and fallen violently in moments of political storm. Its future, therefore, is darkly problematical, if its past is to be taken as precedent. The Assembly of 1870 —met, in a time of tremendous crisis, to settle the destiny of the nation by deciding the question of peace or war—so long as they were led by the sagacity and resolution of Thiers, acted with admirable promptness and with wise patriotism. But, when peace was secured, and Thiers, placed at the head of the government, could no longer be always present in the Tribune to command them to harmonious action, they were quickly broken up into factious camps, and their passions hurried them into follies and excesses which remind us of the impotent unwisdom of the Assembly of 1789. During the struggle with the Commune they were eagerly alert to embrace every opportunity of meddling with the conduct of the war; and only the indefatigable vigilance and immovable determination of the Executive chief prevented them from wrecking the cause of good government by their idle interference. But it was after the suppression of the Commune that the character of the Assembly most conspicuously appeared. In all their work there was manifest, from that time forward, a lamentable want of ability. They sought to usurp the functions of the administration. Their energy found food in the work of a Decentralization Committee, whose object seems to have been to centralize power in the hands of the Legislature whilst taking it away from the Executive; in the inquiries of committees of investigation into everything which should not have been investigated:—such as the acts of the late Government of Defence, and the conduct of the generals during the war. The only point in which all parties seem to have harmonized was in their advocacy of centralization; those who fought for decentralization doing so, apparently, only to cripple the administration or to cloak other designs. With this Assembly originated the measure which provided that the mayors of all cities of over twenty-thousand inhabitants should be nominated by the Executive from the members of the elective municipal councils, as well as the act with reference to the mayors of towns having less than that number of inhabitants which I have already noticed. To this further step towards centralization they were driven by the fear that the demand for local self-government made by such towns as Lyons, Marseilles, Toulouse, and others of equal importance, signified a wish for complete independence, and that to grant to these cities elected mayors would be to constitute so many independent republics! Such fears are themselves instructive. To us, who look upon local autonomy as one of the stoutest and most essential girders of every free state, they open the French temper to its inmost fold. French representatives dare not trust their constituents with powers of self-rule; will the sovereignty of the Legislature which they constitute be a blessing to France? We would suppose not; and we know that the work of these representatives did *not* do them or their country honor. Had not M. Thiers been among them to command, they would have pulled France in ruins about their own feet with hasty passion. As it was, they did all they could to hamper their brave chief in his struggle with the Commune; and, finally, drove him from office, to place executive authority in the hands of a soldier of the Empire, through whom they hoped to gather the reins of absolute power into their own itching palms.

With the constitutional triumph of the Republicans over Marshal McMahon and the election of M. Grévy to the presidency, the Republic may be said at last to have become an actuality, and undoubtedly her present constitution is the best France has ever had. But it is daily jeoparded by the weight of centralization which it carries. In its possibilities of abuse the centralized authority of the present Republic seems scarcely to fall below the despotic system of the last Empire. Each department is ruled by a prefect and a sub-prefect who are the appointees of the Executive. These officers are clothed with all the essential powers of masters. The prefect is *ex-officio* president of the Council General of his department. His prerogatives range from the supervision of municipal administration to the espionage of private club life. Under such a system, local autonomy must of course be confined within narrow limits. The machinery of despotism still stands, ready for use or abuse. And centralization exposes France to her oldtime danger. Paris, when the seat of centralized power, may make herself mistress of France. It is a significant fact, one which has been often noted, and as often deplored, that Paris has given France almost all her 'revolutions.' Paris pulled down Louis Philippe's throne as it had done that of Louis Sixteenth. Almost every crisis has been of her making, almost every government, her creation. Her size and wealth and commercial preëminence would naturally make her power vast in a small and compact country like France; but, had she not been the centre of a complex and complete system of centralization, she could hardly have thrust a change of governments even upon the passive, unresisting people of the more rural departments. Were local self-government strongly built up everywhere throughout the borders of France, she could no more set up new rulers over the nation than could Bordeaux. Every department, every city, every commune would be a centre of united and organized resistance. Paris could no more uproot the institutions of France than New York could establish a Caesar to rule over us, or London place a dictator on Victoria's throne. She would then be only one small part of a great system. If her mob were to hunt the monarch from her streets, he might still be secure of the support of the rest of France; if they drove Parliament from its halls, their humiliation would only be the more complete and overwhelming when, from another and securer seat, that Parliament dictated the terms of their submission. Paris would be powerless. But as the seat of a great centralized government, she may easily control the destinies of the nation. She might overturn or utterly destroy the central authority; and, with that authority, the whole official fabric must inevitably fall. The host of officials who rule the country by virtue of the authority of a central government are impotent when that government has fallen and its authority no longer exists. They are incapable of concerted, united action. When their master is gone, they are isolated and helpless. Paris, the capital, has knocked away the headstone of the corner, and the whole structure of government falls heavily in ruins. Paris is now again the seat of government and we can, therefore, never wholly dismiss our fears for the safety of the Republic until centralization has been exchanged for complete local self-government.

Socially, the French people are far from where they were a century ago. The social revolution has passed further on than the political. The feudal nobility, the ruling aristocracy of the old monarchy, has passed quietly away, leaving nothing of their onetime glory but its forms: the name and affectation of rank, and the *bourgeoisie*, having come to share more largely in political power than they have hitherto been able to do, have pressed up to a higher plane of importance and of intelligence. But it is to be feared that the French *bourgeois* is not of the stuff of which trustworthy citizens are made. His habits of thrift, however admirable in themselves, surely tend to eat away every faculty or aspiration which cannot be harnessed in their service, and must inevitably affect his political spirit. His whole soul is wrapt up in saving; his energies are frittered away in the smallest tricks of economy. Careless of others and of their opinions and cares, he focuses all his powers on the economy of his own household. He isolates himself, that he may have no other expenses than those which are necessary to the support of his immediate family. He can scarcely be called part of the community in which he lives. The American or Englishman makes money partly, sometimes mainly, that he may become a more respected and influential member of the class or community of which he forms a part; and he has, in natural consequence much immediate interest in the affairs of his community. He has a constant eye for public business. The ordinary French *bourgeois*, on the other hand, has no time or inclination to care for public or private interests other than his own—is a mere observer of matters of government. He can scarcely conceive the possibility of living for the public weal.

Still more important than the *bourgeoisie*, in a political point of view, is the class below it. The large estates of the ancient nobility have come, by a slow process which began before the Revolution came, into the possession of a thriving peasantry. Indeed France's main strength, certainly the main-stay of the Republic, is this large and enlarging class of peasant landowners—the promise of a yeomanry such as arose in England after the Black Death had broken the power of the great landholders; and which has since fallen into weakness and decay under a pernicious system of game and tenantry laws. The almost marvellous thrift and industry which signalize the daily life of the French peasantry can scarcely find a parallel among modern nations; unless, indeed, the lower classes of China equal them in capacity for work and careful frugality of living. Then, too, contrary to general opinion, they are eminently independent. Neither the counsels of his priest nor the strenuous influence of his most powerful neighbors can turn the peasant farmer from the course into which his prejudiced preferences have led him. When the rich and titled seek to lead him the terrible memories of the servitude and suffering of the *ancien régime* rise up in bitterness against them. The priest fights in vain against that cold indifference to the authority of the Church which seems as characteristic of the men of the peasantry as of the men of the upper classes. There is now, therefore, little doubt that the peasantry are growingly republican. It is natural that they should be so. Inclined always to hurry in a direction opposite to that which the classes pretending to the mastery of rank almost universally take, they find republicanism most determinedly hostile to Legitimist and Bonapartist alike, and are, on that account primarily, glad to subscribe to its faith; however little of that faith they understand, or care to know. Thus far, republicanism wins their sympathy. Their experience of its rule has, moreover, shown them that under the Republic, no less than under king or emperor—nay much more than under these—there is permanence of peace and security of property—the blessings which of all others they value, and have reason to value, most highly. The more strenuously the forces of the Church, or of the aristocracy, labor to sow the seeds of opposition to the Republic, that the harvest of despotism may grow up to their own profit, the larger swell the Republican ranks. The spirit of loyalty to any dynasty has long been dead in the hearts of the French people, and has been supplanted by a spirit of total indifference to the person or the pretensions of any claimant to the throne, however great his name or lineage, which must chill the enthusiasm of Legitimists or Bonapartists into discouragement.

This is the bright side of the character of the French peasantry. There is a darker. They are pitifully, almost hopelessly, ignorant. And their ignorance is all the more shameful because it is assiduously cultivated and openly gloried in. Every peasant father sternly discourages in his son any fondness for pursuits higher than those of the class into which he has been born. He instinctively feels that any knowledge beyond the traditions of his class will unfit his son for the small duties of the little farm and draw him away into other spheres of life. He will be lost to his family. The peasant youth is, therefore, carefully barred by parental authority, if not by his own preferences, from the possibility of education. Its ignorance seems in some sort essential to the integrity of the class, which seems, therefore, impelled to shut itself off from all light from without by the instincts of self-preservation. It is plain, of course, that as long as this veil of ignorance shuts the peasantry off from all rational instruction, keeping them in the darkness of their superstitions and prejudices, their influence upon politics cannot be healthy. They will adhere to any particular policy or party only because their prejudices cry out against other policies and their hatred burns towards other parties, not because they have any intelligent love for the government to which they lend their support. However thrifty, honest, and naturally intelligent they may be, they will remain so thickly hedged about with ignorance that neither reason nor persuasion can reach them, until the land is so flooded with the light of education that they cannot but let some ray of it in. It may be matter of rejoicing that they have thrown in their lots with republicanism; but the fact must be recognized that they are its allies only by a sort of happy chance. They are glad and steady in their support of the Republic now, while it is firm and prosperously powerful. But there can be no assurance that they will stir themselves to save it in the hour of peril, which may come to it only too easily and speedily. They are stolid; they are hardly spurred to decisive deeds; they are incapable of concerted action. Their energies are over-weeded with the habit of acquiescence in whatever *is*. If an emperor or a monarch is forced upon them, they may move restlessly and discontentedly under his yoke, but they will scarcely rouse themselves to cast it violently and suddenly off. Their mental horizon is bounded by the routine of their every-day life. Education is the only force that can break their lethargy away and wake them into life. The French people can be ripened for self-government only by the sun-light of education.

Until lifted out of the depths of their ignorance, the French people can never see far enough ahead to value the political privileges of the present moment, or to perform zealously their daily political duties. It is, therefore, as manifestly to the interest of the Republican party to advance and perfect education by every means within their power as it is to the interest of the royalist and imperialist factions to foster the apathy which is born of ignorance. And the Republican leaders seem fully awake to this fact. The Republican party, as it is the only party which at all understands self-government and its needs, is also the only one which has any rational ideas or definite purposes as to the advancement of popular education, upon which the health and endurance of self-government depend. Their advocacy of educational reform is, moreover, in the main, brave and resolute. They alone seem courageous enough to leave the Roman Catholic Church out of all plans concerning matters with which of right that hierarchy should have nothing to do. But *any* treatment of the question of educational reform is thickly beset by many and serious difficulties. It is the rock upon which the power of the Republicans is now most in danger of suffering shipwreck. Any party which purposes snatching all power of conferring civil degrees from the Romish clergy and placing the national education upon an entirely undenominational basis—any party which, in other words, is openly favorable to the establishment of a system of thorough-going "lay" education— throws itself against the opposition of the large majority of French mothers. For, as we are told by that acute observer and graceful writer, Mr. Hamerton, who has reason to know France so well, "The clergy are universally anti-Republican, simply because they know that a Republican government will never restore the Pope to his temporal throne, and that it is likely to establish secular education and religious equality in France; and the women of the more influential classes at least are humbly and cheerfully subservient to the priesthood. It can easily be realized that to carry an educational measure in the face of determined, unreasoning, fanatical opposition from all the women of the nation, from all that portion of society to which is assigned, as of right, the supreme control of the young, whom education is intended to reach, is no easy task even for the sturdiest and most resolute. It is here, therefore, that we come directly to the consideration of that influence of the Church of Rome which I have already alluded to as the religious factor in French politics.

The power of the Church in French politics, like every other factor in the political life of France, is fully understood only when we turn upon it all the lights of the revolutionary epoch, viewing the present power of the clergy as it has been developed from the pre-revolutionary system which recognized Papal authority in matters of state. The times when cardinals were statesmen and kings the servants of Rome are not far separated, in spirit from the times when a Romish priesthood can clog the designs and shackle the hopes of a great and powerful party. And it might be hard to prove that the Church of Rome had any stronger hold upon the affections of the French people in the days when Richelieu was building up the powers of the monarchy and framing and directing policies than she has now in these later days of republicanism. It may be true, that before Voltaire made mockery at sacred things a polite amusement the priesthood may have been able to count more surely on the adherence and obedience of Frenchmen; because the rule of the Church, rooted and grounded in the habits of a people easily led by a power which appealed so strongly to their imaginations, had never yet been seriously shaken; and even since Voltaire broke away the national habit which had been so often mistaken for reverence, skepticism and indifference to the claims of the Church have not grown to very much more alarming proportions. Open atheism is rare in France. Indifference, at least on the part of the male portion of the population has long been widespread, almost universal. But, although the power of the Church has managed to out-live all the changes of the century, and still finds, we are told, firm rootage in the life of a people to whom its pomps and pageantries are dearer than anything which could be devised in their stead—to whom marriage is barbarous and death unhallowed in the absence of those solemn ceremonies which wear the garb of ancient custom and claim the sanction of a thousand years; although the Church is dear to the ignorant among the people, because it is all that remains to them of the magnificence of their ancient life; although the duties of the confessional and of the solemn and stately daily service are inseparably knit into the affections of thousands of Frenchwomen; although everywhere the Romish hierarchy has made itself a necessity and *therefore* a power in the lives of most Frenchmen, it would be an ignorant blunder indeed to suppose that the clergy can turn the political opinions of even the lowest classes into the channel of their own partialities. Most Frenchmen support the Church in the performance of its ordinary functions as their necessary and accustomed minister in things spiritual; but they are indifferent to its authority in matters temporal; and this indifference amounts to independence in matters political. On questions of politics the ordinary Frenchman heeds the opinion of his priest as little as he regards that of his wife, the priest's most ardent friend and supporter. American and English writers go strangely astray when they argue upon the assumption that the combined influence of "the nobility" and the clergy is sufficient to turn the scale of the popular vote to the side upon which the weight of that influence is cast. There is an unconquerable antagonism between the old nobility and the humbler ranks, their onetime slaves; and the omnipotence of the Church in questions of religion bows in weakness before questions of public policy. But the heads of the Church have been prudent and wise and far-sighted enough to stand out of the way of the advance of that social and political change which they were quick to recognize as inevitable, as they have been quietly strong to hold those points at which they knew themselves to be powerful. Of all the institutions of the pre-revolutionary society, therefore, the Church alone has preserved the integrity of its power. It is still a great force in France, as any such institution must from its very nature be. [See Hamerton's "Around My House"][1]

But, if the clergy are thus impotent in political affairs, why did their opposition keep the Ferry laws hanging so long in the balance?[2] Possibly—nay probably—if those laws had been submitted to the popular vote they would *not* have been long denied a triumphal acceptance. But the question of educational reform in France is by no means a purely political one—nor yet is it a question of mere expediency. To reform her system of education is to secularize it, to throw down in great part ecclesiastical privileges and foundations and set up a complete organization of "lay education." M. Ferry designed taking away from the Church the right

1 Philip G. Hamerton, *Round My House, Notes of Rural Life in France in Peace and War*, 2nd ed. (London, 1876), Brackets WW's. (Eds.' note.)

2 WW refers here to two bills introduced in the Chamber of Deputies by Jules Ferry on March 15, 1879. One established a Superior Council of Public Instruction and certain academic councils. The other, much more important, was a bill for "freedom of teaching." Its central provision was Article 7 forbidding teaching in public or private schools by members of "unauthorized" religious orders, which struck hardest at the Jesuits. These bills were under debate while WW was writing "Self-Government in France," hence he used the present tense while writing this paragraph. The bill for "freedom of teaching" having passed the Chamber on July 9, 1879, WW apparently then put this paragraph into the past tense, even though this measure had not passed the Senate and in fact never did. For an account of Ferry's struggles for this legislation in 1879, see Alfred Rambaud, *Jules Ferry* (Paris, 1903), pp. 94-123.

of conferring civil degrees—which are necessary, in France, to all professional men—and shuting out such unauthorized societies as that of the Jesuits altogether and finally from the right of instructing French youth. This question is one, moreover, to be decided by the votes of the Legislative Assembly; and the Church numbers a larger proportion of political adherents among French representatives than she can reckon upon among their constituents. Those who still cherish the hope of a third empire, or the re-enthronement of the house of Orléans dare not dash their chances of ecclesiastical support by running directly athwart the most earnest desires of the priesthood of Rome; and many sincere Republicans are easily overawed by any organized antagonism on the part of the Roman authorities, while some are bound, by private interests, to the Roman clergy. Then, too, it was not the forces of the Church alone which M. Ferry found arrayed against him when he laid his scheme before the Assembly. In their opposition to his measures the clerical party found some powerful allies among men with whom they had little else in common. Very many thoughtful Republicans have declared their entire disapproval of those clauses of M. Ferry's bill which strike at the Jesuits, because they see that, by striking at the principle of religious toleration, they strike at Republicanism itself. The Church of Rome can henceforward make herself a power in French politics only when, as in the recent struggle over educational reform, she has right on her side.

The future of France is problematical. There is no disguising the fact that her liberties are still insecure. They rest upon habits of revolution. Frenchmen are unaccustomed, unreconciled to constitutional government. They are unskilful in manipulating the machinery of constitutional reform. Destruction is more natural to them than amendment. If the policy of the government displeases them, their first impulse is to destroy it. Party government is, in the eyes of most Frenchmen, a strange device. They do not altogether understand it; and they do not more than half like it. It is an exotic. Parliamentary government is an unpracticed art in France. For more than a century its *forms* have been observed; and Frenchmen have long known the semblance of legislative deliberation and the formalities of legislative sanction of a sovereign's acts. But not until now have they known the reality of legislative sovereignty; they have come into its exercise inexperienced in its difficulties and untrained in its duties. They are not, indeed, untrained in the laws of parliamentary procedure, or entirely undisciplined in its methods. Their familiarity with its forms has steadied their habits and taught them to put bounds to their passions. But their *power* is new; and it is the newness of their liberties which constitutes their insecurity. France has really never before enjoyed free institutions; this is her first season of education in liberty, its rights and its duties. Self-government is as yet only an experiment with her, and its exercise cannot for many years become firmly established in the habits of her people. Indeed republicanism itself is on trial. Hitherto it has been, in the thoughts of Frenchmen, a synonym of anarchy and bloodshed. They remember that the vilest of Parisian revolutionists have committed the most hideous crimes in its name; that when the power of the first Napoleon, and the throne of Orléans, fell they were made to tremble under the terrible despotism of a power which bloodthirsty wretches hailed as a 'Grand Republic.' No reasonable man can wonder that Frenchmen have hated and dreaded republicanism. Democracy, as far as their experience of it had seen, had proved itself incapable of moderate, orderly, wise, and stable rule. The Conservative Republic now established in their midst— the conservative republicanism now ruling the National Council— is a new revelation to them. The present Republic is of quite another sort from those 'republics' which have mocked them in their darkest days; and they are beginning to become reconciled, if not attached, to the present order of things. They find their energies quickening in the bracing air of self-government. But liberty has been thrust suddenly upon them—upon a people unprepared to receive it because of densest ignorance and because of habits of servitude; upon a people who can hardly be proved to have desired more than a just master. Louis Eighteenth was not dethroned because France was tired of his rule. The universal testimony of acute observers and eminent statesmen such as de Tocqueville, and others of like stamp, who were eyewitnesses of the fall of the Orléans throne, is, that the vast majority of the French people— even a majority of the citizens of Paris—were well satisfied with his government and hostile to a republic. Again and again had a considerable majority declared its consent to the administration of Guizot. The overthrow of the monarchy was, therefore, the work of a minority of the people of Paris, and was made possible only by the weak irresolution of the monarch himself. Nor did France cast out Louis Napoleon because she desired a republic. He had proved himself an incapable and tyrannical self-seeker, and he naturally fell when the calamity of a war which he had himself courted burst upon his throne. The Republic was established upon the ruins of his empire because it was, under the circumstances, the only practicable form of government. The French people would certainly not have consented to the rule of any of those who were then candidates for the French throne; and a republic seems to have been adopted simply because it would make no one man master. A ruler who was at once just and acceptable and available could not be found; and the expedient of having no ruler was, in such a case, a perfectly natural one. With the Bonapartists and Orleanists, the Republic was a time-serving strategy. They hoped by its means to prepare a way for some despot of their own naming. Each hoped to outwit the other and to shield behind a pretence of republicanism their plans of despotism. But Providence has built up the Republic beyond their ability to destroy, and has made it an instrument for the pulling down of their power and the blasting of their hopes.

Many competent witnesses unite in bearing testimony to the fact that France was not ripe for a Republic in 1871. "We have no public life in France," wrote M. Taine in 1870, signifying the completeness of Imperial supervision; and we naturally ask ourselves, how can a nation so long denied any voice in public affairs pass at once to a wise and temperate use of plenary power? "Words are events in France," says Jules Simon, after having participated in the establishment of the Republic; and this one sentence very cleverly epitomizes the French political mood. How often have words caused a revolution in restless France; while events of the gravest import have created scarce a ripple on the people's passions! And the reason is as simple as the fact is manifest. Hitherto, the part of the people in the government of France has been the part of revolution. They have never governed, except to overthrow the government; and words—words that appealed to their imaginations or to their passions—have been the goads which have driven them to action. Until now they have learned how to do nothing but overthrow; and, in arousing them to a work of destruction, words of passion were events. And is it possible that a people thus easily moved to violence, sometimes by a single word, has come calmly and moderately to rule itself through a sovereign Legislature? Questions like this must continue to puzzle us until time has worked out their answers. It is, of course, inevitable that many grave perils should threaten the future of self-government among a people whose traditions and habits bind them to servitude. But to those of us who look to the Republic to regenerate France it is sadly discouraging to hear a keen and well-informed observer of French society declare, that, "even after the nominal establishment of the Republic," "men of good social position, who declared themselves on the side of representative government, lost caste by it." Such a tone in society is almost as gloomily unpropitious as the disheartening division of parties in France; where three great factions war perpetually against one another; two of them vying with each other in the endeavor to re-enslave their countrymen; the third alone a friend of free institutional liberty. Until two great national parties, each alike the friend and earnest upholder of the Constitution, and each divided from its rival only as to questions of general policy and administration within the bounds of that Constitution, grow up to clear the field of all smaller rivals, of all factions or dangerous foes of the Republic, there can be no safety. Certainly while republican principles are looked upon as vulgar by fashionable society, and the government persistently and systematically plotted against by parties whose success is its destruction, liberty must stand in constant jeopardy.

But whilst there are these doubts and fears which we cannot clear away from the future of France, there are also many facts of past achievement and many indications of future safety, to cheer her friends and encourage her statesmen. We have already seen that a large majority of the French people are uniting in support of the Republic. Some among the higher classes, who claim rank, and many among the clergy, who arrogate to themselves divine authority, are the only real enemies of free government. The middle and lower classes are gradually finding out that, in securing to them the enjoyment of peace and protection and substantial liberty, the Republic can and will do more for them than any other government has ever done; and, as they come to realize this fact, they will also come to love and support the Republic for its own sake. And the large majority of Frenchmen are, beyond a reasonable doubt, independent enough to continue in its support against all opposition. If only education can so take hold upon them as to shake them loose from their prejudices, that they may comprehend the principles upon which republicanism rests, and consent to its rule because of a conviction of its right to rule and its ability to secure the blessings of freedom, the Republic may become so stablished that none but an omnipotent hand can compass its destruction. The power of the franchise can never safely be entrusted to those whose ignorance has not been broken by a ray of knowledge for generations and only deepens as the years come and go. How can a nation walk in the dark without many a heavy fall?

The permanence of her present form of government is, above all things else, necessary as the condition of such popular political education as France now needs; for until such rights as that of the sovereign franchise have become habitual they stand in constant peril. As I have already said, there seems to be every reason to believe that the habits of the French are still revolutionary. Until now they have known no constitutional remedy for bad government; and their tendency to adopt violent remedies is assiduously fed by Imperialist and Legitimist intrigues and by the malevolent influence of the Church of Rome. Such a danger is, however, self-corrective; time is its sure remedy. Every perilous crisis passed is strength gained. And France has already come safely and triumphantly through three seasons of severe trial. The Commune assailed her liberties, and was conquered; Thiers was driven from the executive chair, but his very enemies were compelled to proclaim the Republic and elect a president under a liberal constitution; and, finally, Marshal McMahon, the hope of revolutionists, was forced to yield to a constitutional Opposition and give place to one of the staunchest and ablest of French Republicans. The election of M. Grévy to the presidency, in October 1878, was the final establishment of the Republic. These were stirring changes. And it is for us an instructive fact that these great changes were made possible in France by just such a system of ministerial responsibility as we consider unsafe and unsteady, and impracticable on this side the sea. France has Cabinet government. Her ministers, acting under an elected President, resign upon defeat; indeed recent events would seem to show that, under her present Constitution, the President himself will often find it expedient, if not necessary, to resign, when he finds himself out of harmony with the majority of the Assembly. And yet this delicate system of official responsibility works without serious strain in passionate, inexperienced France. It carries her safely and peacefully through crises such as would only a few years ago have hurried her into revolution. Its strength is further stablished by every trial. Not once since 1870 has France turned aside from the paths of constitutional progress; not once has she paused in her pursuit of secure liberty. Assuredly these are cheering facts and the destinies of the nation brighten in their light. If this Conservative Republic can hold its power and continue to secure the blessings of peace and liberty to the French people until another generation, which has never known any other rule, comes into active political life, its future is secure. Experience will then have built up the people in habits of constitutional observance. If the Republic be once overthrown, it is impossible to predict what will follow. If it remain, its safety will be secured by the gradual breaking away of centralization and the final establishment of local self-government.

This is a most critical juncture in the history of France. It is a new starting-point in her career. Imprudence on the part of representatives unused to possessing and unpracticed in exercising sovereign legislative powers is more to be feared than any folly on the part of the people at large; for any wild or unthoughtful step of the present majority in the Assembly might unsettle the government fatally, finally. Liberty is, however, slowly coming to be understood in France. It is no longer a mere abstraction, an unsubstantial phantom born of a disordered fancy. "How false is the conception, how frantic the pursuit, of that treacherous phantom which men call Liberty!" exclaims Ruskin. "There is no such thing in the universe. There can never be. The stars have it not; the earth has it not; the sea has it not; and we men have the mockery and semblance of it only for our heaviest punishment. The enthusiast would reply that by Liberty he meant the Law of Liberty. Then why use the single and misunderstood word? If by liberty you mean chastisement of the passions, discipline of the intellect, subjection of the will; if you mean the fear of inflicting, the shame of committing, a wrong; if you mean respect for all who are in authority, and consideration for all who are in dependence; veneration for the good, mercy to the evil, sympathy for the weak;—if you mean, in a word, that Service which is defined in the liturgy of the English church to be 'perfect Freedom,' why do you name this by the same word by which the luxurious mean license, and the reckless mean change;—by which the rogue means rapine, and the fool, equality; by which the proud mean anarchy, and the malignant mean violence? Call it by any name rather than this, but its best and truest test is, Obedience." We may trust that the time is forever past for France when liberty means license and violence, and enthusiasm means passion; and that the time has come when she may safely enter upon the paths of obedience to just and equal, because self-imposed, laws, administered under the protecting shadow of free institutions. As friends of France, we may be permitted to express the hope—a hope which time is fast ripening into conviction—that it will no more be necessary for her great Revolution to lapse into other convulsions, but that steadily and calmly and temperately, but resolutely, she will, by wise reform, by liberal legislation and patient administration, through the discipline of experience, come into the enjoyment of the rights and privileges of well-adjusted and carefully-guarded self-government —the liberty of self-imposed obedience—that liberty of which Tennyson has said,

"Her open eyes desire the truth.
The wisdom of a thousand years
Is in them. May perpetual youth
Keep dry their light from tears,

That her fair form may stand and shine,
Make bright our days and light our dreams,
Turning to scorn with lips divine
The falsehood of extremes!"

WWhw MS. (WP, DLC).

To Robert Bridges

Dear Bobby,   Walhalla, South Carolina, Sept., 4th/79

Just think of this being September without there being an immediate prospect of our seeing each other! It makes me feel *very* far away from you. Within another month we will both be hard *at work* again—you writing, I digging away at the Law. The University opens on the first of October; so, after the end of this month, address me at University of Virginia, Albemarle County, Virginia —the University has a post office of its own. Until then I will probably remain here in Walhalla, just without the Blue Ridge. Horse Cove soon lost its attractions for us: as the food became miserable, and the comforts insufficient as the cool September nights came on; so we jolted back over the twenty-five miles of rough mountain road to this pleasant village; where we are most comfortably— even delightfully—lodged in a very agreeable private family. We are out of the town itself, yet near enough to it for convenience. It is just a pleasant walk from the house on the hill here to the Post Office, which is near the centre of the town. The window by which I am now writing commands a very attractive view of the village below, and of the blue mountains beyond. Walhalla is in the northwestern corner of South Carolina. It was originally settled by Germans, whose square, unornamental houses are scattered here and there throughout its length:—for it is all length, consisting of one long and wide street, probably about two miles long. It is somewhat of a Summer resort, and its climate is certainly very delightful indeed.

Yes, I've heard twice from the *"Cow."*[1] When she last wrote she was pasturing in Harford [Howard] County with Mr. Webster's stock. He and "Dan'l" have been having some high old times. The house was so full of company that the Colonel was obliged to stable the *"Cow"* in an out-house, whose comforts she was sharing with James Edwin and Dr. McLean from New York. Hiram describes it as "a little house on Col. W's place."—not definite, but suggestive. At a grand meeting of the Archery Club, Hiram was capt. of the "Strangers' target" "and didn't hit the thing at all"; while *"Dan."* carried off the second prize by "a complete tare" &c., &c.—Such is the frivolous life he is leading, while his father is looking for a business opening for him "down town." Frank, instead of going to Princeton, has gone into business: so his elder brother goes to Princeton this month to dispose of his room and furniture. Pitney is polling law; the Heathen is having a good time in Germany; and Shippensburgh[2] has not been heard from. You see, his letter is full of news, which I am giving you at second hand, in the fear, the while, that you have already heard it.

Pete wrote me his third letter just before sailing;[3] since then he has been as silent as he is distant.

The French article is done, and has gone to Boston, to take its chances with the *International* men. I hope it will be as fortunate as was its predecessor—the article on Cabinet Government. It is not as good as it might be—far from it, of course. It has not enough *glow* about it. What little fire it has in it burns feebly and fitfully at best, and is scarcely such as will impart its warmth to others; but Mr. Lodge may like it better than I do. I'm glad you like the plan of it; you are not, however, exactly right about the *bourgeois* and peasant contrast. Those two classes are, as far as I am able to find out, very much *alike* in their main characteristics, differing from each other more in *degree* than in *kind*. The differences which do exist between the two classes seem due in great measure to the deep ignorance of the peasant which is *absolute*, even the *comparative* enlightenment of the *bourgeoisie* being to it as light to darkness.

I have written so much that I have read little, having had time to read a portion of the third volume of *Green's History of the English People* and half (one volume) of McCarthy's *History of Our Own Times* only, besides my reading on the French question, which was not as extended as it should have been. After leaving Princeton, I did not have access to all the desirable books. I'll miss our library there in more than one way. I had read all the books which seemed most essential, however, and contented myself, perforce, with digesting and recasting the facts and thoughts I had, extracted from a few *wordy* Frenchmen and a still smaller number of partial outsiders. Hamerton was my chief stand-by in my study of the French *people*; and he did me much service. Now that most of the writing that I have mapped out for the Summer is accomplished, however, I will probably read hard—though without much plan—for the rest of the vacation; though that *rest* is now small enough.

I'm sure I appreciate your scraps of confidential information about the *tenmile* lass. She must truly be an exceedingly interesting and attractive maiden, if *your* descriptions of her can be trusted. I begin rather to suspect you, old boy, when you say that she is, although "bookish" enough, not, in your opinion, of such stuff as would make a good old maid. Do you mean that you contemplate becoming a "victim of connubiality"? I should be very circumspect in my behavior towards a young lady who considers Aeschylus, untranslated, as enjoyable *Summer-reading*! Such tastes awe me!

I've had no chance of attaching myself to any fair maid this Summer. At the Cove, alas! although there was every advantage of *situation* that a lover might desire, there was no one to love!—except one young damsel who was as harmless as she was unattractive. I visited two very pleasant girls *here* the other afternoon, but haven't had time yet to develope any interesting friendship. I'm still a poor lone laddie with no fair lassie! I'm reserving all my powers of charming for the Virginia girls, who are numerously represented around the University, I have heard. Do you think that Law and love will mix well? I should imagine that each was a perfect *antidote* for the other. Taken each in judicious quantities, they may do me much good. I am afraid, however, that I might get so entangled at the hands of some girl there that I would find it hard to confine my practice to *mock court*

Father is in the North taking his usual vacation trip. Rest and change are essential to him. He is one of the hardest workers I ever saw, and certainly earns his vacation. He has been at Saratoga for the past two weeks, where he has, he writes us, rec'd very much attention from numerous distinguished clergymen, summering there. He preached there last Sabbath and afterwards, among many others, a stiff, stately, tall, puritanical chap came up to him and said: "In the name of the Congregational ministry of New England now sojourning in this city, I offer you my hearty thanks for your admirable sermon. I am from Boston, sir."—the old fool! I suppose he had been busily framing that elaborate address all through the services. Father also met *Dad,* who, it seems, has drifted in that direction from Lake George. He assured father that his son was "one of the gems of the last Senior class"! Imagine how the perspiration must have rolled off his face while he was in the agony of giving such "taffy" as that! Even Dad can *bootlick* desperately upon occasion, it would seem.

As the frost begins to herald chill mornings I will expect to see the old weaver make his appearance, Bobby, in *Harper's*, *Scribner's*, or the *Atlantic*. If you do yourself justice, it will easily command a place in any one of them.

What in the world has become of Charley?[4] I haven't heard a word from him; and neither has any one else as far as I can learn. He must be up in the New England mountains. That's the only supposition that's possible, except the one that he has forgotten us all: which none of us will readily believe.

There's no news here, personal or otherwise,—except that I've "blocked out" my siders and now have a pair which are on a fair way to become quite *distingue*—compared with which yours—much bragged of, of yore—were but as a fleeting shadow! They will soon rival the "Doctor's" celebrated pair. Please give my regards to your family. I don't know them by introduction; but I do know them by reputation.   Your loving friend, Thos. W. Wilson

ALS (Meyer Coll., DLC).
  [1] H. Woods, Jr., to WW, July 25, 1879, and H. Woods, Jr., to WW, Aug. 16, 1879, ALS (WP, DLC).
  [2] R. Bridges.
  [3] H. Godwin to WW, July 12, 20, and 31, 1879, all ALS (WP, DLC).
  [4] C. A. Talcott.

Marginal Notes

J. R. Green, *History of the English People*, Vol. III.

Transcript of WW
Shorthand Comments

P. 6:

If the older claims of freedom had been waived in presence of the dangers which so long beset even national existence, the disappearance of these dangers brought naturally with it a revival of the craving for liberty and self-government. And once awakened such a craving found a solid backing in the material progress of the time, in the up-growth of new social classes, in the intellectual developement of the people, and in the new boldness and vigour of the national temper. The long outer peace, the tranquillity of the realm, the lightness of taxation till the outbreak of war with Spain, had spread prosperity throughout the land. Even the war failed to hinder the enrichment of the trading classes.

[c. Sept. 4, 1879]

Such a craving once awakened will find its issue in liberty; and here is the difficulty with the French people at this time (1879): in all their striving after freedom from despotism, they have no fit intelligence for *self-government*—they do not know its meaning.

P. 19:

Home, as we conceive it now, was the creation of the Puritan.

A noble creation!

Vol. III, 127

In the general enthusiasm which followed on the failure of the Spanish marriage, Eliot had stood almost alone in pressing for a recognition of the rights of Parliament as a preliminary to any real reconciliation with the Crown. He fixed, from the very outset of his career, on the responsibility of the royal ministers to Parliament as the one critical point for English liberty.

This is the cornerstone of liberty in every state which combines a legislature with an executive.

P. 140:

When the Commons met again in January, 1629, they met in Eliot's temper. The first business called up was that of religion. The House refused to consider any question of supplies, or even that of tonnage and poundage, which still remained unsettled though Charles had persisted in levying these duties without any vote of Parliament, till the religious grievance was discussed. "The Gospel," Eliot burst forth, "is that Truth in which this kingdom has been happy through a long and rare prosperity. This ground therefore let us lay for a foundation of our building, that that Truth, not with words, but with actions we will maintain!" "There is a ceremony," he went on, "used in the Eastern Churches, of standing at the repetition of the Creed, to testify their purpose to maintain it, not only with their bodies upright, but with their swords drawn. Give me leave to call that a custom very commendable!"

Here is the clear ring of true metal!

P. 194:

. . . he [Pym] saw too that in Parliament itself the one essential part was the House of Commons. On these two facts he based his whole policy in the contest which followed. When Charles refused to act with the Parliament, Pym treated the refusal as a temporary abdication on the part of the sovereign, which vested the executive power in the two Houses until new arrangements were made. When the Lords obstructed public business, he warned them that obstruction would only force the Commons "to save the kingdom alone." Revolutionary as these principles seemed at the time,

In every representative government, in which the governing power is vested in a council of popular representatives, the execution of the laws alone being left to the executive, complete supremacy, a supremacy which may not be gained by any, will in the end be successfully usurped they have both been recognized as bases of our constitution since the days of Pym. The first principle was established by the Convention and Parliament which followed on the departure of James the Second; the second by the acknowledgement on all sides since the Reform Bill of 1832 that the government of the country is really in the hands of the House of Commons, and can only be carried on by ministers who represent the majority of that House.

It was thus that the work of Pym brought about a political revolution greater than any that England has ever experienced since his day. But the temper of Pym was the very opposite of the temper of a revolutionist. Few natures have ever been wider in their range of sympathy or action. Serious as his purpose was, his manners were genial and even courtly; he turned easily from an invective against Strafford to a chat with Lady Carlisle; and the grace and gaiety of his social tone, even when the care and weight of public affairs were bringing him to his grave, gave rise to a hundred silly scandals among the prurient royalists. It was this striking combination of genial versatility with a massive force in his nature which marked him out from the first moment of power as a born ruler of men.

P. 239:

The old loyalty, too, clogged their enterprise; they shrank from the taint of treason. "If the King be beaten" Manchester urged at Newbury, "he will still be king; if he beat us he will hang us all for traitors." To a mood like this Cromwell's reply seemed horrible; "If I met the King in battle I would fire my pistol at the King as at another."

by the legislature, and the executive be dwarfed despite all carefully conceived devices of preserving a perfect balance between the several departments. The executive must, in any such system, inevitably sink to the position of a mere servant of the legislature, without will or power of its own, unless it be constituted by the executive committee of the legislature's more popular branch. Then its policy may be definite and independent. If he had no other claims to genius, his recognition of this principle would be sufficient to establish Pym's right to be considered a great statesman. Its recognition in this country will be the earnest of better days. (1879)

Horrible crime no doubt, but utterly right.

From William Francis Magie, with Enclosure

My dear Tommy,   [Princeton, N. J., c. Sept. 12, 1879]

I have been deputed to forward the enclosed, which as you may perceive is from the hand (or brain) of Mr. W. R. Wilder. We had so many fellows in town that we got up a class meeting after chapel—first in the Lit. Room & then in my old room in East, where the document was signed & songs and cheers indulged in ad lib.

We then took a look at our ivies which are flourishing, all walked to the cemetery & inspected Dutton's[1] tomb-stone—after which cheerful sight we adjourned to supper. The names of all of our class who have been in Princeton since I got back are on the other sheet, except Sam Alexander's & Sage Archer's. Sage had to go off on the train just before we had our meeting. Sam only was here on Wednesday. . . .

I want to add or repeat my congratulations to you on your splendid success. I hardly thought when we used to sit in front of your fire & talk up the English government, that your views would so soon be put out in public: I was waiting for you to get in Congress first. But I see the results of hard work & lively discussions, for both of which you don't have to wait for Congress. The Princetonian boys are proud as they can be, & say they will give you a good puff in their next number. . . .

Your affec. friend   W. F. Magie.

ALS (WP, DLC) with WWhw notation on env.: "Ans 9/26/79."
[1] La Forrest Dutton, '79, died Oct. 14, 1875.

E N C L O S U R E

From Abram Woodruff Halsey *et al.*

Dear Tommy,   Princeton, Sept. 11, 1879

Your debut in the International Review has inspired a meeting of the late lamented Class of '79. The subscribers, brave men & true, in Princeton assembled, tender you our heartiest congratulations on being the dad of this our first intellectual baby. With three cheers for the baby, its dad and '79, we are

your classmates,

A. W. Halsey	G. A. Brandt
William R. Wilder	E. A. Stevens.
W. Harman Wills	Thos. Henry
J. L. Leeper.	Robt. Morrison.
Hiram Woods, Jr.	C. W. Riggs
Richard T. Jones	W. F. Magie
Theodore M. McNair	Edward W. Sheldon.
Alfred J. McClure,	
Chalmers Martin	
Jno. Thompson Kerr.	

ALS (WP, DLC).

Marginal Notes

Albert Stickney, *A True Republic* (New York, 1879)[1]

Transcripts of WW Shorthand Comments[2]

P. 105:

The English people remove the minister who commands their armies, not because he does his work well or ill, but because his ideas on the Church Liturgy are not what they should be.

[c. Oct. 1, 1879]
A very notable sophistry.

P. 112:

How sound a doctrine [nullification] was this, and how far did the true interests of the people demand a contest over it?

It was urged by the supporters of the doctrine of nullification that these States had been originally, and were still, sovereign States; that all the powers they had not given to the general government by the Constitution had been by them retained; that they had never, by the Constitution, given to the general government the power of coercing a State; and that if a State should declare null and void any act of the national Legislature, the national executive had no right to enforce any such nullified law against the State or its citizens.

Yes, but this was a doctrine honestly held, and with no insignificant show of reason. It was held, moreover, by great masses of the people. If true, it was worthy to defeat parties.

Pp. 114-15:

In the case of a government imposed by force upon a people against its will, most men do not question the right of that people to forcibly resist arbitrary and oppressive acts. But here was the case of a government made by the people of those States themselves, a Constitution assented to by them, which provided peaceable and lawful means for its own modification, and even for ending its existence. The Legislatures of three-fourths of the States could, by the terms of the Constitution itself, amend it in any way, and of course they could amend it in such a way as to provide for the release of any one, or more, or all of the States from its obligations. In other words, the Constitution itself provided the means by which there might be such a thing as peaceable secession. And can it be argued that there could be, in law, under the Constitution, such a thing as forcible secession?

All very clear. But if Mr. Stickney would understand the basis of the argument upon which nullification rests he should read Calhoun's speeches. If after reading them [he fails] to pronounce nullification an absurdity— others may.

P. 116:

This whole doctrine of nullification, which subsequently grew into rebellion, would never have been heard of, had it not been for the existence of parties and the needs of party contests. The whole question was one which never should have been raised. It was not a practical question.

It is absurd to say "If there were no parties." Were not parties inevitable upon questions arising in connection with the formation of the Constitution? Before the Constitution was formed during the debates upon its formation, there was a party of "State Righters" whose power is seen in the constitution of the Senate. Was it to be expected that this power would be equaled by the adoption of the Constitution to which they were opposed?

P. 116:

There being at the time no other "issue," as it is called, on which people could be excited, there being no practical question on which there was any real division of existing interests, this doctrine of State Rights was conjured into being, made a war-cry, and on it was developed a great party combination, which was in after years the nucleus for resistance to any and all unpopular measures of the national government.

Nonsense! It was older than the Constitution itself.

P. 131:

Whatever may be the theory of political parties as they should be, wherever there are many offices and many elections, the natural and certain result is that these party organizations, as a fact, are used for the purpose of carrying elections and not measures. Parties do not elect men to put into action certain principles; they use principles as battle-cries to elect certain men.

That is not only the working of party rule, it is the theory of party rule as it actually exists. Any other statement is only the theory of party rule as men wish it might be.

Under Cabinet government platforms must mean something: certain measures must be and are to secure elections. Without the care of others there can be no carrying of elections. What Mr. Stickney says is very true with reference to the working of the Government by irresponsible Congressional committees.

1 WW's copy not found. From a copy of the same edition in NjP.
2 All transcripts by Chandler Sexton from WW's copy at one time in possession of John T. Winterich. See J. T. Winterich to R. S. Baker, March 24, 1928 (RSB Papers, NjP).

A Political Essay

[c. Oct. 1, 1879]

Congressional Government

Our present system of government, though it does not find its rootage so widely in the hidden soil of unwritten law, is almost as much a growth as is the English constitution. Those who deem our Constitution as still, in spirit at least, what its framers left it or what its early interpreters and defenders represented it to be, have surely been unobservant of that vast body of prescriptive custom which has sprung up about it and which is daily controlling the operations of government. Like Magna Charta and the Bill of Rights, the Constitution of the United States is now only the centre of a system of government which embodies many principles that find no clear recognition in its text, which bears many features that have no beginnings in its simple outlines, and which exercises many functions that can claim no evident sanction in its plain provisions.

In other words, the Constitution takes none but the first steps in organization. It simply lays a foundation of principles. It provides, with all possible brevity, for a Federal government having, in its several branches, executive, legislative, and judicial powers. It vests the executive authority in a single man, for whose election and inauguration it makes carefully specific provision, and whose powers and privileges it defines with all possible clearness. It places distinctly enumerated powers of legislation in the hands of a representative Congress, outlining the organization of its two Houses, definitely providing for the election of their members, whose number it regulates and the conditions of whose choice it names. It establishes a Supreme Court with ample authority of Constitutional interpretation, prescribing the manner in which its judges shall be appointed and the conditions of their official tenure.

Here the Constitution's work of organization ends; and the fact that it goes no further is its chief strength. The moment it went beyond first principles and elementary provisions, at that moment would it lose elasticity and adaptability. The nation could not grow, the governmental system could not develop, without snapping the Constitution asunder. If that Constitution could not daily

adapt itself to the conditions of a healthful progress, it must pass
away, to be remembered as only one landmark of a great nation's
advance, an historical monument, an interesting device of a by-
gone day. Our Constitution has proved strong and lasting, therefore, because of its simplicity and of its limited scope. It is a
corner-stone, not a complete building. It is a root, not a perfect
vine.

We are, indeed, far from the starting point of our constitutional
history—farther in spirit than in time. The Constitution has not
become the supporting pillar of the vast system which we call
our national government without itself undergoing important
changes. It has been at many points "amended." Then, too, by the
definite and final victory of one or other of the original compromis-
ing parties, to whose mutual concessions it owed its birth, it has
been cleared of many of the compromises of which it was at first
so full. There have been many sharp and many bitter controversies between rival schools of constitutional construction—controversies issuing now in the triumph of one, again in the success
of the opposite, body of interpreters—controversies which have in
reality added to the Constitution by building up the Federal government in privileges which were granted to it, if indeed really
granted at all, only by doubtful inference from the Constitution's
more ambiguous clauses. Such, for example, is the right of Congress, now firmly established by long practice, to vote appropriations for "internal improvements." Doubts which formerly clouded
the meaning of the Constitution, or were thought by ingenious
reasoners to cloud it, have been scattered: either by the fierce
winds of war—as in the settlement of the doctrine of secession—or
by the milder forces of discussion.

In short, as already implied, the Constitution now rests upon
other foundations than those which its original designers builded.
It may be a more explicit and more consistent instrument than
they left it, but it is not the same. Indeed they did not expect it,
many of them did not wish it, to remain as they had made it. They
saw its imperfections as clearly as any since their day have seen
them. But they trusted that time would weed out its inconsistencies and clear up its intricacies, leaving its principles free to
grow and strengthen. And their hopes were not vain. Time has
stablished the greater principles of the Constitution. But time has
done other work as well—work which they probably did not foresee
and which they probably would not have desired. It has developed
from the simple system they gave us a complex machinery of government whose existence they could not possibly have forecast,

and whose creation they could hardly have prevented, had they anticipated it.

The genesis of our present scheme of Congressional rule was natural, though not inevitable. Our earlier statesmen recognized the possibility, and feared the probability, of the encroachment of one branch of the government upon one or both of its coördinate branches. They believed that the time might come when the Executive would have to be fortified against the domineering of the Legislature; when the privileges of the Legislature would have to be vindicated against the usurpations of the Executive; or when the powers of the Supreme Judiciary would have to be hedged about with defences against the ambitions now of the Legislature, now of the Executive. They probably perceived, too, that, in adopting forms of representative government and conveying to a popular parliament so large a grant of sovereignty, they were at least leaving a way open for Congress to assume still larger powers within the sphere of the general government and arrogate to itself imperial authority.

It is the present custom of unthinking newspaper writers, insincere demagogues, and utopian philosophers to denounce, in tones of righteous wrath, what they call "the tyranny of partisan majorities," and at the same time, almost in the same breath, to speak the praises of "true representative government." They do not dream that they are laughably inconsistent the while. Representative government is only another name for government by partisan majorities; and if such government be really nothing better than tyranny, this at least can be said for it: that it is a tyranny which the Englishman boasts to have established: a tyranny which other nations have come to regard as the freest form of government the world has ever known, and are wont to consider the stoutest girder liberty can have; a tyranny which we have deliberately chosen to live under, and which has enabled us to live in comparative peace and happiness, through a century of unexampled prosperity. Party government is partisan government: and representative government is party government. We are governed by party majorities in our municipal affairs; we are ruled by partisan majorities in our State concerns; we are reigned over by partisan majorities in our national administration. This 'tyranny' is what we have been accustomed to call *self-government,* and is a thing which is surrounded with great traditions and glorious memories. A system of government which is founded in party rule may be a defective one, but it is the best that human wisdom has yet been able to devise.

But is there no justification for this condemnation of party rule as we feel its operations on this side the sea? Surely here the rule of partisan majorities *is* tyranny. Here representative government exists, many are beginning to fear, in form only, not in reality—or, if in reality, not in its purity or in its fullest effectiveness. Every day we hear men speak bitterly or despondingly of the decadence of our institutions, of the incompetence of our legislators, even of the insecurity of our liberties. It is not only a few theorists here and there, it is not merely one or two morbidly apprehensive patriots who thus only peal in our ears the notes of the tocsin which is forever echoing in their own disturbed and panic-struck brains. The whole nation seems at times to be at least vaguely and inarticulately alarmed: restlessly apprehensive of impending danger. Not many years ago it required no little bravery to question the principles of our Constitution; now every scribbler may declare it a failure unchallenged, and many wise heads are nodded in acquiescence. And we are not at liberty to turn our noses to high heaven at this spreading conviction. When grave and thoughtful and perspicacious and trusted men among us begin to agree in laughing at those "Fourth of July sentiments" which formerly were thought to hallow the lips of every, even the greatest, statesmen and orators who gave utterance to them, we may not answer them with Fourth of July arguments. If we cannot agree with them we must be ready with a reason for the faith to which we hold, opposing fact to fact, argument to argument. We may not say, "these are the glorious works of our ancestors, let not profane voices be lifted up against them or profane hands seek to compass their destruction;" we may not assert, "defects there must be in any human system, times of corruption and oppression cannot be staved off by any device of man: we have inherited a larger measure of liberty than ever any nation was blessed with before: wisdom bids us let well enough alone." Men might not fling their taunts so lightly and so freely at these sacred institutions of ours were there not a wide-spread conviction that these institutions have become corrupted and made the means of personal aggrandizement by designing men whose self-seeking has converted the service of their country into a money-making *trade*. However much we may question the reasonableness of such a conviction, we cannot now doubt its existence.

And, as for my single self, I admit that it has more than a color of reason in it. Party government has become in these United States a galling tyranny—a tyranny which is all the more hateful because it wears the forms of free government and does it[s] work of ruin under authority of a Constitution which was intended to secure the American people beyond a peradventure in the enjoyment of that civil liberty which is the heritage of our race. Self-government has become with us government by a narrow oligarchy of party managers; legislation, a scheme of party aggrandizement. Our commerce, which, if left to its natural growth, would soon surpass that of any other nation in vigor and luxuriance, is stunted in some of its branches in order that others may grow great unnaturally; every wind of party policy plays fast and loose with our finances. Matters of business are left to men utterly ignorant of the first principles of business; every year we are startled by new and radical changes in our common and statute law—changes made without regard to prudence or precedent. Government is become a game of which the governed are only spectators.

Now this is a dark picture; but it is drawn in all truth and soberness. It contains much shame, much sorrow, much discouragement. But to the brave it suggests no disheartenment or dispair. We are, beyond question, fallen upon times of grave crisis in our national affairs: but I am as confident that these things will be remedied as I am that they need remedy,—for I know that they affect the liberties of the Anglo-Saxon race.

Our duty is plain. We must not belie our blood by standing, idle and passive spectators, while our institutions fall into degradation. We must devise adequate and speedy remedies. And many thoughtful men *are* beginning to bestir themselves in behalf of the public weal. Discussion concerning the ills which now beset and distress us is assuming definite shape and a determined voice. It has passed from incoherent wails and passionate exhortations into calm suggestions of remedy and more or less wise, considerate, and statesmanlike plans of reform. Its echoes are heard even beyond sea. We find Englishmen speculating on a possible change of governmental forms in America. Men know that the Anglo-Saxon is not prone to change. He is stubbornly conservative. When, therefore, foreigners find us, who have hitherto put such eager and implicit faith in our own institutions, listening now not only tolerantly but even respectfully and with earnest attention, if not with open approval, to propositions which look toward radical changes in those institutions, they naturally presage momentous political movements, and recognize the possibility of a great political revolution. When Americans become disgusted with their own government, startling changes are a-making. And are they not becoming disgusted with it?

Perhaps one of the most significant of the recent symptom of growing dissatisfaction is the publication of Mr. Albert Stickney's incisive essay on the present prostitution and the capital needs of our system.[1] Mr. Stickney speaks in a manner which is conspicuously candid and manly; and he writes in style which is eminently clear and pointedly direct. He covers the ground of his subject thoroughly, brushing away the more patent follies of hereditary monarchy with vigor; exhibiting the defects of constitutional royalty, or "parliamentary government," with clearness and discrimination; demonstrating the weakness of our present form of government with distinctness and strength; exposing the heart-rottenness of party rule among us with a just and dispassionate, but unsparing hand; examining the business principles on which he conceives true government to rest with quiet common-sense and sober practical sagacity; and naming the radical remedies which he advocates with unhesitating candor and scrupulous consistency.

As Mr. Stickney himself confesses, the changes which he urges—and which are changes of principle, not merely of form—are not such as are likely to meet with ready acceptance. But he offers his suggestions confidently to the consideration of his countrymen. He trusts that his logic, if it be as unerring as he believes it to be, will work its way into the convictions of the less thoughtless among the people; and, whilst regarding anxiously the present, he does not despond as to the future. He does not anticipate any crisis to which our conservative common-sense and Anglo-Saxon spirit will be unequal. He is certainly bold enough in his propositions. He throws his doctrines right in the teeth of all the traditions of our race. The palm tree is not less native to the poles, the thistle not less native to the region of the oak, than is his scheme to our political temper and habits.

Concisely stated, the course Mr. Stickney urges is substantially this: *Permanence in office during good behavior for all public servants*[.] The term system he would have finally done away with. The President should, he thinks, be elected by the people, through an Electoral College which "should meet, deliberate, and vote, at one time and in one place," and which should "be the judge of the elections and qualifications of its own members, as either House of Congress is." With the President alone should abide the privilege, upon him alone should devolve the duty, of appointing the heads of the several executive bureaux; with these executive heads alone should abide the privilege, on them alone should devolve the

---

[1] "A True Republic," by Albert Stickney; New York, Harper Bros., 1879. [WW's note.]

duty, of appointing their subordinates; and each official should be responsible for the manner in which his duties are performed to his immediate superior and to none other, save only the supreme Legislature. The legislative Houses should be elected as now; but their members should retain their seats during good behavior. To these Houses should the President be responsible. They should have the power of removing him "for any misconduct or for any failure on his part to give good and satisfactory results." But, "if not removed for misconduct or inefficiency, he may hold office for life." Besides, "the absolute control of the money" and "the absolute power, in its supreme discretion, of making *all necessary laws, and of regulating the duties of all public officials,*" the national Legislature should have "the absolute power of removing, by a two-thirds vote, for any cause in its judgment sufficient, any government official." The Supreme Judicial system should retain all the essential features of its present organization.

This is, I believe, as clear and accurate an outline of Mr. Stickney's plan of reform as can be given in a few words. His proposals can scarcely be misunderstood or misrepresented, with such bold clearness and fearless distinctness are they made; and those persons who have resolutely nursed the conviction that our institutions are the most perfect work of man will be nettled to find with what rigorous logic he sustains his startling propositions. Grant that its foundations are solid and complete, and the superstructure of his argument seems to stand perfect and indestructible. Admit his premises, and it seems no easy task to escape his conclusions. He never flinches. He never hesitates to go whithersover his reasonings seem to lead.

But I take issue with Mr. Stickney at the very outset of his argument. He assumes that party government is essentially subversive of true liberty, and totally inconsistent with good, and efficient, and vigorous administration. If party government must necessarily be what he conceives it to be—the organized rule of a body of men who are banded together, upon grounds not of principle or of public policy but of personal gain, for the carrying of elections in their own selfish interests—I must at once subscribe to his opinion that it is, and always will be as long as it is suffered to exist, an unmitigated and intolerable evil, and must heartily join him in the hope that it may soon be so thoroughly torn from its rootage that it may have never again a chance of life. It is only too true that party government has in this country sunk into degradation even such as this. But it is my present purpose to show that there is a method which, whilst it essentially involves party rule, is nevertheless a method which may not only deprive this rule of its depravity but even exalt it to a position of most salutary authority.

I suppose that the caucus system may now be considered the central and most essential feature of party government in these United States. Caucuses made up of all the busy party schemers and all the unscrupulous local office-holders meet in every election district, in every village in this broad land, to nominate the most available local partisans for the local offices. Conventions determine in every Congressional district upon the candidates of each of the two great national parties; and conventions decide upon the candidates for the Presidential chair. Every elective office in this country, whether it be local, state, or federal, is, as a rule, filled by a caucus nominee. But nomination is not the only function of the party caucus. The nation's very legislation is itself determined in caucus. Party resolutions, which afterwards find a place in the journals of Congress, and party policies, which afterwards are embodied in statutes and take effect in the administration of the government, are first framed within the closed doors of the party caucus. If any doubt arises as to the proper course to be taken in regard to any pending measure, it is sought to be dispelled, not by thorough and patient debate on the floor of Congress, before the eyes and within the hearing of the country, but by the secret consultations of supreme party conferences—conferences which free the individual partizan's conscience from all suspicion of personal responsibility and concentrate the voice of party against the time for actual voting. The Congressional caucus is thus the crowning triumph of our system of party government, and the chiefest mocker of our liberty.

But it is hard to see one's way clear to agreement with those persons who regard the caucus system as a mere fungus-growth, which has formed on the decayed and decaying portions of our government. It would, rather, seem to be, if not a healthy, at least a natural out-growth of the governmental plant our fathers planted. It was a development necessitated by the complete separation of the legislative and executive branches of our system. This will, I think, clearly appear upon a careful examination of the functions and powers of the national Legislature and a candid survey of the conditions under which those functions and powers are exercised.

Congress is the *supreme* ruling power in the government of the United States. Notwithstanding the paper safe-guards set up by the Constitution, notwithstanding the precise limitations of its prerogatives contained in its original written organization, Congress had the hand of power—the power of the purse and of the law—given to it, and it has stretched forth that hand to brush away all obstructions to the free exercise of its will, and has assumed imperial control of all matters within the scope of the general government. It was natural that it should do so. Under Anglo-Saxon forms of representative government, it was inevitable that it should do so. And, were its powers of absolute control exercised under proper conditions and by proper means—means and conditions which we shall in a moment consider—its doing so would be in the highest degree promotive of liberty. Congress began and has prosecuted its work under peculiar disadvantages. It was originally so constituted that it was not practicable for it to act with unity of design or definiteness of purpose. For it was so organized as to render all leadership next to impossible. There could scarcely be upon its floor any man or any body of men possessing at once the ability and the authority to guide its actions and give tone to its deliberations. A man of brilliant argumentative force and conspicuous wisdom might derive temporary sway over the wills of his fellow-Congressmen by means of his eloquence or temporary authority by virtue of his wisdom; but, however transcendent his worth, however indisputable his fitness for the post, he could not in any sense constitute himself the *official* leader of the House, nor could his fellow-members clothe him with such supremacy. Yet there was an undeniable necessity that the duties of this absent official leadership should be entrusted to some one.

If the earlier Congresses did not formally recognize this necessity, they at least felt and acted upon it. They naturally and properly shrunk from the idea of vesting the control of their legislative acts in any one man or in any clique of men. They, therefore, adopted—with equal naturalness and propriety, it would seem at first sight—the plan of entrusting all important business to the action of Standing Committees: a system of committee control which has since been brought to marvellous perfection and amazing completeness.[2] Fearing the waste of time which would be involved in the unrestricted discussion of the numberless propositions which would be thrown upon the Congress, were all its members given free license to bring in what bills they might choose to introduce, and recognizing, moreover, the insurmountable practical difficulties that would attend all attempts to compress such an ever-accumulating mass of legislation into a few simple, con-

[2] I have already had occasion to describe this system elsewhere. See *International Review* for August 1879, pp. 147-160. [WW's note.]

sistent, and deliberately-framed measures by the instrumentality of free debate on the part of several hundred members, our early legislators entrusted the preparation of all bills relative to the principal subjects of legislation to a number of Standing Committees. In the House of Representatives this plan is rigidly adhered to. Every bill introduced by a private member—that is, by any member who is not acting in behalf of some one of the committees—is, by an imperative rule of the House, at once and without debate, without even an opportunity of explanation being vouchsafed the mover, referred to the appropriate Committee. These Standing Committees constitute, therefore, the legislative machinery of the House. They are given the right of initiative. From all the bills submitted to them they may cut out a policy to their own liking; or they may frame measures for the consideration of the House without regard to any of these bills.

Except on such extraordinary occasions as those on which a suspension of the rules of the House is granted by a two-thirds vote, these several committees do accordingly exercise supreme control over the action of the House in regard to the several branches of legislation touching which they have original supervision. And so stingy of its time is the House that the privilege of debate, even upon the measures fathered and introduced by the Committees, is jealously circumscribed. A limited time—say an hour or two—is allowed for their discussion, the floor being first given, as of right, to members of the reporting Committee, and then to such other members of the House as shall have gained the Committee's consent to use such scraps of the allotted time as may be snatched after the official speakers shall have yielded the floor. Our representatives seem, indeed, to have taxed their ingenuity in devising means for preventing thorough discussion of matters of legislation, although one of the highest and most essential functions of a representative assembly is the open, free, and tireless discussion of its business. Our chiefest representative body carefully, by many and intricate rules of its own making, deprives itself of the privilege of debate, and makes a special two-thirds vote necessary to gain its own consent to the performance of its own highest duty.

It would be hard to conceive of a system more utterly at variance with the true principles of representative government as understood by our English fore-fathers in centuries long gone, and as professedly practiced by ourselves in the century of independence just past, than is this system of Committee government. But its worst feature, its damning fault, is secrecy. The most im-

portant subjects of legislation are discussed and often definitively
settled within the closed doors of Committee rooms, in the unapproachable privacy of Committee conferences. And yet, although
almost omnipotent, these Committees are irresponsible. Let us
take an example. The House's Committee of Ways and Means, together with the Senate's Finance Committee, virtually control all
matters that relate to the national revenues. And, although these
two committees cannot always or often act in harmony with each
other, they nevertheless originate, for the most part, our entire
financial policy. But they are in no wise (except in a very shadowy
way) responsible for the success or failure of that policy. Their
schemes may be mutilated, or accepted entire, by the House, with
which alone rests the accountability. The Secretary who is charged
with the execution of their plans is certainly not answerable. He
is granted no discretion save at such points as the Committees may
carelessly or inadvertently have left open to him some loophole
of evasion. We may well shake off our lethargy and wake to determination of reform when we find our liberties jeoparded by a
system which thus involves the hidden discussion of public business, the well-nigh private direction of public affairs by small
and unbound Committees of Congress, and which lays the responsibility for mistakes of policy, however mischievous or disastrous
such mistakes may prove, nowhere but at the doors of a body
which from its very nature and constitution is not and cannot be
directly or immediately punishable.

But let us not hastily condemn the men who originated this system nor pronounce its conception folly. Without some such machinery Congress would have been as helpless as a rural mass-
meeting. Unless official leadership were vested in some person, or,
as is the actual case, in some small and manageable body, Congress must have drifted aimlessly in a course of hap-hazard legislation. As I have already intimated, it would, under the circumstances, have been manifestly unwise, conspicuously hazardous,
to have entrusted the privilege and duty of constructing all important measures to any one man or any one body of men. To
bestow this privilege and this duty upon a great many distinct and
independent committees must, therefore, have seemed at once the
most feasible, the most convenient, and the wisest possible plan.
Indeed the committee system still seems to many the least imperfect legislative mechanism that can be devised. These forty odd
principal committees are each assigned a special subject of legislation; and they cannot collude to lead the nation's representatives
astray; they cannot combine to usurp every prerogative of legisla-

tion—for they together make up a majority of the House, and it would be the extreme of paradox to speak of the majority conspiring to deceive itself, or combining to usurp its own powers.

And in this last fact it is that the Congressional *caucus* takes its root. There is no *cohesive* principle in the action of the Committees. There is nothing to give a definite direction to their acts, nothing to give unity and consistency to their policy. They may, and often do, work at cross purposes. They tend towards disintegration. They of course represent, at least in their majorities, the dominant party in Congress. If that party therefore, is to have any distinct policy, it cannot expect this policy to originate with its committees, for they cannot act with that oneness of purpose which is made possible only by prevised combination. The party, therefore, whenever, in critical times of doubt, it is desirable to assure itself of its own unity of purpose, to clear away all uncertainties of plan, or to decide all questions of expediency, must itself come together in committee. It does, in fact, often do so. It has frequently constituted itself a committee: and that committee is the *Congressional caucus.*

It is customary to denounce the whole caucus system as one vast fraud, as a mechanism devised by designing men to deprive us of our liberties by circumscribing our freedom of choice in the selection of our representatives, and establishing the omnipotence of political Jobbers. As a matter of fact, it seems to have originated with wise and honest men. It was hit upon as a natural, convenient, and fair means for enabling local parties to decide between the claims of rival candidates within their own ranks. The voters of a party met together and nominated a candidate from among the several aspirants for the suffrages of the party, and were thus tided over the dangers of a split or scattering vote by uniting in the support of their single nominee. Amongst a sparse rural population such a system might operate admirably. In fact it did work efficiently and beneficially in the earlier years of its trial, so long as the citizens of the electoral districts had the time and the inclination to attend nominating assemblies. As soon, however, as population thickens business competition confines men to their daily work almost to the exclusion of other affairs. The driving trade of great cities does not admit politics to their thronged marts. The bustle of busy days drives all interests but that of bread-earning or money-massing from men's minds. The village shopman may spare an evening to the business of nomination; the city merchant cannot. Accordingly as civilization advances and populations condense and businesses multiply and the steps of commerce quicken, the duties of the caucus are left to the idle and the selfishly interested.

Then, too, the system evidently had in it from the first the seeds of corruption. Scheming publicans could easily combine to thrust unwelcome candidates upon men unprepared to meet and thwart parliamentary trickery. Shrewd men who were guiltless of scruples would soon learn to turn the helplessness of mass-meetings to their own advantage. Not much underhand management would be necessary to pack a caucus with subsidized, and therefore devoted henchman. Whilst, therefore, we recognize the one-time utility and purity of this system, and whilst we are able to perceive that its growth was at once natural and inevitable, we are equally impressed with the fact that it has come to be one of the most stupendous and monstrous political evils that has ever existed. Mr. Stickney justly regards it as the essence of party tyranny, saying that the English, in adopting it, as they are beginning to do, "are just entering on that blessed era in the progress toward free government, the era of party tyranny." No one whose voice is worth hearing now denies the monstrous and the growing iniquity of this system which is bringing decay upon our cherished institutions and mockery upon our dearest liberties. And by far the most disheartening fact connected with this perplexing and portentous evil is that our most provident publicists can suggest no adequate remedy. The wisest of them see no help anywhere but in the possibility that the promptings of patriotism will draw our better citizens to the primaries, there to withstand the iniquitous doings of the mercenary jobbers of "machine" government. They see that, now that it has struck its roots so deeply and widely into our political life, it is well-nigh impossible to cut this organized tyranny at once and entirely away. Indeed we cannot destroy it; we must take its power away. I believe that, although we cannot kill the serpent now, we can, at least, extract his fangs. We cannot rid ourselves of the caucus, but we can constrain it to do our bidding. We can harness it in our service.

We have now seen that Congress, the imperial power of the general government, is composed of men who are the nominees of packed conventions; that it in reality transacts the people's business privately by means of Committees; that the policy of its ruling majorities is at critical moments determined upon in the secrecy of party caucuses. It has, in a word ceased to exercise that most essential function of a representative legislature, the function of debate: and it has fallen into the neglect of this its highest privilege and paramount duty from the inexorable necessities of its organization.

Can any one doubt that public debate upon all questions of public business is the cardinal feature of representative government? It is free, prolonged, exhaustive discussion alone that can instruct constituencies as to the nature of the bills which are passed and as to the real bearings and import of questions which are decided. It is the play of debate alone that can definitively settle the principles which should govern all legislation or particular legislative acts. It is the fire of universal criticism alone that can test the quality and burn away the crudities of measures which have been devised in the seclusion of the study or evolved from the compromises of disagreeing committee-men. It is the glare of publicity alone that can frighten trickery and corruption from legislative halls. When the whole nation is audience to their deliberative conclusions, legislators give heed to their ways. But when legislation is degraded into silent assent to the dictation of bodies of men who meet and conclude in privacy—be those bodies committees or caucuses—representative government is become a farce, and law-making a fraud. A great people might as well entrust their sovereign powers to a secret council as to a representative assembly which refuses to make debate its principal business.

But this neglect of its greatest duty on the part of Congress we have seen to have been the necessary result of its organization. It is completely isolated from the coördinate branches of the government, the Executive and the Judiciary. It must, therefore, direct its own business as best it may. It must turn its own helplessness into strength by giving to some the privileges and the authority of official leadership. It must convert its own clumsiness into facility and promptness by a division of labor among committees of its members. Like other mass-meetings, it must appoint a few to draw up its resolutions.

Where, then, is to be found a remedy for the accumulating evils of this system of caucus government and committee legislation? Beyond all comparison the most immediate, the most effective, and the most available corrective may be found in a *simplification of the present plan of committee rule*. Give the privilege of initiative in legislation and the prerogatives of official leadership, which are now enjoyed by the Standing Committees of the House and Senate, to one small committee whose members shall be the heads of the several executive departments and *shall constitute the President's cabinet*. In a word, select the members of the Cabinet from the party majority in Congress and constitute them that committee of the Houses which is needed.

This would, at first sight, seem to be a violent innovation, and, as William Wirt once said, "innovations, however correct in themselves, never fail to startle those who have grown grey in a veneration for the existing order of things." But, in real truth, such a change, instead of an innovation, would be only the perfecting of that system of legislative control which now daily operates in Congress—only a convenient simplification of the Committee system. The Standing Committees of Congress *now* virtually dictate the administration of the executive departments. The Secretary of the Treasury is the executive servant of the financial committees of the two Houses; the Secretary of War lives under the behests of the Military Committees, as does the Secretary of the Navy under those of the Naval Committees. The Secretary of State is under the constant surveillance of the Senate Committee on Foreign Relations. So complete is the servitude of the Secretaries that they may not presume to advise the committees by whom they are directed unless their advice be specially and formally requested. Yet, manifestly, no committee appointed by either House can have so full, so intimate, or so exact a knowledge of the operations and needs of the department whose policy they are set to direct as has the head of that department. They cannot discern so well as he the lines of administration which are practicable or the means of management which are available. They do not have to find their way through the practical perplexities of the daily business of the department; nor can they appreciate the complexity of the internal machinery of administrative economy. They are not in a position to weigh—they can scarcely reckon—the thousand minor considerations which sway the determinations of administrative officers in the conduct of their official business. In short, Committees of Congress have no adequate means of ascertaining those very needs of the departments which it is their duty to supply by legislation. Certainly, then, the heads of the departments would, beyond a peradventure, be better able than any committee now known to give intelligent guidance to legislative supervision of executive administration.

Nor would such an union of legislative and executive functions in a single committee constituted as I have suggested jeopard the independence of the Executive or derogate from the privileges of the Legislature. As chiefs of the executive bureaux, they would surely be interested in preserving and fortifying the prerogatives of the Executive. As official leaders of their party in Congress, they would as surely be zealous to protect the rights and vindicate the authority of the Houses. They *would* not infringe upon the powers of the Executive, because they would be personally concerned in the preservation of its prestige; they *could* not coërce Congress, even if they would.

Evidently Committee government clashes roughly with the true principles of free government. Free government is self-government. Self-government we have accomplished by representative government. Representative government—or, as we have learned to call it, parliamentary government—is the legislative rule of the people acting through representatives. If the people have any rights as regards the action of these representatives in Legislature assembled, they most assuredly have the right to require that every act of legislation shall be the act of the whole body, and not of a small number of its members only; they have the right to require full, free, and frequent discussions of all legislative plans and of every legislative measure; they have the right to demand for each representative the privilege, within reasonable limits, of proposing any bill which he may see fit to introduce and of obtaining a candid debate and a direct vote upon its merits.

But we have seen that all these manifest rights are defeated by the Committee system now in actual operation: Cabinet government would secure them beyond a chance of defeat. Suppose this Cabinet-committee seated in Congress, clothed with all the privileges of membership and invested, moreover, with the prerogatives of initiative in legislation, and you have supposed all the circumstances necessary to make full, free, and frequent parliamentary debates the chief prerequisite of well-guarded party rule—as will presently be made most clearly to appear.

Of course such a system as the one here proposed would involve the *responsibility* of the Cabinet-committee for the success or failure of any policy which they might inaugurate or support. No reasonable person can believe that any Cabinet officer who identified himself with any pending measure would consent to continue in office after the majority whom he would be supposed to represent had signified its disapproval of his course by a formal vote. If he did not, under such circumstances, at once resign, he would forfeit all claim to manly independence. By continuing in office he would be consenting to aid in administering a policy of which he was known to disapprove. By so doing he would lose the respect of all honorable opponents and the support of all conscientious friends. He would be sacrificing his principles to an unworthy love of office. He would be preferring mere place to integrity. He would be openly professing his willingness to do the bidding of his opponents rather than forego the empty honors of conspicuous station. He would soon be shamed into retirement, were he susceptible of shame. Were no place left for shame, he would be forced to quit his place by the very scorn of the Houses.

And, in the exercise of their functions as an executive Committee of the Houses, this Cabinet-committee would, from considerations of policy, be always *united* in responsibility. They would stand or fall *together* in the event of the acceptance or rejection of any measure to which they had given their joint support. Otherwise, they would be no better leaders than any one of the present Standing Committees. They would cease to act in the character of a *committee*. The Houses would not be guided by their counsels. The differences, and disputes, and antagonisms of the council-board would be renewed and heated in the debates on the floor of Congress. Their personal spites would flame out in constant collisions among themselves. They would dispute the leadership with one another. The guidance of the deliberations of the House would be in the hands of several independent, and perhaps antagonistic, chiefs who would, on account of their divisions of opinion on questions of legislation, be miserably incompetent to act together as constitutional advisers of the President upon questions of administration.

Then, too, to allow them such mutual independence would be to deprive the proposed system of Cabinet government of one of its chief benefits. The most admirable and valuable principle of such a system would be that of *responsible leadership*. The Houses should have an accepted and responsible leader in the person of the chief minister of the Cabinet, the Secretary of State. He, or some one of his colleagues, must be the recognized head of the Cabinet, or else Congress will drift helplessly and carelessly, as it does now, for want of some one man to guide its counsels by the authority of his position and the power of his abilities.

And such chief would necessarily be the ablest member of his party in the Houses. Under such a system the Cabinet would be made up of the foremost men of the majority in Congress—men foremost in political influence not only, but in statesmanlike qualities as well. They would live by debate. Their own power would depend upon their ability to vindicate their policy and their party in the burning contestation of public discussion. No party would brave the trial of debate under the leadership of puny weaklings. They would demand that their very strongest champions be put forward to silence the objections and repulse the attacks of their antagonists. The very best material of the party majority would, by a law of selection made absolutely necessary by the conditions of parliamentary warfare, find its way into the Cabinet. The battles must be directed by the generals, not by irresponsible privates.

But some objector relying on Macaulay may say that this would be at best but a leadership of artful dialecticians; that those who can most skilfully gloss over the defects of a cause with a varnish of rhetoric will be the triumphant chiefs of Cabinets; that men who can bear down the opposition of more thoughtful but less ready opponents by the overwhelming rush of eloquent declamation will command the highest seat at our council-board; that we will have a reign of sophists rather than of wise men; that the affairs of the nation will be directed, not by the advice of statesmanlike counsellors, but by the wagging of ready tongues. These are assuredly the objections of ignorance. Sophistry cannot walk thus openly in the cloak of wisdom and truth unchallenged and undiscovered. The leader of a great legislative assembly "must show what he is," not merely say what he would seem to be. Besides meeting his fellow-members, his many watchful adversaries in debate, he must prove himself "able to guide the House in the management of its business, to gain its ear in every emergency, to rule it in its hours of excitement." Subtle word-play, dialectic dexterity, rhetorical adroitness, passionate declamation cannot shield him from the searching scrutiny to which his principles and his plans will be subjected at every turn of the proceedings of the Houses. Clumsy provisions, inadequate policies, untenable principles cannot thrive in the open air of publicity. A charlatan cannot long play the statesman successfully while the whole country is looking critically on. He may act his part admirably in Congress —but the country at large sees none of his theatrical displays, and looks only to his deeds. And in the House itself, a single quick, piercing question from a keen antagonist may be his betrayal. Business routine will tear the thin covering of plausibility from the shams of his policy. Not the words of his mouth alone, not adroit manipulation of opposing factions only, can secure him the highest place in his party: he must be first in statesmanship as well as in partisan manoeuvre. Few persons have any just conception of the informing and unmasking disclosures of thorough debate. Under a Cabinet-committee parties must live by debate: parties which live by debate must live by the espousal of definite policies: and parties which live by the espousal of definite policies are workers of the greatest blessings to a free state.

May we not now find our way to the solution of the caucus prob-

lem? How cure the diseases of that system? Is not the cure at
hand? We have seen that the conditions of party rule would be
such under Cabinet-committee government as to render it imperatively necessary for each party to keep upon the floor of Congress the ablest men they can draw into their ranks; that the
victory would be to the strong in political principle. The struggle
would still be to carry elections; but elections would then be won
by an appeal to argument. Party platforms *must* mean something
when the party leaders are made responsible chiefs in the Legislature. One has only to picture to oneself the discomfiture of Cabinet
ministers who have faithlessly relinquished their avowed policy
and are by their unfaithfulness exposed to the bitter taunts and
the fierce assaults of eager opponents, to realize the purifying and
constraining power of debate. The leaders of the opposition know
that the success of their own party, the chances of their own accession to power, depend on their ability to undermine the influence of the ministers. What a terrible weapon in their hands would
be the broken promises of their antagonists! How rash would be
the ministers who sought to gain the suffrages of the people under
false pretences! Despised platforms would make stout party cof-
fins. Caucus managers would be ruled by stern party necessities—
necessities which would require that the party's ablest men be
nominated for seats in Congress. They would not dare, under such
circumstances, to send incompetent tricksters and wire-pulling
schemers to Congress to damn their party by displays of folly and
demonstrations of political double-dealing in the conduct of legislation.

I know that it will be said that these assertions rest upon the
unwarrantable presumption that constituencies can be brought
to choose their representatives with regard only to the principles
which they advocate. The masses, some assert, cannot be brought
to exercise intelligent discretion. From this opinion I utterly dis-
sent. I believe, with Mr. Stickney, that when the shackles of party
coercion are removed, the people's choice will be deliberate and
wise. Did space permit, many facts of our past political history
might be added to those which Mr. Stickney has instanced in support of this opinion. But, granting that the majority of our constituencies are incapable of exercising a discriminating choice
of representatives—that is, a choice based upon considerations of
political principle—caucus managers would still be under the inevitable necessity of nominating for seats in Congress the very
best man within their election. The success of their party would
turn upon the issues of the debates at Washington. Cabinet minis-

ters would, as has been already shown, court discussion as the only means of vindicating their policy or of furthering such legislation as they favored. The opposition would seek debate as its best opportunity for effective attack. Both parties must, therefore, muster men strong of intellect and cogent of speech, and not merely a numerous force of silent and submissive voters.

No one at all experienced in the workings of large deliberative assemblies can fail to see that under a plan of responsible government such as I suppose no corrupt designs on the part either of ministers or of the opposition would escape discovery in the processes of patient and searching debate. And to suppose that the proof of evil and underhanded purposes on the part of a political party would not result in the overthrow of that party's leaders in the Houses and the rejection of its candidates at the polls, would be to suppose a state of moral, and therefore political, decay which would preclude all possibility of good and free government and would be premonitory of ruin quickly to come. Corrupt men would, therefore, be drags upon their party in Congress; and caucuses would not readily consent to send such to serve as their party's betrayers.

I have now put myself in a position to explain clearly the reasons why liberal statesmen should not give their approval to the governmental changes which Mr. Stickney proposes with so fair a show of reason. In the first place, they could not, of course, for one moment assent to any scheme that would make the tenure of the *representative* office permanent. Mr. Stickney suggests, as we have seen, that the legislative power of the United States be vested in a Senate and House of Representatives *whose members shall be elected for life.* He would thus violate the plainest principles of law and of business by creating an irrevocable agency. The foundational principle of representative government is the principle of agency. The people rule through their representatives as through agents. Free government is such government as enables a people to govern itself—not such as delegates all the powers of government to a body of agents whose agency is revoked only by death. Such a system would cover the most sacred principles of self-government with ridicule; would declare all the greatest political achievements of our Anglo-Saxon race mere illusions. To denominate such a system representative government would be a patent solecism.

Again, what practical advantages would result from allowing the heads of the executive departments to hold their offices during good behavior? A Congress of life-seated representatives would be under the necessity of resorting to the committee system no less than have been the Congresses of the past. We have seen that some such system was and is a necessary device; and there would assuredly be no less imperative need of such a device because members were elected for life. The policy of the executive bureaux would still be directed by Congressional Committees. These Committees would dictate as freely to Cabinet officers who held their offices during good behavior as they now do to those who hold them for four years only. During good behavior? What would be the criterion of such good behavior? Their uprightness and efficiency in carrying into effect policies prescribed by Congressional Committees. And who would be the judges? Congress itself. Is it quite evident that this would be a very material improvement upon the present clumsy tyranny?

Mr. Stickney insists, however, that only such permanent heads, only men who are thus encouraged and enabled to devote their whole lives to the service of the state, are competent to manage the multifarious and complicated affairs of the executive departments. But what scope will there be for knowledge and experience so long as Congress remains the imperial power in the government and continues to command all the proceedings of the departments? How large a province is left for a Secretary's discretion? As far as regards the subordinate officers of the government, I recognize the value of Mr. Stickney's suggestion. I am convinced that the effectiveness of the departments depends on the permanence during good behavior of all their subordinate officers and employees. Undoubtedly these departments, no less than great commercial houses, should be organized upon recognized business principles. Each one of their corps of officials should be responsible to his immediate superior, and all should be subordinate to a permanent chief, who should himself, in turn, be subject to the supervision of the Secretary of the department and removable, for delinquency, inefficiency, or malfeasance, by the President, upon the advice of the Secretary. But the functions and discretion of these permanent officials should not and could not extend beyond the direction of the general business of the departments and the execution of the plans of the cabinet or of Congress.

What would be the gain of making the Secretaryships of the departments tenable during good behavior? We have seen the alternative which presents itself. If Cabinet ministers are to be excluded from Congress, they must remain merely the executive servants of its Committees, bowing meekly and with as good a grace as they can assume, to their mandates. If, on the other hand, they are to be admitted to the privileges of leadership in the Houses, their tenure of office cannot be permanent: for such permanence is incompatible with the principle of responsibility to Congress for the opinions which they entertain and avow. The choice, then, lies between two systems: Either the chiefs of the executive bureaux must be subject to the guidance of irresponsible Committees which are in no way connected with the bureaux, and whose members are appointed according to no rational rule of selection, or the policy of the departments must be determined by legislation directed by ministers who are themselves identified with the departments and who are, consequently, familiar with their needs and possibilities. It is not difficult to decide which of these two systems is the preferable one.

Mr. Stickney makes much of the objection that ministers who are of necessity constantly absorbed in the business of legislation and in the marshalling of their party forces in the daily tilt of debate, have not the time, however strong may be their inclination, to master the duties of their departments or properly to exercise the functions of their official trusts. This objection is an evident one, and is as weighty as it is evident. We must, however, remember that, at every turn in our endeavor to solve this tremendous and perplexing problem of government, we are confronted by the inexorable necessity of compromise. It is, I am persuaded, far better to have the affairs of the departments controlled, however indirectly, by men who are identified with their interests and are in constant communication with subordinates who have spent their lives in the administration of their business, than by numerous disconnected and unharmonious bodies of men who have no direct means of learning what would be wisest in the administration of executive affairs, and who are only too often indifferent as to the results of the policy they thus ignorantly recommend. As long as we continue to have representative government—and long may we continue to enjoy its inestimable and inimitable blessings!—so long will the Legislature remain the imperial and all-overshadowing power of the state. As long as the Legislature does so remain, so long will it be impossible to check its encroachments and curb its arrogance at the same time that we preserve the effectiveness and independence of the Executive—unless some link of connection be constituted between these two branches of the government, some bond which will neutralize their antagonism, if it will not actually harmonize their interests. Such a bond would the Cabinet-committee be—a body which would, from its very nature and offices, be at once jealous of the pretensions of the Houses and of the usurpations of the Executive; zealous at once to defend and to restrain both; identified with the interests of both, in entire sympathy with the self-seeking ambition of neither.

This is evidently not a matter of theory, but a question of practice. I might admit the theoretical perfection of the organization of government which Mr. Stickney would have us make trial of; but I would, at the same time, be compelled, unless I chose wilfully to shut my eyes to notorious facts and my ears to the plainest teachings of experience, to believe in the utter futility of such an experiment. An Executive with departments organized upon the same rules which determine and regulate the officering of a great commercial establishment would be the best possible *were that Executive its own master*. But, under the conditions of representative government, it cannot direct its own concerns. The Legislature is its overlord in fact, if not in theory. Its affairs are completely at the disposal of the Houses. Such being the indisputable and unavoidable facts, the introduction of a responsible ministry is the only expedient by which representative government can be rendered both beneficent and efficient without prejudice to either the executive or the legislative branch of the government. So long as Congress continues master and remains isolated from the Executive, the question as to whether or not it be better that Cabinet officers and their subordinates should hold office during good behavior or for a definite term of years will be a mere matter of detail.

There is another matter—another matter of detail—involved in the adaptation of the system of Cabinet-committee government to our peculiar institution, the Presidency, which may lead us into concurrence with Mr. Stickney at one point at least. By whom is this Cabinet-committee to be appointed? Shall they be appointed by the Houses, whose official leaders they will be, or by the President, whose official advisers they will remain? It makes little material difference to which this power be given. The President, if the choice of ministers be left to him, must select them from the ranks of the ruling majority within Congress. He could not, of course, be permitted to constitute his Cabinet of men who were not already representatives in Congress; for to allow him that privilege would be to vest in him the unconstitutional and most dangerous power of creating members of Congress. For, in order to exercise the functions of official leadership in the Houses, Cabinet ministers must possess all the privileges and be bound by all the duties of full membership. The President's choice being, therefore, necessarily limited to members of Congress, would really be determined by Congress. He would in all cases be practically obliged to appoint the *leaders* of the majority: and the *fact* of leadership would, of course, be beyond his control. It would be decided almost entirely by personal talent and declared by the tacit, spontaneous, and almost unconscious suffrages of the Houses.

Obvious considerations of policy would seem to point to the Executive as the proper appointing power: for he might exercise this right with more promptitude than the Houses, and with as little opportunity of abuse as they. And, such duties being assigned the President, he should hold his office during good behavior, or for long terms. Otherwise, we would be exposed to all the perils of instability. There would be no permanent centre to our system, no central pillar of support.

But loud outcry of ridicule against the introduction of responsible Cabinet government into these United States is made by those who think it impossible for a partisan President to live upon even tolerable terms with a Cabinet made up, as Cabinets might often be, from the ranks of the opposite party. But to a man of sense—nay, even to a man of ambition—it would surely seem preferable to preside over the deliberations of a body of men who have the power of determining, in great degree, the course of legislation, who are the recognized and authoritative leaders of an imperial Legislature, rather than over a body of chief clerks whose discretionary powers are limited and insignificant in comparison. At the head of a council-board whereat sit the commanding leaders of the dominant party in the state, he might, if a man of parts, of personal force, exercise no inconsiderable influence upon the policies of the nation; as chief of an isolated and virtually powerless council, his opportunities and privileges are few, his achievements trifling. If a weak man, he will, under any and every circumstance, be only a tool in the hands of others.

Moreover, as *permanent* head of the Executive, the President would be lifted above the passing caprice of party spirit. He would in a measure become identified with his office. He could afford to appoint Cabinet officers with impartiality, and would be in a position to throw the weight of what influence he might be able to exercise on the side of steady conservatism, looking neither to this party nor to that for his cue. The even course of administration might, it is true, ever and again be disturbed by changes of presidential temper or freaks of presidential whim. But such personal vagaries could never work so great or so irreparable injury as would the vagaries of the Houses, were the appointing power left in their hands. Every consideration, indeed, would seem to point to the wisdom of making the President's tenure of office *permanent*—permanent, that is, so long as he conducted himself with honor and fidelity. In the Presidency so constituted would be the head stone of the official system. The line of permanent officials would terminate in the permanent chief.

So long as Congress remains the supreme power of the state, it is idle to talk of steadying our policy and cleansing our politics by keeping the executive and legislative branches of our government separate, isolated. Congress will command and will enforce its commands on the Administration. Its chiefs will be our rulers. Our only hope of wrecking its present clumsy misrule lies in the adoption of responsible, Cabinet-committee government. Let the interests of the Legislature be indissolubly linked with those of the Executive; let those who have authority to direct the course of legislation be those who have a deep personal interest in building up the legislative departments in effectiveness, in strengthening law and in unifying policies; whose personal reputation depends upon successful administration; whose public station originates in the triumph of principles; whose dearest interests turn upon the vindication of their wisdom and the maintenance of their integrity. Let those who are our leaders in fact be such in name as well, that they may be made to answer, and answer quickly, for their every purpose.

Such are some of the considerations which demonstrate the feasibility of thorough and effective reform in legislative administration and indicate the direction which such reform should most properly take. Other considerations of a more general and quite as conclusive a nature might be added, did space permit and the scope of this article sanction their discussion here. Of these perhaps the most powerful to carry conviction is the probable growth of statesmanship which would be induced by the establishment of Cabinet-committee government. The highest type of statesmanship is the *constructive*, that which is exhibited in the conception and execution of policies, in the building up of uniform systems of law and the establishment of great principles of legislation. The United States has been poor in genius for such great work. Since the death of the last of that illustrious line of statesmen whom the great work of achieving freedom and constructing a Constitution called to fame, there has been scarcely one worthy of their mantle. Even the great genius of Webster was a genius for defence and interpretation rather than for accomplishment and construction. The strength of his intellect and the power of his eloquence were spent mainly in the defence and exposition of the Constitution and gave him no permanent authority in the direction of administration and the guidance of constructive legislation. His mission was an exalted one and in its accomplishment he displayed a genius that was transcendent and an eloquence that was inimitable; but neither his genius nor his eloquence was the instrument of large achievements in the higher workmanship of creation. Calhoun, finding no place for personal leadership in legislation, was fain to turn to a work of destruction. It would seem that by holding out in the future such opportunity for the exercise of personal influence in the direction of legislation and such chance of attaining to high place in legislative councils and commanding authority in legislative deliberations as Cabinet-committee government would afford, a place would be made for the higher works of statesmanship where there now is none: none in the functions of the President, none in the duties of the Cabinet, none in the offices of the Chairman of Committees, none in the commission of the President of the Senate, none within the province of the Speaker of the House. Where there is no room for the exercise of statesmanship, none will be exercised. But where every condition of government invites the ambitious to leadership and inclines to give weight to individual genius and authority to individual opinion, there statesmanship in all its greater exhibitions must and will exist.

How ignorantly many American republicans have claimed the sanction of Montesquieu's high authority in support of a system which has studiously isolated the legislative and executive branches of government. Montesquieu drew all his political maxims from the practice of England. Her constitution was the fountain of never-failing illustration for him. And the hinge principle of that constitution is the linking together of the legislative and executive branches by that strange, subtle, sagacious device, the Cabinet-committee. The *powers* of the executive and of the Parliament are distinct, separate, and uninterchangeable; their interests are, however, united. They are mutually independent, and yet harmonious in coöperation. They turn upon the same hinge, but never slam rudely against each other.

Patrick Henry, that prince of patriots and primate of orators, endorsed upon the resolutions which he moved in the Virginia House of Burgesses in 1765—those memorable resolutions which spoke the first words of revolution—these words of eloquence and wisdom: "Whether this (independence) will prove a blessing or a curse, will depend upon the use our people make of the blessings which a gracious God hath bestowed on us. If they are wise, they will be happy. If they are of a contrary character, they will be miserable—Righteousness alone can exalt them as a nation." Our wisdom is now, in these later days of our independence, to be put anew to the test. I trust in Anglo-Saxon instincts; I believe in the American people. Times of crises are come: evils stare us everywhere in the face: remedies must be found, and that speedily. And remedies will be found, and applied.

Some there be, indeed,—many, it is to be feared—who shrink from facing and are weak to overcome the difficulties of government by which we find ourselves environed. So long as they can ward off actual anarchy and secure temporary peace and comparative prosperity by any makeshift, they are obstinate in shutting their eyes to all dangers awaiting them and in shouting lustily, to deafen and confound their own consciences, "let well enough alone!" Mr. Horace White, writing, in blind optimism, to the *Fortnightly Review*,[3] has added his voice to this cowardly plea. Does Mr. Horace White really think that our governmental methods are "well enough"? Are a shameful Civil Service, rotten public morals, awkward administration, and clumsy, blind legislative tyranny "well enough"? Are finances which are the laughing-stock of the world "well enough"? Is a high carnival of demagogy "well enough"? Is a long future of subjection to caucus rule and partisan dictation "well enough"? Are all these things well enough to let alone when a remedy is within easy reach? The spirit of the master-workmen of the Revolution has passed away, America has lost her breed of noble blood, the age of independence is gone and that of slavery is come, wisdom has departed from us and mocking folly reigns in her stead, if we sit thus idly, thus cowardly, by while our liberties are waning and our institutions are decaying. We will not so solve the problem.

T. Woodrow Wilson

[3] See *Fortnightly Review* for Oct. 1879, article, "Parliamentary Government in America." [WW's note.]

WWhw copy (WP, DLC). WW probably wrote this essay soon after reading Albert Stickney's *A True Republic*, not long after his arrival at the University of Virginia, perhaps in October 1879. The flyleaf of WW's copy of the book, according to Mr. Winterich, who once owned it, was inscribed "T. Woodrow Wilson Oct. 1879." (See J. T. Winterich to R. S. Baker, March 24, 1928 [RSB Papers, NjP].) WW, in a letter to Robert Bridges, Sept. 18, 1880, wrote: "I've been occupying some of the hotter hours of the days for the last week in copying an article which I wrote last year at the University. It is a further discussion of the subject of my article which appeared in the *International Review* last Summer. . . ." WW made a number of penciled revisions, which are not included, probably in the summer or autumn of 1882.

The text here printed is at least WW's second draft of this essay. He apparently sent a copy of his first draft to JRW at some time during the autumn of 1879, and JRW made certain revisions. (See JRW to WW, c. Dec. 13, 1879.) WW may have made another draft soon afterward, or he may have waited until September 1880 to revise the copy that his father had edited. In any event, it seems certain that the text printed above is not the version referred to in JRW to WW, c. Dec. 13, 1879.

From Charles Andrew Talcott

My dear Tommy:—   Utica [N. Y.] Oct. 1   1879
I received No. 6 of the Princetonian today and learned from it that your article had been published in the August number of the International. I sent today for the magazine and expect much pleasure and profit from the perusal of your contribution. I congratulate you upon your success. I know that it is but the beginning of exertions, which will win honor for yourself and influence the politics of our Country. . . .

                    Yours sincerely   Charles Talcott

ALS (WP, DLC) with WWhw notations on env.: "10/8/79"; "Ans 10/12/79."

From Janet Woodrow Wilson

My darling Son,   Wilmington N. C—Monday Oct 6th [1879]
We were rejoiced at the reception of your very sweet and satisfactory letter yesterday. I am very glad to hear that you are so well pleased with what you have seen of the "University" for I feared you would be disappointed. I do hope you will continue to find things satisfactory. But I am considerably disturbed at what you tell me of your room. You cannot be comfortable in such a place as that. I want you to give me all particulars as to your *bed*. Cant you get the people who furnish your room to give you a better bedstead? Also anything else that is needed to make it comfortable? That should be tried first. What pieces of furniture did you get? Have you any carpet? I want to find out what we can send from here in the way of comforts. You can find from your fellow-students what you have a right to claim from your land lord. And I hope you wont make the mistake we made while in the mountains —in being so very modest about asking for things we had a right to. Since the *room* itself is a nice one, of course it can be made comfortable, some way or other. Do they furnish you sheets? By the way have you any of your sheets with you. Please write me about all these little things very particularly. I am anxious to hear about your boarding house[1]—or rather, about the kind of eating you have.

The mail that brought us your letter yesterday, brought two letters for you. I took off the envelope of one that I might enclose it in this. The other I will send in another envelope by this same mail

Your father is still suffering from cold. He was able to preach only once yesterday but he is gradually improving. Josie is well—but still grieving for you. I wont try to tell you how I miss you, my darling. I cant think about it quietly yet.

I do not intend this for a letter, dear. I must write a note to each of your sisters before the mail closes. I have not found it possible to write letters sooner—but cannot put it off longer. I continue to feel unusually well—and am trying to be very careful. I am glad you like Jimmie.[2] My love to him. Papa & Josie unite with me in fondest love to you, my precious boy.

Lovingly Yours, Mother

ALS (WP, DLC) with WWhw notation on env.: "10/8/79."
  [1] WW's signature appears in "The Register of Students vol. 3, 1879-80," the matriculation book, University of Virginia (ViU), with the date Oct. 2, 1879, which he put down by mistake instead of his birthday, added above it. In the same place he noted that he was boarding with Mrs. Ross. In the following year he boarded with Mrs. Massie.
  [2] James Hamilton Woodrow, son of Dr. James Woodrow, and student at the University of Virginia.

Classroom Notebook

[c. Oct. 9, 1879-Jan. 29, 1880]

Inscribed on front page (WWhw): "International Law"
Contents: WWsh notes with WWhw headings on Professor Stephen O. Southall's[1] course on equity, mercantile, international, and constitutional law, consisting of notes on thirty lectures. The front page begins with the third lecture. The first, second, eleventh, fourteenth, eighteenth, twentieth, twenty-fifth, and twenty-eighth lectures are on the verso pages. Subjects covered included the nature, rights, and duties of national states, including neutral rights and duties, the right of intervention, belligerent rights, and admiralty jurisdiction and prize courts. Transcript of WWsh notes on Lecture 25 on the laws of neutrality printed at Jan. 17, 1880.

(WP, DLC).
  [1] Professor of Civil, International, and Constitutional Law and Equity, University of Virginia.

From the Minutes of the Jefferson Society[1]

Jeff. Hall Oct 18, 1879

House called to order at 7 P.M. Pres. Gibson[2] in the chair. After the roll call the following gentlemen were elected members, Messrs Holcombe,[3] Robinson,[4] Daniel,[5] Wilson, Marshall,[6] McLemore,[7] Martin.[8] . . .

Lecture Eighth   11/4/79

Right of Intervention .
Dr Wheaton

(1) ... 1793 ...

Grounds of Intervention

(2) ... 1724/

(3) ... Holland and Belgium 1830/ ... 1. Mackintosh ...

(4) ... Spanish ... ( ) ... (.)

... 1820 ...

(a) ...

(β.) ...

*A Page from Wilson's Notes Taken in Professor Southall's
Course in International Law*

Bound ledger book (ViU).
    1 The Jefferson Society, founded in 1825, was one of the two literary and debating societies at the University of Virginia.
    2 Braxton D. Gibson, '80. The University of Virginia catalogues for this period did not list students by class. The numerals given indicate the latest date of the student's last session, or as indicated, the year of his latest degree. Thus WW, who took no degree and withdrew in December 1880, is listed in the *Directory of Living Alumni of the University of Virginia, 1921, Alumni Bulletin of the University of Virginia,* xiv (April 1921), No. 2, as of the class of 1881.
    3 Edward W. Holcombe, '81.
    4 Henry McD. Robinson, '80, a law student; or Richard A. Robinson, '82 a student in Greek and moral philosophy.
    5 Walter T. Daniel, LL.B., '80.
    6 John T. Marshall, LL.B., '80.
    7 Britain S. McLemore, '82.
    8 Alfred M. Martin, Jr., '80; or James L. Martin, '80, both in law.

From Janet Woodrow Wilson

My darling Son,   Wilmington—[N. C.] Monday Oct. 20th 79.

We received your letter in which you acknowledged the receipt of the boxes and also gave an account of the furnishing of your room. It gives me great satisfaction, dear, to think of your being so comfortably, and even elegantly lodged. I can easily understand your feeling with regard to your expenditure of your money —and I feared that you might regret the loss of your coveted books. But if I were you, I would take all the enjoyment possible in your pleasant surroundings—and regard your purchases as a good *permanent investment.* I would advise you not to think of *selling* your furniture at the end of your term at the University but to keep it for future use. In this way you will avoid the great loss that would be otherwise inevitable. We are delighted to think that you are comfortable, dear boy. You must tell us as soon as you can just how you look in your room. The idea of your concealing anything from *us,* through the fear of being misunderstood! You know your father's trust in you, is perfect—and you do not think mine is less so, I am sure. I am writing hastily, my darling—because your father leaves tonight for Synod[1]—and it is not a great while before he must start. . . .   Yours lovingly, Mother

ALS (WP, DLC) with WWhw notation on env.: "Ans."
    1 The Synod of North Carolina met in Statesville, Oct. 22-25, 1879.

From the Minutes of the Jefferson Society

Jeff. Hall Oct 25, 1879
House was called to order President Gibson in the chair. . . . The following question was chosen for to-night three weeks "Is the Government of Great Britain better adapted to promote the wel-

fare of society than that of the U. S.?["] There were appointed as debaters

Affirmative	Negative
Messrs. Andrews[1]	Messrs. Robinson
Thom[2]	Daniel
Holcombe	Wilson. . .

[1] Charles L. Andrews, M.A., '81.
[2] P. Lea Thom, '80, shown in the Jefferson Society "Roll Book 1856-86" (ViU) as "Final President" for the session 1879-80.

From Janet Woodrow Wilson

My darling Son,   Wilmington. N. C. Tuesday Oct 28th [1879]

I received your "financial letter" last week—and would have answered it at once, if I had had *funds* to forward to you—but of course had to wait till your father's return. He came home this morning—is quite well, and had a pleasant time at Synod. The members of Synod have gotten to understand him as much as they are capable of doing—and he rules them completely without making them conscious that he is doing so! Your father sends you a checque for fifty dollars—thirty for your suit—and the rest for incidental expenses. I think your idea of a "monthly allowance" a capital one—it is the only satisfactory way. When one knows that he has a certain amount to spend and no more, it is an easy matter to regulate his expenses accordingly.

I am so sorry to hear that you are not quite well, dear. Do be careful and not neglect your health. We were much amused at your downsetting of Mr. Bruce.[1] I think he must be a puppy.

Your father says "Of *course* we approve" of your having joined the Greek society you speak of.[2] He only wishes you *could* have belonged to the one he is a member of!

It is late. I have only time to get this into the office. We love you with all our hearts—and confide in you perfectly—and are very proud of you besides. God bless you my darling.

Lovingly Yours   Mother.

ALS (WP, DLC) with WWhw notes (probably used in teaching a child) on env.
[1] William Cabell Bruce, born March 12, 1860. Student at University of Virginia, 1879-80; LL.B., University of Maryland, 1882. Admitted to bar, 1882, and practiced law in Baltimore. Member, Maryland Senate, 1894-96. Member, United States Senate, 1923-29. Author of *Benjamin Franklin* (1918), which won the Pulitzer Prize, *John Randolph of Roanoke* (1923), and other books. Died May 9, 1946. The reference to Wilson's "downsetting" of Bruce is obscure.
[2] WW had just been initiated, on Oct. 25, 1879, into the Phi Kappa Psi Fraternity. He was active in the group from the start and, as he wrote Bridges on Feb. 25, 1880, he represented his chapter at a "grand convention" of the fraternity in Washington, D. C., that month. "Bro. Wilson, delegate to the G. A. C.," the minutes of Alpha Chapter at the University of Virginia for Feb. 28, 1880, read, "made a

verbal report of his trip and was listened to with marked attention." WW was elected General President of Alpha Chapter in the autumn of 1880. Charles W. Kent, "Woodrow Wilson's Undergraduate Days at Virginia Alpha," in Harry S. Gorgas and James D. Campbell, *Centennial History of the Phi Kappa Psi, 1852-1952* (2 vols., Binghamton, N. Y., 1952) II, 168-74.

From Hiram Woods, Jr.

Dear Tommy,   Baltimore, Oct. 28, 1879.
    I haven't time to write much this morning, but must send me [*sic*] my hearty welcome to ΦΚΨ. A note from the University this morning tells me of your membership. Let me hear from you soon, and tell me something about the workings of your chapter.
    In haste,   Fraternally Yours,   Hiram Woods, Jr.

ALS (WP, DLC) with WWhw notation on env.: "Ans."

Two Letters from Janet Woodrow Wilson

My dear child—   Wilmington N. C. [c. Nov. 4, 1879]
    Why don't you write, my darling? If you are sick, you would surely telegraph us at once. I wrote you last week, enclosing checque for fifty dollars—did you receive the letter and enclosure? . . .
    God bless you my darling. Have you written to your Auntie?[1] If not, please do so at once. It will be a comfort to me to know that you are in communication with her.   Yours lovingly   Mother

    [1] Marion Woodrow Bones.

My darling child—   Wilmington, N. C. Thursday [Nov. 6, 1879]
    Your father wishes to send you the enclosed article on Burke—as he thinks it will interest you—and I enclose with it an article on N. Year calls—thinking that if you chanced to make any the coming N. Year, you would like to be posted as to the latest etiquette belonging to such occasions. . . .
    We are so glad to hear that you are quite well again. We are all quite well and correspondingly happy—and our hearts are as full as ever of love for our darling Tommy.
                                Lovingly Yours   Mother

ALS (WP, DLC). The second letter was written on verso of Dr. J. H. Durham to [JRW?], ALS, Oct. 31, 1879.

To Robert Bridges

Dear Bobby,   University of Virginia, Nov. 7th 1879
    If you only knew how difficult it is for me to snatch any time for letter writing from my exacting task-masters in the Law you

would not wonder—as I know you must have been wondering—at my long delay in answering the letter from you which I found awaiting me upon my arrival here.[1] That letter was doubly welcome and was ravenously devoured. It and a letter from Pete[2] came like old friends among hosts of strangers. I only knew *two men* in the University for the first two or three days of my stay here. I verily believe that I would at that time have been willing to give two years of my life for a few weeks—or even a few days— reunion with old 'Seventy-nine. Your letter was, under the circumstances a veritable blessing. The moments spent in its perusal were only less enjoyable than the same time spent in your actual company would have been. *Now* I know lots of fellows and am member of a fraternity—the ΦΚΨ. I have made several friends: Indeed I'm beginning to believe that it don't take me long to make friends, although I used to think myself so reserved as to be hard to become acquainted with. This chapter of our fraternity has at present only eight members, including myself. It contains some very fine fellows. I joined the ΦΚΨ because I knew before coming here that it was a first class fraternity. I would not have joined any of which I had previously known nothing. I tell you of these matters, Bobby, as my nearest friend, because I know that anything which so immediately concerns me will be of interest to you. In short, I treat you in such matters as I know you would treat me under like circumstances. I only wish that I could get you into the University here—if only for a month or two—if for no other reason, that I might be instrumental in getting you into ΦΚΨ, that thus I might be instrumental in creating still another bond of union between us. Not that our friendship *needs* any such artificial strengthening; but I would like that we should be bound together in every possible way.

I have not yet fully decided whether or not I like the University. The course in Law is certainly as fine a one as could be desired. Prof. Minor,[3] who is at the head of the "school," is a *perfect* teacher. I can say with perfect sincerity that I cannot conceive of a better. All the schools are, indeed, as far as I can learn, conducted with equal thoroughness and vigor and ability. But to *like* an institution one must be attracted by something besides its methods of instruction. This place is, of course, totally different from Princeton in almost every respect, and I find myself unable to compare the two institutions at all. The fellows are divided into innumerable groups of friends. There are no bonds such as *class* bonds to bind the men together. You meet and know a man just as you might meet and know a fellow-merchant on some Great Corn Exchange. The tendency in such a community as this is towards *disintegra-*

tion. Of course, living within common limits and pursuing like ends, students are necessarily thrown together and have many sympathies in common. But there is nothing to supply the place of class feeling—and no college feeling exists, except in a vague sort of way. This is the unattractive side of the place. It has many attractive features for an older class of men such as those who attend the professional schools here. There is a great deal of freedom here. You are free to do just as you please. The place is *extensive*, both materially, having long and picturesque ranges of buildings, and mentally, there being every variety of mental activity. Study is made a serious business and the loafer is the exception. Every one has the highest regard for culture and scholarship. There is on all sides an intelligent interest in matters of learning and a keen appetite for literary pursuits—I don't altogether understand the place yet. I can't at once accustom myself to hearing careless fellows like Nancy Minor[4] or Bland Ballard earnestly discussing their studies outside of the class room. But of this I am convinced, that there's no pretence about the place. It is in real truth an University. Every branch is made a specialty. A man is thought to be doing well if he graduates on two tickets—i.e. on two subjects: Latin and Greek, for instance—in one year. And there is certainly more thorough work done here than I had ever expected to see done by young men. And the place is cosmopolitan—as far at least as the South is concerned. There are men here from all parts of the South and East—some from the West, and one feels that the intellectual forces of the South are forming here. Indeed this University is looked upon throughout the South much as Oxford or Cambridge is regarded in England or Harvard in New England.

I'm fairly *itching*, Bobby, to hear the result of your "prospecting" visit to New York. I saw by the *Princetonian* that you had passed through Princeton, and I know that your plans must have taken some new turn by this time. Please write me at once. *I don't want* you to stay at home—I want you to go to work, for the sooner you begin the sooner you'll *succeed.* But don't tell your mother that I want you to leave home. She would'nt like me as much as I hope she does now in consequence of your *mis*representations! But if you *do* stay at home you *must* write, Bobby. Wake the old weaver. I don't want to miss an introduction to him and his *daughter* now that you've interested me in them. When you are working, creating, there is no very immediate danger of your dreaming or moping your senses away. Then, too, with the *auburn-haired* at your door, and *another* not far away, you wont be apt to make your books your *exclusive* companions, you old rascal!

At last I've heard from Charlie.[5] He's working *hard* at Law, is well; was simply silent. He's inveterately lazy as to letter-writing, that's all. The latest from Pete is from Cordova, Spain. It's damn the *Spanish* this time. He says there's no romance about *dirty* women. According to his account the women of Spain never *wash*, for fear of cracking their beautiful skins. Chang writes from Rochester that he is about to plunge into Law.[6] The Cow is taking Chemistry and Physics in Johns Hopkins.[7]

Bobby, I'm going to write to you whenever I can without regard to answers from you, and will expect you to do the same by me. It would be unpardonable in *us* to stand on ceremony in this regard. With much love   Your sincere friend   T. Woodrow Wilson.

P.S.   Don't think my signature affected. I sign myself thus at mother's special request, because this signature embodies *all* my family name.   Yours faithfully   T. Woodrow Wilson

ALS (Meyer Coll., DLC).
¹ R. Bridges to WW, Sept. 30, 1879, ALS (WP, DLC).
² H. Godwin to WW, Oct. 15, 1879, ALS (WP, DLC).
³ John Barbee Minor, born June 2, 1813. A.B., University of Virginia, 1834. Professor of Common and Statute law, University of Virginia, 1845-95. Died July 29, 1895. He was one of the greatest American legal scholars and teachers in the nineteenth century. WW later referred to Minor as one of the most remarkable men he ever knew and, next to his father, his greatest teacher. R. S. Baker, *Woodrow Wilson*, I, 112.
⁴ Henry L. Minor, Princeton, '79.
⁵ Printed in part at Oct. 1, 1879.
⁶ W. B. Lee to WW, Nov. 1, 1879, ALS (WP, DLC).
⁷ H. Woods, Jr., to WW, Oct. 21, 1879, ALS (WP, DLC).

Marginal Notes

John B. Minor, *Institutes of Common and Statute Law* (4 vols., Richmond, 1876-1879).¹	Transcripts of WW Shorthand Comments

Vol. I, 162:

Lastly, if slaves cannot be *made,* either *jure gentium,* from captivity in war, nor *jure civili,* by purchase for a price, it is manifest that no one can be a slave *by birth.* (1 Bl. Com. 423; Montesq. Sp. L., B. XV, c.2; Vat. B. III, 152; 1 Hargr. Jur. Ex. 12 & seq.) In its *origin,* therefore, slavery cannot be justified; but when once instituted, and when slaves constitute a considerable part of the population of a State, the continuance of the institution may, and generally will become a necessity, because more injury would result to the body politic from its precipitate abolition than from its maintenance.

[c. Nov. 10, 1879]
How about its *gradual* abolition? Surely there is some statesmanlike way of ridding a state of such a curse as slavery is—a curse to industry and a curse to morals.

Vol. I, 171:

The colony of Liberia was founded by the wise forecast of Virginia statesmen chiefly, as the best medium of ameliorating the condition of things growing out of slavery, and with the hope that it would at the same time diffuse the light of Christian civilization through the dark places of Africa.

This scheme has been a lamentable failure, however, to all appearances. Dew.

1 The first volume of this series has WWhw signature on the flyleaf; WWhw notation, p. 1: "Begun Oct. 3rd, 1879. Re-begun Oct. 4th 1880"; and WWhw notations (reading dates), p. 588: "12/11/79," "12/15/80," "3/2/82."

From Janet Woodrow Wilson

My darling Son,   Wilmington [N. C.] Nov. 18th [1879]

. . . We received your sweet letter this morning. I am sorry that you dont find more congenial friends at the University—but I feared that you could not replace your Princeton friends there. Do you hear from your old friends? Did you receive the letters I forwarded to you from them? Your father read the Bruce article in the Magazine you sent this morning.[1] He says he will write you with reference to it "very soon." I know you will be glad to hear it.

Do you see anything of Prof. Venable?[2] Is he as lazy as he used to be, I wonder?

You tell us nothing about one thing that is of great importance. What sort of *eating* have you? I am anxious to know. Is your food wholesome? I have feared that your silence on the subject was rather an unfavorable sign. . . .

Your father & Josie unite with me in fondest love to you.

Mother.

ALS (WP, DLC).
1 William Cabell Bruce, "John Randolph: A Sketch," the *Virginia University Magazine*, XIX (Oct. 1879), 7-42.
2 Charles S. Venable, Professor of Mathematics, University of Virginia. He had taught at the University of South Carolina in Columbia, where he knew WW's parents.

From Charles Andrew Talcott

My dear Tommy:—   Utica [N. Y.] Nov. 19 1879

I read your article in the August International and liked it very much. I congratulate you heartily. Any triumph you win is a source of sincere gratification to me. It is so now, I hope it will be so always.

Life at the University must be a strange experience to you after the somewhat stringent laws of Princeton. It seems to me that the course of life and system of instruction which you describe are better suited for one who has had a previous collegiate training than for a beginner fresh from preparatory school. You enjoy a great privilege in being able to listen to such a man as Minor. I sometimes greatly feel the need of instruction. It takes a smart man even to interpret some parts of Blackstone. . . .

Yours sincerely   Charles Talcott

ALS (WP, DLC) with WWhw notation on env.: "Ans 1/1/80."

From Joseph Ruggles Wilson, with Enclosure

My dearest Son—   Home [Wilmington, N. C.,] Nov 19 1879

Your letters afford us great satisfaction and give us real pleasure[.] You are evidently studying amid difficulties—certainly in an uncongenial mental atmosphere:—and you deserve much credit for your uncomplainingness and your unyielding good spirits. I am disposed to think that, if not half the battle of professional life, at least that portion of it which the artillery commands, is won by first a manful declaration of independence as to surrounding circumstances, especially where these circumstances are where *duty* requires us to stand and fight. The body is taught to shrink from every exposure to a changing breeze; but even the body may so clothe its more sensitive parts as to defy all of Fahrenheit's ups and downs. The mind may in this respect take a lesson from its servant. Because things and persons about you however are new and somewhat distasteful even—they are not, on that account, necessarily repulsive. They may be deserving of study as an unexpected phase of life. Or, they may, at an unlooked for hour, expose to view something valuable in which we are ourselves deficient,—or—possibly—may reveal to us the unpleasant but salutary thought that we have all along been setting up a distorted standard, and that here is a corrective. At any rate, you do well to conform to what is around you and in contact with you—so far at least as to gather, out of it all, what good you still need in the composition of yr. character. Above all, darling son, guard against the temptation of imagining yourself to be perfect, and that whatever does not measure well by T. W. W. is to that extent defective. I do not fear however, on your part, an egotism so gross—yet it is proper to plant a post here, on which "Dangerous" is labell[ed]. Your descriptions of yr companions are admirably touched—but are they not just a little bit acid? Indeed, you seem to feel this yourself. What we sometimes call "sham" may be mere affectation—the difference between these being suggested by that between hypocrisy

& self-deception. The one ought to be unsparingly denounced, the other to be unboundedly pitied. Be assured I have never seen *either* in you. Is it because love blinds me? No: I would rather believe it is because you have an innate nobility which is too genuine for shamming and too broad for affecting.

I have read Bruce's article, with care. It is certainly good—and very good—for a youth who is, I suppose, not far out of his teens[.] Did the reader however, not know Randolph's character, and know it *even better* than this writer, it would be hardly possible for him to understand the "sketch." No information is imparted—no large portrait is drawn—we have only a deftly colored caricature. Some of the sentences are quite fine. Some of the sentiments are just and well put. But as to this being a portrait of the real Randolph! Why, the boy mistakes R's chief glory for his principal shame—i.e., his view of the federative feature in the constitution, which he predicted would become the all-in-all of its entire face, which recent events are rapidly showing to be already the fact—& in this prescience (shared by Calhoun) it was that his advocacy of States' rights was grounded—a kind of rights which, if subverted, will leave us a prey to every political danger—will be a shearing of the republic of its locks and leave it in the lap of some anarchical Delilah for a destructive enemy to bind. These rights are all, or nearly all, that render our gov't. *peculiar.* These gone, it becomes like any other republic which has been both the surprise and the contempt of history. And yet, Bruce speaks of R's adherence to the doctrine of States' rights as "merely an extension of egotism." The whole tone of the piece is away from my taste: and would be had Webster written it[.] It is, however, a commendable composition without reference to its matter. Yet what do you say of a figure like this: "tinged with its lofty austerity" How, with what color does austerity *tinge!* There are other queer slips of rhetoric I had intended to point out.—If you fear to enter the arena with him, you are a goose.

I must now close. I am not at all well—but weller than I was. Yr mother wrote you to-day. God bless you, my beloved Thomas, & this benediction is from us all.   Your affc   Father.

ALS (WP, DLC) with WWhw notation on env.: "From Father."

E N C L O S U R E

From Janet Woodrow Wilson

[c. Nov. 19, 1879]

Papa wishes me to ask you what you have done with your

French piece? Have you made any effort to have it published? If not, he wishes you would try to do so at once. Dont forget to tell us about it, dear?

Unsigned note in JWW's hw (WP, DLC).

From the Minutes of the Jefferson Society

Jeff. Hall, Nov. 22nd 1879.

The House was called to order at the usual hour. The inauguration of officers being first in order, Mr. B. L. Abney,[1] of South Carolina took the chair as President, and Mr. Jno. B. Adger,[2] of South Carolina was installed as Vice-President. After a few appropriate and impressive remarks by Mr. Abney in taking the chair, Mr. T. Woodrow Wilson was appointed Secretary; . . .[3]

Benj. L. Abney Presdt   T. Woodrow Wilson Sec'y.

[1] Benjamin L. Abney, '80.
[2] John B. Adger, M.A., '80.
[3] His handwritten minutes of the proceedings cover the period November 22, 1879–January 3, 1880, and also the date of February 28, 1880.

From Janet Woodrow Wilson

My dearest Son,   Wilmington. N. C. Nov 26th 79.

We received your letter to your father yesterday morning. Upon reading it he said he wondered if you thought he had meant in his letter to say that *you* were *hard* in your judgement of others—that if so you were mistaken—as it is very far from the truth. I assured him that you would perfectly understand that he did not mean that. . . .   Yours lovingly,   Mother

ALS (WP, DLC).

Two News Items in the *Virginia University Magazine*

[Dec. 1879]

Collegiana: The Exhibition at the Gymnasium

[An account of an evening of gymnastics, at which WW awarded the prizes.] . . .

When all was over Mr. Wilson, in that happy manner so preëminently possessed by that gentleman, made a perfect little medal-delivery speech. One he gave to Mr. Beckwith,[1] the rest, a whole handful, to Mr. Phister.[2] Speaking of delivering medals reminds us to say to our readers how much we regret to inform them that we were unable to obtain from Mr. Wilson the speech that he delivered in the Washington Hall on the occasion of delivering the medals to the victorious in the Fall games. Mr. Wilson had not written out his speech and therefore could not give it to us. We feel as if this much of an explanation is due, as we are aware of the general wish to have the speech in the *Magazine*. . . .

¹ John F. B. Beckwith, '80.
² Thomas R. Phister, '80.

Collegiana

University Glee Club.—1st tenor—Wilson, Kent;¹ 2d Tenor—Emmet,² Blackstone;³ 1st Bass—Guigon,⁴ DuBose;⁵ 2d Bass—Stokes,⁶ Patterson,⁷ Leader, J. Duncan Emmet.

The above organization was successfully formed on November 1st. . . .

Printed in the *Virginia University Magazine*, xix (December, 1879), 190-95.
    ¹ Charles W. Kent, born Sept. 27, 1860. M.A. University of Virginia, 1882; Ph.D., University of Leipzig, 1887. Professor of English and Modern Languages, University of Tennessee, 1888-93; Professor of English, Rhetoric, and Belles Lettres, University of Virginia, 1893-1917. Prolific author; editor, *Library of Southern Literature* (15 vols.), 1909-10. Died Oct. 5, 1917.
    ² J. Duncan Emmet, M.D., '80.
    ³ John W. G. Blackstone, '81.
    ⁴ Alex B. Guigon, '80.
    ⁵ George P. DuBose, '81.
    ⁶ Sylvanus Stokes, '81.
    ⁷ Archibald W. Patterson, LL.B., '82, author of *Personal Recollections of Woodrow Wilson and Some Reflexions upon His Life and Character* (Richmond, 1929).

From Joseph Ruggles Wilson

[Wilmington, N. C.] Saturday [c. Dec.] 13th [1879]
My dearest Son

I return by this mail yr. MSS.¹ I have read all the pages twice—with great care. You will notice some verbal alterations which I think you will approve—more to vary the phraseology than to improve the sentences. In one place I have pinned a paragraph which ought, I think, to take the place of that marked with brackets. At that point there ought to be a very clear setting forth of what is to follow. Indeed the only objection I can find to the article is obscurity here and there, owing to the transitional humps being covered somewhat, and in part due to a want of careful paragraphing—i.e. there ought to be a paragraph begun wherever there is a change of subject, in advance of argument. I must say, however, that the entire piece is characterized by remarkable vigor both of expression and of thought, and is deserving of a place in any quarterly of the land. You may be sure that this is my *candid* judgment. In transcribing I would alter it very little were I you. Only study paragraphing. Put those sentences into one paragraph

which *express and finish* a thought. You will thus make the reasoning clearer, and cause it to be read with greater pleasure.

Believe me, it is capital, and increases, if anything could do so,
my respect for my precious boy. . . .   Your affc father

ALS (WP, DLC).
[1] Almost certainly WW's "Congressional Government," printed at Oct. 1, 1879.

From Janet Woodrow Wilson

My precious Son—   Wilmington, N. C. Dec 15th 79
. . . You made a curious use of your *"Christmas"* money—buying
shoes and paying washing bills! Will you be able to go over to
Staunton?[1] As Christmas comes on Thursday, it seems to me that
you might get permission to go over on Wednesday & return on
Monday—without any disadvantage to your studies. What do you
think? . . .   Yours lovingly   Mother

ALS (WP, DLC).
[1] Mr. and Mrs. James W. Bones had moved there.

From Joseph Ruggles Wilson

My dearest Son—   Wilmington, [N. C.] Dec. 22, 79
I hardly know what to advise touching the publication of yr.
articles.[1] The N. American declines with gentlemanly politeness,
at least.[2] Would it be worth while to try the Southern Review, formerly issued at Baltimore (Bledsoe editor) but now at Richmond,
editor unknown to me? It would *pay* little or nothing for these
fruits of yr. brain, except perhaps pay a *compliment*. However, let
us be not discouraged [I say "us" for I feel identified with you][3]—for,
looking at the matter with a cold impersonal eye, is it not a little
fast for a young man—would it not be for *any* man as young as
yourself, be possessed of what genius he might—to expect that he
and his ideas should *at once* be acknowledged by the very first
magazines of the land? *Intrinsic* merit has only a poor chance[.]
Names tell, whether their owners write sense or nonsense. That
you will be known by-and-by, in literary circles[,] I have very little
doubt: if you desire to be. I hesitate though, my precious one, to
advise a mere literary career such as you seem to dream about now
and then. At any rate, *far, far* better conquer the law, even through
all its wretched twistings of technical paths of thorn, than suffer
aught to turn attention away from this which is probably to be yr.
meat & drink. And, to say truth, I love to think of your grappling
with those difficulties which your present course of study is throw-

ing in your way; because I know how much stronger you will every day get, how much compacter yr. mental strengths will become, by the conquests you are achieving. Therefore, do not, I entreat, let existing opportunity slip from your grasp. Meanwhile, though, write and write and write—not always about big subjects but sometimes about little ones—not always in the discussion of principles but often of dry practical details. One of the finest of works, and which has made its author immortal, is on "The Hand" by Bell.[4] It is not the man who throws *mountains* that does the most execution, but rather he who has learned the cunning of the sling which, with smooth pebbles from the brook, kills giants. Even mosquitoes are more potential than elephants. Daniel Webster had a mind as condescending for practical particulars as he had for soaring amid the sublimities of unlimited thought. Verb. Sat. [*Verbum satis sapienti est*] Try the Richmond Mag., if you cannot do better. . . .

                                        Your affc   father

P.S. omitted. ALS (WP, DLC).
   [1] "Self-Government in France" and "Congressional Government."
   [2] JRW refers here to "Self-Government in France."
   [3] Brackets JRW's.
   [4] Sir Charles Bell, *The Hand, Its Mechanism and Vital Endowments, As Evincing Design* (Philadelphia, 1835).

To Harriet Woodrow

Dear Hattie,   [Staunton, Va., c. Dec. 30, 1879]
   I missed the train this afternoon, so here I am, still enjoying freedom from Law, instead of being hard at work over my books as I had expected to be by this time. Of course I was glad to be left, since it was through no fault of mine, but only through the fault of uncle James' watch. An accident afforded me a few more hours respite, without compelling me to take the responsibility of extending my absence from the University.
   I would have given a great deal for another glimpse of you to-day. I expect to have so few opportunities of seeing you before you graduate that I covet every chance. But I knew that I could not see you to-day without interfering with the performance of your duties at the Seminary—and this I did not feel at liberty to do, simply for my own pleasure. I called on Mrs. and Miss Crawford this evening during study hours, and it was a great temptation to beg for another sight of you. But I've contented myself with sending you this note with as much love as it can carry and another good-bye.
                         Your loving cousin   T. Woodrow Wilson

ALS (WC, NjP).

To Charles Andrew Talcott

My dear Charlie,   University of Virginia, Va., Dec. 31st 1879

I rec'd your letter, written on the 19th of Nov., promptly and enjoyed it more than you would readily believe; and now, on the last day of never-to-be-forgotten '79, I sit down to answer it. The Law is indeed a hard task-master. I am struggling, hopefully but not with not *over*-much courage, through its intricacies, and am swallowing the vast mass of its technicalities with as good a grace and as straight a face as an offended palate will allow. I have, of course no idea of abandoning this study because of its few unpleasantnfeatures [*sic*]. Any one would prove himself a fool, to be sincerely pitied by all wise men, who should expect to find any work that is worth doing easily done, accomplished without pain or worry; who should turn away from hard study to pursue disappointment in some other direction. Still one may be permitted an occasional complaint, if for no other purpose than to relieve his feelings. To relieve my feelings, therefore, I wish now to record the confession that I am most terribly bored by the noble study of Law sometimes, though in the main I am thoroughly satisfied with my choice of a profession. I think that it is the want of *variety*, principally, that disgusts me. Law served with some of the lighter and spicier sauces of literature would no doubt be at all times to us of the profession an exceedingly palatable dish. But when one has nothing but Law, served in all its dryness, set before him from one week's end to another, for month after month and for quarter after quarter, he tires of this uniformity of diet. This excellent thing, the Law, gets as monotonous as that other immortal article of food, *Hash*, when served with such endless frequency. I'm trying to do some writing, however, at odd intervals and do scraps of reading as I can, and hope thus to tide over these months of preparation for practice with profit and success.

I can't say that my liking for life at the University increases as my acquaintance with it grows. My judgment of the place is about this, that it is a splendid place for the education of the *mind*, but no sort of place for the education of the *man*. In other words, if we regard students as mere studying machines, with ambition or pride or necessity for motive power, this is a fine machine shop; but if we are inclined to suspect that man was not intended to live by the accumulation of knowledge alone, but by the satisfaction of his *heart* needs as well, then this institution is more or less of a failure. A man has every opportunity here of learning as much of language and science and philosophy and law as he can well cram into his head during an ordinary college course, but his opportunities for *moral* growth and intellectual invigoration such as we used to gain in our intercourse with the dear boys who were accustomed to meet after prayer meeting in No. 9 East Witherspoon are fewer and further between than the proverbial angel's visits. You are perfectly right in your estimate of the place. It *is* "better suited for one who has had a previous collegiate training than for a beginner fresh from preparatory school." Such beginners not infrequently work more damage than advantage for themselves[.] I've been unable to find *any* thoroughly congenial companions here and content myself with study and an occasional turn with my pen. I'm going to take an early opportunity to draw a few pen pictures of some of my acquaintances which I think may amuse you.

No, Bob. Bridges aint "turning out loves, marriages, and deaths" as you suppose. Have you heard from the canny Scot since his postal card, signed Droch, requested you to "hollo" down? I had a long letter from him a few weeks ago. The old boy is reading nine hours a day—and reading, what do you suppose? Why nothing more nor less than *Political Science*. The dear fellow spends his mornings with Montesquieu, Leiber, Woolsey, Kent, and such like dignitaries, and has become their enthusiastic pupil. His afternoons, and such evenings as are not spent with some fair enslaver, he devotes to history and lighter literature. He is not only not writing, but is determined not to write for some time—until he's well stored in fact. Stories and verses are become for him, I imagine, things of memory, a reminiscence. This is a new and healthy turn in the dear old dreamer; don't you think it a happy sign?

I hear from Pete occasionally. He is a very faithful correspondent. The poor fellow was, when he last wrote, in a fever of uncertainty about what occupation he should follow and cursed himself most pitilessly for his fickleness. Now it's painting, again it's sculpture; now drawing, again writing. He'll come out all right in the end, I'm sure. He has too much of fine stuff and sturdy sense beneath all his crazy fancies to allow of his throwing himself entirely away anywhere.

I have just returned from Staunton, Va., the place where I was born twenty-three years ago—where four flourishing female schools are situated. At the largest of these schools I have this year five cousins,[1] so you may imagine that I had a delightful time. I was absent a week—*taking* that much holiday. We are given only Christmas day, but are not questioned severely if we take numerous vacations. Only *persistent* neglect of college duties exposes one to the danger of being "requested to withdraw."

Now, Charlie, just remember that one of the greatest enjoyments I have here is the receipt of letters from my Princeton classmates and friends, of whom you are chief; and with this in your mind you will, I'm sure, find time to write frequently to

Your sincere friend   T. Woodrow Wilson

ALS (photostat in RSB Coll., DLC).
1 The fifth cousin, in addition to the four mentioned at June 2, 1879, note 2, was Mary Charlotte Woodrow, daughter of Dr. James Woodrow.

From Janet Woodrow Wilson

My precious Son,   Wilmington N. C. Jan. 5th 1880.
I have been so happy in thinking of you as so content and happy in the society of dear relatives & friends, that I have forgotten that it was necessary for me to *write* as usual—sending my letters to the University—in order that your pleasure might not be marred by anxiety about us. We have received your letter giving an account of your great enjoyment of your visit in Staunton. I am *so glad* that you went to your Auntie's, dear—and that you had such a very pleasant time. Your visit has been as great a relief to my feelings as it can have been to yours, I think. I could not bear to think of your remaining at the University during the holiday week —having no break in your long nine months of study. We were much interested in your account of the cousins. I would love dearly to see them. . . .   Lovingly, yours   Mother

P.S. omitted. ALS (WP, DLC).

From Hiram Woods, Jr.

Dear Tommy,   Baltimore, Jan. 10, 1880.
. . . Your letter brought me the expected news that you were getting a good share of the University popularity. I hope some time to come down to the Univ. and see you for myself. I fully understand how you must feel toward those intensely self-satisfied "Literati" you speak of. My experience with the men at J. H. has been a very similar one. A more self-satisfied, conceited and essentially *freezing* place and men than there are at this same Univ. would be hard to find. Pres. Gilman[1] is "active"—especially with his tongue. Give him a chance, and he'll talk you blind about the goodness of Johns Hopkins, the extra ability of *"our own men,"* the cost of the instruments in the Laboratories, the splendid facilities for "W-e-i-r-r-k-e" (does that give any idea of his pronunciation?), the great power *we* are to be in Balto., the solemn responsibility

the young men of Md. are under to take advantage of these rare opportunities, etc, etc, etc—ad nauseam. He has been through all this to me about 5 times. He strongly reminds me of Ridge's advertisement of his "great African Polar bear, captured on the west coast of Chili, only one now living." Don't talk about the peculiarities of Jimmy after you meet this man. What he needs is a good Princetonian or Harvard Lampoon. It would do him more good than any thing else in the world. . . . Let me thank you for speaking of "That Lass o' Lowries."[2] I read it Christmas. It is certainly absorbing. Write to me soon, Tommy, and tell me about yourself & any of our fellows you have heard from. All send their love.

Your Sincere Friend & Bro. in ΦΚΨ,   H. Woods, Jr.

ALS (WP, DLC).
  1 Daniel Coit Gilman, president of The Johns Hopkins University.
  2 A novel by Frances Hodgson Burnett, published in 1877.

From Joseph Ruggles Wilson

My precious Son   Wilmington [N. C.], Jan. 12, '80
Enclosed please find $54.00 amt of bill for board to April 1st 1880

I am glad that you had so good a time with yr relatives in Staunton. Blood is not always friendship; but when it is it is the best.

Yr. Prof. Minor is a trump. He talked to you like a gentleman of the good oly [old] style. I have no doubt he was perfectly truthful in all he said about you, as you were in all you told him about us. . . .   Your affc   Father

ALS (WP, DLC).

Notes on Professor Southall's Lecture on International Law

[c. Jan. 17, 1880]

Lecture Twenty-five

. . . Neutrals: There are 2 species of neutrality

(a) Ordinary or perfect neutrality which every sovereign state is entitled to with respect to wars in which it is not concerned.

(b) A conventional or qualified neutrality such as that maintained by Belgium which has been declared neutral by all the great powers of Europe so that she can offer no treaties of alliance in contravention thus declared.

Assaults cannot be carried on within the territories of a neutral state and captures made therein are illegal and the neutral power will insist upon all restitution! Their own prize courts will restore them if they get possession of them. A man of war will not be allowed to lie just within neutral waters and make captures just behind these boats nor will it be allowed to over land the territorial border, nor to make preparation within neutral territory for actual war without it.

Immunity from capture extends to armed vessels of the state, but private merchantmen, though within national character as property, are not considered part of its territory; and it is allowed to a belligerent agent to enter upon neutral commercial vessels upon the high-seas with view of finding out

(a) If they be really neutral

(b) If there be enemies' goods on board

(c) If there be any contraband of war on board

Neutral vessels have the right to trade with either belligerent provided they do not deal in contraband or sell to blockaded ports; but either belligerent may overhaul such vessels and take any enemies' goods off of them, paying the neutral carrier freight. So, on the other hand, if a neutral merchant puts his goods upon a belligerent vessel, the opposite belligerent has a right to capture that vessel, but no right to the neutral goods unless they be contraband and must therefore restore the neutral goods at some convenient port or cruise them to the port of their destination and charge freight.

It will be remembered that the Decl of Paris has made a change in these rules. It is declared by the second section "that a neutral flag covers enemies' goods, except contraband". This treaty has thus modified to those who have signed it, or who may sign it, the laws of international usage. It in effect establishes among them the principle "that free ships make free goods" except contraband but the opposite maxim, "that enemies' ships make enemies' goods" is not embodied in it and this is no part of international law. The privilege of neutral flags covering enemies' goods, whether established by the powers' declaration or by their treaties, is not extended to fraudulent use of that flag so as to cover enemies' property in the ship itself as well as in the cargo.

Contraband goods are always liable to capture without payment of freight. They are said to be infectious, for they contaminate all the residue of the cargo *so far as it belongs to the owner of the contraband*, though it be absolutely harmless.

Contraband is whatever is directly useful in war and it therefore varies from time to time as the arts of war change. Agricultural productions, it is said, may become contraband when purpose of one belligerent is reduce his adversary by starvation. The United

States are disposed to think that provisions may be contraband when sent to military post, or naval supplies intended directly for the navy—but when intended for general consumption they are not contraband. This has been the subject of much controversy between the United States and England. Such questions are generally settled by treaty.

Transcript of WWsh classroom notes in notebook described at Oct. 9, 1879.

From Janet Woodrow Wilson

My darling Son,   Wilmington, N. C. Monday—Jan. 19th [1880]
   Your father wrote you last Monday—enclosing funds. Did you receive it? I think you must have done so just after you mailed yours of last Wednesday. I am so sorry to hear of your "blue" fit. I suppose it was natural though—in the way of re-action—after your refreshing & delightful visit to near relatives & friends. But, dear child, I dont feel satisfied that you should only write to us when you feel bright & happy. It would be a relief to you to write when you are blue—and tell us all about it—don't you think so, dear. I cannot see that you have the least reason to be blue—quite the contrary—but then I know that the "blues" are *never* reasonable. Quite the contrary also, as far as I have seen. I had a letter from your Uncle James Bones the other day—a very nice letter. He says they enjoyed your visit extremely—that you "captivated all their hearts." He says the nicest sort of things about you—and ends by expressing his conviction that you are "*sure* to succeed." . . .
                                Lovingly   Mother
I enclose a letter from Josie that was written week before last. He had no envelope at the time he wrote—laid it aside & forgot all about—but I think you will enjoy it all the same now.

ALS (WP, DLC) with WWhw notes on env. Enc.: Joseph R. Wilson, Jr. to WW, Jan. 11, 1880.

From Joseph Ruggles Wilson

My most dear Son—   Wilmington, [N. C.] Jan. 27, '80
   I am sorry to know, from the tone of your few last letters, that that imp "the blues" has been at the inside of you. What business he had there is more than I can conjecture, except to have you fight with and conquer him—as every growing man has at times to do, and as I think *you* have done this time. Let him not again enter. He is from beneath. I need not say to you that his exorcist is found in the cultivation of a hopeful disposition. Would that I had bestowed more attention upon this article of culture. My life might

have been greatly stronger by being greatly happier. But, mistakenly, I have nearly always chosen the dark sides of probabilities at which to look. It will not do. It is irrational. It is sinful, even. It hobbles one's powers as with chains. It makes one timid, too, as one is apt to be in the night:—because it gives one over to his fancy. I beg of you, therefore, that you will strive ag't. despondency as you would with a deadly foe: aye, pray against it as you would for some great salvation. One of the dangers of a young man like yourself—thoughtful, aspiring, conscious of certain stirrings of ambition, and anxious to succeed even where success is hardest—one of your dangers arises from the tendency to *look in* too much and too far: to become too subjective: in short to be too self-conscious. The introverted eye is apt to get tears into it, where is little or no sun to dry them. It does not do to analyze feelings too much. Nor is it wise to be often weighing one's abilities, to ascertain whether they have in them the hard stuff out of which intellectual conquest will come. The true method for knowing oneself and what he is fit for, is to grapple with things outward—is to attack and conquer difficulties of whatever kind that may come up—is to learn to defy circumstances even those that seem most adverse. In your present case, you ought to throw, to pour yourself into your daily studies as if they were your very life: thinking of almost nothing besides, except God and your friends. The law *is*, I see, trying your mettle—and alas! occasionally you have been tempted to cry out, 'you are too hard for me, away with your iron limbs!' Your cure therefore for imaginary broodings is always at hand. It is in conquest. It is to make what is dry in yr. studies moist by hook or by crook. It is to get at the bottom of those principles of justice,—the bottom where many deep and refreshing wells are of which great lawyers have drunk and become what they were. But, dearest one, I have the firmest confidence in yr future. Only make each day fruitful in success and all else will be taken care of.

I need not explain that I am not in the least blaming you. Far from it. I *could not* do so, my precious son, my precious friend. . . .

Your affectionate   Father

ALS (WP, DLC) with WWhw note on env.: "What does *South*[hall] lecture on in connection with the *Federalist*"

From the Minutes of the Jefferson Society

Hall of Jefferson Society, Jan'y 31st 1880—

The Society met at the usual hour, President Adger in the chair, and proceeded to the regular order of business. . . . Mr. T. W.

Wilson was then nominated and unanimously elected orator of the Society for the following month. . . .

From James Wilson Woodrow

Dear Cousin Tommie   Chillicothe [Ohio] Jan. 31st 1880

You have probably wondered at my long delay in answering your interesting letter, but to tell the truth, I felt quite a dread of writing to one who has been so long a collegiate student, and who, it seems to me, must be very critical.

What you call a "full account of myself," can be given in a very few words. At present I attend the Chillicothe High School in the next to the highest class. I intend to leave school at the end of the year, however, if not before, in order to begin my preparation for college. Do not be afraid that I attempt to enter too young, or unthoroughly prepared. By the catalogue which you kindly have taken the trouble to send, I see that in order to be examined in the large amount of Latin and Greek, required, it will take several years of hard study. I began Greek a few days ago, reciting to our pastor Dr. Biggs. . . .

You do not seem to be so fond of the University as of Princeton. Perhaps you have gotten to like it better, by this time. It is very pleasant for Hattie, at all events, to be able to see you every now and then. . . .

Affectionately, your cousin Jas. W. Woodrow

ALS (WP, DLC) with WWhw notation on env.: "Ans."

Marginal Notes

The Federalist on the New Constitution (Hallowell, Maine, 1852).

Transcript of WW Shorthand Comments

P. 67 (No. XV):

It is true, as has been before observed, that facts too stubborn to be resisted, have produced a species of general assent to the abstract proposition, that there exist material defects in our national system; but the usefulness of the concession on the part of the old adversaries of federal measures, is destroyed by a strenuous opposition to a remedy, upon the only principles that can give it a chance of success.

[c. Feb.-May 1880]
These very words might be *now* employed with respect of our present government. (1880)

P. 70 (No. XV):

Those who have been conversant in the proceedings of popular assemblies; who have seen how difficult it often is, when there is no exterior pressure of circumstances, to bring them to harmonious resolutions on important points, will readily conceive how impossible it must be to induce a number of such assemblies, deliberating at a distance from each other, at different times, and under different impressions, long to cooperate in the same views and pursuits.

> The wit of this remark strikingly illustrated by committee government in our present Congress.

P. 101 (No. XXII):

One of the weak sides of republics, among their numerous advantages, is, that they afford too easy an inlet to foreign corruption. A hereditary monarch, though often disposed to sacrifice his subjects to his ambition, has so great a *personal* interest in the government, and in the external glory of the nation, that it is not easy for a foreign power to give him an equivalent for what he would sacrifice by treachery to the state.

> The same true of Cabinet ministers.

Pp. 154-55 (No. XXXV):

There is no part of the administration of government that requires extensive information, and a thorough knowledge of the principles of political economy, so much as the business of taxation. The man who understands those principles best, will be least likely to resort to oppressive expedients, or to sacrifice any particular class of citizens to the procurement of revenue. It might be demonstrated that the most productive system of finance will always be the least burdensome.

> Memorandum:
> This might be applied in discussion of the principle of our adoption of cabinet government in this country; how can such knowledge be best secured and best employed under republican forms?

P. 156 (No. XXXVI):

Nations in general, even under governments of the more popular kind, usually commit the administration of their finances to single men, or to boards composed of a few individuals, who digest and prepare, in the first instance, the plans of taxation; which are afterwards passed into law by the authority of the sovereign or legislature. Inquisitive and enlightened statesmen, are everywhere deemed best qualified to make a judicious selection of the objects proper for revenue; which is a clear indication, as far as the sense of mankind can have

> Cabinet government again.

weight in the question, of the species of knowledge of local circumstances, requisite to the purposes of taxation.

P. 224 (No. XLVII):

From these facts, by which Montesquieu was guided, it may clearly be inferred, that in saying, "there can be no liberty, where the legislative and executive powers are united in the same person, or body of magistrates;" or, "if the power of judging, be not separated from the legislative and executive powers," he did not mean that these departments ought to have no *partial agency* in, or no *control* over the acts of each other. His meaning, as his own words import, and still more conclusively as illustrated by the example in his eye, can amount to no more than this, that where the *whole* power of one department is exercised by the same hands which possess the *whole* power of another department, the fundamental principles of a free constitution are subverted.

No just view of the constitution of England can be obtained if the cabinet, that connecting link between the legislative and executive[,] be left out of view. In the persons of the ministers the executive is actually the governing force in the legislature—much to the advantage of both departments.

P. 239 (No. XLI):

But the great security against a gradual concentration of the several powers in the same department, consists in giving to those who administer each department, the necessary constitutional means, and personal motives, to resist encroachments of the others.

This means a motive is best supplied by a responsible Cabinet.

P. 270 (No. LVIII):

But will not the house of representatives be as much interested as the senate, in maintaining the government in its proper functions; and will they not therefore be unwilling to stake its existence or its reputation on the pliancy of the senate? Or if such a trial of firmness between the two branches were hazarded, would not the one be as likely first to yield as the other? These questions will create no difficulty with those who reflect that in all cases, the smaller the number, and the more permanent and conspicuous the station, of men in power, the stronger must be the interest which they will individually feel in whatever concerns the government. Those who represent the dignity of their country in the eyes of other nations, will be particularly sensible to every prospect of public danger, or of a dishonorable stagnation in public affairs.

Cabinet government again.

P. 270 (No. LVIII):

One observation, however, I must be permitted to add on this subject, as claiming, in my judgment, a very serious attention. It is, that in all legislative assemblies, the greater the number composing them may be, the fewer will be the men who will in fact direct their proceedings.

This is not the case under committee government.

P. 289 (No. LXIII):

Responsibility, in order to be reasonable, must be limited to objects within the power of the responsible party; and in order to be effectual, must relate to operations of that power, of which a ready and proper judgment can be formed by the constituents.

Cabinet government again.

P. 321 (No. LXX):

There is an idea, which is not without its advocates, that a vigorous executive is inconsistent with the genius of republican government. The enlightened well-wishers to this species of government must at least hope that the supposition is destitute of foundation; since they can never admit its truth, without, at the same time, admitting the condemnation of their own principles. Energy in the executive is a leading character in the definition of good government.

! As if a weak executive is not inconsistent with government of any kind.

P. 360 (No. LXXVIII):

That inflexible and uniform adherence to the rights of the constitution, and of individuals, which we perceive to be indispensable in the courts of justice, can certainly not be expected from judges who hold their offices by a temporary commission.

Periodical appointments, however regulated, or by whomsoever made, would, in some way or other, be fatal to their necessary independence. If the power of making them was committed either to the executive or legislature, there would be danger of an improper complaisance to the branch which possessed it; if to both, there would be an unwillingness to hazard the displeasure of either; if to the people, or to persons chosen by them for the special purpose, there would be too great a disposition to consult popularity, to justify a reliance that nothing would be consulted but the constitution and the laws.

How fully has this been verified by the later experience of popular state constitutions which provide for election of state judges by a popular vote.

Classroom Notebook

[Feb. 5–May 15, 1880]

Inscribed on cover (WWhw):

"Constitutional Law Professor Southall University of Virginia."

WWsh notes with WWhw headings taken in Professor S. O. Southall's course in equity, mercantile, international, and constitutional
law, consisting of notes on twenty-eight lectures with the heading
and date (but no notes) for a twenty-ninth lecture. Subjects covered
included the origins, framing and debates over ratification of the
Constitution of the United States and problems of constitutional interpretation. Transcript of WWsh notes on Lecture 10 on the nature of
the Union printed at March 9, 1880.

(WP, DLC).

From Joseph Ruggles Wilson

My dear Son   Wilmington, [N. C.] Feb 5 1880

. . . I was pleased with yr letter received this morning. I would
say to you let the "practise" be for the future. Law as a science is
what you are *now* after. Master that, and all else will fall into line
in due time. Theology does not, in this respect, differ from Law.
Hard study conquers the science—common sense conquers the
practise. All are well, and all join me in immense love to our darling faraway.   Your affc   Father

ALS (WP, DLC).

From the Minutes of the Jefferson Society

Hall of Jefferson Society, Feby 6th/80.

The House was called to order at 7 o'clock by the president, Mr.
Adger. The roll was called, absentees noted & the Minutes of the
previous meeting read & approved. There being no debate the Report of the Question Committee was submitted & the following
question selected for two weeks hence: "Would a restriction of the
suffrage ameliorate our political condition?" To be debated on the
Aff by Messrs. Williams[1] & Neg. Messrs. Woods,[2]

Wilson	Youmans,
Hampton, G.	Browning. . . .

[1] Christopher H. Williams, LL.B. '82, or George G. Williams, '80; possibly Egbert
P. Williams, M.D., '81.

[2] The others, besides WW, were Samuel B. Woods, '80, George McD. Hampton,
'80, Pringle T. Youmans, '81, and William C. Browning, '81.

From Janet Woodrow Wilson

My precious Son,   Wilmington N. C. Thursday–[Feb. 19, 1880]

I have just put up the Scrap book of engravings and will send it to the P. O. at once. I tried to put it up so that it will not be injured. I have only time to write a hurried note. Tommy dear, I am so distressed that I cannot find the books you wished sent to you[.] I looked over every one of those you left in the closet. Have you any idea where they can be? What sort of *looking* books are they? I will look again of course–for I cant be satisfied till I find them. Are you sure you did not take them with you? Please drop me a few lines at once, if you can tell me just where you think they are. If you want them much, I will see if I can get them down street[.] I am glad you liked your cravats. If you will send me one of your old ones that is soiled–and will tell me what colors you want, I will make you some for Spring. By taking the old one to pieces, I can make them *exactly* like it.

We are all quite well. We think of you constantly, and love you so dearly, my darling. God bless you.

Lovingly yours   Mother.

ALS (WP, DLC).

To Robert Bridges

Dear Bobby,   University of Virginia, Va., Feb. 25th 1880.

When I take out your last letter and look at the date of it (Dec. 6th)[1] I'm inclined to be heartily ashamed of myself for my apparently unpardonable delinquency in the matter of our correspondence. I know that you *seem* to have every reason to be seriously offended with me; and, if I did not know what implicit trust may be placed in your friendship, I would be afraid that you *are* offended. You can't imagine how provokingly busy I have been. Not that the *amount* of work that I have had to do is more than I can accomplish by diligent application. But the time is so divided here that one's work is spread over the twenty-four hours in such a way that the intervals of leisure, though not infrequent, are very short–no one of them seeming half long enough to allow of my writing a letter such as I would want to write to you. To-day, however, I have much more time at my disposal than I have had for some weeks, and so I'm going to write you a long letter, Bobby; and hereafter I'm going to content myself with short notes, rather than let lag a correspondence which I value more highly than any other.

Do you remember the figure with which you opened your last letter to me—the fancy about the mirage—about those blessed college days of ours passing away into a mere bright memory? Well, there's more truth than "taffy" in that, Bobby. As regards all but the old crowd, those Princeton days already seem very far away from me indeed, sometimes. But the memory of that dear old crowd can never die. Its influence was permanent. Why, Bobby, my love for you, and for "the Cow," and for Charlie, and for "the Doctor," and for Daniel was and *is* as real and as intense as ever one brother felt for another—and my affection for "Pete" and "the Heathen" was scarcely less warm—only less because I did not learn to know them so soon. And it was just this love that made the pang of parting so bitter. To know that we must all change and, because of the change in ourselves, cease to know one another, was as sad a thought as ever I had

Your last letter was a veritable ray of light. Of course I never thought that you were doing yourself justice in regarding yourself a "dreamer." You allowed yourself to be what, naturally, you were not. I always thought that you had a poetical *temperament,* but your *mind* I knew to be preëminently *logical.* When, therefore, I read your sketch of the singularly delightful course of reading you have been taking, I was positively delighted: and my delight had a large element of selfishness in it, I suspect. Your dreamings, Bobby, your ecstasies over Hawthorne's weird imaginations, were the only things concerning which I did not find myself in complete sympathy with you. But you are now pursuing studies which tally so exactly with my tastes—and which I cannot help regarding as so perfect[l]y suited to your own talents—that I feel like writing you a letter of thanks and congratulation. It's my sincerest hope that our friendship may be life-long—and it's my brightest dream that you and I will someday be co-laborers in the great work of disseminating political truth and purifying the politics of our own country. You are already far ahead of me in your readings on political science, but when I get out of this treadmill of the law I intend to devote every scrap of leisure time to the study of that great and delightful subject, and I may thus overtake you and go along with you. No, indeed, I don't find it at all hard to conceive of you as absorbed in these subjects: and I have a plan to propose. Let's *correspond* often and at length upon any topics of history or political science that may suggest themselves to us as susceptible of discussion. In this way we may benefit ourselves in more ways than one: we will not only clear and settle our beliefs, but, what is almost as desirable, we will grow together and keep up our acquaintance with each other. I am dependent on intellectual sympathy, and if we diligently follow the course I propose we may build up a friendship that will be more valuable to us in the future than all the knowledge of books. This plan is awkwardly put, I know; but you know what I mean. Let's keep our minds and hearts open to one another and the college friendship which we look back upon with happy recollection will ripen into a fellowship even more blessed and profitable. This is no sudden idea, Bobby. It's not a mere fancy. I believe that it can be proved feasible. It's not a mere visionary hope; but a real definite desire and purpose. You'll have to lead me for the present in our investigations, for I have no time here for anything but *law*: but I hope the profit of the plan will be none the less on that account. I'll make up in enthusiasm what I lack in knowledge for the present.

I have just returned from a delightful trip. The ΦΚΨ grand convention met in Washington just a week ago and I went down as a delegate from our chapter here. As you may imagine, during the two or three days of our meeting, I met a great many fine fellows from all parts of the country. It was a[s] fine a set of young men as I would care to meet. But my chief satisfaction was in seeing Hiram once more. He was down as one of the representatives of the Johns Hopkins chapter. After the sittings of the convention were ended I went over to Baltimore with Hiram and spent Friday, Saturday, and Sunday with him. I really had no business to neglect my studies here and run off on a pleasure trip as I did. But the temptation was too great to be resisted. I saw the Doctor. He is looking as well as I ever saw him. The work he is doing seems to agree with him most thoroughly. Both Hiram and he are working as hard as ever men worked, I imagine. You know "the Cow" began to show some symptoms of ability for hard study while he was under Cornwall.[2] Well, since then that ability seems to have been wonderfully developed. The old heifer is genuinely enthusiastic over Physics, and Biology, and Anatomy. And what the "Doctor" don't know about the latter seems to be rubbed out long ago. Why those two chaps talked medicine in my presence at such a rate that I went to sleep in self-defence.—and woke to find them not the least bit repentant of the torture with which they had been inflicting me in my defencelessness. They discussed all the minute operations of this system of ours very much as I propose that we shall discuss the more abstruse questions of political science. I only wished that I had had some fellow law student along that I might have talked them deaf on the technicalities of the law—for I believe that I've been studying law almost as hard as they have been studying medicine. But in spite of their ill-treatment of me, my visit was simply delightful. Some of the old Princeton spirit came over me, and it was a rude breaking of the spell to have to come back here to the grind once more. The only drawback to my enjoyment was the fact that I did not see *Dan*. We telegraphed for him to come down, but his answer was: "Am fearfully sorry, but can't possibly come." I suspect that his father is making Dan'l work and wont consent that anything should break in upon his studies or interfere with the formation of the regular habits which he is beginning to form. I know that not to be allowed to come was as great a trial to him as not being allowed to see him was to me.

I can't say that my liking for the University increases as my acquaintance with it becomes more intimate. Socially it is, in my opinion, a great failure. There's no college life here, as *we* know college life. It's a splendid place to educate the mind, but no place to educate the man. I suppose that the facilities offered here in most of the departments, and especially in the professional schools, for the acquisition of accurate knowledge are scarcely equalled anywhere in the country. But the men here do little but work; they work too much—and notwithstanding all only a small minority get through the examinations. In Chemistry last year, for instance, seventeen were graduated out of a class of one hundred and seventeen! And it's very much the same in many others of the schools. Out of the sixty men who are applying for their degrees in law this year probably less than fifteen will succeed in obtaining them.

My dissatisfaction with the life and customs here may arise from the contrast which is here presented to class life at Princeton. It certainly has not been caused by any want of success on my own part in meeting a great many nice men and forming several very pleasant friendships. And I've had some small successes in other ways. I've gained some reputation as a speaker in the Jefferson Society here. By special request I delivered the medals won in the Fall athletic games, before a large audience of students in a large hall here; after having served as judge in the games themselves. About a month later I delivered the prizes won in the gymnasium contest, immediately upon the close of the contest, to quite a considerable assemblage of ladies and gentlemen, including several of the professors. In the literary societies here we have no essay-reading and speaking such as we used to have in old Whig. The principle exercise is *debate*. On the first Saturday evening of each month, however, an oration is delivered by some member specially elected as "monthly [orator] for—Jan, Feb, March," or whatever the month may be. I am to deliver the March oration. Since my return from Washington I have found, much to my surprise and dismay, that at the meeting which took place during my absence, it was moved and unanimously carried that, inasmuchas several young ladies had expressed a desire to be present when my oration is to be delivered, the society be upon that evening thrown open to visitors! And upon the strength of this resolution, several of my friends have expressed a determination to invite their young lady friends to be present. I'm thoroughly scared. I took no very special pains with my oration and I'm beginning to tremble for its reception. It's too late either to retreat or to write another speech now. I'm fairly entrapped. My speech is on John Bright,[3] who, I hope, "needs no introduction to an intelligent audience." It will probably occupy half an hour or more in its delivery, possibly three quarters of an hour. It's the fashion here to make long speeches. I tell you these things about myself by way of setting you an example. The fuller your letters are of *yourself* the more acceptable will they prove.

I've been keeping my resolve about visiting Staunton frequently. You know I have five cousins there at school. Besides I know lots of people there. It's my birth place and is full of old friends and acquaintances of my family's. I left there when I was quite small. But I'm made much of because I'm my father's son: and I'm made much of with all the cordial warmth of Virginia hospitality. I can leave here on Saturday at noon and, spending Sabbath there with my uncle and cousins, get back here on Monday morning without have missed a single lecture. You may be sure that I've several times made the trip.

But, Bobby, I'm going to stop. If I don't give my pen pause here I may write on until after mail time. Bobby, do return good for evil by writing soon to your

Devoted friend   T. Woodrow Wilson

ALS (Meyer Coll., DLC).
    [1] R. Bridges to WW, Dec. 6, 1879, ALS (WP, DLC).
    [2] Henry B. Cornwall, Professor of Analytical Chemistry and Mineralogy at Princeton.
    [3] Printed at March 6, 1880.

From Charles Andrew Talcott

My dear Tommy:—   Utica [N. Y.] F'eby 26, 1880—
    . . . I must confess that I took great satisfaction, a wicked satisfaction perhaps, in your expression of discontent concerning the

study of the law. Your letter arrived at a time when I was very much discouraged; while I heartily endorsed your sentiments, I took great pleasure in knowing that you were a fellow sufferer. Misery certainly loves company. The law is certainly a harsh task-master; but even when I am most rebellious against its tyranny I cannot help reverencing its wisdom. . . .[1]

Ever affectionately Yours   Chas. Talcott

ALS (WP, DLC) with WWsh and WWhw notations on env.: "Received [WWsh] 3/1/80"; "Ans 5/26/80."
[1] For further extracts from this letter, see WW to C. A. Talcott, May 20, 1880, note 1.

From the Minutes of the Jefferson Society

Jeff. Hall Feb. 28th 1880.
. . . The debate was upon the question, "Would a restriction of the suffrage ameliorate our political condition?" The question was discussed in the Affirmative by Messrs Wilson, and G. McD. Hampton; on the Neg. Messrs. Youmans and Browning. . . .

Jeff. Hall March 6th 1880
. . . The monthly oration being next in order Mr. Wilson delivered an eloquent oration with John Bright as his subject. Mr. Wilson inspired by the bright eyes and approving smiles of many fair visitants delivered his oration with an earnestness and vigor that drew down much well deserved applause. . . .

A Biographical Essay

[[March 6, 1880]]
John Bright.

In every effort of comprehension we are made painfully conscious of the narrow compass of man's boasted powers of mind. As, when we stand before some one of the greater master-pieces of architecture and bestow our admiration upon its grand outlines, its multiform and uniform strength and grace, its swift and high-bending arches, its massive supports, its slender summits, we miss the careful carving of its cornices, the laborious polish of its marbres [marbles], or the modest beauty of the exquisite forms of stone, which in cold counterfeit of man, guard its portals or stand their solemn, silent sentry on its towers—so, when we contemplate the great movements of recorded history and attempt to take in the broader scope of events and follow the main lines of civilization's "journey with the sun," we overlook, in our wide survey, the inner lives of individual nations, the special workings of separate forces, the events of individual epochs, the controlling influence of individual men—in our endeavor to put ourselves in sympathy with *mankind*, we have ceased to sympathize with *man*. The reverse is scarcely less true. If we would bestow our attention upon some *one* event, we find ourselves divorcing it from its necessary connection with *other* events and regarding it in nakedness and isolation. If we could study the character of some one *man*, though that man be our nearest neighbor or our closest friend, we are in constant danger of separating *him* from his surroundings, holding him responsible for what circumstances have made him, reckoning him debased by frailties not his own, or exalted by greatness which was not born with him but thrust upon him. Fortunately, however, when we seek to familiarize ourselves with the characters of those men whom it is our habit to call *great*—such men as have led thought or conceived philosophies or framed policies—we are relieved from this embarrassment by one saving circumstance: we find every truly great man identified with some special cause. His purposes are steadfastly set in some definite direction. The career which he works out for himself constitutes so intimate a part of the history of his times that to dissociate *him* from his surroundings were as impossible as it would be undesirable.

It is, then, under peculiar advantages that we undertake an examination of the character and career of John Bright. Certainly no man ever won for himself a more definite position or a more certain place than has he. He has attained to honored age, absolutely without deviation from the principles of his youth. His life has inseparably interwoven itself with all the greater events of later English history. His name has become synonymous with liberalism. Since his entrance into public life, no great political reform has been accomplished which he has not powerfully helped to triumphant completion. Not since then has there been any considerable scheme of political reformation which has not been set to the music of his eloquence—or any great cause of advancement which has not been at some point carried on the shoulders of his strength.

From his very birth he has imbibed free political principles. He was born some sixty-nine years ago in the busy village of Rochdale, and was bred in the most thriving parts of thrifty Lancashire —the modern home of liberal politics in England. For modern English liberalism seems to have been born in the manufacturing districts, in the inner heart of Britain, in those busy counties in which

Nottingham, Sheffield, Leeds, Manchester and Liverpool are clustered. Nothing could have been more natural than that the clouds of conservative prejudice should have first broken away in these homes of industry. As civilization advances and the steps of commerce quicken, men are more and more massed in great centres of industrial enterprise; and it is in there [these], where similarity of occupation, activity of intercourse and community of feeling kindle quick sympathy among large bodies of men and rouse to active intelligence whole classes of society, that broad and generous ideas of governmental polity find their firmest rootage and their sunniest seasons. It were next to impossible that such principles should find their earliest acceptance in agricultural communities or rural neighborhoods. There, where every condition of disintegration, and not one of union, is present, combined and aggressive action is looked for in vain. Political purposes are not there easily communicated; new political doctrines are not there readily sown. There men's thoughts run as slowly as their plows; men's purposes are as sluggish as their beasts of burden. It were perhaps equally idle to look for political impulse to come from the mining districts. There, where every day is spent away from the light of the sun, men's minds seem as ill-lighted as the deep galleries in which they wearily ply the pick. Their only reform is in riot. They crave license, not liberty.

Trade, indeed, is the great nurse of liberal ideas. Men who deal with all the world *cannot* sympathize with those whose thoughts do not reach beyond the limits of their own immediate neighborhood. The ordinary English farmer knows no world greater or more remote that the nearest market town. The English manufacturer sells his goods in Calcutta, in Valparaiso, in Hong Kong, it may be. When he wishes to buy, the cheapest market is the nearest; when he desires to sell, the dearest is the nearest. Accordingly when we see the cotton-printers and spinners of Manchester the first to uphold the doctrines and spread the gospel of Free Trade, we find no room for surprise. The earliest stirring of the great agitation which looked towards the establishment of Free Trade, were felt about the year 1836. Manchester and her industrial sisters had recently been enfranchised by the Reform Act of 1832, and the famous Anti-Corn-Law-League was one of the first and greatest manifestations of the potential influence which the manufacturing and trading classes were beginning to assume. This stupendous Free Trade movement found its ablest directors and its foremost leaders amongst the merchants of Manchester and its vicinity—leaders who afterwards became the doctors of what came to be known as the "Manchester School" of politicians. Zeal for rational principles of trade changed simple unambitious men of business into diligent politicians, transformed them into orators, exalted them into statesmen. Foremost among these, by reason of zeal, by reason of worth, by reason of intelligence, was Richard Cobden, a cotton-printer of Manchester. His exalted character and persuasive eloquence made him the directing genius of the great drama of agitation set afoot by the League. In economical legislation his talents proved themselves beyond comparison brilliant and sovereign. But it was not permitted him long to survive the great League he had so successfully led. His life ended suddenly upon the triumphant completion of his life-work. He died the greatest apostle of Free Trade—and men now scarcely remember that he was anything else.

The name of John Bright was scarcely less prominently connected with the work and mission of the League than that of Cobden. *His* first step in public life was, like Cobden's, a step to the leadership of the forces of Free Trade. It were not possible or desirable upon this occasion to consider in detail, or even in general outline, those Corn Laws against which the League organized its forces. Suffice it to say that, passed in 1815, their effect had been virtually to exclude all foreign corn from the markets of Great Britain, under the silly pretense of "protecting" home produce, and that it was against this short-sighted policy that the forces of Free Trade made their determined stand. Never before or since has peaceful political agitation been more thoroughly organized or more shrewdly conducted. Every mail-bag that left Manchester was full to overflowing with Free Trade tracts; no conceivable method of schooling the people in the doctrines of sound economy was neglected. From channel to channel, from Tweed to Thames, its principles were preached with all the dint of demonstration, all the power of persuasion, all the energy of eloquence. Immense bazaars evidenced its enterprize and contributed to its wealth. Unrivalled fairs and unnumbered mass-meetings drove its designs to completion. It was a vast movement of thought. Every day added to its increasing strength. Every wind brought news of its accumulating triumphs. It was in this work that Mr. Bright first tried his mettle. It was in this cause that he first developed his genius for affairs. His singleness of aim and energy of purpose and nobility of conception first discovered themselves in the direction and control of this stupendous machinery of propagandism. His character is of strong and elastic fibre such as is toughened and strengthened by every test. It partakes of all the sober thoughtfulness, the warm and intense earnestness, and the noble straightforwardness of that sturdy sect, the Quakers, from whose loins he is sprung—that sect which long ago, under the energetic leadership of that sterling pioneer and singularly genuine man, William Penn, penetrated the wilds of our thriving northern neighbor and laid the first foundations of that illustrious commonwealth whose unsurpassed industries are driving European manufacturers from their won markets. Mr. Bright carried to the public platform and into Parliament a political creed no less simple and no less openly avowed than the religious creed of his sect. And this creed was perfected before it was promulgated. Not until his thirtieth year did he actively participate in public affairs. His liberalism was then mature. His opinions were fullgrown and fruiting. His convictions were rooted and grounded in his very nature. And these convictions are vivid beliefs such as constitute the very essence of practical statesmanship, when united, as they are in him, with an undeviating purpose and a will which knows no discouragement and no defeat. These are rare gifts to be crowned with the rarer gift of eloquence. The campaigns of the League were preëminently speech making campaigns. The gospel of Free Trade was a preached gospel. Every public hall in England had rung with the appeals of its heralds and the cheers of its disciples. In this school was Mr. Bright trained. In the proclamation of this gospel were first developed his marvellous powers of public speech—powers which were first manifested in broken sentences and harsh tones, giving little promise of those grand passages of eloquence and that voice of unrivalled sweetness, variety and strength which have since won for him a place among the very greatest of English orators. These powers were not slow of growth. They grew with his energy and kept pace with his purposes. No orator ever more signally illustrated the truth that eloquence is not of the lips alone. Eloquence is never begotten by empty pates. Grovelling minds are never winged with high and worthy thoughts. Eloquence consists not in sonorous sound or brilliant phrases. *Thought* is the fibre, thought is the *pith*, of eloquence. Eloquence lies in the thought, not in the throat. It was as the expression of his high impulses and strong purposes and sagacious plans and noble courage that John Bright's oratory became a tremendous agency in the world of politics. It is persuasion inspired by conviction. "Out of the abundance of his heart" his mouth speaks. Public speech was the instrumentality by means of which his mind struck its overwhelming blows at political prejudice. His words were tapers, which, lit at the fire of his convictions, first made visible and then dispelled the darkness of political selfishness and social tyranny. He has, moreover, the physical, as well as the mental and spiritual, gifts of the orator. His frame is large and strong; his face is open, truthful and attractive; his features are clearly-cut and mobile—almost articulately expressive. No storm of indignation or scorn sweeps through his mind that does not throw its deep shadows across his face; no bright hope or light humor plays through his thoughts but looks cheerily out at his eyes; no firm resolve possesses his heart but speaks in his dilated nostril or straight-set lip; no passion burns within him but vibrates in the silvery tones of his voice. His voice, indeed, is his most perfect physical gift. It is described by those who have heard him speak as for the most part calm and measured in its tones, but with peculiar vibrations of unspeakable power, answering to the movements of scorn, indignation, pathos or pity that stir his thoughts. It has been likened, in its play of varied tones, to a peal of bells. It is such a voice as easily finds its way to the hearts of listening multitudes—such as reaches with easy compass the farthest limits of vast assemblies—such as relieves statistics of their monotony and sets argument to music. In words which the late Lord Lytton used concerning Ireland's great orator [Daniel O'Connor], we might say, when standing beneath the sounds of his voice as they rose to the rafters of Manchester's great Free Trade Hall, and fell thence on the ears of the eager listeners who filled the vast spaces of its floor:

> "And as I thought, rose the sonorous swell
> As from some church tower swings the silvery bell;
> Aloft and clear from airy tide to tide,
> It glided easy as a bird may glide.
> To the last verge of that vast audience sent,
> It played with each wild passion as it went;
> Now stirred the uproar—now the murmur stilled,
> And sobs or laughter answered as it willed.
> Then did I know what spells of infinite choice
> To rouse or lull has the sweet human voice.
> Then did I learn to seize the sudden clue
> To the grand, troublous life antique—to view
> Under the rock-stand of Demosthenes,
> Unstable Athens heave her noisy seas."

I suppose that it is Mr. Bright's supreme self-restraint that is the chief charm of his delivery. The broad and *silent* river is more suggestive of power than the hurrying, *noisy* mountain stream which every pebble makes boisterous or complaining. The deep and *quiet* breathings of the sea seem more impressive evidence of strength than the spray that is dashed on high as if the monster were shaking his huge sides with laughter. The heavy storm-cloud is more imposing and awe-striking as it sweeps the distant horizon with its quick flames, uttering its thunders in suppressed mutterings, and rolling its billowy lengths in majestic panorama before our eyes, than when it overspreads the entire sky in wild outbreak, deafening us with its sudden peals and drenching us with its hasty rains. So the orator who maintains complete sovereignty over his emotions is a thousandfold more powerful and impressive than he who "saws the air" and "tears a passion to tatters." Emotional demonstrations should come from his audience, not from the orator himself. So, we read of Mr. Bright that he seldom gesticulates; he never shouts. His passions he never allows to master him. He holds himself well in hand. Even at his moments of greatest power and most consummate achievement he is speaking calmly, but not without the deepest emotion—it is, as has been beautifully said, the calmness of white heat.

Mr. Bright's diction is as self-restrained as the orator himself. It is characterized by simple dignity and supple strength. It has none of the superb imagery or the sublime plenitude of Burke's gorgeous rhetoric; it has none of the pithy passion and "pregnant brevity" of Chatham's oratorical sword-thrusts; it has none of the smiling smoothness of Canning's bright sentences. But it has the Saxon bone and sinew. It is lithe and muscular. It is straightforward and natural, but not rugged. It is scholarly, but never pedantic. His refined taste and natural good sense put him above the silly affectation of mere rhetorical glitter. He has escaped that error which so many have allowed to possess them—the error of confounding sound with sense, of reckoning eloquence by the number of syllables. His sentences have the easy, spontaneous flow of conversation; yet they follow each other in close connection, hastening the progress of the thought and clearing the way for the apprehension. The power of his style is indisputable. Even upon the printed page it retains its sovereignty. One has but to read it to feel its charm. The periods are often unskilfully turned. The clauses are sometimes loosely thrown together. There is no dash or swiftness in the movement of the style. And yet, although you cannot always admire it from an artistic point of view, you must always allow its power to engage the attention and to lead the thoughts. It is, undoubtedly, what he says, rather than his manner of saying it, that gives him his supreme control over his hearers and his readers. Yet we are fain to admit, that nobility of sentiment seems all the more noble, strength of principle all the stronger, and mastery of thought all the more masterful when conveyed in a style of such simplicity and clearness that not crystal itself could transmit the light of thought more cloudlessly.

Mr. Bright never received a classical education. In breadth of scholarship he cannot, of course, be for a moment compared with Mr. Gladstone, with acrid Robert Lowe, with Sir William Harcourt, or with several of the more prominent and gifted Conservatives. But his attainments as an *English* scholar are preëminent. Our own language has been the special object of his untiring study. The rich stores of our own English literature he has explored with careful research. The Bible, Milton, and Shakspere have been his most constant companions. And is not this fact pregnant with suggestion? From these noble sources have come, no doubt, his simplicity of creed, his earnest morality, his singleness of principle, his steadfastness of purpose, his breadth of sympathy. From the Bible his unhesitating truthfulness and exalted sentiment; from Milton, his quiet, brave integrity; from Shakspeare, his knowledge of English human nature and his touching eloquence! His character illustrates with peculiar aptness that striking remark of Richter's: "Feelings come and go like light troops following the victory of the present; but principles, like troops of the line, are undisturbed and stand fast."

As I have already said, Mr. Bright's liberalism had attained its growth before he entered public life. His convictions were matured. His purposes were definitely formed. He started, consequently, some forty years in advance of his age—and this fact exposed him to the flings of the unthinking—to the ridicule of the majority of his countrymen, who could not keep pace with his thoughts or sympathize with his designs. Like all who have dared to anticipate the growth of wisdom, or ventured to hasten on before the slow-advancing forces of public opinion, he was assailed with the bitter taunt of *radicalism*. To this day you may hear the echoes of the fierce accusations which were long ago hurled at him by haughty, hating tories whose hatred was born of fear. You may hear heedless observers even *now* speak of John Bright as "the great radical." His voice was raised at first, as now, always in behalf of the people, and men were quick to call him "agitator" and "demagogue." No one, however, who knows anything clearly about the actual history of events in England since

the formation of the Anti-Corn-Law League can now seriously
entertain any other opinion of Mr. Bright than that his statesmanship has been as consummate as his oratory. Take down a volume
of his speeches and look over the table of subjects upon which
he has most frequently and most powerfully spoken. He has identified himself with every enlightened and subsequently triumphant view of policy both at home and abroad. Free Trade, an extended and purified suffrage, a just and liberal land system, a
perfected finance, a worthy, manly, Christian foreign and colonial policy—all have found in him a steady friend and an un-
wearied advocate. Look further than the index to his speeches.
Follow the lines of his eminently statesmanlike plans of administration—plans, almost all of which have now come to their full
harvest—and then tell me if you do not find in these at once the
seeds and fruits of an enlightened *conservatism*. Wisdom is always conservative. John Bright a demagogue and a radical! If
constant and consistent support of the policy dictated by a clearsighted liberalism, if a strenuous and unyielding opposition to the
encroachments of power, and the oppressions of prejudice, and
the tyranny of wealth, be demagogy, then has he indeed been the
chiefest of demagogues! If an early and clear recognition of those
principles of administrative reform which have now received the
sanction of law and the vindication of experience be radicalism,
then has he indeed been the fiercest of radicals. It is a matter of
demonstration that he has uniformly been found among the earliest and most ardent supporters of all those great measures
which are now regarded as the most admirable fruits of the legislation of Great Britain during the last forty years. And his view
has gone still further. He has looked beyond the present even and
has from the very beginning of his career been eager to urge and
powerful to prove essential such a change in the laws regulating
the tenure of English land as would remove the unhappy restraints of primogeniture and facilitate the breaking up of the
vast single estates which now damn England to agricultural stagnation—such a change as would make possible the creation of
numerous small estates and the existence of a large and enlarging class of small land-owners—a yeomanry not less glorious than
that of bright days of power long gone by: days when stout bow-
strings sped victorious arrows on many a field of battle—a yeomanry such as would build up old England in strength, infuse
new youth into her political system, and secure to her a fresh
lease of power and influence. Such a change must come, if England is not to die: and its coming will be but a fresh vindication

of John Bright's political prescience and far-reaching statesmanship. He is always pressing on to those great reforms which he
knows the future must bring forth.

Well, his countrymen are tardily coming to understand Mr.
Bright. Now that they have come to think in most points as he
has all his life been thinking, they cannot well *help* understanding him. He has been translated into their own thoughts and desires. The "Times" newspaper, for many years his most uncompromising foe and loudest denouncer, has now much generous
praise for the man and much genuine respect for his opinions.
But it exclaims with impatient self-complacency, that he is still
bigoted, intolerant of everything that savors of opposition to the
hitherto triumphant progress of liberal ideas! He cannot, it com-
plains, give his opponents their due meed of credit and praise.
He can see nothing good in whatsoever comes from the Conservative party. The "Times" is not far wrong. Mr. Bright *is* positive
and obstinate in his opposition to the policy of the present conservative government—to the Beaconsfieldism of these later days
of brilliant failure abroad. Tolerance is an admirable intellectual
gift: but it is little worth in politics. Politics is a war of *causes*:
a joust of principles. Government is too serious a matter to admit
of meaningless courtesies. In this grand contestation of warring
principles he who doubts is a laggard and an impotent. Shall we
condemn the statesman because in this intense strife, in which he
fights, not for empty formulas or unpractical speculations, but
for the triumph of those principles which are in his eyes vitally
essential to the welfare of the State in whose service he is spending and being spent—because in the very heat of this battle he
does not stop to weigh out careful justice to his foe? He grants
him all the privileges, he extends to him all the courtesies, of
war. He acknowledges, it may be, his integrity of character and
his uprightness of purpose. But is he to stultify himself by praising that against which he vehemently protests and strenuously
fights? Absolute identity with one's cause is the first and great
condition of successful leadership. It is that which makes the
statesman's plans clear-cut and decisive, his purposes unhesitating—it is that which makes him a leader of States and a maker
of history. I would not for a moment be understood as seeking to
lend any color of justification to that most humiliating and degrading precept, "Party, right or wrong." This is the maxim of
knaves, or of fools. The idea *I* would press upon you is as far separated from this as is the east from the west. I would urge that
entire identity with the cause—with the principle—you espouse

wherein alone abide strength and the possibility of success. Party? What is it? It is only a convenient—it may be an accidental—union of those who hold certain great leading principles in common. It is a mere outward sign of agreement. Is it the *party*, then, to which men of thought owe and pay allegiance? No. It is to the *principles*, of which party is the embodiment. The man, therefore, who adheres to any party after it has ceased to avow the principles which to him are dear and in his eyes are vital; the man who follows the leadings of a party which seems to him to be going awrong, is acting a lie, and has lost either his wit or his virtue. With wicked folly such as this Mr. Bright most assuredly cannot be changed [charged]. Never until very recent years has he acknowledged fealty to either of the great parties which divide English public opinion. Hitherto he has himself led a small detached party of progress. Only within the last few years has he announced his adherence to the Liberal party. That great party has come to adopt all the greater of those principles whose promotion has been his life-work—and now that his principles are its principles, he is a Liberal.

I have not attempted to sketch the career of John Bright. I have advisedly avoided doing so—not only because the materials for such a sketch are meagre and insufficient, but also because such a sketch would involve a review of all the political movements that have stirred England since 1840—a review which might prove tedious and would certainly too far trespass upon your patience. I have sought simply to display the more conspicuous traits of his character: to represent him as possessing in an eminent degree those qualities of eloquence and single-minded devotion which are the only lasting powers in the warfare of politics: such qualities as the great statesmen of our Revolution so gloriously exemplified; such qualities as Webster and Calhoun so nobly illustrated.

But I am conscious that there is one point at which Mr. Bright may seem to you to stand in need of defence. He was from the very first a resolute opponent of the cause of the Southern Confederacy. Will you think that I am undertaking an invidious task, if I endeavor to justify him in that opposition? I yield to no one precedence in love for the South. But *because* I love the South, I rejoice in the failure of the Confederacy. Suppose that secession had been accomplished? Conceive of this Union as divided into two separate and independent sovereignties! To the seaports of her northern neighbor the Southern Confederacy could have offered no equals; with her industries she could have maintained no rivalry; to her resources she could have supplied no parallel. The perpetuation of slavery would, beyond all question, have wrecked our agricultural and commercial interests, at the same time that it supplied a fruitful source of irritation abroad and agitation within. We cannot conceal from ourselves the fact that slavery was enervating our Southern society and exhausting to Southern energies. We cannot conceal from ourselves the fact that the Northern union would have continued stronger than we, and always ready to use her strength to compass our destruction. With this double certainty, then, of weakness and danger, our future would have been more than dark—it would have been inevitably and overwhelmingly disastrous. Even the damnable cruelty and folly of reconstruction was to be preferred to helpless independence. All this I can see at the same time that I recognize and pay loving tribute to the virtues of the leaders of secession, to the purity of their purposes, to the righteousness of the cause which they thought they were promoting—and to the immortal courage of the soldiers of the Confederacy. But Mr. Bright viewed the struggle as a foreigner. He was not intimately enough acquainted with the facts of our national history or with the original structure of our national government to see clearly the force or the justice of the doctrine of States-Rights. That doctrine to him appeared a mere subtlety—a mere word-quibble. He saw and appreciated only the general features of the struggle. Its object was none other than the severance of a union which he saw was essential to the prosperity of the South no less, nay, even more, than to the progress of the North—its severance for the avowed purpose of perpetuating an institution which *we* now acknowledge to have been opposed to the highest interests of society. Surely we cannot say that he erred in withstanding a suicidal course such as this. However much he may have mistaken the purposes of secession and the characters of its leaders—and he *did* sadly mistake these—he at least saw what *we* now see to have been to our truest interest; and no one who will examine his public utterances on the subject can fail to be convinced that he opposed the efforts of the Confederacy for the sake of the South, no less than for that of the North. He was a friend of the Union, not a partisan of the abolitionists. When others were predicting the destruction of the Union he exclaimed in sudden eloquence: "I cannot believe, for my part, that such a fate will befall that fair land, stricken though it now is with the ravages of war. I cannot believe, for my part, that civilization, in its journey with the sun, will sink into endless night in order to gratify the ambition of the leaders of this revolt, who seek to 'wade through slaughter to a throne, and shut the gates on mercy to mankind.' I have another and far brighter vision before my gaze. It may be but a vision; but I will cherish it. I see one people, and one language, and one law, and one faith over all that wide continent, the home of freedom, and a refuge for the oppressed of every race and of every clime." Have we not abundant reason to thank God that his happy vision has been realized; that union *still* binds us together in strength, and that the fresh promptings of brotherly love are leading us on to a still closer union in which all that is dark in the past shall be forgotten, all that was wrong forgiven, and the future shall be ripe with promise of achievements as yet unequalled?

I am fully aware that I have laid myself open to the charge of having pronounced an eulogy upon John Bright. I have not stopped to display those small faults of temper and those minor deflections from principle which mar his life as like faults mar every human life. I have allowed myself to believe that these things may be left out of our estimate of the great orator and statesmen without violence to justice or infidelity to truth. I have ventured to utter the few poor sentences and inadequate thoughts to which you have been so indulgent as to listen, with this single intent: that the unhesitating truthfulness, the exalted sentiment, the quiet, brave integrity, the broad sympathy, the sincere purpose, and the splendid daring of devotion which seem to adorn the character of John Bright may be to you as, I trust, they have been in some sort to myself, a pattern and an inspiration. The lesson of his life is not far to seek or hard to learn. It is, that duty lies wheresoever truth directs us; that statesmanship consists, not in the cultivation and practice of the arts of intrigue, nor in the pursuit of all the crooked intricacies of the paths of party management, but in the lifelong endeavor to lead first the attention and then the will of the people to the acceptance of truth in its applications to the problems of government; that not the adornments of rhetoric, but an absorbing love for justice and truth and a consuming, passionate devotion to principle are the body and soul of eloquence: that complete identification with some worthy cause is the first and great prerequisite of abiding success. Such are the crowning ornaments of the character of him in whom the elements are so mixed, "that Nature might stand up and say to all the world, This was a man." Such are the gifts and graces we must foster; such is the panoply of moral strength we must wear —we who are the builders of our country's future—if we are to preserve our institutions from the consuming rusts of corruption, to shield our liberties from the designs of enemies within the gates, and to set our faces towards the accomplishment of that exalted destiny which has been the happiest, brightest dream of generations lately passed away, and which may, we still may trust, be the crowning experience of generations soon to wake.

Printed in the *Virginia University Magazine*, XIX (March 1880), 354-70.

From Janet Woodrow Wilson

My precious Son,   Wilmington, N. C. March 6th [1880]
. . . I want to ask you, dear—if your father should decide that it is better that you should not return to Wilmington—that Josie & I should join you at the end of your term, instead, in Virginia—how would you like it? Your father says he has set his heart upon my taking a little trip with him late in the summer. And your Auntie[1] thinks we may get accommodations at Mrs. Fultz's, where she expects to spend the summer months—the same place they were last summer. Now, if Mrs. F. *can* accommodate us—& Josie & I were to meet you in the way proposed—and then at the proper time—say in Sep.—leave Josie with you for a little while—What do you think? How would it do? Tell me frankly. . . .
God bless you my darling. We all love you dearly—*dearly*.
Your father desired me to enclose the P. O. order for $10, you will find within.   Lovingly yours   Mother

ALS (WP, DLC) with WWhw notations on env.: "Ans." and "I believe that its solution depends upon the accident of the first arrangement of the numbers."
[1] Mrs. James W. Bones.

Notes on Professor Southall's Lecture on Constitutional Law

Lecture Tenth   3/9/80
The Congress of '76 represented distinct colonies, its members voted by states. They did not venture upon the Declaration of Independence until the members of Congress obtained special instructions and authority from their respective legislatures by which they were sent. Otherwise the Declaration of Independence would have been made at an earlier period. The Declaration of Independence is styled "In Congress 4th of July." "The unanimous Declaration of the 13 states of America." It announces that these states, as *free and independent states,* may make war, contract alliances, and do all other things that free and independent states may rightfully do. The legality of that Declaration and its substantive suc-

Reasons for thinking that the *Const.* was *formed* by the *people* of the *several states* and not by the *whole people.*

cess was proclaimed by both the preliminary and final articles of peace with the mother country, in which Geo. III (in 1783) acknowledged that the United States (naming the 13 consecutively) were free and independent states and he treated with them as such. Annual Register (1783 '84).

The Articles of Confederation were assented to by each state for itself; at first Congress voted by states. The Articles provided that no change should be made therein except with the consent of every state. Under these Articles each state retained its sovereignty and independence in the most absolute terms. The same fact is further proved by the deed (bearing date about March '84) by which Virginia ceded the Northwest Territory to the United States under terms which were accepted by Congress declaring [her to be a] sovereign state etc.

The convention which formed the present Constitution was first convoked by the *states* Maryland and Virginia. Under their invitation 5 states met at Annapolis the others having failed to attend; they recommended a general assembly of delegates from the states to meet in May '87 with view of making the necessary changes in the Constitution, and which when made had to be submitted to Congress (by the terms of the calling of the convention) and confirmed by the legislatures of every state. (See Federalist paper 39). The Act of Congress approving this call and proposing the convention made the same provision, that it was to be submitted to Congress and ratified by the states. The Convention which framed the Constitution was composed of delegates from the state legislatures and they all in this convention voted by states, each having one vote. The Constitution which was adopted under [these] terms provided "that the ratification of 9 states shall be sufficient for the establishment of this Constitution *between the states so ratifying the same.*"

Again in the attestation clause of the Constitution the language is as follows "Done in Convention by the unanimous consent of the states present, the 17th day of September in the Year of our Lord 1787 and of the Independence of the United States of America the 12th, in witness whereof we have hereunto subscribed our names etc." In 3 Dal. 199, Chief Justice [?] Chase declared that the Declaration of Independence was not one of joint and collective sovereignty but of the sovereignty of each particular state and that he regarded Virginia as being an independent sovereign state from *June 1776.*

The Constitution was referred to the conventions elected by the people for the purpose in each separate state, each convention purporting to act and to adopt the Constitution for its respective state solely. The Constitution went into practical effect as to the 11 states which adopted it in March of '89. North Carolina and Rhode Island had not then adopted the Constitution. North Carolina adopted it in 21 November '89; Rhode Island not until the 29th of May '90 so that until then they were out of the union.

In as much as the Constitution was to go into operation among any 9 states that might have adopted it, by taking the 9 smallest states it was extremely doubtful if you could have a majority of the people of the United States—and the Constitution would have been adopted by an actual minority of the people of the United States. On the other hand if 5 states had rejected it (leaving only 8) the Constitution would have failed; the 5 smallest states had a population of somewhere about 1/7 of the whole (approximately) so that near about 6/7ths of the whole voting population of the union might have voted for the Constitution and yet it might have been defeated. This shows that the Constitution was not adopted by *one people* acting as a mass for in that event a majority ought to have control, stead of 1/7th. Although the Constitution says, therefore, in its preamble "We the people of the United States" yet that phrase when read in the light of the history of the times shows that by the people was meant not one aggregate mass but the different people of each state acting for their states.

The resolution of the convention for its submission required that it should be laid *before Congress* "and be submitted to the convention delegates chosen in each state by the *people* thereof" and that each convention should indicate its action to Congress (3 Mad. Pap. 1570-1).

Transcript of WWsh classroom notes in notebook described at Feb. 5, 1880.

From Joseph Ruggles Wilson

M[y]. R[evered]. S[on].   Wilmington, [N. C.] Mar 24, '80.
. . . I am pleased that your "Bright" oration produced so fine an impression. I am not, however, surprised. Your consent to have it published was well enough. I dare say it will *read* admirably; for there are some kinds of orations which can bear the cold scrutiny of the eye: that kind, viz: which treats of historical characters and events, characters and events that are in their nature *permanent*. It is only that sort of oration which deals with the passions more than with the understanding that ought not to be subjected to the printer's ink. Of course every spoken speech must suffer, more or less, from being taken away from the thunders of utterance

and placed within the quiet book. Yet not all so suffer to an equal extent.

I have myself (as your Mother has perhaps told you) had a species of triumph on the wave of a wonderfully popular lecturing hour.[1] Enough compliments have been showered upon me to last me during the residue of my natural life.

I am glad that you have had some social enjoyment, under the Venable auspices:—and I suspect that you got more out of it than you are willing to confess! . . .

Your own most affectionate   Father

ALS (WP, DLC) with WWhw notation on env.: "Ans 3/28/80."
  [1] JRW delivered a lecture entitled "Success" before a large audience at the Wilmington Opera House on March 8, 1880. For a report, see Wilmington *Morning Star*, March 9, 1880.

A Biographical Essay

[April 1880]

Mr. Gladstone, A Character Sketch

There is something passing strange in the presumption of those who undertake to write the biographies of living men; and yet one cannot help admiring their audacity and thanking them for their doing. For there is an indescribable charm about such works. Our interest in the characters and careers of men who have, so to speak, shared our times with us, and who are still active forces in the world, is naturally livelier than those from whom we are separated by long spaces of time, whom historians have canonized, and whose memory, even in the thoughts of the vast majority of their own countrymen, is grown as dim as their biographies are dusty. These latter do not seem so nearly of our own flesh and blood. Our sympathy with men whose deeds are of the present moment, whose names are every day set in the newspapers, or vibrated along the wires with the news of the hour, is prompt; our curiosity concerning them and their doings is alert; our appetite for every bit of information regarding them is keen; and we devour what is written about them with a zest such as accompanies our perusal of few other books.

In writing a biography of Mr. Gladstone, Mr. Barnet Smith has, therefore, accomplished a work which is both indiscreet and acceptable. In publishing a work which seems to be receiving the praise of critics of every type and temper, he appears to me [to] have proved at once his intrepidity, his indelicacy, and his shrewd appreciation of the public taste. I have not yet been able to obtain a copy of Mr. Smith's book; but, following afar off the example of Gibbon, who represents himself as always, before opening any book which he was about to read, sitting himself down to write all that he knew and thought about the subject of which it treated; and that also of Mr. John Morley, who, himself in imitation of Gibbon, prepared his mind for the perusal of Trevelyan's Life of Macaulay by writing his admirable essay on the character and genius of the brilliant historian, I sit down to formulate the few crude impressions which have been made upon my mind by the character and career of the great member for Midlothian.

Every one is, of course, more or less familiar with the principal events of Mr. Gladstone's life. Rumors, at least, of so large a career must have found their way to every corner of the world where any news is ever allowed to come. One could hardly avoid knowing the main outlines of a life which has filled and is filling so large a space in the history of so great a nation as our kinsmen beyond the sea. And news of Mr. Gladstone has long been peculiarly abundant. Even the editors of country newspapers, in displaying to their admiring readers the political situation of England, with all the temerity of ignorance and all the wordy reserve of those who are under the driving necessity of filling space without saying anything, handle his name with careless familiarity. His fame has introduced him into the pages of a novel, even, where his name has, doubtless, smiled to find itself.

Mr. Gladstone has himself done much to acquaint the whole English-speaking world with his thoughts and purposes. Literary labors have filled all the intervals of his active work in Parliament and on the hustings. He has written almost as incessantly as he has spoken—has written not only upon themes political, but upon problems of physics, subtle questions of literary criticism, debatable church dogmas, clouded ecclesiastical history, and mooted matters of ethics as well. He has spread all the lineaments of his mind upon printed pages. One might, I suppose, trace all the principal steps of his mental progress in his published writings, beginning with the essay on Church and State and coming down to his latest contribution to the discussion of the borough franchise. For through all these writings run sincerity and candor, like the outcroppings of veins of precious ore. He never clouds his convictions with vague expressions. No one is more fearless than he in emphasizing the variance between the mature liberalism of his age and the idealistic toryism of his youth. And it is just this transparent candor and thoroughgoing good faith that make what he has written so valuable an aid in the study of his character.

His occasional and miscellaneous writings have recently been collected and published in a set of neat little volumes entitled "Gleanings of Past Years." The publication of a series of essays from the pen of a great living statesman would under any circumstances be a notable event in the literary world. We turn to the perusal of such writings with the eagerness and zeal which naturally spring from the interest we have learned to feel in their author as we have watched his conspicuous career and traced his ruling influence in the counsels of his country. And, indeed, Mr. Gladstone's essays are not of such a character as to win very wide popularity entirely on their own intrinsic merits. They borrow greatness from the hand that wrought them. Mr. Gladstone's written style is ponderous. It has little of that bright glow which so lights up and beautifies his speeches; there is none of the swift strength and conquering dash which are the power of his oratory. It is at once a curious and an instructive fact to students of many of the greater orators, that the mastery of thought, of expression, and of method which makes their onset so terrible and their influence so imperial on the platform or in the Senate, deserts them in the closet; and they take up their pens only to multiply stiff phrases and awkward periods. That Mr. Gladstone is not without power even in the use of the pen is abundantly proven by the moving and moulding influence of his great political pamphlets; and these recently collected literary miscellanies have much strength both of thought and of rhetoric. But, as compared with his speeches, they seem of small value; and we are, therefore, inclined at first to think that they might, without risk of injustice, be neglected in our estimate of his intellectual gifts. They are as immeasurably inferior to his many masterful speeches in the House of Commons as is Charles Fox's "History of England" to his great argument on the Westminster Scrutiny.

Still, their value as contributions to the question to which they relate is unquestionable; and their value as contributions to his mental history is, as I have already intimated, inestimable. We would by no means be willing to lose even these lesser works of the greatest English Liberal. They throw a side light upon his character which adds much to its distinctness. His character is one of such grand proportions, of so complex a structure, and of so unique a build that we cannot fully appreciate it until we have viewed it from both sides, and in all lights. And I do not know of any one among modern statesmen whose character is worthier of the study and the imitation of the young men of a free country than is Mr. Gladstone's. His life has been one continuous advance,

not towards power only—fools may be powerful; knaves sometimes
rule by the knack of their knavery—but towards truth also the
while.

William Ewart Gladstone was born in Liverpool in the year
1809. He comes of sturdy Scotch stock; and his mind and body
alike are cast out of strong Scotch stuff. We can easily imagine
what sort of youth his was. He must have been a sober, thoughtful
boy, full of spirits without being boisterous; eager and impetuous
without being imperious; a leader in sport as in study; straight-
forward in everything, even in his hatreds; half-souled in nothing,
not even in his faults. He is old now; he is turned of seventy, and
these are still the leading traits of his character—traits which bear
the ratification of a long and intensely-lived life; which may almost be said to bear the seal of completion. For his active life
may reasonably be thought to be rapidly nearing its close. And
it is because we thus stand near his grave that we may venture
an estimate of his character. The few years that remain to him
cannot materially change a character which has been a-making
for seventy years of busy living.

And just here we seem to have happened upon the chiefest and
most instructive peculiarity of his career: his convictions have
steadily grown towards truth, as the flower grows towards the sun;
his character has developed and gathered strength year by year
and day by day, slowly, as the oak waxes great and strong. He has
all his life been *a-making*. His character will not be entirely complete until death has placed the capstone.

It has been remarked as an interesting circumstance that the
county Lancashire has produced three of the most eminent English statesmen of later years, the late Earl Derby, Mr. Gladstone,
and Mr. Bright; and it may, further, prove worthy of at least a
passing notice that these three men have each typified in his career
a prominent phase of later political history. Lord Derby was a
living type of that reäction against liberalism which followed upon
the accomplishment of the first decisive measures of parliamentary reform and the repeal of the Corn Laws. Sprung from a
family all of whose traditions were strongly Whig, he was among
the first to join the revolt against triumphant Whigism. Mr. Gladstone's career from its first chapter to its last, illustrates the breaking away of the older forms of English Conservatism and the advance of English public opinion to higher plains of principle and
freer and more rational methods of policy. In his youth an unbending Tory, he stands in his old age in the forefront of liberalism. Mr. Bright, in his freedom of faculty, his fearless spirit of in-

quiry, and his creed of common-sense, is a conspicuous type of the spirit of the England of to-day.

Perhaps the most vital characteristic of Mr. Gladstone's nature is his keen poetical sensibility. By poetical sensibility I do not mean an imaginativeness which clothes all the common concerns of life with poetical forms or weds the mind to those things which are picturesque rather than to matters of practical business, to fancies rather than to the interests of ordinary everyday life, to images rather than to fertile purposes. I mean, rather, breadth of sympathy such as enables its possessor to take in the broader as well as the pettier concerns of life, with unconscious ease of apprehension and unfailing precision of judgment; to identify himself with interests far removed from the walks of his own life; to throw himself, as if by instinct, on that side of every public question which, in the face of present doubts, is in the long run to prove the side of wisdom and of clearsighted policy; such a sympathy as makes a knowledge of men in him an *intuition* instead of an experience. Such a faculty is preëminently poetical, raising men above experience, as it seems to do, and enabling them to guide the policy of a government, almost before they can be truly said to have learned to manage the affairs of their own households. And yet it is quite as evidently an intensely practical faculty. Great statesmen seem to direct and rule by a sort of power to put themselves in the place of the nation over whom they are set, and may thus be said to possess the souls of poets at the same time that they display the coarser sense and the more vulgar sagacity of practical men of business.

Had Mr. Gladstone not been endowed with these peculiarities of disposition, he would in all probability have remained unknown to the world, obscurely intrenched behind the unqualified dogmas of his early toryism, whence no one in the hurry of the liberal triumphs which have since been accomplished would have troubled himself to dislodge him. His early education was such, one would have thought, as totally to unfit him for active participation in public affairs. Six years he had spent at Eton in the study of Horace, Virgil and Homer. By the latter all the poetical depths of his nature were strongly stirred. In the superb imagery of the blind bard, and in his vigorous sympathy with man and with nature, young Gladstone's mind found what was but fuel to its own flames. From Eton he went to Oxford and there passed through further drill in the classics and the abstract mathematics. From Oxford he went almost immediately to Parliament. He entered public life with no experience but in poetical feeling and in abstract thought, and with no opinions but those of stubborn conservatism in which he had from his early youth been schooled by his father. He launched himself in public life by writing a pamphlet which was at once a manifestation of his poetical feeling and a vindication of his traditionary tory principles. In this pamphlet he sought to bolster up the union of Church and State by founding it upon a divine foreordination which had constituted the State a moral being, in conscience bound to uphold the true faith by the strength of its temporal arm and to aid in the dissemination of the verities of the true religion by the sanction of its laws and the active coöperation of its ministers. But he did not allow himself to remain long bound by the shackles which he had forged for himself, and for all who might be ready to follow him, in his argument on Church and State. He had commenced life with predilections simply, not with intelligent convictions. His first contact with the cooler atmosphere of practical politics, however, roused him to a new activity. His idealistic theories of state action were dispelled by the necessity for resolving the actual problems of administration as mists are chased from the valleys by the sun.

Mr. Gladstone's mind embodies in strange, and on the whole grand, combination the faculty of poetic sympathy which I have already indicated and the colder qualities of reason. His reason leads and his catholic sympathy impels. When once contact with the practical problems of government had begun to break away the foundations of his early ardent, air-built theories, the progress of transition was rapid and certain. He came gradually to allow full credit to the severe and inexorable processes of his keenly logical mind. And as soon as his mind was awakened his sympathetic affections enlisted his whole nature in the search after truth, fusing his reasonings and communicating their heat to the powers of his will. He was fairly launched on his voyage towards the farthest waters of liberalism. His future course was inevitable. Henceforward he became the embodiment of the liberal tendencies of his nation.

The stages of this development are easy to trace. As long as Mr. Gladstone remained a "private member" of the House of Commons, speaking from the back benches, unemployed in solving the practical problems of actual administration, left to the guidance of his uncorrected, untutored theories, he continued wedded to his speculative opinions. For nine years, from 1832 to 1841, he stood steadily by that transcendental theory of government which, in 1838, he published to the world in his pamphlet on Church and State. For a few months in 1834 he had held office as under-secretary for the colonies in the short-lived, make-shift ministry of Sir Robert Peel. But this short experience has not been sufficient to break in upon his speculations. During this period of preparation, we find him withstanding with his usual vehement determination all attacks on the property of the Irish Church, setting his face sternly against the abolition of religious tests in the Universities, and opposing with consistent zeal the removal of the civil disabilities of the Jews. Whenever his carefully avowed opinions were put to the test, he was ready to uphold them to the last iota.

But in 1841 he was called to the duties of active administration, taking office under Sir Robert Peel, first as Vice-President and later, as President of the Board of Trade. He was rudely shaken from his reveries by the urgent duties and active business of his official trust. The education of his youth—the education of the schools—was corrected by the education of hard work. The student was awakened to the actual direction of practical affairs. His abstract theories broke at once and completely down. Actual contact with urgent, crowding questions of practical legislation roused his mind from its ideal fancies and addressed it to the real work of government. Among the measures introduced by the ministry of Sir Robert Peel were what are known as the Maynooth College grant and the Queen's University Bill. The Maynooth Bill proposed to add to the grant which had already been made to the Roman Catholic College of Maynooth, an institution founded specially for the education of young men for the Roman Catholic priesthood; the Queen's University Bill embraced a scheme for "establishing in Ireland three colleges, one in Cork, the second in Belfast and the third in Galway, and to affiliate these to a new University to be called the 'Queen's University in Ireland.' The teaching in these colleges was to be purely secular." Manifestly both these measures were utterly incompatible with the pronounced convictions of the young President of the Board of Trade. The first proposed to extend the aid of the State to the maintenance of a religion which was not its own—which had for generations been at open enmity with that Church which he had declared it to be the sacred duty of the State to cherish and maintain to the exclusion of every other; the second founded what the opponents of the scheme derisively denominated "godless colleges" under the care and sanction of public law. The first gave support to an alien church; the second excluded all religion from a State institution. Upon the introduction of these measures into Parliament, Mr. Gladstone immediately resigned his position in the Cabinet. But he supported both bills. He had resigned not because he could not give his assent to the actions of his colleagues, but because he wished his change of opinion to be raised above all suspicion of interested motives. He wished to proclaim his change of ground and at the same time to demonstrate his own sincerity. He would not have it thought that his convictions were altered from love of office. He was convinced, not seduced. The fact [is] that his roused faculties had discovered to him the fact that his former position was no longer tenable. He found his principles irreconcilably at war with all the stronger tendencies, with all the healthier impulses of the day. And he quickly and bravely acknowledged the discovery. "He was not," he protested, "to fetter his judgment as a member of Parliament by a deference to abstract theories." Upon this ground his mind began its searchings and fearless examination of all the principles he had hitherto confessed. Once enlisted in this pursuit of truth his eager mind found it impossible to stop at half measures. He cut himself loose, not suddenly but surely, from the preconceived prejudices of his inexperienced years and addressed himself to the task of rational resolution of the problems of government. As far as I can see, the transition was a short one. His liberalism matured and strengthened rapidly. He at once placed himself at the side of those men against whom he had heretofore contended. His conversion was not an isolated one. He left the Conservative ranks with his great master, Sir Robert Peel. He had joined Peel in dealing the blow of Free Trade at the tories; and both men alike now fell under the hatred of the "betrayed" party. Their companionship in liberalism would probably have been continued had not death put a sudden period to the life of the master, and left the pupil to the devices of his own mind.

Mr. Gladstone exhibited at every turn his changed views. In 1841 he strenuously opposed the Ecclesiastical Titles Bill, which forbade Roman Catholic Bishops to assume local titles within the kingdom, as a silly act of mere intolerance. In 1852 he took office, as Chancellor of the Exchequer, in the Aberdeen Coalition ministry, sitting beside Russell and Palmerston. Later, from 1860-1866, he devoted his magnificent financial talents to the service of a thorough-going Liberal administration, carrying out the economical policy of the party whose principles had now finally enlisted him in its service, in a series of budgets unrivalled in their display of knowledge and ability. And finally, within our own easy recollection, from November, 1868, to February, 1874, he, as Prime Minister, led Parliament through that period of magnificent legislation during which the Irish Church was disestablished; the tenure of Irish land was made freer and juster; cheap education was secured to all the population of the kingdom; purchase in the army, with all its attendant abuses and corruption was abolished; the endowed schools were reformed and reconstructed; religious tests were done finally away with at the Universities; and all the serious complications of foreign affairs were amicably and honorably resolved— a period which enthusiastic liberals have, not without some show of truth, exultingly called the "golden period" of English liberalism.

Many persons would be inclined to reckon his an inconsistent course. I cannot so regard it. His career seems to me to have been what it has been principally because of the unhesitating logic of his mind and the simple candor of his nature. When he had been roused from the dreams and speculations of his student mood, and had begun to think and act in the temper of a practical man of business, his keen perceptions, his quiet determination, and his resolute conscientiousness irresistibly urged him to the acceptance of the farthest conclusions of his reason. Few men stand in their old age where they stood in their youth. The untested opinions of the early life do not always or often stand the trial of experience. In public life especially, so varied and varying are the conditions of government, their purposes must be trimmed to possibilities. Men who have early given their undivided attention to practical affairs and who enter public life, if they enter it at all, long after the temper and habits of the schools, have worn off, are generally among the few who begin their career with fixed opinions and matured convictions, which no change of circumstance can alter, and no discouragement defeat. Such a man was Richard Cobden; such a man is John Bright. The latter has passed through a long period of public service with unaltered views, and has lived to see his earliest avowed principles receive the amplest vindication and the fullest ratification. And yet his career has in reality fewer elements of grandeur, no greater flavor of sincerity, and no more of the rigor of consistency than distinguish Mr. Gladstone's life. The contrast between these two men is a remarkable and instructive one. The resemblances between their characters are equally interesting. Both are preëminent in eloquence; both are conspicuous for the noble sincerity and high-strung morality of their characters; both are engaged heart and soul in the pursuit of the highest interests of their country; and both find these interests wrapped up in the principles of the Liberal party which they lead. But, though they both now stand together in close friendship and common leadership, they have reached their present position by very different, widely-separated, ways. Their minds are of different cast. Mr. Gladstone has reasoned his way to the light; Mr. Bright seems to have been born in the light. Mr. Bright began in practice, Mr. Gladstone in study. Study has brightened and expanded Mr. Bright's faculties; practice has collected and concentrated and directed Mr. Gladstone's powers. The one is a man of intuitions, arriving at his conclusions apparently without the aid of laborious processes of ratiocination; the other is a man of large heart and larger reason, quickly and fearlessly, though carefully and cautiously, following the steps of his logic. The one has been all along advanced; the other, advancing. The one has led—led thought; the other has commanded—commanded legislatures and cabinets.

The question of consistency is not a question of absolute fixedness of opinion. One can hardly help pitying one who is incapable of changing his opinions; though, of course, it is scarcely less difficult to withhold one's admiration from that man who has all along adopted the conclusions of truth. It seems to me that right and truth are the proper standards in this matter. He who proves his mind so free from the shackles of prejudice and the blinds of bigotry as to be ready at every turn to abandon its former positions of error or mistake for the new positions of truth and right, and who, moreover, follows the leadings of his progressing convictions without thought of turning back, is no less consistent—consistent with the true standards of consistency—than is he who has from the first occupied the advanced posts of inquiry whither the other has just arrived. If immutability of belief be the criterion of consistency, then let us taunt scientists with fickleness because their investigations have brought them far beyond where they were, even within the short memory of men; let us sneer at all governments which are not despotisms; let us laugh at civilization because it did not stop in the darkness of the middle ages.

Our own century, though perhaps not so deeply scarred by revolutions as many of those which have preceded it, has been richer than they in true political progress. Old systems have been purified; new systems have been set up. Europe has already gone far towards the abandonment of her old despotisms. Austria and Hungary are struggling towards the full and final establishment of free institutions, based upon a limitation of royal power; Germany has vested in a freely elected representative body much real authority; France is experiencing for the first time in her history, and after many blind searchings for liberty, the blessings of a rational system of government, which, though defective in parts, is based upon well-tested principles; even the hideous outbreaks of violence by which Russian nihilism is disgracing itself are manifestations of a revolt against absolutism which has the germs of honorable patriotism in it. In England reform has made such rapid strides that the Conservatives of to-day stand about where the Liberals, or Whigs, of fifty years ago stood. Parliamentary representation has been thoroughly reformed; the suffrage has been extended as far as prudence permitted; the prerogatives of the Crown seem to have been finally hedged about with every safeguard that the most suspicious patriot could demand; commerce has been freed from harassing restrictions; in everything English statesmen seem to have turned their faces towards the light of practical wisdom instead of hiding them longer in the darkness of prejudice. And it is just this spirit of advance, this emancipation from the narrow views of policy which have heretofore too often influenced British legislation, which is, as I have already said, typified in Mr. Gladstone's career. Once an eloquent advocate of the union of Church and State, he has himself disestablished the Church of Ireland, and startled his countrymen with hints of the advisability and probable necessity of separating the Church of England from the Crown; at one time an unbending tory, he has assisted in rudely breaking down some of the most cherished principles of the tory creed by the establishment of free trade; he has flung tolerance in their intolerant faces; he has overwhelmed their schemes of extended dominion by proving them plans of multiplying the burdens of an already overburdened kingdom; he has laughed to scorn the doctrine that concessions to foreign powers when England is in the wrong are inconsistent with British dignity; that only arrogant pretensions are consistent with British prestige; that England is to interpose in behalf of tyranny and despotism whenever Russia, or any other one of her "natural enemies," espouses the cause of self-government and freedom. And in all these things he has been true to his principles. Not even his bitterest foes have ever breathed any suspicion of his insincerity. His aim has always been to serve justice and truth, and in his search for these he has not hesitated or been ashamed to abandon the crude theories of his youth for the more rational principles to which the experience of his maturer years has brought him.

It is hard satisfactorily to analyze such a character as Mr. Gladstone's. Its structure is so complex that one is puzzled to know where its mainspring is to be found. His mind has all the indescribable attributes of genius, and consequently baffles all investigation of its constitution. Some clue to its qualities might be found in the subjects of study to which he has most constantly

devoted his attention. The poems of Homer, as they were the companions of his Eton days, have also been the objects of his life-
long study. He has pondered nothing more thoroughly than the
conceptions of the blind bard, whose creations are to him as real
as though they were flesh and blood. He seems to have found exquisite enjoyment in exploring the recondite subtleties of the
Greek language, and inexhaustible pleasure in the possession of
that "golden key that could unlock the treasures of antiquity, of
a musical and prolific language that gives a soul to the objects of
sense, and a body to the abstractions of philosophy." He has undoubtedly found in this harmonious instrument of thought a spirit
akin to his own. It is his power to give "a soul to the objects of
sense" that has made him one of the greatest financiers the world
has produced; and it is his capacity for giving a body, not to the
abstractions of philosophy, but to the higher impulses of the English race that has given him his power on the platform and his
preëminence in Parliament.

It is only by indirect clues such as this that we can find our
way to the secrets of a nature such as Mr. Gladstone's. For the
principal qualities of his mind are warrior qualities—the qualities
which display themselves in action. We know little clearly of the
characters of the great soldiers of history, save only their battle-
field traits. It is what they did rather than what they were that
constitutes their fame. So Mr. Gladstone's life has been eminently
one of bold action, and it is by his deeds that we are obliged to
read the character of the doer. His mind is habitually militant,
and all that he has written and said, save only his Homeric criticisms, has been written and said not so much to communicate
thoughts as to urge arguments and impart purposes. His has been
a greatness of deed, a greatness embodied in acts of Parliament
and measured by epochs of national progress; a greatness of imperial administrative talent and of sovereign constructive ability.
Of course the greatness is in the man himself and it is his nature
which thus towers above the ordinary level of mankind. It is the
grandeur of the statesman that makes his statesmanship grand,
just as, to liken the finite to the infinite, it is the sublimity of the
divine power that gives grandeur to the works of nature. It is Mr.
Gladstone's lofty qualities of heart, his earnest and practical piety,
and his magnificent gifts of intellect that lend distinguished merit
to his acts of legislation. But men find it hard to separate him from
what he has done just as they find it hard to know anything of
Wellington but that he won Waterloo, or of Marlborough than
that he won Blenheim. And when one sits down, pen in hand, to

write of the character of a great statesman his view is apt to be confined to volumes of statutes and Minutes of Parliamentary proceedings. This genius of acting is no more to be defined than it is to be acquired. And so far are we from being able to appreciate the nature of men from what we see them do in public, that we are surprised to learn that Macaulay had intense domestic affections and was capable of romping with children and of devoting himself to the quiet, unpretentious offices of love in the service of his sister—that he did anything but entertain others with brilliant passages of conversation, bright, incisive essays, overflowing with information and keen criticism, and with picturesque history, full of paradox tricked out in charming rhetoric. So far are we from being able to interpret the characters of men by the greater works of their hands, that we seem to see only the sterner, more practical side of Mr. Gladstone's nature when we regard only his public acts, and find it next to impossible to conceive of him as calming his leisure moments by drawing forth soothing harmony from an organ, as busying his great mind, in intervals of rest, with the practical work of a farm—as doing anything but gravely deliberating upon the great affairs of national administration or passing busy nights in Parliament in the eager contest of debate or the earnest work of legislation.

If, because of the masterful success of his financial administration and the consummate ability of his government, we do not wonder that his countrymen have accorded Mr. Gladstone a prominent place among the very first of English statesmen, still less can we be surprised, in view of his wonderful gifts, that he has won a place among the greatest orators. If the passionate intensity, which enters so largely into the texture of his character, lends so much of force, so much brilliant boldness, to his plans of administration, what overwhelming power it must impart to his oratory! Passion is the pith of eloquence. Not the passion which hurries into extravagance, nor that which spends itself in vehement utterance and violent gesticulation, but that which stirs the soul with enthusiasm for the truth and zeal for its proclamation. It is this that marks the difference between the accomplished speaker and the consummate orator. The difference lies not so much in the diversity of intellectual gift as in the texture of soul. Both England and America are full of good speakers. Every country where discussion holds a place as one of the chief factors of government and where the lecture platform and the electoral hustings, as well as the pulpit and the bar, afford ample opportunity for the cultivation and display of the art of public speech, can boast hosts of pleasing and popular speakers. But in the United States no man is now recognized as the greatest orator in the nation, no one has had to fall upon his shoulders the mantle of Henry, of Clay, or of Webster; and in England only two of a nation of lawyers and of public men are universally acknowledged to have had their lips touched with the fire of the highest eloquence. In this rare preëminence Mr. Bright and Mr. Gladstone stand alone, differing from other orators not in felicity of rhetoric, purity of diction, and mastery of thought, so much as in mental temper. As steel differs from steel in temper, so are the minds of these men of finer metal than those of their rivals in oratory. The instrument they use is not a keen rapier of wit, which can cut floating veils of fancy with delightful skill, or flash the sharp destruction of satire from its burnished blade—such are the tricks of Beaconsfield's brilliant oratory; nor is it of the ordinary steel of striking rhetoric, sharp phrase, and keen argument—of such are the weapons which Robert Lowe and Sir William Harcourt employ. It is a two-edged sword that can split fine hairs of distinction with no less precision than it can search out the heart of an opponent's plea, that can make the dexterous passes of dialectic fence with the same readiness with which it can cleave the defences of prejudice.

It is as an orator that Mr. Gladstone most forcibly appeals to our imaginations. He has certainly been one of the most prolific of English orators. The streams of his eloquence are perennial. His speeches extend their influence beyond the hour of their speaking, their charm beyond the tones of the speaker's voice. They move when read only less than they moved when heard. Even when set in the cold and quiet print they seem full of life and warmth and vigor. When reading a report of one of his great arguments one seems to catch the spirit of the "cheers" which break the column with their parentheses, and to hear echoed plaudits in his own heart. It is not every one, however, I imagine, that would enjoy a perusal of Mr. Gladstone's speeches. A literary critic could scarcely commend their structure; tastes of superrefinement and exalted ideals would hardly find room for admiration of their plans. Theirs is not the beauty of form or of movement, of grace or of symmetry; but the beauty of grand proportions and of rugged strength—that beauty which approaches to grandeur: to a grandeur which is not the grandeur of art but the grandeur of nature. To one who can enter into the spirit of that keen warfare between principles, the warfare of political discussion, there is real music in these speeches—more than in the measured beauty of Ruskin's exquisite style or in the bolder strains of Canning's ornate rhetoric. For one whose imagination is roused more quickly by the tread of armies and the strokes of the sword in battle than by the quiet loveliness of green fields or the majestic sweep of some silent river which does not rebel against its banks, these speeches must possess a powerful attraction. The progress of Mr. Gladstone's arguments is like the sweeping flight of an eagle from crag to crag and summit to summit.

The style of these speeches is peculiar—peculiarly vicious according to the judgment of some. Certainly it is not a style such as would provoke imitation. The sentences, most of them, are long, clause being heaped on clause, parenthesis added to parenthesis, until the very skill of the orator in extricating himself successfully and grammatically excites our wondering admiration. Their strength is a compound strength: the strength of accumulated force. Every now and then, however, the light and heat of these sentences are focused in a single phrase: their meaning concentrated in one short period which must have struck the hearer like a sudden blow. And the meaning of the orator shines clearly through his most involved sentences. They sometimes seem interminable, but they seldom seem obscure. They are powerful weapons in Mr. Gladstone's hands; they could scarcely be handled by any other. Bruce's sword was powerful to work destruction in Bruce's hands; to others its weight would have been but a burden. I suppose that these massive sentences are the natural extemporaneous expression of a mind which is full to overflowing.

But Mr. Gladstone's spoken style is not uniform—not uniform even in its defects, still less in its beauties. His genius as an orator most conspicuously manifests itself in his power of adapting his style to the audience he is addressing. One day he is speaking to a meeting of the most intelligent and learned members of his constituency, and his style is one of measured calmness, his treatment following the leadings of a strict, though eloquent, logic. The next day, perhaps, he meets the farmers of the country side upon the hustings, and the style is changed. It is aflame with earnest persuasion and glowing with passionate sentiment. He is speaking like an Englishman to Englishmen, with eager patriotism and a fire of high resolve. He is convincing his hearers by persuading them. There is always, however, whatever the audience he is addressing, the same foundation of conviction and the same transparency of truth. Though the treatment be diverse, there is no diversity in the beliefs, no crookedness in the counsels, of the orator. The soil may differ, now spread in calm beauty, now piled in great heights, but under all and supporting all are the primitive, unchanging granite veins of conviction.

According to all accounts, the delivery of the orator is in keeping with the style of the orations, is chiefly marked by its power. The personal appearance of the speaker strikes the eye. A London correspondent of the Philadelphia *Press* has thus happily described Mr. Gladstone as he looks since age has begun to creep upon him: "In personal appearance Mr. Gladstone is an active, lithe, muscular man, rather tall, and of well-proportioned frame. His face and figure have that clear-cut contour which generally indicates several generations of intellectual activity and personal leadership. . . .[1] The face is scholarly, cultivated, its outlines boldly defined by the meagreness of muscle which distinguishes the intellectual athlete. There is not an ounce of superfluous flesh on it. The thin lip and wee cut mouth and chin betoken firmness, determination, and endurance. Seventy summers have sat lightly on him, but the years have brought their blessing of rest, and his face in general wears the repose of strength and experience, strongly lined with the record of struggle and thought." I do not suppose that photographs and engravings can convey any very faithful portraiture of such a face. Still all photographs of Mr. Gladstone display the same general cast of feature, and satisfy more or less precisely the description of the correspondent. It is altogether a remarkable face, and the features seem such as would be modified by every current of feeling. The deep eye and quivering muscles answer to every tone of the marvellous voice. If Bright's voice rings like a peal of bells, Gladstone's pierces like a trumpet call or thrills with tones like an organ's.

Upon the hustings Mr. Gladstone overwhelms opposition and seldom fails to compel victory. Once or twice he has had to meet vast assemblages of excited and angered men on Blackheath, who greeted him with jeers and hisses; but never did he fail to change their jeers into cheers, their hisses into applause, their anger into enthusiasm, their enmity into support. At first his voice was raised in accents of conciliation which calmed the passions of his hearers as they rung out above all the fierce vociferations of excited hatred; at last the same voice's calls of command and persuasion were borne aloft above the resounding echoes of redoubled cheers. The exordium broke like harshest discord on the ears of the listeners; to the peroration their own approving cheers were the inspiring refrain.

[1] Elision WW's.

But it is in Parliament that Mr. Gladstone's eloquence is said to be most masterful. There his victories have been unnumbered, his first triumph dating from that memorable night in November, 1852, which has so often been the theme of description; that night when first he was pitted against Disraeli in the direct combat of debate; that night on which, by one splendid leap, he attained to the highest achievements of eloquence. The memory of that night must often recur to men who then sat in Parliament as among their most stirring recollections. It was an occasion of crisis. In February, 1852, the government of Lord John Russell had been broken by the clash of factions in the House of Commons. The storms of 1847, when the great Free Trade victory had been won, had not yet cleared finally away, and Parliament was divided into several hostile and jarring parties: into Peelites, protectionists and Whigs. Even in the Whig ranks there was defection and division. Palmerston had been dismissed from the Foreign Office and driven into opposition. Ever since the entrance of the Russell ministry into office their administration had been characterized by hesitation, vacillation, and general ineffectiveness. Their fall in February, 1852, was, therefore, natural, though at the time not generally expected. They were succeeded by a ministry under the leadership of Lord Derby, in which Mr. Disraeli held the office of Chancellor of the Exchequer and fulfilled the functions of leader of the House of Commons. But if Lord John Russell had been harrassed by the cross fire of irreconcilable factions, much more was Lord Derby fettered by the uncertain support of a make-shift coalition. An appeal was taken to the country in behalf of the new government, and the new government was condemned. The new Parliament met in November, 1852. It speedily became evident that the new ministers must go. The first important business of the session was Mr. Disraeli's financial statement. Driven about by the winds of faction, anxious to conciliate two discordant interests, that of the tory farmers who were clamoring for protection, and that of the Free Traders who were demanding a formal sanction of their policy, the Chancellor of the Exchequer submitted a budget which satisfied nobody. He was immediately attacked by an overwhelming force of Free Traders, Whigs and Peelites, and the great debate to which I have alluded set in. It has been described as a splendid display. On that November night, in a House full to overflowing with eager and excited listeners—members who were unable to find seats on the floor, gathering without the bar or in the galleries of the House—Mr. Gladstone won his first great victory over his life-long opponent. Mr. Disraeli had spoken long and with consummate skill: with all the vigor of desperation and all the eloquence of determination. It was past midnight, the clock upon the towers of St. Stephen's had struck the hour of two, when Mr. Gladstone, without previous preparation, sprang to the floor to answer him. The cheers which had followed Mr. Disraeli's strangely powerful defence had scarcely died away when Mr. Gladstone rose. It would be a bold pen indeed that would essay a description of the place and the scene. And yet it was a scene upon which the imagination would fain linger. The hall of the House of Commons is not a large one. The cushioned benches on which the members are crowded rise in close series on either side of a central aisle at one end of which stands the Speaker's chair. Below his chair are the seats of the clerks and the broad table at either side of which, on the front benches nearest the Speaker, sit the Ministry, and the leaders of the Opposition, the former to the Speaker's right, the latter to his left. Above the rear benches and over the outer aisles of the House, beyond "the bar," hang deep galleries. It seems a place intended for hand to hand combat; and on that chill, damp November morning, it witnessed a combat such as had seldom awakened its echoes before. The slender form of the eager orator rose in striking outline and bold relief from amidst the mass of earnest, upturned faces; from amongst the figures bent in postures of absorbed attention; from beneath the forms which leaned from the galleries as if intent to lose not one syllable of the speaker's rushing speech, not one accent of the voice which was ringing its magnificent changes on the sentiments of his heart. For two hours did that marvellous voice fill the crowded spaces with its silvery vibrations, now breaking the hushed stillness of the chamber with its stirring tones, anon raising its clearer peals above the resounding cheers of the fired audience. The orator's own apparent calmness was in strange contrast with the strong excitement of his hearers. His eye was touched, no doubt, with fire, and his lips livid with expression in their quivering partings; but his nerves were steadied like iron; only an occasional twitching of the muscles of his face to indicate the stupendous movings of the spirit within. It seems to have been with him one of those supreme moments when all the nervous tremors of self-consciousness are gone from the presence of the exalting and transforming inspiration of a cause. If Mr. Disraeli had dazzled, Mr. Gladstone had triumphed. The House divided about four o'clock, and the government was left in a minority of nineteen.

This was, as I have said, the first of Mr. Gladstone's great oratorical triumphs. It won for him an undisputed primacy among

English orators. Afterwards Englishmen came to regard John . Bright as the greatest of English orators; but by none other in his own day, if even by him, has Mr. Gladstone been eclipsed. Gladstone and Bright will probably be remembered by future generations as peers, rather than as rivals, in eloquence. Certainly no man was ever more unfailingly and uniformly eloquent than Mr. Gladstone. Even during his service as Prime Minister, when the requirements of the daily conduct of business in the House of Commons called him daily and hourly to his feet, his reputation for eloquence never dimmed. His very explanations of matters of dry routine business made members turn interested and attentive towards himself. His poetic sensibilities manifested themselves here in communicating to matters of form and legislative detail, the life and light of his own mind. If he was sometimes betrayed by the very facility with which he could speak into weary lengths of explanation and perplexing fullness of statement, there were at least corresponding lengths of interest and compensating plenitude of illustration. He seemed sometimes to waste his riches on trivial subjects; but when the subject was great the orator was supreme. He exalted matters of detail; but he at least never failed to master in all their breadth and scope the great concerns of national legislation and to magnify his consummate powers by the skill of his dealings with the weightier interests of the great empire he was set to rule.

The astonishing achievements and successes of Mr. Gladstone's Midlothian campaign—the news of whose triumphant issue has just reached us as I write—seem a fitting culmination to his career as a statesman. His party is victorious and the very mention of his name is cheered by vast mass-meetings in every part of the kingdom. Beaconsfield is beaten; the brilliant reign of charlatanry is at an end; and the future lies with that great party whose loved and trusted leader is Mr. Gladstone. Providence has been pleased to brighten his declining years with a new assurance of victory to the cause in whose name he has spent the magnificent energies of his nature; and if this be the last work of his life, surely no happier time could come for the closing scenes of the career of a man whose fame has not been bounded by continents or seas; whose works have been the works of progress; whose impulses have been the impulses of nobility; whose purposes have been the purposes of patriotism; whose days have been blessed by a genius which has been fired by devotion, tempered by discretion, purified by piety, and sanctified by love.   Atticus.

Printed in the *Virginia University Magazine*, xix (April 1880), 401-26.

News Item in the *Virginia University Magazine*

[April 1880]

Collegiana

On Friday, the 2d of April, was held the first of the annual debates for the medals given by the Jeff. In anticipation of a large crowd the Wash. Hall[1] had been procured for the occasion, and punctually at half-past three the President took the chair and rapped the large audience to order. The Secretary then read the following question: "Is the Roman Catholic element in the United States a menace to American Institutions?" and amid much applause Mr. Bruce came forward to open for the affirmative. The gentleman first addressed himself to giving a succinct account of the giant strides made by the Catholic Church in this country in the last two or three decades, noticing the fact that in Europe, since the first staggering blow struck it by the Reformation, it has been steadily regaining lost ground, and to-day holds sway over countries which at one time were Protestant. The rapid advance in the United States has been due not to an increase in the number of immigrants, for that has declined in the last decade, but to large accessions from among native Americans, gained by an active proselytism. In face of these facts the gentleman went on to consider whether the Catholic Church of to-day is as active, as rapacio[u]s, as bigoted, and as intolerant as formerly. In connection with this was considered the Irish element which constitutes so large a portion of the immigrants who land yearly in New York. These next to the German socialists are the most violent and extreme, and bring with them neither capital nor trade but a bitter hatred for that country with which we are connected by the closest commercial ties. Along with these immigrants inevitably come a long train of ecclesiastics, trained in the habits of the strictest obedience to the higher ecclesiastical authorities. The Irish keep to themselves, form a large portion of the dangerous mobs of New York, and unlike the docile negro or the passive Mongolian, they are bold, daring and aggressive. We are unable to oppose any statutory provisions to the advance of the Catholic Church; our only hope is in the opposition of the Protestant churches. The Catholic Church has for some time doubled the number of its churches in every decade, and at this rate will soon become the

[1] The Washington Society, founded about 1833, was the other literary and debating society at the University of Virginia. For the outcome of this debate, see the documents at May 3, 1880 and the Editorial Note immediately following that date.

prevailing religion of America. We must then consider whether the character of the Catholic Church has changed. It has been urged that she is no longer the church of the Middle Ages, that more enlightened ideas prevail, and that she is fully in accord with the liberal opinions of to-day. But in face of all this we have the encyclical letter issued in 1864 which denounces those who would subordinate the ecclesiastical to the civil authority, declares that freedom of conscience is not one of the rights of man, declares the renewal of the Inquisition necessary and fixes forever in the Pope the doctrine of infallibility. This was agreed to by Manning and others. Do we see any relaxation here? These principles, moreover, have been carried into active practice. Let a man once believe firmly in the doctrine of infallibility, and he will hold in contempt the civil authority. What is that power which can punish for a few months or years, compared with that which can damn a soul for all eternity! The Catholic Church creates an atmosphere in which freedom of thought cannot exist. The opposition of the Catholic Church to freedom of thought is its opposition to Protestantism. It places the Pope and the king so high above the rest of mankind that the people are debased and degraded. The Protestant churches are the allies of political freedom; the Catholic Church, its opposer; says our great declaration, all men are by nature free and equal; says the Catholic Church, equal only in this sense, that all must bow to the papal decrees. The constitution guarantees religious toleration; the syllabus says only her church must be allowed. Here exists an opposition which can never be reconciled. In conclusion, Mr. Bruce, after pointing out the hopeless conflict and antagonism between the doctrines of the Catholic Church and the ideas of freedom and liberty in which we have been reared, said "The fires of Smithfield have long been quenched and I can forgive the cruelties of an honest intolerance; I can forget the story of ecclesiastical sin and shame, but never can I forget or forgive the opposers of the advancement of human knowledge, the foes of democracy."

Mr. Bruce having concluded, the Secretary read the first gentleman's name on the negative, and Mr. Wilson came forward to reply to the argument of Mr. Bruce as well as to open for the negative.

Mr. Wilson said that this was a discussion which called in question the vitality of Anglo-Saxon institutions; of institutions which had stood the tests of centuries. The object of the opposite side (the affirmative) was to prove "that it is in the power, as, in their opinion, it is in the desire of the Jesuits of the country to overturn" these institutions which have so long stood against all assailing forces. In this debate we should, he said, have nothing to do with Roman Catholicism as a religion: we were to deal with it as *a policy*. He maintained that its political ascendancy over Anglo-Saxon peoples was made violently improbable by all teachings of history. He entered into a brief sketch of the history of Roman Catholic dominion, showing how in the past it had been bounded by the Rhine and the Weser, never having found firm rootage among the German races. "Where Roman generals had found abiding victory impossible, Romish priests found enduring success scarcely less impracticable." The priestly polity had gained no permanent foothold in Northern Germany, and had been predominant as a political power in England whither the sturdy races of North Germany had migrated, only until the breaking away of the feudal system and the full growth of the national spirit. The exemption of the Teutonic races from papal dominion had, he said, been no mystery. Their very natures, their most characteristic institutions, were utterly incompatible with the rule of Rome. The Romish Church could, he continued, maintain its supremacy only over those nations whose governments were centralized, and where the seat of power could be successfully won and held. As an example he adduced France, which had been under the Romish yoke until it had put on habits of self-government. He recounted the manner in which Romanism had been hunted from self-governed England, and asked if the success of papal aggression was to be greater here in America where self-government had obtained its highest development? This question was, he declared, answered by Dr. Brownson, an eminent Roman Catholic of New England, who had admitted the teachings of his church to be utterly incompatible with American civilization, and its success a return to second childhood; by Mr. Cartwright, who had shown that all the governments of Europe were arraying themselves against the Society of Jesus; by Lord John Russell who had shown how all the nations of the Continent had rejected the doctrines of the Syllabus; by the Roman Catholic bishops of the United States who had protested against the claim of infallibility and temporal power, asking "how they are going to live under the free constitution of their Republic and maintain their position of equality with their fellow-citizens after committing themselves" to these principles; and by the leaders of the Liberal Catholics who were raising the standard of revolt within the church's own pale. These were, he said, the teachings of the past and the signs of the present: but the question was (Mr. Wilson said) one entirely of the future. The dangers of the situation are, he was free to admit, very grave: the aggressive claims of the Papal authorities no one can deny—and they had, as Mr. Gladstone had so well shown, grown and accumulated since the Middle Ages. All the proofs of insolent pretensions heaped up by the other side he fully allowed: their premises were unimpeachable but their conclusions utterly unwarrantable. The question was whether America was to be Romanized or Rome Americanized? He had shown the answer of the past: that of the present was no less satisfactory and conclusive. In proof of this he quoted several exceedingly striking cases in which the pretensions of the Romish authorities to the control of civil affairs by interference with the civil rights of Romish communicants had been summarily met and punished in the law courts of several States. These were the lessons of the law that had met the priestly powers at every turn. They were hedged about with the courts of law and told so far shall thou go and no step further. Such were the corroborations of the past which gave confidence to American statesmen and meaning to the opposition of American Roman Catholics to the aggressions of the Papal See. He did not anticipate the victory of Rome because the danger was proclaimed and we forearmed; because of the historical prejudices against Roman Catholic authority which were peculiar to our race; because of our spreading and enlarging and strengthening common-school system which is throwing about us the safeguards of enlightenment; because of the unassailable defences of *self-government*. Our liberties are safe until the memories and experiences of the past are blotted out and the Mayflower with its band of pilgrims forgotten; until our public-school system has fallen into decay and the nation into ignorance; until legislators have resigned their functions to ecclesiastical powers and their prerogatives to priests. . . .

Printed in the *Virginia University Magazine,* XIX (April 1880), 445-50.

From Joseph Ruggles Wilson

My dearest son—   [Wilmington, N. C.] 2nd April 1880
    You will find enclosed P. O. order for $10.00.

    I am sorry to hear of your continued "cold." That climate does not, somehow, agree with you. How would you like to study for one year at home? With the impulse you shall have received, might you not be prepared to profit by a private course? Think what a joy it would be to me, and to all of us! Then the kind of food you are compelled to bolt—it is horrible that dyspepsia should be the inevitable upshot of such boarding. Have you no alternative? Is there no possibility of change in the arrangement? If not, I will *insist* upon your staying at home next year—because health is the all in all of your earthly life, the sine qua non of successful study:—a poor commonplace, but none the less important to be considered, *practically*: for out of such poorness comes richness.

I am glad you have a chance to hear an "orator" now and then. The breed has pretty nearly run out, though. *Thought* is not considered essential, in these last days: only intonation and gesture. In fact the thinner one can make his public utterances the more easily are they swallowed and the more likely, from an "appreciative" audience, to elicit the loud hurrah. . . .

Your affectionate Father

ALS (WP, DLC) with WWhw notation on env.: "Ans 4/7/80."

To Harriet Woodrow

My sweet Rosalind,   University of Virginia, April [c. 14] 1880.

I took that remarkable and delightful letter[1] of invitation from my P. O. box immediately upon my return and devoured it with immense zest. Perhaps I would have enjoyed its perusal more if I had received it before I left; but I hardly could have enjoyed its refreshing nonsense more thoroughly than I did. My only regret was that I could not regard it as a fresh invitation which I was at liberty to accept. If the "two disconsolate damsels" enjoyed the visit of their "chosen Knight" as much as he did, they were amply repaid for the trouble of his entertainment! I learn to love my sweet cousins more and more warmly the more I see of them; and if they return only a small part of the love I bear them, I may well be content.

I hope that you have heard from dear uncle Thomas[2] before this. I could not help sharing much of your anxiety about him, and have ever since my return been wishing for news from him.

It seemed for several nights after I got back as if I was not to be allowed to return to my regular habits any more. On Monday night I was out serenading until after one o'clock. I went down town—about a mile and a half, you know—about half past ten o'clock with the Glee Club, and sang at several places, serenading friends of the other members of the Club, not my own, for I don't know any of the young ladies in town. We had a very jolly, amusing time, listening to the tittering at the windows and collecting in the dark the flowers that were thrown to us, with cards of thanks &c., &c. Being followed by idle listeners collected on the way is rather annoying under such circumstances and makes one feel as if he were taking part in an itinerant show. But we were in good voice—my voice seems to return as soon as I leave Staunton—and were in the humor of singing and, altogether, had quite a jolly time. On the way back we stopped at a restaurant and prepared ourselves for bed by taking some refreshment in the shape of ice cream &c; then we sang one or two rousing choruses, and crawled to bed at the wee small hours. Next day when we were going around with half-open eyes, serenading seemed to have lost all its charms for us.

Then on Tuesday night came the big party at Professor Venable's. It was quite a grand affair—quite grand, that is, for Charlottesville. The old place very seldom sees a full-dress entertainment. I don't know that "a man" has any better time in a low-cut vest and swallow-tailed coat than in ordinary dress; but then he feels as if the occasion were something out of the ordinary run and at least tries to persuade himself that he is really having a splendid time. I don't often have an opportunity to wear my dress suit; so, when I do wear it, I put it on with the determination to be hugely entertained. And I *was* well entertained at the Venable's. The company was quite large. There were more young ladies present than I would have thought it possible to collect in this vicinity. Of course there were "*men*" in superabundance, though not so many as to make the young ladies absolutely inaccessible. I was careful not to allow myself to be introduced to any whom I was not sure of finding entertaining; but still I talked to quite a number and managed to talk a great deal without saying anything. The entertainment, which was on the 13th of April, Thomas Jefferson's birthday, was brought to a close about three o'clock by the ceremony of cutting an immense cake, which had Jefferson's name, with the date of his birth, very prettily raised on it in colored icing. The cake contained a small gold coin, with the same inscription on one side of it, which after much distributing of slices by lot, fell to one of the young ladies present. I met Miss Sexton, but not the smaller damsel with her.

Do you remember the story I told Jessie, and which she repeated to you, about the student here who had the adventure with the robber and came so near being seriously stabbed? Well, I came back to hear a new and very startling version of the adventure. The "fellows" were very much exercised over this terrible experience of young Towle's here right in our midst and determined, in a mass-meeting held to consider the matter, to procure the services of a detective and discover and punish the thief whoever he might be. Accordingly they sent to Richmond for a detective, who came up and conducted his investigation while I was in Staunton. He discovered—what, do you think why, that Towle had *himself* stolen his roommate's money, was his own stabber, and had roused his neighbors by firing at an imaginary robber with blank cartridges. In short, Towle had carefully gotten up and acted out the scare in order to cover his own rascality! He left college immediately upon being discovered, and nothing further will be done about the matter.[3]

There's a romantic side to the story, too. It seems that he spent most of his own and of the stolen money in taking rides with a girl in town with whom he was very much in love and who was, moreover, devoted to him after a fashion[.] She is very young, not grown, and is reported to insist still upon believing and having others believe in Towle's innocence. She is inconsolable over his forced departure.

The delay of the mails which occurred while I was in Staunton was occasioned by a very interesting wreck of a freight train only a few hundred yards from the University. It was a complete smash-up, caused by a mis-placed switch, I believe. The cars were piled about in a most remarkable manner, one being thrown bodily up a bank some ten or twelve feet in height, and others smashed into all sorts of inconceivable shapes. No one was seriously hurt, however, as far as I know.

When are you going to have another picture of yourself taken, Hattie? I want one *very* much. The one I have don't remind me of you as you really are. I liked the one you last had taken ever so much. Couldn't you get a copy of *it* for me?

Tell Jessie, please, that I am going to write to her this week, if possible: and give her loads of love from me. She is a wonderfully fine girl, Hattie. Give my love to Marion and Lottie and tell them that "Jamsie"[4] seems perfectly well. Remember me to all my friends and make up as sweet messages as you can for my "Wabbit,"[5] for Marion, and for "little sister."[6]

I would like to let my pen run on for a page or two more, even at the risk of running into nonsense, but I must stop. I've scarcely had time to *wink* leisurely since my return or I would have written sooner.

Please write *very* soon and tell me all about uncle Thomas. If you knew how much pleasure your letters give me you'd write as often as possible. With unbounded love,

Your loving cousin   Tommy.

ALS (WC, NjP)

¹ This letter is missing, as, indeed, are all of Hattie's letters to WW during 1880 and 1881.

² Her father, Thomas Woodrow, Jr.

³ Amos N. Towle, '80, upon motion of Professor Minor at the faculty meeting of April 20, 1880, was expelled; see bound ledger (ViU), "Faculty Minutes, U. of Virginia 1879-1884," p. 104.

⁴ Marion Woodrow and her sister, Mary Charlotte (Lottie), were daughters of Dr. James Woodrow and sisters of James Hamilton Woodrow (Jamsie).

⁵ Hattie Woodrow.

⁶ Marion McGraw Bones and "little sister," Helen Woodrow Bones, were daughters of James W. Bones.

From Marion Wilson Kennedy

My dearest brother;—   Augusta, [Ark.] Apr. 15th/80.

. . . Your letter was an exceedingly pleasant surprise. I had not felt the least bit offended by your long silence, dear Woodrow, but I will have to confess I was a little bit hurt by it. It looked as if you were *forgetting us.* You need not take the trouble to contradict *that,* for of course I knew well enough it was not so. Please try to find time to write us a note once in a while, dear brother. We are teaching our boys to call you uncle Woodrow now, as mother says you like that name best; and I do not think it will be difficult to do, as they call their baby brother by that name always. . . .

                            Lovingly your sister, Marion.

ALS (WP, DLC) with WWhw notation on env.: "Ans 5/25/80." Also on env.: WWhw and WWsh notes.

From Joseph Ruggles Wilson

My very dear son—   Wilmington, [N. C.] Ap. 17, 1880

I have so many letters to write, these days, that I am in danger of neglecting even *you.* Yours of the 14th was received yesterday, and was as cool water to a thirsty soul. Your capacity for uprooing seems to be enlarging, judging from the wee small hours into which your social engagements draw themselves out. But you cannot go far wrong when it is only to the Professors' homes that you betake yourself. You refer to "Glee Club" serenading: in [*sic*] infer from this that you are practising your voice in singing out-of-doors music. This is well—for thus will you strengthen and give larger compass to your vocalism. He who purposes to become a successful public speaker *must* have a large sustainable voice, and, as far as possible, a *musical* voice. Nothing—not even sense—tells upon the popular ear like resonant searching tones of oratorical utterance. And one reason why oratory has, in this country, so grievously declined, is the neglect of cultivation in the art of voicing. . . .

That case of yr. self-tortured student resembles the negro's at West Point, about which Congress is making such a fool of itself. I have very little doubt of the fact that the base fellow did his own mutilating. . . .[1]   Your affectionate Father.

ALS (WP, DLC).
[1] West Point Cadet Johnson C. Whittaker, a Negro, was found in his room on April 6, 1880, bloody and unconscious, his arms and legs bound, beaten, his hair cropped and ears split. A military board of inquiry, after taking evidence for nearly two months, found him guilty on May 29 of self-infliction or of conniving with an accomplice. A resolution in the United States House of Representatives calling for the facts was blocked by a member from South Carolina, Whittaker's home state, while legislation was proposed in the Senate to protect Negro cadets and midshipmen from the "brutal" hazing allegedly tolerated at the service academies. JRW reached his own verdict more than a month in advance of that of the board of inquiry. See the *New York Times* almost daily from April 8, 1880, through its final editorial of May 31, 1880.

Correspondence Concerning the Award of Medals

Univ. of Virginia, May 3, 1880.

Messrs. Editors,—As there seems to be some misapprehension on the part of the friends of the medallists as to the wherefore of the committee's decision, I beg you to publish their letter to me.

Respectfully, J.F.B. Beckwith.

J.F.B. Beckwith, Esq., Chairman[,] Committee Jefferson Society:

Dear Sir:—The Committee of the Faculty selected by your Society to judge of the debates for the prizes of the Society, beg leave to report as follows:

While the general character of the debates in question has been very creditable to the speakers and to the Society they represent, two of the contestants have shown remarkable excellence. Being required to decide between these gentlemen, our committee is of opinion that the medal intended for the best debater should be awarded to Mr. Bruce. In deciding that the position of orator to the Society, with the other medal bestowed therewith, should be awarded to Mr. Wilson, our committee desires to express very high appreciation of his merits, not merely as a speaker, for which this honor is bestowed, but as a debater also.

Very respectfully, J. W. Mallet, Chairman of Committee.[1]

Printed in the *Virginia University Magazine*, XIX (May 1880), 524-25.
[1] The committee, elected the previous December on motion of Bruce to select the "prize debater and orator," consisted of John W. Mallet, Professor of General and Applied Chemistry and Pharmacy, James Cabell, Professor of Physiology and Surgery, and Charles Venable, Professor of Mathematics. (Minutes of the Jefferson Society for Dec. 20, 1879).

EDITORIAL NOTE
WILSON'S DEBATE WITH WILLIAM CABELL BRUCE

The editors have noted some confusion in the reminiscences and other accounts that have dealt with the puzzling and somewhat irregular awards following the debate participated in by Wilson and Bruce. First, the constitution of the Society then in effect provided a single gold medal for "its best Debater" (Article VII). It provided for the election in April of an Orator to speak his oration at the end of the academic year; but there was no medal or other prize (Article IV). And it further provided, in joint action with the then two other literary societies (there was but one other, the Washington Society, in Wilson's day), a gold medal to be awarded at the same time to the "author of the best contribution to the *Magazine*" (Article VI). Nevertheless, by Wilson's time, as A. W. Patterson records in *Personal Recollections of Woodrow Wilson* (pp. 14-16), a medal for oratory was given, and these two medals had "for years" been annually given and regarded in practice as first and second prizes for the annual debate.

In these circumstances it is more than likely that the orator's medal seemed distasteful to Wilson, and the committee chairman's remarks in the nature of a sop. Patterson (p. 15) notes that Wilson was at first disposed to decline the orator's medal, saying that "he made no pretensions to oratory; that he was a debater or nothing; and that his acceptance of such a trophy would be absurd." Patterson also says that Wilson's friends, although aggrieved, persuaded him to accept the medal. Wilson never referred to the award afterward, unless his prompt attempt to reform these procedures in the new constitution of the Jefferson Society in the next academic year was such a reference.[1]

Wilson's chagrin may have been intensified the following month when Bruce received a gold medal for his "John Randolph: a Sketch" for the best contribution to the *Virginia University Magazine* in the academic year 1879-80. Francis H. Smith, Professor of Natural Philosophy, in presenting the medal to Bruce gave "unstinted praise . . . to those excellent articles on John Bright and Mr. Gladstone, written by Mr. T. Woodrow Wilson of North Carolina."[2]

[1] See documents at Oct. p. 10, 14, Nov. 17, Dec. 4, 17, 1880, Jan. 16, 1881; and the Editorial Note immediately following Dec. 4, 1880.
[2] *Virginia University Magazine*, xx (Oct. 1880), 51.

Notes for a Debate on the Monroe Doctrine

[c. May 4, 1880]

The Monroe Doctrine is no longer the Doctrine of Monroe. [*] in its later applications and in its present sphere of affairs beyond [?] the intended meaning of the declaration of policy made by Mr. Monroe in his message of 1823. I cannot [?] believe indeed that Mr. Monroe were he now living would himself sanction all the interpretations which have been drawn from these evolutions of the declaration which are almost lost amidst numerous other mat-

ters which [* *] the message. And yet it is in its later—in its latest
—conception that we must take this doctrine and must now deal
with it. At various stages of the history of our foreign relations
it has been reconsidered by the executive and it is of course in
the light of these successive executives' dicta that we must learn
the meaning it at present bears. We have in this discussion nothing immediately to do with the concerns of the year '23 the birth-
year of the doctrine[.] We are concerned properly and only with
these possible events which shall bear a date from this time on.

Transcript of WWsh notes on env. of Marion Wilson Kennedy to WW, April
15, 1880. Some of the shorthand outlines are indecipherable because Wilson's
notation, "Ans 5/25/80," was written over them. This is a draft of the introduction to WW's speech in a debate with William Cabell Bruce on the subject "Was the Monroe doctrine founded upon a wise policy?" The Jefferson
Society Minutes are silent about this contest, and it is possible that it was a return
match between WW and Bruce. That the debate occurred between May 6 and May
14, 1880, is evident from JRW's letters to WW of these dates. Bruce, in his *Recollections* (Baltimore, 1936), pp. 68-80, recalls the debate on the Monroe Doctrine
and comments graciously on his relationship with WW at the University of Virginia, particularly their rivalry in debate.

From Janet Woodrow Wilson

My precious Son,   Augusta, Arkansas[1] Wednesday May 5. [1880]
. . . The reason I have not fulfilled my promise as to our summer plans, is, that I have scarcely known what to say. Since I
have been away from your father so much, I do not think it will
be *possible* for us to carry out our plan of going on to meet you at
the end of the session. So I suppose you will have to come to us, my
darling. Besides, do you know, I think it would be cruel to deprive
dear papa of all help & comfort in that way—in the preparation of
his Minutes. I am sure you feel that—for you have spoken of it. As
to going to Europe—there is no hope for this summer. The trouble
is, as to that matter, your father dont care to go but I haven't given
up as to the future. Your father has to prepare a paper for the
"Pres[byterian] Alliance" in Sept.—which meets you know in
Phila.[2] . . .
    God bless you my darling sweet boy. All unite in *unbounded* love
to you. I will tell you *all about everything* again
                              Lovingly yours   Mother

ALS (WP, DLC) with WWhw notations: "Advantages of Senate"; "We promise";
"HOME." Also brief WWsh notes with Arabic numerals and Greek letters.
    1 JWW was visiting her daughter, Marion Kennedy.
    2 JRW was a delegate to the Second General Council of the Presbyterian Al-
liance that met in Philadelphia Sept. 23-Oct. 3, 1880. He commented on a paper
by the Rev. George Fisch, D.D., of Paris on "Recent Evangelistic Work in Paris."

Two Letters from Joseph Ruggles Wilson

My very dear Son—   Wilmington, [N. C.] May 6, 1880

You will find what is good for $20 enclosed. My expenses have been unwontedly great during the past year and it becomes us all to be closely sparing in our outlays. I hope that you will never feel ashamed to economise in little things.

I had sent the $54 to Mr. Peyton[1] before your last letter reached me.

I noticed, in yr. last month's report 6 absences from one of your recitations. Is not this about 1 in 4? If so are you getting the full benefit of your expenditures? You will understand, my precious boy, that it is only love that evokes these shadows to throw across yr. path. We *must* be true to each other all around, if our affection be sincere. I enjoy yr. letters exceedingly, and, fortunately, can sympathize with you in the sentiments you express touching matters and persons. I share your pleasure in witnessing the reinstatement of Gladstone[.] He is likely to be embarrassed by a too numerous following: and so, the wheel being too big, may go into tangential pieces from its own motion. It is a remarkable fall for Beaconsfield who, one short year or so ago, was at the top of England and deafened by popular hurrahs. You are assuredly right, too, as to the Monroe doctrine, and I hope you will make this appear in the approaching discussion. . . .

I am your affectionate   F

P.S. omitted. ALS (WP, DLC) with WWhw note on env.
[1] Green Peyton, Proctor of the University of Virginia.

My very dear and ever dearer son— Wilmington, [N. C.] May 14 80

I am sorry to learn of your recent under-the-weather-ness; but then I am rejoiced to know that you are now higher up as to your physical barometer. You ought to have made such a change as to your boarding accommodations as would have proved anti-dyspeptic; but I suppose it is too late for this session. "Better luck next time."

It is queer that, since it came off, you have never referred to your *debate*, at least in letters to me:[1] nor did you send me a copy of yr. magazine article as you promised.[2] Did you not succeed in the former, and were copies of the latter too much in demand to enable you to procure an extra one? I would exceedingly like to have full particulars of said debate, and to enjoy the pleasure of reading and admiring said essay. . . . Believe in my most affectionate confidence   Your own more so   F

ALS (WP, DLC) with WWhw notes on env.
1 The record is silent about the outcome of the debate on the Monroe Doctrine.
2 "Mr. Gladstone, a Character Sketch."

To Charles Andrew Talcott

My dear Charlie,   University of Virginia, May 20th 1880.

Our term is fast drawing toward its close, which already seems
to me tediously delayed. In one month more, on the first of July
namely, I'll once more be free for a short Summer vacation. My
examinations, which this year are few, are already over and for
the few remaining weeks of the term my duties will be comparatively light, leaving me pretty much a gentleman of leisure—for
which, in view of the hot weather and of the hard work through
which I've been grinding my way for the past eight or nine months,
I am abundantly thankful. For the work *has* been hard and unremitting, affording only the smallest scraps of leisure and the
fewest opportunities for anything but perusal of law, law, law.
Hence my long and seemingly unreasonable silence, Charlie,
which I am now so glad to break. If you knew how often you have
been the subject of my thoughts, and of my praises in the presence
of others, you could not feel hardly concerning my neglect of you
in the matter of letter-writing. You know that I am far from being
demonstrative, Charlie, and not given to making many *professions*; but allow me to say, that I look back upon our college companionship and friendship with unqualified pleasure, and regard
our intimacy there as the most valuable single element of my
course at dear old Princeton. And in proportion to the warmth of
feeling with which I look back upon our association there[,] would
be my grief were anything *now* to be allowed to come between us
to break it off. You know the political dreams I used to indulge
in? Well, don't be afraid, I aint going to bore you with any more
lengthy disquisitions on reform &c. &c. But those indistinct plans
of which we used to talk grow on me daily, until a sort of calm
confidence of great things to be accomplished has come over me
which I am puzzled to analyze the nature of. I can't tell whether
it is a mere figment of my own inordinate vanity, or a deep-rooted
determination which it will be within my power to act up to. At
any rate, *you* are always prominently associated in my mind with
all these schemes. It's on this account, I guess, that I always fall
to writing of them when I sit down to write to you.

I was very much obliged for your description of the Conkling
Convention for the nomination of delegates for Chicago[1]—I was
about to say that I *enjoyed* it: but that would not have been true.

One can never enjoy reading of anything which is his country's curse. But I don't believe that such a state of things will be tolerated much longer. You know this convention system is not so old as one would be led to suppose from the amount of mischief it has worked. The country is, I hopefully believe, gradually waking to a full knowledge—and hence an unutterable disgust, of its methods—and things are rapidly ripening for a radical change which will soon be imperatively demanded. Let us hope that the change will be for the better. I believe that it will, if our English blood be not altogether corrupted by the infusion of foreign elements. The more open and notorious these corrupt methods of party management, the sooner the deliverance, and the more tremendous the indictment against them.

I can't say that my love for the University increases as my stay is prolonged. There's no *college* life here, as *we* know college life, at all. It's simply a place where men happen to have congregated for study—and for nothing else. But still I cannot sufficiently admire Professor Minor's methods of instruction; and I try to appreciate my advantages in spite of other things which are less admirable. Charlie, would it be impossible for you to come here next year? You could, after having studied law, as you have, for a year with your brother, easily get through the whole course in one year. Many men do it without previous study—by sheer dint of regular habits and systematic work. To have you here would be a positive *blessing* to me! And I'm sure such a course would greatly advantage you. Besides it would shorten the necessary term of preparation for you, wouldn't it?

I have taken some time this year for speaking and debate in our literary society, the Jefferson, and have derived considerable benefit from so doing. The Jefferson can't compare with old Whig. Its exercises are rather languid and its discipline quite loose. There are comparatively few men who care to take from their studies enough time to do faithful work in debate, &c. But on the whole it is a very good society and at least affords one an *opportunity* to accomplish a good deal. Much to my surprise I've acquired the reputation of being the best debater and one of the best speakers in the University—because there are so few of either, I presume. I intimate to them quite broadly—to the fellows here, that is—that they don't know what good speaking is, and enlarge upon the merits of the man whom I regarded as the best speaker—though, possibly, not the best eloqutionist,—in '79, one Charlie Talcott, trying to give them some idea of his style—not by imitation, but by description. Since Christmas I have delivered an oration on

John Bright before the society which was published in the Magazine; and have written an essay on Gladstone for the same publication—both of them rather lengthy productions as neither the time of orations nor the length of essays is limited. The oration occupied about fifty-five minutes in its delivery; and the essay covers some twenty-six pages of the Magazine[.] I will try to send you copies of both. The rest of my history for this year is summed up in the word *law*. Understand, Charlie, I am giving you these particulars about myself, because I would do as I would be done by. I want a letter full of *yourself* in return.

Several times since Christmas I have broken the monotony of constant study by a trip of a day or two—generally Saturday and Sabbath—up to Staunton, my birth-place, which is only about forty miles distant, where a great many old friends of my family live, and where several of my cousins are studying—at one of the female schools for which Staunton is famous through all the South. I've enjoyed these trips immensely, especially as my cousins are very sweet girls, and their surroundings peculiarly interesting. I have an aunt living in Staunton at whose house I stay when there —and the pleasures of the trip are thus secured without the ugly objection of an hotel bill.

I have not had much news from the fellows lately—principally because I have neglected them one and all myself, in not writing to them. Pete Godwin was the last heard from.[2] After much travelling about in Europe, after many plans exploded, and many hopes defeated, after much harassing doubt as to the exact work he was to set himself to do, the crazy boy has at last settled himself in the purpose to become what we all thought him best fitted to be, a professional art critic. His spirits are much lighter in consequence of the determination. Doubt made him very gloomy and crazier than ever. He expected when he wrote to return home in August next. His address is, Care J. I. Morgan & Co, London.

From Bridges I have not heard in several months. I don't know what can be the matter with the dear old Scot.

I saw Hiram in February last. Since graduating we have both become members of the ΦΚΨ fraternity, as I beli[e]ve I told you, and we met at a fraternity convention in Washington in the latter part of February. I needn't say *how* we met or how intensely we enjoyed the meeting. He persuaded me to go over to Balto. with him to spend a day after the adjournment of the convention. We telegraphed for Daniel but his father would not let him come—much to our vexation[.] Mr. Webster has Daniel at work in his office, and having determined upon his studying systematically, wont let anything distract his attention if he can prevent it. He's right, of course, but I was sadly bored at missing a sight of Dan'l when I was so near him. I have not heard from Hiram since my visit.

From the rest of the boys not a word, except an occasional "personal" in the *Princetonian* which you must have seen.

Charlie write *soon*. Don't feel *obliged* to write a *long* letter. Write often, if it be only a few lines: and I will promise to do likewise no matter what interferes.

Your loving friend   T. Woodrow Wilson

ALS (photostat in RSB Coll., DLC).

1 This refers to Talcott's long letter of February 26, 1880, written from Utica, N.Y., the day after the Republican state convention had met there and chosen seventy delegates to the Chicago national convention. Senator Roscoe Conkling of New York, having arrived at Utica by train the evening of February 24 to an artillery salute, dominated the convention and prevailed upon it to bind all the delegates for General Grant at Chicago. (*New York Times*, Feb. 26, 1880.) Talcott's letter analyzed "the manner in which the politicians gained possession of the convention," and continued in pessimistic vein: "The question of right never arose, the one object at which they aimed was the control of the convention. . . . I left the convention indignant because of the tyranny I had seen enacted and conscious that similar wrongs are committed in every convention of each party. One need not look further for the cause of the deterioration in statesmanship. Here we can find the reason why cunning and intrigue are substituted for sagacity and foresight in the highest councils of the nation."

2 H. Godwin to WW, Mar. 20, 1880, ALS (WP, DLC).

From Joseph Ruggles Wilson

My dear Son—   Wilmington, [N. C.] June 5, 1880

Your pain-giving letter has just been received. I have, all along, had fear lest your frequent absences from recitation would end in grief, and tried to warn you. You certainly acted most imprudently in leaving the grounds unpermitted, and it seems to me that the faculty would be deserving of censure if they should overlook so gross a breach of discipline. But, then, I will add this—that, come what will, *you possess our confidence*, because we well know your *character*: a blessed knowledge which you have confirmed us in by your straight-forward confessions of juvenile folly.

I have not the heart to write you a long letter. My main object is to assure you of my continued love and trust, and yet to condemn what you have done. It is just because of my love that I have always tried to be faithful in telling you the truth about yourself and yr doings.

God bless and utterly reform you. Your own   Father

ALS (WP, DLC) with WWhw notation on env.: "Ans 6/7/80."

From Janet Woodrow Wilson

My darling son,   Wilmington N. C. June 5 '80

We received yours of June 3rd this morning. I need not try to tell you how distressed I am at the possibility of any disgrace coming upon *you*. Your father has written you & sent his letter to the P. O. I dont know what he wrote—for he is in one of his dark moods today—but whatever it was, you may be sure he loves & trusts you with all his heart. I was going to write you today—to warn you of your danger—for we received your report yesterday which I enclose. But surely they will not be so cruel as to take such extreme measures without previous warning. Dont exasperate them by showing any resentment, my darling. Acknowledge your fault remind them that you were not aware that you were guilty of breaking any fixed rule. Please go to Mr. Venable and get him to use his influence in your behalf—for your fathers sake. Explain the whole circumstances to him. I beg you to do everything in your power to avert this great calamity.

I love you with all my heart, my precious darling boy—and trust you perfectly. I have felt worried as to the effect of your frequent absences from the U—but did not suppose there was this sort of danger. May God bless my darling—and bring good out of this trouble. Josie sends unbounded love.   Lovingly   Mother

ALS (WP, DLC) with WWhw notation on env.: "Rec'd 6/9/80." Enc.: Printed report of James F. Harrison, M.D., Chairman of the Faculty, University of Virginia, June 1, 1880, on T. W. Wilson. Handwritten comments opposite "Common and Statute Law, Prof. Minor," in columns "Absent" and "Remarks": "9 times! 6 times excused. A very intelligent & appreciative student, but suffers greatly by reason of his absences." Handwritten comments opposite "Equity, Mercantile and Internat'l & Cons'l Law, &c., Prof. Southall": "4 [,] 3 excused." The faculty minute book for 1879-84 lists WW under "delinquents in the several schools" as of Jan. 1, 1880, as absent 3 times from "Commercial Law, Equity, &c" (p. 73) and under date of June 1, 1880, as absent 3 times from "Common and Statute Law" (p. 104). At no time does WW appear in the faculty minutes as subject to admonition or discipline.

From Joseph Ruggles Wilson

My dear Son—   [Wilmington, N. C.] Monday June 7th 1880

Your second letter touching the unhappy state of yr. relations with the faculty has been received. I fully agree with you that dismissal or suspension w'd. be a punishment out of proportion with the offence; but that some angry notice was taken of it was only proper—and all the more so, in your present case, because (1) you are worth saving & (2) your absences have been so frequent heretofore. In the May report occur such words as these: a good and appreciative student, but much injured by absences.

Granted that these, or most of them were "excused," yet *all* were not: about ¼th were not: and now that, in the face of these damaging absences the faculty see you taking the law into your own hands, *altogether* what could they do unless say we must part, for there cannot be two lawmakers here? Now, dearest, do not think that I am thus heaping coals of fire upon your already ashes-covered head. Far from it. Only I desire that you and I should look the whole matter squarely in the face—I say "you and I"—for, believe me, we are as truly identified—*my* heart at least being the judge—as if we were one and the same person. What *you* have done, therefore, I feel as if *I* had done—and my head bows and my heart saddens accordingly. Truly thankful am I that you have not sought to conceal aught from me, or to minify the evil—but that you have, like a man (may I add, like a Woodrow-Wilson?) fully set it all forth—aye, even exaggerating it against yourself! Well, then, let us now dismiss the matter altogether. Be sure that you are not less dear to me, or less in my confidence as your father and friend, than you have always been. It would take *very* much more than this—excuseless as it is—to impair that trust in you which, if I could give it up, would render me wretched for the residue of my life. You were foolish, not criminal. You were too independent, forgetting authority, and the necessity for it. Your head went agog. Let it lead you to mistrust it.

My own precious son, I love you, and believe in you. God bless you now and ever: and that He may do so, seek more and more His guidance who is yr. *supreme* father

Your affc.   (earthly) Father.

ALS (WP, DLC) with WWhw notation on env.: *"Rec'd 6/9/80."*

From Marion Woodrow Bones

My dearest Tommy—   Staunton   Va   June 14th '80.

I write to you tonight because I feel in rather better spirits tonight than I have done for a week or so; and as my letter may find you somewhat depressed, I do not wish to increase it. Hattie told us of the trouble you had gotten into by your visit to us, and of the serious consequences you at first feared; but I hope that is all over. I wish, with you, that the session were out, so that you might be relieved of what must be very tiresome and unsatisfactory. . . . Your loving Auntie.

ALS (WP, DLC) with WWhw notations on env.: "Rec'd 6/16/80"; "Ans 6/16/80."

From Janet Woodrow Wilson

My precious Son, Wilmington N. C., June 18–80.

. . . Dont grieve any more over your mistake in the matter of going to the S[taunton] Commencement—for after all, it was only a mistake of a very innocent kind. I only grieved over it because of the threatened consequences to *you*, and your *future* which are so precious to me. Dr. H[arrison] would have been right in seriously *warning* you—he was wrong and cruel, it seems to me in *threatening* you as he did[.] (I honestly believe he did it though, thinking it was best for you) But dont think any more about it, my precious darling.

I want to speak of one thing more. Is it not possible for you to get different boarding for next year? Could you not get a room at one of the Professors houses, where you would likely get decent food? If you continue as at present, your stomach will be ruined for life. If you can secure a room now, you could use your own furniture still you know—could place it there at once. Sister A[nnie] has a boarder who has furnished his own room. . . .

Lovingly yr   Mother

ALS (WP, DLC).

Newspaper Report of a Wilson Speech

June 30, 1880

The Jefferson Literary Society held its final celebration Tuesday night, June 29th, in the public hall of the University. Webber's Washington band furnished the music. Mr. P. Lea Thom, of Baltimore, Md., presided. . . . The exercises were formally opened by prayer by Dr. Vaughan,[1] chaplain to the University. Thereafter the president presented the debater's medal to Mr. W. C. Bruce, of Charlotte county, Va. . . .

The president then presented the Orator's Medal to Mr. T. W. Wilson, of North Carolina. In doing so he said it was to be regretted that the University of Virginia had no Chair of English; that elocution was entirely neglected. Other colleges had. He then referred to the fact that Princeton had such facilities, and that the two students who in late years had been educated there and then strove for collegiate honors in our University had both been successful. The first was Mr. Wooten,[2] of Texas; the second, Mr. Wilson. He then introduced Mr. Wilson, who expressed a lively sense of the delicacy of his position, since the assemblage no doubt was present to hear rhetorical speaking. He did not indulge in rhetoric; he said he was just learning to speak. But he would present some thoughts which had perhaps not occurred to his auditors. Without further preliminaries he spoke, in substance, thus:

The Jefferson Society was indeed once a literary society, but it is not now. Her journals contain entries bright as the records of immortality, but the case is altered now. Outside aids in keeping up its membership are resorted to. The Society seems a machine to elect officers—an organization whose duty it is to meet and adjourn. The Washington Society if not dead sleepeth. It has proposed to renew its life by the excitement and stimulus of elections. I do not taunt my Society, though its day of usefulness is nearly over (but this condition of affairs goes far beyond our Society). The conditions which gave it and like organizations life have passed away. The scholastic standards have been raised. Our fathers and grandfathers graduated at sixteen—we in maturity. And yet in maturity we discuss such question as "Did Mary, Queen of Scots, deserve her fate?" "Which was the greatest General Napoleon or Caesar?" "Was the execution of Charles I justifiable?" &c., &c. These are the whole stock in trade of the average debating society. They are adopted and readopted, debated and redebated to the exclusion of questions of real vitality. Development and progress demand that specialties be studied. College societies, if not vain and useless affairs, must prepare us for life. Life and its demands are different from what they once were, the societies must be different—they must be practical schools. In this death of old affairs I see signs of happy promise—it prefigures a new birth and better existence. Oxford has a political debating society organized and conducted like great national assemblies, where its members learn to express themselves fluently and readily on any great question of public policy. It is said that Cabinet ministers regard these debates as indicating the real state of opinion among the thoughtful classes. Cambridge has a like society. Yale and Harvard have, too. I hope we may not hesitate to follow such lead. Our Society is not dead, though its death as a literary order can only be delayed, not hindered. I look forward to the day when it will give practical training to lawyers and public men of the honester sort. It may be objected by older people than I am that I am young, and forget that passions will be excited in political debates; that, like religious questions, they should be left undebated. I answer that passions are excited only when we are ignorant and prejudiced. The habitual discussion of political measures is as necessary as any scholastic course. Questions that appeal to the heart rather than the reason are out of date now. Not much longer will Mason and Dixon's line mark a separation in political

convictions. Principle will rule. Students are not too young. Ignorance is the principal disqualification. If passions arise it is because
they did not let principle rule and proof decide. The danger of
our Government now is that it has become a government of caucus
rather than free discussion. Free discussion must liberate us from
political bondage. In it the mind learns to move without leading
strings. Youth is no disqualification. Fox led the House before he
was thirty. In his twenties Pitt was in the Ministry, &c. Referring
to the fact that there were heresies among old congressmen in
such a matter as currency, whose laws are commonplaces in lec-
ture-rooms and among students, he said we might conclude that
age was a disqualification. Many were ready to sneer that many
a young man had gone out from college with like views, and yet
had changed nothing—not even themselves. Why? They had a
larger stock of boast than reason in store.

This speech, from which artificial declamation was conspicuously absent, was pronounced by many who heard it as the best
which has been delivered by a student here for many a year. It
was a far better speech than the first medalist made, who evidently
could not have fulfilled the promise his speech gave before the
committee when he contested for and received the first honor over
Mr. Wilson. . . .

Printed in the Richmond *Daily Dispatch*, July 1, 1880.
  [1] The Rev. Clement R. Vaughan.
  [2] Dudley G. Wooten, Princeton, '75.

To Eleanor A. Smith[1]

Miss Ellie,   House F.[2] June 30th [1880]
    I send the basket as you requested. I cannot sufficiently thank
you for the good will of which the flowers were the, to me, more
than gratifying token. Only busy packing prevents my returning
the flowers in person. I will give myself the pleasure of calling
later in the day.   With sincerest regard   T. Woodrow Wilson

ALS (Tucker-Harrison-Smith Coll., ViU). WWhw address on env.: "Miss E. A.
Smith At Home."
  [1] Eleanor A. Smith, daughter of Francis H. Smith, Professor of Natural Philosophy from 1858-59. In 1880 she assisted her mother whose house was hospitably
open to the University community. She was one of two young women who, with
WW and Charles W. Kent, of the Glee Club, sang as a quartet. She married Fielding D. Miles, on Dec. 23, 1886, and Professor Charles W. Kent on June 4, 1895.
  [2] In his first year WW occupied room 158 in this house, one of six brick cottages
known as Dawson's Row, at the west end of the lawns and ranges.

Marginal Notes

James E. Therold Rogers,
ed., *Speeches on Questions
of Public Policy by John
Bright* (2 vols., London,
1868).

Vol. I, 123-47: [Bright's
speech of March 13, 1865,
on Canadian-American-
British relations.]

Transcripts of WW Short-
hand Comments

[July 19, 1880]

No one who clearly understands the
real causes and true nature of the
American Civil War of 1861-65 can
read Mr. Bright's cruel unjust censures
of the course pursued by the Southern
states and his flings at the character
of the people of the South without the
keenest pain. He forgets that England
was solely responsible for the introduction of slavery into America and that
circumstances almost beyond her control led to its continuance in the
Southern states. He evidently knows
nothing of the history of the *constitutional* struggle between sincere advocates of states' right of secession and the
as sincere champions of national
sovereignty, and seems never to have
realized the fact that slavery was only
an *indirect* cause of the Civil War a
great constitutional question itself a
vital issue. From his point of ignorant
view he was right in denouncing a
policy whose only object seemed to him
to be the perpetuation of slavery—
though its real object was the vindication of what seemed to be constitutional
rights. He was ignorant, and, on the
ground of ignorance, may be forgiven
what were, I am convinced, uninten-
tional misrepresentations. But in a man
of his situation and of his great talents
ignorance cannot easily be excused.
To *me* the Civil War and its terrible

scenes are but a memory of a short day.
I have reached maturity at a time when
the passions it stirred have cooled and
when it is possible even for those
who were actual participants in its
transactions to judge its issues without heat and almost without prejudice.
In this calmer period I can clearly
see that the suffering of the Confederacy
was an inestimable [?] blessing, that
the doctrine of states rights was a danger settled, and that the abolition of
slavery was, even for us, a lasting
benefit. I am also ready to forgive,
though I cannot excuse, the ignorance
of Mr. Bright's cruel denunciation.
If once he was unjust, we can the more
easily forgive him in view of his otherwise invariable advocacy of justice
and truth.

T. Woodrow Wilson
7/19/80
Wilmington, North Carolina

Vol. I, 282-83:

We know the cause of this revolt [se-
cession of the southern states], its purposes, and its aims. Those who made it
have not left us in darkness respecting
their intentions, but what they are to
accomplish is still hidden from our
sight; and I will abstain now, as I have
always abstained with regard to it, from
predicting what is to come. I know what
I hope for,—and what I shall rejoice
in,—but I know nothing of future facts
that will enable me to express a confident opinion. Whether it will give freedom to the race which white men have
trampled in the dust, and whether the
issue will purify a nation steeped in
crimes committed against that race, is
known only to the Supreme. In His
hands are alike the breath of man and
the life of States. I am willing to commit to Him the issue of this dreaded
contest; but I implore of Him, and I be-
seech this House, that my country may
lift nor hand nor voice in aid of the
most stupendous act of guilt that history
has recorded in the annals of mankind.

That "stupendous act
of guilt" consisted in seeking to uphold upon con-
stitutional grounds a system which England herself
had suffered to be estab-
lished in America. See page
147.

Articles for the Wilmington *Morning Star*

[c. *Aug. 20, 1880*]

The Education of the People

[I]

We purpose addressing to our fellow taxpayers of the State, to-day and hereafter as space may permit, a few words of practical advice on the subject of the education of our youth—a topic which all must admit to be of present interest and of supreme importance. In doing so we shall not dwell at any great length upon the intellectual advantages which never fail to follow in the train of education. Nor shall its moral blessings be made the direct theme of our discussion. That it brings light to the understanding and strength to the moral sentiments few persons can with any fair show of reason refuse to allow. And the practical value of quickened faculties does not need the establishment of proof. A mind that knows how to think and where to find whatever information it does not already possess, and a sense of right and wrong which has been shown the way to truth and wh. does not need a spur to make it go aright are worth more than capital on a farm, are more valuable than all party prizes at the polls, and are of more service than the gift of eloquence in the conduct of legislation. Since these are conclusions from wh. very few people will demur, we have a very firm foundation on wh. to rest our argument for the extension of education and on wh. to build the simple, practical suggestions as to the best means for its perfection to wh. we shall seek to confine ourselves.

Education, fellow citizens, is a matter of government. Its extension and the perfection of its means should be the care of govt. Why? Because it is essential to good citizenship—as we shall presently try to prove—and because, from the very nature of organized society—that is, from the very nature of *states*—it cannot safely be left to chance[,] private enterprise or endeavor. There is no principle to which a people ought to be more stubborn in sticking than this, that government ought never to be allowed to do that for its citizens wh. they can as well, or better, do for themselves: and from this doctrine naturally and irresistably flows this other, that government should be urged, and if possible compelled, to do that for its people which they can *not* do as well or better for themselves. Under this latter class of objects comes education. It is the height of unwisdom to leave it to chance or to charity. Education whose object is the enlightenment of an entire community, of a whole people, is good only when it is uniformly good:

it can be uniformly good only when uniformly organized: it can be uniformly organized only by some power which has authority in all parts of the state: the only such power is government. This is no hard and hidden matter. Every plain man can see that a big undertaking can be accomplished only by a big power, and that the duty of educating say a million and a half of people cannot be successfully discharged by any possible accumulation of private means, or by any probable organization of private individuals, however large or however wealthy.

It is one of the glories of American institutions that this duty of government to educate its subjects was first fully recognized and systematically performed in America. It is one of the most creditible manifestations of Southern liberality of temper and opinion that we were not ashamed to borrow our systems of education from New England, with whose people we had so little else in common; but it will be far from creditible to us if now, while brighter prospects are opening to us in other things, we suffer this most valuable of systems to languish for want of proper support.

If, then, the support of education be the business of government—as every thinking man must allow that it is—the means of its support is *taxation*. But taxation is our tender point, and has always been the ground of our quickest rebellion. We don't want to pay unless we know what we are paying for and that it is worth the expense and it is natural and right that we should not. Before urging upon our fellow-taxpayers, therefore, the necessity of greater outlay upon education, we shall, as time permits, ask and answer the questions:

I I

How, then, does education benefit the state? In ways almost without number; but principally and most plainly by making for it good citizens and by increasing its material prosperity. Education is one of the highest and most effective *police* agencies. It will at once appear evident to every one who bestows any thought upon the matter that *idleness* is the mother of a great host of the lesser crimes from which communities suffer and for whose punishment they are compelled to keep constantly open court; of those less heinous offences against law which are prompted by reckless desires rather than by vindictive motives, by the appetites and the passions rather than by malice. Stealing and burglary, street fighting and drunkenness, mischief-making and thievery of all kinds, are the special temptations of the idle. They persuade themselves that society owes them a living, and, in order that idleness may bring them an income, they turn sharpers and professional cheats. There is no legitimate way in which the habitually idle can make dollars and cents, so they dare to make them in defiance of right and the law. And idleness is the eldest child of ignorance. The ignorant have no fertility of resources within themselves. Their powers are undeveloped. When employment in the simpler and lower sorts of manual labors fail them, they are utterly at a loss whither to turn for work. There is nothing else that they can do. Idleness is forced upon them, and they must steal or starve. And, of course, when the uneducated are in the majority the idle must greatly multiply in numbers. Education and religion are the only police that can relieve the mayors of our towns from the labors of the daily sittings of their courts, that can lessen the number of magistrates and lighten the cares of jailors, that can give us "undisturbed sleep within unbarred doors." The industrious are always peaceful and law-abiding: the idle are always restless and in mischief. Unless there is a multiplicity of industries there must be many idle; and there cannot be a multiplicity of industries except among a people of active thoughts and many resources within themselves, that is among an educated people. A community always ignorant, must be always poor and slothful.

But it is not only by lessening the number of criminals and securing the peace of society that education raises up good citizens for the state. It has a special value for free states in its power to bring into being intelligent voters. It assuredly needs no elaborate proof that a government which depends entirely upon the popular will, as does ours, will be better and more providently conducted if that will be an intelligent one. There is no more solemn problem for the South to solve than that of how to make universal suffrage a safe, rather than a damning and revolutionary method of rule. The presence of so vast a number of uneducated colored voters at our polls, of voters driven about by every wind of fear, passion, or prejudice, should not make us weakly despond, or cowardly despair, but resolutely resolve to raise these men from ignorance and rescue them from prejudice by the only effective, the only possible means, within our reach—by education, thorough, untiring, undiscouraged instruction. Intelligent property-holding men amongst [us] have been known weakly, unbecomingly, discreditably to hold aloof from political matters and stay away from the polls 'because it was no use for the educated to vote so long as the ignorant were in the majority and must decide the election'! As long as this is their mood things will remain as they are. As soon as they determine to submit to taxation that thorough education may be made universal a brighter, more prosperous time will have set in. Party passion feeds on ignorance and will rule as long as ignorance exists for its support. One of the chief arguments for education is that upon it the safety and health of popular institutions depend. It is the only charm that can free us from the curse of rule by parties whose strength is reckoned by mere numbers and not by the preponderance of intelligence and superiority of principle.

If, then, education is an effective police agent and a blessing to free political institutions, need the people of a free State and a free Union stop to answer in words the question does education pay?

I I I

The education of its youth is the sure means of increasing a state's material prosperity. Not only does it raise up a law-respecting, peace-loving class of citizens, fitted for the duties and strengthened for the responsibilities of a free franchise; it also adds to the variety and the vigor of its industries. Let any one ask himself what is one of the chief influences that builds cities. It is not advantages of location alone. Excellence of position first locates towns, no doubt, but it is not this only that builds them and makes them grow into cities. It is the gathering together of the intelligent. Association quickens the faculties and stimulates enterprize. Where large numbers are brought together all cannot find support in the same pursuits. All cannot be grocers or dry goods merchants, unless all are content to trade without profit. Men are impelled to multiply means of money-making. If they cannot trade they may manufacture for the trader. If they can neither manufacture nor trade, they may construct the manufacturer's factories and fit his machinery; they may rear the trader's storehouses and build his dwelling. Thus association spurs men on to devise new means of livelihood and leads directly to a division of labor and an accumulation of wealth. And the growth of the town attracts capital not only from its immediate neighborhood but from a distance as well, and its increase is hastened and its prosperity secure. Intelligence builds cities then. Ignorance has no devices of its own. It cannot manufacture. It cannot invent. It has no skill to command and to profit by. It can at best only dig or carry mortar or lay bricks, and help the educated to add to their fortunes.

Ignorant communities never have many sources of support; and when those few fail, starvation stares these in the face and they have no hope but in charity. Such communities are often, like the Irish, almost entirely agricultural; and when their crops fail famine is their common lot. The prime advantage of education, therefore, is the activity which it imparts to the mind. It gives men something to fall back on. If one occupation is overcrowded, they are not forced to beg from the charitable: they can turn to other pursuits and earn an honorable liv[e]lihood by other means.

It is a common remark that no two minds are made in all respects alike. One is by nature fitted for one kind of exercise, another for another. But ignorance condemns all to exist upon a common level. Education, on the contrary frees them, each to follow his own bent, and gives him the means as well as the opportunity to follow it to good purpose. It is this which makes all industrious communities industrious. It leads one to invent, another to conceive and carry out great improvements, another to establish great manufacturing industries, another to devote himself to the mining of the earth's mineral treasures, another to employ himself in constructing great public works—railways, canals and the like—in order to give the greater facility to commerce and offer the greater prizes to capital, and still others to pursue the pleasures and extend the blessings of a refined and enlightening literature. It is education more than anything else that has made the contrast between the wealth and enormous prosperity of the North and the comparative poverty of the South. For it is education mainly that has enabled the North to multiply its industrial pursuits almost without limit and strengthen and improve them almost beyond example. The South has no fewer blessings than she in the way of natural advantages. Water power without stint, mineral resources in rich abundance, a climate that does not freeze with its cold nor scorch with its heat, but which blesses with health— all seem to invite to industry and wealth. But enterprize is lacking. And enterprize is spurred by education, is born of enlightenment. Without enlightenment and the enlargement of the moral ties it cannot exist. Enterprize means *activity* of all sorts; and men who know nothing can do little. For them enterprize is a thing impossible.

In short, in the words of that great common-sense philosopher, Carlyle, "Human education is a thing of earnest facts, of capabilities developed, of habits established, of dispositions dealt with, of tendencies confirmed and tendenc[i]es repressed." It is "to develope the man into *doing* something" and cannot but be invaluable to human society.

Is it now necessary to consume time and words in answering the question, Does education pay?[1]

WWhw MS. (WP, DLC). WW repeated his title before each article. These repetitions have been omitted.

1 These three sections may have been written over the period of several weeks. JRW made several deletions and additions in the third section. They have been omitted. WW sent these articles to the editor of the Wilmington *Morning Star*, William H. Bernard, between about August 20 and September 29, 1880, for Bernard rewrote them, using WW's first article for an editorial in the *Morning Star* on August 26, WW's second for an editorial published on Sept. 7, and WW's third for an editorial printed on Sept. 30, 1880. Bernard followed WW's text closely, revising only lightly and giving WW no credit for his efforts. For example, compare the following first paragraph of Bernard's editorial on September 7 with the first paragraph in WW's first section:

"As we stated in a former article we purpose from time to time considering the subject of the education of the people. This is a topic which all must admit to be of present interest and of supreme importance. We shall not dwell at any great length upon the intellectual advantages which never fail to follow in the train of education. We shall not make its *moral* blessings the direct theme of our discussion. That it brings light to the understanding and strength to moral sentiments few persons with any fair show of reason can refuse to allow. The practical value of quickened faculties does not need the establishment of proof. A mind that knows how to think and where to find whatever information it does not possess already, and a sense of right and wrong which has been shown the way to truth and which does not need a spur to make it go aright are worth more than capital on a farm; are more valuable than party prizes at the polls; and are of more service than the gift of eloquence in the conduct of legislation. Since these are conclusions at which very few, if any, intelligent persons will demur, we have a very solid foundation on which to rest our argument for general education, and on which to build the simple, practical suggestions as to the best means for its perfection."

For WW's later comments on this series and Bernard's failure to credit him with the authorship, see WW to R. Bridges, March 15, 1882, Vol. 2.

To Robert Bridges

Fort Lewis, Green Valley, Virginia, Aug. 22nd 1880.
My dear Bobby,

Your letter[1]—so welcome because so long hoped for—addressed to Wilmington was forwarded to me at the University and, soon after reaching home, I received the copy of your paper which you sent me. The present is really the first leisure time I have had for writing since the receipt of either. The University session, beginning, as it does, on the first of October, does not close until the first days of July; and your letter found me busy with all the little, time-absorbing duties that come with the approach of Commencement. A University Commencement is so entirely different from a Princeton Commencement that you may be interested in a brief description of it.

On Sabbath there is no baccalaureate, but, instead, a sermon before the Young Mens' Christian Association by some invited divine of distinction. We had Dr. Stewart Robinson,[2] from Louisville, Ky, who, you remember, preached at dear old P. last year. My experience of his preaching on that occasion rather lessened my desire to hear him this time—so during the sermon I found a cool place outside to spend the hour of its continuance. On Monday morning there is a "German" in the *Library*, a large handsome room with a spacious floor just suited for dancing, and heavily-loaded galleries of serried bookshelves; on Monday evening the "Final Celebration" of the Washington Literary Society, and, afterwards, a promenade concert very much *à la* Princeton, the grounds being decorated and illuminated with Chinese lanterns. On Tuesday morning, another "German"; on Tuesday evening, the Final Celebration of the Jefferson Literary Society (to wh. yours truly belongs), and another promenade concert. On Wednesday morning another "German"; on Wednesday evening, the "Joint Celebration["] of the two literary societies, when they are addressed by some invited orator—this time by ex-governor [Richard B.] Hubbard of Texas, just returned from the Democratic Convention at Cin[cinnati]. On Thursday there is the distribution of diplomas (but no speaking by the graduates) and an address by some alumnus before the society of alumni. Thus ends these days of *dancing and monotony.* I would have escaped the bore if I had not had a part to play on Tuesday night. I had been so fortunate in the contests in the Jefferson Society as to receive at the close of the session the fifty dollar medal as "their best orator for the session of 1879-80," and at the Final Celebration had to speak as annual orator of the Society. I'm not a good speaker yet by any means, Bobby, but I've worked hard during the past year to perfect myself in the art and now speak much better than I ever did at dear old Princeton. I spoke this last time to certainly the most brilliant audience I ever saw and received more congratulations on my speech than were at all good for me. The Richmond papers were full of praises and even the New York papers spoke very highly of its subject and style.[3] I tell you these things, Bobby, just as I would expect you to tell me all your good luck—because I know it will gratify you, and not because I wish to glorify myself in your eyes. I am happy in the knowledge that I am secure in your estimation without recommending myself to it.

I can hardly describe to you the queer sensations that were produced by the perusal of your letter or the conflict of thoughts it aroused. Of course I enjoyed the letter, as I enjoy everything from you. But the news it contained absolutely startled me. I had, of course, all along been thinking of you as staying quietly at home with your books, your evenings spent in pleasant company—with your living friends, as your days were spent in the companionship of the dead who yet live in their works; and you can easily imagine my surprise at receiving a letter from you dated Rochester and containing such an account of hard, driving work, and experiences

of wh. I can form only a faint conception.[4] My first feeling was one
of chagrin and disappointment. Of course I knew that you expected
to become a journalist and that every one who enters journalism
must be content to undergo the preliminary discipline and the
preparatory drudgery of reporting. But some how I had always
hoped that *you* might escape such trying experiences and be allowed always to pursue higher literary work. To be sure this was
all a hope, resting on no positive expectation of its proving practicable. But it was a hope that I had continued to cherish and which
was rudely and painfully broken by the news contained in your
letter. After re-reading it, however, I began to incline to agree with
you in thinking that such employment was just what would prove
of most advantage to one of your disposition just as [at] this time
of life, since it was calculated to sharpen the edge of the practical
faculties and to properly subordinate the contemplative. And certainly all the time, mixed even with my first disappointment, there
was a strong feeling of gratification at your having secured a desirable place in a pleasant city, with an old friend [W. B. Lee], and
with every prospect of quick success. And, Bobby, if I doubted at
first of the result of the experiment you are making, my misgivings were dispelled by the reading of the marked article you sent
me.[5] I don't know that it shows an improved *style*—I always did
think your style admirable, and if there is any step towards *improvement* in this article it seems to me to be in the direction of
simplicity. But the *great* improvement I noticed was in the absence of all mataphysical analysis and reflection in the treatment
of a subject wh. so evidently invited the one and tempted to the
other. I think the sketch perfect, Bobby, and its perfection consists in its peculiar vividness, its studied simplicity, and its sug-
gestiveness. It is so true to life that this one scene tells a whole
story and reaches near to the height of art by being full of writing between the lines, by suggesting to each reader reflections
which just fit his own mood and frame of mind and which could
not have been put in words by the writer without disappointing or
repelling readers of other moods and different frames of mind.
This is very awkward, obscure criticism, Bobby, but I know that
you will understand what I mean and be able to supply what I
have been unable to express. I know this much that I took as
much interest in that piece as if I had written it myself.

I am Summering off in the country here fifteen miles from the
rail-road, with only two mails a week to acquaint me with whatever may be going on in the world outside. This is a delightful
country of pure mountain air, splendid country fare, very com-

fortable accommodations, and every facility for free, healthful, invigorating exercise. I am here with a family party and am spending the time in the quiet way which best suits my tastes and most rests me after a college term. I spend part of the day reading and the rest of it rambling, and rowing on the pretty little stream which runs almost at the foot of the hill on which this house stands. I wish you were here to enjoy country life with me, Bobby. Do write whenever you can catch a moment of leisure. Dont be ashamed of patch-work letters. I enjoy them all the same for they bear the savour of our old friendship, just as well as if they were more elaborate.

I have heard not a word from any of the rest of "the gang" for this long time past, and am utterly in the dark as to their doings or even their whereabouts. I have neglected them in the matter of correspondence and have, in consequence, and no doubt deservedly, been neglected in like manner by them.

With much love to the Heathen and a great deal for yourself,

Your very sincere friend   T. Woodrow Wilson

ALS (Meyer Coll., DLC).
 [1] R. Bridges to WW, May 30, 1880, ALS (WP, DLC).
 [2] The Rev. Stuart Robinson, D.D., pastor of the Second Presbyterian Church of Louisville.
 [3] A search of the New York newspapers failed to reveal any reports of WW's speech of June 29, 1880.
 [4] Bridges had written that he had accepted an editorial position on the *Rochester Democrat and Chronicle* and was working fourteen hours a day.
 [5] It is missing.

From Janet Woodrow Wilson

Saratoga Springs. Wednesday Aug 23. [1880]

My darling Woodrow—

I am going to make a desperate effort to *call* you Woodrow from this time on. The truth is, I have learned to love the name we have called you ever since your baby-hood so much, that I have found it hard to resolve to give it up. But "Tommy" is certainly an unsuitable name for a grown man—and besides, I always wanted to call you Woodrow from the first. You will not think that it sounds less loving? . . .   Lovingly Your Mother.

P.S. omitted. ALS (WP, DLC).

From Robert Bridges

Dear Tommy,   Rochester, [N. Y.] Aug 31st '80
. . . I often think of you at your scholarly pursuits and envy you. I am so glad that you tell me of what you have done and of your

success. I never have the least doubt, Tommy, that you will realize your ideal. You pursue it systematically and are never swerved to one side by circumstances. If you have life and health you will accomplish all that you have planned. Will and work will accomplish anything and you have them in a remarkable combination. I wish I had a tenth of their power. . . .

I have written you a long rambling letter, old fellow, like one of our triangle talks. Don't let us drift apart, Tommy. Although we have only written once in five or six months, yet I know we have not forgotten each other. Not a day passes but I think of you and Pete. I don't believe a man ever had two such congenial friends as I had in college. You were very different, and each filled a place in my heart that the other could not—or no one ever can. It is very pleasant to look back upon, and I shall always keep the memory fresh. It is sad, very sad, my friend, to think that the old life will never be a reality again. Good-bye, old fellow, and don't forget,

Your Friend   Bob Bridges.

ALS (WP, DLC) with WWhw notations on env.: "Rec'd Sept. 10th 1880"; "Ans. Sept. 18th 1880."

To Robert Bridges

Dear Bobby,   Fort Lewis, Bath Co., Va., Sept. 18th 1880

I can't tell you how much good your "long, rambling letter, like one of our triangle talks," did me! It gave me almost as much pleasure as one of those walks themselves, which I shall never forget, and which I often look back upon with such a longing. However large a place I may have filled in your friendship at college, Bobby, it can't have been larger or more secure than that which was kept for you in *my* heart; and, if I can judge by my own feelings, there is little danger of our drifting apart. Our *characters* were for the most part formed before we left dear of [old] Princeton, and as long as we remain what we were then, we will always be the same to each other.

And yet, after all, you are a little mistaken in your estimate of me, old fellow. Do not imagine that I am never discouraged. I hope that I'm never *conquered* by discouragement; but I'm absolutely ashamed of the weak fears and the unmanly dispair which have seldom failed to come after my numerous failures. I tell you one thing, Bobby, I'm absolutely dependent on sympathy—the sympathy we were able to feel in each others' work at Princeton was to me the most blessed part of the rare intercourse we enjoyed there; and the lack of any such sympathy has been just the hardest trial I've had to bear at the University[.] There are no men like 79's to be found there.

Have you heard anything from Charlie lately? I wrote to the rascal about two months or more ago, but never a word have I heard from him this long time past. I wrote to Pete some time since—about the time I wrote my last letter to you—directing to the care of the *Evening Post*, but have gotten no answer as yet. I'm afraid the dear old crazy is vexed with me for my shameful dilatoriness in correspondence. He has a perfect right to be, I must confess, but I sincerely hope it is not so—but that my note did not reach him, or he did not read it. How I envy you the expected pleasure of an early visit from him!

I'm deeply interested in your reporting experience, Bobby, and enjoy every detail of it. I agree with you entirely in thinking that it promises you very great benefit. Are you going to stick to it? You dropped a hint in one of your letters to the effect that, after having tried reporting long enough to reap all its advantages, you might turn to the law or elsewhither. Have you any definite plans? I *know* you'll succeed, whatever you go into, and I'd be only too glad to see you try the profession in which I'm going to try my fortunes.

Although my law course is drawing near its end, I don't know yet where I will practice. My desires point to Baltimore or Philadelphia, but I don't know yet whether there can be found a really good opening for me in either place. I want to begin in some large city, where there is at least *opportunity* for great things to be accomplished, whether I'm equal to their accomplishment or not. Where there's no room for ambition there's less incentive to great exertions; don't you think so?

I find this beautiful Virginia farm on which I'm staying a very interesting place indeed. It has a history of its own which suggests very many reflections. Its low lands, lying, between two high ranges of hills, along a lovely river bottom, was granted to one John Lewis by George III and continued in the Lewis family until March of last year when it passed into the hands of the present owner, a jovial, good-hearted, easy-going farmer and cattle-raiser named Fultz, with whom I am boarding. He bought at Commissioners' sale. The property had been wasted through the profligacy and unthriftiness of a bachelor of the old family, into whose hands it had come and had to be sold for debt. How hard that such an estate should pass out of the family, whose it had been for a hundred years or more, in such a manner! The Lewis' had held in this part of the country just such a position of respectibility and influence as a wealthy English squire occupies and had played just such a leading part; and their poverty is now all the more mortifying and harassing. Those that remain of them now live upon an adjoining farm, in comparative comfort, but in greatly reduced circumstances.

I've been occupying some of the hotter hours of the days for the last week or two in copying an article which I wrote last year at the University.[1] It is a further discussion of the subject of my article which appeared in the *International Review* last Summer and is, in my opinion, superior to the first. Whether it will meet with similar success is another and a very much more doubtful question. I sincerely hope that it will not have the same sad fate which overtook the piece I wrote on French politics. That went a begging among the big reviews—was a complete failure in the matter of finding a publication, and is now put away in all the decency of burial. This present paper deserves a better fate, I hope, but is not likely to meet a better.

My quiet life out here gives me no news to tell, and I brought very few books—only "Webster's Great Speeches," two volumes of Bright's speeches, a Bible, and Bacon's Essays. I wanted to keep away from books and in the open air as much as possible. And I certainly found very few books here, outside of Macaulay and a few others that every one seems to have. My principal literary amusement has been the study of *pronunciation*. I am here with an aunt[2] who is an exceedingly interested student of things literary—as indeed of all things valuable and instructive—and quite an acute critic withal, without being a writer herself or having any the slightest taint of *blue-stockingism* about her. Well, with her I've been ransacking Worcester, whom we both bow to as the highest authority, from whom there can be no reasonable appeal. And I can tell you many of our old methods of pronunciation have been rudely overthrown; for instance, we have drilled ourselves into saying squālor, sōmbre, izolate, &c. &c. I never before fully realized what a fund of instruction and what a store of information there is to be found in Worcester unabridged.

The time not spent in such literary pastimes, I spend out of doors generally. Yesterday I walked over to Green Valley, our post office, for the mail. It is about four miles distant and to walk both ways over a hilly and rocky mountain road I found considerable exercise, but not too much to be enjoyable.

The University term does not begin until the first of October, so my vacation loaf is not over by some two weeks yet, and those two weeks I intend to enjoy to the top of my bent. If only there were some fair damsel out here to beguile my leisure moments, my contentment would be supreme.

I want you to give my warmest love to Chang. I know that he feels hurt at the way I've treated him in regard to corresponding. My time at the University was so engrossed by my studies that I neglected all my correspondents, occasionally even my family. Since the term closed I've hesitated about writing to Chang just because of my dislike to appear as one who fortifies a friendship by tardy excuses. I sincerely hope he is not offended. I wouldn't loose his regard for the world. Give him loads of love, if he'll take them. How I would like to deliver my message in person!

Bobby, please write to me whenever you can. My letters from you I treasure up as things of great value

Your loving friend,   Tommy.

ALS (Meyer Coll., DLC).
  1 "Congressional Government," printed at Oct. 1, 1879.
  2 Marion Woodrow Bones.

From Harold Godwin

My dear Tommy:—   Roslyn L. I. Oct 2d 1880.
   . . . I quite agree with you about the Democratic ticket and party. It is curious to see the Republicans in their death struggle. The last kick is the old saw of *protection* and I think that they will loose as many honest votes by it as ever they can gain. . . .

Ever   H. G.

ALI (WP, DLC) with WWhw notation on env.: "Ans 10/12/80."

To Harriet Woodrow

University of Virginia, Va., Sept. [Oct.] 5th 1880.
My precious Cousin,

The first evening of my return to University quarters cannot be better spent than in writing a letter to you. Mother and Josie left Charlottesville this morning at three o'clock. They came on with me from Fort Lewis on last Thursday, and since then I've been spending all of my time that was not occupied with University duties in town with them. It is only to-night, therefore, that I find myself settled in my new quarters—for they are new quarters, my present room being some distance from the one I occupied last session, and, on the whole, much more pleasantly situated.[1]

I feel right lonely and disconsolate to-night at being left to plod out another long weary session, and am greedy enough to wish for another long letter from you to brighten me up. If your trying delay at Huntington produced no other good result, it at least brought a great pleasure to me in the shape of your letter. What was the subsequent history of your delay? I've wondered every day since the receipt of your letter how long you were compelled to drag out your stay there, and whether you were still kept away from home. I sincerely hope that by this time you have been at home long enough to forget all about your fatigue.

Now, Hattie, there is not a bit of news or of anything that would specially interest you to write about from this stupid place, so I'm going to run the risk of tiring you by writing about things in general which interest me, and about yourself and myself in particular. And, in the first place, I want you to promise to write to me as often as you can. I know of nothing that I dread more intensely than the possibility that we should drift apart now that we are separated without any immediate prospect of seeing each other soon again. I'm a great believer in free correspondence. As for myself, I suspect that one might find out almost, if not quite, as much about me from my letters as by associating with me, for I am apt to let my thoughts and feelings slip more readily from the end of my pen than from the end of my tongue. The only difference is that by associating with me one might discover my unamiable traits much more clearly than from what I have deliberately written. At any rate, however it may be with myself in this respect, since we cannot see each other this Winter, I can ask no greater favor than that you will write me frequent letters full of yourself —and I hope that you wont think that I'm asking too much.

Hattie, why didn't you tell me of the annoyance to which you were subjected last Winter in consequence of my too frequent visits to Staunton? If I had for one moment so much as dreamed of such a thing, I would have foregone the pleasure of those trips rather than have you irritated as you must have been by the reports of idle gossips. If I had known of it in time to prevent it by staying away, I certainly should have done so. But, of course you could not have told me of such a thing! I was about to say that I wished I *had* known it, in order to have kept you from such a disagreeable experience: but I would be representing myself as much more unselfish and selfsacrifising than I am, if I were to pretend to wish that I had known what would have deprived me of all the enjoyment I derived from the opportunity of seeing you sometimes, last Winter. I hope you will excuse my referring to this matter again. I was unwilling to dismiss it finally without assuring you that I knew not one word of it until I reached home and heard what Maggie Williams had said, for I didn't want you to think me so entirely selfish.

I suppose that by this time Aunt Marion is in Staunton with Jessie.[2] When we left Fort Lewis she intended to go to Staunton on Monday, yesterday. She will remain there several weeks, to superintend the making of Jessie's Winter dresses by Miss Rapp, and to have a dress made for herself, by the same lady. She has promised, after her duties in Staunton are accomplished, to return home by way of Wilmington and pay mother a visit of some days. Won't that be nice? Of course I have heard frequently from Jessie since she returned to school, once directly through a letter to myself, and several times indirectly, through letters to Aunt Marion and one to Josie and Marion jointly. She is devoting herself enthusiastically to her music, giving it *six hours* a day. I am afraid, judging from a schedule of her daily engagements which she sent me, that she is confining herself *too* much, and has taken more work than she can successfully perform all Winter long. But her vigor of body don't seem to promise to desert her very soon. She says that she proves her strength by numerous *pillow* battles with her three room-mates, in which she invariably vanquishes them single-handed; and she gives very ludicrous descriptions of frolics after the gas is turned off—frolics in which the chief fun seems to be in falling over chairs and other small obstacles. She and her room-mates have invested in cheese cloth (whatever that may be) curtains trimmed with red for the windows of their room and have succeeded in drawing from Miss Baldwin[3] the opinion that theirs is the prettiest room in the school.

I need not tell you how much we all enjoyed Aunt Helen's and Wilson's[4] visit to Fort Lewis. I can say for myself that it was a rare treat. I only wished that they could have staid longer, though I am afraid that for them a longer stay at Fort Lewis would not have been very entertaining

Is it finally determined that you are to go to Cincinnati this Winter? I am very anxious to learn what your plans are. Although I know so little about it myself, I can easily understand how music would become an exceedingly fascinating as well as useful study and I am sure that a thorough mastery of it is worth even the sacrifice of another year away from home. Don't you think that some of these days you might turn teacher and teach me a little about music? We had a good deal of enjoyment this Summer in singing. Mr. Brown has an excellent bass voice and he, Aunt Marion, Jessie, and I constituted ourselves a quartette and sang a great deal, confining ourselves to sacred music for the most part and trying no very ambitious pieces. Aunt Helen told me of your singing, and gave me some further particulars, as to your costume, &c, of the operetta. How I would have liked to have heard it! Do you really like to sing?

Most of my friends of last year are back, and, in spite of the many *new* faces I see every day, everything seems painfully natural here. My fraternity has a large membership here this year and I am trying to forget my lonliness by entering on its work with renewed vigor. The literary society has not yet reorganized, but that's a small matter to me this year, for I cannot hope to take as active a part in it this year as I did last. My law studies will, I am afraid, compel me to be a silent member most of the session—though there's no telling how soon I'll be tempted into making a speech. I'm going to be a systematic visitor of the young ladies this Winter. This will be my last college year and next Winter I will be obliged to go out into society. So this year I must put myself in training. I am afraid that I am sadly deficient in social accomplishments. I can't talk without anything to say. In fact I'm always inclined to be *mum* just when I am most anxious to appear to advantage by making myself interesting. There are very few girls around here that I care to visit, in fact there's not a single one who has any special attraction for me. But I must learn to visit those who don't interest me as well as those who do.

Sister Marion wrote me some weeks ago that brother Ross was to preach for the Maysville (Ky) people last Sabbath, the first Sabbath in October. Wouldn't it be fine if he were to move there? He will certainly go somewhere very soon, for his health, as well as sister Marion's and the children's has been very much impaired by the terrible malaria of the region of Arkansas where they now are.

Did you know that John Vanmeter[5] is here at the University? I saw him, you know, at Staunton with his sister, but I did not recognize him as he rode up in the omnibus with me, nor until he registered just before me at the hotel. I have not yet introduced myself to him, but I fully intend doing so as soon as I can make an opportunity, for I know how hard it is for a new student to get acquainted here; and besides I want to know him, because he is from Chillicothe. I'll have to explain to him who I am, which will be rather embarrassing, but I won't mind that much.

It's after bed-time, and I was up very early this morning, so I must say good-night. I'm afraid that you have already found these queer square pages very long and very full of nothing, and wont be sorry to see this *last* one. I've written this rambling epistle because I felt like having a talk with you and wanted to send you a big message of love.

With much love to uncle Thomas, Aunt Helen, Wilson, Tommy, and the sweet baby.[6]   Your loving cousin   T. Woodrow Wilson

ALS (WC, NjP).
  [1] Room 31 West Range.
  [2] Mr. and Mrs. James W. Bones had recently moved back to Rome, Ga.
  [3] Mary Julia Baldwin, head of Augusta Female Seminary, 1863-97.
  [4] Hattie's mother, Helen Sill Woodrow, and her brother, James Wilson Woodrow.
  [5] John I. Vanmeter, '81.
  [6] Hattie's parents and brother Wilson and her second brother, Thomas R. The baby was either her sister Helen or her third brother, Herbert H.

From Joseph Ruggles Wilson

My darling son   Wilm[ingto]n [N. C.] Oct. 5 1880
  . . . Please, my precious boy, do not allow your thoughts to be depressed as I fear they are. Let the future care for itself is both the dictate of Scripture and of good sense. The *present* is enough for any ordinary mortal to bear; and *it* being well cared for, what comes after will need *no* care. I beg of you to study this year *law only* & leaving general literature to the cobwebs[.] I have begun the needful preliminaries as to your prospective settlement in one of the larger cities. But, nothing would delight me more than to have you at home for a year or so after your University course shall have been completed. Any how do not fear. You can afford to trust in God, and He has so fitted His providences to your case that you can afford also to trust yourself.

  Prof Venable spoke of you in the highest terms. . . .
                    Affectionately   Your Father

ALS (WP, DLC) with WWhw miscl. notes and figures on env.

From Janet Woodrow Wilson

My darling son,   Wilmington N. C. Friday Oct. 8. [1880]
  Your cheerful & hopeful letter of yesterday, which we received today, gave us much happiness. I am so relieved to hear that you are feeling so much better. I *hoped* that you would feel very differently after you got settled, and regularly to work—but I *feared* that you were going to have a spell of sickness. You can imagine the relief given by your sweet letter received this morning. By the way, what a comfort such prompt communication is! . . .
                    Yours lovingly   Mother.

ALS (WP, DLC) with WWhw notation on env.: "Ans 10/12/80."

From the Minutes of the Jefferson Society

Jefferson Society Oct 9th/80

The first meeting of the Society for session '80-'81 was held Oct. 9th, Mr. Wilson in the chair. Election of Officers being first in order of business, upon nomination by Mr. Lefevre[1] of Mr. T. W. Wilson for President, the latter gentleman was unanimously elected to that office. Mr. Pringle T. Youmans was then nominated & elected vice president & Mr. C. W. Kent Treasurer. Mr. Wilson gave notice that he would at some future time introduce a reso- lution to appoint a committee for revising our constitution. . . .

T. Woodrow Wilson, Pres.   A. W. Patterson, Sect'y.

[1] Walter S. Lefevre, '81.

To Charles Andrew Talcott

My dear Charlie,   University of Virginia, Va., October 11th 1880

Your welcome letter of Sept. 4th[1] has just reached me. Our ses- sion don't open here until the first of October, and your letter, reaching here before I did, was forwarded by our postmaster to Wilmington, while I was absent from home, in the Virginia moun- tains, where I've spent the greater part of my vacation. My Sum- mer was very delightfully passed. During August and Sept. I was at a private place in the country, among mountains that afforded every variety of the finest scenery, where there was opportunity for the enjoyment of every amusement the idle might desire or the adventurous might wish for. I spent almost the whole of each day out of doors, rambling through the woods, climbing all sorts of places, or rowing—about as fast as a Princeton crew—on a very picturesque little river. I scarcely looked into a book the whole vacation through. One or two of Webster's and one or two of Bright's speeches were the extent of my reading, outside of the few newspapers which a tardy semi-weekly mail brought, with news that was stale to the outside world, no doubt, but which was new and very eagerly devoured by our party. Yes, my interest in politics, so far from having abated, seems keener than ever, per- haps because my rustication has for so many weeks shut me off from all accurate knowledge of the course political events were taking. You ask me to write you my ideas on the present condi- tion of politics; but I am inclined to think that nothing but the power of prophecy would enable one to throw any *light* on this subject just at present. I believe that we are nearing the close of a period of *transition,* and what exactly is to come I do not suppose that any man would be able to say. I firmly believe that the Republican party, as a party, is doomed to speedy death. Did you read Lyman Trumbull's big speech, delivered in Ill. this Summer? It's quite an able thing of its kind and fully repays perusal. Trumbull was, you know, before the war came on, a Democrat. When the war came, he acted with the Republicans: since the war he has returned to his former allegiance. In the speech to which I refer he enters into a somewhat elaborate review of his conduct by way of explanation and self-justification—and self-*glorification*; and it is in the course of this review that he brings out the striking and instructive fact, that the Democratic party to-day stands just where the Republicans stood before the war, advocates of identically the same principles, representatives of exactly the same—or, at least, very similar purposes. Meanwhile, the Republican party has been going through not only a process of transformation which has proved a process of degradation, but also through a process of disintegration. We now have, therefore, the strange and ominous spectacle of, on the one side, a party departed utterly from the principles of its one-time greatest leaders, at war with itself, its only creed one of hatred for a section of their own country and their own people, and about to have torn from it its last title to regard—the possession of power:—on the other side, a party, turned from its early beliefs, allying itself, in its pursuit of power, with every damnable heresy—with Greenbackers as with protectionists—whose only claim to respect is that it is less impure than its opponent, whose chief recommendation is that its leader is pure, upright, able, and resolute! If this be a true picture, how can one help believing that such a state of things is premonitory of some great change to come—only the confusion of the elements which precedes a great change of weather? So the conclusion of the whole matter is that I wait, ignorantly, but hopefully and patiently for the setting in of a period of change of parties and of more orderly progress—when reason may get some show of a hearing and passion will quit the boards—or, at least, be relegated to a more subordinate part. It's taken a great many words for me to explain that I know nothing about the matter, hasn't it?

I heard from Pete Godwin the other day.[2] He is in New York again and is by this time at work, serving an apprenticeship in the art department of the Eve. Post, some day, no doubt, to be promoted to the Art Critic's chair. His duties now seem chiefly to consist in compiling notes from foreign newspapers, later on to issue in work in theatres, concert halls, artist's studios, etc.

He's the same old crazy, with only a few more sober ideas in his pate.

I need not say that I enjoyed your letter hugely, and will wish very much for another. I'm hard at work once more on the law, and begin to see my way through its mazes at times a little more clearly. With as much love as ever

Your sincere friend   T. W. Wilson

ALS (photostat in RSB Coll., DLC).
1 C. A. Talcott to WW, Sept. 4, 1880, ALS (WP, DLC).
2 An extract is printed at Oct. 2, 1880.

From the Minutes of the Jefferson Society

Hall of Jefferson Society, Oct 16th 1880.

. . . Mr. Dabney[1] moved that a committee be elected to draught a new constitution & Bylaws—Tabled.

1 Richard Heath Dabney, born March 29, 1860. M.A., University of Virginia, 1881; student, universities of Munich, Berlin, and Heidelberg, 1882-85; Ph.D., University of Heidelberg, 1885. Taught, New York Latin School, 1881-82. Professor of History, Indiana University, 1886-89; Adjunct Professor of History, University of Virginia, 1889-96; Associate Professor of History, same institution, 1896-97; Professor of History, same institution, 1897-1938; Dean, Graduate School, same institution, 1905-23. Died May 16, 1947.

From Joseph Ruggles Wilson

My precious son—   Wilmington [N. C.] Tuesday, Oct. 19, 1880

Your welcome letter dated the 17th (Sunday!) reached me this morning. It gave me real pleasure as all your letters do. Perhaps you are getting to believe yourself rather [more] aged than you are, and thus to look around upon life as one who has somewhat tediously tried it, only to find it wanting. I would rather have you, dear one, kindle the fires of hope until they blaze to the skies, than sit down over any ashes of the past however commemorative to sigh over the fires that are now gone out. What I mean is: rejoice in the fact that you are so soon to face those realities which are already beginning to give place to their anticipative dreams—and to find out for yourself what they *truly* are and what pluck is in you to meet and to exchange fists with them. Expect success and not failure. Say to the future, 'others have conquered you and so will I—God helping me, the odds shall be on my side.' Do not think that you have written gloomily because I am thus responding. I am only reading between the lines where the true meaning usually is—and there I discern a face of solicitude, and hear sighs of anxiety, and perceive regrets that what has been may not be again. Am I wrong? Perhaps I am, and am only substituting my own fancy for imagined yours. . . .

Whilst in N. York & Phila. I laid the train for your future so far as I could. That is, I know with whom to correspond with reference to it when the time for action shall have come nearer. Prof Venable has promised to help us—who has a high opinion of your merits. Don't fear, my darling boy, but fill up the passing hours with study as if all depended upon—*now*,—as indeed it does. . . .   Love   Your Father

ALS (WP, DLC) with WWhw notation and scribbling on env.

From the Minutes of the Jefferson Society

Jeff. Hall, Oct. 23d 1880
. . . Mr. Dabney's motion, tabled at the preceding meeting, was brought up & upon motion Mr. Wilson vacated the chair to explain the object object [*sic*] of the motion & showed the urgent necessity of revising the Constitution & Bylaws. The Committee for the purpose was then elected, co[n]sisting of Messr Lefevre & Andrews, with Mr. Wilson as ex officio chairman. . . .

From Janet Woodrow Wilson

My darling Son,   Wilmington, N. C. Nov. 5th 1880
. . . Your father was so pleased by your last report. I wish you could have seen his face when he read the only words written— "never"—"never"—under the "absent" head, you know—they seemed so emphatic—triumphant in fact. . . .

Your own loving Mother

ALS (WP, DLC) with WWhw notation on env.; "Ans" and WWhw and WWsh notes.

From Robert Bridges

Dear Tommy: Rochester, N Y, Nov. 13th 1880 1. a m
. . . I am looking for your article[1] in the International. It will be a great question in the near future and you will have the inside track. Stick to it, old boy, it will make you famous sometime. I think you ought to settle in the South. You would have more chance there at the start. You are known. Your country is growing rapidly. You will go up with it. The fact is in an overcrowded profession in one of our northern cities a young man does not rise

in merit, so much as in influence and trickery. I see all sides of
life in my reporting and am not impressed with the dignity of a
modern city-bar. This is a hasty letter but none the less from
Your Old Friend   Bob Bridges.

ALS (WP, DLC) with WWhw notation on env.: "Rec'd 11/17/80."
1 "Congressional Government."

From Joseph Ruggles Wilson

My darling son   Wilmington, [N. C.] Nov 19, '80.
. . . I am glad that your studies are keeping your head above the
waters of despondency. You did well to take those lessons in Elocution. Rules—mere rules—are not worth much in teaching one
how to speak, but *principles* are everything; and I trust from what
you write that your instruction has given you these fully and in-
telligibly. . . . Your own   Father

ALS (WP, DLC) with WWhw and WWsh notations on env.

From the Minutes of the Jefferson Society

Hall of Jefferson Society, Novr 20th 1880.
The Society was called to order at the usual hour by President
Wilson & after the roll call & reading of Minutes, proceeded to
the election of officers for the ensuing term. Upon nomination by
Mr. Youmans, Mr. Lefevre was unanimously elected president,
Mr. Gaines[1] vice-president. . . .

1 Clement C. Gaines, LL.B., '82.

Hall of Jefferson Society, Nov. 27th 1880.
The society was called to order at the regular hour by the President, Mr. Wilson. The secretary being absent Mr. Blair[1] was requested to supply his place pro tem. After the calling of the roll &
the reading & approval of the minutes of last meeting, the President yielded the Chair to Mr. Lefevre & the Vice-Pres. elect, Mr.
C C. Gaines took the vice P's chair. . . .
Mr. Wilson reported in behalf of the Constitution committee
that the com's work was nearly completed & that they expected
to submit their report at the next meeting. . . .

1 Joseph P. Blair, M.A., '81.

Hall of Jefferson Society Dec 4th 1880
. . . The report of the Constitution committee followed. A motion
that the House go into a committee of the whole for the considera-

tion of the report, was carried. Mr. Dabney was appointed Chairman of the committee, & reported the adoption of the Preample & Art I. His report was adopted by the house. . . .

EDITORIAL NOTE
THE CONSTITUTION OF THE JEFFERSON SOCIETY

The constitution of the Jefferson Society printed below was, as entries from the minutes of the Society have already indicated, the fruit of Wilson's initiative and the work of a committee of which he was the chairman. Although it is impossible to determine Wilson's role in the drafting of the new constitution in every respect, the editors have concluded that it is fundamentally and essentially a Wilsonian document and merits a place in the printed record of his writings.

The Jefferson Society adopted its first constitution in the year of its founding, 1825. It was revised from time to time. The last revision before the drafting of the constitution of 1880 appears to have been the one made during the academic year 1858-59. The fire of 1895 in the Rotunda at the University of Virginia destroyed the Society's minute books down to 1875 and many other records, and the copy of the constitution of 1858-59 survives only because it had been separately printed in 1860.[1] The editors have concluded from internal and other evidence that Wilson and his colleagues used the constitution of 1858-59 as the basis for their new constitution.

The constitution of 1858-59 was a brief and incomplete document of seven articles, to which were appended forty-one by-laws. Through the latter were scattered, almost at random, substantive provisions more appropriate in the constitution itself. The text of the constitution of 1880 reveals that Wilson and his committee systematically transferred substantive matters from the by-laws of the old constitution to the new frame of government, thus restricting their own new by-laws to procedural regulations. They did not hesitate to add new provisions and to eliminate others.

From a detailed comparison of the two constitutions, the following points about Wilson's role in drafting the document of 1880 emerge:

1. The conciseness, order, and structure of the new constitution reflect Wilson's consistent passion for these qualities.

2. The elaborate governmental machinery established by the new constitution also reflects an important Wilsonian concern. The constitution of 1880 created no fewer than four new committees—a Ways and Means Committee, a Conference Committee, a Judicial Council, and a Final Committee—and gave them functions either wholly new or functions that had hitherto been exercised in whole or in part by individual officers.

3. The new constitution's considerable diffusion of executive power among the committees of the Society may show the young Wilson feeling his way toward the concept of a collective executive like the British Cabinet. At the same time, the new instrument greatly enlarged the powers of the house, for example, by new provisions for

[1] *Constitution of the Jefferson Society of the University of Virginia, Founded 1825* (Charlottesville, 1860).

appeal from executive rulings and requiring approval of disbursements by the whole Society rather than by a committee of three.

4. Clearly Wilsonian was the new constitution's striking emphasis upon and specific provisions for encouraging debate. The provision in Article V for debate by the full membership following the set debate and before the vote was taken was new. Also new were the interesting provisions in Articles V and VIII prohibiting use of parliamentary tactics to end debate before ten-thirty and stipulating that no Final President and Vice President or Medalist could be elected who had not participated in a certain number of debates. It is also worth noting that whereas oratory preceded debating in the old constitution's confused provisions for prizes, debating took precedence in the new.

5. One innovation in Article VI established a new medal for the "second-best" debater, thus regularizing the procedure followed in making the Bruce-Wilson awards in 1880.[2] This was the Society's choice among the three solutions proposed by the constitutional committee. However, it was not Wilson's first choice. As C. W. Kent to WW, Feb. 23, 1881, and R. H. Dabney to WW, March 14, 1881 (both in WP), make clear, Wilson strongly preferred a single award for the best debater. This one of the three proposed solutions was defeated by one vote. Provision for a second medal proved to be the only solution obtainable without splitting the Society. A concession to Wilson's point of view was the proviso that a single medal would be awarded when there were only two contestants.

6. The most direct evidence of Wilson's involvement is the clear reflection in Article VII, concerning the *Virginia University Magazine*, of his strong convictions about the proper constitution and duties of an editorial board. Here Wilson is applying lessons learned and policies advocated while managing editor of *The Princetonian*:[3] in creating a board of editors to choose and serve with an editor-in-chief; in lengthening the term of the editor-in-chief of the *Virginia University Magazine* from three months in the old constitution to one academic year; in greatly increasing the powers of the editor-in-chief; and in stipulating that no editor could serve who had not demonstrated competence by publishing at least one prose article in the *Magazine*; and in eliminating the old constitution's requirement that the winner of the prize for the best contribution to the *Magazine* had to deliver an oration, thus avoiding confusion of literary with oratorical skill.

[2] See the Editorial Note following documents printed at May 3, 1880.
[3] See, e.g., WW's editorial of April 4, 1878, and the news item of Oct. 24, 1878.

A New Constitution for the Jefferson Society[1]

REMARK.   [c. Dec. 4, 1880]

"THE JEFFERSON SOCIETY OF THE UNIVERSITY OF VIRGINIA" was organized on the 14th day of July, 1825, in Dormitory No. 7, on the

[1] *Constitution and By-Laws of the Jefferson Society, of the University of Virginia. Founded 1825. Published by Order of the Society* (Charlottesville, 1881).

West Lawn. Its first Constitution was drawn up by Edgar Mason of Maryland, James H. Lee, of Virginia, and W. C. Minor, of Missouri. Its present Constitution was framed by a Committee appointed during the session of 1880-81, consisting of

T. WOODROW WILSON, of North Carolina, *Chairman.*
WALTER S. LEFEVRE, of Maryland.
CHARLES LEE ANDREWS, of Maryland.

FORM OF INITIATION.

The President shall request the initiate (or initiates) to come forward and sign the Constitution, and shall then read to him (or them) the following:

Sir–(or Sirs)–You have voluntarily become a member (or members) of the Jefferson Society, and I have, in its name, to lay you under the most solemn injunctions to obey and uphold its Constitution, to observe all propriety as a member and a gentleman; and to advance, by strict adherence to duty, the welfare of our organization.

CONSTITUTION.

PREAMBLE.

We, the members of the Jefferson Society of the University of Virginia, in order to form a more perfect organization, provide for our common improvement in the art of debate, promote general culture amongst ourselves and those around us, and drill ourselves in all those exercises which strengthen for the free duties of citizenship, do ordain and establish this Constitution for our government.

ARTICLE I.

MEMBERSHIP.

Sec. 1. Only students in regular attendance upon one or more of the schools of the University of Virginia and not members of any other similar organization in this institution shall be eligible as regular members of this Society.

Sec. 2. The duties and privileges of regular membership in this Society, once assumed, can be renounced only by resignation, under the conditions and in accordance with the rules hereinafter set forth, and by the final termination of a member's connection with the University of Virginia as a student.

Sec 3. All the privileges of membership, except that of voting on Society business, shall be extended to alumni of the University of Virginia who have been members of the Society.

Sec. 4. The privilege of attendance upon the meetings of the Society shall be accorded to its honorary members, to regular members of the Washington Society of the University of Virginia, and to none others except by a special resolution agreed to by a vote of two-thirds of the members present.

Sec. 5. To the privileges and dignity of honorary membership this Society may elect such eminent persons as it may deem worthy of its courtesy.

Sec. 6. For the election of regular members of this Society a vote of two-thirds of the members present at any regular meeting shall be required.

Sec. 7. For the election of honorary members of this Society a vote of four-fifths of the members present at any regular meeting shall be required.

ARTICLE II.

OUTLINE OF GOVERNMENT.

Sec. 1. The executive government of this Society shall be vested in a President, a Vice-President, a Treasurer, a Committee of Ways and Means, a Committee of Conference, a Judicial Council, a Final Committee and a Question Committee.

Sec. 2. The President shall be elected by a majority of the members present at a regular meeting of the Society to serve for a term of three months.

Sec. 3. The Vice-President shall be chosen in the same manner and for the same term as the President.

Sec. 4. The Treasurer shall be elected in the same manner as the President, to serve during the academic session

Sec. 5. The Committee of Ways and Means shall consist of the Vice-President, as chairman *ex-officio*, and of two other members appointed by the President to serve during a presidential term.

Sec. 6 The Committee of Conference shall consist of five members appointed by the President to serve during the academic year.

Sec. 7. The Judicial Council shall consist of the President, the Vice-President and the Treasurer.

Sec. 8. The Final Committee shall be appointed by the President in February of each year, to serve during the remainder of the academic session, and shall consist of two members from the State of Virginia and one member from each of the other States represented in the Society; but in no case shall it consist of less than ten members.

Sec. 9. The Question Committee shall consist of two members appointed by the President to serve six weeks.

Sec. 10. The President shall appoint, to serve during his term of office, a Secretary and an Assistant Secretary; and shall appoint monthly a Sergeant-at Arms.

ARTICLE III.

DUTIES OF OFFICERS.

Sec. 1. *The President.*—The President shall preside over all meetings of the Society and of the Judicial Council, to preserve order and decorum; shall construe and enforce the Constitution and By-Laws of the Society and the rules of practice, subject always to an appeal to the Society itself; shall appoint the Secretary, the Assistant Secretary, the Sergeant-at-Arms, the non-official members of the Committee of Ways and Means, the Committee of Conference, the Final Committee, the Question Committee, all special committees ordered by the Society, and all officers *pro tempore*; and perform all other duties usually pertaining to his office.

It shall be his duty to convene the Society whenever requested to do so by a writing signed by *five* regular members.

He shall have no vote save a casting vote.

It shall be his privilege to take part in any of the regular debates of the Society, after having called the Vice-President to the chair *pro tempore*.

Sec. 2. *The Vice-President.*—The Vice-President shall be *ex-officio* chairman of the Committee of Ways and Means and member of the Judicial Council. In the absence of the President, he shall occupy the chair and exercise all the functions of presiding officer.

Sec. 3. *The Treasurer.*—The Treasurer shall receive and take charge of all the funds of the Society, keeping, in a book provided for the purpose, a careful and minute account of all receipts and disbursements, which account he shall submit to the Committee of Ways and Means at their regular meetings. He shall make no disbursements except such as shall have been approved by the Committee of Ways and Means and reported by that Committee to the Society. He shall report at each regular meeting of the Society a list of all fines imposed within the two preceding weeks, with the cause and date thereof, and an account of all moneys received and paid out since his last report, with receipted bills for all payments exceeding one dollar. His reports must be submitted in writing, in a book provided for the purpose, and shall, after adoption, be filed, together with all accompanying receipts, with the Secretary. He shall also submit at the end of each presidential term a full and exact written report of the financial condition of the Society which report he shall leave with the Committee of Ways and Means to be incorporated in their next regular report to the Society.

Sec. 4. *The Secretary.*—The Secretary shall keep a careful record of the proceedings of the Society; shall conduct its correspondence; shall carefully preserve all its records and all documents that may be entrusted to his care; shall transcribe, in a book kept for the purpose, all amendments and additions to this Constitution and to the By-Laws of the Society; shall read the appointments for debate; and shall perform all the duties naturally incident to the office of recording and corresponding Secretary.

Sec. 5. *The Assistant Secretary.*—The Assistant Secretary shall perform the duties of the Secretary in the absence of the latter; shall call the roll; shall keep an alphabetical list of the members of the Society, from which he shall, at each regular meeting, furnish the Secretary with the list of the appointments for debate for the third ensuing meeting; shall aid the Secretary, when no tellers are appointed, in taking the vote by ballot; and shall, at the close of each meeting, furnish the Treasurer with a list of the absentees from each roll-call.

Sec. 6. *The Sergeant-at-Arms.*—It shall be the duty of the Sergeant-at-Arms to see that no person enter the Hall of the Society during its meetings who is not privileged to be present by the provisions of this Constitution contained in Secs. II and III of Article I; to see that the Hall is suitably prepared for the meetings of the Society, and is left in proper condition after adjournment; to note all cases of disorder and neglect of duty, recording them, with the prescribed fines annexed, in a book to be provided for the purpose, reading them at the close of the meeting during which they have been incurred, and transmitting a list of them to the Treasurer immediately upon adjournment; and to act as the President's ministerial officer in enforcing order.

He may, with the consent of the President, appoint, when necessary, one or more temporary assistants to aid in enforcing order.

ARTICLE IV.

DUTIES OF COMMITTEES.

Sec. 1. *The Committee of Ways and Means.*—The Committee of Ways and Means shall meet in the Hall of the Society every Saturday evening immediately after the adjournment of the Judicial Council. It shall be their duty carefully to audit and examine at these their regular meetings, the accounts of the Treasurer; to act upon all bills presented by him and upon all disbursements which he shall report as necessary or expedient; to attend to the supplying of all necessaries for the Hall, and to the furnishing, heating and repairing of the Hall; and to act as executive committee of the Society in carrying out all business not entrusted to any other committee. It shall, further, be their duty to report to the Society, at each regular meeting, upon all motions submitted to their consideration since their last report, upon the condition of the Treasurer's accounts, and upon all outlays by them deemed advisable; and no disbursements ordered by them shall be made by the Treasurer unless and until their report upon such orders shall have been adopted by the Society.

Sec. 2. *The Committee of Conference.*—It shall be the duty of the Committee of Conference to act in conjunction with similar committees appointed by the Washington Society, upon all matters, regular and incidental, requiring the joint action of the two Societies.

Sec. 3. *The Judicial Council.*—The Judicial Council shall meet in the Hall of the Society every Saturday evening immediately after the adjournment of the Society. It shall be their duty to hear and act upon all excuses for fines and upon all offers of resignation of membership; and they shall hear no excuses for fines which have been standing for more than two weeks, saving in the case of members who have been unable to submit their excuses within that time on account of sickness or absence from the University. From their decisions an appeal shall in all cases lie to the Society itself. It shall be the duty of the Treasurer to embody the action of the Judicial Council in his weekly reports to the Society.

Sec. 4. *The Final Committee.*—The Final Committee shall take entire charge of all matters that concern the Final Celebration of this Society.

Sec. 5. *The Question Committee.*—It shall be the duty of the Question Committee to submit at each meeting of the Society two questions for the regular debates three weeks thereafter; and after the submission of their report it shall be the privilege of any member to propose a quession to be voted on, if seconded by any member of the Society, along with those offered by the Committee.

ARTICLE V.

REGULAR EXERCISES.

Sec. 1. From an alphabetically arranged roll of the members of the Society, which it shall be the duty of the Assistant Secretary to prepare, the Secretary shall divide the members of the Society into six classes containing as nearly as possible an equal number of members; and these classes shall be appointed for debate in regular order.

Sec. 2. Each question for regular debate shall be selected, from the questions submitted as hereinbefore provided, by the class which is to debate it; and a majority of the members thereof who are present when choice should be made, shall have power to select. In case of a tie, the President shall have the casting vote. In case of a failure to choose on the part of the class, the choice shall be left to the Society.

Sec. 3. After the discussion by the regularly appointed debaters, the question shall be open to the house for debate. During the discussion thereof a motion for the previous question or a call for a vote shall not be in order before half-past ten o'clock. At the close of the regular debate, the vote of the Society shall be taken by yeas and nays upon the question.

Sec. 4. At the first regular meeting of the Society in each month, except June, a member shall be elected to deliver an oration before the Society one month thereafter.

ARTICLE VI.

THE MEDAL.

Sec. 1. At the close of each session two medals, ranking respectively as first and second, shall be given by the Society to the two best debaters. But whenever there are but two contestants no second medal shall be given.

Sec 2 These medalists shall be chosen by a committee of three members of the Faculty of the University of Virginia who shall be elected by the Society at its first regular meeting in November of each year.

Sec. 3. At the first regular meeting in April and at the first regular meeting in May respectively there shall be a debate to be participated in only by the contestants for the medals; and at these meetings the aforesaid committee of the Faculty shall sit as judges.

Sec. 4. The decision of the Electoral Committee, which shall be final, shall be rendered within one week after the May debate.

Sec. 5. After the last regular meeting in February the contestants for the medals shall meet to select a question for their first debate. After this first debate they shall choose a question for their second debate.

Sec. 6. The medals thus awarded shall be publicly presented by the President of the Society to the successful contestants on the night of the Final Celebration of the Society, when each of the medalists shall deliver an oration.

Sec. 7. The form of the first medal, which shall be of gold and of the value of fifty dollars, shall be circular, its diameter not less than one inch and three-quarters. It shall bear on its face, enclosed in a wreath of laurel, PRESENTED BY THE JEFFERSON SOCIETY TO————

AS THEIR BEST DEBATER, SESSION 18–. Underneath this inscription there shall be engraven the Greek letters "ΦΠΘ." On the reverse shall be a representation of the University of Virginia, surmounted by the coat of-arms of Virginia beneath the motto of the Society, HAEC OLIM MEMINISSE JUVABIT; and, following the circumference, the words, UNIVERSITY OF VIRGINIA, JUNE (OR JULY)–,   18–.

Sec. 8. The second medal shall be in all respects like the first except that on its face instead of the words "AS THEIR BEST DEBATER," it shall bear the words, "AS THEIR SECOND-BEST DEBATER."

ARTICLE VII.
THE MAGAZINE.

Sec. 1. There shall be at least eight numbers of the Magazine issued during each collegiate year, of which the first shall be published in October.

Sec. 2. The editors of the Magazine shall be six in number. Of these, three shall represent the Jefferson and three the Washington Society. They shall be elected annually, the Jefferson Society making choice of her representatives at the regular meeting of the Society in January of each year. Of the corps of editors thus chosen by the two Societies, five shall have charge of the literary department of the Magazine and the sixth of its financial and other business; and the election of this business editor shall fall alternately to the two Societies. If, at any time, the Jefferson Society have not her full complement of editors, the Society shall, after due notice, proceed to complete it by election.

Sec. 3. The literary editors of the Magazine shall, in January of each year, select from their own number an editor-in-chief; and if at any time the office of editor-in-chief become vacant, it shall be their duty immediately to fill it by election. The editor-in-chief shall have entire control over both the literary and business management of the Magazine[.] He shall have power to allot their work to the other editors and to accept or reject all articles offered for publication.

Sec. 4. When requested to do so, the editors shall preserve strict secrecy as to the authorship of contributions; and no contributions shall be accepted for publication in the Magazine which has previously appeared in print.

Sec. 5. The business editor shall have control, under the editor-in chief, of all business matters connected with the Magazine, such as its financial management, its subscription lists, its advertising department, and the mailing and distribution of its issues. He shall, at the end of each three months of his term of office, make to each Society, through its Secretary, a report, exhibiting the exact condition of the Magazine as regards the concerns under his management.

Sec. 6. No member shall be eligible for the position of literary editor of the Magazine who has not had at least one prose article of his own composition accepted for publication in the Magazine.

Sec. 7.–*The Magazine Medal*–This Society shall at the beginning of each session, through its Committee of Conference, join with the Washington Society in choosing a committee of three members of the Faculty of the University of Virginia to select the best literary production contributed to the Magazine during the session by a member of either Society; and to this number the two Societies shall jointly award a gold medal of the value of fifty dollars. This medal shall be publicly presented by the Chairman of the aforesaid committee of the Faculty at the Final celebration of that Society to which the recipient of the medal may belong,

ARTICLE VIII.

RULES OF ELECTION.

Sec. 1. No one shall be entitled to vote for any officer of this Society or for any editor of the Magazine unless he shall have been a member of this Society for two weeks previous to the election.

Sec. 2. No member who is indebted to the treasury of the Society shall be qualified to vote for Final President or Vice President, or be eligible for either of those offices.

Sec. 3. No member may be Final President or Vice-President or Medalist of this Society unless previous to election (or previous to his appearing before the electoral committee of the Faculty, in the case of the Medalist) he shall have spoken on at least two separate occasions before the Society, either as monthly orator or on a question chosen for regular debate.

ARTICLE IX.

THE BADGE.

The badge of this Society shall be of gold in the shape of a scroll, three-quarters of an inch wide. On its face shall be engraven the following: U. V. JEFF. Soc., two pens crossed, 1825, and the initial letters of the three Greek words, "Φιλοι, Πατρις, Θεος."

ARTICLE X.

RESIGNATION OF MEMBERSHIP.

Whenever any member wishes to resign he shall signify his desire in writing to the Judicial Council, stating his reasons, and, upon obtaining the acquiescence of the Council and paying all his dues to the Society, may be permitted to withdraw. If the consent is withheld, he shall have the privilege of appeal to the Society.

ARTICLE XI.

CHANGES IN CONSTITUTION AND BY-LAWS.

Sec. 1. All motions and resolutions affecting the Constitution or By-Laws of this Society and all resolutions proposing appropriations of Society funds shall be submitted in writing and pass through three readings and a Committee of the Whole; and not more than two readings shall be taken at one sitting of the Society.

Sec. 2. A vote of two-thirds (⅔) of the regular members of the Society shall be necessary to amend this Constitution; but a vote of two-thirds (⅔) of the members present at any regular meeting shall be sufficient to amend the By-Laws.

Sec. 3. Two-thirds (⅔) of the members present at any meeting of the Society may, by a single vote, suspend, for that sitting, any provision of the By-Laws.

BY-LAWS.

ARTICLE I.

MEETINGS.

Sec. 1. This Society shall meet every Saturday evening during the session at seven o'clock P. M., from October to April, and at half-past seven from April to June.

Sec. 2. If, after having been properly requested to do so, the President fail to call a meeting of the Society, a quorum of members may convene it, after having given twenty-four hours' notice of the time at which the meeting is to take place, and of the purpose for which it is called. Notice posted upon four of the college bulletin-boards shall be sufficient.

Sec. 3. Optional attendance on the meetings of the Society shall be allowed to all applicants for degrees and to members living one mile from college at the discretion of the Judicial Committee.

ARTICLE II.

MEMBERS EXCUSED FROM DUTY.

Sec. 1. Members of less than two weeks standing shall be excused from all duties except attendance on the meetings of the Society.

Sec. 2. Members shall be excused from all duties for one week before and four days after each of their examinations.

ARTICLE III.

DUES AND FINES.

Sec. 1. Each member shall pay to the treasury of the Society *Ten Dollars* initiation fee, and an annual tax of two dollars and a half every subsequent session that he is a regular member.

Sec. 2. The roll shall be called at the opening and close of each meeting, and members shall be fined twenty-five cents for unexcused absence from each roll-call.

Sec. 3. Each member failing to debate the question upon which he has been regularly appointed shall be fined fifty cents.

Sec. 4. Every officer and every member of a committee who fails promptly to perform his official duty shall be fined *one dollar*.

Sec. 5. Any member elected monthly orator who fails to perform his duty as such shall be fined *one dollar*.

Sec. 6. Any member guilty of disorder shall be fined twenty-five cents, the Sergeant-at-arms being judge of what constitutes disorder.

Sec. 7. *Special Fines—*

(1) For passing between President and member speaking, twenty-five cents.

(2) Leaving the Hall without permission, twenty-five cents.

(3) Persisting in resolutions, motions, or remarks ruled out of order, fifty cents.

(4) Absence from Hall on leave for more than twenty minutes during meeting, twenty-five cents.

ARTICLE IV.

DEBATE.

Sec. 1. It shall be the duty of the Secretary to re-arrange, from time to time, the classes for debate with a view to keeping the numbers in the several classes as nearly as possible equal. He shall also separate each class into two divisions, one division consisting of the first, third, fifth, &c., on the roll of the class, the other, of the second, fourth, sixth, &c.

Sec. 2. *Manner of Choosing Question for Regular Debate.*—The President shall call upon the Secretary to read the questions which have been submitted in accordance with Article IV, Sec. 5 of the Constitution, and, after the reading of each question, shall inquire if it is seconded by any member of the class appointed to debate the question which may be chosen. He shall then take the vote of the said class upon each question thus seconded. The first of these questions which shall receive the votes of a majority of the class he shall declare chosen. If none of them is chosen by the class, the selection of a question shall fall to the House.

Sec. 3. After the choice of question the Secretary shall read in alphabetical order the names of the members of the class which is to debate the question chosen. He shall then give the privilege of the choice of sides to each member of the class in succession until one declares his preference. The side thus chosen shall be debated by the division to which the mamber making choice belongs.

Sec. 4. Each member of the class appointed for debate shall, at the meeting for which he is appointed, have the privilege of speaking twice upon the question chosen. The Secretary shall call upon the appointed debaters in order, naming alternately those allotted to the affirmative and those allotted to the negative. In this order he shall twice call upon each appointed debater.

Sec. 5. Members not regularly appointed to debate shall have the privilege of speaking twice on each regular question after its discussion has been thrown open to the house; on all other questions also each member shall be allowed to speak twice.

ARTICLE V.

QUORUM.

One-third of the members of the Society shall constitute a quorum for the transaction of all business.

ARTICLE VI.

ORDER OF BUSINESS.

1. First Roll-Call.
2. Reading and adoption of minutes of last meeting.
3. Installation of officers.
4. Nomination, election and initiation of new members.
5. Election of officers.
6. Monthly Oration.
7. Debate.
8. Report of Question Committee and choice of question.

9. Announcement of class to debate and determination of sides.
10. Treasurer's report.
11. Reports of committees, Ways, Means, Conference, etc.
12. Extraordinary and unfinished business.
13. Motions and resolutions.
14. Reading of class to debate within one, two, and three weeks, with announcement of sides and questions.
15. Notices of elections.
16. Report of Sergeant-at-Arms.
17. Second Roll-Call.
18. Adjournment.

ARTICLE VII.
MISCELLANEOUS BUSINESS.

Sec. 1. All motions and resolutions must be submitted in writing, in a blank book provided for the purpose and kept at the desk of the Secretary. They must be signed by the movers and read by the Secretary in the order in which they are submitted

Sec. 2. The President shall give notice of every election at least one week before it is to take place.

Sec. 3. To adjourn the Society before the regular business has been transacted shall require a vote of two-thirds of the members present; and no member who has voted for adjournment shall be allowed to move it again during the same meeting.

Sec. 4. *Call for Yeas and Nays.*—At the request of *five* members the vote shall be taken by *yeas* and *nays*.

Sec. 5. The rules of parliamentary practice as set forth in "Roberts' Rules of Order" shall govern the proceedings of this Society in all cases in which they are not inconsistent with its Constitution and By-Laws.

Sec. 6. Any student of the University who was a member of this Society previous to the session of 1880-'81, but is not now one, may reconstitute himself an active member by signing the Constitution and subjecting himself to the payment of the annual tax.

Sec. 7. Blank books shall be provided by the Treasurer for the reports of each of the standing committees, of the Secretary, of the Treasurer, and for all other uses called for by the Constitution or By-Laws.

Sec. 8. At the meeting in April, at which the first medal debate takes place, and immediately prior to the debate, Article VI of the Constitution shall be read by the President to the Electoral Committee of the Faculty.

ARTICLE VIII.
PREVIOUS ACTS NOT HEREIN CONTAINED.

All motions and resolutions affecting the Constitution and By-Laws of this Society previously passed, and not herein contained, shall be and are hereby *repealed*.

From Janet Woodrow Wilson

My darling child,   Wilmington. N. C. Dec. 9th '80
   I *have* been very anxious about you—and your letter received
this morning scarcely relieves my anxiety—for it reveals to me,
more fully, how very serious your cold has been, not only, but
still is. How did you take the cold dear? Had the want of your new
flannels anything to do with it, I wonder! Do write at once and
tell me *very particularly* how you are. You speak of your health in
a way that fills with me uneasiness. You have always been so well,
apparently—never had any sickness—or, as far as I know—any
weakness of any kind—during your childhood. And you did not
take cold, easily, either. Is it that your confinement in a close room
makes you more liable to colds? If so do find out how to prevent
this—for these colds are ruinous and most dangerous. Are you
much troubled by indigestion this session? As to your Moot Court—
If I were you I would not get Prof. M[inor]'s ill-will for the sake
of anything less than principle. So much is involved in his favor
or disfavor that I would sacrifice a good deal to avoid the latter.
Dont you think it would be wise and proper for you to go to him
and explain that you had no idea of any opposition on his part—
but had understood him to grant his free permission to do as you
pleased in the matter—and consequently supposed that you were
acting with his approbation—and express willingness to abandon
the thing, if he desires you to do so. This course would be no
humiliation to you—for while you are under a Prof. you are in
honor bound to study your profession as *he* thinks best. At the
same time I do not hesitate to say that his conduct in the matter
is simply contemptible. You have nothing to blame yourself with
in the matter. You know it is not uncommon for *old* professors to
think that anything out of the way of the old routine is simply
ruinous. But his want of candor in the matter is unpardonable. . . . Your Mother.

ALS (WP, DLC).

From the Minutes of the Jefferson Society

                    Hall of Jefferson Society Dec 11th 1880
   The Society was called to order at the usual hour by the Pres.
. . . Upon the motion of Mr Wilson the debate was postponed one
week & the report of consideration of the report [*sic*] of the constitution committee was made the special order of the night. A
motion that the house go into a committee of the whole was car-

ried, & Mr Dabney was appointed chairman of the Committee. . . .
Mr. Dabney, Chairman of the Com. of the Whole[,] report the
adoption of Arts II, III, IV, & V of the new constitution, & the rejection of Sec I of Art VI. His reported was adopted by the house.
Moved that the constitution com. be instructed to report some plan
for awarding two medals. Carried. . . .

From Janet Woodrow Wilson and Joseph Ruggles Wilson

My precious boy— Wilmington, N.C. Tuesday Dec. 14th [1880]
Yours of the 13th was received this morning—and we are made
exceedingly uneasy by its contents. It would have been very wrong
for you to have concealed your present condition from us. Well,
my darling—your father desires me to say to you that taking your
state of health into consideration—the amount of work pressing
upon you—together with the unavoidable fear that haunts you that
you may miss your degree—through some whim of the Professor,
or what not—he thinks—we both think—that it is *your duty to come
home*. He does not say you *must*—but he *urges* you to do so. It is
absolutely necessary that your general health be attended to *at
once*. This climate is less trying than the one you are in. Then
you can rest awhile—before you resume your reading at home. We
will fix you up so snugly. And we have a *beautiful horse* which
you can ride whenever you please. You cannot fail to get strong
and *well if* you *only* come home.

Dear, dear Son
Your mother has expressed my sentiments pretty exactly—only
not so strongly as I could wish. It does seem to me that the state
of your health *absolutely* requires your return to us. If you can,
therefore, get the authorities to refund what has been paid for
from January 1 to July—which they ought to do by reason of yr
illness,—or, whether they are dishonest enough to retain it still,
my precious boy, *pack up and leave*. It will not do to make fun
any longer of your "cold" as you mildly term it.
                         Your affc   Father

Your father has not written more strongly than I *feel*
                    Lovingly your   Mother

ALS (WP, DLC) with WWhw notation on env.: "Ans."

From the Minutes of the Jefferson Society

Hall of Jefferson Society Dec 17th 1880

... It was moved & carried that the Society go into Committee of the whole to consider the report of the constitution committee. Mr. Gaines was appointed Chairman of the Com. of the whole & reported that the three systems for awarding 2 medals, proposed but [by] the constitution com., had been rejected. . . . On motion of Mr. Harwood[1] the report of the Constitution Com. was called for. It was moved that 1st plan proposed for awarding 2 medals should [be] adopted. Lost. A motion that society go into Com of the whole was lost. Under head of report coms, Arts VII, VIII, IX, X, XI of the report of the con. com. were adopted. On motion of Mr. R. H. Gaines[2] the com. were thanked for the manner in wh. they had discharged their duty. On motion of Mr. Wilson the society proceeded to the nomination of the electoral committee. . . .

[1] Thomas F. Harwood, LL.B., '81; or, less likely, John T. Harwood, '83, an academic student.
[2] Richard H. Gaines, '83.

From Janet Woodrow Wilson

My precious Son,   Wilmington, N. C. Tuesday [c. Dec. 21, 1880]

We received your letter, containing your decision with reference to leaving the University day before yesterday. It was a great disappointment to us—particularly to your dear father—he so greatly fears that your health will not hold out. I had not allowed myself *fully* to expect you—but still I was hoping for your return more than I knew of—till we received your answer—& yet— I cannot help thinking you are *right* in remaining—in refusing to give up—*if* you are quite sure that *you are not risking your future health* in continuing your course at the University. *Pride* leads you to the determination to sacrifice your health rather than give up the contest. But you know you dare not do this because it would be *wrong*. On the other hand if you can continue your course *without* endangering your health, it will certainly be of advantage to you in every way—not *least* in giving you perserverance and self-reliance. Now, my dear, you will promise us that if you find your health & strength giving way, you will let us know—& *come* home. I am sure you will not let your *pride* lead you to risk your future health & happiness—will you, my precious boy? . . .

What do you hear from Hattie, dear? I find your father has a great admiration for her—and, my darling, you need fear nothing in the way of *disapprobation* from him—any more than from me—

with regard to any hopes you may indulge in reference to your future. He has no prejudices which would be in your way in the least—and you can rely upon his wishing with all his heart, what you wish in the matter. . . .[1]

Good bye, my beloved child. May God bless & keep you, and make you happy & strong. With love unbounded from Papa, Josie & myself   Your own Mother

ALS (WP, DLC).
[1] This paragraph offers the earliest intimation that WW was growing serious in his affection for his first cousin. He began a correspondence during his senior year at Princeton and continued it spiritedly under the mounting stimulus of his occasional visits from Charlottesville to Staunton where Hattie was at school; but only those three letters to her which are printed in this volume, and six to follow in Vol. 2, were preserved by her from the correspondence of this early period. An Editorial Note in Vol. 2, following Sept. 25, 1881, will deal with WW's proposal to Hattie.

From the Minutes of the Jefferson Society

Hall of Jefferson Society Jan 15th 1881

Roll call. Approval of minutes of last meeting. Moved that election of officers be postponed until adoption of new constitution. Carried—. On motion Society went into a committee of the whole. Mr. Dabney was appointed chairman. Com. reported the adoption of that system which provided for a 1st & 2nd Debator's medal, & the adoption of all the By Laws; & the adoption of the constitution as a whole. There not being ⅔ of members present, the constitution as a whole could not be adopted in the society. . . .

A sufficient number being present now, the new constitution was brought up and adopted as a whole. . . .

News Item from the *Virginia University Magazine*

[Jan. 1881]

We regret to announce that Mr. T. W. Wilson, Orator of Jeff. Society 1880, has left the University on account of his health. Last session he distinguished himself as a writer and as a debater. His articles on John Bright and Gladstone were complimented very highly by the *Magazine* committee. His able speech at our last commencement pleased all, and from our distinguished orator, Ex-Gov. [Richard B.] Hubbard, it elicited the remark, "that young man will be an honor to his State." This session he gave most of his attention to the study of law, and was looked upon by the whole class as one of "the surest men for B. L."[1] We sincerely wish that he may speedily recover.

Printed in the *Virginia University Magazine*, xx (January 1881), 250.
[1] Bachelor of Laws.

EDITORIAL NOTE
WILSON'S WITHDRAWAL FROM THE
UNIVERSITY OF VIRGINIA

Wilson's departure from the University of Virginia, sudden though it was, had actually been a matter of family discussion since early April 1880. Dr. Wilson had then suggested that, for reasons of health, his son might continue his legal studies at home during the academic year 1880-81.[1] The letters permit us to reconstruct what followed.

Wilson, in April 1880, must have rejected his father's suggestion and affirmed his determination to return next year and finish his course at the University. He did so, and the question of withdrawal lay dormant until the following December, when his ill health again aroused the serious concern of his parents.[2] By December 14, 1880, both were insisting that Wilson come home at once.[3] His mother's letter of a few days later[4] shows that he was still determined to stick it out.

The sequel can be filled in from the extant documents. Wilson suddenly decided, not only to go home, but also to withdraw from the University. His departure must have occurred on about Christmas Eve and so suddenly that he had no opportunity to say good-by to anyone or go through the formality of requesting permission. The minutes of the faculty for January 1, 1881, merely record his withdrawal but give no date.

Actually, Wilson himself explained the circumstances and reasons for his withdrawal in letters which will be printed in Volume 2. His doctor in Wilmington had examined him during the Christmas vacation and found, as he wrote to Richard Heath Dabney on February 1, 1881, that his digestive organs were "seriously out of gear" and urged him not to return to the University. To Hattie Woodrow he had already written on January 19, 1881: "But it was very hard to leave. The chief regret I had was that I was compelled to end my college days abruptly. I hated to say good-bye to college life, which, after all, is about the happiest, because the freest from care, that one can lead. . . . My hopes for the future prevent my regretting more than is proper that the past *is* the past."

[1] JRW to WW, April 2, 1880.
[2] JWW to WW, Dec. 9, 1880.
[3] JRW and JWW to WW, Dec. 14, 1880.
[4] JWW to WW, c. Dec. 21, 1880.

INDEX

NOTE ON THE INDEX

THE special problem posed by the many different kinds of documents in this series, as well as by the breaking up of constituent items to conform to the strict chronological order of printing, have motivated the structure of the table of contents. This, it is hoped, will facilitate the location of items which, by conventional listing in the order of printing might, like a needle in a haystack, be lost. The arrangement adopted also eliminates the need for duplicate coverage, in contents and in index, of certain documents, like letters. Letters are listed in the contents alphabetically by name, and chronologically for each name, by page. The subject matter of all letters is, of course, indexed. The Editorial Notes are likewise grouped in the contents under a common heading, but are listed, as are Wilson's writings and speeches, chronologically by page, and not alphabetically by title. The writings and speeches, however, are also carried by title in the index to accommodate normal index references to them. The index in general covers significant references to books and articles in text or notes, but does not furnish bibliographical information or cover routine documentation.

Footnotes, editorial notes, and descriptive-location notes are indexed. Page references to footnotes which place a comma between the page number and "n" indicate reference to both text and footnote, thus: "624,n3." This form gives the page where the subject entry appears. On the other hand, absence of the comma indicates reference to the footnote only, thus: "55n2." In this case the page number indicates where the footnote appears. The letter "n" without a following digit signifies an un-numbered descriptive-location note.

An asterisk before an index reference designates identification or other particular information. Re-identification and repetitive annotation have been minimized to encourage use of these starred entries. The cross-references to them should prove helpful in identifying persons referred to by nicknames or by fragments of family names. The index will usually supply the fullest known forms of names of persons of more than casual interest, and, for the Wilson and Axson families, relationships as far down as cousins.

Wilson's reading can be traced through appropriate entries in both index and table of contents, except, in this volume, in the cases of his *Index Rerum* and his Marginal Notes, where his own arrangement of the material here printed promotes easy reference. For this reason the content of these items is not indexed.

Though it is desirable that the index to a volume devoted to Wilson's formative years should guide the reader to expressions of his developing opinions and beliefs, the temptation to over-analyze has been resisted in the interest of proportion. Accordingly, selected opinions and beliefs are indexed under appropriate subheadings within the main Wilson entry; but this treatment has not excluded the use of broad, general headings in the main body of the index for subjects like the South, the civil service, and the committee system in Congress. Occasionally opinions expressed by a correspondent are included where these appear to supplement or reflect views expressed by Wilson in letters which are missing.

INDEX

Adams, Anne, *see* Wilson, Anne Adams
Adams, Herbert Baxter, WW on, 15,n20
"Adirondack" Murray, *see* Murray, W. H. H.
Advocate (Harvard), 436
Aiken, Charles Augustus, *191,n1
Alexander, Samuel, *240,n4, 545
Alligators, the, list of members of, *412,n1
American Cyclopaedia, gift of, from JRW to WW, 233
American Whig Society ("Hall," "Whig," "Lit"), *75,n1, 81,n1, 136,n1, 137, 145,n1, 197,n1; building repairs, 316,n1, 319; endowment of, 380-82, 413; J. N. Beam's history of, 382n3; sophomore oratorical contest in, 240, 250,n1; WW's activities in: 78, 240, 253, 269, 292, 296, 315-16, 319, 328, 355, 377, 380-81,n1, 425, 435; elected historian of, 292; reads history of, 382,n3. *See also* Junior Oratorical Contest and Lynde Debate
Anderson, J. Monroe, *30,n4, 36,n1
Anti-Corn-Law League, 610, 616
Archer, Robert ("Sage"), *321,n1, 545
Atlantic Monthly, 17, 273
"Atticus," 241, 307, 354n, 624
Atwater, Lyman Hotchkiss ("Dad"), 12, 13, *132,n1, 357,n1, 369, 386,n4, 399, 541
Augusta Female Seminary, *486,n1
Axson, Ellen Louise, fiancée of WW, WWshL (draft) to, 13

Bagehot, Walter, his *English Constitution*, 492; influence of, on WW, 493,n5
Baker, Alfred B., *138,n2
Baker, Felie (or Melie) S., *see* Woodrow, Melie (or Felie) Baker
Baker, Melie (or Felie) S., *see* Woodrow, Melie (or Felie) Baker
Baldwin, Mary Julia, *680,n1
Ballard, Bland, Jr., *378,n1, 431, 582
Barr, Frank, cousin of WW, 259
Beam, Jacob N., *see* American Whig Society
Beckwith, John F. B., *587,n1, 651
Beecher, Henry Ward, 457
Bellamy, John D., *157,n1, 165, 182
Bernard, William H., *671n1
Black, James S., *178,n2
Blake, John Rennie, *30,n1, 41, 67
Bland silver bill, 357, 500
Bones, Helen Woodrow, first cousin of WW, *650n6
Bones, James W., uncle-in-law of WW, *39n4, 66,n2, 257,n1, 292, 297, 440,n6, 589n1, 590, 596, 607, 650n6, 682n2

Bones, Jessie Woodrow, first cousin of WW, *38,n4, 159, 215, 257,n1, 279, 282, 286, 292, 323, 451, 487n2, 649, 680,n2
Bones, Marion McGraw, first cousin of WW, *487n2, 649,n6
Bones, Marion Woodrow, maternal aunt of WW, *39,n10, 66,n2, 263,n2, 292, 451,n1, 580,n1, 589n1, 593, 621,n1, 657, 677,n2, 680,n2
Bowery Boys, *133,n1, 134
Brackett, Cyrus Fogg, *259,n1
Bradford, Gamaliel, proposes seats for cabinet members in Congress, 492,n2
Brandt, Gustav A., *545
Bric à Brac, *293,n1
Bridges, Robert, 13, 17, *284,n1, 304; his college room, 514n2, 592, 657; on editorial elections, *360,n1, 423
Brooke, Francis J., *31,n2
Brown, William, *305,n2
Bruce, William Cabell, *579,n1, 584,n1, 586; debates with WW: 643-46, 651,n1, 653n, 661
Bryan, William S. Plumer, *32,n2, 70
Bryant and Stratton business college, 30, 53

Cabell, James, *651n1
cabinet government, as alternative to legislative domination, 498; proposed, and described, 561-64, 570-71; separation of powers, and, 502. *See also* Bradford, G.
Caledonian Games, *145n1, 379
Calhoun, J. C., *65,n1, 166
Caligraph typewriter, used by WW, 16, 17
"Cam," *see* Cameron, H. C.
Cameron, Henry Clay ("Cam"), *191,n1, 193, 222n1, 330, 382
Cane spree, 195-96,n1; note on, *217,n1, 365,n1; WW's victory over a freshman in, 197, 200, 201-202
Carmina Princetonia, *466n
caucus system, 555, 565-66
Chadbourn, George, *166,n1
Chamberlain, Daniel H., *233,n2
Chambers, Andrew A., *194,n1, 199
Chambers Building, *see* Davidson College
Chancellor Green Library, *139,n1
"Chang," *see* Lee, W. B.
"Chapel Stage," *220,n1, 224, 229
"Charley," "Charlie," *see* Talcott, C. A.
Charlotte Female College, 306n1
"Citizen, A," 150-51
civil service, 568, 574
Cliosophic Society, *75n1, 145,n1
College of New Jersey, *see* Princeton University